Rhetorical Theory by Women
before 1900

Rhetorical Theory by Women before 1900

An Anthology

Edited by Jane Donawerth

ROWMAN & LITTLEFIELD PUBLISHERS, INC.
Lanham • Boulder • New York • Oxford

ROWMAN & LITTLEFIELD PUBLISHERS, INC.

Published in the United States of America
by Rowman & Littlefield Publishers, Inc.
4720 Boston Way, Lanham, Maryland 20706
www.rowmanlittlefield.com

12 Hid's Copse Road
Cumnor Hill Oxford OX2 9JJ, England

Excerpts from Plato's *Menexenus* reprinted by permission of publishers and the Loeb
Classical Library from *Plato: Menexenus, Volume IX*, translated by R. G. Bury,
Cambridge, Mass.: Harvard University Press, 1929

Excerpts from Cicero's *De Inventione* reprinted by permission of publishers and the Loeb
Classical Library from *Cicero: De Inventione, Volume II*, translated by H. M. Hubbell,
Cambridge, Mass.: Harvard University Press, 1929

Excerpts from Nancy Lee Swann's *Pan Chao* reprinted with permission, © East Asian Library and the
Gest Collection, Princeton University.

Excerpts of Sei Shonagon's *Pillow Book* reprinted by permission of the publishers from *The Pillow Book
of Sei Shonagon*, translated and edited by Ivan Morris, 2 vols., New York: Columbia University Press,
1967. First published in Great Britain by Oxford University Press, 1967. A later edition was published
in the United Kingdom by Penguin Books, 1970.

British Library Cataloguing in Publication Information Available

Library of Congress Cataloging-in-Publication Data

Rhetorical theory by women before 1900 : anthology / edited by Jane Donawerth.
    p. cm.
    Includes bibliographical references and index.
    ISBN 0-7425-1716-0 (alk. paper) — ISBN 0-7425-1717-9 (pbk. : alk. paper)
    1. Rhetoric. 2. Women and literature. I. Donawerth, Jane, 1947–

PN173 .R435 2002
808'.001—dc21

                                                                    2001048524

Printed in the United States of America

∞™ The paper used in this publication meets the minimum requirements of American National
Standard for Information Sciences—Permanence of Paper for Printed Library Materials, ANSI/NISO
Z.39.48-1992.
Manufactured in the United States of America.

This anthology is dedicated to the many women who have taught me and, so, given me a voice, especially my mother, Hazel Kendrick Donawerth, who taught me elocution; my grandmother, Rhonda Smith Kendrick, who taught me how to use a dictionary; Doris Lusk, who taught me French before school every morning; Madeleine Doran, who taught me Renaissance rhetoric; and Virginia Walcott Beauchamp, who started me on feminist scholarship.

Contents

CONTENTS

Preface

When I first studied the history of rhetorical theory in graduate courses at the University of Wisconsin–Madison in 1972–1973, I received excellent training in the men of the canonical tradition of rhetoric but read no women theorists. When I first taught the history of rhetorical theory at the University of Maryland–College Park in 1982, I taught no women theorists. I didn't know there were any. Like Elizabeth Minnich, I thought that rhetoric, the art of public speech and argument, a foundation of men's education in the West for three thousand years, was an art from which women were excluded.[1]

For the second graduate course I taught in history of rhetorical theory, I included a new assignment for students: an oral and written report answering the question, "Who was the first woman rhetorical theorist?" At that time no women were included in the anthologies or the histories of rhetoric, and none examined in journal articles. I expected my students to find no one before the twentieth century, and then we would discuss the reasons for the exclusion of women from public speaking until this century, as well as the restriction of the higher levels of education to men until the mid-nineteenth century. Contrary to my expectations, however, my students did find women who were rhetorical theorists and teachers of rhetoric. They argued that we should simply broaden the boundaries of what is meant by rhetoric to include all forms of discourse and communication. This broadening occurred historically in the field of rhetoric, for we now study a range of communication arts, not simply public speaking.

That first year my students found Margaret Fell and Pan Chao, and another student made an interesting argument for Sappho. The second year they found Aspasia and Mary Astell and Mary Augusta Jordan, and in the meantime I'd found Gertrude Buck and Hallie Quinn Brown. So they proved me wrong, and I began planning this anthology. That was over fifteen years ago.

In this anthology I have chosen to follow the conventions of the field of history of rhetorical theory rather than the conventions of the field of literature. I have not provided critical editions of these texts that list and compare readings and retain original spelling and punctuation. Such literary editing practices would produce a very irregular format, since I include many translations. Printers and editors supplied spelling and punctuation until the eighteenth century, especially for women writers, and thus it seemed unnecessary to stick to original spelling and punctuation. I have provided the best translations I could find, accurate editions of excerpts based on a single copy text, and large numbers of annotations. A line of three periods (. . .) indicates that the editor has left out a few words. A long line of periods (. . . . . . .) indicates that the editor has left out one or more lines of verse. An ornament (ornament) indicates that the editor has left out a large section of the author's original work.

In the last ten years, many scholars have called for an expanded tradition, or canon, for the history of rhetoric.[1] In this anthology I present the broadest possible selection of women rhetorical theorists before 1900 and not a narrow selection of Britons and Americans. I have so far found no non-Western theorists after the tenth century, and none outside the English language after the seventeenth century. I will continue this search in anticipation of the second edition of this volume. It seemed important, however, to get this group of interesting theorists published, so that many courses can include them and we can start thinking more broadly about the history of rhetoric.

I wish to thank all my students from English 607, Readings in the History of Rhetorical Theory before 1900, and Honors English 399, Gaining the Right to Speak: Women and the History of Rhetorical Theory. I especially thank Richard Fravel for introducing me to Aspasia, Shirley Logan for finding Pan Chao, Marc Hirrel for advising me about Sosipatra, Betsy Kulamer for locating Margaret Fell, Christina Godlewski for suggesting Mary Astell, and Liza Child for mentioning Hannah More and Maria Edgeworth. Stephanie Lenkey, especially, and the other students of English 489, Gender and the History of Rhetorical Theory, helped me very much on my French translations of Madeleine de Scudéry's works. Carole Breakstone was a very adept research assistant, annotating several selections. I am especially grateful to my daughter, Kate Scally, for typing two sections, and my son, Donnie Scally, for indexing.

I thank Virginia Beauchamp—mentor, friend, and longtime supporter of this project—for her aid. Thanks also go to my colleagues Bob Coogan, Sue Lanser, and Linda Coleman, as well as Virginia, who carefully read early drafts of this book and provided encouragement. I am grateful to Eleanor Kerkham for suggesting that I look at Sei Shonagon's works and to Michael Olmert and Stephane Pillet for help in identifying lines of verse. I thank Dave Sebberson for trying out selections with his students, and Andrea Lunsford for her generous advice on the project and suggestions for reorganizing the introduction. I am deeply appreciative of the improvements suggested by the anonymous reviewers at Rowman & Littlefield, and I thank acquisitions editor Brenda Hadenfeldt for the many ways she has expedited the process of preparing the manuscript, as well as Erin McKindley for her editorial expertise and patient thoroughness.

I appreciate the sabbatical, the semesters off from banked leave, and the Graduate Research Board Fellowship at the University of Maryland that helped me work my way through the research, editing, and translation of this volume. I have been lucky in having a particularly supportive group of colleagues at the University of Maryland who teach and research in the field of rhetoric and composition. In addition to those already mentioned, I want to thank Jeanne Fahnestock, Shirley Logan, Carla Peterson, and Leigh Ryan. I also count myself extremely fortunate to be surrounded by scholars in the field of feminist rhetoric and composition studies who are generous with encouragement and advice, especially Cheryl Glenn, Susan Jarratt, Nan Johnson, Jackie Royster, John Schilb, Lucy Schultz, and Jack Selzer.

Finally, I wish to thank the staff of many libraries, including McKeldin Library of the University of Maryland (especially Betty Day), the Folger Shakespeare Library of Washington, D.C., the Library of Congress, and the Hallie Quinn Brown Library of Central State University in Wilberforce, Ohio. I am very appreciative for the computing, xeroxing, and printing done by the office staff of the Department of English of the University of Maryland, especially Janet Duncan, Betty Fern, Lynne Hamilton, Betty Wineke, and Isabella Moulton. And last, heartfelt thanks go to my family—Woody, Kate, and Donnie.

Notes

1. Elizabeth Minnich, "A Feminist Critique of the Liberal Arts," in Liberal Education and the New Scholarship on Women (Washington, D.C.: Association of American Colleges, 1981), 23–38.

2. See James Berlin, "Revisionary History: The Dialectical Method," in *Rethinking the History of Rhetoric: Multidisciplinary Essays on the Rhetorical Tradition*, ed. Takis Poulakos (Boulder: Westview Press, 1993), 135–51; Patricia Bizzell, "Opportunities for Feminist Research in the History of Rhetoric," *Rhetoric Review* 11, no. 1 (Fall 1992): 50–58; Carole Blair, "Contested Histories of Rhetoric: The Politics of Preservation, Progress, and Chance," *Quarterly Journal of Speech* 78 (1992): 403–28; Jane Donawerth, "Transforming the History of Rhetorical Theory," *Feminist Teacher* 7, no. 1 (Fall 1992): 35–39; and John Schilb, "The History of Rhetoric and the Rhetoric of History," *Pre/Text* 7 (1986): 11–34.

Introduction

This anthology documents a great diversity of women's rhetorics across many cultures. I began this research in concert with my students because no women were included in the anthologies of the rhetorical tradition. I expected us to find few women who wrote rhetorical theory before 1900. Instead, we found many. Women have taught rhetoric from the sophistic era of ancient Greece to modern times, from Aspasia to Gertrude Buck. Women from China and Japan, as well as Europe and the United States, have published works on conversation, letter writing, and preaching: witness Pan Chao and Sei Shonagon. Women have written advice on rhetoric addressed to women (like that of Mary Astell), to men (like that of Christine de Pizan), and to mixed audiences (like that of Madeleine de Scudéry and Frances Willard). Some rhetorical theory by women, like Gertrude Buck's, looks very like that produced by their male contemporaries; some, like that of Lydia Sigourney, is quite different. Some rhetorical theory by women, like Jennie Willing's deconstruction of women's role of listener, deserves to be called "feminist"; some, like that of Hannah More, seems to reinforce society's rigid gender roles.

At the same time as I was collecting rhetorical theory, many feminists were revising the history of rhetoric to include women's speeches and writings. Besides Karlyn Kohrs Campbell's (1989) important anthology and critical study of the speeches of nineteenth-century United States women, there are several collections of essays on the history of women's rhetoric: Carole Levin and Patricia A. Sullivan's (1995) on Renaissance women and rhetoric, Andrea Lunsford's (1995) on women's rhetoric from ancient Greece to contemporary France, Molly Wertheimer's (1997) remarkably inclusive collection on rhetorical activities of historical women from ancient Egypt to the nineteenth-century United States, and Christine Mason Sutherland and Rebecca Sutcliffe's (1999) on changes in the history of women's rhetoric. Challenging the conception of the rhetorical tradition as entirely masculine, Cheryl Glenn (1997) examined women's rhetoric from Aspasia to Anne Askew. Catherine Hobbs (1995) edited a volume on writing instruction for females in the nineteenth-century United States, and Lucy Schultz studied the rise of composition in elementary school classrooms (often under women's tutelage or in records of female students). Shirley Logan edited an anthology (1995) and published an analysis (1999) of nineteenth-century African American women's rhetoric, emphasizing abolition, women's rights, antilynching, and racial uplift; Carla Peterson (1995) studied the traveling African American women speakers and writers in the North in the mid-nineteenth-century United States; and Jackie Royster (2000) uncovered traces of the relationship between literacy and social reform for nineteenth- and twentieth-century African American women. Carol Mattingly (1998) analyzed temperance rhetoric by women in the nineteenth century, and Nan Johnson (2000) examined the limited rhetorical space for women in the nineteenth century. Most recently, Susan Kates (2001) described the history of rhetorical education for women and their resulting activist rhetorics from the mid–nineteenth to the mid–twentieth century in the United States. Patricia Bizzell and Bruce Herzberg (2001) took advantage of this growth in scholarship to add several women to their anthology of the classical tradition of rhetoric.[1] The present anthology will find a hospitable place in this body of feminist scholarship but will bring to it new information about the theorizing that women have done about communication.

This introduction offers *a* history, not *the* history, of rhetorical theory by women. A history is not just facts and events but always an interpretation, always a way of seeing facts and events. So, before I begin to tell stories about women's rhetorical theory, we must consider two questions: What is rhetoric? and What kind of history should I write?

Definitions of Rhetoric and Rhetorical Theory

What is rhetoric? The history of the definition of this term runs from fairly narrow and specialized to quite broad. Cicero, following the sophists, argues that oratory, or rhetoric, allows the speaker "to be able through speaking to take over an assembly of men, to draw their minds to you, to lead their desires wherever you desire, or divert them from whatever you wish."[2] As Chaim Perelman summarizes this classical tradition, rhetoric is "the art of speaking well—that is, the art of speaking (or writing) persuasively."[3] Indeed, Perelman sees all discourse as aimed at convincing an audience, even if it is the "universal audience" posited by rationalist philosophy. Writing long before Cicero, Aristotle had qualified the equation of rhetoric and persuasion by defining rhetoric as seeing "the available means of persuasion."[4] Quintilian answered Plato's attacks against the unethical procedures of the sophists by defining rhetoric as *bene dicendi scientiam*, the art of speaking well, or the good man speaking well (*bonus*).[5] In more recent times, Kenneth Burke has urged broadening the range of rhetoric from persuasion to "identification," the rhetor's claim to unity with the audience. Lloyd Bitzer has encouraged us to further consider "rhetorical situation," the exigence and collocation of events that call rhetoric into existence.[6] Recently James Murphy suggested "advice to others about future language use" as a good definition of rhetoric.[7] As the term "rhetoric" has changed in meaning, what counts as rhetoric has also changed, from the formal public speaking of ancient Greece—political, legal, and celebratory speech making—to any spoken or written form of nonliterary discourse (and many would include a great deal of literary discourse).

In the institutionalization of the term "rhetoric" we can see that this movement takes in the whole range of communication. For thousands of years, "rhetoric" was one of the "trivium," the three arts of speech (grammar, rhetoric, and logic) that were the backbone of education for the privileged, literate class in Europe. In the nineteenth century, under the pressure of professional specialization and increased use of writing to persuade, grammar was relegated to elementary education, logic became a formal specialized study, and rhetoric was divided between English departments, which taught composition, and speech departments, which taught public speaking. Over the last twenty years, many "speech departments" have become "communication departments," indicating a further broadening of the field.

What counts as rhetorical theory has thus changed radically in the last twenty years. Consider, for example, George Kennedy, the dean of scholars of the history of the study of rhetoric. In *Classical Rhetoric and Its Christian and Secular Tradition from Ancient to Modern Times* (1980) Kennedy assumed a fairly circumscribed definition of rhetoric and rhetorical theory: "Neither in India or China," he claimed, "did rhetoric become a separate discipline with a fully developed theory, its own logical structure, and a corpus of pragmatic handbooks."[8] Kennedy here defines rhetoric as an art of persuasion emphasizing logic, which was developed by privileged men of the European and American tradition in textbooks for privileged men. By this definition, the works by the women in this volume would not count as rhetorical theory any more than those by Indian and Chinese linguists and philosophers.

In his most recent book, *Comparative Rhetoric: An Historical and Cross-Cultural Introduction* (1998), Kennedy argues for a much broader definition of rhetoric and rhetorical theory:

> Some might argue that "rhetoric" is a peculiarly Western phenomenon, a structured system of teaching public speaking and written composition, developed in classical Greece, taught in Roman, medieval, renaissance, and early modern schools, and with some revisions, still in use today. . . . [But] "Rhetoric" in [a] broader sense is a universal phenomenon . . . for individuals everywhere seek to persuade others to take or refrain from some action, or to hold or discard some belief. . . . The conceptualization and discussion of something analogous to what we call "rhetoric" occurred in other early literate cultures besides the Greek: in ancient Egypt and ancient China, for example, where there were even something resembling handbooks of good speaking and good writing.[9]

Even here, Kennedy is circumscribing a definition for rhetoric based on persuasion or conviction, and, so, he offers a definition less broad than that of many scholars.

A definition of rhetorical theory as "the art of communication through oral, written, or visual discourse" would better cover what is taught by many speech, communication, and English departments and what is designated "rhetoric" in scholarly journals. These broader definitions of rhetoric as an "art of communication" and rhetorical theory as "an extended treatment teaching an aspect of the art of communication" form the basis for the selections of rhetorical theory by women in this anthology. I have chosen texts that are nonfiction, whole texts or large sections of texts devoted to advice on communication, and, where possible, texts or sections of texts not included in Bizzell and Herzberg's anthology (which in its second edition includes a few women theorists). I have excluded fiction, although not all literary forms (such as verse, which from Lucretius on has often been used for scholarly nonfiction materials). I have not included pieces with random paragraphs on communication, except in the cases of Sei Shonagon and Margaret Cavendish, where the forms are constituted by unrelated paragraphs or short sections; this criterion for selection also tends to exclude most fiction. I did not limit myself to textbooks and handbooks, however, because the history of women's education did not always include textbooks and handbooks.

When considering women theorists, we need a broader definition of rhetoric. Because women were often denied rhetorical education in the men's tradition, and because they did not have the rights to preach, to make political speeches, or to defend themselves in law courts, women's rhetoric doesn't fit the public speaking model. Many women theorists do not even treat argument or persuasion. But some do. Thus a broader definition—art of communication—will allow us to examine women's writings on communicating in conversation and letter writing, as well as public speaking and all forms of written discourse.

Once we set up these criteria, women's theory enriches our study of the history of rhetoric because we can see that many of them emphasize conversation as a model for public as well as private discourse, collaboration with the audience in the creation of meaning, and dialogic forms for teaching and reflecting about rhetoric.

Writing a History of Women's Rhetorical Theory

James Berlin reminds us that rhetoric is "never simply a set of disembodied principles that state the way language is used for purposes of persuasion or communication," but also "a set of strictures regarding the way language is to be used in the services of power" in a particular culture at a particular historical moment.[10] That brings us, then, to history. In a classic essay from a decade ago, Patricia Bizzell called for more feminist research in the history of rhetoric, urging that we become "resisting readers . . . of traditional rhetorical history and the white-elite-male-authored texts it canonizes," that we "look for women who have done work similar to the work done" by these canonical men, and that we "look in places not previously studied for work by women that would not have been traditionally considered as rhetoric," perhaps thereby redefining "the whole notion of rhetoric."[11] I started out thinking that looking for women theorists before 1900 would be so unfruitful that it would help clarify for me the misogynist tradition of classical rhetoric. I learned that many women had indeed written rhetorical theory: advice on persuasion, even textbooks on rhetoric. Robert Connors has argued that women in the nineteenth and twentieth centuries transformed the teaching and theory of rhetoric "from cold, distanced demanding lecture-recitation teaching and agonistic competition" to "a personalized editorial coalition and, at its most progressive, an irenic, nurturing partnership between teacher and student."[12] But further, as I traced women's texts to their nearest cousins, and as my students found texts that, they argued, need to be termed "rhetorical theory," I discovered that I could no longer feel comfortable with the handbook definition of rhetoric; that, indeed, women's theory did not always look like the men's theory I was used to; that women's theory often takes conversation as a model for public discourse in ways I had never found in the classical men's tradition of rhetoric.

History of rhetoric requires self-conscious choices about what to include and how to frame the texts. Recently, many scholars have reflected and debated on these issues. Reviewing some of their reflections will help us to understand what kind of choices may be made in selecting and writing about women's rhetorical theory, and so also remind us that the selections and the topics treated in this introduction are indeed choices, not necessary truths.

The major issues examined by revisionary and feminist scholars of history of rhetoric that have influenced me include the following:

- History legitimates a viewpoint that includes political and ideological assumptions.
- Historians are rhetoricians who construct texts, not just inspired discoverers of evidence.
- Histories are dangerous if they rely on myths of continuity, heroic men and women, and progress.
- The best histories strive not to glimpse universality but to locate theories and events in specific historical and material circumstances.
- The best histories do not tell a single story, leaving out information that does not fit, but stress multiplicity and diversity.

I have been especially influenced by the work of James Berlin, Carole Blair, Susan Jarratt, and John Schilb. Let us examine these issues more closely.

History Legitimates a Viewpoint That Includes Political and Ideological Assumptions

Schilb advises us that the drive to historicize is also the drive to legitimate a discipline.[13] One of my purposes in this volume is to lend further legitimacy to the growing body of scholarship on women and rhetoric. This drive to legitimize can be a handicap when a historian does not reveal the underlying assumptions of his or her choices, for the result may be "partial historical accounts," according to Blair.[14] But we can solve this problem, Susan Jarratt reminds us, if we explain our position, not only in terms of our assumptions but also in terms of the feminist conception of "standpoint," that is, where we come from.[15] It is important, then, for me to let my readers know that I was born into a white working-class family on its way up to middle-class status in the Midwest, and that I'm now a tenured professor at an eastern university. I went to college during the intellectually tumultuous 1960s and was an affirmative action hire. When I came to this university, I could go for days in my large department without seeing another woman faculty member.

Historians Are Rhetoricians Who Construct Texts, Not Just Inspired Discoverers of Evidence

Schilb reminds us that historians are "shapers of texts," not "passive recorders of a naked reality." They construct plots and tell stories ("History," 13). Blair points out that theories are also texts or discourses to be analyzed rhetorically, and histories are themselves rhetorical ("Contested Histories," 416–17).

The texts included in this volume are selections, and each selection itself tells a certain kind of story. From Mary Augusta Jordan, for example, I have selected discussions of conversation and letter writing (which link Jordan to the previous century's conduct book rhetoric for women), as well as Jordan's initial chapter on "correctness" (which speaks to the mainstream masculine rhetorical tradition). Regarding Frances Willard, I followed the generic expectations for an anthology, choosing a more coherent chapter written solely by Willard, even though her text is a collage of many writers defending women's preaching.

Histories Are Dangerous If They Rely on Myths of Continuity, Heroic Men and Women, and Progress

Berlin cautions that we must not repeat the fallacious plot of "heroic rhetoricians with the courage and wisdom to change" ("Revisionary History," 138). Blair advises us that we should avoid "the theme of deterministic progress" ("Contested Histories," 416). Carole Spitzack and Kathryn Carter, and Barbara Biesecker warn that we must not turn rhetorical history into a story of "great women speakers."[16]

I have tried to resist the linear plot of progress in this anthology and this introductory history by offering overlapping and discontinuous strands. There are gaps in this history that I cannot explain. Perhaps we will discover other writings by women that make connections across these gaps, but, alternately, we may finally be left with a discontinuous history. The history of women's defenses of public speaking, especially preaching, overlaps with both the history of conduct book rhetoric by women and early textbooks by women, sometimes in the same text.

Christine Sutherland has warned that "this search for ourselves is potentially dangerous" (*Changing Tradition*, 14). I have resisted the push to make this a feminist herstory, by pointing out that the history of feminist theory and the history of women's rhetorical theory diverge at times and by including excerpts like Christine de Pizan's advice to men on eloquence, rather than her much more fragmentary advice for women on persuasion.

The Best Histories Strive Not to Glimpse Universality but to Locate Theories and Events in Specific Historical and Material Circumstances

Schilb proposes that histories of rhetoric are better if they situate the texts they discuss among "a great variety of sociopolitical factors," tracing "discontinuity" as often as "convergence" ("History," 21, 28).[17]

This anthology is organized to locate theories in specific historical circumstances in two ways: by offering several historical tours from different perspectives of the theories in the introduction and by analyzing the writers' life and works historically in the introduction to each selection.

The Best Histories Do Not Tell a Single Story, Leaving Out Information That Does Not Fit, but Stress Multiplicity and Diversity

Berlin suggests that we need "multiple and disparate rhetorics, rather than any single, universal, and timeless formulation" ("Revisionary History," 135). Blair agrees, cautioning that plural is not necessarily multiple ("Contested Histories," 419). James Berlin further urges that "in writing rhetorical history it is not enough to locate and consider rhetorics that reproduced the ideology of the established power structure," for there is always "opposition"; there are always "competing rhetorics" ("Revisionary History," 144–45). Jarratt urges that feminist histories of rhetoric tell not only "women's history" but also give "gendered analysis" ("Speaking to the Past," 192). And Jackie Royster and Jean Williams point out the danger of erasing narratives of African American composition studies in sweeping histories of rhetoric and composition.[18] Schilb concludes that we should avoid trying to "boil rhetorical history down to a particular set of cherished texts."[19]

Schilb cautions, however, that even if we cannot write a "pure, thoroughly objective" history ("History," 25), we must not give up writing histories. Berlin adds that we can still group rhetorics into categories by "systemic principles," as long as we historicize them ("Revisionary History," 135).

In this collection, I offer representative texts, not masterworks. Unlike most of the histories of "the" rhetorical tradition, this one does not include selections based on what was most popular in the national press—such a criterion would have meant that African American rhetoric, for example, would have gone unrepresented, since Hallie Quinn Brown printed her rhetorical theory locally in Ohio. Nor did I look only at college composition texts, since many, many women did not go to college. In this introduction, I trace threads of similarity or partial continuity rather than opt for a more coherent story. My divisions of historical period are discontinuous at times, overlapping at others. I tell the story three times through, once focusing on women's experience, once focusing on the connections to the masculine tradition, once focusing on the connections to the history of feminist theory. I include texts that fall outside any of these continuities, for example, Christine de Pizan's advice, which troubles the assumption that all women concern themselves with conversation and collaboration, or Maria Edgeworth's parody of conduct books and rhetorical handbooks.

As already noted, my history is just one version of history. Now that the texts in this anthology are available, there will be many more versions. I hope that you the reader will begin to make your own interpretation, your own history of the involvement of women in rhetorical theory. And furthermore, we will have occasion to explore the utility of these newly recovered theories in interpretation. As Carole Blair recommends, "A rhetorical theory's worth is its capacity to render rhetorical practices understandable" ("Contested Histories," 420).

A History of Women's Rhetorical Theory and Teaching of Rhetoric

History always tells a story or makes an argument, since so many interpretations are possible and a choice must be made. I agree with Linda Nicholson that it is dangerous for us to make claims about women in patriarchal societies in general, but we can make claims about groups of women in specific historical contexts. Nicholson argues that such histories offer an "elaboration of a complex network of characteristics, with different elements of this network being present in different cases." We must make claims through careful attention "to the historicity of any patterns," Nicholson suggests, but we must look beyond patterns "for the places where such patterns break down."[20]

In women's rhetorical theory, I discern several patterns that seem to have historical beginnings and endings while overlapping with other patterns. This is not a neat history that progresses through one era with one set of characteristics and then another with a different set of characteristics. Rather, groups of women have certain goals for communication, and these seem to arise under certain historical circumstances. Some women who write rhetorical theory do not fit into any of these groups, especially the early ones (or perhaps I just do not yet know enough to see the patterns). The patterns I see include these groups (stars indicate women included in this anthology):

- early exceptions to women's exclusion from rhetoric:
  Aspasia,* Arete, Pan Chao,* Sosipatra, Sei Shonagon*

- 1300s to 1700s women with humanist education:
  Christine de Pizan,* Margaret Cavendish,* Bathsua Makin,* Madeleine de Scudéry*

- 1700s to 1900s writers of conduct book rhetoric:
  Hannah More,* Maria Edgeworth,* Lydia Sigourney,* Eliza Farrar,* Florence Hartley

- 1800s to 1900s teachers of elocution:
  Hallie Quinn Brown,* Genevieve Stebbins,* Anna Morgan*

- 1800s to 1900s teachers of composition:
  Sara Lockwood,* Harriet Keeler and Emma Davis,* Gertrude Buck*

- 1600s to 1900s defenders of public speaking for women:
  Margaret Fell,* Phoebe Palmer, Jennie Willing,* Frances Willard,* Mary Augusta Jordan*

Let us begin, then, with the early women who seem to be exceptions to the exclusion of women from the arts of communication in European and Asian traditions.

Early Exceptions to Women's Exclusion from Rhetoric

In a short dialogue by Plato, the *Menexenus*, Socrates attributes a speech containing advice on rhetoric to Aspasia, who lived during the fifth century B.C.E. She is described in several ancient sources as having taught sophistic rhetoric to her partner, Pericles.[21] Historians generally agree that the speech in its present form, because it mentions events after her death, could not have been written by Aspasia.[22] But because other ancient writers document her teaching rhetoric, I count Aspasia as a sophistic rhetorician. If not actually written by her, then the speech may reflect the tenets of the sophistic theory she taught. (Plato wrote parodies of the speeches of famous sophists in other dialogues.) Aspasia is important to include in this volume because many recent scholars of the history of rhetoric have written about her as a teacher of rhetoric who was lost because later rhetoricians lacked faith in women's abilities. They see Aspasia as a symbol of a new, more inclusive way of looking at the history of rhetoric (Glenn, *Rhetoric Retold*).

Like Gorgias, Isocrates, and other early Greek sophists, the speaker in the speech attributed to Aspasia comments on the speech-making process, particularly epideictic speeches (speeches of praise). Such speeches should arouse virtue, defined as the courage to perform noble military deeds; such speeches should touch hearers by employing the dead soldiers as examples; and such speeches must be organized "naturally," relating first the birth, then the training, then the nobility of the exploits, of the men it praises. We have relatively little advice on speech making from any of the sophists. What is attributed to Aspasia in Plato's dialogue fits very well with what other sophists were teaching. Perhaps because Aspasia was of foreign birth, she was exempt from the Athenian constraint against women studying or employing rhetoric.

We have records of (but no writings by) two other women who taught sophistic rhetoric. Arete, from the fifth century B.C.E., perhaps a contemporary of Aspasia, is alternately credited with running a school of sophistry after her father Aristippus died or teaching sophistry to her son, Aristippus.[23] Sosipatra, a mystic and sophist, taught philosophy and eloquence in Asia Minor in the fourth century C.E., first at Ephesus and then in Pergamon.[24] In contrast, we have no records of Roman women who taught rhetoric, although we know of women who were models of good speech and good conduct to their sons. Such a comparison suggests that sophistry, broadly speaking, was more conducive to women's education and development than other ancient rhetorical traditions. This comparison also suggests, surprisingly, that despite the severe restraints on Athenian women, ancient Greece and its colonies were perhaps more hospitable to women's intellectual development and more supportive of their voices than ancient Rome and its empire.

The passages on "womanly words" in Pan Chao's brief Chinese treatise on the education of women, written in the first century C.E.,[25] thus stand as the earliest authenticated work by a woman on rhetoric. Pan Chao taught eloquence to the empress and her ladies at the Chinese court, and so the East almost certainly preceded the West in admitting women to the arts of communication, especially since Aspasia came from Asia Minor. Pan Chao's advice centers on the harmonious negotiation and accommodation required of the wife, living as daughter-in-law in the extended family of her husband, according to ancient Chinese custom. Pan Chao's theory requires that a woman honor and esteem her husband by avoiding licentious talk and vulgar language, by refusing to quarrel or gossip, and by humbly exchanging only respectful words with her husband's family. Pan Chao, too, seems an exception, since few women received much education in China until the eighteenth century. She served as court historian, standing in for her brother. Perhaps she achieved her exceptional status as her brother's replacement.

In tenth-century Japan, Sei Shonagon served as lady-in-waiting at the court of the Japanese empress. Intertwined with other reflections in her diary or miniessay collection, *The Pillow Book* (c. 1000), are dozens and dozens of passages recording her advice on conversation, letter writing, and preaching. Her conception of a woman's role in speech is as liberal as Pan Chao's is restricted, but she emphasizes what we today might call "interpersonal communication." Sei Shonagon's courtly women had to cover their faces or stand behind screens when men entered the room, but they were encouraged to express their decided opinions with wit and acumen, and to compete in court contests of elegant poem and letter writing. Sei Shonagon's reflections offer advice for aristocratic women and men on the form and politics of discourse in this court society, where even small errors might end a career. Her advice on conversation emphasizes the importance of correct speech and ritual politeness for courtiers and for the women who served both male and female courtiers. Her comments on preaching cover reverential audience behavior as well as the priest's delivery. Her suggestions for letter writing focus not only on the mechanics (selection of paper, calligraphy, presentation) but also the collaborative and dialogic nature of Japanese letters: women help each other to write their letters, and letters are always written with care for the audience (not only the individual recipient, but his or her servants and superiors, as well).

It is especially difficult to discern patterns in these early writings on communication by women from Asia and Europe, since they are widely separated by culture and time. In Europe and Asia Minor sophistry was particularly supportive of women's learning, even in rhetoric. Seemingly the East, more so than the West, bred cultures that encouraged women's rhetorical theorizing (unless there are a great many treatises now lost). A thousand years ago women seem to have been constrained by their roles to value collaborative, conversational rhetoric more than men did. Beyond that, conclusions are risky. Since so few women participated in rhetorical culture (three women in two thousand years), strictures against them seem to have been effectively enforced.

Humanism and a Renaissance of Rhetoric for Women

In fourteenth- to eighteenth-century Europe many women claimed rhetorical and humanist education for women and published their own theories of rhetoric. The recovery of classical languages and manuscripts, as well as a turn toward humanist education centered on rhetoric, enabled some women (while generally excluding women) to argue for women's rights to education and speech.

In fourteenth- to fifteenth-century France, Christine de Pizan was one of the first women to make the Renaissance her own. She traveled with her father from Italy to France, bringing along some of the Italian rhetorical and scientific knowledge that would in later centuries foster the full development of the European Renaissance. Other scholars have described Christine's advice to women on persuasion when public speech was not an option.[26] In this anthology, I include sections from her *Book of the Body Politic* (1404–1407) in which she describes the varied rhetorical skills that men should possess, especially princes and merchants. In this unusual treatise, a woman forthrightly uses her classical learning to advise the men around her (her "superiors") on the elements of eloquence and the skills of persuasion. Christine recommends to her betters a rhetoric built on performance. It is charismatic, attentive to demeanor and delivery, and solidly based on a deductive logic used for display as much as persuasion. To her fellows in the bourgeoisie, she recommends a circumspect rhetoric of negotiation, with one eye always on the hierarchy. Especially interesting is that Christine excludes the lower classes and the knights (who need only fighting skills and loyalty) from the rhetorical knowledge she requires in the prince and the bourgeoisie.

In seventeenth-century Europe, many women defended in print the right of women to participate in the rhetorical education that defined elite culture, and some women advocated giving women broad powers of public speaking, especially in preaching. Since rhetoric was central to humanist education, these women all seem to have been influenced by humanism. In seventeenth-century Europe a group of women were all writing at once on similar issues in the same culture.

I have not yet found any sixteenth-century rhetorical theory by women, but the works of Christine de Pizan were translated and printed frequently during this period, especially in France and England. In seventeenth-century England, Margaret Cavendish, Margaret Fell, Bathsua Makin, and Mary Astell issued calls for rhetorical roles and education for women, and in France, Madeleine de Scudéry developed a rhetorical theory that included conversation and letter writing for salon culture.

In *The Worlds Olio* (1655), Margaret Cavendish, Duchess of Newcastle, surveys a broad range of rhetorical topics dispersed throughout her idiosyncratic encyclopedia. She cites class and social responsibilities for aristocratic women against the early modern requirements that good women pursue silence as a virtue, and she gives her opinion on orators, invention, girls' schools, the physiology of speech production, "what discourses are enemies to Society," and "of speaking much or little." Cavendish is not herself a Greek or Latin scholar but has read translations of classics and humanists. She is interested in contemporary empiricists' ideas about speech, adopting the empiricist concept of the mind as a tabula rasa (blank slate) on which experience impresses itself. She combines this interest with a sophistic emphasis on language as the bond of society, adapting both to an ideal of communal private rather than individual public performance: "social discourse . . . like music in parts." She is further concerned in her writings to defend women against misogynistic attacks on their lack of intelligence or their misuse of language.

In *An Essay to Revive the Antient Education of Gentlewomen* (1673), Bathsua Makin defends women's rights to rhetorical education, domestic persuasion, and limited public speech. One of the most learned humanists in Europe at the time, she combs the classics and outlines a history of women and rhetoric. She is writing in the tradition of the pamphlet controversy about women, praising and defending women's abilities while arguing for the benefits of women's education and their right to speech. She is most concerned that women participate with men as equals in their married conversation—in the larger Renaissance sense of mutual exchange.

In France, in treatises from the 1640s to the 1680s, Madeleine de Scudéry set out the first fully elaborated early modern theory of rhetoric by a woman. In the preface (perhaps coauthored by Madeleine's brother Georges) and one speech by "Sapho to Erinna" of *Les Femmes*

Illustres (1642), de Scudéry encourages women to educate themselves and to seek social status through their writing rather than their beauty. In dialogue essays in *Conversations* (1680) and in *Conversations Nouvelles* (1684), as well as earlier in some of her novels, de Scudéry lays out a rhetoric of conversation (and also letter writing) for the salon culture of Renaissance France, a theory that includes (or even centers on) women. De Scudéry imagines a world of leisure in which intellectual exploration and construction of community are carried on primarily through conversation. She thus takes conversation as a model for public as well as private discourse. Central to her theory, then, is the "agreeable," remaining sensitive to one's audience's interests, entertaining and not imposing one's views on the group. Esprit—spirit or wit—must never come before sensitivity to one's friends in conversation. Even in letters one must appear to be easy and natural, as if conversing, rather than show off the education that such a performance requires. Women are naturally better than men at letter writing because modesty requires them to communicate less directly, and such indirection is a quality of artistic writing.

In *A Serious Proposal* (1694–1697) Mary Astell proposes a women's college that includes a rhetorical curriculum focused on women's tasks of persuasion (encouraging other women to good) and private intercourse with their husbands. Astell addresses women and imagines an all-women school or household in which women educate one another in all the arts, including writing. Astell's Enlightenment rhetoric emphasizes reason. She argues that the good writer allays the passions instead of arousing them so that reason may have priority, and she arranges content according to logical methods. The good writer puts herself in the place of the reader and aims for clarity in style and use of figures. While Astell specifically denies women the right to preach or address public assemblies, she allots them the right to persuade through reasoned writing, a much broader power in her burgeoning print culture.

These fourteenth- to eighteenth-century women draw on their humanist education to argue for women's right to speak and write. They employ the idea of a Renaissance of women's rhetoric from classical or biblical antiquity as a rhetorical strategy for supporting rhetorical education for all women. Educated in languages and rhetoric, Bathsua Makin, Madeleine de Scudéry, and Mary Astell made their living by teaching and writing. These women radically revised classical rhetoric by centering their theories on conversation rather than public speech. The importance of audience in their theories anticipates recent interest in collaboration as a value in communication.

Conduct Book Rhetoric for Women

In conduct books written by men for women in the Renaissance, women are enjoined to be "chaste, silent, and obedient."[27] Many women of eighteenth- and nineteenth-century Europe and America appropriated the conduct book and, within this genre, developed theories of communication for women. Whereas earlier conduct books advised parents to give daughters limited education and encourage silence as a virtue, these conduct books written by women advised parents to offer their daughters extended learning, including rhetoric, and to teach them skills of conversation, writing (especially letters), and reading aloud. Except for Edgeworth's parodic essay, this body of theory incorporates the culture's separate spheres gender theory more rigorously than did women drawing on earlier humanist traditions. Indeed, some of these women seem to be constructing and not merely drawing on the theory of separate spheres.

Hannah More taught in a successful school for girls that she helped found. In a chapter entitled "Thoughts on Conversation" in *Essays on Various Subjects* (1777) for young girls, and in a chapter called "Conversation" in *Strictures on the Modern System of Female Education* (1799)—even in a mock-heroic poem, "The Bas Bleu, or Conversation" (1783–1786)—Hannah More developed a theory of conversation that enforces conservative gender roles for women—separate spheres for men's and women's speech, women cast in the role of good listeners and speaking especially on moral causes. Within that restricted sphere, however, More makes enthusiastic arguments for giving a rigorous education to girls. In this way, she seems much like Pan Chao: both concede a limited or inferior role to women in society in exchange for increased education. However, More is a product of her historical English culture and the anti-French London salon culture of the Enlightenment, just as Pan Chao was of her imperial Chinese context. Rather than the freedoms to be well educated and to direct the course of conversation that de Scudéry foregrounds, More emphasizes constraints on women's speech and writing. More makes powerful arguments that the role of listening in conversation is essential to conversation. And she sets out a witty and extensive analysis of faults of conversation, from gossip to exaggerating for dramatic effect to talking too much about oneself.

Maria Edgeworth, a contemporary of More, taught the Edgeworth brothers and sisters and wrote textbooks for home schooling with her father. In her witty "An Essay on the Noble Science of Self-Justification," appended to *Letters for Literary Ladies* (1795), she parodies the rhetorical manual of her male contemporaries, as well as conduct literature for women. In this essay, she playfully advises wives how to influence and manipulate their husbands through speech, argument, and theatrics, despite their subordinate gender role. Her essay thus falls in a long literary tradition of satire against shrews—women who talk too much and boss their menfolk around. More daringly, it also parodies the categories of Enlightenment men's rhetoric, from the sublime to wit, from sophistic exercises on both sides of an argument to the best use of logical fallacies. In this way, Edgeworth also offers advice on rhetoric—by her negative example decrying not only the selfish individual who manipulates others through her rhetoric but also the eighteenth-century men's theory that recommends manipulating and dominating an audience through psychological and aesthetic techniques.

In the 1830s, in *Letters to My Pupils* and *Letters to Young Ladies*, the New Englander Lydia Sigourney, influenced heavily by Hannah More and corresponding with Maria Edgeworth, published advice for her pupils in girls' schools on conversation and letter writing. By Sigourney's time, this genre of conduct book rhetoric for women has become a women's tradition of rhetorical theory. To Hannah More's theory of conversation and letter writing for women, Sigourney adds suggestions for rigorous training in reading aloud (essential for parlor entertainment in nineteenth-century middle-class society) and extensive collaborative training of the memory through girls' reading societies. In addition, she presents women's discourse, while lying outside public speaking, as important in the realm of public influence. This is especially true in her discussion of women's conversation with men, for she advises that women's rhetoric must be used for moral uplift, since women have enormous influence over young men. This influence must be used to reinforce republican virtues—simplicity, thrift, industry—and requires women to be well educated in the rhetorical skills of clear thinking, broad knowledge, ethical perspicuity, and elegant language.

Sigourney's contemporary, Eliza Farrar, wrote a conduct book for ladies, *The Young Lady's Friend* (1836), which included advice on conversation, letter writing, and reading aloud. She also published *The Youth's Letter-Writer* (1840), a textbook for home schooling in which (following the Edgeworth design for textbooks) an interesting story about a boy's visit away from home propels the characters through lessons in letter writing, mainly taught by the oldest daughter in the family. In these books, Farrar imagines a society in which republican virtues are transmitted and the daily business of American society is conducted largely through conversation and letter writing, and a society is influenced profoundly by women's teaching and communication skills. Farrar extensively analyzes the role of sympathy in rhetoric for women. In both Sigourney's and Farrar's texts, it is apparent how important education outside schools was to the fields of composition, rhetoric, and speech in the nineteenth-century United States.

The tradition of conduct book rhetoric for women continued through the nineteenth century. Florence Hartley, in *The Ladies Book of Etiquette and Manual of Politeness* (1870),[28] treats conversation and letter writing, explaining conversation as a particularly feminine accomplishment that exercises creativity and sympathy, and posing letter writing as central to familial and social community and to women's role of moral and social influence. As we shall see, Mary Augusta Jordan also incorporates topics from this conduct book tradition.

Although conservative on gender roles, the women who wrote conduct book rhetoric were progressive on teaching rhetoric to women. Their emphasis on the moral goal of speech stood later nineteenth-century female rhetoricians in good stead. The right to public speech for women was gradually won as women speakers championed moral causes, especially, in the United States, the abolition of slavery. Before public speech by women was accepted, however, the women of the first half of the nineteenth century used their skills in conversation to influence the men of their families, and they organized letter-writing campaigns on political issues, such as the oppression of Native Americans. This conduct book rhetorical theory by women emphasizes the conversational, collaborative nature of these women's skills.

Parlor Entertainment and Elocution for Women

Nineteenth-century women also participated in the development of elocution as a branch of rhetoric. Elocution is the study of the artful delivery of speech or poetry and includes training the body and voice. With the introduction of sentimental culture and the accompanying development of rhetoric as reception theory (education in taste in reading, writing, and speaking) a new parity between men and women arose.

The French teacher François Delsarte, who died young but whose theories were popularized by his widow, was extremely influential in this movement because he united sentimentality and physical training in his conception that proper training in rhetorical delivery recapitulates a spiritual trinity of body, mind, and soul. In the United States, Delsarte's theories of the discipline and spirituality of elocution were popularized not only by men but also by many female disciples and teachers.

Hallie Quinn Brown, an African American born to freed parents in Philadelphia, migrated with her family to Canada during the Civil War. Later she returned to study and then teach at Wilberforce College for blacks in Ohio. She was a trained elocutionist who toured with concert companies (groups who performed spirituals or songs and dramatic readings) and later by herself. In about 1880 she published *Bits and Odds*, a volume of selections for recitation as dramatic readings, with a tiny preface on elocution that I have included in this anthology. Her selections show that she used classics (Shakespeare), humor (Irish, German, and African American dialect pieces), and abolitionist writings (poetry and prose) to offer a varied program that had a political purpose. Brown published most of her works by having them printed locally and then distributing them herself to her students as textbooks. (African Americans had difficulty getting published by national presses in the nineteenth century.)

Brown privately printed *Elocution and Physical Culture* sometime before 1908 (from the date on the preprinted cover). Her textbook outlines a whole course in physical training for elocution, along with reflections on the moral and mental use and benefits of this training. I have included much of this pamphlet because it is very rare. For her students at Wilberforce, Brown laid out in *Elocution* a progressive set of physical exercises with a rationale that linked them to the intellectual and moral purposes of the art. While current historians of speech tend to see elocution as a corruption of public speaking, as delivery divorced from content, Brown and her contemporaries saw it as an art form, like dance or choral singing, that used the body for aesthetic performance and moral enlightenment. For example, Brown suggests that "good reading and speaking is *music*." She combines detailed instructions for exercises of posture, voice, and gesture, with lessons on the physiology of speech and summaries of the theories on delivery of rhetoricians from Cicero to Delsarte. Brown insists that expression be natural and conversational, that emotion inhabit every expression, that sincerity be the hallmark of the true artist, and that delivery depend as much on the "moral tone" as on physical technique and emotional inflection.

Genevieve Stebbins was a student of Steele MacKaye, who had studied under Delsarte. Stebbins pursued her studies in Paris and Oxford, even seeking out a Hindu in England to learn breathing and meditative exercises. Her handbook, *The Delsarte System of Expression* (1885), was one of the most popular elocution texts and went through many editions. It represents itself not as a textbook by Genevieve Stebbins but as a recovery of Delsarte's teachings after his death, as a dialogue between teacher and students set in New York City, and as a letter from a teacher to pupils. It combines many repetitive physical exercises with romanticized treatment of elocution theory that moralizes and idealizes it as a pathway to the soul. For example, when Stebbins teaches posture, she explains that the "torso represents the moral element," and so leaning toward an object may symbolize attraction; leaning away from the object, repulsion; and standing before the object, humility. *The Genevieve Stebbins System of Physical Training* (1898) was a handbook for teachers that outlined physical exercises for use with students and posed a psychological rationale in sentimental terms. The body, Stebbins argues, expresses emotional, mental, and spiritual states through a semiotic code, a system of signs. But the reverse, by a natural analogy, may also be true: expressing emotional, mental, and spiritual states will help the person feel them. Thus students who go through Stebbins's drills learn self-control. Physical exercises stimulate their mental state, mental well-being, and even moral values such as courage. This analogy between physical and mental states goes back to the Greek idea that music might arouse bravery in warriors, and it is substantiated in contemporary mental self-help regimens that advise lots of physical exercise to avoid depression. In Stebbins's *System*, which concentrates on the very basic beginnings of training, the exercises graduate from techniques of posture, poise, and breathing to gymnastics and creative movement. Stebbins arranges her final series of exercises as analogies to European dance forms and Greek and Roman statues, claiming that adopting these postures and movements will stimulate a bodily understanding of culture and its spiritual values, even in small children. Stebbins's feminist slant is clear in one exercise—the Amazon drill, where schoolgirls assume the warlike poses of the Amazons of Greek friezes.

In later years, English composition, public speaking, rhetoric, dramatic acting, and physical education (especially gymnastics) split into separate arts. But in late-nineteenth-century elocution they were intermingled. Elocution prepared students to select appropriate literary and political writings, read them with clarity and force, express the ideas and emotions with the body, and enact the voices within these readings. Hallie Quinn Brown represents an elocutionist whose works move in the direction of modern speech communication as a discipline. Brown is preparing her students for reading aloud, platform speaking in activist causes, and preaching. Genevieve Stebbins represents the trend of elocution to develop into physical education (including creative movement and modern dance). Anna Morgan toured as an elocutionist after training at the Hershey School of Music in Chicago and then returned to Chicago as a teacher of elocution, first at the Chicago Conservatory and then in her own studio. Morgan represents the trend of elocution away from more general rhetoric to the branch of dramatics.

Anna Morgan's *An Hour with Delsarte* (1889) epitomizes the aesthetic benefits of elocution for women. Although she uses the universal male pronoun to address the reader, sketches of her female students illustrate the volume, and she ends by recommending the career of acting to women. She offers her women students self-cultivation—aesthetic physical training that makes students comfortable with their bodies and enables them to express themselves vocally and physically. For nineteenth-century women, who were bound up in corsets, petticoats, tight sleeves, and constricting collars, who were encouraged to sit still, be quiet, and mind their manners, to be able to move and speak with confidence were enormous achievements. Morgan encouraged naturalistic acting and simplified staging. Although she saw elocution as detailed, intellectual, and requiring frequent practice, Morgan justified the art as based on natural principles. Thus she gave women the ability to conceive of movement and voice as their natural right. Morgan adapted Delsarte's principles of vital, mental, and emotive states to give her female students the sense that their physical, intellectual, and emotional selves were rightly linked. These individual competencies should be used for communal welfare, as her illustration of a poor girl captioned "'Tisn't pleasant to have no place to sleep" suggests. Morgan imagined, and many nineteenth-century women took her imagination to heart, that the "material," the body, should express the "immaterial," the soul or goodness of a person. Such a philosophy allowed women to picture themselves as capable, graceful, and in control of their own bodies, able to speak out with emotional as well as intellectual messages.

Elocution helped give nineteenth-century women a voice. Elocutionists used the words of others, but they selected the message and arranged the material. Elocutionists addressed domestic, school, or church audiences more often than public political assemblies, but they had great influence over those audiences. Although elocution sentimentalized the literature and political rhetoric it adapted for performance, it was this sentimentality that made its message so powerful for nineteenth-century culture. Its importance to the history of rhetoric lies in the ways it revised the canon of delivery, urging a conversational tone and a collaboration among writer, speaker, and listener of the works performed.

Textbooks in Composition and Rhetoric

Gradually women's education extended past elementary school to normal school or female academies and, late in the nineteenth century United States, to college. This was a great achievement for women, who had been arguing for advanced education for over two centuries. Once women were educated at an advanced level, women teachers became numerous. Once women teachers were common, they began writing textbooks for their students. Thus, in the second half of the nineteenth century, many, many composition and rhetoric textbooks were written and published by women. These textbooks have largely escaped the notice of the historians of rhetoric. Some, addressed to normal school rather than college students, were deemed unsophisticated; none were popular enough to be used much in men's colleges, which far outnumbered women's colleges. But they deserve attention in the history of rhetoric because they so clearly represent the democratic edge of composition theory, addressed to new audiences of first-generation students (see Schultz, *Young Composers*). Hallie Quinn Brown, whose texts were discussed in the last section on elocution, could just as easily have been placed here. Although her first work, a collection of readings, seems to have been aimed at a larger audience, her second, *Elocution and Physical Culture*, was a privately printed textbook for her Wilberforce College students, all of whom were first-generation college students.

Sara E. Husted Lockwood taught English at Hillhouse High School in New Haven, Connecticut. She wrote a textbook for high schools and academies, *Lessons in English* (1888), and coauthored a revision of it for "higher schools," *Composition and Rhetoric* (1901), with Mary Alice Emerson, a college professor at Carleton College. We can see in these textbooks that the barrier between high school, academy, normal school, and college was quite permeable. Many girls' schools allowed their students to finish high school and do a short course of college. My own grandmother, Rhoda Smith Kendrick, is a case in point. She finished high school at age seventeen and then took a six-week course at Morehouse College in order to teach in Indiana. Was that course advanced placement high school, teacher training, or college?

Lockwood's *Lessons in English* was a culmination of nineteenth-century American directions in composition. Its purposes were to develop "critical literary taste" and to acquire the "power of thought and facility of expression." It shared with many texts a belletristic substratum, and with many others a traditional classical interest in logic and rhetoric turned toward written composition. In addition, the examples and assignments revolved around the "classics" of American literature, mainly Longfellow and Whittier. In this book Lockwood covered the new knowledge of the history of the language and the old science of classification of figures from rhetoric. For example, she combines exercises in sentence combining with classical paraphrase to teach sentence structure and style. Lockwood's history of the language is quite modern and multicultural, citing English words from Hindu, Polynesian, Spanish, and Hebrew, as well as Latin, Greek, and French. The thematic format of the section on composition combines newer trends on teaching business and formal letter writing with older trends (stretching back to Aphthonius and Erasmus) of teaching amplification from allusion, character, apostrophe, and antithesis. The section on invention (and there is one) is a reworking in modern guise of the commonplaces. If the topic is paper, one must ask about manufacture, composition, invention (where, when, by whom), uses, kinds, advantages, forms, even etymology. But the section on kinds of essays is quite modern, divided into personal narrative, historical narrative, fiction, and description. It is capped with a research paper that is a critical biography of an American poet. I own a copy book of my grandmother's that outlines just such a research paper, although the information seems to come from lecture rather than textual sources. Lockwood's textbook, then, offers something for everyone. It achieves a very respectable compromise among the many traditions of rhetoric and composition.

Based on their many years' experience teaching in Cleveland, Ohio, Harriet L. Keeler and Emma C. Davis, in *Studies in English Composition* (1891–1892), offer a summary of the rhetorical tradition for high school and private preparatory school students. This book, meant to be used through the four years of high school, instructs teachers to show students how to write and speak and to provide them with a guide in the process. It urges teachers to pay more attention to the "spirit and thought" of student writing than to its "technical dress." Keeler and Davis are very concerned to give their students proper models, which they draw from United States writings, literary and rhetorical: Lowell, Webster, Hawthorne, Emerson, Whittier, Longfellow, Jewett. They offer chapters on narrative, description, letters, book reviews, and persuasion, as well as chapters on word choice, grammatical errors, sentence structure and paragraphing, rhetorical figures (only a handful), and style (emphasizing clarity, unity, strength, and harmony). They also include chapters on versification and public speaking for teachers who want their students to try all forms of oral and written discourse. Theirs is a fairly shallow summary of the rhetorical tradition, but a summary nevertheless. They are not disciples of the current-traditional school that place emphasis on grammatical correctness and organizational form.

Gertrude Buck, who received her Ph.D. under Fred Newton Scott at the University of Michigan and taught at Vassar College (a women's college), represents a woman whose career directly parallels that of male rhetorical theorists of the time. She taught college, wrote textbooks aimed at a mixed audience of male and female students, and made a living from writing and teaching composition (and to some degree speech). Still, Buck does not fit easily into mainstream men's rhetoric of her time period, current-traditional rhetoric, which emphasized correctness and form. She seems quite aware that she is writing new kinds of textbooks for new kinds of students and consequently draws on contemporary scientific ideas about developmental psychology, language, and pedagogy, as well as the rhetorical tradition. In 1899 Gertrude Buck and Elisabeth Woodbridge together published *A Course in Expository Writing*. Gertrude Buck also brought out *A Course in Argumentative Writing* (1899), another textbook, and *The Metaphor*, a philosophical treatise addressed to a scholarly audience. Her article "The Present Status of Rhetorical Theory" was published in 1900.

In *The Metaphor*, a revision of her dissertation, Buck outlines a theory of language that threads its way through her textbooks. She understands a metaphor not as a shortened form of the simile but rather as a stage before the process of abstraction and differentiation is completed in simile. The function of metaphor is not clarity but communication and stimulation: the audience experiences a release of tension when the writer or speaker struggling to express herself offers this articulated resemblance to bring form to what was before inchoate. In Buck's theory, language is social, and the audience, as well as the speaker or writer, has a vital role. It is not the writer alone who creates a metaphor, but the writer in concert with the audience. For Buck, language is in the process of evolutionary development for the entire society and for the individual speaker; understanding and therefore education are based on an evolutionary psychological model rather than a mechanistic one.

These principles of social purpose, psychological effect, and evolutionary development of language are also apparent in Buck's textbooks. In *A Course in Expository Writing*, Buck offers advice on the related forms of writing, description, and exposition. She bases this advice on several premises: that the basic purpose of all language is the firm and precise communication of ideas; that humans are all basically rational and, while unique in their experience, share a fund of commonsense knowledge based on experience; that learning a process is easier if broken down into manageable pieces; that expression, even in description and exposition, is a psychological process; and that the teacher must be a *real* audience who responds to the effects of the student's writing rather than merely condemning it.

In *A Course in Argumentative Writing*, Buck defines argument not as persuasion but as recreating in the mind of the hearer or reader "the train of thought or reasoning which has previously led you to this conclusion." Buck teaches strategies of argument in an order that she believes parallels human development: from less abstract sensory experience (induction) to abstracted, more differentiated experience (classification and deduction, analogy). Rhetoric supplements logic by considering the audience and thus introducing psychological responses into rhetoric, for the speaker must imaginatively put herself in the place of the person addressed. Buck further encourages a progressive pedagogy, recommending topics of direct interest to students, based on their experiences, and debate in class so that students collaboratively develop ideas and argumentative strategies for later written pieces.

Until the nineteenth century, women published their ideas about communication not in the handbook form of men's rhetoric but in dialogues, novels, essays, epistles, and conduct books. In the last quarter of the nineteenth century, for the first time, women write handbooks and textbooks of composition, rhetoric, and elocution—the same forms used by men. Much of what they write is a reworking of the rhetorical tradition. But they write for an audience that includes women, and they frequently include ideas and emphases from earlier works by women on conversation as a model for other discourse and collaboration between speaker and audience in the construction of meaning.

Defending Public Speaking

During the second half of the nineteenth century, women defended public speaking and wrote handbooks for their students more vigorously than in previous centuries, although this strand of rhetorical theory by women begins at least as early as Margaret Fell's treatise in support of women's preaching. Rhetorics that advocate public speaking for women, much more than the composition texts, are arguments for women's rights. Women can maintain the fiction in writing, even published writing, that they are not speaking publicly. This group of works defending women's public speaking is more diverse, including rhetorics aimed at the general population in support of women's preaching, at young working women, and at adult women in their own homes who wanted more knowledge about speaking and writing. Preaching, extended by sentimental culture into the broader area of morality, is the area in which women first won rights to public speaking and where most defenses of public speaking were mounted. By the end of the nineteenth century, this area was available to women, and women were nearly full citizens in oratorical culture, even though they had yet to win the right to vote.

In *Women's Speaking Justified* (1666), the Quaker Margaret Fell urges her Anglican audience to allow women to preach on the basis of scriptural authority. Especially troublesome for this religious society was Saint Paul's injunction against women speaking in church. Fell refutes interpretations of his teaching as forbidding all women to preach. She seems influenced by humanists in her comparative use of multiple translations of the Bible to establish interpretations of biblical passages and thus scriptural authority. She constructs a tradition of women's preaching through a self-conscious reinterpretation of the Bible, arguing that the conversations that women have with each other in the Bible about faith constitute preaching. She revises her contemporaries' understanding of the story of Eve to make the original woman a partner in human enterprises, including speaking, and she argues that the feminine imagery for the early church in the New Testament amounts to permission for women to become full preaching members of that church.

Born into a Methodist family, Phoebe Worrall Palmer inherited the inclusivity accorded women preachers in early Methodism. She became an important speaker at revival meetings, at first for women's audiences only but after 1839 for men, too, in Canada as well as the United States. In her long treatise, *The Promise of the Father* (1859), and her short pamphlet summary of it, *Tongue of Fire on the Daughters of the Lord* (1859),[29] Palmer refutes Paul's command against women's preaching by situating it historically. She cites many nineteenth-century Quaker and Methodist women who speak publicly and convert souls to Christianity, redefining preaching not as public oratory but as witnessing—telling the good news of the gospel. Although I do not include selections from her work, she is important as an influence on Frances Willard, whose argument for women's preaching is represented here.

The chapter entitled "Talking" in Jennie Fowler Willing's *The Potential Woman* (1881) is a combination of radicalized conduct book rhetoric for women and a defense of women's preaching. Jennie Willing was a Canadian who moved to Illinois with her parents. Self-educated, she grew up to be an ardent reformist and activist. Like many other nineteenth-century female speakers (such as Hallie Quinn Brown), Willing received training in public speaking at a Chautauqua. She helped found the WCTU (Women's Christian Temperance Union); was a board member of Evanston College for Ladies, where Frances Willard taught; was a professor of English at Illinois Wesleyan University, campaigned for suffrage for women, and was a licensed Methodist preacher who shared duties with her husband, also a minister. *The Potential Woman* is a handbook for young working women that offers practical guidance in various useful subjects: hygiene, economics, homemaking, and communication. In the first half of "Talking," Willing analyzes the misogyny that prevents women from learning how to participate in public discussion and speech making, argues for women's right to speak, recommends learning correct speech from grammars and dictionaries, and proposes lots of reading in order to enrich conversation. In the second half of the chapter, Willing argues for women's right to preach, citing passages in the Bible that support women's prophecy; refutes Paul's injunctions against women's speaking in church by a historical interpretation; gives examples of women who are both good mothers and noted preachers; and advises self-conscious study of public speaking as well as constant study of the Bible for female preachers.

Ironically, we probably owe Frances Willard's great defense of women's preaching to the actions of Jennie Willing's brother, who forbade women to conduct their own evening prayers when he took over as president of Northwestern University, which also housed Evanston College for Women, where Willard was dean of women. Willard founded the WCTU, participated in the campaign for women's suffrage, and helped develop effective techniques of social protest and public demonstration for women in the WCTU, as well as teaching members public speaking and parliamentary procedure.

Willard's *Woman in the Pulpit* (1889) is structured as a collaborative argument in favor of women's preaching. Two chapters summarize Willard's own arguments, the first refuting Paul's injunctions against women speaking in church (as historically necessary for a small group of women but not to be applied to women in general), the second supporting women's preaching by historical and biblical examples and by arguments that women's voices are physically competent with proper training; that preaching is particularly appropriate to women because of their natural moral leadership; that motherhood is not in conflict with spiritual guidance of others; and that God calls women as well as men to preach. But these two chapters are nestled in the middle of several others. Around her own arguments, Willard builds a communal structure suggesting a national republican citizenry in favor of women preaching: letters from twenty-one men and eleven women with their own arguments in favor of women's preaching. Willard prefaces her volume with several letters by famous male preachers encouraging women's preaching. In other chapters she includes men's letters and women's letters. She concludes her volume with a hostile refutation of her own argument (which was initially published in a journal) and then a male preacher's refutation of that hostile letter. She lets other voices speak along with hers and in so doing overcomes the competitiveness of argument that taxed feminist theorists, creating a collaborative structure, a community forum, in which consensus can ostensibly be reached.

Mary Augusta Jordan's *Correct Writing and Speaking* (1904) stands at the end of our tradition chronologically, but not logically. It could have been placed in a number of categories. Its passages on women's conversation and letter writing, as well as its publication in the Woman's Home Library Series, make it a candidate for inclusion with the nineteenth-century American conduct book rhetorics for women. Its summation of belletristic rhetoric combined with the new science of linguistics on the history of the English language, as well as the status of the author as a first-generation college woman who eventually becomes a professor at a women's college, suggests that it be considered a college composition textbook aimed at women who did not have the privilege of college education. Its explicit passages on public speaking for women inclined me to place it in this category, since few texts by women dealt with that topic earlier.

Jordan's general thesis also supports placing the book with handbooks of public speaking. In a book titled *Correct Writing and Speaking*, Jordan argues, against the current-traditional trend of masculine composition and rhetoric at the end of the nineteenth century, that there is no one correct standard English, and she uses all of canonical literature, as well as the new linguistics, to do so. Jordan nevertheless suggests that one can speak a better rather than a worse English by reading widely and carefully choosing models to imitate.

In the short section specifically on women's public speaking, Jordan comments on the idea that the age of public speaking is coming to an end and suggests that it is taking a new form. Rather than the powerful individual imposing his eloquent will on the community, Jordan sees American public speaking as a form in which the community organizes itself. "Community spirit" requires expression, often at a banquet but frequently with the real possibility of changing society for the better. The public speaker draws on "the reserve of sympathy and common living" that he or she shares with the audience. Women thus need training in public speaking as much as men but rarely receive it. Consequently, she suggests, women should seek out vocal training and should develop wider intelligence as well as feminine sympathy in order to be ready for the obligations of the communal orator that she envisions. Women do not need to feel immodest in roles of public leadership, then, since what is required of the public speaker is to help the audience interpret and know itself "in terms of something else than prejudice, or passion, or lazy self-indulgence." The public speaker must be, in fact, a spiritual leader, and women had long been arguing for the benefits of women's religious leadership. They must help preserve and direct the "spiritual energy" of the audience. Here Jordan reflects influence by the elocutionists, as well as the women activists of the nineteenth century.

Thus we see how the early defenses of women's preaching gradually broaden to take in all forms of women's public speaking: arguments by Fell, Palmer, and Willard for women's participation in religious persuasion lead to Willing's and Jordan's arguments for women's speaking in general. In making these arguments, these female theorists agree to reformulate preaching along the lines of conversation—personal testimony rather than public oration. They further continue the development in women's rhetorical theory of the emphasis on dialogic speech, meaning as collaboration between speaker and audience. Such theories are the ground on which women turn their rhetoric toward activism in the nineteenth century.

Connections to the Classical Tradition(s) of Men's Rhetoric

Although I have just separated out women's rhetorical theory to give a historical overview of it, women's theory was not separate from the dominant discourse of men's rhetorical theory and pedagogy. Women, like men, were teachers of rulers because of their schooling in rhetoric and their success as rhetorical theorists. Not only Aristotle and Quintilian, but also Pan Chao, Christine de Pizan, and Hannah More taught rulers or wrote handbooks dedicated to princes: Aristotle taught Alexander; Quintilian and Pan Chao held remarkably similar posts at imperial courts; Christine de Pizan, like Erasmus, wrote on the education of the Christian prince and did not leave out rhetoric; and Hannah More dedicated a treatise on women's education to her monarch's daughter.

A comparison of Pan Chao and the Roman rhetorician Quintilian is instructive. Roughly contemporary in the first century, Quintilian and Pan Chao both taught eloquence, and both were eventually supported by imperial posts at the court of their emperors (although Pan Chao was not allowed to take the title for the post because she was a woman). Both had an influence on education that extended at least to the eighteenth century. Although Quintilian's system formed a model for much of late Roman and early modern European education for boys, Pan Chao's modest goal of more literate education for women, though discussed, was not adopted until the eighteenth century in China. They share a similar emphasis on the development of moral character through education, but the traits Quintilian attributes to the good man speaking well are very different from those that Pan Chao advocates for the respectable woman making herself agreeable.

A crucial difference thus results from the differences in material and social conditions among men and women in Rome and China. Quintilian's theory explores the rhetoric that the Roman man will use in public places, especially the law court, while Pan Chao's theory explores the rhetoric that the Chinese woman will use in private, since she is excluded from most public roles. Quintilian gives advice on how to persuade large groups, while Pan Chao gives advice on how to get along in a domestic situation. Indeed, Quintilian says that "there would be no such thing as eloquence, if we spoke only with one person at a time" (I:55; I.ii.33). Pan Chao, on the other hand, concentrates on the eloquence necessary to such intimate conversations, especially for a daughter-in-law living with an extended family dominated by the mother-in-law, but including sisters-in-law and other relatives, as well as the husband. When we compare Pan Chao and Quintilian, one outside and one a mainstay of the classical tradition, we discover that *both* adapt their theories to their gender and to their cultural institutions.

Michel de Certeau has argued that one cultural reading practice followed by subordinate groups is "poaching," stealing from the dominant culture, but making what one takes more suitable nourishment for oneself.[30] According to de Certeau, few readers are passive consumers. Many of the women who write rhetorical theory seem to have this relationship of "poacher" to the canonical male philosophers and rhetoricians of their cultures. Aspasia was a sophist who was influenced by male sophists. Her suggestion that epideictic praise follow the order of birth, education, and achievements was taught by other sophists and had earlier origins. Pan Chao's emphasis on the silence, harmony, and subservience of wifely speech echoes Confucian theories that some historians of rhetoric maintain are a basis for an early Chinese rhetoric. But both Aspasia and Pan Chao use that very knowledge borrowed from a masculine tradition to argue against its exclusion of women—Aspasia in the fragment of philosophical debate where she interrogates the nameless wife (reported in Cicero), and Pan Chao in her argument that women must receive as much education as men in order better to serve men.

De Scudéry adapts ideas from Aristotle, Quintilian, and especially the sophists to salon conversation, where women wielded power. In her free translation of concepts from the classical masculine tradition of public speaking to a rhetoric of Renaissance French salon conversation for men and women, de Scudéry seems most influenced by Aristotle's division of sophistries into mistakes of words and matter, and the sophists' emphases on the civilizing power of speech and *kairos*—timeliness and decorum. Cavendish and Astell, in very different ways, adapt contemporary empiricist ideas to their conceptions of speech. Cavendish argues for a simplified version of John Locke's idea of the mind as a tabula rasa (blank tablet) on which experience writes ideas, an epistemology that forms the basis for later empiricist rhetoric by men. But she adapts this theory to the exploration of women's supposed inferiority, questioning that ideology. Astell cites the Port-Royal logic and rhetoric of her French male contemporaries. But Astell is also highly influenced by the nonempiricist Augustine, especially by his Platonic conviction of the power of truth in itself to be persuasive. Still, neither the Port-Royal rhetoricians nor Augustine use conversation in the manner of Astell—as a model for all communication, the writer as friend speaking to the reader as neighbor.

In the late eighteenth and early nineteenth centuries, women are influenced by men's theories in a more negative way. As women such as Hannah More, Lydia Sigourney, and Eliza Farrar begin writing conduct books for women, they adapt the tradition to their own aspirations, but they cannot entirely escape the rigid constraints on women that are part of the rhetorical form they have chosen. Conduct books by men, as far back as the late Middle Ages and the Renaissance, warn sternly against women's speech and education, suggesting that women's best virtues are chastity, silence, and obedience. Requiring women to be silent leaves little room for them to speak or even write. More, Sigourney, and Farrar resist the genre they are taking over by requiring education for women, as well as training in conversation and letter writing. But they also are influenced by the genre in the many negative prescriptions they advance for women's speech: women must not talk too much; they must never gossip; they must not exaggerate or flatter; they must not parade their knowledge. Felicitously, however, this framework also allows these conduct book theorists to develop a crucial aspect of conversation theory: the role of the listener. If women must generally be silent, they can be influential as good listeners who support intellectual and moral discussion by their attentiveness and silent encouragement.

In both conduct book rhetoric and elocution, women take advantage of ideas of the psychology of sympathy, developed by male philosophers in the eighteenth century and adapted to rhetoric by George Campbell. Sympathy, for Sigourney and Farrar, gives special importance to women's role in conversation. Sympathy, according to elocutionists such as Brown and Morgan, creates a bond between speaker and audience, even in the delivery of others' words.

Once women begin writing textbooks for normal schools and colleges, men continue to influence women's theories, even as women transform men's theories to their own purposes. Hallie Quinn Brown frequently cites her debt to Delsarte as she adapts his elocution of theater and parlor entertainment to her different purposes of black preaching and activist performance for mixed audiences. Lockwood's synthesis of classical and belletristic rhetoric is characteristic of the nineteenth-century men's rhetorics and composition textbooks that Nan Johnson has studied in her history of American rhetoric.[31] Gertrude Buck was strongly influenced by Fred Newton Scott, also a composition theorist, but she seems more his partner than the passive receiver some histories of rhetoric imply (a point made by JoAnn Campbell).[32] And Mary Augusta Jordan synthesizes William James's and John Dewey's new developmental psychology with traditional masculine belletristic literary rhetoric, and further combines them with the scientific analysis of speech in the new linguistics. Jordan also draws on the nineteenth-century tradition of conduct book rhetoric by women. All these women were probably more influenced by the theory of the masculine classical tradition than by any female precursors or contemporaries. But all these women also adapted (or subverted) this tradition to women's uses.

Not all the women included in this volume were predominantly influenced by men. By the nineteenth century there is a strong sense that women need speaking and writing skills that differ from men's, and there existed a theory of separate gendered spheres of influence that supported such a move. Lydia Sigourney and Eliza Farrar might be said to be much more influenced by More and Edgeworth than by men of the classical tradition, even when their ideas at times echo that masculine tradition. Frances Willard may very well have been more influenced by Quaker women's claims for women's right to preach than by any part of the masculine sermon rhetoric tradition.

In addition, all these women differed from men in one crucial aspect: their sense that they needed to defend themselves for asking to speak and write for a public audience. Especially important here was the biblical pronouncement by Paul that women should not speak in church: "Let you women keep silence in the churches: for it is not permitted unto them to speak; but they are commanded to be under obedience, as also saith the law. And if they will learn anything, let them ask their husbands at home: for it is a shame for women to speak in the church" (1 Timothy 2:11–12, King James Version). Since so many of these women were devout Christians, this passage and the masculinist ideology it supported in church and society posed a considerable obstacle to women's right to speak in public, or even to their education in rhetoric.

From the seventeenth century on, however, there was a lively tradition of refuting Paul. Women latched onto the humanist techniques of biblical interpretation that argued for reading the Bible literally only when that is the most appropriate reading. Otherwise, biblical words must be read metaphorically, or with consciousness of the historical context. Margaret Fell, in her refutation of Paul's dicta, does both. She argues that here, as elsewhere in the Bible, "women" is a metaphor meaning the church in general, or at least those churchgoers who had not studied enough and not yet received "the light." She further argues that Paul was speaking historically to a particularly troublesome group of women who needed this particular regulation. Elsewhere Paul welcomes women into the church, praising Lois and Eunice for their teaching of Timothy, and promising all Christians that their sons and daughters will prophesy. In "The Letter Killeth," the first chapter of *Woman in the Pulpit*, Frances Willard attacks a literalist reading of the Bible in general, seeing it as serving the status quo in an un-Christian way. She claims that the New Testament legitimates women's public speaking in support of the church in over forty passages and denies it in only two, the two most often quoted. Jennie Willing inveighs against "false literalism" and argues quite firmly that Paul's injunction was only for that place and that time, and not beyond. She feels that the inner call to preach for selected women vastly outweighs the injunction of Paul, especially considering the number of women called to Christian service recorded in the Bible.

But even women who are not arguing for preaching feel called to acknowledge Paul's restrictions. Astell points out that women must not preach but then suggests that preaching is not the most effective way to persuade someone to Christianity—catechism (one-on-one discussion, study, and examination) is more persuasive. Hannah More reads Paul and social strictures more literally, acknowledges women's inferiority, and suggests that their religious role must lie in conversation and silent support. However, More is also one of the founders of the radical Sunday school movement that frequently was in trouble for allowing women to read the Bible and expound scripture to children and working-class adults.

Connections to the History of Feminism

Feminism and rhetorical theory by women sometimes run in the same channel and sometimes diverge into separate strands. What qualifies as "feminist" depends on the culture and era. In general, I term anyone from the seventeenth century and earlier arguing for women's education as "feminist," with the understanding that the word "feminist" was not used before the nineteenth century. During the eighteenth century, marriage reform is the touchstone of the "feminist" (along with continued demands for education). And it is not until the nineteenth century that women who may be called "feminist" begin to concentrate on demands for property rights and suffrage.

Not all feminist writers wrote rhetorical theory, and not every female rhetorical theorist was a feminist. Pan Chao's *Lessons for Women*, from first-century China, might be called the first work of feminist theory, as well as the first work of rhetorical theory by women, because she not only argues for formal education for women but also makes suggestions for a theory of domestic communication for women. Although Pan Chao constructs a place in which women can speak, that place is confined to the family, and the role she gives women is the gendered one of obedient servant and peacemaker.

After Pan Chao, however, the strands of feminist theory and rhetorical theory by women diverge. Sei Shonagon, from tenth-century Japan, writes rhetorical theory but does not challenge the mores of her day. She was born into a culture and a class that valued education for women and encouraged her to develop communication skills and to comment on the strategies and aesthetics of letter writing, preaching, and conversation. Even Christine de Pizan keeps her rhetorical theory and her feminist theory mostly in separate places. She hardly comments on communication by women in *The City of Ladies* or *The Treasure of the City of Ladies* but defends women's virtue and abilities to reason and govern. She discusses princes' and merchants' eloquence in *The Book of the Body Politic* but hardly mentions women.

A history of feminist theory remains to be written. Feminists haven't yet sorted out what to do with the early defenses of women. From the late Middle Ages until at least the eighteenth century, there were numerous popular pamphlets and treatises that either blamed or praised women, called the *querelle des femmes* on the Continent and the "pamphlet controversy about women" in England. It is not clear whether or not we should call "feminist" these works, by Christine de Pizan, Jane Anger, Rachel Speght, and many others, usually written to counter misogynist tracts blaming women and to defend women as virtuous and as equal or superior to men. These treatises in the pamphlet controversy seem "feminist" in their countering of misogyny but conservative in their essentialist defenses of women as superior to men, and their celebration of traditional virtues, especially chastity, in women. The rhetorical treatises by women often share with these pamphlet defenses of women the celebration of women's traditional virtues of modesty and silence but less often assume an essentialist view of gender (since they recognize that changing the education of women will change their gender roles considerably). The treatises arguing for women's rhetorical theory seem to form a strand that is separate from the early defenses of women, except for Bathsua Makin's, in which the long catalogues of women who were excellent rhetoricians or logicians imitate the long catalogues in the pamphlet controversy of women who were virtuous or famous.

In seventeenth-century Europe, feminist theory and rhetorical theory run in the same channel: defenses of the rhetorical education of women and of women's rights to speak, especially to preach. Margaret Cavendish, Bathsua Makin, Madeleine de Scudéry, and Mary Astell all defend women's right to a humanist education that includes rhetoric, and all develop complex theories about communication that include women's participation. Margaret Fell, who does not explicitly make an argument for women's education in humanist knowledge and rhetoric, does demonstrate remarkable knowledge of the Bible and argues for women's right to preach.

In the eighteenth century, when "feminist" writers are calling for marriage reform as well as education for women, rhetorical theory and feminist theory run in separate channels again. At the end of the century, Mary Wollstonecraft does not theorize rhetoric or communication for women in her *Thoughts on the Education of Daughters* (1787), offering only a paragraph against women's gossip, a paragraph against taking dress as a topic of conversation, and a page on writing for mainly functional reasons. Indeed, Wollstonecraft expresses ambivalence about the value of extended education for women of some classes, who will marry husbands who feel anxiety about learned women. Yet Wollstonecraft's *A Vindication of the Rights of Woman* (1792) is a feminist classic. Hannah More, who is not "feminist" in sentiments or goals, expresses antipathy for Wollstonecraft in many of her writings and yet develops an elaborate argument for women's education in many treatises, and a full rhetorical curriculum for the girls she teaches and addresses. This condemnation of Wollstonecraft continues through much of the early conduct book rhetoric, including that by Lydia Sigourney and Eliza Farrar.

The nineteenth century saw the full politicization of women, and the development of a movement by women who called themselves "feminist." Women organized to claim citizenship rights, property rights, and the vote, as well as to support national causes such as abolition, Native American rights, humane treatment of the insane, and laws against the sale and consumption of alcohol. In the second half of the nineteenth century, feminism and rhetorical theory by women again merge and overlap. Jennie Willing and Frances Willard are WCTU activists who teach women public speaking and parliamentary procedure as part of their grass-roots organization program to make the sale and consumption of alcohol illegal. Both are also feminists, campaigning for the right of women to vote, and both are involved in the formal education of women in rhetoric at college level. Finally, both write eloquent defenses of women's preaching. Hallie Quinn Brown was a self-named feminist, an ardent activist for civil rights causes, and also an elocutionist who addressed an international audience in her speaking tours and performed abolitionist as well as literary readings. In addition, Brown taught elocution at Wilberforce College and wrote textbooks for her students. Gertrude Buck, too, was a feminist who campaigned for the vote for women and published many textbooks. This integration of feminism and rhetorical theory for women is quite understandable in the second half of the nineteenth century, when women have at last begun to use public speaking to promote campaigns for women's rights.

But let's stop and reconsider. In this history of the relationship of feminism and rhetorical theory, I have carefully separated out women whose theories and politics outside their theories did not fit the current leading edge of feminism. It is useful to remind ourselves that not every woman who worked in women's education was a feminist. Mary Augusta Jordan wrote against women's suffrage, for instance. Still, before 1900, women's education was a feminist issue. Would it be better to conceive of this history as two strands of feminist thought, one concentrating on the promotion of education for women, including rhetoric, the other branching out into other issues from the eighteenth century on? Perhaps some of you will think that it is better to call both of these sets of writings "feminist," and to think of the differences between "feminists" and women who write rhetorical theory as debates within the course of feminism.

Finding a Voice

As diverse as theories of communication by women may be, women's theories seem to differ from men's in one central aspect: most take conversation rather than public speaking as a model, seeing all communication as collaborative or dialogic. This makes sense, since all these women were restricted to a domestic sphere different from men's by their culture.

Elizabeth Minnich, in a groundbreaking essay, criticized the rhetorical tradition of liberal arts as a tradition that defined what was "manly" and excluded women. Aristotle, she reminds us, not only wrote the first extended, organized treatise on rhetorical theory in the West, but also justified slavery and argued that women are by nature inferior. Minnich comments, "Given the influence of Socrates, it is fascinating that rhetoric became an art, a liberal art, but conversation did not. It seems always to have been considered both too trivial and too dangerous (sort of like women). . . . Conversation remains a largely private art; we do not have a tradition of teaching it. . . . [Conversation is an] exchange between people that actively involves both . . . [so that] each speaker takes the other into account, asking questions, seeking words and ways to speak that can be heard by the other, listening with as much seriousness as speaking."[33] This anthology shows that women before Minnich recognized the neglect of conversation in the rhetorical tradition and added their own theories explaining it.

We have seen how Pan Chao developed a theory of communication adapted to the ancient Chinese household, in which a wife must create social relationships with her sisters-in-law, mother-in-law, and husband. She must harmonize in her conversation with many others. We have seen how Sei Shonagon described elegant conversation in her journal as a guide for herself and for others at the court of tenth-century Japan, giving an equal place to women in valuing aesthetic appreciation, as well as wit and gossip in speech. In seventeenth-century France, Madeleine de Scudéry devoted several dialogue essays to conversation and helped to establish this form as an important instrument of social and moral influence for both men and women.

While Hannah More followed de Scudéry in emphasizing the importance of conversation, she severely restricted the role that women could play. In the process, however, she theorized in new ways the possible faults of conversation (like the faults of spoken and written composition that men's rhetoric had long employed), and developed guidelines for good listening skills. In the nineteenth century Lydia Sigourney, Eliza Farrar, and Mary Augusta Jordan followed More in discussing conversation and developing it as an art of communication especially important for women, who might collaborate to employ its influence when they lacked other means of political or social power. Furthermore, they sentimentalized the art, linking it to women's role as guardian of home and morals. Midcentury activist Jennie Willing radicalized this conduct book rhetoric of conversation for women by disputing the role of good listener as flattery and offering women the nobler role of preacher. As Karlyn Kohrs Campbell pointed out, all rhetorical genres were gendered masculine initially because women were not allowed to speak publicly, and rhetorical theory initially covered only public genres.[34] All of these women are important to the history of rhetoric because in our time rhetoricians and linguists have acknowledged conversation as a vital communication skill and dialogue as a basis for rhetoric and pedagogy, and we need to know what their forerunners had already developed as guidelines.

Women taught and theorized conversation as an art. But women who wrote rhetorical theory also used conversation as a model for other forms of communication and thus anticipated modern theories of composition in important ways. The use of conversation as a model is central to Margaret Fell's defense of women preaching, *Women's Speaking Justified*. Fell is able to create a scriptural tradition of women preaching only because of her redefinition of preaching as conversation—testimony, prophecy, and advice, rather than public lecture. In the Quaker institution of the Meeting, preaching is reconceived as sharing rather than lecturing, in private rather than public space. Fell, however, sees a further connection to women's lived experience: most of her examples concern what later Protestants call "witnessing," women talking to their friends and families about the spiritual events in their lives. Fell's contribution to sermon rhetoric, then, depends not only on her inclusion of women but also her use of conversation as a model for speech. Using the Bible as the authority for women's preaching, she must also redefine "preaching" to include advice and comfort spoken privately.

Many women in this anthology take conversation as a model for all communication, allowing us to identify this as characteristic of women's theory. Sei Shonagon's theories and Japanese culture of her time took letter writing as an extension of daily conversation and gift exchange. Madeleine de Scudéry tells us that letters of gallantry between friends of the opposite sex should be "a conversation between absent persons." Mary Astell suggests that good writing occurs when the writer as "friend" addresses the reader as "neighbor." In the preface to *Bits and Odds*, Hallie Quinn Brown tells her pupils that their goal must be to learn "varieties of natural expression." Gertrude Buck uses oral debate as a prewriting exercise for her college students. Again and again in these treatises, the good speaker writes as she speaks.

These theorists do not mean public speaking, but the natural and spontaneous easiness of daily conversation.

What does this emphasis on conversation, collaboration, and dialogue add to our conception of rhetoric? Both Cicero, at the center of the masculine European rhetorical tradition, and Madeleine de Scudéry, on its margins, celebrate the civilizing power of speech. Following the Greek sophists, Cicero represents language as the force that led humanity out of the wilderness into civilization, a political force through public speech that allowed peoples to make laws for themselves. Adapting Cicero to salon conversation and seventeenth-century France, Madeleine de Scudéry represents language as the bond that holds society together, not through public speaking but through the conversation that educates and plants morality daily in ordinary people. In eighteenth-century England, George Campbell sees public speaking and writing, especially preaching, at the center of rhetoric and outlines many ways that speakers (who are superior in education to their listeners) may manipulate their mass audience through the mechanics of human psychology. A contemporary of Campbell, Hannah More, despite her conservatism, at the center of rhetoric places conversation, skills of listening and sharing ideas, where the listener is equal to or sometimes even superior to the speaker. As a group, then, women theorists bring a model of communication based on conversation, collaboration, and dialogue to our understanding of the history of rhetoric. Even when women develop a theory of public speaking for women, the model of conversation for speech remains. In *Elocution and Physical Culture* Hallie Quinn Brown warns her students that they must be "as earnest and sincere upon the platform as we are in private conversation," and even in public recitation the reader must "speak to the individual, not to the multitude." Mary Augusta Jordan warns her students not to manipulate their audience: "The audience is not to be dominated, cajoled, or bullied," Jordan insists. "It is to be interpreted, and made to know its own self in terms of something else than prejudice, or passion, or lazy self-indulgence." Thus the speaker for Jordan is less a manipulator than a facilitator, in dialogue with her audience. This conception of conversation as a model for all communication is important because our current theories of communication, especially with the advent of radio, television, and video, often depend on such a model. Today we are in conversation with many parts of the globe.

Notes

1. Karlyn Kohrs Campbell, ed., *Man Cannot Speak for Her*, 2 vols., Contributions to Women's Studies, no. 101 (New York: Greenwood Press, 1989); Carole Levin and Patricia A. Sullivan, eds., *Political Rhetoric, Power, and Renaissance Women* (Albany: State University of New York Press, 1995); Andrea Lunsford, ed., *Reclaiming Rhetorica: Women in the Rhetorical Tradition* (Pittsburgh: University of Pittsburgh Press, 1995); Molly Wertheimer, ed., *Listening to Their Voices: Essays on the Rhetorical Activities of Historical Women* (Columbia: University of South Carolina Press, 1997); Christine Mason Sutherland and Rebecca Sutcliffe, eds., *The Changing Tradition: Women in the History of Rhetoric* (Calgary: University of Calgary Press, 1999); Cheryl Glenn, *Rhetoric Retold: Regendering the Tradition from Antiquity through the Renaissance* (Carbondale: Southern Illinois University Press, 1997); Catherine Hobbs, ed., *Nineteenth-Century Women Learn to Write* (Charlottesville: University Press of Virginia, 1995); Lucille M. Schultz, *The Young Composers: Composition's Beginnings in Nineteenth-Century Schools* (Carbondale: Southern Illinois University Press, 1999); Shirley Logan, ed., *With Pen and Voice: A Critical Anthology of Nineteenth-Century African-American Women* (Carbondale: Southern Illinois University Press, 1995); Logan, "We Are Com-

ing": The Persuasive Discourse of Nineteenth-Century Black Women (Carbondale: Southern Illinois University Press, 1999); Carla Peterson, *"Doers of the Word": African-American Women Speakers and Writers in the North (1830-1880)* (New York: Oxford University Press, 1995); Jacqueline Jones Royster, *Traces of a Stream: Literacy and Social Change Among African American Women* (Pittsburgh: University of Pittsburgh Press, 2000); Nan Johnson, "Reigning in the Court of Silence: Women and Rhetorical Space in Postbellum America," *Philosophy and Rhetoric* 33, no. 3 (2000): 221–43; Carol Mattingly, *Well-Tempered Women: Nineteenth-Century Temperance Rhetoric* (Carbondale: Southern Illinois University Press, 1998); Susan Kates, *Activist Rhetorics and American Higher Education, 1885–1937* (Carbondale: Southern Illinois University Press, 2001); Patricia Bizzell and Bruce Herzberg, eds., *The Rhetorical Tradition: Readings from Classical Times to the Present*, 2d ed. (Boston: St. Martin's Press, 2001).

2. Cicero, *De Oratore*, ed. E. W. Sutton and H. Rackham (1942; reprint, Cambridge, Mass.: Harvard University Press, 1967), I.viii.30 (my translation).

3. Chaim Perelman, "Rhetoric and Philosophy," *Philosophy and Rhetoric* 1 (1968): 15.

4. Aristotle, *Aristotle on Rhetoric: A Theory of Civic Discourse*, trans. George A. Kennedy (New York: Oxford University Press, 1991), 35.

5. Quintilian, *Institutio Oratoria*, ed. H. E. Butler (1920; reprint, Cambridge, Mass.: Harvard University Press, 1969), II.xi.34 (my translation).

6. Kenneth Burke, *A Rhetoric of Motives* (Berkeley: University of California Press, 1969), 19–23; Lloyd Bitzer, "The Rhetorical Situation," *Philosophy and Rhetoric* 1 (1968): 1–14.

7. James J. Murphy, "Conducting Research in the History of Rhetoric: An Open Letter to a Future Historian of Rhetoric," in *Publishing in Rhetoric and Composition*, ed. Gary A. Olson and Todd W. Taylor (Albany: State University of New York Press, 1997), 188.

8. George Kennedy, *Classical Rhetoric and Its Christian and Secular Tradition from Ancient to Modern Times* (Chapel Hill: University of North Carolina Press, 1980), 7.

9. George Kennedy, *Comparative Rhetoric: An Historical and Cross-Cultural Introduction* (New York: Oxford University Press, 1998), 3.

10. James A. Berlin, "Revisionary History: The Dialectical Method," in *Rethinking the History of Rhetoric: Multidisciplinary Essays on the Rhetorical Tradition*, ed. Takis Poulakos (Boulder: Westview Press, 1993), 142.

11. Patricia Bizzell, "Opportunities for Feminist Research in the History of Rhetoric," *Rhetoric Review* 11, no. 1 (Fall 1992): 51.

12. Robert J. Connors, "Women's Reclamation of Rhetoric in Nineteenth-Century America," in *Feminine Principles and Women's Experience in American Composition and Rhetoric*, ed. Louise Wetherbee Phelps and Janet Emig (Pittsburgh: University of Pittsburgh Press, 1995), 71.

13. John Schilb, "The History of Rhetoric and the Rhetoric of History," *Pre/Text* 7, nos. 1–2 (1986): 12.

14. Carole Blair, "Contested Histories of Rhetoric: The Politics of Preservation, Progress, and Change," *Quarterly Journal of Speech* 78, no. 4 (November 1992): 403.

15. Susan Jarratt, "Speaking to the Past: Feminist Historiography in Rhetoric," *Pre/Text* 11, nos. 3–4 (1990): 198–201.

16. Carole Spitzack and Kathryn Carter, "Women in Communication Studies: A Typology for Revision," *Quarterly Journal of Speech* 73, no. 4 (November 1987): 405; and Barbara Biesecker, "Coming to Terms with Recent Attempts to Write Women into the History of Rhetoric," *Philosophy and Rhetoric* 25, no. 2 (1992): 144. In her essay, Barbara Biesecker also attacks Karlyn Kohrs Campbell's anthologies of women's rhetoric for choosing to celebrate the individual rather than collective rhetorical practices. Although I see how one can write a history avoiding the dangers of individualism (Shirley Logan, Carla Peterson, Susan Kates, and Carol Mattingly have recently done so), I don't see how an anthology, by definition a collection of writings attributed, in Western culture and Eastern, to specific authors, can do so. Despite its focus on individuals at the expense of collective groups, anthologies enable us to look at otherwise inaccessible texts for ourselves. Otherwise we have to take the word of the historian—another individual author.

17. See also Berlin, "Revisionary History," 136.

18. See Jacqueline Jones Royster and Jean C. Williams, "History in the Spaces Left," *College Composition and Communication* 50, no. 4 (1999): 563–84.

19. John Schilb, "Future Historiographies of Rhetoric and the Present Age of Anxiety," in *Writing Histories of Rhetoric*, ed. Victor Vitanza (Carbondale: Southern Illinois University Press, 1994), 131.

20. Linda Nicholson, "Interpreting Gender," *Signs* 20, no. 1 (1994): 99–100.

21. When I quote a text in the introductions that are included in the anthology, the version I quote is the one used in the anthology. On Aspasia, see Madeleine Henry, *Prisoner of History: Aspasia of Miletus and Her Biographical Tradition* (New York: Oxford University Press, 1995); and Cheryl Glenn, "sex, lies, and manuscript: Refiguring Aspasia in the History of Rhetoric," *College Composition and Communication* 45, no. 2 (May 1994): 180–99.

22. See Henry, *Prisoner*; and E. F. Bloedow, "Aspasia and the 'Mystery' of the *Menexenos*," *Wiener Studien*, n.s. 9 (1975): 32–48.

23. Guy Cromwell Field, "Aristippus," in *The Oxford Classical Dictionary*, ed. N. G. L. Hammond and H. H. Scullard, 2d ed. (1970; reprint, Oxford: Clarendon Press, 1976), 111.

24. Eunapius, *Lives of the Philosophers and Sophists*, trans. W. C. Wright (1921; reprint; Cambridge, Mass.: Harvard University Press, 1961), 411–19.

25. On Pan Chao, see Nancy Lee Swann, *Pan Chao: Foremost Woman Scholar of China, First Century A.D.* (1932; New York: Russell & Russell, 1968).

26. Bizzell and Herzberg, *Rhetorical Tradition*, 488–93; Jenny R. Redfern, "Christine de Pisan and *The Treasure of the City of Ladies*," in *Reclaiming Rhetorica: Women in the Rhetorical Tradition*, ed. Andrea Lunsford (Pittsburgh: University of Pittsburgh Press, 1995), 73–92.

27. Suzanne W. Hull, *Chaste, Silent, and Obedient: English Books for Women 1475–1640* (San Marino, Calif.: Huntington Publications, 1982, 1988).

28. Florence Hartley, *The Ladies Book of Etiquette and Manual of Politeness* (Boston: Lee & Shepard, 1870).

29. Phoebe Palmer, *Promise of the Father* (1859; reprint, New York: Garland, 1985); and Palmer, *Tongue of Fire on the Daughters of the Lord* (1859), in *Phoebe Palmer: Selected Writings*, ed. Thomas Oden (Mahwah, N.J.: Paulist Press, 1988), 35–57.

30. Michel de Certeau, "Reading as Poaching," in *The Practice of Everyday Life*, trans. Steven F. Randall (Berkeley: University of California Press, 1984), 165–76.

31. Nan Johnson, *Nineteenth-Century Rhetoric in North America* (Carbondale: Southern Illinois University Press, 1991).

32. Joann Campbell, ed., *Toward a Feminist Rhetoric: The Writing of Gertrude Buck* (Pittsburgh: University of Pittsburgh Press, 1996).

33. Elizabeth Kamarck Minnich, "A Feminist Critique of the Liberal Arts," in *Liberal Education and the New Scholarship on Women: Issues and Constraints in Institutional Change*, Report of the Wingspread Conference (Washington, D.C.: Association of American Colleges, 1981), 26.

34. Karlyn Kohrs Campbell, "Gender and Genre: Loci of Invention and Contradiction in the Earliest Speeches by U.S. Women," *Quarterly Journal of Speech* 81, no. 4 (November 1995): 479.

Aspasia

Fifth century B.C.E.

Aspasia was born sometime after 470 B.C.E. in Miletus, a colony or ally of Greece in Asia Minor. She came to Athens about 450 B.C.E. and was perhaps the younger sister of the wife of an Athenian citizen, Alcibiades, who had spent exile in Miletus and was grandfather of the notorious Alcibiades. Thus Aspasia was in Athens a *metic*, a resident alien, whose children were denied citizenship. She was perhaps a teacher of rhetoric in Athens, and her house seems to have been a place where philosophers, poets, and artists met to discuss intellectual issues. She may have been a courtesan. Aspasia lived with Pericles after he divorced his Greek wife. Most probably she was his *pallake*, or concubine, and biographers assume that Pericles Jr. was Aspasia's son. After his two sons by his first wife died, Pericles successfully appealed to the assembly to have Pericles Jr. granted citizenship and status as his heir. Aspasia has been praised as a partner in Pericles's great speeches, as well as in his political ambitions and artistic patronage in Athens. Consequently, she was a favorite target of the comic poets. She may have been prosecuted for impiety by the comic poet Hermippus and defended by Pericles (since women were not allowed to speak on their own behalf in Greek courts), or this episode may only have been dramatic fantasy. After Pericles's death in 429 B.C.E., Aspasia married (or, more probably, was contracted as concubine) to Lysicles and is supposed to have had a son by him. Her son by Pericles became an Athenian general and was executed after the battle of Arginusae. A figure on the margins of Greek society because of her Milesian origins, Aspasia moved to the center in the sophistic reconstruction of society under Pericles. Indeed, her ethnicity and her gender seem to have cancelled out each other: her gender made her less dangerous as a foreigner than a man would have been, and her foreign birth placed her outside some of the rigid restrictions on Greek aristocratic women.

Aspasia's teaching of rhetoric is discussed in Plato, Plutarch, Cicero, Quintilian, and in lost dialogues by Aeschines Socraticus and Antisthenes. In Plato's *Menexenus*, which is excerpted here, Socrates and Menexenus discuss Athenian funeral orations, Socrates joking about the emotional effect of the inflated rhetoric: "every time I listen fascinated I am exalted and imagine myself to have become all at once taller and nobler and more handsome." As an example that "it is no difficult matter to win credit as a fine speaker" when "a man makes his effort in the presence of the very men whom he is praising," Socrates offers to repeat an oration that Aspasia taught him. The oration, in praise of the men who have died in battle in the service of Athens, examines in great detail the mythic and recent history of Athens, inflating the accomplishments and revising the motives so that they appear in their best light. The final section is a moving appeal to living citizens to emulate their fallen heroes. It is impossible for Aspasia or Socrates to have composed the entire speech because it treats history that neither could have known. Perhaps none of the speech was composed by Aspasia, since Menexenus twice makes a point of suggesting that Socrates is really the author, and because throughout the speech Athenians are praised for their racial purity as Greeks, whereas Aspasia as a Milesian was initially denied citizenship for her son. Some readers, following the lead of Menexenus, dismiss the possibility of Aspasia's writing speeches at all: "Aspasia . . . deserves to be congratulated if she is really capable of composing a speech like that, woman though she is." Other readers argue that Plato wrote the speech to parody and attack the sophists' rhetoric and teachings, in much the same way that he included the speech by Lysias in the *Phaedrus*, and that he chose Aspasia because she was "one of the chief architects of that rhetoric" (Bloedow 48, Glenn passim). Plutarch, who criticizes Pericles for allowing Aspasia to influence him, nevertheless argues that "in the *Menexenus* of Plato, even though the first part of it be written in a sportive vein, there is, at any rate, thus much fact, that the woman had the reputation of associating with many Athenians as a teacher of rhetoric" (71; xxiv.4).

Along with the negative portrait of Aspasia in the *Menexenus* survives a positive one recorded by Cicero and Quintilian. They quote the lost dialogue of Aeschines, apparently one that showed Aspasia operating in the role of the Socratic philosopher, questioning a woman about the good life. Cicero (but not Quintilian) then continues the anecdote with Aspasia questioning Xenophon along parallel lines (reprinted in this volume). Especially significant is Aspasia's inclusion of the woman in her theorizing, Aspasia's addressing herself to another woman as her audience. As Cheryl Glenn points out, we know Aspasia only from "fragments and references in the works of male authors" (Glenn 182). But we do have this astonishing account that suggests that under an extremely repressive gender system allowing Athenian wives no education beyond domestic matters and little travel beyond the domicile, Aspasia created a place where she could discuss the good life not only with men, but also with other upper-class women, where she presumably, from many accounts, also taught her theory of sophistic rhetoric. I include this material by male writers about Aspasia because we have no early surviving treatises by women, because the advice on rhetoric that Aspasia gives in the speech attributed to her may very well have been what she taught (even if the speech is not hers), and because Aspasia has become too important a figure in feminist scholarship on the history of rhetoric to leave out.

For further information, see E. F. Bloedow, "Aspasia and the 'Mystery' of the *Menexenus*," *Wiener Studien*, n.s. 9 (1975): 32–48; Theodore Cadoux, "Aspasia," in *The Oxford Classical Dictionary*, ed. N. G. L. Hammond and H. H. Scullard, 2d ed. (1970; reprint, Oxford: Clarendon Press, 1976), 131–32; Cheryl Glenn, "sex, lies, and manuscript: Refiguring Aspasia in the History of Rhetoric," *CCC: College Composition and Communication* 45, no. 2 (May 1994): 180–99; Madeleine Henry, *Prisoner of History: Aspasia of Miletus and Her Biographical Tradition* (New York: Oxford University Press, 1995); Susan Jarratt and Rory Ong, "Aspasia: Rhetoric, Gender, and Colonial Identity," in *Reclaiming Rhetorica: Women in the Rhetorical Tradition*, ed. Andrea A. Lunsford (Pittsburgh: University of Pittsburgh Press, 1995), 9–24; George Kennedy, *The Art of Persuasion in Greece* (Princeton: Princeton University Press, 1963); Nicole Loraux, *The Invention of Athens: The Funeral Oration in the Classical City*, trans. Alan Sheridan (Cambridge, Mass.: Harvard University Press, 1986), 264–70, 321–27; Plutarch, "Pericles," in *Plutarch's Lives*, trans. Bernadotte Perrin (1916; reprint, Cambridge, Mass.: Harvard University Press, 1951), 3:69–73; Quintilian, *Institutio Oratoria*, trans. H. E. Butler (1921; reprint, Cambridge, Mass.: Harvard University Press, 1966), 2:286–89 [V.xi.28–29]; Rosamond Kent Sprague, ed., *The Older Sophists* (Columbia: University of South Carolina Press, 1972), 41–42; Jennifer S. Uglow, ed., *The International Dictionary of Women's Biography* (New York: Continuum, 1982), 27.

From *Menexenus*

By Plato

SOCRATES. From the agora,[1] Menexenus, or where from?

MENEXENUS. From the agora, Socrates, and the council chamber. . . . I went to the council chamber because I had learned that the council was going to select someone to make an oration over the dead; for you know that they propose to arrange for funeral rites.

SOCRATES. Yes, I do. And whom did they select?

MENEXENUS. Nobody: they postponed it 'til tomorrow. I fancy, however, that Archinus will be selected, or Dion.

SOCRATES. In truth, Menexenus, to fall in battle seems to be a splendid thing in many ways. For a man obtains a splendid and magnificent funeral even though at his death he be but a poor man; and though he be but a worthless fellow, he wins praise, and that by the mouth of accomplished men who do not praise at random, but in speeches prepared long beforehand. And they praise in such splendid fashion that, what with their ascribing to each one both what he has and what he has not, and the variety and splendor of their diction, they bewitch our souls; and they eulogize the state in every possible fashion, and they praise those who died in the war and all our ancestors of former times and ourselves who are living still; so that I myself, Menexenus, when thus praised by them feel mightily ennobled, and every time I listen fascinated I am exalted and imagine myself to have become all at once taller and nobler and more handsome. And as I am generally accompanied by some strangers, who listen along with me, I become in their eyes also all at once more majestic; for they also manifestly share in my feelings with regard both to me and to the rest of our City, believing it to be more marvelous than before, owing to the persuasive eloquence of the speaker. And this majestic feeling remains with me for over three days: so persistently does the speech and voice of the orator ring in my ears that it is scarcely on the fourth or fifth day that I recover myself and remember that I really am here on earth, whereas 'til then I almost imagine myself to be living in the Islands of the Blessed—so expert are our orators.

MENEXENUS. You are always deriding the orators, Socrates. And truly I think that this time the selected speaker will not be too well prepared; for the selection is being made without warning, so that the speaker will probably be driven to improvise his speech.

SOCRATES. Why so, my good sir? Each one of these men has speeches ready made; and what is more, it is in no wise difficult to improvise such things. For if it were a question of eulogizing Athenians before an audience of Peloponnesians, or Peloponnesians before Athenians, there would indeed be need of a good orator to win credence and credit; but when a man makes his effort in the presence of the very men whom he is praising, it is no difficult matter to win credit as a fine speaker. . . .

MENEXENUS. And do you think that you yourself would be able to make the speech, if required and if the council were to select you?

SOCRATES. That I should be able to make the speech would be nothing wonderful, Menexenus; for she who is my instructor is by no means weak in the art of rhetoric; on the contrary, she has turned out many fine orators, and among them one who surpassed all other Greeks—Pericles, the son of Xanthippus.

MENEXENUS. Who is she? But you mean Aspasia, no doubt.

SOCRATES. I do; and also Connus the son of Metrobius; for these are my two instructors, the one in music, the other in rhetoric. So it is not surprising that a man who is trained like me should be clever at speaking. But even a man less well taught than I, who had learned his music from Lamprus and his rhetoric from Antiphon the Rhamnusian,[2]—even such a one, I say, could none the less win credit by praising Athenians before an Athenian audience.

MENEXENUS. What, then, would you have to say, if you were required to speak?

SOCRATES. Nothing, perhaps, myself, of my own invention; but I was listening only yesterday to Aspasia going through a funeral speech for these very people. For she had heard the report you mention, that the Athenians are going to select the speaker; and thereupon she rehearsed to me the speech in the form it should take, extemporizing in part, while other parts of it she had previously prepared, as I imagine, at the time when she was composing the funeral oration which Pericles delivered; and from this she patched together sundry fragments.

MENEXENUS. Could you repeat from memory that speech of Aspasia?

SOCRATES. Yes, if I am not mistaken; for I learned it, to be sure, from her as she went along, and I nearly got a flogging whenever I forgot.

MENEXENUS. Why don't you repeat it then?

SOCRATES. But possibly my teacher will be vexed with me if I publish abroad her speech.

MENEXENUS. Never fear, Socrates; only tell it and you will gratify me exceedingly, whether it is Aspasia's that you wish to deliver or anyone else's; only say on. . . .

SOCRATES. Nay, then, I must surely gratify you; for indeed I would almost gratify you if you were to bid me strip and dance, now that we two are alone. Listen then. In her speech, I believe, she began by making mention of the dead men themselves in this wise:

"In respect of deeds, these men have received at our hands what is due to them, endowed wherewith they travel their predestined road; for they have been escorted forth in solemn procession publicly by the City and privately by their kinfolk. But in respect of words, the honor that remains still due to these heroes the law enjoins us, and it is right, to pay in full. For it is by means of speech finely spoken that deeds nobly done gain for their doers from the hearers the meed of memory and renown. And the speech required is one that will adequately eulogize the dead and give kindly exhortation to the living, appealing to their children and their brethren to copy the virtues of these heroes, and to their fathers and mothers and any still surviving ancestors offering consolation. Where then could we discover a speech like that? Or how could we rightly commence our celebration of these valiant men, who in their lifetime delighted their friends by their virtue, and purchased the safety of the living by their deaths? We ought, in my judgment, to adopt the natural order in our praise, even as the men themselves were natural in their virtue. And virtuous they were because they were sprung from men of virtue. First, then, let us eulogize their nobility of birth, and second, their nurture and training: thereafter we shall exhibit the character of their exploits, how nobly and worthily they wrought them.

"Now as regards nobility of birth, their first claim thereto is this—that the forefathers of these men were not of immigrant stock, nor were these their sons declared by their origin to be strangers in the land sprung from immigrants, but natives sprung from the soil living and dwelling in their own true fatherland; and nurtured also by no stepmother, like other folk, but by that mother-country wherein they dwelt, which bore them and reared them and now at their death receives them again to rest in their own abodes. Most meet it is that first we should celebrate that Mother herself; for by so doing we shall also celebrate therewith the noble birth of these heroes.

"Our country is deserving of praise, not only from us but from all men, on many grounds, but first and foremost because she is god-beloved. The strife of the gods[3] who contended over her and their judgment testify to the truth of our statement. . . . And a second just ground of praise would be this—that during that period in which the whole earth was putting forth and producing animals of every kind, wild and tame, our country showed herself barren and void of wild animals, but chose for herself and gave birth to humanity, who surpasses all other animals in intelligence and alone of animals regards justice and the gods. And we have a signal proof of this statement in that this land of ours has given birth to the forefathers both of these men and of ourselves. For every creature that brings forth possesses a suitable supply of nourishment for its offspring; and by this test it is manifest also whether a woman be truly a mother or no, if she possesses no founts of nourishment for her child. Now our land, which is also our mother, furnishes to the full this proof of her having brought forth humanity: for, of all the lands that then existed, she was the first and the only one to produce human nourishment, namely the grain of wheat and barley, whereby the race of humankind is most richly and well nourished, inasmuch as she herself was the true mother of this creature. And proofs such as this one ought to accept more readily on behalf of a country than on behalf of a woman; for it is not the country that imitates the woman in the matter of conception and birth, but the woman the country. . . . And after [this produce] she brought to birth for her children the olive, sore labor's balm. And when she had nurtured and reared them up to adult estate, she introduced gods to be their governors and tutors, . . . and they set in order our mode of life, not only in respect of daily business, by instructing us before all others in the arts, but also in respect of the guardianship of our country, by teaching us how to acquire and handle arms.

"Such being the manner of their birth and of their education, the ancestors of these men framed for themselves and lived under a civic polity which it is right for us briefly to describe. For a polity is a thing which nurtures men, good men when it is noble, bad men when it is base. It is necessary, then, to demonstrate that the polity wherein our forefathers were nurtured was a noble one, such as caused goodness not only in them but also in their descendants of the present age, among whom we number these men who are fallen. . . . One man calls it "democracy"; another man, according to his fancy, gives it some other name; but it is, in very truth, an "aristocracy"[4] backed by popular approbation. Kings[5] we always have; but these are at one time hereditary, at another selected by vote. And while the most part of civic affairs are in the control of the populace, they hand over the posts of government and the power to those who from time to time are deemed to be the best men; and no man is debarred by his weakness or poverty or by the obscurity of his parentage, or promoted because of the opposite qualities, as is the case in other states. On the contrary, the one principle of selection is this: the man who is deemed to be wise or good rules and governs. And the cause of this our polity lies in our equality of birth. For whereas all other states are composed of a heterogeneous collection of all sorts of people, so that their polities are also heterogeneous, tyrannies as well as oligarchies, some of them regarding one another as slaves, others as masters; we and our people, on the contrary, being all born of one mother, claim to be neither the slaves of one another nor the masters; rather does our natural birth-equality drive us to seek lawfully legal equality, and to yield to one another in no respect save in reputation for virtue and understanding.

"Wherefore the forefathers of these men and of us, and these men themselves, having been reared up thus in complete freedom, and being nobly born, achieved before all men many noble deeds both individual and national, judging it their duty to fight in the cause of freedom alike with Greeks on behalf of Greeks and with barbarians on behalf of the whole of Greece. The story of how they repulsed Eumolpus[6] and the Amazons,[7] and still earlier invaders, when they marched upon our country, and how they defended the Argives against the Cadmeians[8] and the Heraclidae against the Argives,[9] are stories which our time is too short to relate as they deserve, and already their valor has been adequately celebrated in song by poets who have made it known throughout the world. . . . These exploits, therefore, for these reasons I judge that we should pass over. . . , but those exploits for which as yet no poet has received worthy renown for worthy cause, and which lie still buried in oblivion, I ought, as I think, to celebrate, not only praising them myself but providing material also for others to build up into odes and other forms of poetry in a manner worthy of the doers of those deeds. And of the deeds whereof I speak the first were these.

"The Persians were in command of Asia, and were enslaving Europe, when they came in contact with the children of this land, our own parents, of whom it is right and proper that we should make mention first and celebrate their valor. But if we are to celebrate it fitly, in order to visualize it we must place ourselves, in thought, at that epoch when the whole of Asia was already in bondage to the third of the Persian kings. . . . Thus the minds of all men were enslaved, so many were the mighty and warlike nations which had fallen under the yoke of the Persian empire.

"Then Darius, accusing us and the Eretrians of having plotted against Sardis, dispatched fifty myriads of men in transports and warships, together with three hundred ships of war, and Datis as their commander; and him the king ordered to bring back the Eretrians and Athenians in captivity, if he wished to keep his own head. He then sailed to Eretria against men who were among the most famous warriors in Greece at that time, and by no means few in number; them he overpowered within three days, and lest any should escape he made a thorough search of the whole of their country. And his method was this. His soldiers marched to the limits of Eretria and posted themselves at intervals from sea to sea; then they joined hands and passed through the whole of the country, in order that they might be able to report to the king that not a man had escaped out of their hands.[10] With the same design they sailed off from Eretria to Marathon, supposing that they would have an easy task in leading the Athenians captive under the same yoke of bondage as the Eretrians.

"And while these actions were being accomplished in part, and in part attempted, not one of the Greeks lent aid to the Eretrians nor yet to the Athenians, save only the Lacedaemonians (and they arrived on the day after the battle); all the rest were terror-stricken and, hugging their present security, made no move. It is by realizing this state of affairs that we can appreciate what manner of men those were, in point of valor, who awaited the onset of the barbarians' power, chastised all Asia's insolent pride, and were the first to rear trophies of victory over the barbarians; whereby they pointed the way to the others and taught them to know that the Persian power was not invincible, since there is no multitude of men or money but courage conquers it. I, therefore, affirm that those men were the begetters not merely of our bodies but of our freedom also, and the freedom of all the dwellers in this continent; for it was the example of that exploit of theirs which fired the Greeks with courage to risk the later battles in the cause of salvation, learning their lesson from the men of Marathon.

"To them, therefore, we award in this our speech the first prize for valor, and the second to those who fought and won the sea-fights off Salamis and at Artemisium.[11] And . . . the achievement I shall mention is that which was, in my judgment, the noblest that they performed. . . . For whereas the men of Marathon had only proved to the Greeks thus much— that it was possible to repel the barbarians by land though few against many—yet the prospect in a sea-fight remained still doubtful, and the Persians still retained the reputation of being invincible by sea, in virtue of their numbers and their wealth, their naval skill and strength. For this, then, the men who fought those sea-fights merit our praise, that they delivered the Greeks from the second of their fears, and put an end to the terrors inspired by multitudes of ships and men. . . .

"The exploit at Plataea[12] I put third both in order and in merit of those which secured the salvation of Greece; and in this exploit, at last, the Lacedaemonians cooperated with the Athenians.

"By the action of all these men the greatest and most formidable danger was warded off, and because of this their valor we pronounce their eulogy now, as our successors will in the time to come. But, in the period that followed, many cities of the Greeks were still in league with the barbarian, and of the king himself it was reported that he was purposing to renew his attempt against the Greeks. Wherefore it is right that we should make mention also of those men who put the finishing touch to the work of salvation executed by their predecessors by sweeping away the whole of the barbarian power and driving it clean off the seas. These were the men who fought the sea-fight at the Eurymedon,[13] the men who served in the expedition against Cyprus, the men who voyaged to Egypt and to many another quarter[14]—men whom we ought to hold in memory and render them thanks, seeing that they put the king in fear and caused him to give his whole mind to his own safety in place of plotting the destruction of Greece.

"Now this war was endured to the end by all our citizens who warred against the barbarians in defence of all the other Greek-speaking peoples as well as themselves. But when peace was secured and our city was held in honor, there followed the usual consequence which the successful suffer at the hands of men; for it was assailed by jealousy first, and after jealousy by envy; and thereby our city was plunged against its will into war with the Greeks. . . . Our men won a victory after a two day's battle at Oenophyta,[15] and rightfully restored those who were wrongfully exiled. These were the first of our men who, after the Persian war and now helping Greeks against Greeks in the cause of freedom, proved themselves men of valor and delivered those whom they were aiding; and they were the first to be honored by the state and laid to rest in this tomb.

"Later on, when there was widespread war, and all the Greeks had marched against us and ravaged our country, most evilly requiting our city, and our men had defeated them by sea and had captured their Lacedaemonian leaders in Sphagia,[16] although they had it in their power to destroy them, yet they spared their lives and gave them back and made peace, since they deemed that against their fellow Greeks it was right to wage war only up to the point of victory, and not to wreck the whole Greek community for the sake of a city's private grudge, but to wage war to the death against the barbarians. . . .

"This peace was followed by a third war, as formidable as it was unexpected, wherein many brave men lost their lives and now lie here. Many of these reared up numerous trophies of victory in Sicily.[17] . . . Many others of them fought in the sea-fights in the Hellespont, where in one single day they captured all the enemy's ships,[18] besides winning many other engagements. But what I have termed the formidable and unexpected character of the war lay in this, that the rest of the Greeks had arrived at such a pitch of jealousy towards this city that they even brought themselves to solicit privately the aid of their deadliest foe, the very king whom they had publicly expelled with our assistance, inviting a barbarian as their ally against Greeks; and dared to range against our city the united forces of all the Greeks and barbarians.[19] And then it was that the strength and valor of our state shone out conspicuously. For when men fancied that she was already reduced by war, with her ships cut off at Mytilene, her citizens sent sixty ships to the rescue, manning the ships themselves and proving themselves indisputably to be men of valor by conquering their foes and setting free their friends;[20] albeit they met with undeserved misfortune, and were not recovered from the sea to find their burial here.[21] And for these reasons we must remember and praise them always; for it was . . . due to them that men formed the conviction regarding our city (and it was a true conviction) that she could never be warred down, not even by all the world. And in truth it was by our own dissensions that we were brought down and not by the hands of other men; for by them we are still to this day undefeated, and it is we ourselves who have both defeated and been defeated by ourselves.

"And after these happenings, when we were at peace and amity with other states, our civil war at home was waged in such a way that—if men are fated to engage in civil strife—there is no man but would pray for his own state that its sickness might resemble ours. So kindly and so friendly was the way in which the citizens from the Peiraeus and from the city consorted with one another, and also—beyond men's hopes—with the other Greeks; and such moderation did they show in their settlement of the war against the men at Eleusis.[22] And the cause of all these actions was nothing else than that genuine kinship which produces, not in word only but in deed, a firm friendship founded on community of race. And of those who fell in this war also it is meet to make mention and to reconcile them by such means as we can under present conditions—by prayer, that is and by sacrifice—praying for them to those that have them in their keeping, seeing that we ourselves also have been reconciled. . . .

"After this, when peace was completely reestablished, the city remained quiet, granting forgiveness to the barbarians for the vigorous defence they had offered when she had done them injury, but feeling aggrieved with the Greeks at the thought of the return they had made for the benefits she had done them, in that they joined themselves to the barbarians, and stripped her of those ships that had once been the means of their own salvation, and demolished her walls as a recompense for our saving their walls from ruin.[23] Our city, therefore, resolved that never again would she succor Greeks when in danger of enslavement either by one another or at the hands of barbarians; and in this mind she abode. Such then being our policy, the Lacedaemonians supposed that we, the champions of liberty, were laid low, and that it was now open to them to enslave the rest, and this they proceeded to do.

"But why should I prolong the story? For what followed next is no tale of ancient history about men of long ago. Nay, we ourselves know how the Argives, the Boeotians and the Corinthians—the leading states of Greece—came to need our city, being stricken with terror, and how even the Persian king himself—most marvelous fact of all—was reduced to such a state of distress that eventually he could hope for salvation from no other quarter save this city of ours which he had been so eager to destroy. And in truth, if one desired to frame a just accusation against the city, the only true accusation one could bring would be this—that she has always been compassionate to excess and the handmaid of the weak. And in fact, on that occasion, she proved unable to harden her heart and adhere firmly to her resolved policy of refusing to assist any in danger of enslavement against those who wronged them; on the contrary, she gave way and lent assistance. The Greeks she aided herself and rescued them from slavery, so that they remained free until such time as they enslaved each other once more. . . . We, and we alone, could not bring ourselves either to hand . . . over [the Greeks on the continent to the King of Persia] or to join in the agreement. So firmly-rooted and so sound is the noble and liberal character of our city, and endowed also with such a hatred of the barbarian, because we are pure-blooded Greeks, unadulterated by barbarian stock. For there cohabit with us none of the type of Pelops, or Cadmus, or Aegyptus or Danaus, and numerous others of the kind, who are naturally barbarians though nominally Greeks; but our people are pure Greeks and not a barbarian blend; whence it comes that our city is imbued with a whole-hearted hatred of alien races. None the less, we were isolated once again because of our refusal to perform the dishonorable and unholy act of surrendering Greeks to barbarians. Yet truly in this war also we suffered the loss of valiant men—the men who had difficult ground to cope with at Corinth and treachery at Lechaeum;[24] valiant, too, were the men who rescued the king and drove the Lacedaemonians off the seas. These men I recall to your memory, and you it becomes to join in praising and celebrating men such as these.

"And now we have related many of the noble deeds done by the men who are lying here, and by all the others who have died in defence of their city; yet far more numerous and more noble are those that remain unmentioned; for many days and nights would not suffice were one to relate them all in full. Wherefore it is right that every man, bearing these men in mind, should exhort these men's children, just as in time of war, not to fall out of rank with their fathers nor to give way to cowardice and beat a retreat. And I myself for my own part, O you children of valiant men, am now exhorting you and in the future wheresoever I shall encounter any of you, I shall continue to remind you and admonish you to be zealous to show yourselves supremely valiant. But on this occasion it is my duty to record the message which your fathers, at the time when they were about to risk their lives, enjoined us, in case any ill befell them, to give to those who survived them. I will repeat to you both the words which I heard from their lips and those which they would now desire to say to you, if they had the power, judging from what they actually said on that occasion. You must, however, imagine that you are hearing from their own lips the message which I shall deliver. This, then, is what they said:

"'O children, that you are born of valiant sires is clearly shown by the facts now before you: we, who might have ignobly lived choose rather to die nobly, before we bring you and those after you to disgrace, and before we bring shame upon our own fathers and all our earlier forebears, since we deem that life is unworthy to be lived for the man who brings shame upon his own, and that such a one has no friend among gods or man, either here on earth, or under the earth when he is dead. Wherefore you must bear in mind our words, and whatsoever else you practice you must practice it in union with valor, being well assured that when divorced from this all possessions and pursuits are base and ignoble. . . . For these reasons make it your endeavor, first and last and always, in every way to . . . exceed, if possible, both us and those who went before us in renown; but if not, be well assured that if we vanquish you in virtue our victory brings us shame, whereas, if we are defeated, our defeat brings happiness. And most of all would we be the vanquished, you the victors, if you are careful in your conduct not to trade upon the glory of your ancestors nor yet to squander it, believing that for a man who holds himself of some account there is nothing more shameful than to find himself held in honor not for his own sake but because of the glory of his ancestors. In the honors which belong to their parents, the children truly possess a noble and splendid treasure; but to use up one's treasure, whether of wealth or of honor, and bequeath none to one's children, is the base and unmanly act of one who lacks all wealth and distinctions of his own. And if you practice these precepts you will come to us as friends to friends whensoever the appointed doom shall convey you hither; but if you neglect them and play the coward, you will be welcomed graciously by none. Let such, then, be the words we address to our children.

"'Those of us who have fathers or mothers must counsel them always to bear their calamity—if so be that such has befallen them—as cheerfully as possible, and not join in their lamentations; for in sooth they will need no further cause of grief; the present misfortune will provide grief in plenty. Rather should we mollify and assuage their sorrow by reminding them that in the greatest matters the gods have already hearkened to their prayers. For they prayed not that their sons should become immortal, but valiant and renowned; and these, which are the greatest of boons, they obtained. . . . Moreover, by bearing their calamities thus bravely they will clearly show that they are in truth the fathers of brave sons and of a like bravery themselves; whereas if they give way they will afford grounds for suspecting either that they are no fathers of ours or that we have been falsely praised. . . . That ancient saying, 'Nothing overmuch' is judged to be a noble saying. . . . That man is best prepared for life who makes all that concerns his welfare depend upon himself . . . for because he puts his trust in himself, he will neither be seen rejoicing nor yet grieving overmuch. Of such a character we request our friends to be, and desire them to appear, even as we now display ourselves as such, being neither aggrieved nor alarmed overmuch if so be that at this present crisis we must die. We beseech both fathers and mothers to pass the rest of their lives holding to this same conviction, and to be well assured that it is not by mourning and lamenting us that they will gratify us most; nay, if the dead have any perception of the living, it is thus that they would gratify us least, by debasing themselves and bearing their sorrows with a heavy heart; whereas by a lighthearted and temperate demeanor they would gratify us most. . . . But to our wives and children let them give care and nurture and devote their minds to them; for thus they will best forget their ill fortune and live a life that is nobler and truer and more pleasing in our eyes.

"'Let this, then, suffice as our message to our kinsfolk. To the city we would add an exhortation that on our behalf they care for our parents and our sons, bestowing on the latter an orderly training, and on the former the fitting nurture of old age; and, as it is, we are well assured that even without our exhortation the city will bestow upon them ample care.'

"Such is the message, O you children and parents of the fallen, which they enjoined upon us to deliver, and which I, with all the earnestness in my power, have now delivered; and I myself, on their behalf, entreat the children to imitate their fathers, and the parents to have no fear for themselves, seeing that we, both privately and publicly, will give nurture to your age and bestow care upon you, wherever one of us meets with one of you. And as regards the care bestowed by the city, of your own selves you know well that she has made laws regarding both the children and the begetters of those who have fallen in the war, to ensure their care; and that the highest authority in the state is instructed to watch over them beyond all other citizens, that the fathers and mothers of these men may suffer no wrong. And the city herself helps in the bringing up of their children, endeavoring to render them as little conscious as possible of their orphaned condition; while they are yet children she stands towards them as a father, and when they arrive at man's estate she presents them with full military equipment and sends them back to their own place, thereby exhibiting and putting them in mind of their fathers' profession by bestowing on each of them the instruments of his father's prowess, while at the same time desiring that he should be auspiciously equipped with arms on commencing his journey to his ancestral hearth, there to rule with power. Nor does the city ever omit to pay honor to the dead heroes themselves, seeing that she herself year by year performs publicly, on behalf of all, those customary rites which are privately performed for each; and moreover, she institutes contests in athletics and horse-racing and music of every kind. And thus, in simple fact, she stands towards the fallen in the position of son and heir, towards the sons in that of father, and towards the parents of the dead in that of guardian, thus exercising towards all all manner of care throughout all time. Laying which to heart, you should bear your sorrow with the greater calm; for thus will you best content both the dead and the living, and tend and be tended with the greatest ease.

"And now that you and all the rest have already made public lamentation for the dead as the law ordains, go your ways."

There, Menexenus, you have the oration of Aspasia, the Milesian.

MENEXENUS. And by Zeus, Socrates, Aspasia, by your account, deserves to be congratulated if she is really capable of composing a speech like that, woman though she is.

SOCRATES. Nay, then, if you are incredulous, come along with me and listen to a speech from her own lips.

MENEXENUS. I have met with Aspasia many a time, Socrates, and I know well what she is like.

SOCRATES. Well, then, don't you admire her, and are you not grateful to her now for her oration?

MENEXENUS. Yes, I am exceedingly grateful for the oration, Socrates, to her or to him—whoever it was that repeated it to you; and what is more, I owe many other debts of gratitude to him that repeated it.

SOCRATES. That will be fine! Only be careful not to give me away, so that I may report to you later on many other fine political speeches of hers.

MENEXENUS. Have no fear: I won't give you away; only do report them.

SOCRATES. Well, it shall be done.

Notes for *Menexenus*

Although I have adopted R. G. Bury's translation from Plato, *Menexenus*, first published in 1929 (reprint, Cambridge, Mass.: Harvard University Press, 1961), I have silently corrected spelling to contemporary usage and punctuation to the conventions of this volume, and I have corrected footnotes against the *Oxford Classical Dictionary*, as well as adding additional material to the notes.

1. The agora was a place of popular assembly, especially for political purposes, usually located in the center of the city, often surrounded by stoas or colonnades.

2. Antiphon, 480–411 B.C.E., was the first of the ten great Attic Orators. Thus Socrates is being ironic, since Aspasia never performed in public, while Antiphon was acclaimed.

3. Athena and Poseidon. See Ovid, *Metamorphoses* VI.70ff.

4. "Aristocracy" means "rule of the best."

5. A reference to the *archontes*, the nine city officials, one of whom was called *basileus* ("king").

6. Eumolpus, a Thracian bard and chieftain, son of Poseidon, was said to have aided the Eleusinians in invading Attica.

7. The Amazons, a mythical race of female warriors in Pontus, were said to have attacked Athens and been driven back to Asia by the hero Theseus.

8. The Athenians were said to have defended the Argives against the Cadmeians in the war of "the seven against Thebes" (of which city Cadmus was the founder).

9. The Athenians supposedly aided "the sons of Heracles" against Eurystheus, King of Tiryns in Argolis.

10. The expedition of Datis took place in 490 B.C.E.

11. These battles took place during Xerxes's invasion of Greece in 480 B.C.E.

12. At Plataea the Persians under Mardonius were defeated in 479 B.C.E.

13. The Athenians, under Cimon, defeated the Persian forces, both by land and sea, at the river Eurymedon in Pamphylia, in 466 B.C.E. (cf. Thucydides i.100).

14. These naval operations (against Persia) took place about 461–458 B.C.E.

15. Athenians fought the Lacedaemonians at Oenophyta in 457 B.C.E. (cf. Thucydides i.108).

16. Sphagia, that is, Sphacteria. These events took place in 425 B.C.E., the seventh year of the Peloponnesian War.

17. The second Sicilian expedition took place in 415–413 B.C.E.

18. This is an exaggeration if the occasion is that mentioned in Thucydides viii.9 ff., when ten empty ships were captured. But possibly the reference is to the victory at Cyzicus, 411 B.C.E., when sixty ships were taken or sunk.

19. This refers to the Spartan treaty with Tissaphernes, 412 B.C.E., and the subsequent cooperation with the Persians against Athens.

20. The battle of Mytilene was fought in 407 B.C.E.

21. At the battle of Arginusae, 406 B.C.E., the crews of twenty-five ships were lost.

22. "The men at Eleusis" are the oligarchical party at Athens who held sway for about eighteen months (404–403 B.C.E.) until ousted by the democrats under Thrasybulus.

23. These formed part of the terms exacted by the Spartans after the battle of Aegospotami, 405 B.C.E.

24. The Corinthian oligarchs were supported by the Spartans, against whom the Athenians fought in 393–392 B.C.E.

From *De Inventione*

By Cicero

In a dialogue by Aeschines Socraticus, Socrates reveals that Aspasia reasoned thus with Xenophon's wife and with Xenophon himself: "Please tell me, madam, if your neighbor had a better gold ornament than you have, would you prefer that one or your own?" "That one," she replied. "Now, if she had dresses and other feminine finery more expensive than you have, would you prefer yours or hers?" "Hers, of course," she replied. "Well now, if she had a better husband than you have, would you prefer your husband or hers?" At this the woman blushed. But Aspasia then began to speak to Xenophon. "I wish you would tell me, Xenophon," she said, "if your neighbor had a better horse than yours, would you prefer your horse or his?" "His," was his answer. "And if he had a better farm than you have, which farm would you prefer to have?" "The better farm, naturally," he said. "Now, if he had a better wife than you have, would you prefer yours or his?" And at this Xenophon, too, himself was silent.

Then Aspasia: "Since both of you have failed to tell me the only thing I wished to hear, I myself will tell you what you both are thinking. That is, you, madam, wish to have the best husband, and you, Xenophon, desire above all things to have the finest wife. Therefore, unless you can contrive that there be no better man or finer woman on earth, you will certainly always be in dire want of what you consider best, namely that you be the husband of the very best of wives, and that she be wedded to the very best of men." In this instance, because assent has been given to undisputed statements, the result is that the point which would appear doubtful if asked of itself is through analogy conceded as certain, and this is due to the method employed in putting the question. Socrates used this conversational method a good deal, because he wished to present no arguments himself, but preferred to get a result from the material which the interlocutor had given him—a result that the interlocutor was bound to approve as following necessarily from what he had already granted.

Note for *De Inventione*

This excerpt is taken from Cicero, *De Inventione*, trans. H. M. Hubbell (1949; reprint, Cambridge, Mass.: Harvard University Press, 1968), 93–95, I.xxxi.51–53.

Pan Chao

c. 48–117

Pan Chao lived during the first and second centuries C.E. under the great Han empire in China (Swann 24, 50). She was a royal historiographer and librarian and a teacher of the empress and other court ladies. Pan Chao came from the wealthy, educated, influential Pan family with many court connections. She herself was well educated, although a girl. She lived most of her adult life as a widow. When her older brother Pan Ku died, the emperor brought Pan Chao to court to finish his work as royal librarian and historiographer. But she was not given her brother's title because she was a woman. She wrote several sections of the *Han shu*, the Han dynastic history and encyclopedia of learning, as well as numerous other treatises and poems. She was also librarian at court, supervising the editorial labors of a staff of assistants and training other scholars in her work. In this capacity, she rearranged and enlarged the *Biographies of Eminent Women* by Liu Hsiang. It is possible that she supervised the copying of manuscripts from bamboo slips and silk onto a recently invented material, paper. She was an adviser to the empress Teng when she became regent, and Pan Chao's son Ch'eng (or Ku) was made a political minister and given an official title because of her influence. Her daughters-in-law collected and edited her works after her death.

According to her epitaph, Pan Chao taught the empress and court ladies "poetry, eloquence, and history" (Swann 44, 52 n. 6). Her *Lessons for Women*, the earliest known treatise on the education of women, and the earliest extant writing on rhetoric by a woman, emphasizes domestic duties and the traditional gender role of Chinese women as serving men and family, but it also presents the argument that girls must be well educated in order to serve. This education, though, follows the principle of the complementary difference of *Yin* and *Yang*, and so eloquence for women is not the same as eloquence for men. Pan Chao's theory requires that women honor their husbands by avoiding licentious talk with them and show esteem by refusing to quarrel. Her advice demands that women eschew vulgar language and gossip, and that they humbly exchange only respectful words with their husband's family. The final aim of such eloquence is not public acclaim but domestic accord, not only with the husband but also with the parents-in-law and the sons-in-law and daughters-in-law who live in the house:

> Words from the heart which agree,
> Give forth fragrance like the orchid.

This treatise on the education of women was dedicated to the daughters in Pan Chao's family but was circulated immediately at court. It was popular for centuries in China as a guide for women's conduct.

For further information, see Nancy Lee Swann, *Pan Chao: Foremost Woman Scholar of China* (1932; reprint, New York: Russell & Russell, 1968); and Jane Donawerth, "Transforming the History of Rhetorical Theory," *Feminist Teacher* 7, no. 1 (Fall 1992): 35–39.

Lessons for Women (First century)

Introduction

I, the unworthy writer, am unsophisticated, unenlightened, and by nature unintelligent, but I am fortunate both to have received not a little favor from my scholarly father, and to have had a [cultured] mother and instructresses upon whom to rely for a literary education as well as training in good manners. More than forty years have passed since, at the age of fourteen, I took up the dustpan and the broom[1] in the Ts'ao family. During this time with trembling heart I feared constantly that I might disgrace my parents, and that I might multiply difficulties for both the women and the men[2] [of my husband's family]. Day and night I was distressed in heart, [but] I labored without confessing weariness. Now and hereafter, however, I know how to escape [from such fears].

Being careless, and by nature stupid, I taught and trained [my children] without system. Consequently, I fear that my son Ku may bring disgrace upon the Imperial Dynasty by whose Holy Grace he has unprecedentedly received the extraordinary privilege of wearing the Gold and the Purple,[3] a privilege for the attainment of which [by my son, I] a humble subject never even hoped. Nevertheless, now that he is a man and able to plan his own life, I need not again have concern for him. But I do grieve that you, my daughters,[4] just now at the age for marriage, have not at this time had gradual training and advice; that you still have not learned the proper customs for married women. I fear that by failure in good manners in other families you will humiliate both your ancestors and your clan. I am now seriously ill, life is uncertain. As I have thought of you all in so untrained a state, I have been uneasy many a time for you. At hours of leisure I have composed in seven chapters these instructions under the title, "Lessons for Women." In order that you may have something wherewith to benefit your persons, I wish every one of you, my daughters, each to write out a copy for yourself.

From this time on every one of you strive to practice these [lessons].

Chapter I
Humility

On the third day after the birth of a girl the ancients observed three customs: [first] to place the baby [on the ground] below the bed; [second] to give her a potsherd[5] with which to play; and [third] to announce her birth to her ancestors by an offering. Now to lay the baby [on the ground] below the bed plainly indicated that she is lowly and weak, and should regard it as her primary duty to humble herself before others. To give her potsherds with which to play indubitably signified that she should practice labor and consider it her primary duty to be industrious. To announce her birth before her ancestors clearly meant that she ought to esteem as her primary duty the continuation of the observance of worship in the home.[6]

These three ancient customs epitomize a woman's ordinary way of life and the teachings of the traditional ceremonial rites and regulations. Let a woman modestly yield to others; let her respect others; let her put others first, herself last. Should she do something good, let her not mention it; should she do something bad, let her not deny it. Let her bear disgrace; let her even endure[7] when others speak or do evil to her. Always let her seem to tremble and to fear. [When a woman follows such maxims as these,] then she may be said to humble herself before others.

Let a woman retire late to bed, but rise early to duties; let her not dread tasks by day or by night. Let her not refuse to perform domestic duties whether easy or difficult. That which must be done, let her finish completely, tidily, and systematically. [When a woman follows such rules as these,] then she may be said to be industrious.

Let a woman be correct in manner and upright in character in order to serve her husband. Let her live in purity and quietness [of spirit], and attend to her own affairs. Let her love not gossip and silly laughter. Let her cleanse and purify and arrange in order the wine and the food for the offerings to the ancestors. [When a woman observes such principles as these,] then she may be said to continue ancestral worship.[8]

No woman who observes these three [fundamentals of life] has ever had a bad reputation or has fallen into disgrace. If a woman fail to observe them, how can her name be honored; how can she but bring disgrace upon herself?

Chapter II
Husband and Wife

The Way of husband and wife is intimately connected with *Yin* and *Yang*,[9] and relates the individual to gods and ancestors. Truly it is the great principle of heaven and earth, and the great basis of human relationships. Therefore the *Rites*[10] honor union of man and woman; and in the *Book of Poetry* the "First Ode" manifests the principle of marriage. For these reasons the relationship cannot but be an important one.

If a husband is unworthy, then he possesses nothing by which to control his wife. If a wife is unworthy, then she possesses nothing with which to serve her husband. If a husband does not control his wife, then the rules of conduct manifesting his authority are abandoned and broken. If a wife does not serve her husband, then the proper relationship [between men and women] and the natural order of things are neglected and destroyed. As a matter of fact the purpose of these two [the controlling of women by men, and the serving of men by women] is the same.

Now examine the gentlemen of the present age. They only know that wives must be controlled, and that the husband's rules of conduct manifesting his authority must be established. They therefore teach their boys to read books and [study] histories. But they do not in the least understand that husbands and masters must [also] be served, and that the proper relationship and the rites should be maintained.

Yet only to teach men and not to teach women—is that not ignoring the essential relation between them? According to the *Rites*, it is the rule to begin to teach children to read at the age of eight years, and by the age of fifteen years they ought then to be ready for cultural training. Only why should it not be [that girls' education as well as boys' be] according to this principle?

Chapter III
Respect and Caution

As *Yin* and *Yang* are not of the same nature, so man and woman have different characteristics. The distinctive quality of the *Yang* is rigidity; the function of the *Yin* is yielding. Man is honored for strength; a woman is beautiful on account of her gentleness. Hence there arose the common saying: "A man though born like a wolf may, it is feared, become a weak monstrosity; a woman though born like a mouse may, it is feared, become a tiger."

Now for self-culture nothing equals respect for others. To counteract firmness nothing equals compliance. Consequently, it can be said that the Way of respect and acquiescence is woman's most important principle of conduct. So respect may be defined as nothing other than holding on to that which is permanent, and acquiescence nothing other than being liberal and generous. Those who are steadfast in devotion know that they should stay in their proper places; those who are liberal and generous esteem others, and honor and serve [them].

If husband and wife have the habit of staying together, never leaving one another, and following each other around within the limited space of their own rooms, then they will lust after and take liberties with one another. From such action improper language will arise between the two. This kind of discussion may lead to licentiousness. Out of licentiousness will be born a heart of disrespect to the husband. Such a result comes from not knowing that one should stay in one's proper place.

Furthermore, affairs may be either crooked or straight; words may be either right or wrong. Straightforwardness cannot but lead to quarreling; crookedness cannot but lead to accusation. If there are really accusations and quarrels, then undoubtedly there will be angry incidents. Such a result comes from not esteeming others, and not honoring and serving [them].

[If wives] suppress not contempt for husbands, then it follows [that such wives] rebuke and scold [their husbands]. [If husbands] stop not short of anger, then they are certain to beat [their wives]. The correct relationship between husband and wife is based upon harmony and intimacy, and [conjugal] love is grounded in proper union. Should actual blows be dealt, how could matrimonial relationship be preserved? Should sharp words be spoken, how could [conjugal] love exist? If love and proper relationship both be destroyed, then husband and wife are divided.

Chapter IV
Womanly Qualifications

A woman [ought to] have four qualifications: 1) womanly virtue; 2) womanly words; 3) womanly bearing; and 4) womanly work. Now what is called womanly virtue need not be brilliant ability, exceptionally different from others. Womanly words need be neither clever in debate nor keen in conversation. Womanly appearance requires neither a pretty nor a perfect face and form. Womanly work need not be work done more skillfully than that of others.

To guard carefully her chastity; to control circumspectly her behavior; in every motion to exhibit modesty; and to model each act on the best usage—this is womanly virtue.

To choose her words with care; to avoid vulgar language; to speak at appropriate times; and not to weary others [with much conversation], may be called the characteristics of womanly words.

To wash and scrub filth away; to keep clothes and ornaments fresh and clean; to wash the head and bathe the body regularly, and to keep the person free from disgraceful filth, may be called the characteristics of womanly bearing.

With whole-hearted devotion to sew and to weave; to love not gossip and silly laughter; in cleanliness and order [to prepare] the wine and food for serving guests, may be called the characteristics of womanly work.

These four qualifications characterize the greatest virtue of a woman. No woman can afford to be without them. In fact they are very easy to possess if a woman only treasures them in her heart. The ancients had a saying: "Is love far off? If I desire love, then love is at hand!" So can it be said of these qualifications.

Chapter V
Whole-Hearted Devotion

Now in the *Rites* is written the principle that a husband may marry again, but there is no canon that authorizes a woman to be married the second time. Therefore it is said of husbands as of heaven, that as certainly as people cannot run away from heaven, so surely a wife cannot leave [a husband's home].[11]

If people in action or character disobey the spirits of heaven and of earth, then heaven punishes them. Likewise if a woman errs in the rites and in the proper mode of conduct, then her husband esteems her lightly. The ancient book, *A Pattern for Women*, [*Nü Hsien*] says: "To obtain the love of one man is the crown of a woman's life; to lose the love of one man is to miss the aim in a woman's life."[12] For these reasons a woman cannot but seek to win her husband's heart. Nevertheless, the beseeching wife need not use flattery, coaxing words, and cheap methods to gain intimacy.

Decidedly nothing is better [to gain the heart of a husband] than whole-hearted devotion and correct manners. In accordance with the rites and the proper mode of conduct, [let a woman] live a pure life. Let her have ears that hear not licentiousness; and eyes that see not depravity. When she goes outside her own home, let her not be conspicuous in dress and manners. When at home let her not neglect her dress. Women should not assemble in groups, nor gather together [for gossip and silly laughter]. They should not stand watching in the gateways. [If a woman follows] these rules, she may be said to have whole-hearted devotion and correct manners.

If, in all her actions, she is frivolous, she sees and hears [only] that which pleases herself. At home her hair is disheveled, and her dress is slovenly. Outside the home she emphasizes her femininity to attract attention; she says what ought not to be said; and she looks at what ought not to be seen. [If a woman does such as] these, [she may be] said to be without whole-hearted devotion and correct manners.

Chapter VI
Implicit Obedience

Now "to win the love of one man is the crown of a woman's life; to lose the love of one man is her eternal disgrace." This saying advises a fixed will and a whole-hearted devotion for a woman. Ought she then to lose the hearts of her father- and mother-in-law?[13]

There are times when love may lead to differences of opinion [between individuals]; there are times when duty may lead to disagreement. Even should the husband say that he loves something, when the parents-in-law say "no," this is called a case of duty leading to disagreement. This being so, then what about the hearts of the parents-in-law? Nothing is better than an obedience which sacrifices personal opinion.

Whenever the mother-in-law says, "Do not do that," and if what she says is right, unquestionably the daughter-in-law obeys. Whenever the mother-in-law says, "Do that," even if what she says is wrong, still the daughter-in-law submits unfailingly to the command.

Let a woman not act contrary to the wishes and the opinions of parents-in-law about right and wrong; let her not dispute with them what is straight and what is crooked. Such [docility] may be called obedience which sacrifices personal opinion. Therefore the ancient book, *A Pattern for Women*, says: "If a daughter-in-law [who follows the wishes of her parents-in-law] is like an echo and a shadow, how could she not be praised?"

Chapter VII
Harmony with Younger Brothers- and Sisters-in-Law

In order for a wife to gain the love of her husband, she must win for herself the love of her parents-in-law. To win for herself the love of her parents-in-law, she must secure for herself the good will of younger brothers- and sisters-in-law. For these reasons the right and the wrong, the praise and the blame of a woman alike depend upon younger brothers- and sisters-in-law. Consequently, it will not do for a woman to lose their affection.

They are stupid both who know not that they must not lose [the hearts of] younger brothers- and sisters-in-law, and who cannot be in harmony with them in order to be intimate with them. Excepting only the Holy Men, few are able to be faultless. Now Yen Tzû's greatest virtue was that he was able to reform.[14] Confucius praised him [for not committing a misdeed] the second time. [In comparison with him] a woman is the more likely [to make mistakes].

Although a woman possesses a worthy woman's qualifications, and is wise and discerning by nature, is she able to be perfect? Yet if a woman live in harmony with her immediate family,[15] unfavorable criticism will be silenced [within the home. But] if a man and woman disagree, then this evil will be noised abroad. Such consequences are inevitable. The *Book of Changes* says:

> Should two hearts harmonize,
> The united strength can cut gold.
> Words from hearts which agree,
> Give forth fragrance like the orchid.
> This saying may be applied to [harmony in the home].

Though a daughter-in-law and her younger sisters-in-law are equal in rank, nevertheless [they should] respect [each other]; though love [between them may be] sparse, their proper relationship should be intimate. Only the virtuous, the beautiful, the modest, and the respectful [young women] can accordingly rely upon the sense of duty to make their affection sincere, and magnify love to bind their relationships firmly.

Then the excellence and the beauty of such a daughter-in-law becomes generally known. Moreover, any flaws and mistakes are hidden and unrevealed. Parents-in-law boast of her good deeds; her husband is satisfied with her.[16] Praise of her radiates, making her illustrious in district and in neighborhood; and her brightness reaches to her own father and mother.

But a stupid and foolish person as an elder sister-in-law uses her rank[17] to exalt herself; as a younger sister-in-law, because of parents' favor, she becomes filled with arrogance. If arrogant, how can a woman live in harmony with others? If love and proper relationships be perverted, how can praise be secured? In such instances the wife's good is hidden, and her faults are declared. The mother-in-law will be angry, and the husband will be indignant. Blame will reverberate and spread in and outside the home. Disgrace will gather upon the daughter-in-law's person, on the one hand to add humiliation to her own father and mother, and on the other to increase the difficulties of her husband.

Such then is the basis for both honor and disgrace, the foundation for reputation or for ill-repute. Can a woman be too cautious? Consequently, to seek the hearts of younger brothers- and sisters-in-law decidedly nothing can be esteemed better than modesty and acquiescence.

Modesty is virtue's handle; acquiescence is the wife's [most refined] characteristic. All who possess these two have sufficient for harmony with others. In the *Book of Poetry* it is written that "here is no evil; there is no dart." So it may be said of [these two, modesty and acquiescence].

Notes

The translated text is taken from Nancy Lee Swann, *Pan Chao: Foremost Woman Scholar of China* (1932; reprint, New York: Russell & Russell, 1968), 82–99. Brackets indicate the words Swann has added for clarity. I have modified punctuation, spelling, and one or two instances of word choice, and simplified the notes to fit the format of the rest of this anthology. My thanks to Shirley Logan for finding Pan Chao. Although under the revised alphabet Pan Chao is Englished as Ban Tzao, I have retained the old spelling because the scholarship on her in English is catalogued under that spelling. Chinese fashion, "Pan" is her surname.

1. To "take up the dustpan and the broom" is a conventional expression for the inferior position of the daughter-in-law in relation to her parents-in-law. While according to tradition fifteen years was the age of marriage for girls, Pan Chao was married at fourteen, and some girls did not marry until their twenties.

2. In Pan Chao's culture, the husband's place was without, the wife's place was within, the home.

3. For his position, Ku Ch'eng would have received two thousand piculs of grain, the gold seal, and the purple robe.

4. Not necessarily only her own daughters, but also the other girls of her extended family by marriage.

5. A potsherd or tile was given to baby girls to play with to signify success at domesticity; potsherds or tiles were used in preparing fibers for weaving nettle hemp or grass cloth, and as weights for the spindle.

6. Worship of ancestors (including mothers) and the wife's role in the ceremonies resulted indirectly in defining and elevating the position of wife and mother in ancient Chinese society.

7. Literally, "Let her hold filth in her mouth, let her swallow insult."

8. Major purposes of marriage were to unite two families (rather than two individuals) in love and to secure the continuance of the family line of ancestral worship.

9. The Chinese philosophical conception of yin and yang, the universe resting on the harmonious balance of opposing principles in nature (male and female, light and dark, summer and winter, etc.), was named and discussed in writings from the fifth century B.C.E. on. In Confucian philosophy, the "doctrine of the mean" connects nature (what heaven has conferred), the way (the path of duty), and education (cultivation of the way). Nowhere do the sayings of Confucius show any interest in teaching women.

10. The *Rites* are three classic Chinese treatises.

11. Not even after the death of a husband does the worthy wife leave her husband's home.

12. Literally, "To become of like mind with one man may be said to be the final end; to fail to become of like mind with one man may be said to be the eternal end."

13. Since the woman goes to live with the husband's family in traditional Chinese culture, discord between the daughter-in-law and the mother-in-law (or between wife and husband's brothers and sisters) can disrupt the marriage as surely as discord between husband and wife; the tragic consequences of discord between daughter-in-law and mother-in-law is a traditional theme of Chinese poetry.

14. Yen Tzû was the favorite disciple of Confucius and an advocate of education for regeneration.

15. Literally, "the people in the same room." In China the daughter-in-law often lived in the same room, but not necessarily the same compartment, with her mother-in-law in the women's courtyard, while the husband had his room up in front in the men's courtyard.

16. Literally, "praises the beauty of her character."

17. In traditional Chinese society, power of control over other sons' wives went to the eldest daughter-in-law.

Sei Shonagon

b. 965?

There is little exact information about Sei Shonagon, one of the most celebrated Japanese writers in the Heian period in the tenth century. She was author of *The Pillow Book* (Makura no soshi, "Notes of the Pillow") and also of several dozen surviving poems. She probably knew Chinese—the mark of the truly educated person, usually reserved for men. During the last decade of the tenth century, she was lady-in-waiting to Empress Sadako (sometimes spelled "Teishi"), consort of Emperor Ichijo. Shonagon retired after the empress died in childbirth in 1000. Shonagon's name is uncertain: she was called "Shonagon" ("minor counselor") at court, but her real name may have been Nagiko. "Sei" refers to the Chinese spelling of her family name, Kiyowara. Her father, Kiyowara no Motosuke, a noted scholar and poet, worked as a provincial official. Some sources record that Shonagon was married in 983 to Tachibana no Norimitsu, a government official; had a son, Norinaga; and parted from her husband in 993. Shonagon is mentioned caustically in Lady Murasaki's *Tale of Genji*. Both Fujiwara no Tadanobu and Fujiwara no Sanetaka may have been her lovers. There are no records of her after 1017. According to one tradition, when her court service ended she married Fujiwara no Muneyo, governor of Settsu province, and had a daughter, Koma no Myobu; according to another tradition, she became a Buddhist nun and died in poverty.

Shonagon began *The Pillow Book* while she was at court but continued it in retirement. It was circulated immediately and for several hundred years in manuscript. First printed in the seventeenth century, it appears in many different versions: the order of entries was changed by scribes, and comments and passages were added, edited, or deleted. *The Pillow Book* is a series of little essays, sometimes only lists, of preferences, observations, narratives; the Japanese call this genre *zuihitsu* (miscellany), and it is not clear whether Shonagon began the genre or followed older Japanese or Chinese models, now lost. Shonagon is witty and gives a detailed, gossipy perspective on court life. She is extremely class-conscious, worshiping the royal family and holding servants in contempt.

The entries in *The Pillow Book* on rhetoric include advice and opinions on conversation, preaching, and letter writing. On conversation, Shonagon advocates pure language and rigorous use of amenities in the sections of advice, but also offers vignettes showing witty repartee and sociable give-and-take among the empress's ladies and between ladies and gentlemen. She especially idealizes the empress as a conversationalist who values sincerity in her ladies, who seeks out and elicits comments from the shy ones (as Shonagon was at first), and who keeps the relationships going with special jokes and sentimental or funny gifts. On preaching, Shonagon requires handsome priests who are well trained in elocution, with excellent memories, as well as attentive, polite audiences who do not come to services to flirt and show off. She is most detailed on letter writing, offering prescriptions for paper, calligraphy, accompanying gift and bearer, and appreciation for the value of letters as gifts of love.

Especially important to Shonagon was the category of "morning-after letters." In Japanese court society, heterosexual sex between courtiers was illicit but frequent. It was guided by elaborate codes: as soon as the man left after a nighttime tryst, supposedly secret but actually quite public because of thin walls and numerous servants, custom required that he send a poem on beautiful paper with a decorative flower or branch to the lady, and that she reply. In a section entitled "Things That Make One Nervous," Shonagon scolds men who are irresponsible about this custom: "When a man who has spent the night with a woman is late with his next-morning letter, it worries not only the woman herself but even people who hear about the matter." Shonagon depicts the meticulous observation of domestic codes of communication as requisite for respect and influence at court: if the gentleman does not respond, everyone will hear about his lack of politeness, and he will suffer a loss of status that might be disastrous to him in court politics. The ideal gentleman lingers for a last few loving words, reluctant to go, and starts his morning-after letter as soon as he arrives home, putting "heart and soul into the calligraphy." He carefully selects a pageboy to carry his message, and he waits eagerly for a reply, reciting Chinese poems and religious meditations.

For further information on Sei Shonagon, see the introduction to *The Pillow Book of Shei Shonagon*, trans. Ivan Morris, 2 vols. (New York: Columbia University Press, 1967); Sen'ichi Hisamatsu, *Biographical Dictionary of Japanese Literature* (Tokyo: Kodansha International, 1976), 88–89; Earl Miner, Hiroko Odagiri, and Robert E. Morrell, *The Princeton Companion to Classical Japanese Literature* (Princeton: Princeton University Press, 1985), 227–28; and Felice Fischer, "Sei Shonagon," in *Japanese Women Writers: A Bio-Critical Sourcebook*, ed. Chieko I. Mulhern (Westport, Conn.: Greenwood Press, 1994), 339–45.

From *The Pillow Book* (c. 1000)

6. Different Ways of Speaking
   A priest's language.
   The speech of men and of women.[1]
   The common people always tend to add extra syllables to their words.

24. Depressing Things

A letter arrives from the provinces, but no gift accompanies it. It would be bad enough if such a letter reached one in the provinces from someone in the capital; but then at least it would have interesting news about goings-on in society, and that would be a consolation.

One has sent a friend a verse that turned out fairly well. How depressing when there is no reply-poem![2] Even in the case of love poems, people should at least answer that they were moved at receiving the message, or something of the sort; otherwise they will cause the keenest disappointment.

Someone who lives in a bustling, fashionable household receives a message from an elderly person who is behind the times and has very little to do; the poem, of course, is old-fashioned and dull. How depressing!

27. Hateful Things

One is in a hurry to leave, but one's visitor keeps chattering away. If it is someone of no importance, one can get rid of him by saying, "You must tell me all about it next time," but, should it be the sort of visitor whose presence commands one's best behavior, the situation is hateful indeed.

A man who has nothing in particular to recommend him discusses all sorts of subjects at random as though he knew everything.

To envy others and to complain about one's own lot; to speak badly about people; to be inquisitive about the most trivial matters and to resent and abuse people for not telling one, or, if one does manage to worm out some facts, to inform everyone in the most detailed fashion as if one had known all from the beginning—oh, how hateful!

One is in the middle of a story when someone butts in and tries to show that he is the only clever person in the room. . . .

One is telling a story about old times when someone breaks in with a little detail that he happens to know, implying that one's own version is inaccurate—disgusting behavior!

A newcomer pushes ahead of the other members in a group; with a knowing look, this person starts laying down the law and forcing advice upon everyone—most hateful.

A man with whom one is having an affair keeps singing the praises of some woman he used to know. Even if it is a thing of the past, this can be very annoying. How much more so if he is still seeing the woman! (Yet sometimes I find that it is not as unpleasant as all that.)

I hate people whose letters show that they lack respect for worldly civilities, w
discourtesy in the phrasing or by extreme politeness to someone who does not deser\
sort of thing is, of course, particularly odious should the letter be addressed to oneseıı.

As a matter of fact, most people are too casual, not only in their letters but in their direct
conversation. Sometimes I am quite disgusted at noting how little decorum people observe
when talking to each other. It is particularly unpleasant to hear some foolish man or woman
omit the proper marks of respect when addressing a person of quality; and, when servants fail
to use honorific forms of speech in referring to their masters, it is very bad indeed. . . .

Sometimes a person who is utterly devoid of charm will try to create a good impression by
using very elegant language; yet he only succeeds in being ridiculous. No doubt he believes
this refined language to be just what the occasion demands, but, when it goes so far that everyone bursts out laughing, surely something must be wrong.

It is most improper to address high-ranking courtiers, Imperial Advisers, and the like simply by using their names without any titles or marks of respect; but such mistakes are fortunately rare.

If one refers to the maid who is in attendance on some lady-in-waiting as "Madam" or
"that lady," she will be surprised, delighted, and lavish in her praise.

When speaking to young noblemen and courtiers of high rank, one should always (unless
Their Majesties are present) refer to them by their official posts. Incidentally, I have been
very shocked to hear important people use the word "I" while conversing in Their Majesties'
presence.

Ladies-in-waiting who want to know everything that is going on.

31. Things That Give a Pleasant Feeling

On a pretty sheet of white Michinoku[3] paper someone has written a letter with a brush
that would not seem capable of making such delicate strokes.

One is in a rather bored mood when a visitor arrives—a man with whom one's relations
are neither too intimate nor too distant. He tells one what has been happening in society,
things pleasant and disagreeable and strange; moving from one topic to another, he discusses
matters both public and private—and all in so clear a fashion that there is no possibility of misunderstanding. This gives one a very pleasant feeling.

One has visited a shrine or a temple with the request that certain prayers be said on one's
behalf. What a pleasure to hear the ritualist or priest intone them in a better voice, and more
fluently, than one had expected!

35. A Preacher Ought to Be Good-Looking

A preacher ought to be good-looking. For, if we are properly to understand his worthy sentiments, we must keep our eyes on him while he speaks; should we look away, we may forget to listen. Accordingly, an ugly preacher may well be the source of sin. . . .

But I really must stop writing this kind of thing. If I were still young enough, I might risk the consequence of putting down such impieties, but at my present stage of life I should be less flippant.

Some people, on hearing that a priest is particularly venerable and pious, rush off to the temple where he is preaching,[4] determined to arrive before anyone else. They, too, are liable to bring a load of sin on themselves and would do better to stay away. . . .

Now a couple of gentlemen who have not met for some time run into each other in the temple, and are greatly surprised. They sit down together and chat away, nodding their heads, exchanging funny stories, and opening their fans wide to hold before their faces so as to laugh the more freely. Toying with their elegantly decorated rosaries, they glance about, criticizing some defect they have noticed in one of the carriages or praising the elegance of another. They discuss various services that they have recently attended and compare the skill of different priests in performing the Eight Lessons or the Dedication of Sutras.[5] Meanwhile, of course, they pay not the slightest attention to the service actually in progress. To be sure, it would not interest them very much; for they have heard it all so often that the priest's words could no longer make any impression.

After the priest has been on his dais for some time, a carriage stops outside the temple. The outriders clear the way in a somewhat perfunctory fashion, and the passengers get out. They are slender young gentlemen, clad either in hunting costumes or in court cloaks that look lighter than cicada's wings, loose trousers, and unlined robes of raw silk. . . . As one would expect from such people, they now make a great show of rubbing their rosaries and prostrating themselves in prayer. The priest, convinced by the sight of the newcomers that this is a grand occasion, launches out on an impressive sermon that he presumes will make his name in society. But no sooner have the young men settled down and finished touching their heads on the floor than they begin to think about leaving at the first opportunity. Two of them steal glances at the women's carriages outside, and it is easy to imagine what they are saying to each other. They recognize one of the women and admire her elegance; then, catching sight of a stranger, they discuss who she can be. I find it fascinating to see such goings-on in a temple.

Often one hears exchanges like this: "There was a service at such-and-such a temple where they did the Eight Lessons." "Was Lady So-and-So present?" "Of course. How could she possibly have missed it?" It is really too bad that they should always answer like this.

One would imagine that it would be all right for ladies of quality to visit temples and take a discreet look at the preacher's dais. After all, even women of humble station may listen devoutly to religious sermons. Yet in the old days ladies almost never walked to temples to attend sermons; on the rare visits that they did undertake, they had to wear elegant traveling costume, as when making proper pilgrimages to shrines and temples. If people of those times had lived long enough to see the recent conduct in the temples, how they would have criticized the women of our day!

✦

47. Unsuitable Things

✦

Ugly handwriting on red paper.

✦

53. It is Hateful When a Well-Bred Young Man

It is hateful when a well-bred young man who is visiting a woman of lower rank calls out her name in such a way as to make everyone realize that he is on familiar terms with her. However well he may know her name, he should slur it slightly as though he had forgotten it. On the other hand, this would be wrong when a gentleman comes at night to visit a lady-in-waiting. In such a situation he should bring along a man who can call out the lady's name for him—a servant from the Office of Grounds if she is in the Imperial Palace, or else some-one from the Attendants' Hall; for his voice will be recognized if he calls her name himself. But, when he is visiting a mere under-servant or girl attendant, such a precaution is unnec-essary.

✦

74. Things That Make One Sorry

✦

A man who is going on a long journey wants letters of introduction to people living in the various places he plans to visit. By means of an intermediary he asks one to write such a letter to an acquaintance in one of these places. One dashes off a letter and sends it to the man be-fore he leaves for his travels. But, when one's acquaintance sees the letter, he becomes annoyed, saying that it is far too casual. Not only does he refuse to give the traveler a reply, but he goes about saying that one is a person of no consequence.

✦

84. Splendid Things

✦

A learned priest is also splendid. It is impressive enough when he reads his breviary by himself, but how much more so when he is among several lectors officiating in the Sacred Readings at one of the fixed periods![6] It is getting dark. "Why haven't they brought the oil?"

says one of the lectors. "How late they are in lighting the lamps!" All the lectors stop reading, but the learned priest continues quietly reciting the scriptures from memory.

85. Graceful Things

An attractive young woman . . . is engaged in writing practice, and the fine, smooth sheets of her notebook are elegantly bound by threads of uneven shading.

A letter written on fine green paper is attached to a budding willow branch.

92. Embarrassing Things

While entertaining a visitor, one hears some servants chatting without any restraint in one of the back rooms. It is embarrassing to know that one's visitor can overhear. But how to stop them?

A man whom one loves gets drunk and keeps repeating himself.

To have spoken about someone not knowing that he could overhear. This is embarrassing even if it be a servant or some other completely insignificant person.

Parents, convinced that their ugly child is adorable, pet him and repeat the things he has said, imitating his voice.

An ignoramus who in the presence of some learned person puts on a knowing air and converses about men of old.

A man recites his own poems (not especially good ones) and tells one about the praise they have received—most embarrassing.

Lying awake at night, one says something to one's companion, who simply goes on sleeping.

93. Surprising and Distressing Things

Someone speaks about things that he cannot possibly know from first-hand experience or in any other way; and he does not give his hearers a chance to object.

117. Shameful Things

A man's heart is a shameful thing. When he is with a woman whom he finds tiresome and distasteful, he does not show that he dislikes her, but makes her believe she can count on him. . . . Yet he is untrue to her not only in his thoughts but in his words; for he speaks badly about her to other women just as he speaks badly about those women to her. The woman, of course, has no idea that she is being maligned; and, hearing his criticisms of the others, she fondly believes he loves her best. The man for his part is well aware that this is what she thinks. How shameful!

When a woman runs into a lover with whom (alas!) she has broken for good, there is no reason for her to be ashamed if he regards her as heartless. But if the lover shows that he has not been even slightly upset by their parting, which to her was so sad and painful and difficult, she is bound to be amazed by the man and to wonder what sort of a heart he can have. Oblivious of his own callous attitude, her abandoned lover carries on a glib conversation in which he criticizes the behavior of other men.

120. Awkward Things

One has allowed oneself to speak badly about someone without really intending to do so; a young child who has overheard it all goes and repeats what one has said in front of the person in question.

133. Distractions at Boring Times

Even during a period of abstinence, if I receive a visit from a man who is witty and good at conversation, I let him come in.

144. Things That Are Unpleasant to Hear
Someone who has an ugly voice yet speaks and laughs without restraint.
A drowsy voice reciting incantations.
Someone who speaks while her teeth are being blackened.
A commonplace person who talks while eating.

147. Things That Make One Nervous

When a man or a woman whom one loathes comes to call, one becomes extremely nervous.

When a man who has spent the night with a woman is late with his morning-after letter,[7] it worries not only the woman herself but even people who hear about the matter.

When a woman produces a letter that she has received from a man one loves oneself, it makes one very nervous indeed.

156. Enviable People

People who have a good hand, who are skilful at composing poems, and who are always chosen first when there is a letter to be written. . . . Several women are attending a lady of quality who wishes a letter to be written on her behalf to an important person. Obviously many of them are suited for the task (it is not likely that *all* her women will have writing as feeble as the tracks of a bird's feet); yet the lady especially summons a woman who is not in the room and, producing her own inkstone, tells her to write the letter. This is bound to make the others envious. The fortunate woman may be one of the older members of the household, whose writing is of the most elementary kind; yet she will set herself to the task with enthusiasm. On the other hand she may be an experienced calligrapher. Perhaps the letter is going to some high court noble; or possibly it is intended to introduce a young woman who is hoping to take service in the palace. The writer is instructed to do her very best, and she begins by carefully selecting the paper.

157. Things That One Is in a Hurry to See or to Hear

A letter from the man one loves.

158. Things That Make One Impatient

A letter has arrived from some beloved person who is far away. One becomes very impatient as one tries to unfasten the rice paste with which it is tightly sealed.

One has to send a return poem in a hurry; yet it takes quite a long time to write and one becomes very impatient. In the case of a love letter one need not usually hurry so much;[8] but when one is exchanging ordinary letters with men or women, speed is essential and one is liable to make slips.

206. Things That Should Be Short

The speech of a young girl.

217. Letters Are Commonplace

Letters are commonplace enough, yet what splendid things they are! When someone is in a distant province and one is worried about him, and then a letter suddenly arrives, one feels as though one were seeing him face to face. Again, it is a great comfort to have expressed one's feelings in a letter even though one knows it cannot yet have arrived. If letters did not exist, what dark depressions would come over one! When one has been worrying about something and wants to tell a certain person about it, what a relief it is to put it all down in a letter! Still greater is one's joy when a reply arrives. At that moment a letter really seems like an elixir of life.

250. Men Really Have Strange Emotions

I remember a certain woman who was both attractive and good-natured and who furthermore had excellent hand-writing. Yet when she sent a beautifully written poem to the man of her choice, he replied with some pretentious jottings and did not even bother to visit her. She wept endearingly, but he was indifferent and went to see another woman instead. Everyone, even people who were not directly concerned, felt indignant about this callous behavior, and the woman's family was much grieved. The man himself, however, showed not the slightest pity.

251. Sympathy Is the Most Splendid of All Qualities

Sympathy is the most splendid of all qualities. This is especially true when it is found in men, but it also applies to women. Compassionate remarks, of the type "How sad for you!" to someone who has suffered a misfortune or "I can imagine what he must be feeling" about a man who has had some sorrow, are bound to give pleasure, however casual and perfunctory they may be. If one's remark is addressed to someone else and repeated to the sufferer, it is even more effective than if one makes it directly. The unhappy person will never forget one's kindness and will be anxious to let one know how it has moved him.

If it is someone who is close to one and who expects sympathetic inquiries,[9] he will not be especially pleased, since he is merely receiving his due; but a friendly remark passed on to less intimate people is certain to give pleasure. This all sounds simple enough, yet hardly anyone seems to bother. Altogether it seems as if men and women with good heads rarely have good hearts. Yet I suppose there must be some who are both clever and kind.

252. It Is Absurd of People to Get Angry

It is absurd of people to get angry because one has gossiped about them. How can anyone be so simple as to believe that he is free to find fault with others while his own foibles are passed over in silence? Yet when someone hears that he has been discussed unfavorably he is always outraged, and this I find most unattractive.

If I am really close to someone, I realize that it would be hurtful to speak badly about him and when the opportunity for gossip arises I hold my peace. In all other cases, however, I freely speak my mind and make everyone laugh.

254. Pleasing Things

Someone has torn up a letter and thrown it away. Picking up the pieces, one finds that many of them can be fitted together.[10]

I am most pleased when I hear someone I love being praised or being mentioned approvingly by an important person.

A person in whose company one feels awkward asks one to supply the opening or closing line of a poem. If one happens to recall it, one is very pleased. Yet often on such occasions one completely forgets something that one would normally know.

I greatly enjoy taking in someone who is pleased with himself and who has a self-confident look, especially if he is a man. It is amusing to observe him as he alertly waits for my next repartee; but it is also interesting if he tries to put me off my guard by adopting an air of calm indifference as if there were not a thought in his head.

255. One Day, When Her Majesty Was Surrounded by Several Ladies

One day, when Her Majesty was surrounded by several ladies, I remarked in connection with something that she had said, "There are times when the world so exasperates me that I feel I cannot go on living in it for another moment and I want to disappear for good. But then, if I happen to obtain some nice white paper, Michinoku paper, or white decorated paper, I decide that I can put up with things as they are a little longer. . . ."

"It really doesn't take much to console you," said the Empress, laughing. "I wonder what sort of a person it was who gazed at the moon on Mount Obasute."[11]

The ladies who were in attendance also teased me. "You've certainly found a cheap prayer for warding off evil," they said.

Some time later, when I was staying at home and absorbed in various petty worries, a messenger brought me twenty rolls of magnificent paper from Her Majesty. "Come back quickly," she wrote, adding, "I am sending you this because of what you told me the other day. It seems to be of poor quality, however, and I am afraid you will not be able to use it for copying the Sutra of Longevity."[12] It delighted me that Her Majesty should have remembered something that I myself had completely forgotten. . . . I was so excited that I could not frame a proper reply, but simply sent Her Majesty this poem:

> Thanks to the paper that the Goddess gave,
> My years will now be plenteous as the crane's. . . .[13]

Then I immediately used the paper I had received to write my collection of notes.[14] I felt a glow of delight and all my worries began to disappear.

268. Bad Things

Vulgar turns of speech are very bad. It is quite remarkable, but from a single word one can tell whether a person is vulgar or distinguished.

This does not mean that I consider my own way of speaking to be necessarily superior to that of others. After all, how should I always know what is good and what is bad? I am not concerned with what other people think but with my own views on the matter.

I do not mind if a man deliberately utters a vulgar expression without attempting to improve it; but I am disappointed if he uses it as though it were his normal way of speaking.

283. It Is Delightful for the Master of a Household
When a group of ladies-in-waiting are on leave from court and have gathered in a room, it is delightful for the master of the household to hear them exchanging flattering remarks about their mistresses and gossiping about the latest news from the palace.

I should like to live in a large, attractive house. My family would of course be staying with me; and in one of the wings I should have a friend, an elegant lady-in-waiting from the palace, with whom I could converse. Whenever we wished, we should meet to discuss recent poems and other things of interest. When my friend received a letter, we should read it together and write our answer.

290. If a Servant Girl
If a servant girl says about someone, "What a delightful gentleman he is!" one immediately looks down on him, whereas if she insulted the person in question it would have the opposite effect. Praise from a servant can also damage a woman's reputation. Besides, people of that class always manage to express themselves badly when they are trying to say something nice.

310. Things That Are Hard to Say
I find it difficult to transmit a long message[15] accurately from beginning to end; and the reply is no easier.

It is very hard to frame a reply to a message one has received from a person with whom one feels ill at ease.

A father hears that his grown-up son has done something that he would not have expected of him.[16] How hard it is to reprimand him to his face!

312. Everyone Should Behave as Elegantly as Possible
Everyone should behave as elegantly as possible—women as well as men. One might imagine that the mistress of a household can commit certain lapses without being criticized. Yet even she is not safe; for as soon as some knowing messenger comes to the house he will hear about her weaknesses and report them to everyone. Still more precarious is the position of a court lady, who is always in the center of things.

314. I Cannot Bear People

I cannot bear people who, without really understanding the subject, join in a conversation about past or recent events and who confuse the issue with their irrelevant remarks.

317. A Young Bachelor

A young bachelor of an adventurous nature comes home at dawn, having spent the night in some amorous encounter. Though he still looks sleepy, he immediately draws his inkstone to him and, after carefully rubbing it with ink, starts to write his next-morning letter. He does not let his brush run down the paper in a careless scrawl, but puts himself heart and soul into the calligraphy. What a charming figure he makes as he sits there by himself in an easy posture, with his robe falling slightly open! . . . As he finishes his letter, he notices that the white robe is still damp from the dew, and for a while he gazes at it fondly.

Then he makes arrangements for delivering his letter. Instead of calling one of the ladies in attendance, he takes the trouble to get up and select a page-boy who seems suitable for the task. Summoning the boy to his side, he whispers his instructions and hands over the letter. The page leaves for the lady's house, and for some time the gentleman watches him disappear in the distance. As he sits there, he quietly murmurs some appropriate passage from the sutras. . . .

Presently he performs his ablutions and changes into a white court cloak, which he wears without any trousers. Thus attired, he starts reciting the sixth scroll of the Lotus Sutra from memory. A pious gentleman indeed—or so one might think, except that at just this moment the messenger returns (he cannot have had far to go) and nods encouragingly to his master, who thereupon instantly interrupts his recitation and, with what might strike one as sinful haste, transfers his attention to the lady's reply.

318. It is Noon on a Summer Day

It is noon on a summer day and the weather is so hot that one does not know what to do with oneself. One keeps waving one's fan, but there is not a breath of cool air; then, just as one is hurrying to put one's hands in a bowl of iced water, a letter arrives. It is written on a sheet of fine, brilliantly red paper and attached to a Chinese pink in full bloom. Without thinking, one lays aside one's fan (which was not doing much good in any case) and imagines how deeply one's friend must feel to have taken all this trouble on such a suffocating day.

326. It Is Getting So Dark

It is getting so dark that I can scarcely go on writing; and my brush is all worn out. Yet I should like to add a few things before I end.

I wrote these notes at home, when I had a good deal of time to myself and thought no one would notice what I was doing. Everything that I have seen and felt is included. Since much of it might appear malicious and even harmful to other people, I was careful to keep my book hidden. But now it has become public, which is the last thing I expected.

One day Lord Korechika, the Minister of the Center, brought the Empress a bundle of notebooks. "What shall we do with them?" Her Majesty asked me. "The Emperor has already made arrangements for copying the 'Records of the Historian.'"[17]

"Let me make them into a pillow," I said.[18]

"Very well," said Her Majesty. "You may have them."

I now had a vast quantity of paper at my disposal, and I set about filling the notebooks with odd facts, stories from the past, and all sorts of things, often including the most trivial material. On the whole I concentrated on things and people that I found charming and splendid; my notes are also full of poems and observations on trees and plants, birds and insects. I was sure that when people saw my book they would say, "It's even worse than I expected. Now one can really tell what she is like." After all, it is written entirely for my own amusement and I put things down exactly as they came to me. How could my casual jottings possibly bear comparison with the many impressive books that exist in our time? Readers have declared, however, that I can be proud of my work. This has surprised me greatly; yet I suppose it is not so strange that people should like it, for, as will be gathered from these notes of mine, I am the sort of person who approves of what others abhor and detests the things they like.

Whatever people may think of my book, I still regret that it ever came to light.

Notes

This excerpt comes from *The Pillow Book of Sei Shonagon*, trans. and ed. Ivan Morris, 2 vols. (New York: Columbia University Press, 1967). I have regularized spelling and format, and I offer only condensed versions of the notes.

1. Women's language was far less influenced by Chinese and contained a larger proportion of "pure" Japanese words and constructions.

2. When one received a poem, it was customary to reply promptly with another poem ringing the changes on some central image. A failure to reply (or at least to have someone reply in one's place) was the height of rudeness. It was permissible not to answer love poems, but this signified that one was uninterested in the sender.

3. *Michinoku*: thick, white paper used for writing love letters, notes, and so on, and normally carried in the breast of one's robe.

4. *Sekkyo*, translated here as "preaching" or "sermon," has the literal meaning of "expound the sutras."

5. *Hakko* (Eight lessons): a series of eight services in which the eight volumes of the *Lotus Sutra* were expounded. Two services were held each day, one in the morning and one in the afternoon. The commentary normally took the form of a catechism, in which one priest would ask questions about important sections of the sutra and another would reply. *Kyo kuyo* (Dedication of sutras) refers to the practice of ordering copies of the sutra to be made and dedicated to some person or institution or to the Three Treasures—the Buddha, the Law, and the Priesthood. After the copy was completed, the sutra would be recited in a special service of dedication.

6. For the purpose of reading the scriptures, the day and night were divided into six periods. Lectors specialized in studying and reciting the *Lotus Sutra*.

7. It was an essential part of Heian etiquette for the man to write a love letter *(kinuginu no fumi)* to the lady with whom he had spent the night; it usually included a poem and was attached to a spray of some appropriate flower *(fumitsuke)*. The letter had to be sent as soon as the man returned home or, if he was

on duty, as soon as he reached his office. The lady was expected to send a prompt reply. If the man failed to send a letter, it normally meant that he had no desire to continue the liaison.

8. The rules for replying to love poems were less rigorous than those governing other types of correspondence.

9. Literally, "people whom one must necessarily love, people whom one must visit."

10. Letters were not considered private.

11. The empress refers to the *Kokin Shu* poem,

> Inconsolable my heart
> As I gaze upon the moon that shines
> On Sarashina's Mount Obasute.

The empress implies that Shonagon manages to comfort herself too easily, and contrasts her with the inconsolable poet who gazed at the moon in Sarashina. In the following lines the other ladies express the idea that Shonagon's method of curing her world-weariness is far too cheap; prayers for warding off evil normally involved making expensive gifts to Buddhist priests.

12. *Jumyo kyo* (Sutra of longevity): a short sutra frequently recited or copied in order to ward off personal dangers and secure a long life.

13. The poem plays on the word *kami*, which means both "deity" (referring to the empress) and "paper." Shonagon refers to her earlier remark that the sight of some good paper makes her feel she can stay a little longer on earth. The crane is a standard symbol of longevity in the Far East.

14. *Soshi*: collection of miscellaneous notes, impressions, anecdotes, and so on, of which Shonagon's *Pillow Book* (Makura no soshi) is an example. Shonagon must have received this paper from the empress well after the notebooks mentioned in section 326, and it seems likely that she had already started writing her *Pillow Book* by this time.

15. Literally, "such things as the message of an [ordinary] person or the message of a superior."

16. Some offense of a sexual nature, explains one of the commentaries. It may have been an injudicious liaison.

17. It appears that Korechika also presented Emperor Ichijo with a quantity of paper (good paper being in short supply even at court) and that the emperor had decided to use his allotment for making a copy of the huge Chinese historical work, *Shih chi*. Korechika became minister of the center in the eighth month of 994; he was forced out of the capital about a year and a half later. Thus it seems improbable that Shonagon started writing her *Pillow Book* before the winter of 994.

18. *Makura ni koso wa shihaberame* (make them into a pillow), that is, a pillow book. Here we have one explanation of the title of Shonagon's book. *Makura no soshi* (Pillow book) referred to a notebook kept in some accessible but relatively private place, and in which the author would record impressions, daily events, poems, letters, stories, ideas, descriptions of people, and so on. Her work is the only extant one of its type and is the oldest surviving book of the typically Japanese genre known as *zuihitsu*.

Christine de Pizan

c. 1364–c. 1430

Christine de Pizan was born in Venice, about 1364, to Tommaso di Benvenuto da Pizzano and his wife, the daughter of his friend Tommaso Mondino di Forlì. Christine's father had been a physician and a lecturer in astrology at the University of Bologna and was a civil servant in Venice when Christine was born. Shortly after her birth, he was invited to become the astrological adviser to Charles V of France. Thus Christine grew up at the French court, with access to the court orchards, gardens, zoo, and, most important, library. The library of Charles V emphasized books on government and science—subjects we can see reflected in Christine's own writings. In 1380, at age fifteen, Christine married Etienne de Castel, a royal secretary who was twenty-five and university educated. Christine, who was self-educated, was taught a notary's hand by either her father or her husband. Christine's father died in 1387, and her husband died during an epidemic while he was on a government mission in 1390. Christine thus had to assume economic responsibility for a double household: her own three children, as well as her mother and a niece.

From 1390 on, Christine made her living through writing, perhaps by copying some manuscripts, but soon by selling her books or by acquiring patronage through strategically placed gifts of her books (the most common system of support for an artist at the time). A woman who was well educated and supported herself by writing was unique at this time. Maintaining her ties with members of the French royal family and acquiring new patrons among the nobility of both France and England, in 1397 Christine was able to place her daughter Marie in a convent with Marie the daughter of Charles VI (where the aunt of Charles VI, Marie de Bourbon, was prioress). In 1398, her son Jean was placed as a companion to the son of the earl of Salisbury in England at the court of Richard II. Her oldest son died sometime between 1398 and 1401.

Christine began by writing poems—ballades—in the 1390s. By 1402, she had assembled over one hundred of them in a collection and continued with her poetry, often giving them as gifts to various nobles on New Year's Day, Valentine's Day, and May Day. Christine published in manuscript and eventually in ornate illuminated manuscripts once she could afford the artists. From 1392 on, Charles VI suffered periodic bouts of insanity, and power resided in one or another of the royal family—who ruled changed from day to day. From 1399 to 1404, Christine primarily cultivated Louis, Duke of Orleans; the king's younger brother; and his Italian princess, Valentina Visconti, as her patrons. In 1403, her poem *La mutacion de fortune* (The mutability of fortune) brought her to the attention of Philip, Duke of Burgundy, the king's uncle, who was aligned politically with the queen, Isabeau of Bavaria. Christine presented Philip with a New Year's copy of the poem in 1404, and he commissioned her to write the biography of Charles V, which she finished that same year. Like Pan Chao, Christine de Pizan was a court historian. In 1402, Christine participated in a debate concerning the *Roman de la rose* (*The Romance of the Rose*) and especially Jean de Meun's part, which was highly erotic and also misogynistic. Christine sent the queen a copy of all the writings in the controversy, including her own, and in 1410 Christine presented a collection of her poetry to the queen. After Philip's death, in 1406, his son and heir, John the Fearless, also Duke of Burgundy, became Christine's patron. The Burgundian family was especially concerned with the humanist themes of history, education of children, and political reform. These formed central interests, along with the defense of women, in Christine's works. She published numerous poems and prose works outlining the proper education of knights and rulers, such as *L'epistre d'Othéa la deese, que elle envoya a Hector de Troye quant il estoit en l'age de quinze ans* (The letter from Othéa the goddess that she sent to Hector of Troy when he was fifteen years old, 1399), as well as treatises that combined social critique with history, such as *L'avision-Christin* (The vision of Christine, 1405–1406). Her most famous works were written as part of the *querelle des femmes*, the controversy about women—*Le livre de la cité des dames* (The book of the city of ladies, 1405) and *Le livre des trois virtues* (The book of the three virtues, 1405), also known as *Le trésor de la cité des dames* (The treasure of the city of ladies).

Christine also eventually sought as patron the dauphin, Louis of Guyenne, son of Charles VI, born in 1396. It is for his education that she wrote *Le livre du corps de policie* (*The Book of the Body Politic*, 1404–1407), represented in this anthology by passages on eloquence from the sections for monarchs and for bourgeoisie. Christine's final decades were troubled by the civil war between the dukes in France, and she dedicated many of her final works to the women whose husbands and sons did not return from these battles, especially to Marie de Berry, Duchess of Bourbon. Tradition says that Christine joined her daughter in the Abbey of Poissy during these last years. One of her final works celebrated Joan of Arc. Christine died sometime in 1430, before Joan of Arc's capture and execution.

The Book of the Body Politic may be placed in a subcategory of the genre of conduct book popular in the late Middle Ages and throughout the Renaissance called "the education of the prince" or "the mirror for princes." Christine's treatise is broader than the usual work in this category, since it treats all the governing estates—princes, knights, clergy, and merchants. In three books, Christine instructs each estate on the virtues necessary to govern well, the education required for this class, and the specific duties and responsibilities to the classes above and below them (including the common people). It is especially interesting that Christine included so much about other estates in a book dedicated to the dauphin. Clearly she wished him to be a model ruler, interested in the welfare of the entire range of his subjects. Christine does not question this hierarchical order, for she sees it as the only way a society might live together harmoniously, joined as a body with each part functioning differently, the prince at its head.

In a hierarchical society, rhetoric is not for all estates. Jenny Redfern has analyzed Christine's views on rhetoric for women in scattered passages in *The Treasure of the City of Ladies*. Christine advises women to cultivate gentle, agreeable, charitable speech. Since women have no power, in order to protect their reputations they must be wary of speaking too freely, and they must learn to use persuasion and the influence of others to achieve their purposes. If they are married to a great man, they must use their special position as an advocate to help others with less power, and they must always urge peaceful solutions, since war harms women and children especially.

In *The Book of the Body Politic*, Christine is equally conscious of the intricacies of the power structure, although in this book she concentrates on the public hierarchy of men. In this hierarchical society, eloquence is firmly attached to class roles. The princes—kings, dukes, all the aristocratic leaders of society—need eloquence to impress and persuade their people to obey their ordinances and live together in an orderly society. Knights, whom Christine compares to dogs, need loyalty and courage but not eloquence. The bourgeoisie or merchants need rhetoric to persuade the commoners to keep quiet and to serve as liaison for the needs of the lower orders to their superiors. Christine describes eloquence for king and nobility through detailed reference to classical sources. She does not mention eloquence as a quality needed for a knight. She reinforces the prohibitions against disorderly speech for middle and lower classes through biblical quotations and invites the merchants to use their persuasive powers both to quell the complaints of the lower classes and to present just complaints to the prince. Rhetoric is thus a privilege of nobility in Christine's view of an ordered society, as well as a useful tool of negotiation for the merchant class, the class to which Christine belonged.

For further information, see Christine de Pizan, *The Book of the Body Politic*, ed. and trans. Kate Langdon Forhan (New York: Cambridge University Press, 1994); Daniel Kempton, "Christine de Pizan's *Cité des Dames* and *Trésor de la Cité*: Toward a Feminist Scriptural Practice," in *Political Rhetoric, Power, and Renaissance Women*, ed. Carole Levin and Patricia A. Sullivan (Albany: State University of New York Press, 1995), 15–37; and Jenny R. Redfern, "Christine de Pisan and *The Treasure of the City of Ladies*: A Medieval Rhetorician and Her Rhetoric," in *Reclaiming Rhetorica: Women in the Rhetorical Tradition*, ed. Andrea A. Lunsford (Pittsburgh: University of Pittsburgh Press, 1995), 73–92.

From *The Book of the Body Politic* (1404–1407)

Part I, Chapter 26
How It Is Fitting That a Prince Be Prudent and Wise in Eloquence

Just as we have said that it is necessary for a prince to be a just judge, and even better that he should love and gather around him wise men and philosophers, so certainly it is quite expedient that he himself be wise and that he be somewhat instructed in the [arts and] sciences so that he knows something about them. . . . And that a prince should be wise is clear from the saying of Plato, as repeated in Valerius[1]—which, though brief, is at the same time very noble and very significant—for Plato said that the world will be fortunate when philosophers begin to rule or kings become philosophers.

And since all knowledge should be part of his learning, one can infer that it is most virtuous for a prince to speak eloquently and to reason wisely and logically. For there is little doubt that well ordered and wise speech issuing from the mouth of a prince is far more deeply considered and more willingly heard than that coming from any other source. And also he is able to profit from it in many cases, for it would be difficult to find a hard heart that is not softened by fair words. For example, it was written of Philostratus that he was so eloquent a man that, notwithstanding the custom of the Ancients, governed by wise philosophers, to live in freedom without a ruler, yet through his fair eloquence, wise and sweet, he was such a man that, even though the wise Solon who upheld liberty opposed him, he was made prince or ruler of Athens. There are enough other examples on this topic to be able to show how oftentimes noble eloquence is a great aid.

But to the noble eloquence that is of a level to be called "Rhetoric," Valerius also added the manner of movement of the body in speaking, and said that when eloquence is conveyed through the wise disposition of graceful movement of the body, it invades the watchers in three ways, for it binds the hearts[2] of some [people] and the ears of others, [and] it seduces and mollifies the eyes of others. It invades the heart, he said, when, through appropriate movement of the body, the speaker represents and recalls to the memory such things as dangers, fortunate and unfortunate events, virtues, vices, examples of brave men, and the effects of advice—by such means [people's] spirits are guided to consent by speaking. Second, the ears of the audience or of those who watch are invaded and captured by agreeable and well moderated pronunciation because it causes great pleasure and great delight. Third, the eyes of those who watch are invaded to such a degree that they heed and ponder the handsome bearing and integrity of the persuader or the speaker. And thus his eloquence is increased by all these means. And by the opposite of these means, he says, speaking is poorly relished and less powerful and yields little effectiveness. For example, Valerius said that one who was named Quintus Ortensius put so much study into graceful movement of the body while speaking, more or as much as [into study of] speaking, that one never knew whether one ran after him to listen to him or to watch him. And thus, said Valerius, sight assists the words of the orator or speaker, and the words assist the sight of the listeners.

Chapter 27
How It Is an Appropriate Thing That a Prince Have Dignified Bearing

And along with graceful speech and seemly movement of the body, it is fitting for a prince to have a handsome shape and a dignified gait and posture. A handsome and lofty performance by a prince is a thing that gives much pleasure to see, not putting on arrogance, but maintaining discretion. And much profit comes to the person who naturally knows how to regulate his deportment or can acquire such skill, if, as is said of the wise Pericles (of whom I have already spoken), he was of such noble shape and carriage that through his wise speech much more than through force, he commanded the Athenians to do as he wished. And then, we can draw examples from the ancients of other countries concerning the handsome fashioning of the prince—that is, the handsome carriage and bearing and skillful movement while speaking delightful and embellished language.

Nor is it right, it seems to me, that we forget our French princes, those, among others, whom we have seen and attended upon, who are very special and excellent to our eyes, adorned with a handsome appearance, as was the very illustrious, knowledgeable, and prudent, wise King Charles, fifth of that name, who has been mentioned formerly, who was without fault, possessed of very great learning. It was beautiful to see his handsome and lordly bearing and to hear his exquisitely ornamented language. And when in council or elsewhere he would lay out an argument or speak at length, he did not fail to put his premises in excellent order, perfect and precise, and to deduce directly from them several points, and then to conclude his pronouncement very notably—just as he demonstrated before the Emperor, his uncle, the time he was at Paris. He enumerated at length before the council the injuries one after the other he had received from the king of England, and then he desired to renew the war (just as I put these things at length in the book of *Feats and Good Manners* that I compiled, in the third part, if I remember, which is near the end of the tenth book).

And his very excellent son Louis, Duke of Orleans, inherited this very notable gift of speaking, without doubt. As everyone knows, it is a marvelous thing to hear him speak in council or any other gathering, [to hear him] guide and steer what he wishes to say through a well-crafted and polished arrangement, such that hypnotized the solemn clerks of the University of Paris, flawless rhetoricians, who discovered themselves marvelling at this force that moved them. For if he first puts forward a question or a proposition on which he wishes to speak, he does not miss any point, [and] he follows all the rules [of logic] that apply in order to arrive at the terms [of his syllogism]. And if he gives a response to anyone, even if the thing before him that has been proposed is strange and composed of many different materials, he does not fail to recall all the main points and sections of the matter, and he responds to each article so appropriately that those who have seen him witness to the miracle of his great memory and his wonderful rhetoric. And along with this is the fashioning and movement of the body so suited to the eloquent language that he is well able to be compared to the famous ancients spoken of before.

And the excellent Duke of Burgundy, Philip, brother to King Charles spoken of before, and uncle to Louis, also had, along with great erudition which made him famous, a very fine speaking ability and a very gracious manner.

Thus concludes my advice concerning the fashioning and adorning of language, how it comes to some by nature more than to others, even those who are noble; it is a sign of good understanding, and firmness of thinking, and constant courage, which qualities often belong to a lofty prince and a valiant man.

Part III, Chapter 6
Concerning the Second Estate of People, Known as the Bourgeois or Merchants

These people ought to be involved in the happenings and needs of the cities where they live so that all things that pertain to trade and to the community are well governed. Because the lower classes do not commonly possess great prudence in words or anything that touches on politics, they should not interfere in the ordinances established by princes. . . . If [the merchants] have a case sometime when the commoners are upset by any burden, they should assemble the wisest and most discreet in deeds and words among them, and go before the prince or before the council to make their outcry in humility and to present their case in a good-natured way, and not let them [the commoners] do anything, because that is the common way to destruction of cities and of peace. As much as is in their power, the merchants should quiet the murmurings of the common people because of the evil that could come to all in the area—by this means they should protect themselves as much as others. And if sometimes the ordinances of princes and of their councils on the surface seem, in their judgment, improper in any way, they should not interpret it the worst way, but should think that what was done was done with good intention, though the causes are not made apparent to everyone. For there is danger in foolishly complaining. "Wisdom knows how to keep silent," said Socrates, the greatest and most commendable philosopher, according to Valerius. Once he was in a place where there were many who talked, speaking evil about the ordinances of the prince, and noticing one of these evil-speakers who came to him, asked why he alone remained silent and all the others spoke. "Because," he said, "I have repented many times of speaking, but not once of remaining silent." It is a much better thing to hush the tongue, from which can come evil and not reward, and the discreet person sees this. The wise Cato said that the highest virtue is to curb the tongue. For he who is close to God, by means of educated reason, knows how to keep silent. And Seneca says, in Book V of his last prose-work, that those who wished to be disciples of Pythagoras[3] had to agree to be silent for five years because, he said, thus they would discover that which they should speak.

Part III, Chapter 7
How Wise Citizens Ought to Remind the Common People of Their Duties[4]

And thus, as it was said [before], the wise should remind the simple and ignorant that they should be silent about that which it is not fitting they should speak, from which great danger could come and no good. And this testimony is written in the book of Exodus, the twenty-second chapter, that the law prohibits complaining, and it says that you may not murmur at all against lords and you may not speak evil against the princes of the people.[5] And this is confirmed by Solomon in the book of Ecclesiastes, the fifth chapter, who says you may not slander the king in your thoughts,[6] that is to say that the subject should not make a wicked conspiracy against the lord. And there is also danger in complaining against and defying the laws of princes, as Justin[7] says in the twelfth book, concerning Alexander. For when [Alexander] had won dominion over Persia, for his great victories, he desired to be saluted in the manner of that place, which was a common manner of worship, as we might say to genuflect or to kneel when speaking, which was not the custom in Macedon or in other regions. But because there was complaining, Callisthenes[8] the philosopher (whom Aristotle had left with Alexander because he was not able to endure the hardship of following him) reproved [Alexander] very bitterly and spoke too much, for which Alexander had him put to death. And it is known, says Valerius, that when Aristotle left Alexander, he left him Callisthenes in his place, who was his disciple and was very wise. Aristotle taught his disciple that he should never speak about the vices of his prince behind his back; and he told him it should not be done for two reasons. The first is that it is not fitting for a subject to speak evil of his lord; the other is that when such words rush from the mouth, then speedily flatterers are ready to report them. And further, he taught him that he should speak little to Alexander, and that when he did speak to him, he would do so mildly. And, consequently, if he kept silent, he would not say anything that could be turned to his disadvantage. And he should not flatter, yet through his merry speech, what he said to him would be acceptable. But this disciple did not learn well the doctrine of his teacher, and so he repented of it too late.

Notes

The selections by Christine de Pizan are my own translations, based on the standard edition, *Le livre du corps de policie*, ed. Robert H. Lucas (Geneva: Librarie Droz, 1967), pt. 1, chaps. 26–27, pp. 80–85; pt. 3, chap. 7, pp. 185–91.

1. Valerius Maximus, a first-century Roman historian and rhetorician, was most famous in the Middle Ages for his *Memorable Deeds and Words in IX Books*.

2. Literally, "spirits of the heart."

3. Pythagoras: Greek philosopher, sixth century B.C.E., famous for his beliefs in reincarnation and number as the basis of the universe.

4. Literally, "concerning what they ought to do."

5. Exodus 22:28 KJV: "Thou shalt not revile the gods, nor curse the rule of thy people."

6. Exodus 10:20 KJV: "Curse not the king, no not in thy thought."

7. Marcus Junianius Justinus, third-century historian, wrote an epitome of Pompeius Trogus's *Historiae Phillipicae*.

8. Callisthenes: fourth century B.C.E., Aristotle's nephew, Alexander the Great's historian, executed by Alexander for participation in a conspiracy.

Margaret Cavendish, Duchess of Newcastle

c. 1623–1673

Margaret Cavendish was the eighth and last child of Thomas and Elizabeth Leighton Lucas. Her father died when she was a toddler. A shy child, Margaret nevertheless stayed often in London with her sister, who was married to Sir Edward Pye. The Lucas family were Royalists and hosted Marie de Medici for two days when she visited her daughter, Queen Henrietta Maria. Many family members were arrested at the beginning of the Civil War disturbances. After their release, they gathered in 1642 at the court in exile in Oxford. With her brothers in the army, Margaret joined the queen's ladies-in-waiting and accompanied her further west and eventually to France. She was separated from her family for eight years. At court she heard of the marquis of Newcastle, a heroic, loyal commander who, never sufficiently supported by the king, retreated to France after his army was slaughtered. They met, fell in love, became engaged secretly, and were married in 1645. Their secrecy and the difference in their class earned them the queen's disfavor.

Margaret began to write in Paris early in her marriage. At first impoverished, Newcastle had secured funds by 1647, was an adviser to the king, and entertained a brilliant circle in exile—Waller, Descartes, Gassendi, Hobbes (who was writing *The Leviathan*). In 1648, because of social unrest in Paris, they moved to the Netherlands and then on to Antwerp. In the meantime, the Royalists and the Scottish army had failed and King Charles was executed in 1649. Prince Charles barely escaped in another defeat in 1651. Margaret returned to England in 1652 to try to negotiate an annuity from her husband's estates in England, but she failed and returned to Antwerp, worried about her husband's health. Although Margaret complains that she was not well educated because she did not have a humanist's training in classical languages, she seems to have been an avid reader, for she imitates and alludes to many works in her writings. She claims, further, to have learned a great deal from her husband and from the writers and philosophers who attended on him. All during this period she continued to write and publish in expensive, subsidized editions, with commendatory poems by her husband as preface. Cavendish was very prolific, publishing poetry, plays, orations, letters, a utopia, philosophical reflections, short romances, and a biography of her husband. Her husband, himself a poet and playwright, adored her and encouraged her writing. Newcastle and his wife returned to England but retired from court to Welbeck, their country estate, in 1660. Newcastle was titled a duke in 1665. Despite the great disparity in their ages, Margaret died before her husband, on December 15, 1673.

In 1655, while in exile during the Interregnum, Cavendish published *The World's Olio*. This work is a cross between a commonplace book (in which students organized their thoughts and ideas from great writers under varied topics), a collection of short essays (a relatively new form in the seventeenth century), and an encyclopedia (a favorite genre of the early humanists). Under a wide range of topics, covering manners, governing, science, and education, Cavendish discusses her own opinions of important philosophical issues of her day. Interspersed through much of the book, in short sections, she sketches her ideas about rhetoric. Her theories seem to be influenced mainly by empiricists in the line of Bacon and sophistic rhetoric as revived by the humanists: she analyzes the physiological production of voice and cautions against verbal excess and attention to words, not things, in speech, in the manner of the empiricists; she argues both sides of the question and qualifies her answers so often as to appear a relativist, like the sophists. She is extremely sensitive to the gendered constraints on speech, but argues her way out of them by establishing "the natural" as the quality most important to eloquence, then establishing women as speakers by nature. She anticipates eighteenth-century rhetoricians in her interest in adding "to inform" as an aim of rhetoric. Like Christine de Pizan, she is hierarchical in her view of who possesses eloquence. But like Madeleine de Scudéry, whom she may have met in Paris, she places conversation at the center of her conception of speech. Like Astell, she does not like sermons. Cavendish further explored oratory and eloquence in *Orations of Divers Sorts* (1662), "The Female Academy" from *Plays* (1662), and *CCXI Sociable Letters* (1664).

For further information, see Sara Heller Mendelson, *The Mental World of Stuart Women: Three Studies* (Brighton, U.K.: Harvester Press, 1987), 1–61; Kathleen Jones, *A Glorious Fame: The Life of Margaret Cavendish, Duchess of Newcastle, 1623–1673* (London: Bloomsbury, 1988); Kate Lilley, ed., introduction to *Margaret Cavendish: The Blazing World & Other Writings* (London: Penguin, 1992); Jane Donawerth, "The Politics of Renaissance Rhetorical Theory by Women," in *Political Rhetoric, Power, and Renaissance Women*, ed. Carole Levin and Patricia A. Sullivan (Albany: State University of New York Press, 1995), 257–72; Donawerth, "Conversation and the Boundaries of Public Discourse in Rhetorical Theory by Renaissance Women," *Rhetorica* 16, no. 2 (Spring 1998): 181–99; Christine Mason Sutherland, "Aspiring to the Rhetorical Tradition: A Study of Margaret Cavendish," in *Listening to Their Voices: The Rhetorical Activities of Historical Women*, ed. Molly Meijer Wertheimer (Columbia: University of South Carolina Press, 1997), 255–71; Anna Batigelli, *Margaret Cavendish and the Exiles of the Mind* (Lexington: University Press of Kentucky, 1998); and Ryan John Stark, "Margaret Cavendish and Composition Style," *Rhetoric Review* 17, no. 2 (Spring 1999): 264–81.

From *The Worlds Olio* (1655)

The Preface to the Reader

It cannot be expected I should write so wisely or wittily as men, being of the effeminate sex, whose brains nature hath mixed with the coldest and softest elements. And to give my reason why we cannot be so wise as men, I take leave and ask pardon of my own sex, and present my reasons to the judgment of truth; but I believe all of my own sex will be against me out of partiality to themselves, and all men will seem to be against me, out of a compliment to women. . . .

True it is, our sex make great complaints that men from their first creation usurped a supremacy to themselves, although we were made equal by nature, which tyrannical government they have kept ever since, so that we could never come to be free, but rather more and more enslaved, using us either like children, fools, or subjects, that is, to flatter or threaten us, to allure or force us to obey, and will not let us divide the world equally with them, as to govern and command, to direct and dispose as they do; which slavery hath so dejected our spirits, as we are become so stupid, that beasts are but a degree below us, and men use us but a degree above beasts. Whereas, in nature we have as clear an understanding as men, if we were bred in schools to mature our brains and to manure our understandings, . . . we might bring forth the fruits of knowledge.

But to speak truth, men have great reason not to let us into their governments, for there is great difference betwixt the masculine brain and the feminine, the masculine strength and the feminine. . . . Men and women may be compared to the blackbirds, where the hen can never sing with so strong and loud a voice, nor so clear and perfect notes as the cock; her breast is not made with that strength to strain so high. Even so, women can never have so strong judgment, nor clear understanding, nor so perfect rhetoric, to speak orations with that eloquence as to persuade so forcibly, to command so powerfully, to entice so subtly, and to insinuate so gently and softly into the souls of men. Or they may be compared to the sun and moon, according to the description in the Holy Writ, which saith, "God made two great lights, the one to rule the day; the other the night."[1] So man is made to govern commonwealths, and women their private families.[2]

To the Reader

I desire those that read any of this book, that every chapter may be read clearly, without long stops and stays, for it is with writers as it is with men: for an ill-affected fashion or garb takes away the natural and graceful form of the person; so writings, if they be read lamely or crookedly, and not evenly, smoothly, and throughly,[3] ensnarl the sense. Nay, the very sound of the voice will seem to alter the sense of the theme; though the sense will be there in despite of the ill voice or reader, but it will be concealed, or discovered to its disadvantage. For, like an ill musician or, indeed, one that cannot play at all, who instead of playing, he puts the fiddle out of tune and causeth a discord, which if well played upon would sound harmoniously, or like one that can play but[4] one tune on all sorts of instruments, so some will read with one tone or sound of voice, though the passions and numbers are different. And some again in reading wind up their voices to such a passionate screw, that they whine or squeal rather than speak or read; others fold up their voices with that distinction, that they make that three square that is four square, and narrow that should be broad, and high that should be low, and low that should be high; and some again so fast that the sense is lost in the race. So that writings, though they are not so, yet they sound good or bad according to the readers, and not according to their authors. And indeed, such advantage a good or ill reader gives, as those that read well shall give a grace to a foolish author, and those that read ill, disgrace a wise and a witty author.

But there are two sorts of readers, the one that reads to himself and for his own benefit, the other to benefit another by hearing it. In the first, there is required a good judgment and a ready understanding; in the other, a good voice and a graceful delivery. So that a writer hath a double desire: the one, that he may write well; the other, that he may be read well. And my desire is the more earnest, because I know my writings are not strong enough to bear an ill reader, wherefore I entreat so much favor as to give it its own countenance, wherein you will oblige the writer to be

Yours,

M.N.[5]

Book I, Part I

Why Men Write Books

Some say men write books not so much to benefit the world, as out of love to fame, thinking to gain them honor of reputation. But surely men are so delighted with their own conceits, especially fine and new ones, that were it a sin or infamy, they would write them, to see their beauty and enjoy them, and so become unlawful lovers. Besides, thoughts would be lost if not put into writings; for writing is the picture of thoughts, which shadows last longer than men.[6] But surely men would commit secret idolatry to their own wit, if they had not applause to satisfy them and examples to humble them, for every several man, if wit were not discovered, would think not any had it but he. For men take pleasure first in their own fancies, and after seek to gain the approving opinions of others, which opinions are like women's dressings: for some will get such advantage in putting on their clothes, who although they have ill faces and not so exact bodies, will make a better show than those that are well favored and neatly shaped with disordered attire; wherein some men are so happy in their language and delivery as it beautifies and adorns their wit, which without it would be like an unpolished diamond. But such difference there is between, that to create a fancy is the nature of a god, but to make neat and new words is the nature of a tailor.

Of Several Writings

Writings that are set forth in books and other ways are of several and different natures: for some, as magistrates and fathers, do reprove and endeavor to reclaim the world and men, as moral philosophers; others as attorneys do inform them, as historians; some as lawyers do plead in the behalf of some former writings, and act against others, as contraversers;[7] some as ambitious tyrants that would kill all that stood in their way, as casuists; some as challengers, as logicians; some as scouts, as natural philosophers, but they bring not always true intelligence;[8] some like hangmen, as the skeptics that strive to strangle not only all opinions, but all knowledge; some like ambassadors that are sent to condole and congratulate, as books of humiliation and thanksgiving; some as merchants, as translators which traffic out of one language into another; some as painted faces, as oratory; some as jubilies,[9] to recreate, rejoice, and delight the spirits of men, as poetry; some as bawds to entice the minds, as amorous romance; some as pits that one must go many fathoms deep to find the bottom, neither do they always reach it, as those that are called strong lines; some as conjurers that fright with their threatening prophecies; some as cutpurses that steal from the writings of others; some as jugglers that would have falsehood appear for truth; some like mountebanks[10] that deceive and give more words than matter; some as echoes which commonly answer to another's voice; some like buffoons that laugh and jest at all; some like flatterers that praise all; some like malcontents[11] that complain against all; and some like God that is full of truth, and gives a due to all deservers; and some like devils that slander all.

Of the Motion of the Thoughts in Speaking and Writing

Those that have very quick thoughts shall speak readier than write because in speaking they are not tied to any style or number.[12] Besides, in speaking, thoughts lie close and careless, but, in writing, they are gathered up and are like the water in a cup, that the mouth is held downward, for every drop striving to be out first, stops the passage; or like the common people in an uproar, that runs without any order and disperses without success, when slow and strong thoughts come well armed and in good order, discharges with courage, and goeth off with honor.

Of Eloquence, Art, and Speculation

Many do seem to admire those writings whose styles are eloquent and, through ignorance, take it for eloquence, commending the method instead of the matter, the words instead of the sense, the paint instead of the face, the garb instead of the person. But hard and unusual phrases are like a constrained behavior: it hath a set countenance, treads nicely, taking short steps, and carries the body so stiff and upright, as it seems difficult and uneasy, like those that think it a part of good breeding to eat their meat by rule and measure, opening the mouth at a just and certain wideness, grinding the meat betwixt their teeth like a clock with so many strokes as make an hour, so many bits makes a swallow. So likewise, if the little finger be not bowed short, and by degrees all their fingers to be joined until the fore-finger and the thumb meet in a round circle, they think all other vulgarly bred. But nature is easy, and art hard, and what resembles nature nearest is most to the life, and what is most to the life is best. But art belongs more to the mechanics and peasants than to the noble and free, and all arts belong more to actions than speculations. And though speculation be nothing until it be put into practice, yet the best actions come from the clearest speculations, for speculations are like the king, to command and rule, practice the slave, to obey and work. But there are more arts and inventions gotten by chance and practice than merely by ingenuity of brain.

Of Orators

I have heard say that orators are seldom wise men, for they study so much of the words, as they consider not the matter, for though method in words may please the sense of the ear, yet not the understanding. For they that will speak wisely must speak the next way to the matter or business, but if it be in such a case as the ear is more to be desired than the understanding, they must speak composedly. For rhetoric is choosing words fitted to such a subject and, though study and society sweetens language, yet if it have not a natural elegance, it shall not work so strongly upon the senses.

What Discourses Are Enemies to Society

Of all discourses, the worst enemy to society is the divulging the infirmities of others, wherein some are so evil-natured in striving to defame others, as they will not only use all their rhetoric to make their faults appear more odious or their virtues less, but will strive to make their virtues seem vices—when to discover infirmities is ignoble, but to lessen virtues is the part of an envious man, which is the nature of a devil. And since union is the bond of society, the discourse should always tend to peace and not to discord; for there is no man but hath virtues to praise, as well as vices to dispraise. And it is as easy to take the better side—I am sure it is more honorable for the speaker, for faults in particular should never be mentioned but in private to themselves, in an admonishing way, otherwise they do but inveterate.

The next enemy to society in discourse is disputation, which affords the least pleasure in society. For first, it is tedious. Next, it is contradictory and begets enemies of friends. And it is a kind of rudeness to contradict strangers, though they should speak nonsense, but logic, which is the art of disputations, should be left to schools, writings, and public theaters, which are appointed places for such discourse. For some say logic is to make truth appear; others that it is to make falsehood appear like truth; and some say, again, that it is to dispute on both sides, and that it makes more discord than it can compose, which discord is the cause of so many writings, and several religions, and factions in the world, which makes men become tigers and vultures to one another, when otherwise they would be like the society of angels.

The last and worst enemy to society is forswearing and blasphemy, for what pleasure or advantage can a man have to blaspheme, which is to curse God, who hath the power to return his curses on his head with horrid punishments. And for swearing, though it be allowed for the confirmation of a truth, and for the keeping of a promise, whereby it is made sacred and religious, yet to make it common is to make it of no effect. Besides, it shows little wit and less memory, that they should want words to fill up their discourse with, but what oaths are fain[13] to supply. And for lying, where there is no truth, there can be no trust; and where there is no trust, there can be no union; and where there is no union, there can be no perfect society, but may rather be called a concourse, which is to meet rather than to unite, where society is the father of peace, the bond of love, the arm of strength, the head of policy, the heart of courage, the hand of industry, and the bowels of charity. And discourse is the life which gives light to the eyes of the understanding, sound to the ears, mirth to the heart, comfort to the sorrowful and afflicted, patience to the oppressed, entertains the time, recreates the mind, refreshes the memory, makes the desires known, and is a heavenly comfort.

The Best Kind of Discourse in Ordinary Conversation

The best kind of discourse in ordinary conversation, and most pleasant, is that which is most various, free, and easy, as to discourse of countries, the natures of soils, situations of cities, and people's laws, customs, and superstitions; what men, women, and beasts were deified; what countries had most and longest wars and peace; what conquerors there were and who they were, what conducts they used in their victories, how they marshalled their forces, and what forces they had; what famous commonwealths-men there were, their policies in governments; the beginning of states, their falls, the causes of their risings and their ruins; what countries were governed by republics or democracy, what by aristocracy, and what by monarchy; what commodities several countries afford for traffic[14] or otherwise; what plantations there are; what men famous for arts and what arts there are; what famous buildings and monuments there are or have been, and who were their founders; what colleges or schools there are or have been of famous and learned men, as philosophers, historians, and of their several opinions; what ancient poets, and who were accounted the best, what countries they were born, bred, or lived in; what punishments or exiles there were, or what faults, what cruelties were put in execution, and by whom, and to whom, and where; what kings governed with clemency, and what by tyranny, and what their factions, their splendors, their decays, their pastimes, and recreations were; what ambassadors there were and their ambassages, from kings to kings, and states to states; what entertainments and magnificencies princes make; what several fashions several countries have in their entertainments and sports, what extravagant garbs and diets; what women famous for beauty and martial exploits; what kind of people can live the hardest, and which live the most luxurious; and for discourses of mirth—songs, verses, scenes, and the like; and for their home discourses, according to their affairs and employments.

And this is better discourse than to backbite their friends, or to curse their foes, or to scandal the innocent, or seditiously to complain against their government and governors, or to speak lasciviously to foul the ears of the chaste. And there is no wit in a clownish discourse. And to speak like a gentleman is to speak honestly, civilly, and confidently. To speak like a wise man is to speak properly, timely, and knowingly, and not conceitedly.

The Four Discourses

There are four kinds of discourses—as foolish, extravagant,[15] nonsense, and rational. And of all, nonsense is the hardest. For to speak foolishly is as if a man should speak to a child, that can have no experience or knowledge of affairs in the world or judgment to distinguish; or to a shepherd, that never saw nor heard many things or reports, but only his sheep and their bleatings; as to ask any questions of battles or governments of commonwealths, or to discourse with statesmen of children's babies, bells, or rattles, which is to speak improperly and not timely. And to speak extravagantly is as if a man were to sell his house, and another should ask him what he should give him for it, and he should answer him in talking of transmigrations and metamorphoses or the like, and so to speak quite from the purpose. But to speak rationally is to ask proper questions, or to answer directly to what he is questioned in, for reason is to clear the understanding and to untie the knots that clear the truth. But to speak nonsense is to speak that which hath no coherence to anything, when there is no words but may be compared to something, and though it hath no reference to what is spoken, yet it might have to what might be spoken. So as it is harder to find out nonsense in words, than reason.

Of Vulgar Discourse

The reason why the vulgar hath not such varieties of discourse is not only because they have not read or heard or seen so much of the world as the better sort hath, but because they have not so many several words for several things. For that language which is most copious, wit flourishes most in. For fancy[16] in poetry without expression of words is but dead. For that makes a language full to have many several words for one thing or sense. And though the vulgar is born and bred with such a language, yet very seldom with variety and choice, being employed in the coarse affairs of the world and not bred in schools or courts where are the most significant, choicest, and plentifullest expressions, which make the better sort not only have finer and sweeter discourse, but fill them full of high and aspiring thoughts, which produce noble qualities and honorable actions; where the meaner sort of people are not only ignorant of the purity of their native language, but corrupteth what they have and being always groveling in the dung of the earth, where all their thoughts are employed, makes their discourse so unsavory.

Of Old Men's Talking Too Much

The reason why old men love rather to tell stories than to hear them is because the outward senses decay sooner than the understanding, and hearing imperfectly wearies them by tedious attention. For though old men many times grow deaf, yet they seldom grow dumb with age, and when one faculty fails, they strive to supply it with another, which makes them commit the error of too much talking.

Of Speaking Much or Little

Those that speak little are either wise men or crafty men, either to observe what was spoken by others, or not to discover themselves too suddenly. And those that speak much are either fools or else very witty men—fools, because they have little to entertain them in their thoughts, and therefore employ the tongue to speak like a parrot by rote, and fools think the number of words helps to fill up the vacant places of sense; but those that have wit, their brains are so full of fancy that if their tongue like a midwife should not deliver some of the issue of the brain, it would be overpowered, and lost in painful throes.

Of the Same Defect in Women

And the reason why women are so apt to talk too much is an overweening opinion of themselves in thinking they speak well, and striving to take off that blemish from their sex of knowing little by speaking much, as thinking many words have the same weight of much knowledge. But my best friend[17] says he is not of my opinion, for he says women talk because they cannot hold their tongues.

Of Silence

It is said that silence is a great virtue. It is true—in a sick person's chamber that loves no noise, or at the dead time of night, or at such times as to disturb natural rest, or when superiors are by, or in the discourse of another, or when attention should be given, or if they have great impediments of speech. And speaking many times is dangerous, infamous, rude, foolish, malicious, envious, and false.

But it is a melancholy conversation that hath no sound. And though silence is very commendable at some times, yet in some cases it is better to speak too much than too little, as in hospitality and the receiving [of] civil visits, for it were better that strangers and friends should think you talk too much than that they should be displeased in thinking they were not welcome by speaking too little. Besides, it is a less fault to err with too much courtesy than with too much neglect. And surely to be accounted a fool is not so bad as to be said to be rude—for the one is the fault of the judger; the other is the fault of the actor or speaker. For civility is the life to society, and society to humane nature.

It is true that there are more errors committed in speaking than in silence, for words are light, and subtle, and airy, as that when they are once flown out, cannot be recalled again, but only to ask pardon with more. And there is an old saying, "to talk much and well is seldom heard." But it cannot be verified in all, for some will speak well as long as there is grounds to speak on, but the length of time makes it sound to the ear as wine tastes to a drunken man when he cannot relish between good and bad. So that it is not only the matter, but the manner, time, and subject in speaking which makes it so hard to speak well or please many, and though it be always pleasing to the speaker to delight others, yet that doth not always please others that he delights to speak of, as there is nothing more tedious to strangers than to hear a man talk much of himself, or to weary them with long compliments. And though civility in that kind ought to be used, yet they should carry such forms and times as not to lose respect to themselves, or to be over-troublesome in long expressions to others. But there is few but loves to hear themselves talk, even preachers. For a preacher that preaches long loves rather to talk than to edify the people: for the memory must not be oppressed in what they should learn, or their reproofs too sharp in what they should mind; for with one word or two of reproof he reforms, half a score undoes again, which makes it a railing instead of exhortation. Neither is it always required for a man to speak according to his profession or employment in the affairs of the world—for it would be ridiculous for a lawyer in ordinary conversation to speak as if he were pleading at the bar. Yet everyone ought to have respect in his discourse to his condition, calling, or dignity, or to the quality of others—for it is not fit that a priest, which either is or should be a man of peace, to speak like a soldier, which is a man of war, or to speak to a nobleman as to a peasant.

Again, there is nothing so much takes away the sweetness of discourse as long preambles or repetitions, and indeed the whole discourse is tedious and unpleasing if it be overlong. Though their tongues were as smooth as oil and run upon the ways of truth, yet too much doth, as it were, overfill the head and stop the ears, for the head will be as the stomach when it is overcharged: it will take surfeit of the most delicious meat, wherefore in speaking judgment is required.

Yet some are so over-wise in the ordering their discourse, as it is not only troublesome to themselves, but a pain to the hearers, having so set and constrained a way of speaking, as if their words went upon hard screws, when there is nothing so easy as speech, for there is no part of man so unwearily active as the tongue. And of the other side, some are so full of talk as they will neither give room nor time to others to speak, and when two or three such persons of this voluble quality or nature meet, they make such a confusion in speaking all together as it becomes a tumultuous noise rather than sociable discoursing, which is a disturbance to society—for discourse should be like music in parts.[18]

Wit Is Free

Some men in striving to show their wits in discourse make themselves fools. For wit must not be struggled withal, and brought, as it were, by the head and shoulders, for as it is natural, so it must have its natural place and time. And a woman, by striving to make her wit known by much discourse, loses her reputation. For wit is copious, and busies itself in all things, and humours,[19] and accidents, wherein sometimes it is satirical, and sometimes amorous, and sometimes wanton—which in all these women should shun. So that in women the greatest wisdom, if not wit, is to be sparing of their discourse.

Of Speech

As eight notes produce innumerable tunes, so twenty-four letters produce innumerable words, which are marks for things, which marks produce innumerable imaginations or conceptions, which imaginations or conceptions begets another soul, which another[20] animal hath not, for want of those marks, and so want [of] those imaginations and conceptions which those marks beget. Besides, those marks beget a soul in community. Besides, words are as gods that give knowledge and discover the minds of men. And, though some creatures can speak, yet it is not natural, for it is like puppets: they are made to walk with screws, that when the screws are undone, the puppets can go no farther; so parrots or the like can only repeat the words they are taught, but cannot discourse, because they know not what it signifieth. But man can speak when he comes to maturity, that is to be man, without teaching, that is, although he doth not learn a language that his forefathers have made, yet he can make one of his own, that is to give marks to things to distinguish them to himself.

Book I, Part ii
Epistle

My company is too dull to entertain and too barren of wit to afford variety of discourse, wherefore I bend myself to study nature. And though nature is too specious to be known, yet she is so free as to teach: for every straw or grain of dust is a natural tutor to instruct my sense and reason; and every particular rational creature is a sufficient school to study in; and our own passions and affections, appetites and desires, are moral Doctors to learn us; and the evil that follows excess teaches us what is bad, and by moderation we find and do so learn what is good, and how we ought to live and moderate them by reason, and discourse them in the mind. . . . But there is a natural education to all, which comes without painstaking, not tormenting the body with hard labor, nor the mind with perturbed study, but comes easy and free through the senses, and grows familiar and sociable with the understanding, pleasant and delightful to the contemplation. For there is no subject that the sense can bring into the mind but is a natural instructor to produce the breeding of rational opinions, and understanding truths, besides imaginary fancies, if they will give their mind time as to think.

But most spend their time in talk rather than in thought. But there is a wise saying—"Think first, and speak after"—and an old saying that "Many speak first, and think after," and doubtless many, if not most, do so. For we do not always think of our words we speak, for most commonly words flow out of the mouth, rather customarily than premeditatedly, just like actions of our walking, for we go by custom, force, and strength, without a constant notice or observation. For though we design our ways, yet we do not ordinarily think of our pace, nor take notice of every several step; just so, most commonly we talk. For we seldom think of our words we speak, nor many times the sense they tend to, unless it be some affected person that would speak in fine phrases.

And though speech is very necessary to the course of man's life, yet it is very obstructive to the rational part of man's mind. For it employs the mind with such busy and unprofitable matters, as all method is run out of breath, and gives not contemplation leave to search and inquire after truth, nor understanding leave to examine what is truth, nor judgment how to distinguish truth from falsehood, nor imagination leave to be ingenious, nor ingenuity leave to find invention, nor wit leave to spin out the fine and curious thread of fancy, but only to play with words on the tongue, as balls with rackets. Besides, a multiplicity of words confounds the solid sense and rational understanding, the subject in the discourse.

Yet to think very much and speak very seldom makes speech uneasy and the tongue apt to falter, when it is to deliver sense of the matter they have, and want of uncustomary speaking makes the orator to seek for words to declare the sense of his meaning or the meaning of his sense. Besides, want of eloquence many times loseth not only rational opinions but conceals truth itself, for want of persuading rhetoric, to raise up belief or to get understanding. So that a contemplatory person hath the disadvantage of words, although most commonly they have the advantage of thoughts, which brings knowledge.

But life being short, those that speak much have not time to think much, that is, not time to study and contemplate, wherefore it is a great loss of time to speak idle words, that is, words that are to no purpose, and to think idle thoughts, that bring no honest profit to the life of man, nor delight for life's pastime, nor news to the knowledge and understanding. But most men speak of common matters and think of vulgar things, beat upon what is known and understood, not upon what ought to be known and understood, but upon known improbabilities, or vain ambitions, or upon that which nothing concerns them, or upon evil designs to work distractions, or upon that which cannot advantage them nor anybody else.

But it is very probable my readers will at this discourse condemn me, saying I take upon me to instruct as if I thought myself a master, when I am but a novice and fitter to learn. I answer, it is easier to instruct what ought to be done than to practice what is best to be done. But I am so far from thinking myself able to teach, as I am afraid I have not capacity to learn.

Yet I must tell the world that I think that not any hath a more able master to learn from than I have, for if I had never married the person I have, I do believe I should never have written so as to have adventured to divulge my works. For I have learned more of the world from my Lord's discourse, since I have been his wife, than I am confident I should have done all my life, should I have lived to an old age. And though I am not so apt a scholar as to improve much in wit, yet I am so industrious a scholar to remember whatsoever he hath said and discoursed to me. And though my memory is dull and slow and my capacity weak to all other discourses, yet when I am in company, I had rather show my simplicity than be thought rude—wherefore I choose rather to speak, though foolishly, than say nothing, as if I were dumb, when I entertain my acquaintance. And though I do not speak so well as I wish I could, yet it is civility to speak. But it is my Lord's discourse that gets me understanding and makes such impressions in my memory as nothing but death can rub it out. And my greatest fear is that I the scholar should disgrace him the master, by the vulgar phrases and the illiterate expressions in my works. But the truth is, I am neither eloquent by nature nor art; neither have I took the accustomary way of often speaking to make my words or letters fluent, not but my tongue runs fast and foolish when I do speak, but I do not often speak. For my life is more contemplary than discoursing, and more solitary than sociable, for my nature being dull and heavy, and my disposition not merry, makes me think myself not fit for company.

Book I, Part iii

A Gentleman's Study

A gentleman should not be ignorant, but know all the good is to be known, and the bad, or else he can hardly know what is best; yet leave the practice of the worst to the inferior. But his study should be Navigation, Fortification, Architecture, Culture, Waterworks, Fireworks,[21] and the like, which studies are profitable to his country, both for strength, plenty, and use, which make a kingdom flourish. For every man should, like a bee, bring honey to the hive, and not, like the effeminate drone, suck out the sweet and idly live upon the heroic labor of others. But to study laws is rather to study division than settlement; to study divinity is rather to study controversy than salvation; to study philosophy is to seek that they cannot find; to study history is to study lies more than lives—where a gentleman should study truth, follow truth, and practice justice. A little rhetoric doth well to clothe his mind in soft numbers, trim it with handsome phrases; and a gentleman should converse with poetry, for poetry sweetens the nature—not softens it, to make it facile, but civilizes it, making it courteous, affable, and conversable, inspiring the mind with high and noble thoughts, which is the way to be enshrined in honorable fame. Like an urn that keeps the ashes of the body from being scattered and lost, so fame keeps good deeds in the urn of memory.

The Pastime of Wit

Wit cheers the heart, refresheth the spirits, delights the mind, entertains the thoughts, sweetens melancholy, dresses joy, mourns with sorrow, pleaseth lovers, excuseth falsehoods, mends faults, begs pardon. Wit is a fine companion, either in private closets, full courts, or in long travels. Wit is neither troublesome, nor chargeable.[22] Wit hath no bottom, but is like a perpetual spring. Wit is the sun of the brain.

Civility from Men Due to Women

Compliments from men to women are as a tribute due to womenkind; for women, fearing they should not be so noble creatures as men, are apt to be out of countenance, as mistrusting some imperfectness in themselves. Wherefore men of noble natures are willing to help the weak, and therefore ought to give our sex confidence by their praises and therefore should be civil to women in having as tender a regard to them as to children. For though women be not so innocent, yet they are as powerless. And it is the part of a noble, heroic nature to strive to oblige the weak. And it is better to be used with cruelty than scorn, or a rude kindness.

Book II, Part i
The Epistle

As for the grammar part, I confess I am no scholar, and therefore understand it not, but that little I have heard of it is enough for me to renounce it. For if I have any wit, it is so little that it would be lost in scholastical rules. Besides, it were worse to be a pedantic woman than a pedantic man, yet so ill it is in man, that it doth, as it were, degrade him from being magnanimous and heroic, for one shall seldom find a generous and valiant heart and a pedantical brain created or bred in one body. But those that are nobly bred have no rules but honor and honesty, and learn in the school of wisdom to understand sense and to express themselves sensibly and freely with a graceful negligence, not to be hide-bound with nice and strict words and set phrases, as if the wit were created in the inkhorn and not in the brain. Besides, say some, should one bring up a new way of speaking, then were the former grammar of no effect. Besides, I do perceive no strong reason to contradict, but that everyone may be his own grammarian, if by his natural grammar he can make his hearers understand his sense. For though there must be rules in a language to make it sociable, yet those rules may be stricter than need to be, and to be too strict makes them to be too unpleasant and uneasy. But language should be like garments, for though every particular garment hath a general cut, yet their trimmings may be different and not go out of the fashion; so wit may place words to its own becoming, delight, and advantage, and not alter language nor obstruct the sense, for the more liberty we have of words, the clearer is sense delivered. As for wit, it is wild and fantastical, and therefore must have no set rules; for rules curb and shackle it and, in that bondage, it dies.

Book III, Part iii

The Inventory of Judgment's Commonwealth, the Author Cares Not in What World It Is Established

Item, That no sermons shall be preached, by reason they do more harm than good, troubling the conscience of the fearful, the heads of the ignorant, and the ears of the wise. But there shall be prayers said in every parish church once a day, and the moral laws, the divine laws, and the national laws, with their threatening punishments and promising rewards, shall be read and repeated once a week.

Item, No children shall speak before their parents, no servants before their masters, no scholars[23] before their tutors, no subject before the prince, but either to answer to their questions, to deliver a message, or to know their will and pleasure, to declare their grievances, to ask pardon for faults committed, or to present a humble request in the most humblest manner, unless they command them to discourse freely to them, yet not without a respect to their presence and authority.

Item, For the generality, none shall speak but to ask rational, dutiful, and humble questions, to request just demands, to discourse of probable arguments, to defend right and truth, to divulge virtue, to praise the meritorious, to pray to heaven, to ask mercy, to move pity, to pacify grief, to assuage anger, to make an atonement, and to instruct the ignorant.

Item, That no woman of quality should receive visits or give visits but in public meetings, nor have any whisperings or private conference, that her actions might have sufficient witness and her discourses a general audience.

❦

Item, Eloquence shall not be employed nor pleaded in amorous discourses, nor to make falsehood to appear like truth; but to dress and adorn virtue that she may be accepted and entertained by those that will refuse and shun her acquaintance if she be clad in plain garments.

❦

Notes

These excerpts are taken from Margaret Cavendish, the Duchess of Newcastle, *The Worlds Olio* (London, 1655), preface, "To the Reader," sigs. B2^{r-v}, C3^v-D2^v, D4^{r-v}, E2^r-E4^r, K4^r-L1^r, N1^{r-v}, O^v, Ec2^r-Ef1^r (Folger copy N873), by permission of the Folger Shakespeare Library. I have modernized spelling and punctuation.

1. "And God made two great lights; the greater light to rule the day, and the lesser light to rule the night; he made the stars also" (Genesis 1:16, KJV). Note that Cavendish deletes "greater" and "lesser"—the relationship between lights, and thus by analogy between men and women, is not hierarchical.

2. Many of the female heroes Cavendish creates in her fiction and plays contradict this principle. Victoria in *Bell in Campo*, Lady Orphant in *Loves Adventures*, and Travellia in *Assaulted and Pursued Chastity* lead armies and excel in oratory. Lady Sanspareile in *Youth's Glory, Death's Banquet* becomes the envy of male scholars for her oratorical skills, and the empress in *The Blazing World* governs a world and conquers other nations with great success.

3. Throughly: opposite of haltingly.

4. But: only.

5. M.N.: Margaret Newcastle.

6. Cavendish is here entering a sixteenth- and seventeenth-century linguistic controversy about spelling: she argues that writing or spelling represents concepts rather than sounds.

7. Contraversers: controversialists.

8. Intelligence: a spy's information.

9. Jubilies: jubilees, songs sung during a jubilee or period of celebration.

10. Mountebanks: quacks who tell stories and perform tricks to sell something not worth buying; charlatans.

11. Malcontents: rebellious, discontented persons.

12. Number: rhythm or meter.

13. Fain: inclined.

14. Traffic: trade.

15. Extravagant: archaic sense of wandering beyond bounds or proprieties.

16. Fancy: imagination.

17. Best friend: Cavendish is referring to her husband.

18. Music in parts, that is, harmonious.

19. Humours: personality traits or quirks (derived from the earlier medical idea that humans were made up of four humours that determined personality).

20. Another, that is, any other.

21. Fireworks: explosives and munitions.

22. Chargeable: expensive.

23. Scholars: students.

Margaret Fell

1614–1702

Margaret Askew, by tradition a descendant of the Protestant martyr Anne Askew, was born in 1614 at Marsh Grange in Lancashire to Margaret Pyper (probably) and John Askew. In 1632, she married Thomas Fell, a lawyer and member of Parliament. From 1649 on, under Cromwell, her husband was an important government official in Lancaster and North Wales and, under the Restoration, a judge in several courts. Judge Fell was an active supporter of religious tolerance. They had nine children, eight of whom grew to adulthood—one son (George) and seven daughters (Margaret, Bridget, Isabel, Sarah, Mary, Susannah, and Rachel). In June 1652, George Fox, then a traveling preacher in the process of organizing the Quaker religion, visited Swarthmoor Hall, where the Fells lived, and converted Margaret and almost her entire household to Quakerism. Thomas Fell was not there and never converted, but he became fast friends with Fox and was a friendly supporter of the religion and an enthusiastic encourager of his wife's activities. For the early years of the movement, while Fox traveled and converted, Margaret Fell became the center and organizer, the "nursing mother" as many letters greet her, who offered her house for local meetings and a resting place for the traveling preachers, who kept them all in touch through continued correspondence, and who helped to formulate important religious doctrines, especially those involving the Quaker marriage ceremony, women's speaking, and later the women's meetings. In her publications at this time, she took as her special task the conversion of the Jews, and two of her pamphlets were translated into Hebrew, almost certainly by the young Spinoza. Although Fell's son was a bitter antagonist of Quakers and also contested his mother's inheritance from his father, all the daughters married Quakers, four of the daughters became preachers, and all were involved in organizing the local meetings where they lived, as well as in supporting Quaker prisoners and their families. After her husband's death in 1658, Fell traveled widely, preaching, visiting meetings and prisoners throughout England, and lobbying Charles II to release Quaker prisoners. She was imprisoned three times for holding Quaker meetings at her house and for refusing to pay tithes or take oaths—in 1664–1668, 1670–1671, and 1683–1684. She was praemunired in 1664, and her estate was confiscated. In 1665, her estate was granted to her antagonistic son. He never took possession, however, and her sons-in-law seem to have settled with him for money so that Swarthmoor might remain in the service of the Quakers, as well as Fell's home. In prison the first time at Lancaster Castle, she employed herself in writing: in 1666 she wrote *Women's Speaking Justified*, along with three other tracts and a public letter to Charles II. In October 1669, after years of friendship, Fell married George Fox, but the couple only rarely lived together, since their preaching and family responsibilities often took them in different directions. After Margaret began to limit her travels, grandchildren frequently lived with her and their aunts at Swarthmoor while their mothers traveled and preached for Quakerism. After George Fox died in 1691, Margaret left her home for London only once more and limited her involvement to local meetings. She died in April 1702, eighty-eight years old.

Women's Speaking Justified, published in 1667, five years before Bathsua Makin's *Essay*, is as direct an argument for women's right to speak as Makin's is a subversive one. Makin's middle-class standing and her liberal views resulted in a more conciliatory rhetorical strategy, while Margaret Fell's upper-class standing and radical sectarian views, as well as her subject matter, encouraged her to preach. Her pamphlet is an argument in favor of women preaching and prophesying in church (which in the seventeenth century was neither customary nor legal). It is addressed to an Anglican audience, since many Quaker women, including Margaret Fell, had been preaching for years. Because she thus confronts the sexual politics of sermon rhetoric, Margaret Fell must be acknowledged as an innovative and crucial voice in the rhetorical tradition of manuals on preaching. Rather than organize her pamphlet along the classical lines of a defense, Fell adopts the ecstatic voice of a sectarian preacher. She begins and ends with the argument that women are equal to men in God's eyes, a historically legitimate Protestant position, and in the middle of her treatise carries this argument to the extreme that women should be allowed, like men, to preach in church, a doctrine of the new Quaker sect that George Fox had already articulated but that she had helped to formulate.

For further information, see Isabel Ross, *Margaret Fell: Mother of Quakerism* (London: Longmans, Green, 1949); Margaret Fell, *Women's Speaking Justified* (1667), published with *Epistle* and *A Warning to All Friends*, compiled and with an introduction by David J. Latt (Los Angeles: William Andrews Clark Memorial Library/University of California, 1979); Elaine Hobby, *Virtue of Necessity: English Women's Writing, 1649–1688* (London: Virago 1988); Bonnelyn Young Kunze, *Margaret Fell and the Rise of Quakerism* (Stanford: Stanford University Press, 1994); and Jane Donawerth, "The Politics of Renaissance Rhetorical Theory by Women," in *Political Rhetoric, Power, and Renaissance Women*, ed. Carole Levin and Patricia A. Sullivan (Albany: State University of New York Press, 1995), 256–72.

Women's Speaking Justified, Proved and Allowed of by the Scriptures (1666)

And it shall come to pass, in the last days, saith the Lord, I will pour out of my Spirit upon all flesh; your sons and daughters shall prophesy. Acts 2:27, Joel 2:28[1]

It is written in the Prophets, They shall be all taught of God, saith Christ. John 6:45

And all thy children shall be taught of the Lord, and great shall be the peace of thy children. Isaiah 54:13

And they shall teach no more every man his neighbor, and every man his brother, saying, Know the Lord, for they shall all know me, from the least to the greatest of them, saith the Lord. Jeremiah 31:34–35

Whereas it hath been an objection in the minds of many, and several times hath been objected by the clergy, or ministers, and others, against women's speaking in the Church; and so consequently may be taken, that they are condemned for meddling in the things of God, the ground of which objection is taken from the Apostle's words, which he writ in his first Epistle to the Corinthians, chapter 14, verses 34–35, and also what he writ to Timothy in the first Epistle, chapter 2, verses 11–12.[2] But how far they wrong the Apostle's intentions in these Scriptures, we shall show clearly when we come to them in their course and order. But first let me lay down how God himself hath manifested his will and mind concerning women, and unto women.

And first, when *God created man in his own Image: in the Image of God created he them, male and female; and God blessed them; and God said unto them, Be fruitful, and multiply: And God said, Behold, I have given you of every herb*, etc. Genesis 1.[3] Here God joins them together in his own Image, and makes no such distinctions and differences as men do; for though they be weak, he is strong: and as he said to the Apostle, *His Grace is sufficient*, and his *strength is made manifest in weakness*, 2 Corinthians 12:9.[4] And such hath the Lord chosen, even *the weak things of the world, to confound the things which are mighty; and things which are despised, hath God chosen, to bring to nought things that are*, 1 Corinthians 1.[5] And God hath put no such difference between the male and female as men would make.

It is true, *the Serpent that was more subtle than any other beast of the field* came unto the woman with his temptations and with a lie, his subtlety discerning her to be more inclinable to hearken to him, when he said, *If ye eat, your eyes shall be opened*. And the woman saw that *the fruit was good to make one wise*; there the temptation got into her, and *she did eat, and gave to her husband, and he did eat also*, and so they were both tempted into the transgression and disobedience. And therefore God said unto Adam, when he hid himself when he heard his voice, *Hast thou eaten of the Tree which I commanded thee that thou shouldst not eat?* And Adam said, *The woman which thou gavest me, she gave me of the Tree, and I did eat. And the Lord said unto the woman, What is this that thou hast done? And the woman said, The serpent beguiled me, and I did eat.* Here the woman spoke the truth unto the Lord—see what the Lord saith, verse 15, after he had pronounced sentence on the Serpent: *I will put enmity between thee and the woman, and between thy seed and her seed; it shall bruise thy head, and thou shalt bruise his heel*, Genesis 3.[6]

Let this Word of the Lord, which was from the beginning, stop the mouths of all that oppose women's speaking in the power of the Lord; for he hath put enmity between the woman and the Serpent; and if the seed of the woman speak not, the seed of the Serpent speaks; for God hath put enmity between the two seeds, and it is manifest that those that speak against the woman and her seed's speaking, speak out of the enmity of the old Serpent's seed. And God hath fulfilled his Word and his Promise: *When the fullness of time was come, he hath sent forth his Son, made of a woman, made under the Law, that we might receive the adoption of sons*, Galatians 4:4–5.

Moreover, the Lord is pleased, when he mentions his church, to call her by the name of "woman," by his prophet's saying, *I have called thee as a woman forsaken, and grieved in Spirit, and as a wife of youth*, Isaiah 54.[7] Again, *How long wilt thou go about, thou back-sliding daughter? For the Lord hath created a new thing in the earth, a woman shall compass a man*, Jeremiah 31:22. And David, when he was speaking of Christ and his Church, he saith, *The King's daughter is all glorious within, her clothing is of wrought gold; she shall be brought unto the King; with gladness and rejoicing shall they be brought; they shall enter into the King's palace*, Psalm 45.[8] And also King

Solomon in his Song, where he speaks of Christ and his Church, where she is complaining and calling for Christ, he saith, *If thou knowest not, O thou fairest among women, go thy way by the footsteps of the flock*, Canticles 1:8, 5:9.[9] And John, when he saw the wonder that was in heaven, he saw a *woman clothed with the Sun, and the Moon under her feet, and upon her head a Crown of twelve Stars; and there appeared another wonder in heaven, a great red Dragon stood ready to devour her child*: here the enmity appears that God put between the woman and the dragon, Revelations 12.[10]

Thus much may prove that the Church of Christ is a woman, and those that speak against the woman's speaking speak against the Church of Christ and the seed of the woman, which seed is Christ; that is to say, those that speak against the Power of the Lord and the Spirit of the Lord speaking in a woman, simply by reason of her sex or because she is a woman, not regarding the seed, and Spirit, and Power that speaks in her, such speak against Christ and his Church, and are of the seed of the Serpent, wherein lodgeth the enmity. And as God the Father made no such difference in the first creation, nor ever since between the male and the female, but always out of his mercy and loving-kindness had regard unto the weak, so also, his Son, Christ Jesus, confirms the same thing; when the Pharisees came to him and asked him, if it were lawful for a man to put away his wife, he answered and said unto them, *Have you not read, that he that made them in the beginning, made them male and female, and said, For this cause shall a man leave father and mother, and shall cleave unto his wife, and they twain shall be one flesh. Wherefore they are no more twain but one flesh. What therefore God hath joined together, let no man put asunder*, Matthew 19.[11]

Again, Christ Jesus, when he came to the city of Samaria, where Jacob's Well was, where the woman of Samaria was; you may read in John 4 how he was pleased to preach the everlasting gospel to her; and when the woman said unto him, *I know that when the Messiah cometh, (which is called "Christ") when he cometh, he will tell us all things; Jesus saith unto her, I that speak unto thee am he*.[12] This is more than ever he said in plain words to [any other] man or woman (that we read of) before he suffered. Also he said unto Martha, when she said she knew that her brother should *rise again in the last day, Jesus said unto her, I am the Resurrection and the Life: he that believeth on me, though he were dead, yet shall he live; and whosoever liveth and believeth shall never die. Believest thou this?* She answered, *Yea Lord, I believe thou art the Christ, the son of God.* Here she manifested her true and saving faith, which few at that day believed so on him, John 11:25–26.

Also, that woman that came unto Jesus with an alabaster box of very precious ointment, and poured it on his head as he sat at meat—it's manifested that this woman knew more of the secret Power and Wisdom of God, than his Disciples did, that were filled with indignation against her; and therefore Jesus saith, *Why do ye trouble the woman? For she hath wrought a good work upon me; verily, I say unto you, wheresoever this Gospel shall be preached in the whole world, there shall also this that this woman hath done be told for a memorial of her*, Matthew 26, Mark 14:3.[13] Luke saith further, *She was a sinner*, and that *she stood at his feet behind him weeping, and began to wash his feet with her tears, and did wipe them with the hair of her head, and kissed his feet, and anointed them with ointment*.[14] And when Jesus saw the heart of the Pharisee that had bidden him to his house, he took occasion to speak unto Simon, as you may read in Luke 7, and he turned to the woman, and said, *Simon, seest thou this woman? Thou gavest me no water to my feet, but she hath washed my feet with tears, and wiped them with the hair of her head: Thou gavest me no kiss, but this woman, since I came in, hath not ceased to kiss my feet. My head with oil thou didst not anoint, but the woman hath anointed my feet with ointment. Wherefore I say unto thee, her sins, which are many, are forgiven her, for she hath loved much*, Luke 7:37 to the end.[15]

Also, there were *many women which followed Jesus from Galilee ministering unto him*, and stood *afar off* when he was crucified, Matthew 28:55, Mark 15.[16] Yea, even the women of Jerusalem wept for him, insomuch that he said unto them, *Weep not for me, ye daughters of Jerusalem, but weep for yourselves, and for your children*, Luke 23:28.

And certain women which had been healed of evil spirits and infirmities, Mary Magdalene, and Joanna the wife of Chuza, Herod's steward's wife, and many others which ministered unto him of their substance, Luke 8:2–3.

Thus we see that Jesus owned[17] the love and grace that appeared in women, and did not despise it, and by what is recorded in the Scriptures, he received as much love, kindness, compassion, and tender dealing towards him from women, as he did from any others, both in his lifetime, and also after they had exercised their cruelty upon him; for Mary Magdalene, and Mary the mother of James, beheld where he was laid: *And when the Sabbath was past, Mary Magdalene, and Mary the Mother of James, and Salom, had brought sweet spices that they might anoint him. And very early in the morning, the first day of the week, they came unto the sepulchre at the rising of the sun. And they said among themselves, who shall roll us away the stone from the door of the sepulchre? And when they looked, the stone was rolled away, for it was very great*, Mark 16:1–4, Luke 24:1–2.[18] *And they went down into the sepulchre* and, as Matthew saith, *The Angel rolled away the stone, and he said unto the women, Fear not, I know whom ye seek, Jesus which was crucified: he is not here, he is risen*, Matthew 28.[19] Now Luke says thus: *that there stood two men by them in shining apparel, and as they were perplexed and afraid, the men said unto them, He is not here; remember how he said unto you when he was in Galilee, that the Son of Man must be delivered into the hands of sinful men, and be crucified, and the third day rise again; and they remembered his words, and returned from the sepulchre, and told all these things to the eleven, and to all the rest*.[20]

It was Mary Magdalene, and Joanna, and Mary the mother of James, and the other women that were with them, which told these things to the Apostles. *And their words seemed unto them as idle tales, and they believed them not*.[21] Mark this, ye despisers of the weakness of women, and look upon yourselves to be so wise: but Christ Jesus doth not so, for he makes use of the weak: for when he met the women after he was risen, he said unto them, *All Hail*, and they came and held him by the feet, and worshipped him, then said Jesus unto them, *Be not afraid, go tell my brethren that they go into Galilee, and there they shall see me*, Matthew 28:10, Mark 16:9.[22] And John saith, when Mary was weeping at the sepulchre, that *Jesus said unto her, Woman, why weepest thou? what seekest thou? And when she supposed him to be the gardener, Jesus saith unto her, Mary; she turned herself, and saith unto him, Rabboni, which is to say master; Jesus saith unto her, Touch me not, for I am not yet ascended to my Father, but go to my brethren, and say unto them, I ascend unto my Father, and your Father, and to my God, and your God*, John 20:16–17.[23]

Mark this, you that despise and oppose the Message of the Lord God, that he sends by women; what had become of the Redemption of the whole body of mankind, if they had not believed the Message that the Lord Jesus sent by these women, of and concerning his Resurrection? And if these women had not thus, out of their tenderness and bowels of love, who had received mercy, and grace, and forgiveness of sins, and virtue, and healing from him, which many men also had received the like, if their hearts had not been so united and knit unto him in love, that they could not depart as the men did, but sat watching, and waiting, and weeping about the sepulchre until the time of his Resurrection, and so were ready to carry his Message, as is manifested; else how should his Disciples have known, who were not there?

O blessed and glorified be the glorious Lord; for this may all the whole body of mankind say, though the wisdom of man, that never knew God, is always ready to except against the weak; but *the weakness of God is stronger than men, and the foolishness of God is wiser than men.*[24]

And in Acts 18, you may read how Aquila and Priscilla took unto them Apollos, and expounded unto him the way of God more perfectly, who was an eloquent man, and mighty in the Scriptures; yet we do not read that he despised what Priscilla said, because she was a woman, as many now do.

And now to the Apostle's words, which is the ground of the great objection against women's speaking, and first, 1 Corinthians 14. Let the reader seriously read that chapter, and see the end and drift of the Apostle in speaking these words: for the Apostle is there exhorting the Corinthians unto charity, and to desire spiritual gifts, and not to speak in an unknown tongue, and *not to be children in understanding, not to be children in malice, but in understanding to be men; and that the Spirits of the Prophets should be subject to the Prophets, for God is not the Author of Confusion, but of Peace.* And then he says, *Let your women keep silence in the church,* etc.[25]

Where it doth plainly appear that the women, as well as others that were among them, were in confusion, for he says, *How is it brethren? when ye come together, every one of you hath a psalm, hath a doctrine, hath a tongue, hath a revelation, hath an interpretation? Let all things be done to edifying.*[26] Here was no edifying, but all was in confusion, speaking together. Therefore, he saith, *If any man speak in an unknown tongue, let it be by two, or at most by three, and that by course, and let one interpret, but if there be no interpreter, let him keep silence in the church.*[27] Here the man is commanded to keep silence as well as the woman, when they are in confusion and out of order.

But the Apostle saith further, *They are commanded to be in obedience, as also saith the Law; and if they will learn anything, let them ask their husbands at home, for it is a shame for a woman to speak in the church.*[28]

Here the Apostle clearly manifests his intent, for he speaks of women that were under the Law, and in that transgression as Eve was, and such as were to learn, and not to speak publicly, but they must first ask their husbands at home, and it was a shame for such to speak in the Church. And it appears clearly, that such women were speaking among the Corinthians, by the Apostle's exhorting them from malice and strife, and confusion, and he preaches the Law unto them, and he saith, *in the Law it is written, with men of other tongues, and other lips, will I speak unto this people,* verse 2.[29]

And what is all this to women's speaking that have the Everlasting Gospel to preach, and upon whom the Promise of the Lord is fulfilled, and his Spirit poured upon them according to his word, Acts 2:16–18. And if the Apostle would have stopped such as had the Spirit of the Lord poured upon them, why did he say just before, *If any thing be revealed to another that sitteth by, let the first hold his peace?* And *you may all prophesy one by one.*[30] Here he did not say that such women should not prophesy as had the Revelation and Spirit of God poured upon them, but their women that were under the Law, and in the transgression, and were in strife, confusion, and malice in their speaking, for if he had stopped women's praying or prophesying, why doth he say, *Every man praying or prophesying having his head covered, dishonoreth his head; but every woman that prayeth or prophesieth with her head uncovered, dishonoreth her head. Judge in your selves, Is it comely that a woman pray or prophesy uncovered? For the woman is not without the man, neither is the man without the woman, in the Lord,* 1 Corinthians 11:3–4, 13.[31]

Also that other Scripture, in 1 Timothy 2, where he is exhorting that prayer and supplication be made everywhere, lifting up holy hands without wrath and doubting: he says in the like manner also, that *women must adorn themselves in modest apparel, with shamefastness and sobriety, not with broidered hair, or gold, or pearl, or costly array*; he says, *Let women learn in silence with all subjection, but I suffer not a woman to teach, nor to usurp authority over the man, but to be in silence; for Adam was first formed, then Eve; and Adam was not deceived, but the woman, being deceived, was in the transgression.*[32]

Here the Apostle speaks particularly to a woman in relation to her husband, to be in subjection to him, and not to teach, nor usurp authority over him, and therefore he mentions Adam and Eve. But let it be strained to the utmost, as the opposers of women's speaking would have it, that is, that they should not preach nor speak in the Church, of which there is nothing here; yet the Apostle is speaking to such as he is teaching to wear their apparel, what to wear, and what not to wear, such as were not come to wear modest apparel, and such as were not come to shamefastness and sobriety, but he was exhorting them from broidered hair, gold, and pearls, and costly array; and such are not to usurp authority over the man, but to learn in silence with all subjection, as it becometh women professing godliness with good works.

And what is all this to such as have the Power and Spirit of the Lord Jesus poured upon them, and have the Message of the Lord Jesus given unto them? Must not they speak the Word of the Lord because of these indecent and unreverent women that the Apostle speaks of, and to, in these two Scriptures? And how are the men of this generation blinded, that bring these Scriptures, and pervert the Apostle's Words, and corrupt his intent in speaking of them? And by these Scriptures, endeavor to stop the Message and Word of the Lord God in women, by condemning and despising of them. If the Apostle would have had women's speaking stopped, and did not allow of them, why did he *entreat his true yokefellow to help those women who labored with him in the gospel?* Philippians 4:3. And why did the apostles join together *in prayer and supplication with the women, and Mary the mother of Jesus, and with his brethren*, Acts 1:14, if they had not allowed, and had union and fellowship with the Spirit of God, wherever it was revealed in women as well as others? But all this opposing and gainsaying of women's speaking has risen out of the bottomless Pit, and Spirit of Darkness that hath spoken for these many hundred years together in this night of apostasy, since the Revelations have ceased and been hid, and so that Spirit hath limited and bound all up within its bond and compass, and so would suffer none to speak, but such as that Spirit of Darkness approved of, man or woman.

And so here hath been the misery of these last ages past, in the time of the Reign of the Beast, that John saw when he *stood upon the sand of the sea*, rising *out of the sea*, and out of the earth, *having seven heads and ten horns*, Revelations 13.[33] In this great city of Babylon, which is the woman that hath sat so long upon *the scarlet-colored Beast, full of names of blasphemy, having seven heads and ten horns; and this woman hath been arrayed and decked with gold, and pearls, and precious stones; and she hath had a golden cup in her hand, full of abominations, and hath made all nations drunk with the cup of her fornication.*[34] And *all the world hath wondered after the Beast, and hath worshipped the Dragon that gave power to the Beast;*[35] and this *woman has been drunk with the blood of the saints, and with the blood of the Martyrs of Jesus,*[36] and this hath been the woman that hath been speaking and usurping authority for many hundred years together.[37] And let the times and ages past testify how many have been murdered and slain, in ages and generations past: every religion and profession (as it hath been called) killing and murdering one another, that would not join one with another. And thus the Spirit of Truth and the Power of the Lord

Jesus Christ hath been quite lost among them that have done this, and this mother of harlots hath *sitten as a queen, and said, She should see no sorrow.*[38] But though her days have been long, even many hundred of years, for there was power given unto the Beast to continue forty and two months, and to make war with the Saints, and to overcome them; and *all that have dwelt upon the earth have worshipped him, whose names are not written in the Book of the Life of the Lamb, slain from the foundation of the world.*[39]

But blessed be the Lord, his time is over, which was above twelve hundred years, and the darkness is past, and the night of apostasy draws to an end. And the true light now shines, the morning Light, *the bright morning Star, the Root and Offspring of David:*[40] he is risen, he is risen, glory to the highest forevermore. And the joy of the morning is come, and the Bride, the Lamb's Wife, is making herself ready, as a Bride that is adorning for her husband, *and to her is granted that she shall be arrayed in fine linen, clean and white, and the fine linen is the Righteousness of the Saints.*[41] The holy Jerusalem is descending out of heaven from God, having the glory of God, and her light is like *a jasperstone, clear as crystal.*[42]

And this is that free woman that all the Children of the Promise are born of, not the children of the bondwoman, *which is Hagar, which [en]genders* to strife and *to bondage, and which answers to Jerusalem which is in bondage with her Children; but this is the Jerusalem which is free, which is the Mother of us all.*[43] And so this bondwoman and her children, that are born after the flesh, have persecuted them that are born after the Spirit, even until now; but now the bondwoman and her seed is to be cast out, that has kept so long in bondage and in slavery, and under limits; this bondwoman and her brood is to be cast out, and our Holy City, the *New Jerusalem, is coming down from Heaven,* and *her Light* will shine throughout the whole earth, even as *a jasperstone, clear as crystal,*[44] which brings freedom and liberty, and perfect Redemption to her whole seed; and this is that woman and Image of the eternal God, that God has owned, and does own, and will own for evermore.

More might be added to this purpose, both out of the Old Testament, and New, where it is evident that God made no difference, but gave his good Spirit, as it pleased him, both to man and woman, as Deborah, Huldah, and Sarah. The Lord calls by his prophet Isaiah, *Hearken unto me, ye that follow after Righteousness, ye that seek the Lord, look unto the Rock from whence ye were hewn, and to the hole of the Pit from whence ye were digged; look unto Abraham your Father, and to Sarah that bare you, for the Lord will comfort Sion,* etc., Isaiah 5.[45] And Anna the prophetess, who *was a widow of fourscore and four years of age, which departed not from the Temple, but served God with fastings and prayers night and day,* she coming in at that instant (when old Simeon took the Child Jesus in his arms) and *she gave thanks unto the Lord, and spake of him to all them who looked for Redemption in Jerusalem,* Luke 2:36–38. And Philip the Evangelist, into whose house the Apostle Paul entered, who was one of the Seven, Acts 6:3, he *had four daughters which were virgins, that did prophesy,* Acts 21.[46]

And so let this serve to stop that opposing spirit that would limit the Power and Spirit of the Lord Jesus, whose Spirit is poured upon all flesh, both sons and daughters, now in his Resurrection; and since that the Lord God in the Creation, when he *made man in his own Image, he made them male and female;*[47] and since that Christ Jesus, as the Apostle saith, was made of a woman, and the power of the Highest overshadowed her, and the Holy Ghost came upon her, and the holy thing that was born of her, was called the Son of God; and when he was upon the earth, he manifested his love, and his will, and his mind, both to the woman of Samaria, and Martha, and Mary her sister, and several others, as has been shewed; and after his Resurrection also manifested himself unto them first of all, even before he ascended unto his Father: *Now when Jesus was risen, the first day of the week, he appeared first unto Mary Magdalene*, Mark 16:9. And thus the Lord Jesus has manifested himself and his Power, without respect of persons, and so let all mouths be stopped that would limit him, whose Power and Spirit is infinite, that is pouring it upon all flesh.

And thus much in answer to these two Scriptures, which have been such a stumbling block, that the ministers of Darkness have made such a mountain of. But the Lord is removing all this, and taking it out of the way.

M. F.

A Further Addition in Answer to the Objection concerning Women keeping silent in the Church: *For it is not permitted for them to speak, but to be under obedience: as also saith the Law. If they will learn anything, let them ask their husbands at home, for it is a shame for a woman to speak in the Church*: now thus as Paul writes in 1 Corinthians 14:34[48] is one with that of 1 Timothy 2:11, *Let women learn in silence, with all subjection.*

To which I say, if you tie this to all outward women, then there were many women that were widows which had no husbands to learn of, and many were virgins which had no husbands. And Philip had four daughters that were prophets—such would be despised, which the Apostle did not forbid. And if it were to all women, that no woman might speak, then Paul would have contradicted himself; but they were such women that the Apostle mentions in Timothy, that grew wanton *and were busy-bodies, and tattlers*,[49] and kicked against Christ. For Christ in the male and in the female is one, and he is the Husband, and his Wife is the Church, and God hath said, that his daughters should prophesy as well as his sons. And where he has poured forth his Spirit upon them, they must prophesy, though blind priests say to the contrary, and will not permit holy women to speak.

And whereas it is said, I permit not a woman to speak, as saith the Law—but where women are led by the Spirit of God, they are not under the Law. For Christ in the male and in the female is one; and where he is made manifest in male and female, he may speak, for *he is the end of the Law for Righteousness to all them that believe*.[50] So here you ought to make a distinction what sort of women are forbidden to speak, such as were under the Law, who were not come to Christ, nor to the Spirit of Prophecy. For Huldah, Miriam, and Hannah were prophets, who were not forbidden in the time of the Law, for they all prophesied in the time of the Law. As you may read in 2 Kings 22, what Hulda said unto the priest, and to the ambassadors that were sent to her from the King: *Go*, saith she, *and tell the man that sent you to me, Thus saith the Lord God of Israel, Behold, I will bring evil upon this place, and on the inhabitants thereof, even all the words of the Book which the King of Judah hath read, because they have forsaken me, and have burnt incense to other gods, to anger me with all the works of their hands. Therefore my wrath shall be kindled against this place, and shall not be quenched. But to the King of Judah, that sent you to me to ask counsel of the Lord, so shall you say to him, Thus saith the Lord God of Israel, Because thy heart did melt, and thou humbled thyself before the Lord, when thou heardst what I spake against this place, and against the inhabitants of the same, how they should be destroyed; Behold I will receive thee to thy Father, and thou shalt be put into thy grave in peace, and thine eyes shall not see all the evil which I will bring upon this place*.[51] Now let us see if any of you blind priests can speak after this manner, and see if it be not a better sermon than any of you can make, who are against women's speaking. And Isaiah, that went to the Prophetess, did not forbid her speaking or prophesying, Isaiah 8.[52] And was it not prophesied in Joel 2 that *Hand-maids should prophesy*?[53] And are not hand-maids women?

Consider this, ye that are against women's speaking, how in the Acts the Spirit of the Lord was poured forth upon daughters as well as sons.[54] In the time of the gospel, *when Mary came to salute Elizabeth in the hill country in Judea, and when Elizabeth heard the salutation of Mary, the Babe leaped in her womb, and she was filled with the Holy Spirit; and Elizabeth spoke with a loud voice, Blessed art thou amongst women, blessed is the fruit of thy womb. Whence is this to me, that the Mother of my Lord should come to me? for lo, as soon as thy salutation came to my ear, the Babe leaped in my womb for joy, for blessed is she that believes, for there shall be a performance of those things which were told her from the Lord.* And this was Elizabeth's sermon concerning Christ, which at this day stands upon record. And then Mary said, *My soul doth magnify the Lord, and my Spirit rejoiceth in God my Savior, for he hath regarded the low estate of his Handmaid: for behold, from henceforth all generations shall call me blessed. For he that is mighty hath done to me great things, and holy is his name; and his mercy is on them that fear him, from generation to generation; he hath shewed strength with his arm; he hath scattered the proud in the imaginations of their own hearts; he hath put down the mighty from their seats, and exalted them of low degree; he hath filled the hungry with good things, and the rich he hath sent empty away. He hath holpen his servant Israel, in remembrance of his mercy, as he spake to his Father, to Abraham, and to his seed forever.*[55] Are you not here beholding to the woman for her sermon, to use her words to put into your Common Prayer?[56] And yet you forbid women's speaking. Now here you may see how these two women prophesied of Christ and preached better than all the blind priests did in that age, and better than this age, also, who are beholding to women to make use of their words.

And see in the Book of Ruth, how the women blessed her in the Gate of the City, of whose stock came Christ: *The Lord make the woman that is come into thy House like Rachel and Leah, which built the house of Israel; and that thou makest do worthily in Ephrata, and be famous in Bethlehem: let thy house be like the house of Pharez, whom Tamer bare unto Judah, of the seed which the Lord shall give thee of this young woman. And blessed be the Lord, which hath not left thee this day without a kinsman, and his name shall be continued in Israel.*[57] And also see in the first chapter of Samuel, how Hannah prayed and spake in the Temple of the Lord, *Oh Lord of Hosts, if thou wilt look on the trouble of thy handmaid, and remember me, and not forget thy handmaid.*[58] And read in the second chapter of Samuel, how she rejoiced in God, and said, *My heart rejoiceth in the Lord: my horn is exalted in the Lord and my mouth is enlarged over my enemies, because I rejoice in thy Salvation; there is none holy as the Lord, yea, there is none besides thee; and there is no God like our God: speak no more presumptuously, let not arrogance come out of your mouths, for the Lord is a God of knowledge, and by him enterprises are established; the bow, and the mighty men are broken, and the weak hath girded to themselves strength; they that were full, are hired forth for bread, and the hungry are no more hired; so that the barren hath born seven, and she that had many children is feeble; the Lord killeth, and maketh alive; bringeth down to the grave, and raiseth up; the Lord maketh poor, and maketh rich, bringeth low and exalteth, he raiseth up the poor out of the dust, and lifteth up the beggar from the dunghill to set them among princes, to make them inherit the seat of Glory; for the pillars of the earth are the Lord's, and he hath set the world upon them; he will keep the feet of his Saints, and the wicked shall keep silence in darkness, for in his own might shall no man be strong; the Lord's adversaries shall be destroyed, and out of Heaven shall be thunder upon them; the Lord shall judge the ends of the world, and shall give power to his King and exalt the Horn of his Anointed.*[59] Thus you may see what a woman hath said, when old Ely the priest thought she had been drunk, and see if any of you blind priests that speak against women's speaking can preach after this manner, who cannot make such a sermon as this woman did, and yet will make a trade of this woman and other women's words.

And did not the Queen of Sheba speak, that came to Solomon, and received the *Law of God, and preached* it in her own kingdom, and *blessed the Lord God that loved Solomon and set him on the throne of Israel, because the Lord loved Israel forever; and made the King to do equity and righteousness?*[60] And this was the language of the Queen of Sheba. And see what glorious expressions Queen Esther used to comfort the people of God, which was the Church of God, as you may read in the Book of Esther, which caused joy and gladness of heart among all the Jews, who prayed and worshipped the Lord in all places, who jeopardized her life contrary to the King's command, went and spoke to the King, in the wisdom and fear of the Lord, by which means she saved the lives of the People of God; and righteous Mordecai did not forbid her speaking, but said, *If she held her peace, her and her Father's house should be destroyed;*[61] and herein you blind priests are contrary to righteous Mordecai.

Likewise you may read how Judith spoke, and what noble acts she did, and how she spoke to the elders of Israel, and said, *Dear brethren, seeing ye are the honorable and elders of the People of God, call to remembrance how our Fathers in time past were tempted, that they might be proved if they would worship God aright; they ought also to remember how our Father Abraham, being tried through manifold tribulations, was found a friend of God; so was Isaac, Jacob, and Moses, and all they pleased God, and were steadfast in Faith through manifold troubles.* And read also her prayer in the Book of Judith, and how the Elders commended her, and said, *All that thou speakest is true, and no man can reprove thy words, pray therefore for us, for thou art an holy woman, and fearest God.*[62] So these Elders of Israel did not forbid her speaking, as you blind priests do; yet you will make a trade of women's words to get money by, and take texts, and preach sermons upon women's words; and still cry out, "Women must not speak. Women must be silent." So you are far from the minds of the Elders of Israel, who praised God for a woman's speaking. But the Jezebel, and the woman, the false church, the great whore, and tattling women, and busy-bodies, are forbidden to preach, which have a long time spoken and tattled, which are forbidden to speak by the True Church, which Christ is the Head of—such women as were in transgression under the Law, which are called a woman in the Revelations.

And see further how the wise woman cried to Joab over the wall, and saved the city of Abel, as you may read, 2 Samuel 20, how in her wisdom she spoke to Joab, saying, *I am one of them that are peaceable and faithful in Israel, and thou goest about to destroy a city and mother in Israel; why wilt thou destroy the inheritance of the Lord? Then went that woman to the people in her wisdom, and smote off the head of Sheba, that rose up against David, the Lord's Anointed: then Joab blew the trumpet, and all the people departed in peace.*[63] And this deliverance was by the means of a woman's speaking; but tattlers, and busy-bodies are forbidden to preach by the True Woman, [to] whom Christ is the husband, to the woman as well as the man, all being comprehended to be the Church and so in this True Church, sons and daughters do prophesy, women labor in the Gospel. But the Apostle permits not tattlers, busy-bodies, and such as usurp authority over the Man, [who] would not have Christ reign nor speak neither in the male nor female; such the Law permits not to speak, such must learn of their husbands. But what husbands have widows to learn of, but Christ? And was not Christ the husband of Philip's four daughters? And may not they that learn of their husband speak then? But Jezebel, and tattlers, and the Whore that denies Revelation and Prophecy are not permitted, which will not learn of Christ. And they that be out of the Spirit and Power of Christ, that the Prophets were in, who are in the transgression, are ignorant of the Scriptures; and such are against women's speaking, and men's too, who preach that which they have received of the Lord God. But that which they have preached, and do preach, will come over all your heads, yea, over the head of the False Church, the Pope; for the Pope is the head of the False Church, and the False Church is the Pope's wife, and so he and they that be of him, and come from him, are against women's speaking in the True Church, when both he and the False Church are called "woman" in Revelations 17,[64] and so are in the transgression that would usurp authority over the Man Christ Jesus, and his Wife, too, and would not have him to reign. But the judgment of the great Whore is come.

But Christ, who is the Head of the Church, the True Woman which is his wife, in it do daughters prophesy, who are above the Pope and his wife and a-top of them. And here Christ is the Head of the male and female, who may speak; and the Church is called *a Royal Priesthood*; so the woman must offer as well as the man, Revelations 22.17, *The Spirit saith, Come, and the Bride saith, Come*. And so is not the Bride the Church? And doth the Church only consist of men? You that deny women's speaking, answer: doth it not consist of women as well as men? Is not the Bride compared to the whole Church? And doth not the Bride say, *Come*? Doth not the woman speak then? The husband is Christ Jesus, the *Amen*, and doth not the False Church go about to stop the Bride's mouth? But it is not possible for the Bridegroom is with his Bride, and he opens her mouth. Christ Jesus, who goes on conquering, and to conquer who kills and slays with the sword, which is the words of his mouth; the Lamb and the Saints shall have the victory, the true speakers of men and women over the false speaker.

The End.

Notes

The title continues, *All such as speak by the Spirit and Power of the Lord JESUS, And how WOMEN were the first that preached the Tidings of the Resurrection of JESUS, and were sent by CHRIST's Own Command, before He ascended to the Father, John 20.17*. The pamphlet is reproduced from Margaret Fell, *Women's Speaking Justified* (London, 1666) (Folger copy F642, copy 1, by permission of the Folger Shakespeare Library). I have modernized spelling and punctuation and regularized Fell's capitalization for emphasis, but I have not changed the verb forms. I thank my students Betsy Kulamer and Will Stofega for proposing Margaret Fell as a rhetorical theorist and April Tassi for her teaching edition of the pamphlet for my classes.

1. Fell's biblical quotations follow roughly the King James Version (1611) but occasionally seem to be corrected against the Geneva Bible (1560); sometimes Fell quotes from the Coverdale Bible (1535). The frequent variations from the King James Version that do not appear in other translations demonstrate that Fell was quoting from memory, occasionally adding, subtracting, or changing words or phrases. Quakers and other religious people in the Renaissance memorized large portions of the Bible. Quoting from memory may have been habitual Quaker practice or it may have been a necessity, since Fell wrote this pamphlet in prison. In either case, it demonstrates Fell's vast biblical knowledge. This quotation comes from Joel 2:28 and Acts 2:17 (Fell or the printer made a slight error). The wording is closest to KJV, but the connection between these two biblical texts is stressed in the marginal commentary of the Geneva. I will not annotate the biblical quotations unless there is a discrepancy between Fell's citation and the King James citation, other than the variation of minor words and dropped phrases that seem to be characteristic of Fell's quotation from memory.

2. KJV 1 Corinthians 14:34–35: "Let you women keep silence in the churches: for it is not permitted unto them to speak; but they are commanded to be under obedience, as also saith the law. And if they will learn anything, let them ask their husbands at home: for it is a shame for women to speak in the church." 1 Timothy 2:11–12: "Let the woman learn in silence with all subjection. But I suffer not a woman to teach, nor to usurp authorization over the man, but to be in silence."

3. Genesis 1:27–28, 29; following more closely KJV but changing and dropping words and a whole sentence. Especially significant, Fell's middle "them" is "him" in both the KJV and the Geneva; the Coverdale Bible reads "created he them." Fell's printer italicized the biblical quotations; where missing, I have supplied italics.

4. 2 Corinthians 12:9; no Renaissance translation that I have located so far uses the word "manifest," but perhaps Fell is responding to the Geneva marginal commentary objecting to the phrasing "made perfect."

5. 1 Corinthians 1:27–28, but leaving out several phrases that associate the weak with what is base.

6. KJV Genesis 3:1, 5–6, 11–13, 15. The word "if" seems to come from the Geneva marginal commentary.

7. Isaiah 54:6.

8. Psalms 45:13–15.

9. The Renaissance termed the Song of Solomon the "Canticles." In her reference to KJV Song of Solomon 5:9 and the one above for Jeremiah 31:22, Fell seems influenced by the Geneva commentary reading the woman in the passages as Jerusalem (i.e., the Church on earth).

10. KJV, Revelation 12:1, 3–4; many words left out. The Geneva gloss equates the woman with the Church.

11. Matthew 19:4–6.

12. John 4:25–26.

13. Matthew 26:10, 13 (also in Mark 14:6).

14. Luke 7:37–38.

15. Luke 7:44–47.

16. Actually Matthew 27:55; Luke 15:40–41; Fell follows Matthew but changes the word order.

17. Owned: acknowledged.

18. Mark 16:1–4; KJV has "bought," not "brought."

19. Matthew 28:2, 5.

20. Luke 24:4–9.

21. Luke 24:11.

22. Matthew 28:10 but Mark 16:7.

23. John 20:15–17.

24. 1 Corinthians 1:25, but the order of sayings is reversed.

25. 1 Corinthians 14:20, 32–34. "The Apostle" is Paul.

26. 1 Corinthians 14:26.

27. 1 Corinthians 14:27–28.

28. 1 Corinthians 14:34–35.

29. 1 Corinthians 14:21.

30. 1 Corinthians 14:30–31.

31. 1 Corinthians 11:4–5, 13, 11. Fell skips all the verses that enjoin female subservience in this chapter and quotes, in her own order, only those verses that might have a more equitable interpretation put upon them.

32. 1 Timothy 2:9, 11–14.

33. Revelation 13:1.

34. Revelation 17:2–4.

35. Revelation 13:4.

36. Revelation 17:6.

37. The Geneva Bible commentary (and many other Protestant commentaries) equate this woman of Revelation with the Roman Catholic Church. They see this passage as a reference to the idolatry of the Catholic Church in its use of religious images and ornate churches, as well as its persecution of Protestants.

38. Revelation 18:7.

39. Revelation 13:8.

40. Revelation 22:16.

41. Revelation 19:7–8.

42. Revelation 21:11.

43. Galatians 4:24–26.

44. Revelation 21:10–11.

45. Actually, Isaiah 51:1–3.

46. Acts 21:9.

47. Genesis 1:27.

48. 1 Corinthians 14:34–35.

49. 1 Timothy 5:13.

50. Romans 10:4.

51. Geneva, 2 Kings 22:15–20.

52. Isaiah 8:3.

53. Joel 2:28.

54. Acts 2:17–18 (quoting Joel 2:28).

55. Luke 1:39–55.

56. This speech of Mary's forms the basis for the Magnificat, a Catholic prayer regularly said at Vespers that remained part of the Anglican Evening Prayers. Fell's wording—"your Common Prayer"—recalls the title of the Anglican directory for church services: The Book of Common Prayer.

57. Ruth 4:11–12, 14. KJV, but one word taken from Geneva.

58. Geneva, 1 Samuel 1:11.

59. Geneva, 1 Samuel 2:1–10.

60. Geneva, 1 Kings 10:9.

61. Esther 4:14.

62. Coverdale, Judith, middle of chapter 8; the Coverdale Bible doesn't have verse divisions.

63. 2 Samuel 20:19, 22. Perhaps Geneva, but it seems to be yet a different translation.

64. The marginal commentary in the Geneva Bible to Revelation 17:4 reads, "This woman is the Antichrist, that is, the Pope with the whole body of his filthy creatures, as is expounded in verse 18, whose beauty only standeth in outward pomp and impudency and craft like a strumpet."

Bathsua Makin

1600–c. 1675

Bathsua Reginald Makin was born in 1600 and named after the biblical Bathsheba. Her father, Henry Reginald, ran a school at Stepney, England, and invented a system of shorthand. Her grandfather had published two books of translated Latin sermons, and her father a broadsheet of Latin poems, as well as manuscript pamphlets on mathematical instruments. At the age of sixteen, through the urging of her father, she published a book, *Musa Virginea* (London, 1616), of Latin, Greek, Hebrew, Spanish, French, and German verse encomia of the reigning Stuart family. In the 1620s, she married Richard Makin, moved to Westminster, and had eight children. Her sister Ithamaria married John Pell in 1632. (Pell has mistakenly been identified by some biographers as Bathsua's brother, but he is her brother-in-law.) By 1640, Bathsua Makin was known as the most learned woman in England, and she had entered court service as tutor to the children of Charles I, especially to the princess Elizabeth. When Parliament took the princess into custody (at the beginning of the English Civil War), Makin was allowed to remain with her as a servant. The princess died in 1650. Makin was allotted a pension for her service under Charles II but could not collect it during the Civil War, or afterward in the Restoration. While her husband was absent during the Civil War and Interregnum, Makin raised their three remaining children on her own.

Makin also tutored the Lady Elizabeth (Hastings) Langham, perhaps until 1652 when Lady Elizabeth married; Makin wrote an elegy at her death in 1664. Makin's husband died in 1659, and her sister, who had helped support her, died two years later. *An Essay to Revive the Ancient Education of Gentlewomen*, her proposal for the education of women, was published in 1673 and indicates in its postscript that she teaches in a school for gentlewomen at Tottenham High Cross, within four miles of London. Her partner in this school was Mark Lewis, who also wrote textbooks and pamphlets. Elizabeth Drake, mother of the bluestocking Elizabeth Robinson Montagu and the novelist Sarah Robinson Scott, was said to have been educated at the academy that Makin founded. Makin died sometime after 1675.

In the humanist tradition, Makin maintained a friendship through correspondence with the Dutch scholar Anna Maria van Schurman, who refers to her in a letter to Simond d'Ewes, published with the English translation of her treatise in support of women's education, *The Learned Maid* (1659). In return, Makin's *Essay* praises Dutch women in general, and van Schurman in particular, as models of proper education for women; indeed, Makin's essay may have been inspired by van Schurman's. Makin shares with van Schurman the proposal that only women with enough time, wealth, and basic intelligence should receive a humanist education, and the qualification that women not use their education for public offices. But Makin's supporting arguments are very different. In her educational theories, Makin was a progressive, influenced by the works of John Amos Comenius, especially his advice on using the vernacular instead of Latin in teaching, and his hopes for universal education as a basis for church and social reform.

According to her *Essay*, Makin seems to have taught her female students rhetoric: "I cannot tell where to begin to admit women, nor from what part of learning to exclude them, in regard of their capacities. . . . I would not deny them the knowledge of grammar and rhetoric, because they dispose to speak handsomely. Logic must be allowed, because it is the key to all sciences." Makin enters this anthology of women and rhetorical theory not only as a teacher of rhetoric, but also as a theorist. Certainly, *An Essay to Revive the Ancient Education of Gentlewomen*, as Paula Barbour argues, is a "plea that England revive the sixteenth-century experiment in the rigorous education of women" (p. iii). But the *Essay* is also a carefully formulated defense of women's speech and of women's right to speak. In this respect, the *Essay* may be read as theory outlining a rhetoric of the politics of speech with regard to gender. This subversive idea counterbalances Makin's qualification that only a few women, those with wealth, superior class standing, and innate intelligence, should be educated. Makin structures her treatise as a set of three letters, one in favor of educating women, one against it, and a lengthy third (presumably by the writer of the first letter) defending women's use of speech as a benefit for all, and resolving the debate in favor of educating women.

In the third letter, after introducing her proposal to educate women and outlining a brief history of educated women who have achieved excellence in learning, Makin also introduces her defense of women's speech. Makin acknowledges that women have little financial or political power, and so they need the advantages derived from persuasion as a power. In her list of women who have excelled in each particular art and science, including Aspasia, Arete, and Margaret Cavendish, she not only furthers her plea for education for women but also ties each discipline to her defense of women speaking. If circumstances put women in the position of head of household, as the late Civil War often did, then Makin is happy to cite those women as models, who "appeared before committees, and pleaded their own causes with good success." She would have women "able to understand, read, write, and speak their Mother-Tongue" and "Learned, that they may stop their ears against Seducers" of their souls who teach religious heresies. With regard to gender and rhetoric, she adopts something of the position that Pan Chao did long before her. If women will not usually speak in public, they need to be taught a rhetoric that will help them in conversation with their husbands and in domestic duties. Limited as it is, this is the argument that two centuries later opened college education to women in England and the United States.

For further information, see Bathsua Makin, *An Essay to Revive the Antient Education of Gentlewomen* (1673), introduction by Paula Barbour, Publication 202 (Los Angeles: William Andrews Clark Memorial Library/University of California, 1980); Jean R. Brink, "Bathsua Makin: Educator and Linguist," in *Female Scholars: A Tradition of Learned Women before 1800*, ed. Jean R. Brink (Montreal: Eden Press Women's Publications, 1980), 86–100; Hilda Smith, *Reason's Disciples: Seventeenth-Century English Feminists* (Urbana: University of Illinois Press, 1982); Frances Teague, "The Identity of Bathsua Makin," *Biography* 16, no. 1 (Winter 1993): 1–17; Teague, *Bathsua Makin: Woman of Learning* (Lewisburg, Pa.: Bucknell University Press, 1997); and Jane Donawerth, "The Politics of Renaissance Rhetorical Theory by Women," *Political Rhetoric, Power, and Renaissance Women*, ed. Carole Levin and Patricia A. Sullivan (Albany: State University of New York Press, 1995), 256–72.

From *An Essay to Revive the Ancient Education of Gentlewomen* (1673)

From the Third Letter, Defending Women's Education

Women Have Been Good Linguists

It is objected against women, as a reproach, that they have too much tongue: but it's no crime they have many tongues; if it be, many men would be glad to be guilty of that fault. The tongue is the only weapon women have to defend themselves with, and they had need to use it dexterously. Many say one tongue is enough for a woman: it is but a quibble upon the word.[1] Several languages, understood by a woman, will do our gentlemen little hurt, who have little more than their mother-wit, and understand only their mother-tongue; these most usually make this objection to hide their own ignorance. Tongues are learned in order to [understand] things. As things were and yet are in the world, it's requisite we learn tongues to understand arts: it's therefore a commendation to these women after mentioned, that they were mistresses of tongues.

There is an ancient copy of the Septuagint,[2] sent from the Patriarch of Alexandria to King James, written by a woman called Tecla,[3] so accurate and excellent, that the authors of the polyglot Bible[4] chose it before all other copies written or printed, to make use of in that impression.[5]

Anna Maria Schurman of Utrecht,[6] (called by Spanhemius, *ultimum naturae in hoc sexu conatum, et decimam Musam,*[7] nature's master-piece among women, excelling the very Muses) hath printed divers works in Latin, Greek, French, and the Persian tongue; she understood the Arabic also. Besides, she was an excellent poet.

Amalasunth,[8] Queen of the Ostrogoths, the daughter of Theodericus, was a great mistress of the Latin and Greek tongues; she spoke distinctly all the barbarous languages that were used in the Eastern empires.

For excellency in tongues most of those persons before mentioned are eminent instances: Maurata, the Lady Jane Grey, and the three Elizabeths, etc.[9]

Women have not been mere talkers (as some frivolous men would make them) but they have known how to use languages, when they have had them. Many women have been excellent orators.

Women Have Been Good Orators

Valerius Maximus[10] tells us of Amesia, a modest Roman lady, when she was accused of a great crime, and ready to incur the sentence of the praetor, she in a great confluence stepped up amongst the people and, without any advocate, pleaded her own cause so effectually, that by the public suffrage she was acquitted from all aspersion whatsoever, and from that time she was called "Androgyne."[11]

Hortensia[12] was equal to her, the daughter of Quintus Hortensius.[13] When a grievous fine was imposed upon the Roman matrons by the tribunes, when all lawyers and orators were afraid to take upon them the patronage of their cause, this discreet lady pleaded before the triumvirate in the behalf of the women, so happily[14] and boldly, that the greatest part of the mulct[15] imposed upon them was remitted.

Some have commended Caia Africana's[16] eloquence: I cannot approve of the use she put it to, but pass her over.[17]

Tullia[18] (by the instruction of her mother Terentia[19]) was counted equal to her father Cicero[20] in eloquence.

Divers of those persons before mentioned were very eloquent, particularly Maurata, Cornelia,[21] and Queen Elizabeth. We may suppose Schurman, and the rest that wrote so elegantly, could also speak eloquently upon a just occasion.

It is objected against poor women, they may learn tongues and speak freely, being naturally disposed to be talkative, but for any solid judgment or depth of reason, it is seldom found in their giddy crowns.[22] I proceed therefore to show they have been good logicians, philosophers, mathematicians, divines, and poets.

Women Have Understood Logic

Logic is the key—those that have this in their heads may unlock other sciences; some women have had it at their girdles,[23] and been very dexterous in disputation.

Hipparchia[24] with one sophism put to silence Theodorus. It was thus: "That which Theodorus is doing, he is not said to do unjustly; if Hipparchia do so, she is not said to do unjustly." This he granted. She proceeds: "But, Theodorus beating himself, is not said to do unjustly; therefore, if Hipparchia beats Theodorus, she is not said to do unjustly." Theodorus makes no reply, but, just like our lazy gentlemen, goes out of the room and says, "Let women mind their spinning."

Margarita Sarocchi,[25] a gentlewoman of Rome, is looked upon as so great a sophister, that she is ordinarily a Moderatix in the Academy at the disputation amongst learned wits, in the most polite parts of learning and philosophy, yea, and divinity, too.

Those who read Schurman's *Dissertations*[26] will conclude she understood the principles and practice of logic very well.

Cecilia[27] did strange things by her great skill in logic—particularly, by solid argument she dissuaded Tiburtius Valerianus's brother[28] from heathenish idolatry to the Christian faith.

Some think I have hardly spoke to the purpose yet; logic disposes to wrangle, a thing women are inclined to naturally. I proceed therefore to show that women have been great proficients in the most solid parts of learning, which require most serious thoughts and greatest judgment; they have been good philosophers, good arithmeticians, good divines, and good poets.

This Kind of Education Will Be Very Useful to Women

1. The profit will be to themselves. In the general they will be able to understand, read, write, and speak their mother-tongue, which they cannot well do without this. They will have something to exercise their thoughts about, which are busy and active. Their quality ties them at home; if learning be their companion, delight and pleasure will be their attendants. For there is no pleasure greater, nor more suitable to an ingenious mind, than what is founded in knowledge: it is the first fruits of heaven, and a glimpse of that glory we afterwards expect. There is in all an innate desire of knowing, and the satisfying this is the greatest pleasure. Men are very cruel that give them leave to look at a distance, only to know they do not know; to make any thus to tantalize, is a great torment.

This will be a hedge against heresies. Men are furnished with arts and tongues for this purpose, that they may stop the mouths of their adversaries. And women ought to be learned, that they may stop their ears against seducers. It cannot be imagined so many persons of quality would be so easily carried aside with every wind of doctrine, had they been furnished with these defensive arms; I mean, had they been instructed in the plain rules of artificial reasoning, so as to distinguish a true and forcible argument from a vain and captious fallacy, [or] had they been furnished with examples of the most frequent illusions of erroneous seducers. Heresiarchs[29] creep into houses, and lead silly women captive, then they lead their husbands, both their children—as the devil did Eve, she her husband, they their posterity.[30]

It is none of the least considerations, that a woman thus educated, who modestly uses her learning, is, in despite of envy, honored by most, especially wise and good men; such a one is admired and even adored by the vulgar and illiterate.

2. Women thus educated will be beneficial to their relations. It is a great blessing of God to a family, to provide a good wife for the head, if it be eminent; and a presage of ruin, when he sends a ranting Jezebel[31] to a soft Ahab.[32]

One Athaliah, married to Joram, plucks ruin upon the house of Jehosaphat.[33] How many families have been ruined by this one thing, the bad education of women? Because the men find no satisfactory converse or entertainment at home, out of mere weariness they seek abroad; hence they neglect their business, spend their estates, destroy their bodies, and oftentimes damn their souls.

The Italians slight their wives, because all necessary knowledge, that may make them serviceable (attainable by institution[34]) is denied them: but they court, adore, and glory in their courtesans, though common whores, because they are polished with more generous breeding.

Many learned men, having married wives of excellent parts, have themselves instructed them in all kinds of learning, the more to fit them for their converse, and to endear them and their society to them, and to make them admired by others. The woman is the glory of the man; we joy in our children when eminent, and in our wives when excellent, either in body or mind.

I have said before how they may improve their children in learning, especially the tongues; I mention it again, because it is a reason of so great weight, that it is sufficient (if there was nothing else) to turn the scale. Tullia had never been so eloquent, had not she had so learned a mother as Hortensia.[35]

The Gracchi, Baptista, Damar, Aristippus, Eustochium (before mentioned) had never been so famous in arts and tongues, had they not been timely taught by their mothers—Cornelia, Constantia, Arete, and Paula.[36]

King Lemuel's wisdom was extraordinary, yet he acknowledges the seeds were sown by the timely instruction of his mother, Proverbs 31.[37] Therefore Solomon charges children to mind the instruction of their mothers, having found so much good by it himself.[38]

Besides, none have so great an advantage of making most deep impression on their children, as mothers. What a prudent and virtuous mother commends by precept and example, sticks long; witness Lemuel and his proverbs, many of which he sucked in with his mother's milk.

Timothy was taught the holy scriptures from a child, by his grandmother Lois, and by his mother Eunice.[39]

We may presume the children of the elect lady were found walking in the truth from their mother's instructions. For they seldom speak the language of Canaan, whose mothers are of Ashdod.[40]

3. Women thus instructed will be beneficial to the nation. Look into all history: those nations ever were, now are, and always shall be the worst of nations, where women are most undervalued, as in Russia, Ethiopia, and all the barbarous nations of the world. One great reason why our neighbors the Dutch have thrived to admiration is the great care they take in the education of their women, from whence they are to be accounted more virtuous, and to be sure more useful than any women in the world. We cannot expect otherwise to prevail against the ignorance, atheism, prophaneness, superstition, idolatry, [and] lust that reigns in the nation, than by a prudent, sober, pious, virtuous education of our daughters. Their learning would stir up our sons, whom God and nature hath made superior, to a just emulation.

Had we sufficient number of females thus instructed to furnish the nurseries of noble families, their children might be improved in the knowledge of the learned tongues before they were aware. I mention this a third time, because it is of such moment and concern.

The memory of Queen Elizabeth is yet fresh. By her learning she was fitted for government, and swayed the scepter of this nation with as great honor as any man before her.

Our very reformation of religion seems to be begun and carried on by women.

Mrs. Anne Askew,[41] a person famous for learning and piety, so seasoned the queen and ladies at court, by her precepts and examples, and after sealed her profession with her blood, that the seed of reformation seemed to be sowed by her hand.

✦

My intention is not to equalize women to men, much less to make them superior. They are the weaker sex, yet capable of impressions of great things, something like to the best of men.

Hercules and Theseus were very valiant; Manalippe and Hyppolite were little inferior to them.[42] Zeuxes and Timanthes were brave painters. So were Timarete, Irene, Lala, Martia, and many others.[43]

For poetry, Sappho may be compared with Anacreon, Corinna with Pindar.[44] Tullia was eloquent like Cicero, Cato's daughter little inferior to himself in the theory and practice of philosophy.[45] Semiramis was like Alexander in magnificence,[46] Tanaquil as politic as Servius Tullius.[47] Portia was as magnanimous as Brutus.[48]

The inference I make from hence is that women are not such silly, giddy creatures, as many proud, ignorant men would make them—as if they were incapable of all improvement by learning, and unable to digest arts that require any solidity of judgment.

Notes

This excerpt is taken from Bathsua Makin, *An Essay to Revive the Antient Education of Gentlewomen* (London, 1673), sigs. B2^r–B3^r, D1^r–D3^r (Folger M309) by permission of the Folger Shakespeare Library. I have modernized spelling and punctuation. I thank Andrew Naprawa and Andrea H. Scopelitis for suggesting to me Bathsua Makin as a rhetorical theorist.

1. "A quibble upon the word" is a pun, or equivocation—"tongue" means not only the physical organ used in speech but also a language. Makin is refuting this customary misogynistic joke about women talking too much.

2. Septuagint: the Greek translation of the Old Testament, supposedly produced by seventy (or seventy-two) Jews in as many days; the Bible of the early Christians.

3. Tecla: the name of an apocryphal early convert of Saint Paul, and so a popular name for subsequent female saints and martyrs. Here she is said to have written out or translated a version of the Septuagint that was later sent to King James I of England.

4. Polyglot Bible: a comparative Bible with different texts in various languages arranged in columns; Makin is probably referring to *The London Polyglot*, edited by Brian Walton, published in 1657 and dedicated (eventually) to King Charles II, King James's grandson.

5. Impression: printing.

6. Anna Maria van Schurmann (1607–1678), Dutch linguist who knew Arabic, Aramaic, Greek, Latin, and other languages; coleader of a religious community much like the Quakers; famous throughout Europe for her learning and her treatise in favor of women's education.

7. Spanhemius: Latin translation of "Spanheim," the name of a family of famous learned men and linguists from Leyden; perhaps Frederick Spanheim (1600–1649), minister and professor of philosophy and divinity first at Geneva, then at Leyden; perhaps his son, Frederic (1632–1705). The Latin may be translated as "known to be the masterpiece of nature in this sex, and the tenth muse."

8. Amalasuntha, or Amalasuenta (died 534), queen of the Ostrogoths in Italy, killed by her husband.

9. Makin mistakenly refers to Olympia Maurata (d. 1555) as a linguist and tutor to the empress of Germany, when it was her father who was the tutor. Lady Jane Grey (1537–1554), an accomplished linguist, was Protestant queen of England for nine days after the death of Edward VI, and was beheaded by Queen Mary, her Catholic successor and the legitimate heir. "The three Elizabeths" famous for their knowledge of languages are Queen Elizabeth I (1533–1603), one of the most successful of English monarchs; Princess Elizabeth and later Queen Elizabeth of Bohemia (1596–1662), daughter of King James I and Anne of Denmark; and Princess Elizabeth (1635–1650), daughter of Charles II, pupil of Makin, devoted student of languages and theology.

10. Valerius Maximus, first-century Roman historian who composed a commonplace book of people and events (organized by topics), popular throughout the Middle Ages and the Renaissance, *Factorum ac dictorum memorabilium libri IX* [Collections of memorable acts and sayings].

11. Androgyne: androgynous, two-sexed person, displaying both feminine and masculine aspects.

12. Hortensia (c. 50 B.C.E.), Roman matron and politician, a great orator, daughter of Quintus Hortensius Hortalus. Makin's account is taken from Valerius Maximus Bk. VIII, ch. iii.

13. Quintus Hortensius Hortalus (114–49 B.C.E.), one of the great Roman orators, friend of Cicero and opponent of Pompey.

14. Happily: fortunately or effectively.

15. Mulct: fine or penalty.

16. Caia Africana (also Afrania or Gnea Africana) pleaded for herself in many lawsuits; according to Valerius Maximus, she frequented the forum, forgetting her place (VIII.iii).

17. Pass her over: leave her out.

18. Tullia (79–45 B.C.E.), married three times, beloved by her father, Cicero.

19. Terentia, first wife of Cicero, involved in politics through her influence, mother of a son and a daughter with Cicero, was divorced by him. She remarried and lived to be 103.

20. Marcus Tullius Cicero (106–43 B.C.E.), greatest of Roman orators, rhetorical theorist, philosopher, lawyer, politician, defender of the Republic, killed by order of Antony.

21. Cornelia (c. 169 B.C.E.), Roman matron, daughter of Scipio Africanus, married to Tiberius Gracchus; famous for her literary salon, for her letter writing, and for educating her sons, the famous Gracchi brothers.

22. Crowns: heads.

23. At their girdles: hanging on or tucked in their belts, at their side, at hand.

24. Hipparchia (c. 300 B.C.E.): Cynic philosopher who married Crates of Thebes.

25. Margarita Sarocchi: Renaissance woman from Rome, member of the Galileo circle, who wrote an unfinished pastoral romance that was published.

26. "Schurman's *Dissertations*" is Anna Maria van Schurman's treatise defending women's education, *Amica dissertatio . . . de capacitate ingenii muliebris ad scientias* [A friendly dissertation concerning the capacity of clever women to learn], published in 1638.

27. Cecilia: Roman martyr of the third century, said to have persuaded her fiancé and his brother to become Christians.

28. Tiburtius Valerianus's brother: Makin has confused the names. Cecilia's fiancé was Valerian; his brother was Tiburtius. Both were martyred.

29. "Heresiarchs" are heretics.

30. See Genesis 3.

31. Jezebel: Tyrian wife of King Ahab of Israel; portrayed as a ruthless oppressor, a worshiper of Baal, who deserved the downfall Elijah prophesied for her. See 1 Kings 18:19; 1 Kings 21; 2 Kings 9:30–37.

32. Ahab: king of Israel (c. 869–850 B.C.E.); in conflict with Elijah over his queen, Jezebel, and her worship of Baal; archetypal villain who allowed Jezebel to order the death of Naboth. See 1 Kings 18, 21.

33. Athaliah: queen of Judah who reigned 843–837 B.C.E.; she usurped the throne and killed the king's sons. Joram: king of Israel, son of Ahab, husband to Athaliah. See 2 Kings 11:1–3. Jehosaphat: king of Judah who reigned c. 873–858 B.C.E., contemporary and ally, then enemy, of Ahab; praised for piety. See 2 Kings 15:24; 2 Chronicles 18, 20.

34. Misprint for instruction?

35. Misprint for Terentia (see notes 18–19).

36. For Cornelia, mother of the Gracchi, see note 21. Constantia Sforza of Milan was married to Alexander; their daughter was Baptista, whose granddaughter was the poet Vittoria Colonna. Dama or Damar (c. 600 B.C.E.) was the daughter of Pythagorus and Theano. In Greece in the fifth century B.C.E., Arete, daughter of the sophist Aristippus, taught her son Aristippus rhetoric and philosophy; this second Aristippus became a Cynic. A woman of wealth, Paula (347–404 C.E.) accompanied Jerome to Palestine in 385. She and her daughter Eustochium, knowledgeable in Greek, Latin, and Hebrew, studied scripture together under the guidance of Jerome, and in later life they founded a convent.

37. Proverbs 31 records the prophecies of King Lemuel's mother, who warns against drunkenness and describes the characteristics of the good wife.

38. The Renaissance generally attributed Proverbs to Solomon, hence his reputation for wisdom. Makin's wording suggests that she is following the Geneva Bible wording for Proverbs 1:8: "My sonne, heare thy fathers instruction, and forsake not thy mothers teaching."

39. As an assistant to Paul, Timothy was sent at various times to Thessalonica, Corinth, and perhaps Philippi to oversee those churches; Lois was Timothy's grandmother and Eunice was his mother; they instructed him in the Christian faith. See 2 Timothy 1:5; 3:14–15.

40. In Nehemiah 13:23–25, the prophet reproves the Israelites who married foreign wives and had children who "could not speak in the Jews' language." The Geneva Bible marginal note interprets this to mean, as Makin also means it, a falling away from true religion.

41. Anne Askew (c. 1521–1546) was burned for heresy by Henry VIII's bishops for her radical Protestant ideas; she left a record of her "Examinations" under torture; John Foxe recorded her inspiring bravery at her death in *The Acts and Monuments* (1563 in English). She was a lady-in-waiting to Queen Katherine Parr.

42. Hercules and Theseus were legendary heroes, famous for their bravery. Hercules, son of Zeus, strongest of all men, had to perform nine labors, the last of which was to steal the girdle or belt of Hip-

polyte, queen of the Amazons, which resulted in a war. Theseus married Hippolyte after besting her in battle.

43. Zeuxes, Timanthes, and Timarete were legendary Greek painters from the fifth to fourth centuries B.C.E. Zeuxes was noted for increased realism and emotional effect, Timanthes for inventiveness. Irene, daughter of Cratinus, Lala Czizena, and Martia were also painters.

44. Sappho, Anacreon, Corinna, and Pindar were Greek lyric poets from the seventh to sixth centuries B.C.E. Sappho, the most famous, is the woman poet whose poetry has been well preserved, although all poems but one are fragmentary, reconstructed from quotations. Sappho is also said to have run a school for girls. Corinna was a contemporary of Pindar and competed with him in poetry contests.

45. Cato's daughter: In the first century B.C.E., Porcia and her father, Cato, are more famous for their politics than their philosophy, although they are also renowned for their Stoic and republican principles, which caused each to commit suicide.

46. Semiramis was queen of Syria in the ninth century B.C.E. and, according to legend, conqueror of Bactria and founder of Babylonia. Alexander the Great of Macedon (356–323 B.C.E.) conquered all of Greece and much of the Middle East.

47. Tanaquil, sixth century B.C.E., was wife of Tarquinius Priscus, an early Roman king. Livy, the Roman historian, records her as a masterful politician. Servius Tullius (578–535 B.C.E.), of slave ancestry, was king of Rome and was credited with establishing many important Roman institutions.

48. A first-century republican, Brutus, ally of Cicero and Cassius, was married to Porcia, Cato's daughter.

Madeleine de Scudéry

1608–1701

Famous for her multivolume, intricately plotted prose romances, Madeleine de Scudéry was the most popular novelist in seventeenth-century Europe. Born into an old family of the upper middle class and lower gentry in Rouen, de Scudéry and her older brother, Georges, were raised by an uncle after their parents died when Madeleine was five years old. Madeleine eventually followed Georges to Paris, where he made a success writing plays and she writing novels, and where their conversational skills in the salons gained them the patronage of many aristocrats, including Mme. de Rambouillet and eventually the king. Georges's first play, *Le Prince Déguisé*, was successfully produced in 1635, and Madeleine published the first of a series of extremely popular novels, *Ibrahim ou l'illustre bassa*, in 1641, under her brother's name, a practice she continued throughout his life. Her other novels included *Artamène ou Le Grand Cyrus* (1649–1653), *Clélie, Histoire Romaine* (1654), and *Mathilde d'Aguilar* (1667). From 1644 to 1647, the brother and sister lived in Marseilles, where Georges had been granted the post of governor of Notre-Dame-de-la-Garde. Georges was elected to the Académie Française in 1650; although Madeleine was eventually awarded a prize for her *Discours de la gloire*, she was never admitted as a member because it was closed to women. During the Frond (1648–1654), Madeleine remained loyal to the king and took no part in the rebellion, although she maintained ties to the disgraced Condé family. Owing to his Condé connection, Georges fled to a city near Le Havre and was married there in 1654. Living alone, Madeleine continued a tradition she began when living with her brother in Paris in 1653, of the Samedis, a weekly salon on Saturdays at her home. Her circle became noted throughout Europe as *les précieux* for its style of conversation and writing, and Madeleine and the other women of her salon were ridiculed in Molière's play *Les précieuses ridicules* in 1659. De Scudéry never married, although she was especially close to Paul Pellisson, with whom she had a Platonic love affair; she burned his letters when he was imprisoned, as secretary to the disgraced Fouquet, in 1661. Perhaps partly through appeals by de Scudéry and her friends, Pellison was released in 1666. De Scudéry was also a close and loyal friend of many women in the salon circles, especially Mme. de Rambouillet, Mme. de Sévigné, and Mme. de Lafayette. After her brother's death in 1667, Madeleine continued to publish but anonymously, never putting her name in her books, although her authorship was an open secret. Throughout her life, she supported herself, and sometimes her brother as well, through her brilliant conversation and writing. She was deaf for the last forty years of her life and died in 1701.

From 1642 to 1684, de Scudéry developed a theory of rhetoric and composition in prefaces, fictional speeches, novels, and dialogue essays on conversation and letter writing, drawing on classical rhetorical principles from Aristotle, Cicero, and the sophists, and adapting them to the circumstances of aristocratic and middle-class women (and men) in the salons of seventeenth-century France. By appropriating rhetoric, de Scudéry was appropriating the Renaissance for women, since rhetorical Latin education was the center of humanist culture. In *Les femmes illustres ou les harangues héroiques* (1642; not included in this anthology), de Scudéry published a series of fictional speeches attributed to women of the ancient world—Cleopatra, Volumnia, Mariam, Zenobia, and others—and argued, especially in the preface (probably written with her brother) and in the final speech, "Sappho to Erinna," that women should aim for social mobility through education and authorship rather than through marriage. In a two-volume set of dialogue essays, *Conversations sur divers sujets* (1680), some of which were excerpted from her novels, she treated conversation, speaking too much or too little, flattery, dissimulation, invention, and wit, modeling her theory of rhetoric on conversation rather than on public speaking. Unlike the classical dialogues on the art of rhetoric by Plato, Cicero, and Augustine, de Scudéry's dialogues feature women speakers who often guide the discussion and sum up the conclusions for the group, acting as models of the art of conversation. For example, in "De parler trop, ou trop peu" (a dialogue I have not included in this volume), de Scudéry's Plotina is a model for all women: "On the subject of speaking agreeably, the charming Plotina speaks as becomes a rational Woman to speak. For all her expressions are noble and natural at the same time; she does not have to search for what she wants to say; there is no constraint in her words; her discourse is clear and fluent; there is a gentle manner in her way of speaking, no affectation in the sound of her voice, a great deal of freedom in her actions [or gestures], and a wonderful coherence between her eyes and her words (which is one thing that contributes to rendering speech most agreeable)" (*Conversations* 108). In *Conversations nouvelles sur divers sujets, dedie'es au roy* (1684), she rounded out her theory of rhetoric and composition by including a dialogue, "On the Manner of Writing Letters," that adapts the *ars dictaminis*, the rhetorical art of writing letters, to her contemporaries; a version of this dialogue was first published as part of her novel, *Clélie* (1654). She offers her own catalogue of kinds of letters: besides the usual forms of letters of condolence, recommendation, business, and congratulation, she includes letters of gossip, polite letters that discourage further correspondence, and, central to her theory, love letters. Women, she argues, are better than men at writing love letters because they are required by their gender roles to mask their feelings, and such disguise is the essence of art. De Scudéry's *Conversations* were used as textbooks in girls' schools in the seventeenth century, and she was so influential that over a century later Hannah More caustically repudiates the influence of the *précieuses* in her own essays on conversation.

For further information, see Nicole Aronson, *Mademoiselle de Scudéry*, trans. Stuart R. Aronson (Boston: Twayne, 1978); Domna Stanton, *The Aristocrat as Art: A Study of the Honnête Homme and the Dandy in Seventeenth- and Nineteenth-Century French Literature* (New York: Columbia University Press, 1980); Elizabeth Goldsmith, *"Exclusive Conversations": The Art of Interaction in Seventeenth-Century France* (Philadelphia: University of Pennsylvania Press, 1988); Elizabeth Goldsmith, ed., *Writing the Female Voice: Essays on Epistolary Literature* (Boston: Northeastern University Press, 1989); Peter Burke, "The Art of Conversation in Early Modern Europe," in *The Art of Conversation* (Ithaca: Cornell University Press, 1993), 89–122; Jane Donawerth, "The Politics of Renaissance Rhetorical Theory by Women," in *Political Rhetoric, Power, and Renaissance Women*, ed. Carole Levin and Patricia A. Sullivan (Albany: State University of New York Press, 1995), 256–72; and Jane Donawerth, "'As Becomes a Rational Woman to Speak': Madeleine de Scudéry's Rhetoric of Conversation," in *Rhetorical Activities of Historical Women*, ed. Molly Wertheimer (Columbia: University of South Carolina Press, 1997), 305–19.

"On Conversation"
From *Les Conversations sur Divers Sujets* (1680)

"Since conversation is the bond of society for all humanity, the greatest pleasure of decent people,[1] and the most ordinary method by which is introduced into the world not only politeness, but also the purest morals and the love of glory and virtue, it appears to me that the company cannot entertain themselves more agreeably, nor more usefully," said Cilenie, "than to examine what people call 'Conversation.' For when men only speak strictly according to the exigency of their affairs, we cannot call it so."

"In fact," said Amilcar, "a lawyer who pleads his cause to his judges, a merchant who negotiates with another, a general of the army who gives orders, a king who speaks of affairs of state in his Council—all this ought not to be called conversation. All these people may be able to discourse well about their interests and business, and yet not have that agreeable talent of conversation, which is the sweetest charm of life, and perhaps more rare than one believes."

"For my part, I don't doubt any of this," replied Cilenie, "but it seems to me that before it can be well defined, wherein principally consists the charm and beauty of conversation, all the people who compose this company should recall the boring conversations that they found the most irritating."

"You have a good point," said Cerinte, "for by observing all that is tiresome, one may better understand what is diverting; and to show [you] an example," she added, "I made a visit to a family yesterday, by which I was so overwhelmed that I thought I would die of boredom. Indeed, do but imagine me in the midst of ten or twelve women, who spoke of nothing else but all their little domestic cares, of the faults of their servants, of the good qualities or vices of their children; and there was one woman among the rest, who spent more than an hour recounting syllable by syllable the first tattlings of a son of hers, who is just three years old. You may judge after that, if I did not pass my time in a lamentable manner."

"I assure you," responded Nicanor, "that I spent my time little better than yourself, since I found myself engaged against my will with a troop of women (whom you may easily guess), who employed the whole day in nothing but speaking well or ill of their clothes, and in lying continually about the price that they cost them. For some, out of vanity, said much more than was correct, as I was informed by the least silly of them all; and others, to be thought clever, said much less—so much so that I passed the entire day in hearing such shallow and senseless matters that it makes me still a little embarrassed."

"On my part," said the lovely Athis, "fifteen days ago I found myself with some ladies who, although they had wit enough, strangely wearied me. For in short, to speak things as they are, these are women who make a practice of being gallant, who have at least one affair each, and an affair that so possesses them that they think of nothing else—so much so that when you are not a part of their intrigues, and find yourself in their company, you become quite embarrassed yourself, and also greatly embarrass them. And indeed, the whole time I was with those of whom I speak, I heard them talking continually without understanding what they said. For there was one on my right who, speaking to one who sat next to her, said that she knew from very good sources, that such a gentleman had broken off with such a lady, and that she had consequently renewed [her amour] with such another. And another on my left, speaking passionately to one lady from among her friends, told her the most foolish stuff in the world. 'After all,' she said to her, in a fret, 'you-know-who ought not to boast that she has deprived me of a gallant, since he whom she believes she has wrenched from me is someone I have driven away. But if the fancy takes me to recall him, I will do it so well that he will never look at her again in her life.' On the other hand, I heard some giving an account of a collation[2] they were treated to, affecting to say that it was paltry, with as much fervor as if they thought to diminish the beauty of the lady on whom it was bestowed, by saying that her lover was not magnificent enough. In short, I must confess, that in my life I never felt so much impatience as I did that day."

"On my part," replied Cilenie, "if I had been in your place, I would have found a means of diverting myself at the expense of the very ones who bored me. But I could not find a way to escape boredom three days ago, with a man and a woman who make conversation on two subjects only: that is to say, the complete genealogies of all the families of Mytilene, and all the estates of these families. For indeed, except on certain occasions, how entertaining is it to hear such gossip for a whole day long: Xenocrates was the son of Tryphon, Clidemus descended from Zenophanes, Zenophanes was the issue of Tyrtaeus, and so of the rest? And what diversion is there, likewise, to hear that such a house wherein you have no interest, wherein you never were, and where you'll never go as long as you live, was built by this man, bought by that, exchanged by another, and that it is at present possessed by a man you do not know?"

"This is not very agreeable, without doubt," answered Alcé, "but it is not nearly as annoying as encountering people who are engaged in some troublesome business, and can speak of nothing else. And in truth, a while ago I met a sea-captain, who claims that Pittacus ought to recompense him for a ship. He held me three hours, not only telling me the reasons he claimed to have for being reimbursed, but also what someone might respond to him [about his claim], and what he could reply. And to make me the better comprehend the losses caused him, he set about telling me in detail what his ship cost him. For that purpose, he told me the names of those who built it, and specified to me all the parts of his ship, one after the other, unnecessarily, to make me understand it was one of the best and dearest of ships, and he had suffered a great deal of injustice."

"It's true," said Amithone, "one feels persecuted encountering that sort of person. But to tell you the truth, those grave and serious conversations wherein no enjoyment is permitted have something so depressing that I never happen into them without being taken with a headache. For the talk is always on the same note. They never laugh, and all is as formal, as if one were at church."

"I agree with what you say," replied Athis, "but I must say, to the shame of our sex, that the men have a great advantage over us, as to conversation. And to prove it, I need only tell the company that, going to Lycidice's house, I found her in her mother's chamber, where was so great a number of women that I was at pains to find a place for myself, but there was not one man. I cannot tell you in what manner all those ladies had their wits addled that day, though some of them were very witty. But I am constrained to avow that the conversation was not very entertaining. For in fact, they spoke only of tedious trifles, and I may say that in my life I never heard so much talking in order to say so little.

"But happening to be near Lycidice, I could easily observe the annoyance she felt. It's true, I observed it with delight, since it made her say a hundred amusing things. As she was very much bored with this noisy conversation, which so much grated upon her humour, one of her kinsmen arrived. And this is remarkable, that though this man had not that elevated wit rarely to be found, and though he was but of the rank of ordinary well-bred people, the conversation changed all of a sudden, and became more ordered, more witty, and more agreeable, though there was no other change in the company, than the arrival of a man who spoke very little. But indeed, without being able to tell you the true reason, they fell to talk of other things; they talked much better; and those same persons who bored me as well as Lycidice, diverted me extremely.

"When the company was gone, I remained alone with Lycidice. She no sooner saw herself at liberty than, passing from her humour of annoyance to cheerfulness, said she to me, 'Well Athis, will you still condemn me for preferring the conversation of men to that of women? And are you not constrained to acknowledge, that whoever would write what fifteen or twenty women say together would make the worst book in the world?' 'I confess,' said I to her, laughing, 'that if the person wrote what I have heard spoken today, it would be a bizarre account.' 'For my part,' said she, 'there are some days that I am so irritated by my sex that I am grieved to the very heart I am a woman, principally when I happen into one of those conversations composed all of dresses, furniture, jewels, and similar things. Not that,' said she, 'I am against their being made a subject of discourse. For indeed, sometimes my hair is well enough arranged, that it is easy for someone to say so, and sometimes my clothes are beautiful enough and well enough made, that it is right someone should commend them. But I would have us speak very little of these sorts of things, and only when speaking gallantly and in passing, without transports and devotion, and not as some women do of my acquaintance, who spend all their lives speaking and thinking of nothing else, and whose thoughts of those things are likewise so full of irresolution that, in my opinion, at the end of their days, they will not have determined to their satisfaction if carnation becomes them better than blue, or if yellow is more advantageous to them than green.'

"I must confess that Lycidice made me laugh, and I found it so much more pleasant since it is true that there is a lady of my acquaintance who employs all her wit only in such things, who never talks of anything else, and who makes her greatest glory consist only in what is piled up around her—that is to say, in the gilding of her palace, in the magnificence of her furniture, in the beauty of her clothes, and in the richness of her jewels.

"After having laughed at what Lycidice said, I wished to defend women in general, and told her I was persuaded there are as many men as ladies whose conversation is scarcely agreeable. 'There are many of them without a doubt,' she replied, 'whose company is insupportable. But there is this advantage, that we can more easily get rid of them, and we are not obliged to treat them with so exact a civility. But Athis, it is not that with which I am concerned. For what I am telling you is that the most amiable women in the world, when they are together in a great number, and without any men, hardly say anything of value, and are more bored than if they were alone. But as for men who are well-bred, it is not the same with them. Their conversation is, without doubt, less enjoyable when there are no ladies than when there are. But commonly, though it is more serious, yet it is more rational and, in short, they can easier be without us, than we without them. In the meanwhile this vexes me more than I can tell you.'

"'For my part,' I answered, 'it seems to me that I could live without boring myself, though I never saw any but my female friends, provided they were all like Lycidice.' 'I'll tell you, if you please,' she responded, 'to requite your civility, I would be as little bored as you, if all my friends were like you. But I must at least add, provided I might see them but one, two, or three at the most together. For to see twelve of them at a time, I would rather see nobody. Yes,' pursued she, with the most pleasing gloominess in the world, 'though there were twelve Athises in the world, I would not wish to see them all together every day, unless they had two or three men with them. For though you never say anything inappropriate, I am sure that if there were twelve of you, you would; or at least, you would speak like the rest, of meaningless things, and make the conversation tedious and boring. In the end,' said she, 'what would you have me say more than that? Unless you are a great hypocrite, you must confess, that something, which I am not capable of explaining, makes a well-bred man rejoice and divert a company of ladies more than the most amiable woman upon earth can do. I'll say more,' added she, 'for I maintain that when there are but two women together, if they are not in friendship with one another, they will divert themselves less, than if each of them talked with a man of wit, though they had never seen him before. Judge after this if I have not reason to murmur against my sex in general.'"

"Those conversations are without doubt very vexing," replied Amilcar, "but there are another kind that strangely trouble me. For I happened to be one day at Syracuse with five or six women and two or three men who have it in their heads that for a conversation to be agreeable, it is necessary to laugh eternally—insomuch that as long as those persons are together, they do nothing but laugh at all they say to one another, even if it is not very amusing. And they make so great a noise that often they are no longer listening to what they are speaking, and then they only laugh because the rest laugh, without knowing the reason. However, they do it as heartily as if they knew what was said. But it is strange that their laughing is really so contagious sometimes, that one cannot help but be taken with their malady. And I found myself one day with those perpetual laughers, who inspired me so forcefully with their laughter, that I laughed almost until I cried, without knowing why I did so. But to speak the truth, I was so much ashamed of it a quarter of an hour later, that all my joy turned, in a moment, into vexation."

"Though there is a great deal of folly in laughing without reason," responded Valeria, "yet I am not so uncomfortable in the company of these sorts of people as I am to find myself with those whose conversation consists of nothing but long, sad, and lamentable stories, extremely tedious. For example, I am acquainted with a woman who knows all the tragic adventures, [whose daily discourse is a book of martyrs[3]], and who spends all her time in deploring the misfortunes of life and in relating lamentable things with a sad and doleful voice, as if she were paid for bewailing all the calamities of the world."

"Let us not pass over so quickly," said Plotina, "the fault of over-long recitations. For in my opinion, one ought to guard against becoming accustomed to perpetually telling stories, as I know some who never speak but of what is past, and are always telling what they have seen, never what they see."

"The truth is," said Amilcar, "that sometimes those eternal story-tellers are very much to be dreaded! Some of them are confused; others too long; some are so troubled that they will never allow themselves to be interrupted; others, on the contrary, interrupt themselves, and at the end do not know what they have said or what they would like to have said. But those who stick to things that no one cares about, and which of themselves are not very pleasant, are the most troublesome of all the tale-telling tribe."

"I know likewise a family," resumed Cerinta, "where the conversation is very irritating; for they never discuss anything but the little occurrences of the neighborhood, which courtiers who come there by chance have nothing to do with, and no understanding of. And I remember well, one day I heard them talk of a hundred little intrigues that did not concern me at all, and the noise whereof extended no farther than the street where they happened to be, and which besides were so little diverting in themselves, that I was extremely bored."

"It is also a great agony," said Nicanor, "to find oneself in a large company where everyone has a secret—principally when you have none—and you have nothing more to do than to listen to the little murmur made by those who converse with each other in whispers. And yet, if they were truly secrets," added she, "I would have patience. But it very often happens that these things which are said with so much mystery are nothing but trifles."

"Likewise, I know other people," joined in Alcé, "who, in my mind, possess a trait at once very irritating and also very agreeable. For they have such a fancy for earth-shaking news in their heads, that they never speak unless it concerns battles, or some siege of a considerable city, or some great revolution in the world; and you would say to hear them, that the gods change the face of the universe only to furnish them with conversation. For unless it concerns such grand and important occurrences, they never speak, and cannot bear [discussing] any other kind. So that without knowing how to sift to the bottom of politics, and without being well versed in history, a person cannot argue with them upon any subject whatsoever."

"It is true," replied Nicanor, "that what you describe is not always agreeable. But those other people, who, without bothering about the major affairs of the world, want to know nothing, when it comes to speak, except private gossip, likewise are very irritating. For you see them always as busy as if they had a thousand affairs, though they have none of any sort except knowing all those of others, in order to go repeat them from house to house, like public spies, who are neither here nor there, except when they can turn it to their advantage as the occasion presents itself. Thus, they do not aim to know things in order to know them, as much as to repeat them to others."

"It is also a great fault," said Cerinta, "to affectedly show all your wit. And I know a man who in the first few visits he makes in places where he wants to please, passes continually from one subject to another, without going deeply into any; and I can assure you without exaggeration, that in an hour I have heard him speak of all things it is possible to speak on, since not only did he tell all that happened at court, but also all that happened in the town. Then he related what he had done that day. He recounted what was said in the places where he had been and asked Arpasia what she had done. Afterward, he teased Melinta about her silence, and then spoke of music and painting. He made several proposals of going abroad, and said so many different things, that a man in the company, taking notice of this great diversity, made others likewise observe it with intention to commend him. 'For indeed,' said he, after having caused it to be noticed, 'there is nothing more tiresome than to find oneself in a conversation with that sort of people who attach themselves to the first thing that is spoken and go so deeply into it, that in a whole afternoon they never change the subject.' For as conversation ought to be free and natural, and all those who compose the company ought to have an equal right to change it as they see fit, it is an irritating thing to meet with those opinionated people who leave nothing to say on a subject, and who are ever harping upon it, no matter what care is taken to interrupt them."

"For my part," said Cilenia, "I am perplexed to hear you all talk as you do. For, after all, if it is not fitting always to talk of science like Damophilus; if it is tedious to converse about all the little cares of a family; if it is not appropriate to speak often of clothes; if it is not judicious to gossip about love affairs; if it is not entertaining to speak only of genealogies; if it is too vulgar to discuss lands sold or exchanged; if it be likewise forbidden to speak too much of our own business dealings; if too great a gravity is not diverting in conversation; if there is folly in laughing too often, and in laughing without cause; if recitations of fatal and extraordinary events are not engaging; if the little tidings of the neighborhood are tedious to those who are not concerned with them; if these conversations of little things that are whispered in the ear are irritating; if those people who converse only of great occurrences are wrong; if those eternal seekers after private tidbits[4] are not reasonable; of what can we speak, and of what must the conversation be composed, to make it both rational and pleasing?"

"It must be composed of all that we have rejected," Valeria agreeably replied, with a smile, "but it must be conducted with judgment. For in the end, though all those people we have mentioned are bothersome, I, however, maintain boldly that one cannot speak but of what they do, and that one can speak agreeably on much that they do not manage well."

"I easily apprehend what Valeria says is true," replied Amilcar, "though it did not seem so to me at first. For I am so persuaded that all sorts of things are proper in conversation, that I do not except any."

"Indeed," added Valeria, "one must not imagine that there are things that are never fit for inclusion. For it is true that there are certain encounters where it is quite proper to say what would be ridiculous on all other occasions."

"For my part," said Amithone, "I confess that I wish that there were some rules for conversation, as there are for many other things."

"The principal rule," replied Valeria, "is never to say anything that offends the judgment."

"But still," added Nicanor, "I would like to know more precisely how you conceive conversation ought to be."

"I conceive," she responded, "that in general, it ought more often to concern the subjects of ordinary, polite conversation, rather than great events. However, I think that nothing is precluded; that [conversation] ought to be free and diversified, according to the times, places, and persons with whom we [converse]; and that the secret is to speak always nobly of small things, very simply of great things, and graciously of the subjects of polite [conversation], without transport and affectation. Thus, though the conversation ought always to be both natural and also rational, I must not fail to say, that on some occasions, the sciences themselves may be brought in with a good grace, and that an agreeable silliness may also find its place, provided it be clever, modest, and courteous. So that, to speak with reason, we may affirm without falsehood that there is nothing that cannot be said in conversation, provided it [is managed with] wit and judgment, and one considers well, where one is, to whom one speaks, and who one is oneself. Notwithstanding that judgment is absolutely necessary in order never to say anything inappropriate, yet the conversation must appear so free as if we rejected not a single one of our thoughts, and all is said that comes into the fancy, without any affected design of speaking more often of one thing than another. For there is nothing more ridiculous than those people who have certain subjects on which they talk wonders, and otherwise say nothing but foolishness. So I would have it appear that we do not know what we are going to say, and yet that we always know well what we are going to say. For if this course is taken, women will not be inappropriately learned, nor ignorant to excess, and everyone will say only what ought to be said to make the conversation agreeable. But what is most necessary to make it sweet and entertaining is that it must have a certain air of civility, which absolutely precludes all bitter retorts, as well as anything that might offend decency. And, finally, I desire that [the ideal conversation] will demonstrate the art of diversion so that gallantry may be uttered to the severest woman in the world; so that a little foolery may be related to grave and serious people; so that science may be spoken of appropriately to the ignorant (if you are forced to it); and, in sum, that wit is able to be adapted to the things that are spoken of, and to the people you speak with. But besides all I have now said, I would have a certain spirit of joy reign [over conversation], which, without partaking of the folly of those eternal laughers who make so great a noise over so small a matter, does, however, inspire in the hearts of all the company a disposition to make everything contribute to their diversion, and not to weary themselves with anything. And I would have both small and lofty things discussed, as long as they are always discussed well, and yet nothing spoken but what is necessary to be said."

"In sum," added Amilcar, "without giving you the trouble of speaking any more upon conversation or making rules for it, it is enough to admire your [conversation], and to do as you do, to merit the admiration of all the earth. For I assure you that I will be rebuked by no one when I say that I never heard you say anything but what was agreeable, courteous, and judicious; and no one knows so well as you the art of pleasing, charming, and diverting."

"I wish," she replied, blushing, "that all you say was true, and that I could believe you sooner than myself. But to show you I cannot believe you, and that I know I am often wrong, I declare ingenuously, that I am very sensible that I have now said too much and, instead of telling all that I think about conversation, I should have contented myself with telling each one of the company what you have just said of me."

After this, everyone opposing each in turn the modesty of Valeria, we gave her so much praise that we almost made her angry. And afterwards, we conducted so polite and cheerful a conversation that it lasted almost until evening, when this charming company separated.

Notes for "On Conversation"

This is my own translation, based on Madeleine de Scudéry, *Les conversations sur divers sujets* (Amsterdam, 1686), 1:1–20 (Folger 171523), compared with *Conversations upon Several Subjects*, trans. Ferrand Spence (London, 1683), sigs. B1ʳ–B11ʳ (Folger 152766), by permission of the Folger Shakespeare Library, and with thanks to the students of my fall 1993 English 489B, Gender and the History of Rhetorical Theory, who edited the Spence translation of this dialogue as a class project; special thanks to Stephanie Lenkey.

1. *Honnêtes gens* are discriminating, honest, decent, polite middle- and upper-class people; "honesty" in seventeenth-century France and England combines virtue and elegance as a standard of taste for polite society.

2. A collation is a light meal.

3. This wonderful comparison was added by the seventeenth-century translator Ferrand Spence.

4. I have translated "nouvelles de cabinet" as "private tidbits": news of the cabinet would be the gossip or secrets one could only tell one's most intimate friends, since they were the ones in French aristocratic society who were admitted to the cabinet, or most private of rooms. We still have in English a form of this expression in "cabinet secrets," although now it means the secrets that only the great political leaders share with their counselors.

"Conversation on the Manner of Writing Letters" From *Conversations Nouvelles sur Divers Sujets* (1684)

A Lady who greatly loved to read, and who was very lazy about writing to her male and female friends, requested one of her kinsmen to send her some books to entertain her in the country. This kinsman (whom I shall call "Cléante"), in order to reproach her polite cerning her perpetual silence, decided to send her some collections of letters, for she h ̲ ̲ ̲ ̲ to him in parting that she would not thank him for the books he would send her until her re-turn, because she disliked writing, being persuaded that she wrote much worse than she con-versed, adding modestly that she did not wish her letters to damage the spirit of their friend-ship during her absence.

Cléante therefore wished to persuade her that people have always written [letters] and an-swered [them]. For this purpose, he sent her all the anthologies of letters, beginning with Mal-herbe, Balzac, Costar, Voiture and, to be brief, all the dead authors, without excepting the epis-tles of the ancients. To these he added those letters by Don Guevar the Spaniard, Cardinal Bembo, Cardinal Bentivoglio and, above all, those of Annibale Caro, whom Montaigne in his time and the wise and famous Chapelain in ours placed above all the other Italian authors.[1] In short, Cléante put together a little library of letters which he sent to her by one of his servants. Since Aminte possessed infinite wit, she well understood this raillery, but she kept her word and did not thank Cléante with a note, and contented herself with sending him this madrigal:

> To Cléante
> Never! I will not change my mind:
> The more I read, the more I find,
> The more I see nothing to write—
> For one must never write behind
> The best, only the best endite.[2]

Cléante found it extremely amusing that Aminte found it easier to reply in verse than in prose, to the extent that he showed this madrigal to Bérise, who was a friend in common to both, and full of wit. And since Aminte was not more than half a day away from them, they de-cided to form a party to go to see her, and to make war on her slothful reluctance to write. They took with them a very amiable woman whom I shall name "Clariste," whose humour was quite different from Aminte's, for she was used to writing two or three notes a day to her spe-cial friends. And this party made their trip two days later.

Aminte received these three persons very agreeably. "If our visit is importunate," Bérise said to her, while embracing her with an elegant and playful air, "blame yourself, because if you had written us, perhaps we would not have come to see you."

"I assure you," replied Aminte, after she had greeted them and invited them into her cabi-net,[3] "I do not repent my silence, for after having read the enormous number of beautiful letters that Cléante maliciously sent to me, I have confirmed my resolution to write only that which is absolutely necessary. And out of all the different styles that I have observed in all these collec-tions of letters, I did not find any of which I was capable, nor any that fit me or that I could im-itate. Without doubt, I saw a thousand beauties, but except for the letters of Voiture, the re-mainder were written for the public, and Balzac and Costar and all the others thought more about posterity than about those to whom they were writing. The greatest part of the love let-ters by these excellent men," she added, "are scarcely fitting to inspire love, and Voiture himself was a thousand times more admirable in his letters of gallantry than in his actual love letters."

"I assure you," repeated Bérise, "that you will write better than anyone else, if you would take the pains to do so, and I find it perfectly amusing that you had to send verses to Cléante rather than thank him in prose."

"The reason," replied Aminte, "is very easy to find, for nothing is simpler than to make up a wicked little madrigal, and nothing is more difficult than to write a pleasant note; and, accordingly, I am a lady perfectly capable of making mediocre verses without shame, but not a witty letter in prose."

Since this party existed only to persuade Aminte to write occasionally to her friends, Clariste told her that all of society wrote letters, some good, some bad, and that it appeared very strange that she alone never wrote to anyone.

"I think," answered Aminte, smiling, "that I shall prove to you the opposite of what you have just said."

"You may well be embarrassed," said Bérise.

"Do you not see," replied Aminte, "that in the works of Sarrazin,[4] who has so much wit, there is not a single letter, and I am still persuaded that if he wrote many, someone would not have failed to include them when printing his poems, as someone did those of Malherb and Voiture."

"Since I have a friend who was his friend," said Cléante, "I am able to assure you that never did a man write more letters than he, and that scarcely ever was there one who wrote better, whether to famous people, such as Balzac, Costar, and others, or to princes or mighty ministers and, above all others, to the ladies. But he hardly ever preserved his letters, so that at his death it was necessary to search for them in the hands of others, not in his study. And when one of his female friends and two of his male friends offered to take care of his works after his death,[5] it did not bind the ladies to whom he had written to release his letters. However, it is a great shame that they have been lost, because the serious and informative ones were very beautiful, and the letters of entreaty were very charming."

"At least," said Aminte, "do you agree with me that women have written less often than men or, if they have replied, they have written badly, for I see very few letters from ladies in the very large number of volumes that you have given me; and since, generally speaking, all people possess vanity, there would have been [printed] answers from the ladies if they had answered well."

"One cannot doubt," objected Clindor, "that there have always been ladies who wrote admirably well, and one can see the incontestable proofs in Voiture himself. But the respect one owes to ladies does not permit one to print their letters without their consent, and they rarely give it from pure modesty."

"For my part," said Clariste, "I, who take an obvious pleasure in receiving letters from persons whom I love, and who do not hate to reply to them, do not make a point of fashioning my notes. I write as I speak, I speak what I think, and provided that I make myself understood, I am content. And I am persuaded that it is never necessary to have too much wit[6] in ordinary letters. Someone has shown me," added Clariste, "a marginal note from a love letter, where that sentiment is well explained. Behold, it is a lady who speaks: 'I forgot to ask forgiveness from you for having wished to have the wit of your writing, for when one does not hate oneself, and one is unhappy, nothing is necessary except tenderness.'"

After Clariste had recited these four lines, Cléante cried, "Ah, Madame, how you have given me great pleasure to commend this sentiment, for it is certain that there is little need to have much wit in notes or letters of love. And that is the reason it makes it so difficult to find letters and notes of this nature, which are perfect: for there is little need at all for grand words; it is also not necessary to speak like the people; neither too much art, nor too much negligence is necessary. There is little need of what one calls 'elegance'[7] yet gallantry, politeness, and passion are needed. And it is finally so difficult to write well about love, because there is nothing which gives one the advantage."

"But for my part," said Bérise, "I do not understand at all why it is any more difficult to write of one thing than another. For in the end I believe that in the case of letters one must simply say what one thinks and say it well. So that when one has wit and judgment, one thinks about each thing pretty much what it is appropriate to think, and consequently one writes what it is appropriate to write. In effect, if I am writing for an important business, I will not write as if I had nothing more than a simple compliment to make; if I send some news, I will not play the wit; if I am composing a friendly letter, I will not express myself in high style; and if I wish to write love letters, I will consult only my heart. That is why you assign such great difficulty to writing letters of this nature."

"In truth," said Aminte, "I hold there are many who write all sorts of letters very well, and there are a few persons who do so perfectly well."

"I fall into agreement," replied Cléante, "but I repeat that among all kinds of letters, those called love letters are the most difficult to compose. And also, [concerning love letters,] there are fewer people who are able to judge well."

"Bérise speaks, however, as if she has found all sorts of letters equally easy to compose," replied Aminte. "However, I believe, as does Cléante, that only one of these sorts requires especial delicacy and judgment."

"But in order to show you what I know," responded Bérise, "and at least I know a little in general about how to compose letters, is it not true that business letters should be precise, that [in them] good sense is more important than eloquence, that they [should] say all that is necessary and nothing else, that one must exclude all superfluous words, be content with only those which are necessary, and try principally to compose that which is orderly and clear? However," she added, "also required is a certain spirit of civility that distinguishes the business letters of polite people from those who are not. It is necessary to listen to others, for I know nothing more insupportable than to write a letter that needs explication, and which muddles things instead of clarifies them."

"However," replied Aminte, "there are many people who believe in listening and who listen not a bit."

"That is not true of Bérise," responded Cléante, "for I assure you that she listens much better than she speaks. That is why it would please me very much to be shown how she thinks that letters of consolation should be composed. For if occasions to write something present themselves often enough," he added, laughing, "I shall compose five or six following her advice, which I shall keep to avail myself of whenever I have such an occasion. Nothing is more contrary to my humour than such letters. Also, I have been tempted a hundred times rather than to afflict myself with this sort of letter to the afflicted, to sooner choose to amuse them than to sympathize with them. In effect, I know so little what it is necessary to say, or what it is necessary not to say, that I can never compose a letter of this nature without writing it more than one time, and without making the same erasures after having put it down in clean copy. That is why the beautiful Bérise will do me a great favor by teaching me how to write [such letters] well."

"In truth," replied Bérise, "you will not have such great trouble, if you share my sentiments; for I can't stand these grand letters of consolation, which never have any purpose, and which do not console anyone. Nevertheless, to listen to the speech of certain people, you would think that their letters have a magical force against affliction, and that those who read them will never again feel any regret for what was lost. Yet I am willing," she added, "to be persuaded once and for all, that it appears that nothing but time seems to console such grief, and it is not the aim of eloquence to interfere in this. And then, to tell you the truth, how is it possible to console people who are not at all afflicted? That is why I find that the best way to compose on these occasions is to compose very short letters of consolation, for to write reasonably, it requires simply that you show the person to whom you write the part you take in his or her grief, without going into long complaints or grand eulogies, and without employing all of morality and useless eloquence."

"It is true," said Cléante, "and you are right. For how can one console, about the death of their husbands, wives who have no need of consolation? And how can one console all sorts of people with whom it would be better to rejoice in order to suit the secret feelings of their hearts, since it is sometimes very convenient to be heirs of those concerning whose death one is supposed to console them. That is why, kind Bérise," added Cléante, "I make a vow never to write letters of consolation that are not short, to let all the morality and all the eloquence rest in peace on these occasions, no longer to compose lengthy exaggerations of the cruelty of death, as do some people, nor any more grand eulogies or long panegyrics, and in short, to be led completely by your sentiments. I do not even ask you," added he, "how one should rejoice with those who have happened on some good thing, for I know how to do that admirably, and I can offer you ten or twelve openings for that kind of letter without counting those said earlier: 'I take part . . .' 'I am so interested in . . .' And other things too vulgar for witty people. But you would give me a rare pleasure, if you would teach me how to compose [properly] letters of recommendation that would provide an introduction [without misunderstanding] for those for whom one speaks, and above all, teach me very precisely how it is possible to make known to those to whom one writes, if one wishes it done exactly how one says it, or if one is scarcely worried at all about it. For when I am away from Paris, I am overwhelmed with these sorts of letters."

"For my part," said Bérise, "when I recommend for some business a person whom I do not much like, I write a letter short and dry; there is still courtesy, and the vocabulary of entreaty is found therein, but it is found there without being supported by anything. On the other hand, when I wish to beg effectively, I first say that the favor I ask is reasonable; I say something good about the person for whom I am entreating; I testify to the friendship I have for her or him; I take upon myself her cause if she is my protégé; I even engage the person to whom I write to render her a service, through a feeling of pride; and for greater certainty, I write her another note [saying] that I stick by everything that I have already written."

"For myself, in particular," said Clariste to Bérise, "I very much wish that you would apprise me how to write to those people with whom one has a business relationship with propriety, and whom you do not esteem enough to give your friendship to, nor to take pleasure in amusing them."

"First of all," replied Bérise, "I would write them as little as I could, for I cannot stand those people who write only in order to write, who voluntarily involve themselves, without any necessity, in receiving letters from people about whom they do not care at all, and who love in general to receive letters from anyone and to write without any selectivity. In second place, when constrained to write in the manner that you mean, I would not put in these kinds of letters all my wit nor my whole friendship; for one assuredly makes a mistake when one writes a very beautiful and very obliging letter to a person of very mediocre merit. That is why it is necessary to have a kind of [lukewarm] civility that one can find when one looks for it, in order to make use of it for these people whom one does not esteem very much, and for whom one does not feel any friendship, when some social reason requires us to write them. And it is necessary to compose these letters, which we have properly called letters of compliment [in our discussions], so that they contain nothing special, nothing good or bad—composed of some words and little content, so that they engage no one, neither those who write them nor those to whom they are written, and so that they have a universal air suitable to nearly every kind of mediocre person, without being especially appropriate to anyone."

"In truth," replied Aminte, "judgment is necessary in everything. For example, one might say that there is nothing easier to write than news. However, one often sees people who write even news very inadequately."

"Those are the people," responded Cléante, "who very often write something without knowing anything, who believe all that anyone tells them, who write without order and without charm, who entertain only themselves by writing those things that one cares nothing at all about, or that are pleasing only to themselves, or that sometimes do not have enough of the attraction of novelty. However, it is certain, too, that it is still not so necessary for a woman to be young to be beautiful, as it is necessary for news to be new to be interesting; and there is nothing more irritating than to receive a long narration of an old adventure."

"Yet it is true," resumed Aminte, "that there are certain sinister happenings that one remembers and repeats from time to time, and which circulate widely as if they had only just happened; these things are assuredly troublesome enough to those who know them, when [correspondents] write them as if well known, if there are no particular circumstances included. But in my opinion, when one composes these letters where one recounts the latest news, one should think up some news that would please the person to whom one writes. For I am sure that there are people who do not love this universal news with which fame is ordinarily burdened, and who do not desire [to hear about] battles won or lost, sieges of cities, fires, floods, shipwrecks, uprisings of people, and other similar great events; there are those also who scarcely care about the great happenings that one finds in the newspapers, who prefer what one calls the news of the "*cabinet*," which are not told except quietly in one's ear, and which are not well known except to worldly, well informed people, who have exquisite judgment and delicate taste. That is why it is very necessary to know the humour and the interests of the people to whom one writes, when one meddles in handing on some news to them. And there are also some things one should never hand on."

"That is right, Madame," replied Cléante, "but what I principally would like Bérise to tell us, since she seems to be already engaged in it, is, in what letters it is permissible to display all one's wit, and in what fashion it is best to display it."

"You know better than I, without doubt," she replied; "but in order to make you realize that I am capable of appreciating the beauty of your letters of gallantry, if you ever write some to me, I will declare to you that the following are the only letters that I do not understand everything about and, with regard to these letters, which I will call 'serious letters,' I could only make mistakes."

"As far as these [serious] letters," responded Cléante, "it is without doubt permissible to avail oneself of a very elevated style; for example, if a lofty official writes to another concerning some important matter, or some learned people were to conduct intercourse through letters, they would employ, appropriately, history, moral philosophy, politics, the poets, and almost the whole power of eloquence."

"About such stuff," said Bérise, "I understand nothing. But letters of gallantry, I understand them admirably. It is proper in these that wit has all one's attention, that there is imagination and the freedom to play, and that judgment does not appear so severe that one may not mingle some agreeable foolishness among things more serious. One is able to rail ingeniously [in these letters]; praise and flattery agreeably find their place in them; in them one speaks sometimes of friendship, as if one were speaking of love; for these letters one searches out novelty; in them one is able also to speak harmless lies; one makes up news, when one knows none; one passes from one subject to another without constraint; and these sorts of letters are properly called a conversation between absent persons. It is necessary to save a place for wit that has a constrained character, that tastes of books and the study, and that is full of gallantry, which one might call the soul of this sort of letters. It is requisite in these letters that the style be easy, natural, and noble—all at once. Yet it is not necessary to refrain from employing a certain art, which makes the trivial, which one would not be able to include in letters of this nature, [following] that most popular proverb, even into the most elevated thing [which one can include]—all in the service of a clever wit, provided that a worldly air reigns throughout. But on these occasions one should keep from using that grand eloquence which is particularly appropriate for speeches, and one should employ another [eloquence] that sometimes conveys a more charming effect with less noise, principally among ladies; for, in a word, the art of speaking well about trifles is not known to all sorts of people."

"I assure you," responded Clariste, "then I can also assure you again, that it does not suit all sorts of people to wish to know that."

"But amiable Bérise," said Cléante, "do us the favor in its entirety, and tell us very precisely how you would wish love letters to be composed."

"Since I have never written any, and never received any," she replied, "I do not know very well what it is I should say. However, since today I feel myself in a humour to talk, I shall not refuse you. But first I shall tell you, in my opinion there are more [kinds of] love letters than you think."

"I agree with you," replied Cléante, "but one should not be astonished if so few love letters are in print, for one does not write the former[8] except to be viewed by the whole world, while one does not write the latter[9] except to be hidden. Those who receive an elegant love letter would be embarrassed to publish it; thus one should not find it strange that one sees so few good ones of this kind. Indeed, to speak truthfully, since there are a great many people who have an abundance of wit, but there are not so many who have an abundance of love, one should also not be surprised that there are fewer fine letters of this kind than of all other sorts; since it is always true that in order to write exactly as necessary about these matters, one must love passionately, and be capable of a certain delicacy of heart and spirit, which makes this passion agreeable, both in conversation and in letters—and all this is rarely found."

"But did someone not say a little while ago," responded Aminte, "that it was not necessary to employ much wit for these occasions?"

"I admit it," answered Bérise, "but do you not think that sometimes it is possible to have a lot? Thus one is able to say also that love letters do not need that fire of wit that necessarily shines in letters of gallantry, yet they require something else in place of that; the heat of passion takes the place of this fire of wit that I spoke of earlier. That is why I find that the true nature of love letters must be tender and impassioned, and that there is something elegant, something spiritual, and at the same time something playful in these sorts of letters, yet always one must adhere to passion and respect. It is necessary that expression in these letters be very tender and very touching, and one must always say those things that move the heart, mixed with those that entertain the spirit. If I am not wrong, one should likewise include a little anxiety, because happy letters get you nowhere in love. It is not that one is not able to encompass joy; but, after all, it must never be a peaceful joy, and when one does not have a subject for complaint, one must make one up."

"You spoke admirably of these things," responded Cléante, "for if you had done nothing else your whole life than to experience love and to write about it, you could not have discussed it better."

"If I have not experienced it," she replied, smiling, "I have friends who have done it for me, and who have taught me what to say about it. But finally, a love letter should have more sentiment than wit; the style should be natural, deferential, and impassioned; and I also maintain that there is nothing proper in composing a letter of this nature that does not move at all because it has been too beautifully written. Also, it is for that reason that there are so few people who can judge love letters well. For in order to be a fair judge, it is necessary to put oneself in the place of those who love; it is necessary to know that it is their hearts that speak; it is necessary to know that those [who write] understand a hundred little things well and others scarcely at all; finally it is necessary to know how to make a very delicate distinction between the gallantry of a letter of friendship and the gallantry of a letter of love. As for the rest," she added, "I heard from a very courteous gentleman that ordinarily women write better *billets d'amour*[10] than do men, and I think he is right. For when a lover has resolved to write openly about his passion, he does not require more art than to say 'I die of love.' But with a woman, since she cannot ever admit so precisely what she feels, and she must keep it a great secret, this love that one can only catch a glimpse of, she delights more than someone who puts himself on display."

"But from what I have seen," said Aminte, "it is necessary that the love letters of a lover and his beloved be different."

"Do not doubt it," responded Bérise, "for love and respect must prevail in the letters of a lover, while virtue, modesty, and fear mingle with tenderness in those of such a beloved as I intend. For I do not meddle in talk about young scatter-brains, who are more forward than men, who speak more than they are spoken to, and who make themselves despised by those who they believe adore them. Nor do I speak about those women who are past youth except in spirit, and to whom an ingrained imprudence has given a ridiculous boldness."

"But my amiable Bérise," responded Cléante, "since you know everything, tell me also whether it is permissible to write long love letters. For I have a friend full of wit, who says that *billets d'amour* must be short."

"To speak of all sorts of notes in general," answered Bérise, "I think that it is good not to be excessively long, but it is just fine, and there is none the worse, if two people who love each other infinitely, who scarcely can speak freely, and who have a thousand little vexations to make each other understand, are only able to write that which they are not able to say easily, and [it would be a shame] if love, which is an exaggerated passion, which causes all things to grow, did not have the privilege sometimes to be able to require the writing of long letters. For how can one encompass a great passion in a few words? How can one put enormous jealousy in a little note, and make another experience all the feelings of a tender heart through only three or four words? For those who write notes of gallantry," she added, "it is easy to make them brief, even where there is a great deal of wit. Because they have their judgment totally at liberty, they may choose what they say, and reject those thoughts that do not please them. But a poor lover whose judgment is disordered may choose nothing; he says everything that comes into his fancy, and may not be selective. For in the case of love, one can never say too much, and one can never believe that enough has been said. Thus I maintain that he cannot stop himself from sometimes composing long letters, so long as they are characterized throughout by the love that begets them. And, to speak sincerely, nothing merits more praise than one exquisite love letter; for finally, despite what I've said earlier, I believe that when one writes [such a letter], one's spirit is so engrossed and so distracted, that it is much more difficult to write well than on any other occasion. As I have said, it is not that the heart should not be involved; but it is that sometimes the heart is so distressed that it does not very well know what it feels."

"But, pardon me," Cléante interrupted, "who are these friends of yours who know so well how to talk of love?"

"She is a confidante in a passion so gallant and so virtuous," replied Aminte, "that if you knew all that she knows, you would not be surprised to find yourself speaking as she speaks. But after all," continued Aminte, "if one is able to commend a beautiful love letter in itself, one must never praise those ladies who expose themselves, or who receive them, or who reply to them; for however innocent the passion that caused them to be written, those who view these sorts of letters are never satisfied [that it is innocent]. And then, to speak truthfully, there is a great deal of indiscretion among men in general, so that no matter how virtuous the tenderness that one has for them, one must never confess it, and much less through letters or through [encouraging] words. That is why, despite all your anthologies of letters, and all these charming precepts of Bérise, I remain unmoved from my first opinion, that I do not like to write."

"That results, no doubt," responded Bérise, "from the fact that you do not care with any affection about your friends, for letters are the only consolation for absence. And likewise, when one is in the same place, the use of notes is a convenience without equal: notes deliver all the messages from the web of people one has employed; one informs others thereby of a thousand little things they would not otherwise know, because one would have forgotten them by the time one saw them. In a word, whoever keeps me from receiving notes from my friends and replying to them deprives me of a great pleasure."

Aminte answered that she would refrain from following her own inclination and that she would instead beg to be allowed to follow hers. The rest of the conversation was very playful and very agreeable; and since Bérise and Cléante found themselves in a [good humour] to entertain them during their return, they overwhelmed Aminte with all sorts of different letters written during the next eight days. Some told her about marriages, and so she wrote to congratulate them. Others told her of people who had died, and so she grieved with their kinsmen. At last she received a bunch of letters on all sorts of subjects, and without letting herself be fooled, to them she did not respond except by a profound silence—which did not entertain her, but did entertain others as a result, for on her return she spoke a thousand charming things to justify it, or to excuse it, which made them all realize that she had written only what she thought, in order to write perfectly.

Notes for "Conversation on the Manner of Writing Letters"

This is my translation based on Madeleine de Scudéry, "Conversation de la manière d'écrire des lettres," in *Conversations Nouvelles sur Divers Sujets, Dedie'es au Roy* (La Haye, 1685) (Folger 171523, Tome II, sigs. B1ʳ–B12ᵛ), by permission of the Folger Shakespeare Library, and with thanks for the vetting of Stephanie Lenkey.

1. François de Malherbe (1555–1628), a French poet and critic, was official poet of Henry IV and Louis XIII, who advocated classical ideals of objectivity and precision of language. Jean Louis Guez de Balzac (1597?–1654) was a French writer whose Latinate sentence structure in his *Lettres* (1624) greatly influenced French prose style. Pierre Costar (1603–1660) was famous for his defense of Voiture and his letters. Vincent Voiture (1597–1648) was a Frenchman of letters who wrote in the *précieux* style of de Scudéry's circle. The "epistles of the ancients" would have included the letters of Cicero and the verse epistles of Ovid and Horace, and perhaps Seneca and Pliny. Don Guevar the Spaniard, Antonio Guevaro (1480?–1545), was a Spanish moralist, novelist, and historian, as well as a bishop. Pietro Bembo (1470–1547), Italian humanist and cardinal in the Roman Catholic Church, wrote in many genres, promoted a classical style, and established Petrarch and Dante as national poets, as well as the Tuscan vernacular as standard for the Italian language. Guido Bentivoglio (1577–1644), member of a powerful Italian family and a cardinal of the Catholic Church, was famous for his histories and letters. Annibale Caro (1507–1566), Italian poet and friend of Bembo, translated the *Aeneid* and was famous for his letters. Michel Eyquem de Montaigne (1533–1592) is still famous for his *Essais*, first published in 1580, in a complete edition in 1595. Jean Chapelain (1595–1674), French critic and poet, founding member of the French Academy, was famous for his epic poem on Joan of Arc (*Pucelle* 1656) and his attack on Pierre Corneille's *Le Cid*.

2. Literal translation:

> No, I will not rouse myself to take this back
> The more I read, the more I admire,
> The more I see nothing to write
> For one should never write
> Unless one writes always well.

3. A cabinet is a small room, often adjoining a lady's or gentleman's bedroom, used in the seventeenth century as a combination sitting room, study, dressing room or boudoir, and even salon to entertain intimate friends.

4. Jacques Sarrazin (1588–1660), French sculptor and painter, was a founder of the Académie Royale and a proponent of neoclassical style.

5. That is, to edit his works.

6. I have translated *esprit* as "wit" here, but it seems to mean in de Scudéry's usage something in between the English word "wit" and the Italian word *sprezzatura* or gallant spirit, with perhaps also the connotations of "fire" or "soul" and "style."

7. "*Bel esprit*," literally, "handsome spirit," but usually translated "wit" or sometimes "spirit" or "gallantry." Since Cléante says gallantry and passion *are* required, I have here translated it as "elegance."

8. All the kinds of letters discussed before love letters.

9. Love letters.

10. *Billets d'amour*: love notes.

Mary Astell

1666–1731

Mary Astell was born in 1666 to gentlefolk: Peter Astell, a coal merchant in New Castle, and Mary Errington Astell, daughter of another wealthy coal merchant. Astell was raised as an Anglican, but her mother came from an old Catholic family. From the age of eight years, Astell was tutored by her Uncle Ralph Astell, a curate at St. Nicholas Church, who let her read in the large church library. Astell's father died when she was twelve, leaving the family poor and the daughter without a dowry to attract a gentleman of her class. At twenty-one, Astell determined to go to London on her own, an astonishing resolution for a woman at this time. She eventually settled in Chelsea, where there was a large community of women. Throughout the remainder of her life she was surrounded by a supportive network of single and widowed female friends on the outskirts of London. Her first patron was Archbishop Sancroft, and two of her early books, in 1695 and 1696, were theological. Her feminist works also appeared in this decade, with five editions of the *Serious Proposal* by 1700, and *Some Reflections Upon Marriage* (a treatise against marriage) in 1701. These works made her famous. The rest of her works were High Tory and Jacobite pamphlets against the Dissenters: throughout she is a conservative defending authority, the Anglican Church, and the Stuart monarchy. Astell withdrew from public life to a great degree after 1709, when she founded a charity school for girls in Chelsea under the auspices of the Society for the Propagation of Christian Knowledge. Astell arranged financial support for the school and oversaw its curriculum and management, perhaps supported by her patrons and friends in Chelsea, Lady Catherine Jones and Lady Elizabeth Hastings. When she was sixty years old, she accepted Lady Catherine Jones's offer to live with her and, after a mastectomy, died there of breast cancer in May 1731. Astell influenced the second wave of eighteenth-century feminism in the 1750s and 1760s, through her friendship with Lady Mary Wortley Montagu, and through George Ballard's biography of her in his 1752 *Memoirs of Several Ladies of Great Britain Who Have Been Celebrated for Their Writings*.

In *A Serious Proposal to the Ladies, Part I* (1694), Mary Astell proposes, as did Bathsua Makin, that women receive a humanist education similar to that of men, but in a women's monastery or college retired from the world. In *A Serious Proposal, Part II* (1697), she outlines a detailed program of study as well as the means for such an education. Astell enters a history of rhetorical theory because, in the second part, she outlines a method of logic and an art of rhetoric that she finds most suitable to women. Rather than the pulpit and political oratory that George Campbell and later eighteenth-century rhetoricians take as their model for communication, where an informed speaker preaches to an uninformed audience, Astell takes conversation, the writer as "Friend" speaking with the readers as "Neighbors." In her use of conversation as the model for discourse she anticipates by two centuries current developments in rhetorical theory.

In her long section on logic, Astell critiques as cumbersome and outmoded the system of syllogistic reasoning, which entangles and obscures instead of clarifying, and offers instead her own "method," in the same way that many logicians after Peter Ramus in the sixteenth century had. The only source that Astell mentions by name is Antoine Arnauld's *L'Art de penser*, the Port-Royal logic, growing out of seventeenth-century French Cartesian philosophy. Her own work is original, a meld of the logical traditions of the sixteenth and seventeenth centuries in Europe. From Ramus and Bacon comes a critique of scholasticism, and from Ramus and Arnauld a desire for a simple orderly method of reasoning. From Aristotle, despite the critique, comes an emphasis on deduction and analogy as the important modes of reasoning. From the classical humanist tradition comes a skepticism about the relation of language to reality that requires wary definition of terms as one goes through a reasoning process, as well as (going back to Augustine's revision of Plato) a faith that each mind has within "a teacher . . . who will if they seriously apply themselves to him, immediately enlighten them so far as that is necessary." From the Cartesians—Pascal, Descartes and Arnauld—comes an emphasis on "clear and evident" principles as the necessary basis of reasoning. But the actual steps of the reasoning process are Mary Astell's own formulation: thoroughly defining and gaining knowledge of the question, subjects, and terms used; setting aside irrelevant issues; ordering thoughts from simple to complex; dividing the subject into parts for examination so that nothing is left unexamined; concentrating on the subject without digression throughout; and treating as truth only what one evidently knows, sometimes settling for probability only.

Astell complements her art of logic with an art of rhetoric. Again she revises according to what she judges appropriate for women, but here she revises not by simplifying but by changing the basis of the art, shifting rhetoric from the model of public oratory to private conversation: "They write best perhaps who do't with the gentle and easy air of conversation." The aim of her rhetoric is thus much less manipulative than many later eighteenth-century rhetorics: rather than excite the passions of the audience to her own ends, she wishes to allay them so that the audience is free to consider the subject without bias. Having relegated invention of ideas to logic, in keeping with Ramistic and Baconian trends in her century, she yet cautions in her rhetoric that "writing . . . is nothing else but the communicating to others the result of our frequent and deep meditations." She treats the major topics of the art of rhetoric, leaving out memory and delivery, as many of the contemporary rhetorics did: she discusses arrangement, imitation, style, self-criticism, ornament, and sophistry. Arrangement she defines as proceeding according to the logical method she had outlined in the earlier section. She recommends imitation as the primary means of learning to speak or write well, and outlines six levels of style (as opposed to the classical three) and the excesses of each that can ruin discourse. Learning to criticize one's own work without bias, she suggests, is the most important step in becoming a good writer, and it is important that we put ourselves in the place of the audience, in order to "consider how such a discourse would operate on us, if we had their infirmities and thoughts about us" (120). She finishes her section on rhetoric by recommending figurative language in order to "clear the mind of a prejudiced reader" (rather than the classical purpose, to excite emotions in the audience in favor of the speaker's cause) and by inveighing against sophistry, for "ornaments are common to falsehood and truth, but clearness and strength of reasoning are not."

But by far her greatest originality and her most eloquent revisions of the art of rhetoric result from her reconception of the relation between writer and reader. In Astell, the audience is granted respect, equality with the speaker, and freedom. At the bottom of Astell's description of the audience is a Platonic—or Augustinian—faith in the attractiveness of truth to all humans. Since the way to be a good speaker is to be a good Christian, to Astell, persuasion results from love. Rather than the power over the audience that knowledge and rhetoric gives the speaker

101

emphasized in classical rhetorics, Astell finally emphasizes the <u>freedom for self</u> that knowledge and rhetoric provide women: without such knowledge "we are their property into whose hands we fall, and are led by those who with greatest confidence impose their opinions on us."

For further information, see Ruth Perry, *The Celebrated Mary Astell: An Early English Feminist* (Chicago: University of Chicago Press, 1986); Christine Sutherland, "Outside the Rhetorical Tradition: Mary Astell's Advice to Women in Seventeenth-century England," *Rhetorica* 9, no. 2 (Spring 1991): 147–63; Jane Donawerth, "The Politics of Renaissance Rhetorical Theory by Women," in *Political Rhetoric, Power, and Renaissance Women*, ed. Carole Levin and Patricia A. Sullivan (Albany: State University of New York Press, 1995), 256–72; Christine Sutherland, "Mary Astell: Reclaiming Rhetorica in the Seventeenth Century," in *Reclaiming Rhetorica: Women in the Rhetorical Tradition*, ed. Andrea A. Lunsford (Pittsburgh: University of Pittsburgh Press, 1995), 93–116; Jane Donawerth, "Conversation and the Boundaries of Public Discourse in Rhetorical Theory by Renaissance Women," *Rhetorica* 16, no. 2 (Spring 1998): 181–99; and Erin Herberg, "Mary Astell's Rhetorical Theory: A Woman's Viewpoint," in *The Changing Tradition: Women in the History of Rhetoric*, ed. Christine Mason Sutherland and Rebecca Sutcliffe (Calgary: University of Calgary Press, 1999), 147–57.

From *A Serious Proposal to the Ladies for the Advancement of Their True and Greatest Interest*

Part II (1697)
Wherein a Method Is Offer'd for the Improvement of Their Minds

V. As nature teaches us logic, so does it instruct us in rhetoric much better than rules of art, which, if they are good ones, are nothing else but those judicious observations which men of sense have drawn from nature, and which all who reflect on the operations of their own minds will find out themselves. The common precepts of rhetoric may teach us how to reduce ingenious ways of speaking to a certain rule, but they do not teach us how to invent them; this is nature's work and she does it best. There is as much difference between natural and artificial eloquence as there is between paint and true beauty. So that as a good author well observes, all that's useful in this art, "is the avoiding certain evil ways of writing and speaking, and above all an artificial and rhetorical style composed of false thoughts, hyperboles, and forced figures, which is the greatest fault in rhetoric."[1]

I shall not therefore recommend under the name of "rhetoric" an art of speaking floridly on all subjects, and of dressing up error and impertinence in a quaint and taking garb, any more than I did that wrangling which goes by the name of "logic," and which teaches to dispute *for* and *against* all propositions indefinitely whether they are true or false. It is an abuse both of reason and address to press them into the service of a trifle or an untruth, and a mistake to think that any argument can be rightly made, or any discourse truly eloquent that does not illustrate and enforce truth. For the design of rhetoric is to remove those prejudices that lie in the way of truth, to reduce the passions to the government of reason, to place our subject in a right light, and excite our hearers to a due consideration of it. And I know not what exactness of method, pure and proper language, figures, insinuating ways of address and the like signify, any farther than as they contribute to the service of truth by rendering our discourse intelligible, agreeable, and convincing. They are indeed very serviceable to it when they are duly managed, for good sense loses much of its efficacy by being ill expressed, and an ill style is nothing else but the neglect of some of these, or over-doing of them.

Obscurity, one of the greatest faults in writing, does commonly proceed from a want of meditation, for when we pretend to teach others what we do not understand ourselves, no wonder that we do it at a sorry rate. 'Tis true, obscurity is sometimes designed to conceal an erroneous opinion which an author dares not openly own, or which, if it be discovered, he has a mind to evade. And sometimes even an honest and good writer who studies to avoid may insensibly fall into it, by reason that his ideas being become familiar to himself by frequent meditation, a long train of them are readily excited in his mind, by a word or two which he's used to annex to them; but it is not so with his readers, who are perhaps strangers to his meditations, and yet ought to have the very same idea raised in theirs that was in the author's mind, or else they cannot understand him. If therefore we desire to be intelligible to everybody, our expressions must be more plain and explicit than they needed to be if we write only for ourselves, or for those to whom frequent discourse has made our ideas familiar.

Not that it is necessary to express at length all the process our mind goes through in resolving a question—this would spin out our discourse to an unprofitable tediousness, the operations of the mind being much more speedy than those of the tongue or pen. But we should fold up our thoughts so closely and neatly, expressing them in such significant though few words, as that the reader's mind may easily open and enlarge them. And if this can be done with facility, we are perspicuous as well as strong; if with difficulty or not at all, we're then perplexed and obscure writers.

Scarce anything conduces more to clearness, the great beauty of writing, than exactness of method; nor perhaps to persuasion, for by putting everything in its proper place with due order and connection, the reader's mind is gently led where the writer would have it. Such a style is easy without softness, copious as that signifies the omission of nothing necessary, yet not wordy and tedious, nor stuffed with nauseous repetitions, which they who do not think before they write and dispose their matter duly, can scarce avoid. The method of thinking has been already shown, and the same is to be observed in writing, which if it be what it ought, is nothing else but the communicating to others the result of our frequent and deep meditations, in such a manner as we judge most effectual to convince them of those truths which we believe— always remembering that the most natural order is ever best, that we must first prepare their minds by removing those prejudices and passions which are in our way, and then propose our reasons with all the clearness and force, with all the tenderness and good nature we can.

And since the clearness and connection, as well as the emphasis and beauty of a discourse, depends in a great measure on a right use of the particles, whoever would write well ought to inform themselves nicely in their proprieties. An *and*, a *the*, a *but*, a *for*, etc., do very much perplex the sense when they are misplaced, and make the reader take it many times quite otherwise than the writer meant it. But this is not a place to say all that this subject deserves; they who would have much in a little may consult an ingenious author[2] who has touched upon it and from thence take hints to observe how these little words are applied in good authors, and how themselves may best use them to express the several postures of their own minds.

In a word, I know not a more compendious way to good speaking and writing, than to choose out the most excellent in either as a model on which to form ourselves—or rather, to imitate the perfections of all, and avoid their mistakes, for few are so perfect as to be without fault, and few so bad as to have nothing good in them. A true judgment distinguishes, and neither rejects the good for the sake of the bad, nor admits the bad because of the good that is mingled with it. No sort of style but has its excellency and is liable to defect. If care be not taken, the sublime which subdues us with nobleness of thought and grandeur of expression will fly out of sight and, by being empty and bombast, become contemptible. The plain and simple will grow dull and abject; the severe, dry and rugged; the florid, vain and impertinent. The strong, instead of rousing the mind, will distract and entangle it by being obscure; even the easy and perspicuous, if it be too diffuse or over-delicate, tires us instead of pleasing. Good sense is the principal thing without which all our polishing is of little worth, and yet, if ornament be wholly neglected, very few will regard us. Studied and artificial periods are not natural enough to please; they show too much solicitude about what does not deserve it. And a loose and careless style declares too much contempt of the public. Neither reason nor wit entertains us if they are driven beyond a certain pitch, and pleasure itself is offensive if it be not judiciously dispensed.

Every author almost has some beauty or blemish remarkable in his style from whence it takes its name; and every reader has a peculiar taste of books as well as meats. One would have the subject exhausted; another is not pleased if somewhat be not left to enlarge in his own meditations. This affects a grave, that a florid style; one is for easiness, a second for plainness, a third for strength, and a fourth for politeness. And perhaps the great secret of writing is the mixing all these in so just a proportion that everyone may taste what he likes without being disgusted by its contrary, and may find at once that by the solidity of the reason, the purity and propriety of expression, and insinuating agreeableness of address, his understanding is enlightened, his affections subdued, and his will duly regulated.

This is, indeed, the true end of writing, and it would not be hard for everyone to judge how well they had answered it, would they but lay aside selflove, so much of it at least as makes them partial to their own productions. Did we consider our own with the same severity, or but indifferency, that we do another's writing, we might pass a due censure on it, might discern what thought was crude or ill expressed, what reasoning weak, what passage superfluous, where we were flat and dull, where extravagant and vain, and, by criticizing on ourselves, do a greater kindness to the world than we can in making our remarks on others. Nor should we be at a loss, if we were impartial, in finding out methods to inform, persuade, and please. For human nature is for the most part much alike in all, and that which has a good effect on us, will generally speaking have the same on others, so that to guess what success we are like to have, we need only suppose ourselves in the place of those we address to, and consider how such a discourse would operate on us, if we had their infirmities and thoughts about us.

And if we do so, I believe we shall find there's nothing more improper than pride and positiveness, nor anything more prevalent than an innocent compliance with their weakness: such as pretends not to dictate to their ignorance, but only to explain and illustrate what they did or might have known before if they had considered it, and supposes that their minds being employed about some other things was the reason why they did not discern it as well as we. For human nature is not willing to own its ignorance; truth is so very attractive, there's such a natural agreement between our minds and it, that we care not to be thought so dull as not to be able to find out by ourselves such obvious matters. We should therefore be careful that nothing pass from us which upbraids our neighbor's ignorance, but study to remove it without appearing to take notice of it, and permit them to fancy, if they please, that we believe them as wise and good as we endeavor to make them. By this we gain their affections, which is the hardest part of our work, excite their industry and infuse a new life into all generous tempers, who conclude there's great hope they may with a little pains attain what others think they know already, and are ashamed to fall short of the good opinion we have entertained of them.

And since many would yield to the clear light of truth were it not for the shame of being overcome, we should convince but not triumph, and rather conceal our conquest than publish it. We doubly oblige our neighbors when we reduce them into the right way, and keep it from being taken notice of that they were once in the wrong, which is certainly a much greater satisfaction than that blaze of glory which is quickly out, that noise of applause which will soon be over. For the gaining of our neighbor, at least the having honestly endeavored it, and the leading our own vanity in triumph are real goods and such as we shall always have the comfort of. It is to be wished that such propositions as are not attended with the clearest evidence were delivered only by way of inquiry, since even the brightest truth, when dogmatically dictated, is apt to offend our readers and make them imagine their liberty's imposed on, so far is positiveness from bringing anybody over to our sentiments. And besides, we're all of us liable to mistake, and few have humility enough to confess themselves deceived in what they have confidently asserted, but think they're obliged in honor to maintain an opinion they've once been zealous for, how desirous soever they may be to get rid of it, could they do it handsomely.[3] Now a modest way of delivering our sentiments assists us in this, and leaves us at liberty to take either side of the question, as reason and riper consideration shall determine.

In short, as thinking conformably to the nature of things is true knowledge, so the expressing our thoughts in such a way, as most readily and with the greatest clearness and life excites in others the very same idea that was in us, is the best eloquence. For if our idea be conformable to the nature of the thing it represents, and its relations duly stated, this is the most effectual way both to inform and persuade, since truth being always amiable, cannot fail of attracting when she's placed in a right light, and those to whom we offer her are made able and willing to discern her beauties. If therefore we thoroughly understand our subject and are zealously affected with it, we shall neither want suitable words to explain, nor persuasive methods to recommend it.

And since piety and virtue should, in spite of the mistaken customs of the age, be the principal theme of a Christian's conversation, that which those who bear that sacred name ought always to regard some way or other, even when it might be unseasonable to speak of it directly, the way to be good orators is to be good Christians; the practice of religion will both instruct us in the theory, and most powerfully enforce what we say of it. Did we truly relish the delights of God's service, we could neither refrain from talking of the pleasure, nor be so ill-natured as not to strive to communicate it; and were we duly warmed with a zeal for his glory and concern for our neighbor's soul, no figures of rhetoric, no art of persuasion would be wanting to us. We should diligently watch for opportunities, and carefully improve them, accommodating our discourse to the understanding and genius of all we could hope to do good to.

Besides, by being true Christians we have really that love for others which all who desire to persuade must pretend to; we've that *probity*[4] and *prudence*, that *civility* and *modesty* which the masters of this art say a good orator must be endowed with, and have plucked up those vicious inclinations from whence the most distasteful faults of writing proceed. For why do we choose to be obscure but because we intend to deceive, or would be thought to see much farther than our neighbors? One sort of vanity prompts us to be rugged and severe, and so possessed with the imagined worth and solidity of our discourse, that we think it beneath us to polish it. Another disposes us to elaborate and affected ways of writing, to pompous and improper ornaments; and why are we tediously copious but that we fancy every thought of ours is extraordinary? Contradiction is indeed for our advantage as tending to make us wiser, yet our pride makes us impatient under it, because it seems to lessen that esteem and deference we desire should be paid us. Whence come those sharp reflections, those imagined strains of wit, not to be endured amongst Christians, and which serve not to convince but to provoke—whence come they but from ill nature or revenge, from a contempt of others and a desire to set forth our own wit? Did we write less for ourselves, we should sooner gain our readers, who are many times disgusted at a well writ[5] discourse if it carries a tang of ostentation. And were our temper as Christian as it ought to be, our zeal would be spent on the most weighty things, not on little differences of opinions.

I have made no distinction in what has been said between speaking and writing, because though they are talents which do not always meet, yet there is no material difference between them. They write best perhaps who do it with the gentle and easy air of conversation; and they talk best who mingle solidity of thought with the agreeableness of a ready wit. As for *Pronunciation*,[6] though it takes more with some auditors many times than good sense, there needs little be said of it here, since women have no business with the pulpit, the bar, or St. Stephen's Chapel. And nature does for the most part furnish them with such a musical tone, persuasive air, and winning address as renders their discourse sufficiently agreeable in private conversation. And as to spelling, which they're said to be defective in, if they don't believe, as they're usually told, that it's fit for them to be so, and that to write exactly is too pedantic, they may soon correct that fault, by pronouncing their words aright and spelling them accordingly. I know this rule won't always hold because of an imperfection in our language, which has been oft complained of but is not yet amended. But in this case a little observation or recourse to books will assist us; and if at any time we happen to mistake by spelling as we pronounce, the fault will be very venial, and custom rather to blame than we.

I've said nothing of *Grammar*, though we can't write properly if we transgress its rules, supposing that custom and the reading of English books are sufficient to teach us the grammar of our own tongue—if we do but in any measure attend to them. And though women are generally accused of writing false English, if I may speak my own experience, their mistakes are not so common as is pretended, nor are they the only persons guilty. What they most commonly fail in is the particles and connection, and that generally through a briskness of temper which makes them forget, or haste which will not suffer them to read over again what went before. And indeed, those who speak true grammar, unless they're very careless, cannot write false, since they need only peruse what they've written, and consider whether they would express themselves thus in conversation.

But for this and for *Figures*, etc., and indeed for all that relates to this subject, I must refer you to an ingenious treatise which handles it fully,[7] and to which I'm obliged in great measure for what little skill I have—observing only that whatever it is we treat of, our style should be such as may keep our readers attent,[8] and induce them to go to the end. Now attention is usually fixed by admiration, which is excited by somewhat uncommon either in the thought or way of expression. We fall asleep over an author who tells us in an ordinary manner no more than we knew before: he who would take must be sublime in his sense, and must clothe it after a noble way. His thoughts must not be superficial, such as everyone may fall into at the first glance, but the very spirits and essence of thinking, the sum of many hours' meditation folded up in one handsome and comprehensive period, whose language is intelligible and easy that the readers may not lose the pleasure of the kernel, by the pain they find in cracking the shell.

The most difficult subject must be made easy by his way of handling it. Though his matter may deserve a meditation, yet his expressions must be so clear that he need not be read twice to be understood; *these* are to be so natural and familiar, condescending to the meanest capacity,[9] while his thoughts are great enough to entertain the highest. He discourses always on a useful subject, in a manner agreeable to it, and pleases that he may instruct. Nothing seems studied in his whole composition, yet everything is extraordinary, a beautiful harmony shining through all its parts. No sentence is doubtful, no word equivocal; his arguments are clear and his images lively. All the ideas he excites in your mind as nearly resemble the thing they represent as words can make them. While the exactness of his method and force of his reason enlighten and convince the mind, the vivacity of his imagination and insinuating address gain the affections and conquer the will. By the weight and closeness of the former, you would take him for an angel, and the tender and affable sweetness of the last bespeaks him a friend. He considers that, as mere flourish and rhetoric are good for nothing, so neither will bare reason dull and heavily expressed perform any great matter, at least not on those who need it most, whose palates being depraved, their medicines must be administered in a pleasing vehicle. Since mankind are averse to their real happiness, he does not only tell them their duty but interests them in it; and thinking it not enough to run them down with the strength of reason, he draws them over to a voluntary submission by the attractiveness of his eloquence. For he has a peculiar turn and air which animates every period, so that the very same truth which was dry and unaffecting in a vulgar author's words, charms and subdues you when clothed in his. He shows no more warmth than may convince his readers that he's heartily persuaded of the truths he offers them; and if it is necessary at any time to make use of figures to give a more lively representation than plain expressions could, to describe his own passions and excite the same in others upon a just occasion, in a word to awaken a stupid and clear the mind of a prejudiced reader, his figures are duly chosen and discreetly used. For he knows that scarce anything speaks a greater want of judgment than the showing concern where there needs none, or is a worse fault in oratory than the polishing a wrong or a trifling thought, the neatness of whose dress may strike with admiration perhaps at first sight, but upon a review it will certainly appear contemptible. And therefore as he does not abound in superfluous ornaments, so neither does he reject anything that can promote his end, which is not his own reputation, but the glory of his God and his neighbor's edification. He considers the narrowness of the human mind, and says all that is necessary but no more; understands it so well as to know what will move and please, and has so much command of himself as to give over when he has done enough. Yet he can exhaust the most fruitful subject without making the reader weary; for when he enlarges, it is in things not words, and he mingles variety without confusion. All the diverse excellencies of different styles meet in his to make up a perfect one: strength and ease, solidity and liveliness, the sublime and the plain. He's neither so lofty as to fly out of sight, nor so humble as to become creeping and contemptible. His strength does not make him rugged and perplexed, nor his smoothness, weak and nice. Though everything is neat, there's not a grain of affectation; he is grateful to the ear, but far removed from jingling cadence. Brief when there is occasion without dryness or obscurity, and florid enough to entertain the imagination without distracting the mind, there's not an antiquated or barbarous word to be found in him. All is decent, just, and natural; no peculiar or affected phrases, whether courtly or clownish, grave or burlesque. For plain and significant language is ever best. We have a mistaken idea of learning, if we think to pretend to it by sending our reader every minute to the dictionary. Words out of the common way are only allowable when they express our sense with greater force than ordinary ones could, or when they are so significant as to ease us of circumlocutions, a hard word which I could not avoid without using half a dozen words.

After all, it may not be amiss to take notice that ornaments are common to falsehood and truth, but clearness and strength of reasoning are not. They who would propagate error usually disguise it in equivocal terms and obscure phrases; they strive to engage our passions, rather than to convince our reason, and carry us away in the torrent of a warm imagination. They endeavor to refute, or if they can't do that, to ridicule the contrary opinion, and think this sufficient to establish their own. Being much better skilled in pulling down former systems than in building new ones, for it requires not great skill to object, and there are many truths which we're very certain of, and yet not able to answer every impertinent[10] inquiry concerning them, their greatest art is in confounding things, in giving a probable air to what they write, in pretending to demonstration where the nature of the truth does not require it, and evading it where it does. An immoral or heretical discourse therefore may be *cunningly* but not *well* writ, for we can never plead for error and vice with true eloquence. We may trick them up in a handsome garb, adorn them with quaint expressions, and give them such a plausible turn as may enable them to do very much mischief; but this is only a fulsome[11] carcass. The substance and life are not there if virtue and truth are wanting.

Notes

The text is taken from Mary Astell, *A Serious Proposal to the Ladies for the Advancement of Their True and Greatest Interest, Parts I and II*, 4th ed. (London, 1701), 116–26; Folger PR 3316 A655 S3 Cage, by permission of the Folger Shakespeare Library. I have modernized spelling and punctuation and regularized format. My thanks to Christina Godlewski for alerting me to Mary Astell as a rhetorical theorist.

1. In the original edition that was copy text for this excerpt, the marginal note (added by either Astell or her printer) reads "*L'art de Penser*, p. 22," a reference to Antoine Arnauld's *L'Art de Penser* (1675), the Port-Royal logic.

2. In the original edition that was copy text for this excerpt, the marginal note (added by either Astell or her printer) reads "Lock, *Of Human Und.*, Bk. III, Ch. 7," a reference to John Locke's *An Essay Concerning Human Understanding* (1690), bk. 3, chap. 7, entitled "Of Particles." Locke defines particles as "the words whereby it signifies what connexion it gives to the several affirmations and negations, that it unites in one continued reasoning or narration." Astell's term "particles" includes conjunctions and transitional phrases.

3. Handsomely: adroitly, cleverly, easily.

4. Probity: integrity, honesty, uprightness.

5. Writ: archaic form of "written."

6. Pronunciation: the rhetorical sense of delivery, rather than the linguistic sense of articulation.

7. In the original edition that was copy text for this excerpt, the marginal note (added by either Astell or her editor) reads "Art of Speaking," a reference to Bernard Lamy's *De l'art de parler* (1675), translated into English as *The Art of Speaking* (1676).

8. Attent: attentive, alert and interested.

9. Condescending: reaching down to the simplest understanding; "condescending" did not have its present negative connotation in the eighteenth century.

10. Impertinent: irrelevant.

11. Fulsome: offensive to the sense of taste.

Hannah More

1745–1833

Born on February 2, 1745, Hannah More was seen as the invalid and genius in a family of four girls. Trained in cooking, sewing, and other home crafts by her mother, Hannah and the other girls were also tutored by their father, a schoolmaster. Alarmed at her brilliance in Latin and mathematics, her father stopped teaching Hannah those subjects as inappropriate to girls, but her mother talked him into continuing Latin. All the sisters attended a local boarding school, studying Latin, Italian, Spanish, and French, and hearing lectures in literature, astronomy, elocution, religion, philosophy, and science. None of the sisters married. Hannah was engaged to William Turner when she was twenty-two and he was twenty years older. Although the marriage was scheduled several times, Turner canceled each time and finally settled a £200 annuity on her that left her financially independent. In 1758, the sisters established a boarding school for girls in Bristol, teaching French, reading, writing, arithmetic, and needlework.

From 1774 on, Hannah became friends in London with the Bluestocking Circle, centered on Elizabeth Montague and her "conversation parties," as well as Elizabeth Vesey, Elizabeth Carter, Hester Chapone, and Frances Boscawen, and including Samuel Johnson, James Boswell, Joshua Reynolds, Fanny Burney, David Garrick and his wife, and Horace Walpole. More published two tragedies—*Percy* (1777), and *Fatal Falsehood* (1779)—which the Garricks produced. She further published a novel, *Coelebs in Search of a Wife* (1808).

Despite extremely conservative ideas on the domestic and subordinate role of women, More was a social reformer who wrote in support of abolition. In her later years, she was also an Evangelical, a reform-minded group within the Anglican Church. In a counter-Methodist move, in the 1790s the More sisters established Sunday schools in impoverished districts, which taught children reading, religion, and hygiene. They also organized parent groups on Sunday evenings to study reading and religion. More and her sisters further established a School of Industry for poor boys, as well as schools in the mining districts of England. Despite her support of the established church, More did not escape controversy excited by the fear of women preaching. More helped found the Religious Tract Society in 1799 and wrote dozens of cheap, popular tracts, conservative fictions treating crucial moral and social issues (such as alcohol, sex before marriage, and unemployment) aimed at the lower classes. More died in 1833, over eighty, but still vigorously championing religion, restrictive gender roles that she herself did not imitate, and conservative, anti-French politics.

More was a prolific rhetorical theorist, including sections on conversation in all of her educational treatises, and some of her moral essays: *Essays on Various Subjects, Principally Designed for Young Ladies* (1777); *Thoughts on the Importance of the Manners of the Great* (1788), *Strictures on the Modern System of Female Education* (1799), and *Hints for Forming the Character of a Young Princess* (1808). She also wrote a mock-heroic poem, "The Bas Bleu, or, Conversation"

(1783–1786), which outlines the qualities of ideal conversation and offers the Bluestocking "conversation parties" as its model. Her rhetorical theory follows eighteenth-century developments in rhetoric in its emphasis on psychology and association of ideas, but centers on conversation for girls and women rather than public discourse for boys and men. She advocates facilitating others' expression of ideas (especially men's) and the feminine role of listening, rather than wit and performance in conversation, but also emphasizes the importance of education and intelligent rather than trivial conversation for women.

In *Essays on Various Subjects*, More adapts her theory to the short essay form for girls, advocating for girls simplicity and candor in conversation, but never wit at the expense or detraction of others. Because much of this essay is repeated in altered or expanded form in *Strictures*, I have not included it in this anthology. In her mock-heroic poem, "The Bas Bleu," More deprecates the *précieuses*, such as Mme. de Rambouillet and Madeleine de Scudéry, who set the taste for the seventeenth-century salon, and outlines a different standard for the eighteenth-century British salon, one that emphasizes knowledge, and high moral purpose rather than play. In *Strictures on Female Education*, More outlines in a longer essay the qualities of the ideal Christian female speaker—simplicity, truth, restrained wit, and a sound education providing knowledge that is never concealed under the guise of feminine innocence. More is better at cataloguing the faults of conversation—inappropriate allusion, assertion rather than proof, competitive display, girls' hiding their intelligence, vanity—than she is at describing its virtues. But in the guise of attacking falsehood in speech, More offers a brilliant analysis of the sophistics of conversation, including taking words out of context, relating half the truth, and changing the meaning of the original words by a new tone or look.

For further information, see Mary Alden Hopkins, *Hannah More and Her Circle* (New York: Longmans, Green, and Co., 1947); M. G. Jones, *Hannah More* (Cambridge: Cambridge University Press, 1952); Christine Krueger, *The Reader's Repentance: Women Preachers, Women Writers, and Nineteenth-Century Social Discourse* (Chicago: University of Chicago Press, 1992), 94–124; Patricia Demers, *The World of Hannah More* (Lexington: University Press of Kentucky, 1996); Charles Howard Ford, *Hannah More: A Critical Biography* (New York: Peter Lang, 1996); *Selected Writing of Hannah More*, ed. Robert Hole (London: William Pickering, 1996); and Jane Donawerth, "Hannah More, Lydia Sigourney, and the Creation of a Women's Tradition of Rhetoric," in *Rhetoric, the Polis, and the Global Village*, Proceedings of the 1998 Rhetoric Society of America Conference, ed. C. Jan Swearingen (Mahwah, N.J.: Erlbaum, 1999), 155–62.

From "The Bas Bleu, or, Conversation" (1783–1786)

Vesey![1] of verse the judge and friend!
Awhile my idle strain attend:
Not with the days of early Greece,
I mean to ope my slender piece;
The rare symposium to proclaim
Which crowned th'Athenians' social name;

Or how Aspasia's parties[2] shone,
The first *Bas-bleu* at Athens known;
Where Socrates[3] unbending sat,
With Alcibiades[4] in chat;
And Pericles[5] vouchsafed to mix
Taste, wit, and mirth, with politics.

. . . .

The vanquished triple crown to you,
Boscawen sage, bright Montagu,[6]
Divided fell; your cares in haste
Rescued the ravaged realms of taste;
And Lyttleton's[7] accomplished name,
And witty Pulteney[8] shared the fame;
The men, not bound by pedant rules,
Nor ladies *précieuses ridicules:*[9]
For polished Walpole[10] showed the way,
How wits may be both learned and gay;
And Carter[11] taught the female train,
The deeply wise are never vain;
And she, who Shakespeare's wrongs redressed,[12]
Proved that the brightest are the best.
This just deduction still they drew,
And well they practiced what they knew;
Nor taste, nor wit, deserves applause,
Unless still true to critic's laws,
Good sense, of faculties the best,
Inspire and regulate the rest.
O! how unlike the wit that fell,
Rambouillet![13] at thy quaint hotel;
Where point, and turn, and equivoque[14]
Distorted every word they spoke!
All so intolerably bright,
Plain common sense was put to flight;
Each speaker, so ingenious ever,
'Twas tiresome to be quite so clever;
There twisted wit forgot to please,
And mood and figure banished ease;
No votive altar smoked to thee,
Chaste queen, divine Simplicity!
But forced conceit, which ever fails,
And stiff antithesis prevails;
Uneasy rivalry destroys
Society's unlabored joys:
Nature, of stilts and fetters tired,
Impatient from the wits retired.

. . . .

Hail Conversation, heavenly fair,
Thou bliss of life, and balm of care!
Still may thy gentle reign extend,

111

And taste with wit and science blend.
Soft polisher of rugged man!
Refiner of the social plan!
For thee, best solace of his toil,
The sage consumes his midnight oil,
And keeps late vigils to produce
Materials for thy future use,
Calls forth the else neglected knowledge
Of school, of travel, and of college.
If none behold, ah! wherefore fair?
Ah! wherefore wise, if none must hear?
Our intellectual ore must shine,
Not slumber idly in the mine.
Let Education's moral mint
The noblest images imprint;
Let Taste her curious touchstone hold,
To try if standard be the gold;
But 'tis thy commerce, Conversation,
Must give it use by circulation,
That noblest commerce of mankind,
Whose precious merchandise is Mind!
. . . .

Enlightened spirits! You, who know
What charms from polished converse flow,
Speak, for you can, the pure delight
When kindling sympathies unite;
When correspondent tastes impart
Communion sweet from heart to heart;
You ne'er the cold gradations need
Which vulgar souls to union lead;
No dry discussion to unfold,
The meaning caught ere well 'tis told.
In taste, in learning, wit or science,
Still kindred souls demand alliance:
Each in the other joys to find,
The image answering to his mind.
But sparks electric only strike
On souls electrical alike;
The flash of intellect expires,
Unless it meet congenial fires.
The language to th'elect alone
Is, like the mason's mystery, known;
In vain th'unerring sign is made
To him who is not of the *trade*.[15]
What lively pleasure to divine,
The thought implied, the hinted line,
To feel allusion's artful force,
And trace the image to its source!
Quick memory blends her scattered rays,

Till fancy kindles at the blaze;
The works of ages start to view,
The ancient wit elicits new.
But wit and parts if thus we praise,
What nobler altars should we raise,
Those sacrifices could we see,
Which wit, O Virtue! makes to thee?
At once the rising thought to dash,
To quench at once the bursting flash!
The shining mischief to subdue,
And lose the praise and pleasure, too!
Though Venus' self, could you detect her,
Imbuing with her richest nectar,
The thought unchaste—to check that thought,
To spurn a fame so dearly bought—
This is high principle's control,
This is true continence of soul!

. . . .

But let the lettered, and the fair,
And chiefly, let the wit beware;
You, whose warm spirits never fail,
Forgive the hint which ends my tale.
O shun the perils which attend
On wit, on warmth, and heed your friend:
Though science nursed you in her bowers,
Though fancy crown your brow with flowers,
Each thought, though bright invention fill,
Though Attic bees each word distil,
Yet, if one gracious power refuse
Her gentle influence to infuse,
If she withhold her magic spell,
Nor in the social circle dwell,
In vain shall listening crowds approve;
They'll praise you, but they will not love.
What is this power, you're loath to mention,
This charm, this witchcraft? 'Tis attention.
Mute angel, yes; thy looks dispense
The silence of intelligence;
Thy graceful form I well discern,
In act to listen and to learn;
'Tis thou for talents shalt obtain
That pardon wit would hope in vain;
Thy wondrous power, thy secret charm,
Shall envy of her sting disarm;
Thy silent flattery soothes our spirit,
And we forgive eclipsing merit;
Our jealous souls no longer burn,
Nor hate thee, though thou shine in turn;
The sweet atonement screens the fault,

113

And love and praise are cheaply bought.
With some complacency to hear,
Though somewhat long the tale appear,
The dull relation to attend,
Which mars the story you could mend;
'Tis more than wit, 'tis moral beauty,
'Tis pleasure rising out of duty.
Nor vainly think, the time you waste,
When temper triumphs over taste.

Notes for "The Bas Bleu"

I have taken the text from *The Works of Hannah More* (New York: Harper & Brothers, 1855), 5:359–71. My thanks to the University of Maryland Rare Books Collection. As in other instances, I have modernized spelling and punctuation but not if change interfered with meter or rhyme. More's note to the title in this edition explains: "The following title owes its birth and name to the mistake of a foreigner of distinction, who gave the literal appellation of the *Bas-bleu* to a small party of friends, who had often been called, by way of pleasantry, the *Blue Stockings*. These little societies have been sometimes misrepresented. They were composed of persons distinguished, in general, for their rank, talents, or respectable character, who met frequently at Mrs. Vesey's and at a few other houses, for the sole purpose of conversation, and were different in no respect from other parties, but that the company did not play at cards."

1. More's footnote to a later reference to Mrs. Vesey in the poem, in a passage that I do not include, states: "This amiable lady was remarkable for her talent in breaking the formality of a circle, by inviting her parties to form themselves into little separate groups." The printer of the American edition adds, "She was the wife of the honorable Agmondesham Vesey, an Irish gentleman and the friend of Burke, on whose recommendation he became a member of Johnson's Literary Club."

2. On Aspasia, see the first entry in this collection.

3. Socrates (469–399 B.C.E.), most famous of all Greek philosophers, noted for his conversational method of teaching and the firm principles that made him accept a death sentence with equanimity.

4. Alcibiades (450–404 B.C.E.), Athenian general and statesman, pupil of Socrates; leader then exiled from Athens, military advisor in exile to Sparta and Samos, recalled to assume an exceptional command at Athens, exiled again and murdered in Phrygia.

5. Pericles (c. 495–429 B.C.E.), partner to Aspasia and frequenter of her salons, brilliant politician and sophistic rhetor, led the program for public building that made Athens the most beautiful city in Greece.

6. John Montagu, Earl of Sandwich (1718–1792), was a British politician; both the sandwich and the Sandwich Islands (later Hawaii) were named for him.

7. Baron George Lyttleton (1709–1773), writer and frequenter of the "bluestocking" salons.

8. William Pulteney, Earl of Bath (1684–1764), statesman and Whig leader.

9. *Précieuses ridicules*: The printer's note says "See Molière's comedy." This refers to Jean Baptiste Poqueline Molière, *Les précieuses ridicules*, a comedy attacking the women who participated in salon culture; it was rumored that Madeleine de Scudéry served as model for these caricatures. See her biography and selections from her dialogues in this collection.

10. Horace Walpole (1717–1797), Earl of Orford, was the youngest son of the famous statesman Robert Walpole; he served in Parliament, wrote a Gothic romance and treatises on a variety of historical and aesthetic topics, frequented the salons, built a Gothic castle, and ran a private printing press at his country house, Strawberry Hill.

11. Elizabeth Carter (1717–1806), poet, contributor under the pen name "Eliza" to *The Gentleman's Magazine*, and famous for her translation of Epictetus, was a bluestocking and attended the London salons.

12. Elizabeth Robinson Montagu (1720–1800), one of the bluestockings, noted for her wit and her salon frequented by Johnson, Walpole, and Burke, wrote *An Essay on the Writings and Genius of Shakespeare* (1769) to defend Shakespeare against Voltaire's criticisms of the poet.

13. In seventeenth-century France, Mme. de Rambouillet, friend of de Scudéry, held a salon at the Hôtel de Rambouillet. More's note explains, "The society at the Hôtel de Rambouillet, though composed of the most polite and ingenious persons in France, was much tainted with affectation and false taste. See Voiture, Menage, etc. The late Earl of Mansfield told the author, that, when he was ambassador at Paris, he was assured that it had not been unusual for those persons of a purer taste, who frequented these assemblies, to come out from their society so weary of wit and labored ingenuity, that they used to express the comfort they felt in their emancipation by saying "*Allons! faisons des solécisme!*" [Come! Let us commit a solecism!—an error in grammar or taste].

14. An "equivoque" is a pun, or play with multiple meanings of a word. By the end of the eighteenth century in England, puns, which had been for centuries considered witty, were considered in bad taste. We still groan at puns, acknowledging eighteenth-century influence. Actually, the précieuse salon did not treasure puns, as we can see from de Scudéry's "Conversations."

15. A Mason is a member of a secret society, the Ancient Free and Accepted Masons, perhaps originating in guilds of the trade of stonemason, based on symbols from apocryphal descriptions of the building of Solomon's Temple, and dedicated to liberal social and religious ideas and charitable works. A Mason refuses to divulge the rituals to the uninitiated. An English Grand Lodge was formed in London in 1717, and the organization spread rapidly through eighteenth-century England.

From *Strictures on the Modern System of Female Education* (1799)

Chapter XIV: Conversation

Hints suggested on the subject. — On the tempers and dispositions to be introduced in it. — Errors to be avoided. — Vanity under various shapes the cause of those errors.

The sexes will naturally desire to appear to each other such as each believes the other will best like; their conversation will act reciprocally; and each sex will appear more or less rational as they perceive it will more or less recommend them to each other. It is therefore to be regretted that many men, even of distinguished sense and learning, are so apt to consider the society of ladies as a scene in which to rest their understandings, rather than to exercise them; while ladies, in return, are too much addicted to make their court by lending themselves to this spirit of trifling. They often avoid to make use of what abilities they have, and affect to talk below their natural and acquired powers of mind, considering it as a tacit and welcome flattery to the understanding of men, to renounce the exercise of their own.

Now since taste and principles thus mutually operate, men, by keeping up conversation to its proper standard, would not only call into exercise the powers of mind which women actually possess, but would even awaken in them new energies which they do not know they possess; and men of sense would find their account in doing this, for their own talents would be more highly rated by companions who were better able to appreciate them. And, on the other hand, if young women found it did not often recommend them, in the eyes of those whom they might wish to please, to be frivolous and superficial, they would become more sedulous in correcting their own habits. Whenever fashionable women indicate a relish for instructive conversation, men will not be apt to hazard what is vain or unprofitable; much less will they ever presume to bring forward what is loose or corrupt, where some signal has not been previously given that it will be acceptable, or at least that it will be pardoned.

Ladies commonly bring into company minds already too much relaxed by petty pursuits, rather than overstrained by intense application; the littleness of the employments in which they are usually engaged does not so exhaust their spirits as to make them stand in need of that relaxation from company which severe application or overwhelming business makes requisite for studious or public men. The due consideration of this circumstance might serve to bring the sexes more nearly on a level in society, and each might meet the other halfway; for that degree of lively and easy conversation which is a necessary refreshment to the learned and the busy would not decrease in pleasantness by being made of so rational a cast as would yet somewhat raise the minds of women, who commonly seek society as a scene of pleasure, not as a refuge from intense thought or exhausting labor.

It is a disadvantage even to those women who keep the best company, that it is unhappily almost established into a system by the other sex, to postpone everything like instructive discourse until the ladies are withdrawn, their retreat serving as a kind of signal for the exercise of intellect. And in the few cases in which it happens that any important discussion takes place in their presence, they are for the most part considered as having little interest in serious subjects. Strong truths, whenever such happen to be addressed to them, are either diluted with flattery, or kept back in part, or softened to their taste; or if the ladies express a wish for information on any point, they are put off with a compliment, instead of a reason, and are considered as beings who are not expected to see and to judge of things as they really exist.

Do we then wish to see the ladies, whose opportunities leave them so incompetent, and the modesty of whose sex ought never to allow them even to be as shining as they are able—do we wish to see them take the lead in metaphysical disquisitions? Do we wish them to plunge into the depths of theological polemics,

And find no end in wand'ring mazes lost?[1]

Do we wish them to revive the animosities of the Bangorian controversy,[2] or to decide the process between the Jesuits and the five propositions of Jansenius?[3] Do we wish to enthrone them in the professor's chair, or to deliver oracles, harangues, and dissertations? To weight the merits of every new production in the scales of Quintilian, or to regulate the unities of dramatic composition by Aristotle's clock?[4] Or renouncing those foreign aids, do we desire to behold them, inflated with their original powers, laboring to strike out sparks of wit, with a restless anxiety to shine, which generally fails, and with a labored affectation to please, which never pleases?

Diseurs de bons mots, fades caractère![5]

All this be far from them! —But we *do* wish to see the conversation of well-bred women rescued from vapid commonplaces, from uninteresting tattle, from trite and hackneyed communications, from frivolous earnestness, from false sensibility, from a warm interest about things of no moment, and an indifference to topics the most important, from a cold vanity, from the overflowings of self-love, exhibiting itself under the smiling mask of an engaging flattery, and from all the factitious manners of artificial intercourse. We *do* wish to see the time

116

passed in polished and intelligent society, considered among the beneficial, as well as the pleasant portions of our existence, and not consigned over, as it too frequently is, to premeditated trifling, or systematic unprofitableness. Let us not, however, be misunderstood; it is not meant to prescribe that they should affect to talk on lofty subjects, so much as to suggest that they should bring good sense, simplicity, and precision into those common subjects, of which, after all, both the business and the conversation of mankind is in a great measure made up.

It is too well known how much the dread of imputed pedantry keeps off anything that verges towards *learned*, and the terror of imputed enthusiasm staves off anything that approaches to *serious* conversation, so that the two topics which peculiarly distinguish us, as rational and immortal beings, are by general consent in a good degree banished from the society of rational and immortal creatures. But we might almost as consistently give up the comforts of fire because a few persons have been burnt, and the benefit of water because some others have been drowned, as relinquish the enjoyments of intellectual, and the blessings of religious intercourse, because the learned world has sometimes been infested with pedants, and the religious world with fanatics.

As in the momentous times in which we live, it is next to impossible to pass an evening in company, but the talk will so inevitably revert to politics, that, without any premeditated design, everyone present shall infallibly get to know to which side the other inclines; why, in the far higher concern of eternal things, should we so carefully shun every offered opportunity of bearing even a casual testimony to the part we espouse in religion? Why, while we make it a sort of point of conscience to leave no doubt on the mind of a stranger, whether we adopt the party of Pitt or Fox,[6] shall we choose to leave it very problematical whether we belong to God or Baal?[7] Why, in religion, as well as in politics, should we not act like people who, having their all at stake, cannot forbear now and then adverting for a moment to the object of their grand concern, and dropping at least an incidental intimation of the side to which they belong.

Even the news of the day, in such an eventful period as the present, may lend frequent occasions to a woman of principle, to declare, without parade, her faith in a moral Governor of the world; her trust in a particular Providence; her belief in the divine Omnipotence; her confidence in the power of God, in educing good from evil, in his employing wicked nations, not as favorites but instruments; her persuasion that present success is no proof of the divine favor; in short, some intimation that she is not ashamed to declare that her mind is under the influence of Christian faith and principle. A general concurrence in exhibiting this spirit of decided faith and holy trust would inconceivably discourage that pert infidelity which is ever on the watch to produce itself; and, as we have already observed, if women, who derive authority from their rank or talents, did but reflect how their sentiments are repeated and their authority quoted, they would be so on their guard that general society might become a scene of general improvement, and the young, who are looking for models on which to fashion themselves, would be ashamed of exhibiting anything like levity, or skepticism, or profaneness.

Let it be understood that it is not meant to intimate that serious subjects should make up the bulk of conversation; this, as it is impossible, would also often be improper. It is not intended to suggest that they should be abruptly introduced, or unsuitably prolonged; but only that they should not be systematically shunned, nor the brand of fanaticism fixed on the person who, with whatever propriety, hazards the introduction of them. It is evident, however, that this general dread of serious topics arises a good deal from an ignorance of the true nature of religion; people avoid it on the principle expressed by that vulgar phrase, of the danger of playing with edge tools. They conceive of it as something which involves controversy, and dispute, and mischief; something of an inflammatory nature, which is to stir up ill humours; as of a sort of party business which sets friends at variance. So much is this notion adopted, that I have seen announced two works of considerable merit, in which it was stipulated as an attraction that religion, as being likely to excite anger and party distinctions, should be carefully excluded. Such is the worldly idea of the spirit of that religion, whose direct object it was to bring "peace and good will to men"!

Women too little live or converse up to their understandings; and however we have deprecated affectation or pedantry, let it be remembered, that both in reading and conversing the understanding gains more by stretching than stooping. If by exerting itself it may not attain to all it desires, yet it will be sure to gain something. The mind, by always applying itself to objects below its level, contracts and shrinks itself to the size, and lowers itself to the level, of the object about which it is conversant; while the mind which is active expands and raises itself, grows larger by exercise, abler by diffusion, and richer by communication.

But the taste of general society is not favorable to improvement. The seriousness with which the most frivolous subjects are agitated, and the levity with which the most serious are dispatched, bear a pretty exact proportion to each other. Society, too, is a sort of magic lantern;[8] the scene is perpetually shifting. In this incessant change, the evanescent fashion of the present minute, which, while in many it leads to the cultivation of real knowledge, has also sometimes led even the gay and idle to the affectation of mixing a sprinkling of science with the mass of dissipation. The ambition of appearing to be well-informed breaks out even in those triflers who will not spare time from their pleasurable pursuits sufficient for acquiring that knowledge, of which, however, the reputation is so desirable. A little smattering of philosophy often dignifies the pursuits of the day without rescuing them from the vanities of the night. A course of lectures (that admirable assistant for enlightening the understanding) is not seldom resorted to as a means to substitute the appearance of knowledge for the fatigue of application; but where this valuable help is attended merely like any other public exhibition, and is not furthered by correspondent reading at home, it often serves to set off the reality of ignorance with the affectation of skill. But instead of producing in conversation a few reigning scientific terms, with a familiarity and readiness, which

Amaze the unlearn'd, and make the learned smile,[9]

would it not be more modest even for those who are better informed, to avoid the common use of technical terms whenever the idea can be as well conveyed without them? For it argues no real ability to know the *names* of tools; the ability lies in knowing their *use*. And while it is in the thing, and not in the term, that real knowledge consists, the charge of pedantry is attached to the use of the term, which would not attach to the knowledge of the science.

In the faculty of speaking well, ladies have such a happy promptitude of turning their slender advantages to account, that there are many who, though they have never been taught a rule of syntax, yet, by a quick facility in profiting from the best books and the best company, hardly ever violate one; and who often exhibit an elegant and perspicuous arrangement of style, without having studied any of the laws of composition. Every kind of knowledge which appears to be the result of observation, reflection, and natural taste sits gracefully on women. Yet, on the other hand, it sometimes happens, that ladies of no contemptible natural parts are too ready to produce, not only pedantic expressions, but crude notions; and still oftener to bring forward obvious and hackneyed remarks, which float on the very surface of a subject, with the imposing air of recent invention, and all the vanity of conscious discovery. This is because their acquirements have not been woven into their minds by early instruction; what knowledge they have gotten stands out, as it were, above the very surface of their mind, like the *appliqué* of the embroiderer, instead of having been interwoven with the growth of the piece, so as to have become a part of the stuff.[10] They did not, like men, acquire what they know while the texture was forming. Perhaps no better preventive could be devised for this literary vanity, than *early* instruction: that woman would be less likely to be vain of her knowledge who did not remember the time when she was ignorant. Knowledge that is *burnt in*, if I may so speak, is seldom obtrusive, rarely impertinent.

Their reading also has probably consisted much in abridgements from larger works, as was observed in a former chapter; this makes a readier talker, but a shallower thinker, than the perusal of books of more bulk. By these scanty sketches their critical spirit has been excited, while their critical powers have not been formed. For in those crippled mutilations they have seen nothing of that just proportion of parts, that skillful arrangement of the plan, and that artful distribution of the subject, which, while they prove the master hand of the writer, serve also to form the taste of the reader, far more than a disjointed skeleton, or a beautiful feature or two can do. The instruction of women is also too much drawn from the scanty and penurious sources of short writings of the essay kind: this, when it comprises the best part of a person's reading, makes a smatterer and spoils a scholar. For though it supplies current talk, yet it does not make a full mind; it does not furnish a storehouse of materials to stock the understanding, neither does it accustom the mind to any train of reflection. For the subjects, besides being each succinctly and, on account of this brevity, superficially treated, are distinct and disconnected: they arise out of no concatenation of ideas, nor any dependent series of deduction. Yet on this pleasant but desultory reading, the mind which has not been trained to severer exercise loves to repose itself in a sort of creditable indolence, instead of stretching its powers in the wholesome labor of consequent investigation.[11]

I am not discouraging study at a late period of life, or even slender knowledge; information is good at whatever period and in whatever degree it is acquired. But in such cases it should be attended with peculiar humility, and the new possessor should bear in mind that what is fresh to her has been long known to others; and she should therefore be aware of advancing as novel that which is common, and obtruding as rare that which everybody possesses. Some ladies are eager to exhibit proofs of their reading, though at the expense of their judgment, and will introduce in conversation quotations quite irrelevant to the matter in hand, because they happen at the instant to recur to their recollection, or were, perhaps, found in the book they have just been reading. Inappropriate quotations or strained analogy may show reading, but they do not show taste. That just and happy allusion which knows by a word how to awaken a corresponding image, or to excite in the hearer the idea which fills the mind of the speaker, shows less pedantry and more taste than bare citations; and a mind imbued with elegant knowledge will inevitably betray the opulence of its resources, even on topics which do not relate to science or literature. Well informed persons will easily be discovered to have read the best books, though they are not always detailing catalogues of authors. Though honey owes its exquisite taste to the fragrance of the sweetest flowers, yet the skill of the little artificer appears in this, that the delicious stores are so admirably worked up, as not to taste individually of any of those sweets of the very essence of which it is compounded. But true judgment will detect the infusion which true modesty will not display; and even common subjects passing through a cultivated understanding borrow a flavor of its richness. A power of apt selection is more valuable than any power of general retention; and an apposite remark, which shoots straight to the point, demands higher powers of mind than a hundred simple acts of memory: for the business of the memory is only to store up materials which the understanding is to mix and work up with its native faculties, and which the judgment is to bring out and apply. But young women who have more vivacity than sense, and more vanity than vivacity, often risk the charge of absurdity to escape that of ignorance, and will even compare two authors who are totally unlike, rather than miss the occasion to show that they have read both.

Among the arts to spoil conversation, some ladies possess that of suddenly diverting it from the channel in which it was beneficially flowing, because some *word* used by the person who was speaking has accidentally struck out a new train of thinking in their own minds, and not because the general *idea* expressed has struck out a corresponding idea, which sort of collision is indeed the way of eliciting the true fire. Young ladies whose sprightliness has not been disciplined by a correct education consider how things may be prettily said, rather than how they may be prudently or seasonably spoken, and hazard being thought wrong, or rash, or vain, for the chance of being reckoned pleasant. The flowers of rhetoric captivate them more than the justest deductions of reason; and to repel an argument they arm themselves with a metaphor. Those also who do not aim so high as eloquence are often surprised that you refuse to accept of a prejudice instead of a reason; they are apt to take up with a probability in place of a demonstration, and cheaply put you off with an assertion when you are requiring a proof. The same mode of education renders them also impatient of opposition; and if they happen to possess beauty, and to be vain of it, they may be tempted to consider that as an additional proof of their always being in the right. In this case, they will not ask you to submit your judgment to the force of their argument, so much as to the authority of their charms.

The same fault in the mind, strengthened by the same cause (a neglected education) leads lively women often to pronounce on a question without examining it: on any given point they seldomer *doubt* than men, not because they are more clear-sighted, but because they have not been accustomed to look into a subject long enough to discover its depths and its intricacies; and not discerning its difficulties, they conclude that it has none. Is it a contradiction to say, that they seem at once to be quick-sighted and short-sighted? What they see at all, they commonly see at once; a little difficulty discourages them; and, having caught a hasty glimpse of a subject, they rush to this conclusion, that either there is no more to be seen, or that what is behind will not pay them for the trouble of searching. They pursue their object eagerly, but not regularly; rapidly, but not pertinaciously; for they want that obstinate patience of investigation which grows stouter by repulse. What they have not attained, they do not believe exists; what they cannot seize at once, they persuade themselves is not worth having.

Is a subject of moment started in company? While the more sagacious are deliberating on its difficulties, and viewing it under all its aspects, in order to form a competent judgment before they decide, you will often find the most superficial woman present determine the matter without hesitation. Not seeing the perplexities in which the question is involved, she wonders at the want of penetration in him whose very penetration keeps him silent. She secretly despises the dull perception and slow decision of him who is patiently *untying* the knot which she fancies she exhibits more dexterity by *cutting*. By this shallow sprightliness, the person whose opinion was best worth having is discouraged from delivering it, and an important subject is dismissed without discussion, by this inconsequent flippancy and voluble rashness. It is this abundance of florid talk from superficial matter, which has brought on so many of the sex the charge of *inverting* the Apostle's precept, and being *swift to speak, and slow to hear*.[12]

For, if the great Roman orator could observe that silence was so important a part of conversation, that "there was not only an art but an eloquence in it,"[13] how peculiarly does the remark apply to the modesty of youthful females! But the silence of listless ignorance, and the silence of sparkling intelligence, are two things almost as obviously distinct, as the wisdom and the folly of the tongue. An inviolable and marked attention may show that a woman is pleased with a subject, and an illuminated countenance may prove that she understands it, almost as unequivocally as language itself could do; and this, with a modest question, is in many cases as large a share of the conversation as it is decorous for feminine delicacy to take. It is also as flattering an encouragement as men of sense require, for pursuing such topics in the presence of women, which they would be more disposed to do, did they oftener gain by it the attention which it is natural to wish to excite.

Yet do we not sometimes see an impatience to be heard (nor is it a *feminine* failing only) which good breeding can scarcely subdue? And even when these incorrigible talkers are compelled to be silent, is it not evident that they are not listening to what is said, but are only thinking of what they themselves shall say when they can seize the first lucky interval for which they are so narrowly watching?

But conversation must not be considered as a stage for the display of our talents, so much as a field for the exercise and improvement of our virtues, as a means for promoting the glory of our Creator, and the good and happiness of our fellow creatures. Well-bred and intelligent Christians are not, when they join in society, to consider themselves as entering the lists like intellectual prize-fighters, in order to exhibit their own vigor and dexterity, to discomfit their adversary, and to bear away the palm of victory. Truth and not triumph should be the object; and there are few occasions in life, in which we are more unremittingly called upon to watch ourselves narrowly, and to resist the assaults of various temptations, than in conversation. Vanity, jealousy, envy, misrepresentation, resentment, disdain, levity, impatience, insincerity, will in turn solicit to be gratified. Constantly to struggle against the desire of being thought more wise, more witty, and more knowing than those with whom we associate demands the incessant exertion of Christian vigilance, a vigilance which the generality are so far from suspecting necessary in the intercourse of common society, that cheerful conversation is rather considered as an exemption and release from it, than as an additional obligation to it.

But society, as we observed before, is not a stage on which to throw down our gauntlet, and prove our own prowess by the number of falls we give to our adversary; so far from it, good breeding, as well as Christianity, considers as an indispensable requisite for conversation the disposition to bring forward to notice any talent in others, which their own modesty or conscious inferiority would lead them to keep back. To do this with effect requires a penetration exercised to discern merit, and a generous candor which delights in drawing it out. There are few who cannot converse tolerably on some one topic. What that is, we should try to find out, and in general introduce that topic, though to the suppression of any one on which we ourselves are supposed to excel. And, however superior we may be in other respects to the persons in question, we may, perhaps, in that particular point, improve by them; and if we do not gain information, we shall at least gain a wholesome exercise to our humility and self-denial; we shall be restraining our own impetuosity; we shall, if we take this course on just occasions only, and so as to beware lest we gratify the vanity of others, be giving confidence to a doubting, or cheerfulness to a depressed spirit. And to place a just remark, hazarded by the diffident, in the most advantageous point of view; to call the attention of the inattentive, the forward, and the self-sufficient, to some quiet person in the company, who, though of much worth, is perhaps of little note—these are requisites for conversation, less brilliant, but far more valuable, than the power of exciting bursts of laughter by the brightest wit, or of extorting admiration by the most poignant sallies of ridicule.

For wit is, of all the qualities of the female mind, that which requires the severest castigation; yet the temperate exercise of this fascinating quality throws an additional luster round the character of an amiable woman; for to manage with discreet modesty a dangerous talent confers a higher praise than can be claimed by those in whom the absence of the talent takes away the temptation to misemploy it. To women, wit is a peculiarly perilous possession, which nothing short of the sober-mindedness of Christianity can keep in order. Intemperate wit craves admiration as its natural element; it lives on flattery as its daily bread. The professed wit is a hungry beggar that subsists on the extorted alms of perpetual panegyric; and like the vulture in the Grecian fable, its appetite increases by indulgence. Simple truth and sober approbation become tasteless and insipid to the palate, daily vitiated by the delicious poignancies of exaggerated commendation. Under the above restrictions, however, wit may be safely and pleasantly exercised; for *chastised wit* is an elegant and well-bred, and not unfeminine quality. But *humor*, especially if it degenerate into imitation or mimicry, is very sparingly to be ventured on; for it is so difficult totally to detach it from the suspicion of buffoonery, that a woman will be likely to lose more of that delicacy which is her appropriate grace, than she will gain in the eyes of the judicious, by the most successful display of humor.

But if it be true that some women are too apt to affect brilliancy and display in their own discourse, and to undervalue the more humble pretensions of less showy characters; it must be confessed, also, that some [women] of more ordinary abilities are now and then guilty of the opposite error, and foolishly affect to value themselves on not making use of the understanding they really possess. They exhibit no small satisfaction in ridiculing women of high intellectual endowments, while they exclaim with much affected humility, and much real envy, that "they are thankful *they* are not geniuses." Now, though one is glad to hear gratitude expressed on any occasion, yet the want of sense is really no such great mercy to be thankful for; and it would indicate a better spirit, were they to pray to be enabled to make a right use of the moderate understanding they possess, instead of exposing with a visible pleasure the imaginary or real defects of their more shining acquaintance. Women of the brightest faculties should not only "bear those faculties meekly," but consider it as no derogation cheerfully to fulfill those humbler duties which make up the business of common life, always taking into account the higher responsibility attached to higher gifts. While women of lower attainments should exert to the utmost such abilities as Providence has assigned them, and while they should not deride excellencies which are above their reach, they should not despond at an inferiority which did not depend on themselves; nor, because God has denied them ten talents, should they forget that they are equally responsible for the one he *has* allotted them, but set about devoting that one with humble diligence to the glory of the Giver.

Vanity, however, is not the monopoly of talents: let not a young lady, therefore, fancy that she is humble, merely because she is not ingenious. Humility is not the exclusive privilege of dullness. Folly is as conceited as wit, and ignorance many a time outstrips knowledge in the race of vanity. Equally earnest competitions spring from causes less worthy to excite them than wit and genius. Vanity insinuates itself into the female heart under a variety of unsuspected forms, and seizes on many a little pass which was not thought worth guarding.

Who has not seen as restless emotion agitate the features of an anxious matron, while peace and fame hung trembling in doubtful suspense on the success of a soup or a sauce, on which sentence was about to be pronounced by some consummate critic, as could have been excited by any competition for literary renown, or any struggle for contested wit? Nor was the illustrious hero of Greece more effectually hindered from sleeping by the trophies of Miltiades,[14] than any modish damsel by the eclipsing superiority of some newer decoration exhibited by her more successful friend.

There is another species of vanity in some women which disguises itself under the thin veil of an affected humility; they will accuse themselves of some fault from which they are remarkably exempt, and lament the want of some talent which they are rather notorious for possessing. This is not only a clumsy trap for praise, but there is a disingenuous intention, by renouncing a quality they eminently possess, to gain credit for others in which they are really deficient. All affectation involves a species of deceit. The Apostle, when he enjoins, "not to think of ourselves more highly than we ought,"[15] does not exhort us to think *falsely* of ourselves, but to think "soberly," and it is worth observing that in this injunction he does not use the word *speak*, but *think*, inferring possibly, that it would be safer to *speak* little of ourselves or not at all; for it is so far from being an unequivocal proof of our humility to talk even of our defects, that while we make *self* the subject, in whatever way, self-love contrives to be gratified, and will even be content that our faults should be talked of, rather than that we should not be talked of at all. Some are also attacked with such proud fits of humility, that while they are ready to accuse themselves of almost every sin in the lump, they yet take fire at the imputation of the slightest *individual* fault; and instantly enter upon their own vindication as warmly as if you and not themselves, had brought forward the charge. The truth is, they ventured to condemn themselves in the full confidence that you would contradict them; the last thing they intended was that you should believe them, and they are never so much piqued and disappointed as when they are taken at their word.

Of the various shapes and undefined forms into which vanity branches out in conversation, there is no end. Out of a restless desire to please, grows the spurious desire to astonish; from vanity, as much as from credulity, arises that strong love of the marvelous with which the conversation of the ill-educated abounds. Hence that fondness for dealing in narratives hardly within the compass of possibility. Here vanity has many shades of gratification: those shades will be stronger or weaker, whether the relater chance to have been an eye-witness of the wonder she recounts, or whether she claim only the second-hand renown of its having happened to her friend, or the still remoter celebrity of its having been witnessed only by her friend's friend. But even though that friend only knew the man, who remembered the woman, who actually beheld the thing which is now causing admiration in the company, still *self*, though in a fainter degree, is brought into notice, and the relater contrives in some circuitous way to be connected with the wonder.

To correct this propensity "to elevate and surprise,"[16] it would be well in mixed society to abstain altogether from hazarding stories, which, though they may not be absolutely false, yet lying without the verge of probability, are apt to impeach the credit of the narrator; in whom the very consciousness that she is not believed, excites an increased eagerness to depart still farther from the soberness of truth, and induces a habit of vehement asseveration, which is too often called in to help out a questionable point.[17]

There is another shape, and a very deformed shape it is, in which loquacious vanity shows itself; I mean the betraying of confidence. Though the act be treacherous, yet the fault, in the first instance, is not treachery, but vanity. It does not so often spring from the mischievous desire of divulging a secret, as from the pride of having been trusted with it. It is the secret inclination of mixing *self* with whatever is important. The secret would be of little value, if the revealing it did not serve to intimate *our* connection with it; the pleasure of its having been deposited with us would be nothing, if others may not know it has been so deposited. When we continue to see the variety of serious evils this principle involves, shall we persist in asserting that vanity is a slender mischief?

There is one offence committed in conversation of much too serious a nature to be overlooked, or to be animadverted on without sorrow and indignation: I mean, the habitual and thoughtless profaneness of those who are repeatedly invoking their Maker's name on occasions the most trivial. It is offensive in all its variety of aspects; it is very pernicious in its *effects*; it is a *growing* evil; those who are most guilty of it are from habit hardly conscious when they do it, are not aware of the sin; and for both these reasons, without the admonitions of faithful friendship, little likely to discontinue it. It is utterly INEXCUSABLE; it has none of the palliatives of *temptation* which other vices plead, and in that respect stands distinguished from all others both in its nature and degree of guilt. Like many other sins, however, it is at once cause and effect; it *proceeds* from want of love and reverence to the best of Beings, and *causes* that want both in themselves and others. Yet with all those aggravations, there is, perhaps, hardly any sin so frequently committed, so seldom repented of, and so little guarded against. On the score of *impropriety*, too, it is additionally offensive, as being utterly repugnant to female delicacy, which often affects to be shocked at swearing in a man. Now this species of profaneness is not only swearing, but, perhaps in some respects, swearing of the worst sort; as it is a *direct* breach of an express command, and offends against the *very letter* of that law which says in so many words, THOU SHALT NOT TAKE THE NAME OF THE LORD THY GOD IN VAIN.[18] It offends against *delicacy* and *good breeding*; for those who commit it little think of the pain they are inflicting on the sober mind, which is deeply wounded when it hears the holy name it loves dishonored; and it is as contrary to good breeding to give pain, as it is to true piety to be profane.

I would endeavor to give some faint idea of the grossness of this offence, by an analogy (oh! how inadequate!) with which the feeling heart, even though not seasoned with religion, may be touched. To such I would earnestly say: suppose you had some beloved friend—to put the case still more strongly, a departed friend, a revered parent, perhaps—whose image never occurs without awaking in your bosom sentiments of tender love and gratitude; how would you feel if you heard this honored name *bandied about* with unfeeling familiarity and indecent levity; or at best, thrust into every pause of speech as a vulgar expletive? Does not your affectionate heart recoil at the thought? And yet the hallowed name of your truest Benefactor, your heavenly Father, your best Friend, who gives you all you enjoy, those very friends in whom you so much delight, those very organs with which you dishonor him, is treated with an irreverence, a contempt, a wantonness, with which you cannot bear the very thought or mention of

124

treating a human friend. His name is impiously, is unfeelingly, is ungratefully singled out as the object of decided irreverence, of systematic contempt, of thoughtless levity. It is used indiscriminately to express anger, joy, grief, surprise, impatience; and what is almost still more unpardonable than all, it is wantonly used as a mere unmeaning expletive, which, being excited by no emotion, can have nothing to recommend it, unless it be the pleasure of the sin.

Among the deep, but less obvious mischiefs of conversation, *misrepresentation* must not be overlooked. Self-love is continually at work, to give to all we say a bias in our own favor. The counteraction of this fault should be set about in the earliest stages of education. If young persons have not been discouraged in the natural, but evil propensity to relate every dispute they have had with others to their own advantage; if they have not been trained to the duty of doing justice even to those with whom they are at variance; if they have not been led to aim at a complete impartiality in their little narratives, and instructed never to take advantage of the absence of the other party, in order to make the story lean to their own side more than the truth will admit; how shall we in advanced life look for correct habits, for unprejudiced representations, for fidelity, accuracy, and unbiased justice?

Yet, how often in society, otherwise respectable, are we pained with narrations in which prejudice warps, and self-love blinds! How often do we see that withholding part of a truth answers the worst ends of a falsehood! How often regret the unfair turn given to a business, by placing a sentiment in one point of view, which the speaker had used in another! the letter of truth preserved where its spirit is violated! a superstitious exactness scrupulously maintained in the underparts of a detail, in order to impress such an idea of integrity as shall gain credit, while the leading principle is designedly misstated! nay, a new character given to a fact by a different look, tone, or emphasis, which alters it as much as words could have done! the false impression of a sermon conveyed, when we do not like the preacher, or when through him we wish to make religion itself ridiculous! the avoiding of literal untruths, while the mischief is better effected by the unfair quotation of a passage divested of its context! the bringing together detached portions of a subject, and making those parts ludicrous when connected, which were perfect in their distinct position! the insidious use made of a sentiment by representing it as the *opinion* of him who had only brought it forward in order to expose it! the relating opinions which had merely been put hypothetically, as the avowed principles of him we would discredit! that subtle falsehood which is so made to incorporate with a certain quantity of truth, that the most skillful moral chemist cannot analyze or separate them! for a good *misrepresenter* knows that a successful lie must have a certain infusion of truth, or it will not go down. All that indefinable ambiguity and equivocation, all that prudent deceit, which is rather implied than expressed, those more delicate artifices of the school of Loyola and Chesterfield,[19] which allow us when we dare not deny a truth, yet so to disguise and discolor it, that the truth we relate shall not resemble the truth we heard! These and all the thousand shades of simulation and dissimulation will be carefully guarded against in the conversation of vigilant Christians.

Again, it is surprising to mark the common deviations from strict veracity which spring, not from enmity to truth, not from intentional deceit, not from malevolence or envy, or the least design to injure, but from mere levity, habitual inattention, and a current notion that it is not worthwhile to be correct in small things. But here the doctrine of habits comes in with great force, and in that view no error is small. The cure of this disease in its more inveterate stages being next to impossible, its prevention ought to be one of the earliest objects of education.

The grievous fault of gross and obvious detraction, which infects conversation, has been so heavily and so justly condemned by divines and moralists that the subject is exhausted. But there is an error of an opposite complexion, which we have before noticed, and against which the peculiar temper of the times requires that young ladies of a better cast should be guarded. From the narrowness of their own sphere of observation, they are sometimes addicted to accuse of uncharitableness, that distinguishing judgment which, resulting from a sound penetration and a zeal for truth, forbids persons of a very correct principle to be indiscriminately prodigal of commendation without inquiry, and without distinction. There is an affectation of candor, which is almost as mischievous as calumny itself; nay, if it be less injurious in its individual application, it is, perhaps, more alarming in its general principle, as it lays waste the strong senses which separate good from evil. They know (though they sometimes calumniate) that calumny is wrong; but they have not been told that flattery is wrong, also; and youth, being apt to fancy that the direct contrary to wrong must necessarily be right, are apt to be driven into violent extremes. The dread of being only suspected of one fault, makes them actually guilty of the opposite; and to avoid the charge of harshness or of envy, they plunge into insincerity and falsehood. In this they are actuated either by an unsound judgment, or an unsound principle.

In this age of high-minded independence, when our youth are apt to set up for themselves, and every man is too much disposed to be his own legislator, without looking to the established law of the land as his standard, and to set up for his own divine, without looking to the revealed will of God as his rule, by a candor equally vicious with our vanity, we are also complacently led to give the latitude we take; and it is become too frequent a practice in the mouths of our tolerating young ladies, when speaking of their more erring and misled acquaintance, to offer for them this flimsy vindication: "That what they do is right, if it appear right to them," [or] "If they see the thing in that light, and act up to it with sincerity, they cannot be materially wrong." But the standard of truth, justice, and religion must neither be elevated nor depressed in order to accommodate it to actual circumstances; it must never be lowered, to palliate error, to justify folly, or to vindicate vice. Good-natured young people often speak favorably of unworthy, or extravagantly of common characters, from one of these motives: either their own views of excellence are low; or they speak respectfully of the undeserving, to purchase for themselves the reputation of tenderness and generosity; or they lavish unsparing praise on almost all alike, in the usurious hope of buying back universal commendation in return; or, in those captivating characters in which the simple and masculine language of truth is sacrificed to the jargon of affected softness, and in which smooth and pliant manners are substituted for intrinsic worth, the inexperienced are too apt to *suppose* virtues, to *forgive* vices. But they should carefully guard against the error of making manner the criterion of merit, and of giving unlimited credit to strangers for possessing every perfection, only because they bring unto company the engaging exterior of urbanity and alluring gentleness. They should also remember that it is an easy, but not an honest way of obtaining the praise of candor, to get into the soft and popular habit of saying of all their acquaintance, when speaking of them, that they are so good! True Christian candor conceals faults; but it does not invent virtues. It tenderly forbears to expose the evil which may belong to a character; but it dares not ascribe to it the good which does not exist. To correct this propensity to false judgment and insincerity, it would be well to bear in mind, that while every good action, come from what source it may, and every good quality, be it found in whomsoever it will, deserves its fair proportion of distinct and willing commendation, yet no character is good, in the true sense of the word, which is not religious.

In fine—to recapitulate what has been said, with some additional hints: study to promote both intellectual and moral improvement in conversation; labor to bring into it a disposition to bear with others, and to be watchful over yourself; keep out of sight any prominent talent of your own, which, if indulged, might discourage or oppress the feeble-minded; and try to bring their modest virtues into notice. If you know any one present to possess any particular weakness or infirmity, never exercise your wit by maliciously inventing occasions which may lead her to expose or betray it; but give as favorable a turn as you can to the follies which appear, and kindly help her to keep the rest out of sight. Never gratify your own humor, by hazarding what you suspect may wound anyone present in their persons, connections, professions in life, or religious opinions; and do not forget to examine whether the laugh your wit has raised be never bought at this expense. Give credit to those who, without your kindness, will get none; do not talk *at* any one whom you dare not talk *to*, unless from motives in which the golden rule will bear you out. Seek neither to shine nor to triumph; and if you seek to please, take care that it be in order to convert the influence you may gain by pleasing, to the good of others. Cultivate true politeness, for it grows out of true principle, and is consistent with the gospel of Christ; but avoid those feigned attentions which are not stimulated by goodwill, and those stated professions of fondness which are not dictated by esteem. Remember that the pleasure of being thought amiable by strangers may be bought too dear, if it be bought at the expense of truth and simplicity; remember that simplicity is the first charm in manner, as truth is in mind, and could truth make herself visible, she would appear invested in simplicity.

Remember, also, that true good nature is the soul, of which politeness is only the garb. It is not that artificial quality which is taken up by many when they go into society, in order to charm those whom it is not their particular business to please, and is laid down when they return home to those to whom to appear amiable is a real duty. It is not that fascinating but deceitful softness which, after having acted over a hundred scenes of the most lively sympathy and tender interest with every slight acquaintance, after having exhausted every phrase of feeling for the trivial sicknesses or petty sorrows of the multitudes who are scarcely known, leaves it doubtful whether a grain of real feeling or genuine sympathy be reserved for the dearest connections, and which dismisses a woman to her immediate friends with little affection, and to her own family with little attachment.

True good nature, that which alone deserves the name, is not a holiday ornament, but an everyday habit. It does not consist in servile complacence, or dishonest flattery, or affected sympathy, or unqualified assent, or unwarrantable compliance, or eternal smiles. Before it can be allowed to rank with the virtues, it must be wrought up from a humour into a principle, from an occasional disposition into a habit. It must be the result of an equal and well-governed mind, not the start of casual gaiety, the trick of designing vanity, or the whim of capricious fondness. It is compounded of kindness, forbearance, forgiveness, and self-denial: "it seeketh not its own,"[20] but must be capable of making continual sacrifices of its own tastes, humours, and self-love; but among the sacrifices it makes, it must never include its integrity. Politeness on the one hand, and insensibility on the other, assume its name, and wear its honors; but they assume the honors of a triumph, without the merit of a victory; for politeness subdues nothing, and insensibility has nothing to subdue. Good nature, of the true cast, and under the foregoing regulations, is above all price in the common intercourse of domestic society; for an ordinary quality, which is constantly brought into action by the perpetually recurring though minute events of daily life, is of higher value than more brilliant qualities which are more seldom called into use, as small pieces of ordinary current coin are of more importance in the commerce of the world than the medals of the antiquary. And, indeed, Christianity has given that new turn to the character of all the virtues, that perhaps it is the best test of the excellence of many, that they have little brilliancy in them. The Christian religion has degraded some splendid qualities from the rank they held, and elevated those which are obscure into distinction.

Notes for *Strictures on the Modern System of Female Education*

This excerpt is taken from the Library of Congress copy of Hannah More, *Strictures on the Modern System of Female Education* (London, 1799), 2:43–96 (LC 1421.M78 1799a). I have modernized spelling and regularized punctuation.

1. John Milton, *Paradise Lost* 2.1.561: in hell, some of the fallen angels pretend to escape their pain in theological dispute, "And found no end, in wand'ring mazes lost."

2. Bangorian controversy: a fierce theological controversy sparked by a sermon preached before the king in 1717 by Benjamin Hoadly, bishop of Bangor, against the authority of a worldly church.

3. Jansenists were followers of the Roman Catholic reform movement begun by the Dutch theologian Cornelis Jansen (1585–1638), which was particularly popular in seventeenth-century France, especially among the Port-Royal scholars and clergy.

4. Quintilian was a famed first-century Roman rhetorical theorist whose *Institutio Oratorium* was used to judge good speaking and writing for all Europeans with a Latin education for hundreds of years. "Aristotle's clock" refers to unity of time (that the events of a play should take place within twenty-four hours), attributed by eighteenth-century aesthetics to Aristotle, although the only unity Aristotle in the *Poetics* stressed was unity of action.

5. A variant of Blaise Pascal, *Les Pensées de Pascal Oeuvres Complètes* (Paris: Bibliothèque de la Pleiades/nrf Gallimard, 1954) 14:1091—"Diseur de bons mots, mauvais caractère"; Jean de la Bruyère misquotes this passage in *Caractères* with "diseurs" plural, but not "caractère" and still "mauvais" instead of "fades"; see *Oeuvres* (Paris: Bibliothèque de la Pleiade/nrf Galimard, 1951) 7:241.

6. William Pitt (1759–1806), prime minister under George III, and Charles James Fox (1749–1806), head of the opposition, were lifelong rivals.

7. In the Bible "Baal" is a Canaanite deity that represents the most heinous form of idolatry.

8. A "magic lantern" was an early form of optical projector that displayed pictures on a wall.

9. Alexander Pope, "Essay on Criticism," l. 327.

10. An *appliqué* is a cutout piece of cloth sewn onto another piece to make a design or picture; "stuff" refers to the cloth that is the background.

11. In a footnote More explains, "The writer cannot be supposed desirous of depreciating the value of those many beautiful periodical essays which adorn our language. But, perhaps, it might be better to regale the mind with them singly, at different times, than to read at the same sitting a multitude of short pieces on dissimilar and unconnected topics, *by way of getting through the book*."

12. "The Apostle" is Paul in James 1:19: "Wherefore, my beloved brethren, let every man be swift to hear, slow to speak, slow to wrath."

13. "The great Roman orator" is Cicero. This remark on silence does not occur in Cicero's rhetorical works.

14. Miltiades (c. 550–489 B.C.E.) was the general who commanded the Greeks who defeated the Persians at the battle of Marathon.

15. Paul is the Apostle who writes in Romans 12:3, "For I say, through the grace given unto me, to every man that is among you, not to think of himself more highly than he ought to think; but to think soberly, according as God hath dealt to every man the measure of faith."

16. The note by More or her printer reads "*The Rehearsal*" and refers to the 1671 play by George Villiers, Duke of Buckingham, in which a character complains about "the new kind of Wits," "fellows that scorn to imitate Nature; but are given altogether to elevate and surprise" (Act I, scene i).

17. In a footnote More explains, "This is also a good rule in composition. An event, though it may actually have happened, yet if it be out of the reach of probability, or contrary to the common course of nature, will seldom be chosen as a subject by a writer of good taste; for he knows that a probable fiction will interest the feelings more than an unlikely truth. Verisimilitude is indeed the poet's truth, but the truth of the moralist is of a more sturdy growth."

18. Exodus 20:7, the Third Commandment.

19. Ignatius Loyola (1495–1556) founded the Society of Jesus, or the Jesuits, who became known as great equivocators in England during the Reformation. More assumes her audience shares her anti-Catholic biases. Philip Stanhope, Earl of Chesterfield (1694–1773), statesman and wit, was known for the worldliness of his advice in the letters to his illegitimate son, published after his death.

20. According to Paul, 1 Corinthians 13:5, it is charity that "seeketh not her own."

Maria Edgeworth

1768–1849

Of Anglo-Irish descent, Maria Edgeworth was born on January 1, 1768. Her mother died when she was very young. Her father, Richard Lovell Edgeworth, was frequently absent, and her stepmother sent her away to school. But when she was brought home from school at age fourteen to help with the many children, Maria served as her father's secretary and accountant, gradually becoming his favorite and his intellectual companion. Influenced by Joseph Priestley, Maria's father was famous for his works on education and the nature of the mind. His pragmatic philosophy of education emphasized children's reasoning capacity, the utility of subjects taught, and the association of ideas. At various times, and especially in her early twenties, Maria was taken on tours of England and Europe with the goal of meeting an eligible young man to marry, but she refused the one offer she had. The Edgeworth family was liberal and supported the French Revolution, as well as education for the poor and religious tolerance in Ireland, where they lived.

By age twelve, Edgeworth was writing short stories and doing translations from French. She had enormous success in the 1790s with children's stories inculcating her father's principles of education, beginning with *The Parents' Assistant* in 1796. *Early Lessons* (1801) begins a series of textbooks for children according to her father's theories, collections that illustrate scientific or moral maxims. She also wrote plays. In the early nineteenth century, Edgeworth was the most popular British novelist—more popular than Jane Austen or Sir Walter Scott, who were her contemporaries. She was most famous for her Irish novels, *Castle Rackrent* (1800), *The Absentee* (1812), and *Ormond* (1817). With her royalties she supported the family (and especially her wastrel brother). She spent some time in London society, but her unpopular father, who accompanied her, prevented her from becoming a center of literary society. The advantage and disadvantage of her father's thorough editing of all her work are much debated in current criticism; the most recent work suggests that the family collaborated in Maria's works during the stages of planning and editing—not only her father, but also her stepmother, Harriet, and her sisters. From the 1820s on, sensitive to critics, Edgeworth wrote mainly for children. Edgeworth died on May 22, 1849.

Maria Edgeworth's "An Essay on the Noble Science of Self-Justification" seems to be descended from satires that parodied conduct book advice, like Jane Collier's *An Essay on the Art of Ingeniously Tormenting with Proper Rules for the Exercise of That Art* (1753) and Jonathan Swift's *Directions to Servants* (1745). Edgeworth satirizes Enlightenment men's rhetoric, shrewish wives, and the traditional British requirement of feminine modesty, silence, and obedience. In a parody of an Enlightenment rhetorical treatise, Edgeworth divides her topic into the two categories of defensive and offensive strategies, and she argues that her aim is to "reduce" her art "to a science" by considering its "axioms" or "maxims." By placing the nagging and blaming of husbands in this traditional structure of rhetorical treatise, Edgeworth highlights the manipulative nature of all rhetoric. In addition, Edgeworth runs through, with delightful superficiality and solemn pompousness, all the catchwords of enlightenment rhetoric. In her treatment of wives' defending themselves from husbands' blame, she mockingly parodies the categories of voice taught in elocution, the attack on the opponents' weaknesses in appeals to ethos, taste as a standard, the requirement of agreeableness for polite conversation, sophistic exercises on either side of an issue (wives should always assume the wrong side, to stay in practice in debate), wit and judgment as qualities of the good speaker, and the Augustinian dictum that the ignorant yet may speak well from God's inspiration. She shows herself most witty when she attacks the sacred idol of Enlightenment rhetoric and aesthetics, the sublime, defined, according to Edgeworth, as "that happy imagination which shall make you believe all you fear and all you invent."

At the same time that she radically critiques the tradition of men's enlightenment rhetoric, Edgeworth also satirizes the nagging wife, a commonplace goal of satire for centuries before her. The means of Edgeworth's satire is novel, however, for she attributes design and technical training to the shrew. Edgeworth's shrew is a craftswoman who turns a husband's criticism of her faults into proof that he no longer finds her agreeable (the thrill is gone!). Her shrew is never caught without an ambiguity and refuses to define on principle. Her shrew unrepentantly arouses her husband's temper or assumes the pose of injured innocence, and milks the audiences with her graciousness by quitting the field whenever she sees her opponent about to triumph—"I give it up—I won't dispute trifles!"

However, Edgeworth's treatise is not finally conservative, condemning wives, since her wives resist conventional strictures. Edgeworth's model is Xantippe, fabled shrewish wife of Socrates. Edgeworth's Xantippe, however, is sister to Aspasia: "In addition to the patience, philosophy, and other good things which Socrates learned from his wife, perhaps she taught him this mode of reason"—by "interrogatories artfully" leading "an unsuspicious reasoner . . . to your own conclusion." Here Edgeworth amusingly turns the manipulative quality of Socratean dialectic against all the men who champion it by attributing its origin to Socrates's shrewish wife.

By the end of Edgeworth's treatise, we have learned not to take virtues and vices at face value, especially the virtues and vices associated by her society with gender. A woman doesn't need to give reasons, Edgeworth innocently claims, in a society where "Silence is the ornament of your sex." Although it is "the duty of a wife to submit," Edgeworth points out, she yet may have her own opinion. The satire of men's rhetoric and women's recriminations ends climactically on the final cause, gender restrictions: "may your husbands rue the hour when first they made you promise 'to obey.'" At the last, shrews ironically turn out to be women who are required to obey against their better judgment and so become angry at an unjust society.

For further information see the standard biography, Marilyn Butler, *Maria Edgeworth: A Literary Biography* (Oxford: Clarendon, 1972); Elizabeth Harden, *Maria Edgeworth* (Boston: Twayne Publishers, 1984); and Jane Donawerth, "Poaching on Men's Philosophies of Rhetoric: Eighteenth- and Nineteenth-Century Rhetorical Theory by Women," *Philosophy and Rhetoric* 33, no. 3 (2000): 243–58.

From "An Essay on the Noble Science of Self-Justification" (1795)

For which an eloquence that aims to vex
With native tropes of anger arms the sex.
Parnell[1]

131

Endowed, as the fair sex indisputably are, with a natural genius for the invaluable art of self-justification, it may not be displeasing to them to see its rising perfections evinced by an attempt to reduce it to a science. Possessed, as are all the fair daughters of Eve, of an hereditary propensity, transmitted to them undiminished through succeeding generations, to be "Soon moved with the slightest touch of blame,"[2] very little precept and practice will confirm them in the habit, and instruct them in all the maxims of self-justification.

Candid pupil, you will readily accede to my first and fundamental axiom—that a lady can do no wrong. But simple as this maxim may appear, and suited to the level of the meanest capacity, the talent of applying it on all the important but, more especially, on all the most trivial occurrences of domestic life, so as to secure private peace and public dominion, has hitherto been monopolized by the female adepts in the art.

Excuse me for insinuating by this expression, that there may yet be amongst you some novices. To these, if there be any such, I principally address myself.

And now, lest fired with ambition you lose all by aiming at too much, let me explain and limit my first principle, "That you can do no wrong." You must be aware that real perfection is beyond the reach of mortals; nor would I have you aim at it; indeed, it is not in any degree necessary to our purpose. You have heard of the established belief in human infallibility which prevailed not many centuries ago, but since that happy period is past, leave the opinions of men to their natural perversity; their actions are the best test of their faith. Instead, then, of a belief in your infallibility, endeavor to enforce implicit submission to your authority. This will give you infinitely less trouble, and will answer your purpose as well.

Right and wrong, if we go to the foundation of things, are, as casuists tell us, really words of very dubious signification, perpetually varying with custom and fashion, and to be referred to and adjusted, ultimately, by no other standards but opinion and force. Obtain power, then, by all means. Power is the law of man; it is his law and yours.

But to return from a frivolous disquisition about right, let me teach you the art of defending the wrong. After having thus pointed out to you the "glorious end" of your labors, I must now instruct you in the equally "glorious means."

For the advantage of my subject, I beg to consider you all, ladies, as married; but those who have not as yet the good fortune to have that common enemy, a husband, to combat, may in the mean time practice my precepts upon their fathers, brothers, and female friends—with caution, however, lest by discovering their arms too soon, they preclude themselves from the power of using them to the fullest advantage hereafter. I therefore recommend it to them to prefer, with a philosophical moderation, the future to the present.

Timid brides, you have, probably, hitherto been addressed as angels—prepare for the time when you shall again become mortal. Take the alarm at the first approach of blame, at the first hint of a discovery that you are anything less than infallible. Contradict, debate, justify, recriminate, rage, weep, swoon, do anything but yield to conviction.

I take it for granted that you have already acquired sufficient command of voice; you need not study its compass. Going beyond its pitch has a peculiarly happy effect upon some occasions. But are you voluble enough to drown all sense in a torrent of words? Can you be loud enough to overpower the voice of all who shall attempt to interrupt or contradict you? Are you mistress of the petulant, the peevish, and the sullen tones? Have you practiced the sharpness which provokes reply, and the continual monotony which effectually precludes it, by setting your adversary to sleep? An event which is always to be considered as decisive of the victory, or at least as reducing it to a drawn battle—you and Morpheus[3] divide the prize.

Thus prepared for an engagement, you will next, if you have not already done it, study the weak part of the character of your enemy—your husband, I mean. If he be a man of high spirit, jealous of command, and impatient of control, one who decides for himself and is little troubled with the insanity of minding what the world says of him, you must proceed with extreme circumspection. You must not dare to provoke the combined forces of the enemy to a regular engagement, but harass him with perpetual petty skirmishes; in these, though you gain little at a time, you will gradually weary the patience, and break the spirit of your opponent. If he be a man of spirit, he must also be generous; and what man of generosity will contend for trifles with a woman who submits to him in all affairs of consequence, who is in his power, who is weak, and who loves him?

⸜⸜⸜

But such a man as I have described, besides being as generous as he is brave, will probably be of an active temper. Then you have an inestimable advantage, for he will set a high value upon a thing for which you have none—time. He will acknowledge the force of your arguments merely from a dread of their length; he will yield to you in trifles, particularly in trifles which do not militate against his authority, not out of regard for you, but for his time. For what man can prevail upon himself to debate three hours about what could be as well decided in three minutes?

Lest amongst infinite variety, the difficulty of immediate selection should at first perplex you, let me point out that matters of *taste* will afford you, of all others, the most ample and incessant subjects of debate. Here you have no criterion to appeal to. Upon the same principle, next to matters of taste, points of opinion will afford the most constant exercise to your talents. Here you will have an opportunity of citing the opinions of all the living and dead you have ever known, besides the dear privilege of repeating continually: "Nay, you never must allow that," or, "You can't deny this, for it's the universal opinion—everybody says so! everybody thinks so! I wonder to hear you express such an opinion! Nobody but yourself is of that way of thinking"—with innumerable other phrases with which a slight attention to polite conversation will furnish you. This mode of opposing authority to argument, and assertion to proof, is of such universal utility, that I pray you to practice it.

If the point in dispute especially be some opinion relative to your character or disposition, allow in general that you are sure you have a great many faults but, to every specific charge reply, "Well, I am sure I don't know, but I did not think that was one of my faults! Nobody ever accused me of that before! Nay, I was always remarkable for the contrary, at least before I was acquainted with you, sir. In my own family, ask any of my own friends;[4] ask any of them; they must know me best."

But if instead of attacking the material parts of your character, your husband should merely presume to advert to your manners, to some slight personal habit which might be made more agreeable to him, prove, in the first place, that it is his fault that it is not agreeable to him: his eyes are changed, or opened. But it may perhaps have been a matter almost of indifference to him, 'til you undertook its defense—then make it of consequence by rising in eagerness in proportion to the insignificance of your object; if he can draw consequences, this will be an excellent lesson—if you are so tender of blame in the veriest trifle, how unimpeachable must you be in matters of importance. As to personal habits, begin by denying that you

133

have any; as all personal habits, if they have been of any long standing, must have become involuntary, the unconscious culprit may assert her innocence without hazarding her veracity.

However, if you happen to be detected in the very fact, and a person cries, "Now, now, you are doing it!" submit. But declare at the same moment that it is the very first time in your whole life, you were ever known to be guilty of it; that therefore it can be no habit, and of course no ways reprehensible.

Extend also the rage for vindication to all the objects which the most remotely concern you; take even inanimate objects under your protection. Your dress, your furniture, your property—everything which is or has been yours—defend, and this upon the principles of the soundest philosophy—these things all compose a part of your personal merit; all that connected the most distantly with your idea gives pleasure or pain to others,[5] becomes an object of blame or praise, and consequently claims your support or vindication.

In the course of the management of your house, children, family, and affairs, probably some few errors of omission or commission may strike your husband's pervading eye; but these errors, admitting them to be errors, you will never if you please allow to be charged to any deficiency in memory, judgment, or activity, on your part. There are surely people enough around you to divide and share the blame—send it from one to another, 'til at last, by universal rejection, it is proved to belong to nobody. You will say, however, that facts remain unalterable, and that in some unlucky instance, in the changes and chances of human affairs, you may be proved to have been to blame. Some stubborn evidence may appear against you, an eyewitness perhaps. Still you may prove an alibi, or balance the evidence. There is nothing equal to balancing evidence; doubt is, you know, the most philosophic state of the human mind, and it will be kind of you to preserve it in the breast of your husband.

Indeed, the short method, of denying absolutely all blameable facts, I should recommend to pupils as the best; and if in the beginning of their career as justification, they may startle at this mode, let them depend upon it, that in their future practice it must become perfectly familiar. The nice distinction of simulation and dissimulation depends but on the trick of a syllable—palliation and extenuation are universally allowable in self-defense; prevarication inevitably follows, and falsehood "is but in the next degree."[6]

Yet I would not destroy this nicety of conscience too soon; it may be of use. In your first setting out, you must establish credit; in proportion to your credit will be the value of your future asseverations. In the meantime, however, argument and debate are allowable to the most rigid moralist. You can never perjure yourself by swearing to a false opinion.

I come now to the art of reasoning—don't be alarmed at the name of reasoning, fair pupils; I will explain to you its meaning.

If instead of the fiery-tempered being I formerly described, you should fortunately be connected with a man who, having formed a justly high opinion of your sex, should propose to treat you as his equal and who, in any little dispute which might arise between you, should desire no other arbiter than reason, triumph in his mistaken candor, regularly appeal to the decision of reason at the beginning of every contest, and deny its jurisdiction at the conclusion. I take it for granted that you will be on the wrong side of every question and, indeed, in general I advise you to choose the wrong side of an argument to defend; while you are young in the science, it will afford the best exercise and, as you improve, the best display of your talents.

134

If, then, reasonable pupils, you would succeed in argument, follow pretty nearly these instructions.

Begin by preventing, if possible, the specific statement of any position or, if reduced to it, use the most *general terms*.

Use the happy ambiguity which all languages, and which most philosophers allow. Above all things, shun definitions: they will prove fatal to you, for two persons of sense and candor who define their terms cannot argue long without either convincing, or being convinced, or parting in equal good humor; to prevent which, go over and over the same ground, wander as wide as possible from the point, but always with a view to return at last precisely to the same spot from which you set out.

I should remark to you that the choice of your weapons is a circumstance much to be attended to: choose always those which your adversary cannot use. If your husband is a man of wit, you will, of course, undervalue a talent which is never connected with judgment: for your part, you do not pretend to contend with him on wit. But if he be a sober-minded man who will go link by link along the chain of an argument, follow him at first, 'til he grows so intent that he does not perceive whether you follow him or not; then slide back to your own station and, when with perverse patience he has at last reached the last link of the chain, with one electric shock of wit, make him quit his hold, and strike him to the ground in an instant. Depend upon the sympathy of the spectators, for to one who can understand *reason*, you will find ten who admire *wit*.

But if you should not be blessed with a ready wit, if demonstration should in the meantime stare you in the face, do not be in the least alarmed; anticipate the blow which you could neither foresee nor prevent. While you have it yet in your power, rise with becoming magnanimity, and cry, "I give it up! I give it up! La! let us say no more about it. I do so hate disputing about trifles. I give it up!" Before an explanation on the word "trifle" can take place, quit the room with flying colors.

If you are a woman of sentiment and eloquence, you have advantages of which I scarcely need apprise you. From the understanding of a man, you have always an appeal to his heart; or, if not, to his *affection*, to his *weakness*. If you have the good fortune to be married to a weak man, always choose the moment to argue with him when you have a full audience. Trust to the sublime power of numbers; it will be of use even to excite your own enthusiasm in debate. Then, as the scene advances, talk of his cruelty and your sensibility,[7] and sink with becoming woe into the pathos of *injured innocence*.

Besides the heart and the weakness of your opponent, you have still another chance, in ruffling his *temper*, which, in the course of a long conversation, you will have a fair opportunity of trying; and if, for philosophers will sometimes grow warm in the defense of truth, he should grow absolutely angry, you will in an inverse proportion grow calm, and wonder at his rage, though you well know it has been created by your own provocation. The bystanders, seeing anger without any adequate cause, will all be of your side. Nothing provokes an irascible man, interested in debate and possessed of an opinion of his own eloquence, so much as to see the attention of his hearers go from him. You will, then, when he flatters himself that he has just fixed your eye with his very best argument, suddenly grow absent: your house affairs must call you hence—or you have directions to give to your children—or the room is too hot, or too cold—the window must be opened, or door shut, or the candle wants snuffing. Nay, without these interruptions, the simple motion of your eye may provoke a speaker: a butterfly, or the figure in a carpet may engage your attention in preference to him; or, if these objects be absent, the simple averting your eye, looking through the window in quest of outward objects, will show that your mind has been abstracted, and will display to him at least your wish of not attending. He may, however, possibly have lost the habit of watching your eye for approbation; then you may assault his ear. If all other resources fail, beat with your foot that dead march to the spirits, that incessant tattoo, which so well deserves its name. Marvelous must be the patience of the much-enduring man, whom some or other of these devices does not provoke. Slight causes often produce great effects; the simple scratching of a pick-ax, properly applied to certain veins in a mine, will cause the most dreadful explosions.

Hitherto we have only professed to teach the defensive; let me now recommend to you the offensive part of the art of justification. As a supplement to reasoning comes recrimination: the pleasure of proving you are right is surely incomplete 'til you have proved that your adversary is wrong. This might have been a secondary, let it now become a primary object with you; rest your own defense on it for further security. You are no longer to consider yourself as obliged to deny, palliate, argue, or declaim, but simply justify yourself by criminating another; all merit, you know, is judged by comparison. In the art of recrimination, your memory will be of the highest service to you; for you are to open and keep an account current of all the faults, mistakes, neglects, [and] unkindnesses of those you live with. These you state against your own (I need not tell you that the balance will always be in your favor). In stating matters of opinion, produce the words of the very same person which passed days, months, years before, in contradiction to what he is then saying. By displacing [and] disjointing words and sentences, by misunderstanding the whole or quoting only a part of what has been said, you may convict any man of inconsistency, particularly if he be a man of genius and feeling, for he speaks generally from the impulse of the moment, and of all others can the least bear to be charged with paradoxes. So far for a husband. Recriminating is also of sovereign use in the quarrels of friends; no friend is so perfectly equable, so ardent in affection, so nice in punctilio, as never to offend. Then note his faults and con them by rote. Say you can forgive, but you can never forget—and surely it is much more generous to forgive and remember than to forgive and forget. On every new alarm, call the unburied ghosts from former fields of battle; range them in tremendous array, call them one by one to witness against the conscience of your enemy, and ere[8] the battle is begun, take from them all courage to engage.

There is one case I must observe to you, in which recrimination has peculiar poignancy. If you have had it in your power to confer obligations on anyone, never cease reminding them of it, and let them feel that you have acquired an indefeasible right to reproach them without a possibility of their retorting. It is a maxim with some sentimental people, "To treat their servants as if they were their friends in distress." I have observed that people of this cast make themselves amends, by treating their friends in distress as if they were their servants. Apply this maxim—you may do it in a thousand ways, especially in company. In general conversation, where everyone is supposed to be on a footing, if any of your humble companions should presume to hazard an opinion contrary to yours, and should modestly begin with "I think—" look as the man did when he said to his servant, "You think! Sir—what business have you to think?"

Never fear to lose a friend by the habits which I recommend. Reconciliations, as you have often heard it said, are the cement of friendship; therefore, friends should quarrel to strengthen their attachment, and offend each other for the pleasure of being reconciled.

I beg pardon for digressing—I was, I believe, talking of your husband, not of your friends—but I have gone far out of my way.

If in your debates with your husband, you should want "Eloquence to vex him,"[9] the dull prolixity of narration, joined to the complaining monotony of voice which I formerly recommended, will supply its place, and have the desired effect: Morpheus will prove propitious. Then, ever and anon, as the soporific charm begins to work, rouse him with interrogatories, such as, "Did not you say so?" "Don't you remember?" "Only answer me that!"

By the by, interrogatories artfully put may lead an unsuspicious reasoner, you know, always to your own conclusion. In addition to the patience, philosophy, and other good things which Socrates learned from his wife, perhaps she taught him this mode of reasoning.[10]

But after all, the precepts of art, and even the natural susceptibility of your tempers will avail you little in the sublime of our science, if you cannot command that ready enthusiasm which will make you enter into the part you are acting, that happy imagination which shall make you believe all you fear and all you invent.

Who is there amongst you who cannot or who will not justify when they are accused? Vulgar talent! The sublime of our science is to justify before we are accused. There is no reptile so vile but what will turn when it is trodden on; but of a nicer sense and nobler species are those whom nature has endowed with antennae, which perceive and withdraw at the distant approach of danger. Allow me another allusion; similes cannot be crowded too close for a female taste, and analogy, I have heard, my fair pupils, is your favorite mode of reasoning. The sensitive plant is too vulgar an allusion; but if the truth of modern naturalists may be depended upon, there is a plant which, instead of receding timidly, like the sensitive plant, from the intrusive touch, angrily protrudes its venomous juices upon all who presume to meddle with it. Don't you think that this plant would be your fittest emblem? Let me, however, recommend it to you, nice souls, who of the Mimosa kind, "Fear the dark cloud, and feel the coming storm,"[11] to take the utmost precaution, lest the same susceptibility, which you cherish as the dear means to torment others, should insensibly become a torment to yourselves.

Distinguish, then, between sensibility and susceptibility, between the anxious solicitude not to give offence, and the captious eagerness of vanity to prove that it ought not to have been taken; distinguish between the desire of praise and the horror of blame; can any two things be more different than the wish to improve, and the wish to demonstrate that you have never been to blame? Observe, I only wish you to distinguish these things in your own minds. I would by no means advise you to discontinue the laudable practice of confounding them perpetually in speaking to others.

When you have nearly exhausted human patience in explaining, justifying, vindicating—when, in spite of all the pains you have taken, you have more than half betrayed your own vanity, you have a never-failing resource, in paying tribute to that of your opponent, as thus: "I am sure you must be sensible that I should never take so much pains to justify myself if I were indifferent to your opinion. I know that I ought not to disturb myself with such trifles, but nothing is a trifle to me which concerns you. I confess I am too anxious to please. I know it's a fault, but I can't cure myself of it now. Too quick sensibility, I am conscious, is the defect of my disposition; it would be happier for me if I could be more indifferent, I know." Who could be so brutal as to blame so amiable, so candid a creature? Who would not submit to be tormented with kindness?

When once then your captive condescends to be flattered by such arguments as these, your power is fixed. Your future triumphs can be bounded only by your own moderation; they are at once secured and justified.

Forbear not, then, happy pupils, but, arrived at the summit of power, give a full scope to your genius, nor trust to genius alone. To exercise in all its extent your privileged dominion, you must acquire, or rather you must pretend to have acquired, infallible skill in the noble art of physiognomy. Immediately the thoughts as well as the words of your subjects are exposed to your inquisition.

Words may flatter you, but the countenance never can deceive you; the eyes are the windows of the soul, and through them you are to watch what passes in the inmost recesses of the heart. There, if you discern the slightest ideas of doubt, blame, or displeasure, if you discover the slightest symptoms of revolt, take the alarm instantly. Conquerors must maintain their conquests, and how easily can they do this, who hold a secret correspondence with the minds of the vanquished? Be your own spies, then. From the looks, gestures, slightest motions of your enemies, you are to form an alphabet, a language, intelligible only to yourselves, yet by which you shall condemn them, always remembering that in sound policy, suspicion justifies punishment. In vain, when you accuse your friends of the high treason of blaming you, in vain let them plead their innocence, even of the intention: they did not say words which could be tortured into such a meaning. No, but "they looked daggers, though they used none."[12] And of this you are to be the sole judge, though there were fifty witnesses to the contrary. How should indifferent spectators pretend to know the countenance of your friend as well as you do—you that have a nearer, a dearer interest in attending to it? So accurate have been your observations that no thought of their soul escapes you; nay, you often can tell even what they are going to think of.

The science of divination certainly claims your attention; beyond the past and the present, it shall extend your dominion over the future; from slight words, half-finished sentences, from silence itself, you shall draw your omens and auguries: "I am sure you were going to say," or "I know such a thing was a sign you were inclined to be displeased with me." In the ardor of innocence, the culprit, to clear himself from such imputations, incurs the imputation of a greater offence. Suppose to prove that you were mistaken, to prove that he could not have meant to blame you, he should declare, that at the moment you mention, you were quite foreign to his thoughts, as he was not thinking at all about you.

Then, in truth, you have a right to be angry. To one of your class of justificators, this is the highest offence, possessed as you are of the firm opinion that all persons, at all times, on all occasions, are intent upon you alone. Is it not less mortifying to discover that you were thought ill of, than that you were not thought of at all? Indifference, you know, sentimental pupils, is more fatal to love than even hatred.

Thus, my dear pupils, I have endeavored to provide precepts, adapted to the display of your several talents. But if there should be any amongst you who have no talents, who can neither argue nor persuade, who have neither sentiment nor enthusiasm, I must, indeed, congratulate them; they alone are the true adepts in the science of self-justification. Indulgent nature, often even in the weakness, provides for the protection of her creatures; just Providence, as the guard of stupidity, has enveloped it with the impenetrable armor of obstinacy.

Let him begin with, "Now, my dear, only listen to reason—" You stop him at once with, "No, my dear, you know I don't pretend to reason; I only say that's my opinion."

Let him go on to prove that yours is a mistaken opinion—you are ready to acknowledge it, long before he desires it. You acknowledge it may be a wrong opinion; but still, it is your opinion. You do not maintain it in the least, either because you believe it to be wrong or right, but merely because it is yours. Exposed as you might have been to the perpetual humiliation of being convinced, nature seems kindly to have denied you all perception of truth, or at least all sentiment of pleasure from the perception.

Should a man with persevering temper tell you that he is ready to adopt your sentiments if you will only explain them, should he beg only to have a reason for your opinion—no, you can give no reason. Let him urge you to say something in its defense—no, like Queen Anne, you will only repeat the same thing over again, or be silent.[13] Silence is the ornament of your sex; and, in silence, if there be not wisdom, there is safety. You will, then, if you please, according to your custom, listening to all entreaties to explain and speak with a fixed immutability of posture and a predetermined deafness of the eye which shall put your opponent utterly out of patience, yet still by persevering with the same complacent importance of countenance, you shall half persuade people you could speak if you would. You shall keep them in doubt by the true want of meaning, "which puzzles more than wit."[14] Even because they cannot conceive the excess of your stupidity, they shall actually begin to believe that they themselves are stupid. Ignorance and doubt are the great parents of the sublime.

His eloquence or his kindness will avail less when, in yielding to you after a long debate, he expects to please you, [but] you will answer, undoubtedly with the utmost propriety, that you should be very sorry he yielded his judgment to you; that he is very good; that you are much obliged to him; but, that as to the point in dispute, it is a matter of perfect indifference to you; for your part you have no choice at all about it; you beg that he will do just what he pleases; you know that it is the duty of a wife to submit, but you hope, however, you may have an opinion of your own.

While I write, new precepts rush upon my recollection; but the subject is inexhaustible. I quit it with regret, fully sensible of my presumption in having attempted to instruct those who, while they read, will smile in consciousness of superior powers. Adieu, then, my fair readers! Long may you prosper in the practice of an art peculiar to your sex. Long may you maintain unrivalled dominion at home and abroad. And long may your husbands rue the hour when first they made you promise *"to obey."*[15]

Notes

This excerpt is taken from Maria Edgeworth, *Letters for Literary Ladies, To Which Is Added, An Essay on the Noble Science of Self-Justification* (London, 1795) (Library of Congress PR4644 .L4 1795). In a few places I have modernized spelling and punctuation.

1. The head quotation comes from a poem, "Hesiod; or The Rise of Woman," in *Poems on Several Occasions* (London, 1722), ll. 61–62, by Thomas Parnell (1679–1718), Irish poet and clergyman, friend of Pope and Swift.

2. "Daughters of Eve" indicates women's inferiority because they have inherited Eve's sin in causing the fall of all humankind; Edgeworth's allusion is taken from Eve's defense of her actions in John Milton's *Paradise Lost* Bk. IX, l. 1143: "To whom soon mov'd with touch of blame thus Eve."

3. Morpheus: god of sleep.

4. Friends: family members.

5. The author's note in the original edition suggests "Vide Hume." Edgeworth is directing the reader to *A Treatise of Human Nature* (1740) by David Hume (1711–1776) and parodying the doctrine of the association of ideas, whereby people are imagined to form complex ideas by the accretion of associations to simple ideas connected together in their experience.

6. "Is but in the next degree": very close. Compare Shakespeare, *Richard II* 1.4.36: "our subjects / next degree in hope."

7. Sensibility: the capacity to entertain deep feelings, taken as a sign of humanity, taste, and privileged class in the eighteenth century.

8. Ere: before.

9. Reference to quotation in headnote.

10. Xantippe, Socrates's wife, was by tradition a shrew, and therefore might comically be said to teach Socrates patience. Socrates, an ancient Greek philosopher of fifth-century Athens whose teachings were recorded by Plato, developed his philosophy in question and answer with his students, called "dialectic." Edgeworth is making fun of the Platonic dialogues in which Socrates seems to be questioning and soliciting answers from students or opponents but is actually leading them, through stages of definitions, to his own conclusions.

11. The Sensitive Plant is a member of a group of plants that move when touched or when shocked by weather. Perhaps the second reference is to poison ivy. The Mimosa belongs to the category of Sensitive Plants. The quotation seems to be a misquotation or allusion to Erasmus Darwin's poem, "The Sensitive Plant," from *The Botanic Garden* (1791), Part II, ll. 247–52:

> Weak with nice sense, the chaste MIMOSA stands,
> From each rude touch withdraws her timid hands;
> Oft as light clouds o'erpass the summer-glade,
> Alarm'd she trembles at the moving shade,
> And feels, alive through all her tender form,
> The whisper'd murmurs of the gathering storm.

12. Shakespeare, *Hamlet* 3.2.1.414: "I will speak daggers to her, but use none."

13. Author's note: "Vide Duchess of Marlborough's apology." On April 3, 1710, Sarah, Duchess of Marlborough, having heard that the Queen had spoken against her, asked to speak with the Queen. The Queen repeated over and over, "Whatever you have to say, you may put it in writing," and "You said you desire no answer and I shall give you none."

14. Alexander Pope, "Epistle to a Lady," from *Moral Essays* (1734), l. 114: "For true No-meaning puzzles more than Wit."

15. In the traditional Anglican marriage service, women promised "to love, honor, and obey" their husbands; needless to say, men did not promise to obey their wives.

Lydia Sigourney

1791–1865

Lydia Sigourney was born September 1, 1791, to Zerviah Wentworth and Ezekiel Huntley in Norwich, Connecticut; she was named Lydia Howard Huntley for the dead first wife of her father. Her father worked as gardener on the estate of Jerusha Talcott Lathrop, who encouraged Lydia's reading. Mainly self-educated, Lydia studied to be a teacher. She was very well read but had to learn painting, embroidery, and the decorative arts in order to teach girls. She opened a school in Norwich in 1811 with her friend Nancy Maria Hyde; Hyde had to stop teaching owing to illness. In 1814, Sigourney moved to Hartford to begin a girls' school in the home of Daniel Wadsworth, who also helped her publish her first book, *Moral Pieces in Verse and Prose* (1815). Although she did not continue to teach after her early years, she was so valued as a teacher that her pupils held annual reunions for fifty years after the school was discontinued. In 1819, Lydia Huntley married Charles Sigourney, a widower with three children, and owner of a hardware business. The business did not prosper, and eventually Sigourney was the main support of the family through her writings. She wrote *Traits of the Aborigines* (1822), a historical epic about the destruction of Native American tribes, and the fictions *Sketch of Connecticut, Forty Years Since* (1824) and *Lucy Howard's Journal* (1857). She published over fifty volumes of verse and became the best-known woman poet in the United States. The Sigourneys had five children of their own, the first three dying at birth, the son dying in his early twenties of tuberculosis, the daughter surviving her mother and overseeing her autobiography, *Letters of Life* (1866). Sigourney traveled to Europe for her health, leaving her family behind. There she met the royalty and famous literati of both England and France. She corresponded with Elizabeth Barrett Browning, Edgar Allan Poe, many American writers, and female educators and social reformers. Maria Edgeworth read and commended Sigourney's works. When Charles Dickens visited the United States, he called on Mrs. Sigourney. Sigourney supported abolition, schools for African Americans, and schools for the deaf, and she protested injustices against the Indians. Until her death she pursued many charitable projects in Hartford and New England, budgeting 10 percent of her income after her retirement for these good works. Sigourney's husband died in 1854, while Sigourney continued in the house in Hartford, a literary celebrity who entertained many important visitors, until her death in June 1865.

Sigourney is best known for her writings. She published sixty-five volumes in the early years of her marriage, anonymously so as not to embarrass her husband with a working wife. She wrote sentimental poetry, magazine columns, and moral essays (often presented as letters) expressing the sober, republican, pious, industrious, and thrifty values of the nineteenth-century United States. Sigourney was a career writer who supported herself and her family, and in her later years she recycled earlier material into collections. We are most interested in her conduct literature, works of education, and moral advice.

In her conduct literature, Sigourney followed Hannah More in creating and teaching a very gendered rhetorical theory. One of the first books Sigourney owned was Hannah More's *Sacred Dramas*, and she quotes More on education and rhetoric throughout her own volumes. Sigourney argued that the natural vocation of females is to teach, and advocates a republican ideal for women, stressing industry, which she interprets to mean self-education (rather than only the household crafts). In two volumes, *Letters to Young Ladies* (1833) and *Letters to My Pupils* (1837), she gives advice on a variety of aspects of rhetoric: conversation, reading aloud as part of parlor entertainment, letter writing, and training the memory (the fifth canon of rhetoric in classical education).

In *Letters to Young Ladies*, which saw over twenty-five editions, Sigourney treats reading aloud, letter writing, and memory. She defends reading aloud as appropriate for women even in a mixed social gathering (men as well as women) because it offers moral instruction and may be viewed as a service to the family. She instructs young ladies on the details of content and format for letter writing and refers them to Eliza Farrar's works. She suggests a systematic reading program to young women as a means of training their memory; in doing so, she revises and updates classical mnemonic systems, adapting them to her society's and women's needs. Rather than practice word-for-word memory, using commonplaces as categories and associating the unknown subjects to be memorized with familiar objects (as in classical rhetoric), Sigourney advises note taking, paraphrasing what you have read to others, and conversation as means to improving memory. She suggests that girls form reading societies and thus helps promote the club movement for nineteenth-century women; her description sounds very close to the model "conversations" actually held by Margaret Fuller and Elizabeth Peabody a few years later in Boston. Finally, she discusses conversation at length, constructing a theory of women's conversation very like Hannah More's. Sigourney warns against the faults of "excessive volubility," flattery, gossip, and exaggeration, and she commends the skill of good listening. Like Madeleine de Scudéry, she proposes the agreeable as a major aim of conversation. Sigourney's contribution to the art of conversation is pragmatic: she adds a section on conversation with young men, suggesting that women should use their influence to promote virtue in those who have power to change society, but also those who will determine, through marriage, the careers of the women.

In *Letters to My Pupils*, Sigourney treats pronunciation and conversation, emphasizing training in enunciation even for women, who do not speak publicly. She suggests that conversation for women should follow three rules of thumb: it should give pleasure; it should be instructive; it should be comforting. She urges that women learn the value of silence as well as the value of speech, like More, emphasizing for women the role of good listener.

In her treatises, Sigourney appropriates the nineteenth-century requirement of gendered spheres of influence in society, and analyzes women's means to power through their limited, private sphere: they can teach, converse, read aloud, write letters. These strategies, in fact, are those of Sigourney and her contemporaries for political purposes, such as abolition and women's rights: since women were denied public speaking, they used teaching and conversation, letter campaigns, and parlor speaking to all-women audiences. Sigourney's careful citation of other women's works in her treatises and her elaborate epistolary networking helped to create a women's tradition of rhetoric in the nineteenth-century United States. While progressive, Sigourney is not a feminist: she thinks that girls must be educated in academic subjects but must also choose the role of modest listener; she thinks that girls must receive training in delivery but should use it only to read aloud to their families. Especially interesting in this regard is Sigourney's treatment of gossip. Because women move in a narrow sphere, they are more prone to character demolition in order to have something to talk about. They must educate themselves in order to have something other than gossip to discuss: "The wide circle of the sciences, the whole range of literature, the boundless world of books open for you sources of conversation as innumerable as they are sublime." Like Hannah More, Lydia Sigourney is a mixture of compliance and resistance to the limitations placed upon women.

For further information, see Gordon S. Haight, *Mrs. Sigourney: The Sweet Singer of Hart-ford* (New York: Yale University Press, 1930); Thomas H. Scherman, "Lydia Huntley Sigourney," in *The Oxford Companion to Women's Writing in the United States*, ed. Cathy N. Davidson and Linda Wagner-Martin (New York: Oxford University Press, 1995), 807; Jane Donawerth, "Hannah More, Lydia Sigourney, and the Creation of a Women's Tradition of Rhetoric," in *Rhetoric, the Polis, and the Global Village: Selected Papers from the 1998 Thirtieth Anniversary Rhetoric Society of America Conference*, ed. C. Jan Swearingen (Mahwah, N.J.: Erlbaum, 1999); and Nina Baym, "Lydia Sigourney," in *American National Biography*, ed. John A. Garraty and Mark C. Carnes (New York: Oxford University Press, 1999), 19:926–28.

From *Letters to Young Ladies* (1833)

Letter VII
Manners and Accomplishments

Reading aloud with propriety and grace is an accomplishment worthy the acquisition of females. To enter into the spirit of an author, and convey his sentiments with a happy adaptation of tone, emphasis, and manner is no common attainment. It is peculiarly valuable in our sex, because it so often gives them an opportunity of imparting pleasure and improvement to an assembled family, during the winter evening or the protracted storm. In the zeal for feminine accomplishments, it would seem that the graces of elocution had been too little regarded. Permit me to fortify my opinion by the authority of the Rev. Mr. Gallaudet:[1] "I cannot understand why it should be thought, as it sometimes is, a departure from female delicacy to read in a promiscuous[2] social circle, if called upon to do so, from any peculiar circumstance, and to read, too, as well as Garrick[3] himself, if the young lady possesses the power of doing it. Why may she not do this with as much genuine modesty, and with as much of a desire to oblige her friends, and with as little of ostentation, as to sit down in the same circle to the piano, and play and sing in the style of the first masters? If to do the former is making too much of a display of her talents, why should not the latter be so? Nothing but some strange freak of fashion can have made a difference."

Fine reading is an accomplishment where the inherent music both of the voice and the intellect may be uttered, for the scope and compass of each is often fully taxed and happily developed in the interpretation of delicate shades of meaning and gradations of thought. Its first element, to be *clearly understood*, is often too much disregarded, so that with some who are pronounced fashionable readers, low or artificial intonations so perplex the listener, as to leave it doubtful whether the "uncertain sound be piped or harped."[4]

Thus it sometimes happens that, in fashionable penmanship, the circumstance that *it is to be deciphered* seems to have been forgotten. "To read so as not to be understood—and to write so as not to be read, are among the minor immoralities," says the excellent Mrs. Hannah More.[5] Elegant chirography[6] and a clear epistolary style are accomplishments which every educated female should possess. Their indispensable requisites are neatness, the power of being easily perused—orthographical[7] and grammatical correctness. Defects in either of these particulars are scarcely pardonable. You are aware that the handwriting is considered one of the talismans of character. Whether this test may be depended on or not, the fact that letters travel farther than the sound of the voice or the sight of the countenance can follow renders it desirable that they should convey no incorrect or unfavorable impression. The lesser niceties of folding, sealing, and superscription are not beneath the notice of a lady. Mrs. Farrar, in her excellent little work on letter-writing,[8] remarks that it is "well to find out the best way of doing everything, since there is a pleasure in doing things in the *best way*, which those miss who think *any way* will do." Do not indulge in a careless style of writing, and excuse yourself on the plea of haste. This nourishes a habit which will be detrimental to excellence. Our sex have been complimented as the possessors of a natural taste for epistolary composition. It is an appropriate attainment, for it admits the language of the heart, which we understand, and rejects the elaborate and profound sciences, in which we are usually deficient. Ease and truth to nature are its highest ornaments, and Cicero proved himself to be no less a master of its excellences than of his more sublime art of eloquence, when he said, "Whatever may be the subject of my letters, they still speak the language of conversation."[9]

Letter IX
Books

All systematic reading should be with a fixed purpose to remember and profit. Cultivate the retentive power by daily and persevering exercise. If anyone complains that she has a weak memory, it is her own fault. She does not take due pains to give it strength. Does she forget the period for meals, the season for repose? Does she forget the appointed hour for the evening party, or to furnish herself with a fitting dress in which to appear there? Does she forget the plot of the last romance, or the notes of a fashionable piece of music? Yet some of these involve detail, and require application.

Why then might not the same mind contain a few historical facts, with their correlative dates? Frankly, because it does not feel the same interest, nor put forth the same effort. Some who are not willing *entirely* to forget what they read, content themselves with making extracts from the books that pass through their hands. But this is not a successful mode of impressing their contents. To form a written memory is like "making to ourselves a graven image,"[10] and suffering the spiritual essence to escape. All reliance on memoranda is a false indulgence to memory. It is keeping her in leading strings,[11] when she should walk erect, like a laborer to the field. It would seem that she shared in the indolence of our common nature, and would willingly accept of any substitute that would relieve her from responsibility. But so important are her functions to the welfare of the immortal mind that she should feel it her duty to be as sleepless as the Roman sentinel, and be made to answer for her sin, if the idea committed to her custody escape.

I am inclined to think memory capable of indefinite improvement by a judicious and persevering regimen. Read, therefore, what you desire to remember, with concentrated and undivided attention. Close the book and reflect. Undigested food throws the whole frame into a ferment. Were we as well acquainted with our intellectual as with our physical structure, we should see undigested knowledge producing equal disorder in the mind.

To strengthen the memory, the best course is not to commit page after page verbatim, but to give the substance of the author, correctly and clearly, in your own language. Thus the understanding and memory are exercised at the same time, and the prosperity of the mind is not so much advanced by the undue prominence of any *one faculty*, as by the true balance and vigorous action of *all*. Memory and understanding are also fast friends, and the light which one gains will be reflected upon the other.

Use judgment in selecting from the mass of what you read the parts which it will be useful or desirable to remember. Separate and arrange them, and give them in charge to memory. Tell her it is her duty to keep them, and to bring them forth when you require. She has the capacities of a faithful servant, and possibly the dispositions of an idle one. But you have the power of enforcing obedience and of overcoming her infirmities. At the close of each day, let her come before you, as Ruth came to Naomi, and "beat out that which she has gleaned." Let her winnow repeatedly what she has brought from the field, and "gather the wheat into the garner" ere she goes to repose.[12] This process, so far from being laborious, is one of the most delightful that can be imagined. To condense is perhaps the only difficult part of it; for the casket of memory, though elastic, has bounds, and if surcharged with trifles, the weightier matters will find no fitting place.

While memory is in this course of training, it would be desirable to read no books whose contents are not worth her care; for if she finds herself called only occasionally, she may take airs, like a froward child, and not come when she is called. Make her feel it as a duty to stand with her tablet ready whenever you open a book, and then show her sufficient respect not to summon her to any book unworthy of her.

To facilitate the management of memory, it is well to keep in view that her office is threefold. Her first effort is to *receive* knowledge; her second, to *retain* it; her last, to *bring it forth* when it is needed. The first act is solitary, the silence of fixed attention. The next is also sacred to herself and her ruling power, and consists in frequent, thorough examination of the state and order of the things committed to her. The third act is social, rendering her treasures available to the good of others. Daily intercourse with a cultivated mind is the best method to rivet, refine, and polish the hoarded gems of knowledge. Conversation with intelligent men is eminently serviceable. For after all our exultation on the advancing state of female education, with the other sex will be found the wealth of classical knowledge and profound wisdom. If you have a parent or older friend who will, at the close of each day, listen to what you have read and help to fix in your memory the portions most worthy of regard, count it a privilege of no common value, and embrace it with sincere gratitude.

Weekly societies, organized on the plan of recapitulation, render very important assistance to those who are earnestly engaged in a course of history. They should comprise but few members, and those of somewhat congenial taste and feeling, that no cause of restraint or reserve may impede the free action of the mind. Three or four young ladies, with one or two older ones, will be found an agreeable and profitable number. Let the system to be pursued and the authors to be studied be a subject of mutual arrangement, and at the stated meeting let each compress the substance of what she has read during the week, relate the principal events with their chronology, and as far as possible mention what was taking place at the same period of time in the annals of other nations. Opinions dissenting from those of the historian should be freely given, with the reasons for such variation, and the discussions which arise will both serve to fix knowledge firmly in the memory, and aid in forming a correct judgment of the character and deeds of those whom history has embalmed. If to read each of the same era or people produces monotony, the history of different nations may be studied, or one can pursue a course of biography, another of mental philosophy, the natural sciences, or theology, and thus vary the mental banquet. From this partnership in knowledge, great increase of intellectual wealth will be derived, while your subjects of thought and conversation will be perceptibly elevated.

Letter XII
Conversation

So great a part of our time is devoted to conversation, and so much has it the power to influence the social feelings and relative[13] duties, that it is important to consider how it may be rendered both agreeable and useful. In all countries where intelligence is prized, a talent for conversation ranks high among accomplishments. To clothe the thoughts in clear and elegant language and to convey them impressively to the mind of another is no common attainment.

Conversation, to be interesting, should be sustained with animation. Warmth of heart must put in motion the wheels of intellect. The finest sentiments lose their force if uttered with lassitude and indifference. Still, the most fluent speakers are not always the most agreeable. Great rapidity of enunciation should be avoided. It perplexes minds of slow comprehension and confuses those which are inured to habits of reflection. It sometimes proceeds from great quickness of perception, and is sometimes an affectation of sprightliness, but will usually be found to produce fatigue, rather than to give pleasure.

A proneness to interrupt others is still more offensive than excessive volubility. Scarcely any brilliance in conversation can atone for this. It is an infraction of the principle of mutual exchange on which this department of social intercourse depends. The term itself conveys an idea, if not of equal rights, at least of some degree of reciprocity in the privilege of receiving and imparting thought. Even those who most admire the fluency of an exclusive speaker will condemn the injustice of the monopoly. They will imagine that they themselves might have uttered a few good things, had they been allowed an opportunity. Perhaps some appropriate remark arose to their lips, but the proper time for uttering it was snatched away. It is possible that regret for one's own lost sayings may diminish the effect of even a flood of eloquence, so that piqued self-love will be apt to overpower admiration, and the elegant and indefatigable talker be shunned, except by a few who are silent from dullness or patient listeners from principle. The encounter of a number of these earnest and fierce speakers, the clamor, the tireless competition, the impossibility of rescuing thought from the confusion of tongues, the utter frustration of the legitimate design of discourse, *to be understood*, would be ludicrous, were it not painfully oppressive to the nerves.

Fluency in conversation must not be assumed as a test of talent. Men of genius and wisdom have been often found deficient in its graces. Adam Smith ever retained in company the embarrassed manners of a student. . . . The conversation of Goldsmith did not evince the grace and tenderness that characterize his compositions. Thomson was diffident and often uninteresting. Dante was taciturn, and all the brilliance of Tasso was in his pen. Descartes seemed formed for solitude. . . . Our own Washington, Hamilton, and Franklin were deficient in that fluency which often fascinates a promiscuous circle.[14] The list might easily be enlarged, but enough instances have been adduced to console those who happen not to excel in this accomplishment, and to assure them that if sometimes constrained to be silent, they are at least kept in countenance by a goodly company.

As Pythagoras[15] imposed on those who would be initiated into his philosophy a long term of silence, so they who would acquire the art of conversation should *first learn to listen*. To do this with an appearance of unwearied attention, and as far as possible with an expression of interested feeling on the countenance, is a species of amiable politeness to which all are susceptible. It is peculiarly soothing to men of eminent attainments or refined sensibility, and is a kind of delicate deference which the young are bound to pay to their superiors in age.

Another mode of imparting pleasure in conversation is to lead others to such subjects as are most congenial to their taste, or on which they possess the most extensive information. From this will arise a double benefit. *They* will be satisfied, and *you* will reap the fruits of their knowledge. This was one of the modifications of benevolence practiced by the late Dr. Dwight,[16] himself one of the most accomplished and eloquent men in conversation whom our country, or any other country, has ever produced. That you may observe this rule with regularity, do not permit yourself to estimate too lightly the attainments of those whom education has less favored than yourself. Among them you will often discover strong common sense, an acquaintance with practical things, and a sound judgment of the plain intent of life, in which minds of greater refinement may be deficient. This meek search after knowledge from the humblest sources is graceful in the young, and the virtuous, however laborious may be their lot or obscure their station, are deserving of such respect, and made happier by it.

Those who would please others should never talk for display. The vanity of shining in conversation is usually subversive of its own desires. However your qualifications may transcend those of the persons who surround you, it is both unwise and unkind to obtrude them upon their notice or betray disregard of their opinion. It is never politic to humble those whom you seek to conciliate. It is a good rule not to speak much of yourself or your own concerns, unless in the presence of friends who prompt these subjects or whose advice you are anxious to obtain. It was among the amiable traits in the character of Sir Walter Scott, never voluntarily to allude to those splendid productions of his genius which were winning the wonder and applause of every clime.[17] There is a politeness, almost allied to piety, in putting out of view our own claims to distinction and bringing forward the excellence of others.

But in studying to render conversation agreeable, let us not forget that it should have a higher object than merely the art of pleasing. It was a noble rule of the celebrated Cotton Mather, "never to enter any company, where it was proper for him to speak, without endeavoring to be useful in it."[18] Mrs. Elizabeth Rowe,[19] who eminently possessed the talent of conversation, and so united it with an amiable disposition, that it was said of her, she was never known to have uttered an unkind or ill-natured remark, made it the means of moral improvement to others, by commending in their presence some persons distinguished by the particular virtue which she desired them to imitate. Thus she often led to the formation of good habits, and by her eloquence, reformed and elevated the characters of those around her.

Avoid exaggeration in discourse. Those of lively imaginations are very prone to this fault. When the addition of a few circumstances or the coloring of a single speech would so embellish a narrative, their veracity is not proof against the temptation.

Spare to use the language of flattery. Truth seems to abandon the guidance of those young persons who indulge much in its dialect. Every habit of hyperbolical expression impairs confidence. Obtain an accurate knowledge of the meaning of words and of the different shades of those reputed synonymous. Much carelessness and superfluous verbiage in conversation might be prevented by a habit of strict definition of terms, and a precise adaptation of them to the facts which are stated, or the sentiments which are conveyed. The study of etymology might not only be brought into daily practical use by ladies, but [also] be rendered a moral benefit. Yet in these days of high intellectual cultivation, in which females so liberally partake, the sacrifice of veracity in common discourse cannot be resolved into ignorance of the import of language so correctly as into the desire of shining or making amusement at the expense of higher things. "It is very difficult," says the excellent Mrs. Hannah More, "for persons of great liveliness to restrain themselves within the sober limits of strict veracity, either in their assertions or narrations, especially when a little undue indulgence of fancy is apt to secure for them the praise of genius and spirit; and this restraint is one of the earliest principles which should be worked into a youthful mind."[20] Without sincerity, the intercourse of the lips will be but "as a sounding brass, or a tinkling cymbal,"[21] and dear, indeed, must be that reputation for wit which is purchased by the forfeiture of integrity.

You are doubtless aware that our sex have been accused of a tendency to remark with severity upon the foibles of character. It has been gravely asserted that we were prone to evil-speaking. *Is it so?* Let us candidly canvass the point. We may have temptations to this vice peculiar to ourselves. We have more leisure for conversation than men. Our range of subjects is more limited. The multifarious pursuits of business and politics or the labors of scientific and professional studies engross their thoughts and necessarily lead them to more elevated and expansive channels. Women, acting in a narrower sphere,[22] examine with extreme ardor whatever falls under their observation or enters into competition with them. When employments weary or amusements fail, *character* is a favorite field in which to expatiate. By nature they are gifted with a facility for reading its idioms. But if they indulge themselves in searching out only its weaknesses—if they form a taste for hunting down its deformities and feeding, like the hyena, upon its fleshless, lifeless carcass—are they not in danger of perverting the tides of benevolent feeling, and of tingeing the fountains of the heart with bitterness?

It is very difficult to ascertain whether the faults of others are presented to us without exaggeration. So little do human beings understand the motives of others that actions may be blamed by men, which the recording angel exults as he writes in the pure record of heaven.

Yet, if we are sure that those whom we hear censured are quite as guilty as they are represented, is not the call on us rather for pity than for punishment? Is it not to be inferred that the community will take care to visit the error with its full penalty, and that it may be safe for us to withhold our smiting, when so many scourges are uplifted? Perhaps, even the measure of Jewish infliction, "thirty stripes, *save one*,"[23] may be transcended, if we add our stroke.

From the danger of evil-speaking there is for you, my dear young friends, many sources of protection. Education has provided you with a shield against this danger. The wide circle of the sciences, the whole range of literature, the boundless world of books, open for you sources of conversation as innumerable as they are sublime. Subjects to which your mothers were strangers are as familiar to your lips as household words. You have no need to dissect character. You have no excuse for confining your attention to the frailties of your associates. What is it to you who wears an ill-assorted ribbon, or a tasteless garment; or who takes the lead in fashion, to you, who can solve, at ease, the most intricate problem of Euclid, and walk with Newton among the stars?[24] What a paucity of judgment, what a perversion of intellect does it discover, to cast away the treasures of education and place yourself on a level with the neediest mind. It is like parting with your birthright, and not receiving even the poor payment of a "mess of pottage."[25] If there has ever been just cause for this serious charge of a love of calumny[26] upon our whole sex, it behooves the young females[27] of the present generation to arise and wipe it away. In those places where danger has been discovered to exist, apply the remedy. Avoid as far as possible all personal conversation. But when character is necessarily the subject of discussion, show yourselves the gentle excusers of error and the advocates of all who need defence. It was once my happiness to associate with some young people who were in love with goodness, and in fear lest the habit of evil-speaking might unawares gain victory over them. They said, "We will form ourselves into a society against detraction. If we asperse any person, or if we neglect to defend the absent when they are defamed, we will pay a fine, to be appropriated to the relief of the poor."[28] Truly, the purse for the poor flourished, and so did the virtues of those lovely and kind-hearted beings. . . .

It is not proposed that you should surrender a correct judgment, or attempt to applaud the vicious. Yet do not testify too much complacency in the condemnation even of those who deserve it. You cannot compute the strength of their temptations, or be positive that you would have offered a firmer resistance. Be tender of the reputation of your companions. Do not suppose that, by detracting from their merits, you establish your own. Join cheerfully in their praises, even should they be called forth by qualities or accomplishments in which you are deficient. Speak with severity of none. . . . Be assured that you testify your discrimination more by discovering the *good* than the *evil* among your fellow-creatures, so imperfect are even the best, so much alloy mingles with earth's finest gold.

We have now inquired, with regard to conversation in general, how it may be rendered agreeable, safe, and subservient to utility. Before we dismiss the subject, let us turn our attention to that modification of it which regards the intercourse of young ladies with those of their own age, among the other sex. This is a point of no minor importance. From your style of conversation and manners, they are accustomed to gather their most indelible impressions, not merely of talents, but of those secret springs which modify feeling, and character, and happiness. Their courtesy yields to you the choice of subjects and induces a general acquiescence in your sentiments. But are you aware that all these circumstances are scrutinized freely in your absence and that, while you are flattering yourself with having dexterously sustained your part, cool criticism may be resolving your wisdom into vanity, or associating your wit with ill-nature?

I would not seek to disguise the degree of influence which, in the radiant morning of your days, you possess over young men. It is exceedingly great. I beg you to consider it in its full import, in all its bearings, and to use it like an angel.

You have it in your power to give vigor to their pursuit of respectability, to fix their attention on useful knowledge, to fortify their wavering opinions, and to quicken or retard their progress in the path of benevolence and piety. You have it also in your power to interrupt their habits of industry and application, to encourage foppishness in dress, to inspire contempt of a just economy and plain exterior, and to lead them to cultivate levity of deportment, or to seek for variety of amusements at the expense of money, which perhaps they can ill afford to spend, and of time, which it is madness to waste. How important, my dear young friends, that the influence thus entrusted to you, be rationally, and kindly, and religiously used.

In your conversation with young men, avoid frivolity. Do not, for the sake of being called sociable, utter sound without sense. There seems implanted in some minds a singular *dread of silence*. Nothing is, in their opinion, so fearful as a *pause*. It must be broken, even if the result is to speak foolishness. Yet to the judicious, the pause would be less irksome than the folly that succeeds it. Neither reserve nor pedantry in mixed society is desirable, but a preference of such subjects as do not discredit the understanding and taste of an educated young lady. Dress, and the various claims of the candidates for the palm of beauty and fashion, with the interminable gossip of reputed courtships or incipient coquetries, are but too prone to predominate. Perhaps you would scarcely imagine that by indulging much in these topics you are supposed to furnish a key to your own prevailing tastes. Still less would you be disposed to believe the freedom of remark to which levity of deportment exposes you, even among those young gentlemen who are most willing to promote it. This disposition to frivolity in conversation repeatedly occupied the elegant and reproving pen of Addison. "If," said he, "we observe the conduct of the fair sex, we find that they choose rather to associate with persons who resemble themselves in that light and volatile humour which is natural to them, than with such as are qualified to moderate and counterbalance it. When, therefore, we see a fellow loud and talkative, full of insipid life and laughter, we may venture to pronounce him a female favorite."[29]

I trust, my young friends, that nothing in your deportment will ever authorize a conclusion like this. Yet, if a young man of good education, refined taste, and elevated morality, chooses in your company trifling subjects or descends often to levity, pause and inquire of yourself, *why it is so?*—whether he supposes this deportment most congenial to you, and what there is in your conduct which might warrant such an opinion.

There were both good sense and knowledge of human nature in the maxims given by a German author to his daughter: "Converse always with your female friends, as if a gentleman were of the party, and with young men, as if your female companions were present."[30] Avoid the dangerous license[31] of conversation, both in variety of subject and freedom of remark. Extreme delicacy on these points is expected by correct judges, and should always characterize an educated young lady.

I would not desire that conversation should be fettered by restraint, or paralyzed by heartless ceremony. But I would have the dignity of the sex maintained by its fairest and most fascinating representatives. I grieve to see folly sanctioned by the lips of beauty.

Conversation need not be divested of intelligence by the vague fear of preciseness or pedantry. It ought to be a delightful and improving intercourse between intellectual and immortal beings. To attain excellence in it, an assemblage of qualifications is requisite: disciplined intellect, to think clearly and to clothe thought with propriety and elegance; knowledge of human nature, to suit subject to character; true politeness, to prevent giving pain; a deep sense of morality, to preserve the dignity of speech; and a spirit of benevolence, to neutralize its asperities and sanctify its powers.

It requires good talents, a good education, and a good heart: the "charity that thinketh no evil," and the piety which breathes good will to man because it is at peace with its Maker.[32] No wonder that so few excel in what requires such rare combinations. Yet be not discouraged in your attempts to obtain so valuable an accomplishment, since it is the medium by which knowledge is communicated, affection enkindled, sorrow comforted, error reclaimed, and piety incited to go on her way rejoicing.

I beseech you, abuse it not. Every night, in the silence of your apartment, let the heart question the lips of their part in the day's doings. Recall the instances in which they have been trifling, profitless, or recreant to the law of kindness, and thus gather deeper contrition for the prayer with which you resign yourself to sleep. Lest this work be done lightly or carelessly, endeavor to make it a faint emblem of that tribunal before which we must all stand at last; and engrave indelibly on your memory the solemn assurance that for "*every idle word, we must give account in the day of judgment.*"[33]

Notes for *Letters to Young Ladies*

These excerpts are taken from Lydia Sigourney, *Letters to Young Ladies* (1833; reprint, New York: Harper & Brothers, 1852), 114–16, 156–61, 186–201. I am grateful to the Rare Book Collection of McKeldin Library of the University of Maryland, College Park. Spelling has been modernized and punctuation regularized.

1. Thomas Gallaudet (1787–1851), American educator, graduated from Yale and Andover Theological Seminary, studied deaf education, and supported the education of women as teachers; his son founded Gallaudet College for the Deaf.
2. Promiscuous: including both sexes, men and women.
3. David Garrick (1717–1779), famous English actor, playwright, and producer of plays, whose direct style replaced declamation; friend and sponsor of Hannah More.
4. I have been unable to locate this quotation.
5. See the section on Hannah More in this anthology.
6. Chirography: the art of penmanship.
7. Orthographical: related to the art of spelling.
8. See the section on Eliza Farrar in this anthology.
9. I have been unable to locate this quotation from Cicero.
10. Exodus 20:4: "Thou shalt not make unto thee any graven image."
11. Leading strings: strings sewn on garments that are held by an adult as a child learns to walk.
12. Ruth 2:17: "So she gleaned in the field until even, and beat out that she had gleaned."
13. Relative: related.
14. Adam Smith (1723–1790) was a famous Scottish economist and moral philosopher whose theory of the division of labor revolutionized economics. Oliver Goldsmith (1730?–1774) was an Irishman who, trained to be a physician, made a living in London as a poet, dramatist, essayist, and novelist. James Thomson (1700–1748) was a Scottish poet who came to London to tutor but became a literary star with his popular, long, pre-Romantic poem *The Seasons*. Dante Alighieri (1265–1321) was a famous Italian poet, author of *The Divine Comedy*, living most of his life in exile for political reasons. Torquato Tasso

(1544–1595) was a famous Italian poet most noted for his long *Jerusalem Delivered*, who spent much of his life in an insane asylum because of a head injury. René Descartes (1596–1650) was an important French philosopher, founder of analytic geometry, a skeptic who wrote the famous principle *Cogito ergo sum*. George Washington (1732–1799) was general of the American revolutionary forces and first president of the United States. Alexander Hamilton (1755–1804) was an American revolutionary who aided in proposing and writing the Constitution and, as first Secretary of the Treasury, laid out a strong financial program for the new country; he was killed by Vice President Aaron Burr in a duel resulting from political disagreements. Benjamin Franklin (1706–1790) was a printer, journalist, inventor, and humorist; he helped draft the Declaration of Independence and became an ambassador to France.

15. Pythagoras (c. 531 B.C.E.), Greek philosopher, founded a religion based on observation of nature and influenced the development of music and mathematics.

16. Dr. Theodore Dwight Jr. (1796–1866), an editor in Brooklyn, was a longtime friend of Sigourney's; they both lost their grown sons about the same time.

17. Sir Walter Scott (1771–1832), a Scotsman, was the most popular novelist of Sigourney's age, famous for such works as *Rob Roy* and *Ivanhoe*.

18. Cotton Mather (1663–1728), an American Puritan minister, was famous for his theological writings, treatises on witchcraft, and books of moral advice.

19. Elizabeth Rowe (1674–1737), English writer, friend of Matthew Prior, Dr. Isaac Watts, and Alexander Pope, author of poetry and moral letters, was famous for her extensive correspondence, as well as her conversation.

20. See the section on Hannah More in this anthology.

21. Corinthians 13:1.

22. Sigourney here invokes the doctrine of separate spheres, popular throughout the nineteenth and early twentieth centuries, which assumes that men and women were biologically designed as beings who spend their lives in separate social spaces (public and private, the family and the world) and perform very separate roles.

23. Sigourney seems to be misremembering Deuteronomy 25:3: "Forty stripes he may give him, and not exceed: lest, if he should exceed, and beat him above these with many stripes, then thy brother should seem vile unto thee." Note Sigourney's subtle anti-Semitism, since she refers to this custom not as Old Testament or historical but as "Jewish."

24. Euclid, who lived in the fourth century B.C.E., was a Greek mathematician who taught at Alexandria, famous for his book on geometry, *The Elements*, which establishes the deductive system of definitions, axioms, and conclusions followed in later mathematics. Sir Isaac Newton (1642–1727), an English mathematician, founded modern physics, invented calculus, and discovered the law of gravity, the three laws of motion, and the relationship of the spectrum to white light. Sigourney here suggests not that girls talk about these men, but that girls who have the intellectual resources to do geometry and study physics don't need to gossip about their friends.

25. Sigourney here refers to the story of Jacob and Esau. Helped in his trickery by his mother, Jacob stole his brother's inheritance in exchange for a "mess of pottage," a bowl of soup; see Genesis 25.

26. Calumny: malicious misrepresentation of another's character.

27. It behooves the young females: it is fitting and advantageous for young women.

28. "Detraction" is literally the "taking away" of reputation; to "asperse" is to cover with harmful charges of wrongdoing; and to be "defamed" is to be harmed in reputation by slander—to have one's fame taken away.

29. Joseph Addison (1672–1719) was an English essayist, poet, and statesman, famous for his contributions to *The Tattler* and *The Spectator*, noted for his gallant but negative views of women. I have been unable to locate this quotation.

30. I have been unable to locate this quotation.

31. License: irresponsible freedom.

32. "Charity [that] . . . thinketh no evil" is Paul's description of Christian love in 1 Corinthians 13:5. "Good will toward men" is the message of the angels at Jesus' birth, which all Christians are required to imitate: see Luke 2:14.

33. Paraphrase of Matthew 12:36.

From *Letters to My Pupils* (1851)

Fitly-Spoken Words

Fitly-spoken words! What are they? Their preciousness has been compared to "apples of gold in pictures of silver," or as some translations render it, "golden oranges in baskets of wrought silver," where the rich hue of the fragrant fruit is heightened by the beauty of its vase. Let us inquire into the nature of those words, which the wise monarch of Israel has thus graphically illustrated.[1]

And first, with regard to their garniture, *fitness of speech*. So much of our time is devoted to oral intercourse, that it is no slight object of education to regulate, and render it effective. It is expected of a well-trained lady that she should converse both agreeably and usefully; and you, my young friends, will desire in this, as in other accomplishments, to give pleasure, in order to do good. On the face of the subject, a clear enunciation is essential. It is what the Roman orator said of action, "the first, the second, the third thing."[2] Beauty of sentiment avails little if marred by an indistinct utterance. Thought loses its weight when the words glide trippingly over the tongue.[3] The upright moralist who classed the "speaking so low as not to be heard, among minor immoralities,"[4] would find but too many in our own generation, to cite before her tribunal. In what you have to say, do not deprive a single syllable of its due sound. It is a species of injustice, both to the word and its hearer. To listen and lose a part is a painful tax on the nervous system. If you have the gift of an unstammering tongue, do not perplex your friends by swallowing a portion of what you seem to address to their ears. Suffer the lips and teeth to have a share in modifying sound, rather than to let it gurgle pitifully in the depths of the throat, or be forced unnaturally through the nasal organs. It has been asserted by some satirical foreigners that one mode of distinguishing an American was by his speaking through the nose. I trust this is a mistake; still, it will do no harm to guard the point, in our own case. A confused utterance is never graceful, and often a fruitful source of misconstruction. There can be little need of multiplying arguments in proof of what must be so obvious to yourselves. Still, I would fain[5] commend strongly to you the beautiful attainment of a fine elocution,[6] as what I desire each one of you, my dear young friends, assiduously to cultivate.

It seems scarcely necessary to caution those so accustomed to the usages of well-bred society against interrupting others in discourse. Yet I doubt not you may have been often annoyed by the bursting in of rude, impatient voices, upon the pleasant interchange of thought. Job's messengers of evil tidings had that bad habit, "while one was yet speaking, there came also another and said."[7] Those whose comprehension has been thus perplexed should avoid inflicting the same inconvenience on their friends. It is an infraction of the privilege of conversation, which implies reciprocity. It cannot therefore be with propriety a lectureship, where some are installed to set forth their favorite subjects, and others to listen with a mouse-like observance. Neither is it a piratical enterprise, to snatch on this side and on that; nor the fierce monopoly of high-sounding lungs, finding bliss in their own selfish exercise; nor a hubbub of unmeaning vociferations, where truth enters only to be trodden down; but the quiet intercourse of minds, to which God has given reason, love of knowledge, kindred sympathies, and the vehicle of language, that they may advance mutual happiness and improvement.

Aim to clothe your thoughts in the best language. By this, I do not, of course, mean an ostentatious style, or those efforts after elegance which reject simplicity. The society of the highly educated, and the art of listening, are a profitable regimen for the young. She who would converse well must learn to listen; as he who would wisely rule must first know how to obey. Reflect ere[8] you speak, whether what you are about to utter is worth saying. This will chasten an undue fluency, and hold in check the tendency to gossiping—that stigma so long affixed to the social intercourse of the fair sex. In olden times, when from a more limited education than we enjoy, their[9] range of subjects was narrower, and the fashions of dress and foibles of character fell more intensely under their observation, this fault might have been more readily forgiven.

Speak in sweet tones. It seems expected of the young and amiable, that their voice should be an echo of the soul's harmony. I think now of one whose varied intonations are like rich music, long to be remembered. And she always speaks with a smile. Would that each one of you would cultivate these attractions. The habit might be easily formed, now, in your forming season. Melody of voice and the bright beaming forth of a radiant spirit are the natural accompaniments of words fitly spoken. They give the last, exquisite polish to that "basket of wrought silver," in which the ripened fruits of thought are beautifully arranged.

Now, what are those *words*, whose rich meaning renders them worthy of such care in presentation? Surely, they must be engines of power. "How forcible are *right* words," exclaimed the Patriarch to whom we have already referred, when to his other sufferings were added the ill-chosen discussions of those friends, to the "opening of whose lips," he had looked for consolation.[10]

Suppose, for the sake of conciseness, we divide our *fitly-spoken words* into three classes: those that give pleasure, those that impart instruction, and those that comfort sorrow.

1. Words that give pleasure. Here, the gentle expressions of kindness and affection deserve a prominent place. Fail not to use them, where they are justly due. They aid in the cultivation of the heart. Taciturnity, or reserve to their promptings, may settle into coldness of character. Spare not to tell those who are bound to you by kindred blood, friendship, or gratitude, how tenderly you love them. The sweetness of domestic intercourse depends much on the frank communication of affectionate feeling.

Encouragement of those who are striving to establish right habits, or overcome wrong dispositions, will give scope for many pleasant words. Warm appreciation of the good deeds of your acquaintance may be so judiciously expressed as not to hurt their delicacy. Some minds are so prone to dejection, and so deficient in proper self-esteem, that frequent allusion to their virtues is medicinal, and an incentive to perseverance and higher attainments in excellence. Yet avoid the dialect of flattery. Like all departures from rectitude, it will weaken confidence in your veracity. It is the false coin of conversation, a counterfeit readily detected. Keep truthfulness, as well as gentleness, ever in view, and regard the apostolic precept, "*to please for edification.*"[11]

2. Words that convey instruction. What a wide field here opens before you. All who have less education than yourselves may be considered, in some degree, as your pupils. Whoever is desirous of knowledge, or unacquainted with its benefits, or enslaved by incorrect habits, or unconvinced of the truths of our holy religion, or unsustained by its hopes, may be the better for your teachings. Yet avoid display and dogmatical assertions and, like the bee singing at her work, hide your precepts in honey. Use judgment and knowledge of human nature in select-

ing the information that you impart. The rules of logic or the axioms of philosophy would be scarcely intelligible to an untrained intellect. I knew a studious boy who persisted in reading his lessons aloud, every evening, to an aged colored servant-woman. If wearied with the labors of the day, she fell asleep, he elevated his voice to a higher key; for "I am determined," said he, "to improve her mind." Probably all the advantage derived from this exercise of classic lore was his own. Perhaps the dreams of the heavy sleeper were scarcely broken, but his perseverance might have found a surer place in the casket of memory for what he desired to commit there.

Knowledge grows by imparting it, as the physical powers, through exercise, gather strength. If the teachers of the intellectual branches share liberally the benefits they communicate to others, in the accumulation of mental treasure and the increase of suggestive thought, will not those, also, who labor to impress moral and religious precepts, deepen within themselves the energies of a pure and consistent example?

3. Words that soothe sorrow. Here, our sex ought to be proficients. They are expected to be comforters. Their tender sympathies are easily awakened, and by the circumstances of their lot in life, kept in frequent exercise. Exert yourselves, therefore, to comfort, according to your ability, all who may come within your sphere of action. Sickness, poverty, and grief, with their infinite variations, will surround you as you walk the path of probation. "Let the moving of your lips" assuage their pain.[12] Sympathy, though it may not remove the load, gives strength to bear it. Soothe the wailing infant and the disappointed child, whose troubles are not the less keenly felt because to us they may seem as trifles.

The trials of your friends and companions, I have already seen that you count as your own. In their deeper adversities, have ever ready for them, in the dialect of love, that best remedy for sorrow, perfect reconcilement to the Ruling Hand. Into their stricken hearts, pour from your own, confidence in the wisdom of omnipotence, trust in its goodness, thankfulness for the discipline of its fatherly school, assurance that what is dark and mysterious here shall be revealed in the land without a cloud, where it shall be brightly seen with angel-ken, how "all things did work together for good, to those who loved God."[13]

Still, there are occasions in human life where silence is more eloquent than speech. If you are observant, you will perceive that in some situations, the sound of the human voice is arrogant and vain. It is so where Nature discloses her majesty—on the heights of solemn mountains, amid the thunder of the fathomless, storm-wrought ocean, or in the presence of the never-resting, glorious Niagara.

There is also a depth of human sorrow, where silence is wisdom. Frail man struggling against the strong surge of adversity, inspires a sensation of that awe which sublimity produces. Classic polytheism asserted that the sight was worthy of the admiration of her deities.

> To me, and to the state of my great grief
> Let kings do homage,

said the desolate mother of the murdered Arthur.[14] You will doubtless come in contact with instances of severe bereavement where words are inadequate. They are even felt to be hazardous. They may touch some chord whose vibration is agony. Then, the tear of silent sympathy, the meek bowing down by the side of the smitten, as if to take a part of the burden that crushes them, is the dialect of true feeling.

There are depths in devotion, where the voiceless thought alone aspires to communion with its Maker. The humbled soul realizes that "He is in His holy temple, and keeps silence before Him."[15] Language, convinced of its poverty, submissively withdraws, or hides its face in the lap of silence.

Beautiful silence! that hast a place in heaven, among the harps that know no dissonance. Far more fitting is it that thou shouldst dwell with us, so often mistaken in our best ministries of speech, and discordant in our highest melodies.

We have considered the fitness of speech; let us not overlook the beauty of well-timed silence. Its holy hush, like pauses in music, heightens the succeeding harmony. Like shades in a picture, it illustrates the design. Like repose to the toil-worn, it gives energy for future action. The long, undeclining day of the arctic regions is said to be oppressive to the nerves. Men yearn for the sober twilight, to temper its intense brightness, and for the shadow of the deep night, lulling weariness to repose.

Learn, therefore, when to be silent, as well as how to speak. Ulysses was called the most eloquent, and the most silent of men.[16] I would have you talk *well*, but not talk *always*. And since by our words, as well as our deeds, we are to be judged, may right words, fitly-spoken, and the holy pauses of well-timed silence, mingle bright memories with your crown of rejoicing at the last great day.

Notes for *Letters to My Pupils*

This excerpt is taken from Lydia Sigourney, *Letters to My Pupils: With Narrative and Biographical Sketches* (New York: Robert & Carter and Brothers, 1851), 44–56. My thanks to the Rare Book Collection in McKeldin Library of the University of Maryland, College Park. I have modernized spelling and regularized punctuation.

1. The "wise monarch of Israel" is Solomon, and the quotation is from Proverbs 25:11.
2. The "Roman orator" is Cicero. For this quotation, see Cicero's *De Oratore* III.lvi.213; Cicero is quoting Demosthenes, the great Greek orator.
3. An allusion to Hamlet's speech to the players in *Hamlet* 3.2.1–4: "Speak the speech, I pray you, as I pronounc'd it to you, trippingly on the tongue, but if you mouth it, as many of our players do, I had as live [lief] the town-crier spoke my lines." Sigourney is ironically reversing Hamlet's meaning—he means "glidingly"; she means "stutteringly."
4. The upright moralist is Hannah More. See the section on More in this anthology.
5. Fain: willingly.
6. Elocution: delivery or pronunciation.
7. Job 1:16.
8. Ere: before.
9. Their: females.
10. The "Patriarch" is Job. See Job 6:25; 16:5.
11. The apostle is Paul. See Romans 15:2.
12. Job 16:5.
13. Romans 8:28.
14. A misquotation, from a nineteenth-century edition of Shakespeare: Constance, Arthur's mother in Shakespeare's *King John* (3.1.70–71), says, "To me and to the state of my great grief, / Let kings assemble."
15. 1 Corinthians 14:28.
16. Ulysses, a Greek king and warrior known for his clever plots and his eloquence, is a major character in Homer's *Iliad* and the hero of the *Odyssey*.

Eliza Farrar

1791–1870

Eliza Ware (Rotch) Farrar was born on July 12, 1791, in Dunkirk, France, to Elizabeth Barker and Benjamin Rotch. Her parents and grandparents were Quakers who had been burned out of the whaling industry in Nantucket by the British in the Revolutionary War. After seeking reparations in England, which they were denied, the family eventually settled in France at Dunkirk and rebuilt their whaling industry. As Quakers, the family had been neutral in the Revolutionary War, and again in the siege of Dunkirk by the British and in the French Revolution. After Eliza's father was almost executed by Robespierre for representing the whalers' grievances to him, they fled France and settled in Great Britain, eventually whaling out of Milford Haven, Wales. Eliza knew French and was educated in England, where the family remained.

Eliza returned to the United States in 1819 and lived with her grandparents in Bedford, Massachusetts. In 1828, she married John Farrar (1779–1853), professor of mathematics at Harvard University. They had no children. Her husband introduced a sweeping reform of the science and mathematics curriculum at Harvard based on French advances. He wrote and published (mostly textbooks) on astronomy, electricity, magnetism, optics, mechanics, and trigonometry. Eliza Farrar traveled across the Atlantic nine times and knew many of the celebrated men and women of both the United States and England: poets and hymn writers Helen Maria Williams and Anna Letitia Barbauld, Benjamin West the painter, prison reformer Elizabeth Fry, Admiral Lord Nelson, novelist and educator Maria Edgeworth, salonnière Mme. Juliette Récamier, founder of the Red Cross Florence Nightingale, astronomer and mathematician Mrs. Somerville, the music-publishing Novello family, singer Clara Countess of Gigliucci, Shakespearean scholar Mrs. Cowden Clarke, factory reformer Harriet Martineau, Sir Samuel Cunard of the steamship line, Swiss novelist Rodolphe Töpffer, the Ladies of Llangollen (Lady Eleanor Butler and Hon. Miss Ponsonby), asylum reformers Sir William Ellis and his wife, lawyer-orators Daniel Webster and Jacob Barker, American transcendentalist Margaret Fuller, and noted historian Delia Bacon. Several years before Margaret Fuller's Conversations (lecture-discussions with a circle of Boston women in Elizabeth Peabody's bookstore), Eliza Farrar helped Delia Bacon set up courses of lectures on history for women, first in Brattle House and then in Farrar's own parlor in Cambridge.

Eliza wrote her first book in England before she was married. She was author of children's literature—*The Children's Robinson Crusoe* (1830), *The Story of the Life of Lafayette* (1831), *John Howard* (1833), and *Congo in Search of his Master* (1854)—and a volume of memoirs (1866), as well as the conduct book dealing with rhetoric and the narrative textbook from which selections have been included in this anthology: *The Young Lady's Friend* (1836) and *The Youth's Letter-Writer* (1840). Farrar died in Springfield, Massachusetts, on April 22, 1870.

Eliza Farrar's works on rhetoric follow closely the English tradition of Maria Edgeworth's enjoyable textbooks and Hannah More's moral conduct book rhetoric for girls. *The Young Lady's Friend* is a conduct book that also treats rhetoric and communication, like Hannah More's and Lydia Sigourney's successful conduct books published before it. It is addressed very specifically to girls between the ages of fifteen and twenty and recommends a lifetime education program for girls, since they are generally taken out of formal schooling sooner than boys. The ideal middle-class young woman for Eliza Farrar knows several languages, is an avid reader not only of novels but also of history and science, manages domestic affairs, sews well, and is adept at conversation and letter writing. In chapters on the relationship to brothers and sisters and to servants, Farrar is concerned about the smooth running of domestic society. Farrar conservatively subscribes to very gendered spheres for young men and women, while assuming that women are quite equal to men in intelligence and rhetorical abilities. Farrar echoes Hannah More on the faults of conversation girls may fall into, but she recommends much wider study in classical and empiricist rhetoric for girls than does More, and continued practice in composition. My selections from *The Young Lady's Friend* have been taken mainly from the section on letter writing, even though there is also a chapter on conversation; the chapter on conversation follows Hannah More's analysis fairly closely.

The Youth's Letter-Writer (1840) tells the story of a young boy, visiting his uncle and family, who is taught to write letters to his family. Chapters cover the mechanics of pens, paper, and handwriting; the conventions of date, address, greeting, and sealing; how to choose, limit, and develop topics; and models of letter writing and good style. All of this is taught while telling stories of the boy's adventures with his cousins, with repeated justification of the necessity of learning to write letters out of kindness to family and friends. One chapter is of special interest, since it demonstrates the democratizing of literacy in the nineteenth-century United States: Anna, the older cousin, teaches the poor farmboy who works for the family how to write letters in order to stay in touch with his distant family. Farrar emphasizes clarity, conciseness, and correct grammar and spelling, but she also represents letters as conversations on paper, gifts to family and friends, and suggests that a good writer will develop an individual voice. She supports exact truth and plainness as American virtues and gives advice on how to write about feelings as well as events.

For further information, see Eliza Farrar, *Recollections of Seventy Years* (Boston: Ticknor & Fields, 1866); "Eliza Ware (Rotch) Farrar," in *The National Cyclopaedia of American Biography* (New York: James T. White, 1906), 13:317–18; Brooke Hindle, "John Farrar," in *Dictionary of Scientific Biography*, ed. Charles Gillespie (New York: Charles Scribner's Sons, 1971), 4:546; Joonok Huh, "Elizabeth Ware Rotch Farrar," in *American National Biography*, ed. John A. Garraty and Mark C. Carnes (New York: Oxford University Press, 1999), 7:737–38; Jane Donawerth, "Hannah More, Lydia Sigourney, and the Creation of a Women's Tradition of Rhetoric," in *Rhetoric, the Polis, and the Global Village*, ed. C. Jan Swearingen (Mahwah, N.J.: Erlbaum, 1999), 155–62; and Donawerth, "Poaching on Men's Philosophies of Rhetoric: Eighteenth- and Nineteenth-Century Rhetorical Theory by Women," *Philosophy and Rhetoric* 33, no. 3 (2000): 243–58.

From *The Young Lady's Friend* (1836)

Chapter XII
Female Companionship

An extensive correspondence among girls of your own age is not desirable—it consumes too much time. But a few correspondents are useful as furnishing inducements for you to practice the art of letter writing. Do not feel bound to write to every girl that begs you to do so, but choose carefully whom you will have in that relation and, when you have a few choice correspondents, do not neglect them and begin every letter with an apology, but write in due season and waste no paper on commonplace excuses. Always notice the contents of your friend's letter, and endeavor to write of those things which will most interest her.

Madame de Sévigné praises her daughter[1] for her attention to dates, which, she says, shows an interest in the correspondence; a dateless letter certainly loses much of its value, and they are but too common.

Remember the liability of a letter to miscarry, to be opened by the wrong person, to be seen by other eyes than those for whom it is meant, and be very careful what you write to the disadvantage of anyone. Praise and admire as much as you please, but beware of blame. Your judgment may be wrong, and you know not when nor where it may come up against you and make you sorry you ever penned it.

Inexperienced letter writers often feel provoked with themselves when they have filled a sheet without touching on some topics that they fully intended to introduce, and perceive that they have spread out one of inferior importance over half their paper. This may be avoided by considering, before you begin, all that you wish to write about, and allowing to each topic its proper space.

If your correspondent require that her letters be kept private from all friends, make it a point of honor to comply with her wishes; only make an exception in favor of your mother, in case she should desire to see the correspondence, for young ladies under age should gracefully acknowledge their parent's right of inspection though, where there is a proper confidence on both sides, it will rarely be enforced.

The more rational and elevated the topics are on which you write, the less will you care for your letters being seen, or for paragraphs being read out of them; and where there is no need of any secrecy, it is best not to bind your friend by promises, but to leave it to her discretion.

A letter, written in a fair, legible hand, without any blots or erasures, and properly folded, sealed, and directed, is one very good index to a lady's character.[2]

The letters of a regular correspondent should be endorsed and filed, as regularly by young ladies as by merchants; this facilitates your reference to any one of them, prevents their being lost, or mislaid, or exposed to curious eyes, saves your table from being strewed, and your lettercase from being crowded with them.

The letters of past years should either be destroyed or carefully locked up with directions on the box, that in case of your death they are to be returned, unread, to the writers or, if that cannot be done, that they should be burnt, unread. This disposal of letters after death is often the only important part of a young girl's last will, and yet this is rarely provided for. It is best to be always so prepared, by making the necessary arrangements whilst in health.

The letters of very young persons rarely have any interest beyond the period in which they are written; they are seldom read after they are a year old, and the idea of keeping them for future perusal is altogether chimerical; life is too short, and too much crowded with novel interests, to allow time for reading over quires of paper filled with the chat of young girls, however good it may have been in its day; and, therefore, the wisest plan is to agree with your correspondent to make each a bonfire of the other's letters when they shall be more than a year old. A year's letters are enough for a memorial of your friend, if she be taken from you and, by keeping the latest, you will have her most mature compositions.

Chapter XX
Mental Culture

However irksome may have been the writing of themes at school, you cannot relinquish the frequent exercise of the mind in composition without neglecting one of the most important means of mental culture. Nothing is a greater help to accuracy of statement and accuracy of thought. Those who are unaccustomed to this exercise may begin by writing down the thoughts of others from memory; a sermon or a lecture, a conversation or a passage from a book will furnish a topic. In the last case, the novice can compare her composition with the original, and so correct it. The more varied the subjects you treat of, the more useful will be the exercise; and if the labor of composition be irksome to you, there can be no stronger proof that your mind requires the discipline. It should be remembered that, however valuable these compositions are as exercises of the young mind, they seldom have any intrinsic merit, and should, therefore, be kept to yourself, and destroyed when they have answered their purpose.

Notes for *The Young Lady's Friend*

These excerpts are taken from the Library of Congress copy of Eliza Farrar [By a Lady.], *The Young Lady's Friend* (Boston: American Stationers/John B. Russell, 1837), 279–83, 425–26. I have modernized spelling and punctuation, in the few instances where that was needed.

1. Marie de Rabutin-Chantal, Marquise de Sévigné (1626–1696) is noted for her fifteen hundred letters to her daughter, full of gossip about literary and social figures and witty commentary, published after her death.

2. In the 1840 edition, Farrar's footnote here reads, "Directions how to do this will be found in *The Youth's Letter Writer* by Mrs. Farrar, published by Bartlett & Raynor, New York."

From *The Youth's Letter-Writer;*
or The Epistolary Art (1840)

Chapter I
Conversation between Henry Moreton and His Uncle on the Difficulty of Letter-Writing.—Henry's First Letter to His Parents.

"How I do hate writing letters!" was the exclamation of a youth of fourteen years of age, as he sat down before a sheet of fine letter paper, prepared to do what he considered the most difficult of all his duties. With an excellent pen, just made for him by his uncle, and good ink, and lines under his paper, and plenty of thoughts in his head, there he sat like one stupefied; and after scrawling over his blotting paper, trying his pen again and again, and waiting so long between each trial that the ink dried in the nib, he threw it down in despair, muttering the foolish wish that the art of writing letters had never been invented.

The name of this perplexed youth was Henry Moreton; he was now on a visit to his uncle, Mr. Charles Price and, having been absent from home ten days, and made a journey of several hundred miles from his father's to his uncle's house, it was highly necessary and proper that he should send his parents a full account of himself since he parted from them. The dreaded task had been deferred 'til his conscience smote him for the delay, and he had now sat down, resolved to write home, but had proceeded no farther than "My dear parents," when he gave up in despair, and expressed the inconsiderate wish above mentioned, loud enough for his uncle to hear. Mr. Price had been observing Henry's dilemma with mingled feelings of amusement and compassion. That a fine, bright boy, who did everything else well for his age, and was full of conversation, and loved his family dearly, should be so puzzled to write a letter, seemed to him at first rather ludicrous. But as Mr. Price saw Henry's face become clouded, and observed how troubled the poor fellow really was, he sympathized very kindly with him, and resolved to help him over his difficulty.

"That is a strange wish of yours, Henry. Have you never reflected upon the great benefits derived from letter-writing? Imagine for a moment what a doleful change it would make in all our intercourse with our fellow beings, if we were deprived of this mode of communicating with them. We will not now stop to consider the stagnation in commerce or the total derangement of public affairs which would take place; we will only remark the effect of such a change upon families and friends. What would you and your brothers and sisters have known of your cousins here, or of me, without the intercourse of letters? We should have seemed like strangers to you, instead of near relations. I doubt whether you would have wished to pay us this visit, but for hearing the letters read that passed between the families; for we have seen each other but seldom for the last dozen years."

"It was cousin Anna's letters to my sister Maria," said Henry, "which made me wish to come and see you. She described you all so naturally, and told us how pleasantly you passed your evenings, and what the boys did in winter, and of their making molasses candy in the study and oversetting the skillet. I fancied I could see it all, and longed to be one of the party; and when your invitation came, I was all ready to accept it."

"This is a case in point certainly," replied Mr. Price; "you can judge of the happiness which our letters give your family, and I can tell you, that here the receipt of a letter from your parents or sister makes every individual in the house happy. Even Neptune wags his tail, and perceives that there is joy among the children. Now if letters written under ordinary circumstances give so much pleasure, think what it must be to a wife to hear from her husband when absent from her on some perilous enterprise, or to a father to receive tidings from a beloved family. Young men who leave their pleasant homes to earn a living in some remote region or to go on long voyages consider a letter from a brother or sister as one of the greatest blessings, whilst those they leave behind are equally indebted to this admirable art. Even when letters do not convey joyful tidings, when they tell us of the sorrows and trials of those we love, there is still a satisfaction in knowing all that has befallen them. Anything is better than ignorance and uncertainty respecting the fate of our friends. Your parents are, at this moment, suffering the pain of uncertainty as to your safety; they know you were to make a long journey and that you were liable to many accidents by the way, and they must feel anxious to hear of your arrival here."

"I know that, uncle, and have felt very uncomfortable on that account; but I do not like to write only this, that I am here, safe and sound. And I do not know how to make up a good letter that will read well and tell them all they wish to know."

"If your father," said Mr. Price, "were to walk into the room this minute, should you be at any loss what to say to him?"

"O no!" exclaimed Henry; "I should tell him everything that happened since we parted. He would ask me questions and I should chatter on, not minding how I told it, but just saying what came uppermost. But in writing a letter, I have no questions to help me, and I must mind how I make my sentences, and say something proper for the *beginning* of a letter, and have a good *ending*, and that's what I know nothing about. I never could write a letter, and I fear I never shall learn."

At this, his uncle could not help laughing, but he went on to assure Henry that the great difficulty he found in letter writing arose from his notions about having a proper beginning and ending, forming set phrases and fine sentences—all which notions were erroneous.

"You cannot," he continued, "begin with anything better than a plain statement of the fact which your friends most wish to hear, or end with anything better than messages of love to your family and an affectionate farewell to your parents. The best letters are the most like the best conversation; and if you will only fancy yourself talking to your father and mother, in a limited portion of time, and therefore consider what they most wish to hear, you may venture to write exactly what you would say to them, and there would be an end of all your difficulties."

Henry's countenance now began to brighten, and he felt encouraged by what his uncle said. He had always fancied there was something peculiar in the composition of a letter, and that it must be as different as possible from conversation; but if he might talk to his parents on paper, he thought he could do that, though he should feel the want of their questions to lead him on.

"You must proceed in this as you do in other things," said Mr. Price; "you must put yourself in the place of others, and think what would be most agreeable to them. You know that the predominant feeling of your parents about you now must be anxiety to hear whether you performed your long journey without any accident, so you can begin with telling them that you arrived here safely. Then they will wish to know how long you were on the road, what inci-

162

dents occurred, and who were your stage companions. And if anything happened to you that would be particularly interesting or amusing to your family, tell them that by all means. When satisfied as to your journey, their thoughts will naturally turn to those you are now with, and they will like to hear how you found us all, and how you have passed your time since you arrived. Now try what you can do at talking on paper."

"Thank you, dear uncle. I feel now as if I knew what I was going about, and could fill a whole sheet with the greatest of ease."

Henry wrote a good running hand for a boy of his age, but it was rather large and, sure enough, he was not long in filling up his paper. He had written upon one of the foldings, and had only the other one left, when he found to his surprise that he had not told half what he had to say. He was so full of the idea that he might *talk on paper*, that he forgot that he could not put as much into a letter as he would say in conversation. He had therefore run out into minute details of his coach companions, which were not very interesting, and had no room for the most amusing of his adventures, for any account of his uncle's family, or how he had spent his time since he arrived. So he concluded his letter very abruptly, saying he had not told the best part of his story because he had not room, but he would put it in his next letter. On reading it over, he was very much dissatisfied with his performance, and complained to his uncle that, in this way of talking on paper, he could say so little; he even doubted whether a well-written letter could be anything like conversation, because his own appeared so poor to him. His uncle encouraged him by saying that his letter would give his parents much greater pleasure than a more studied production, and that the reason it did not satisfy him was because he had not attended to one essential part of his directions, which was to fancy himself talking to his absent friends in a *limited portion of time*, and not run on with trifling particulars which would fill up his paper too fast. "Remember," continued his uncle, "I said that the *best* letters were like the *best* conversation; there may be a fault in your manner of talking, which, when put upon paper, appears doubly conspicuous."

Upon this hint at his way of talking, Henry smiled and said, "I am often told at home that I talk too much and too fast, and that I say the same things over too often. Therefore, uncle, it will never do for me to write as I talk."

"You must correct the faults of both," said Mr. Price; "a little practice in writing upon this plan will help you to improve your conversation and your letters, too. This is a very good beginning. The next time you try, you will choose among your facts, and tell the most interesting only. But you have labored enough for the present in this new kind of exercise. So you had better join your cousins, who are playing ball in the field next the barn, and leave your letter with me to fold and direct. It shall go by tomorrow's mail, and you may be sure it will be a welcome messenger to all the dear ones at home." Henry ran out to play, much pleased at the thought of having done something that would add to the happiness of those he loved so well.

Mr. Charles Price was the father of seven children who had been left motherless when the eldest was but ten years old; and in performing, as far as he could, the duties of both parents, he had learned to give his ready sympathy to the troubles and pleasures of childhood, to understand the workings of the youthful mind, and to minister to it in the happiest way. All children who knew Mr. Price loved and revered him. His conversation was always instructive, and he did his young friends good as much by calling forth their powers as by what he imparted of his own stores of wisdom and knowledge. He knew just how far to tax a child's powers without pressing him too hard. He smiled on every worthy effort, however unsuccessful; and though very direct and sincere in his criticisms, he always chose a time for imparting them when they could best be borne. He felt that the moment when Henry Moreton had just finished his letter and was himself dissatisfied with it, when his mind was tired by the unusual effort he had made, was not the best time for pointing out its numerous defects; but he knew he could give him some instruction in letter writing by criticizing this faulty production, and therefore he took the pains of copying it before he sent it off, that he might at some future opportunity give his nephew the benefit of his criticisms and make him learn by his own mistakes. Henry's letter was as follows, except that we do not copy his verbal inaccuracies.

Oakwood, May ___, 183___.

My dear Parents,

I arrived here safe and well on Friday in last week. I was three days getting here because I did not arrive here 'til ten o'clock at night; and as I left you at four o'clock on Wednesday morning, that may fairly be called three days; and as I was one night on board the steamboat, I may say that my journey took up three days and one night. The last part of the road was very bad, up to the hubs of the wheels. I lost my hat, looking out of the window to see how deep the wheels sank. I got it again, though, by that kind gentleman's stopping the stage and getting the driver to pick it up. But I forget that I have not told you about that gentleman; he was very kind to me all the way, I mean all the way that he was with us, for we did not take him in 'til the last day's journey. But I liked him very much—he was so kind to me, and told so many funny stories. There were two ladies in the stage who would not laugh at any of them, but were so silent and prim that everybody disliked them; at least, I am sure I did, and so did Mr. Smith. They only went a little way. But, dear me! I am telling the last part of my story first; this all happened the last day of my journey. I ought to go back to the beginning, and tell it all in order. Well then, to begin with what happened when I first left you. Nothing particular happened, except that I did not like riding in the dark with so many strangers, and as we passed by a lamp, I tried to see what they looked like, but could only see that they were all men, and most of them were fast asleep. One great fellow kept lolling down upon me, 'til he almost crushed me, and I pinched and poked him, but still he kept on, 'til at last I remembered the pincushion I had in my pocket, and I managed to get a pin out of it, and after a few pricks with that, he waked quite up, and then he fixed himself in a better way, up in the corner, and did not fall down on me anymore. I was packed into the back seat with a whole row of backs before me, which is what I do hate; I wish there were no back seats in a stage, for they always make little fellows like me sit in them, and there I am half smothered, and I cannot see anything. But let me see, where was I before I told about not liking to ride in the back seat? O, I was describing the first part of my journey. Well, there we were in the dark, as I said before; but by degrees it became lighter, and long before we stopped to breakfast, it was broad daylight. I ate my breakfast and paid for it like the other passengers. There was an old gentleman there who offered to pay for me. Now, I don't know whether he meant to give the money for my breakfast, or whether he meant to pay the master of the inn and let me pay him—which do you think he meant, father? I thanked him, and told him I could as well pay for myself. I went to the bar and handed up half a dollar, which was what I saw others pay, and after doing that, I was turning away, but the man called out to me and said, "Here, my son, half of this is enough for your bread-and-milk breakfast." I don't know how he knew that I had eaten only bread and milk, but that is what he said, and he returned me half my money; and I think that was very fair and honorable of him, don't you? Then we all got into the stage again, and this time I got a forward seat, and could look out and see the country. There was a farmer in the stage who knew all the farms by the roadside, and he told us who owned them and how they were cultivated, and he said the season was more backward than he had ever known it, that everything was three weeks behindhand. He showed us one farm, that there had been a lawsuit about and told a very long story about it, and he was called upon as a witness, and there was an appeal, and he had to travel a great many miles about it; but I could not understand what the lawsuit was about, and so I cannot tell you. But I have no more paper, and so I cannot tell you the best part of my journey. I will write that in my next letter. Love to all.

Your affectionate son,

Henry Moreton.

[In Chapter II, Mr. Price gently criticizes Henry's letter sentence by sentence, pointing out places where he could cut out irrelevant or wordy passages, and phrases that could be worded more clearly.]

Chapter X
Letter from Louisa Price to Her Father.—Anna's Observations upon It.—Mode of Announcing Bad News.—Truth Essential to a Correspondence.—The Evils of False Accounts.—Mode of Forming a Good Hand.—Folly of Writing When Angry.

It was now Louisa's turn to write, and all her secret hopes that something would occur that would make as good a subject for a letter as Henry had had were fulfilled. There was a dear long letter from her father to acknowledge, and a most important change in the family to announce. Louisa was a silent, thoughtful child, devoted to books and to her own reveries. She was often seen composing letters to her absent brother, but could seldom be prevailed upon to send them to him or to show what she had written. She was painfully alive to criticism and could ill bear the free discussions and offhand speeches of her brothers and sisters. She had been known to write poetry, but the least observation of others upon what she had been doing would make her burn or efface her lines. She knew that her letter to her father would be regarded as public property in the little community at Oakwood, because Anna's, William's, and Henry's had been; and therefore, she had made a great effort to conceal her repugnance to showing it, and to write such a one as she would like that William should see. He was the "lion in her path"; there was nothing that she dreaded like Willy's criticism, except that he should find out how much she cared for it.

Nobody knew when Louisa wrote her letter; but on the third evening after Henry's epistle was finished, this quiet little girl put hers into her sister's hands, and asked her to seal and direct it. "I suppose I may read it, too," said Anna. "Oh yes, read it aloud for the good of all," added William. Louisa blushingly assented, and Anna read as follows:

My dear father,

We were all made very happy by the receipt of your entertaining letter from New York. We all thought that you would write from Albany, but as you took the night boat, that was impossible. I would say more about your letter, were it not for a great family misfortune which occurred yesterday, and which has made us all so miserable that I cannot write of anything else.

It falls to my lot to inform you of this sad event, so without further preface, I will tell you, at once, what the terrible stroke is. Our beloved Neptune has been taken away from us. He is gone, never to play with us more, and when you come home, that good dog will not be here to welcome you. Yet he is not dead; he still lives to amuse others. He has been torn from us by the hand of man. Captain J___ has given up being a farmer; he is going to sea again, and he sent a man here for Neptune, who said that the captain gave him to you on this condition, that he should have him back again whenever he went to sea. It was a hard condition, I think, and we wish now that he had never given Neptune to us at all. To have such a dear dog with us long enough for us all to become passionately fond of him, and then to lose him! It is too bad—don't you think so, father? William thinks that the captain had a right to take the dog, but that it was very unkind of him to do it. Anna says we ought to feel more for Captain J___, and judge of his feelings for the dog by our own. What do you think about it, Papa? You will feel for us children, I am sure, and as you often say that the happiness of a great many ought to be considered before the happiness of one, you will decide against the captain, and in favor of your unhappy children.

As this one event engrosses all our thoughts and feelings, you will not expect me to write of anything else; so, with love from all the mourners, I remain your affectionate daughter,
Louisa Price.

The children all felt so much about the loss of the dog that they were not at all aware of the extravagance of Louisa's language. Neither did they perceive that there was a little affectation in the style, nor that the manner in which the loss of Neptune was announced was likely to alarm their father extremely.

All this was, however, apparent enough to Anna; and it required great self-command on her part to read the letter through gravely, and keep her thoughts to herself, when William and Henry were praising it. Knowing the sensitiveness of Louisa, and that it was as much as the poor child could bear to show her letter at all, she refrained from all comment upon it, and only considered within herself how she should prevent her father from being alarmed by Louisa's way of announcing the removal of Neptune. As there was a good deal of blank paper left, she asked Louisa if she might fill it up. This request was readily granted, and as soon as Anna was thoroughly engaged in writing, and all fear of further attention being paid to her letter was over, Louisa slipped off to bed.

Henry had watched his cousin Anna's looks, and observed that she did not join in the praises bestowed on Louisa's performance; and therefore, when the timid girl was gone, he asked Anna if she did not think that a very womanly letter, and remarkably well written for a child of twelve years of age.

"I do not admire it so much as I do some children's letters, Henry. Some of the expressions are too womanly. Louisa's letters are not simple enough to please me, but Papa says that her faults are those of a fine mind partially developed, that Louisa must be let entirely alone and never criticized, and that when she grows up she will write better than any of us."

"Well, I like her letter very much," said Henry. "Her manner of announcing the loss of Neptune is fit for a novel; it produces a sort of startling effect."

"Yes, quite too much so," rejoined Anna; "it is enough to frighten Papa, and make him think that one of us is dead at least. I would not on any account let it go so; but fortunately Louisa has begun her letter on the wrong page; I can therefore fold it the other way, and so put all her writing on the two inner pages, and write myself on that one which Papa will read first. In this way, I shall save him from being unnecessarily alarmed. I have heard him say a great deal about the impropriety of frightening people unnecessarily by a startling way of telling or writing a piece of news; I shall like to know what he will say to Louisa's doing it— whether he will think it best to tell her of that fault, or let it alone to cure itself, as he does all the rest of hers. I beg that you and Willy will not say a word to her about her letter."

The boys promised not to speak of it. Henry begged leave to read it again, and then he saw how alarming her beginning was. Anna told Henry that when her father was thrown from his horse and broke his arm, he made her write the account of it to her uncle Moreton three times over before he was satisfied that it was so worded as to give the least possible alarm and anxiety.

"How was it worded at last? Do you recollect, Anna?"

"Yes, I shall never forget it. I began in this way.

"'I write at the request of my father,'—he made me say that, to show that he was alive and in his senses,—'to tell you of an accident he met with yesterday, lest you should hear of it in some indirect and alarming way.'—'*Yesterday*' was put in to show that several hours had elapsed since the event; and saying that we wrote to *prevent his being alarmed* showed that what we should tell would not alarm him."

"Why did not you say 'a trifling accident'?" asked Henry.

"Because that would not have been true, and you know that Papa is truth itself. It was a bad fracture, and he was very much bruised and hurt besides. After breaking the news in this cautious way at the beginning of the letter, he allowed me to go into all the particulars and tell the whole truth about it. Papa does not approve of keeping friends ignorant of the health of those they love. Did you never hear him tell the story of the siege of Dunkirk,[1] and the false letters which the gentlemen there wrote to their absent wives?"

"No, never," said Henry; "I have heard my mother tell about the siege, but she never said a word about any false letters. What were they?"

"They were letters written by the gentlemen who remained in the besieged city, to their wives who fled to Calais to be out of danger. Those who were afraid their wives would return unadvisedly sent them terrific accounts of the siege and represented things as far worse than they really were. Other gentlemen, who had timid wives and had no fear of their coming back, wrote that all was as safe and quiet as if the enemy were a thousand miles off. When the ladies met, they compared these accounts, and found them so contradictory that they knew not what to believe and lost all confidence in their husbands' letters. Meanwhile, our grandfather always wrote the exact truth to our grandmother, and the letters she received were soon the only accounts that were believed by the refugees; and they used to say in French, 'Tell us, Madame Price, what the brave American writes, for our husbands send us nothing but lies.'"

"To be sure, in such a case as that," said Henry, "where there were so many together, any false account would be immediately detected, and then they would not know what to believe. I wonder the husbands had not thought of that."

"Some were perhaps in the habit of deceiving their wives, and never thought of being detected. But in writing, as in speaking, it is not only the best policy to state the exact truth, but it is our duty to do so. In all our intercourse with others, it is of the utmost importance to preserve their confidence, and this cannot be done unless truth is scrupulously adhered to, in writing as well as speaking."

"But there are some cases, Anna," said William, "in which we are not obliged to tell the whole truth; we may hold our tongues, and so I suppose we may sometimes avoid mentioning a subject in a letter."

"Certainly," replied Anna; "there are many such cases. But where our friends are sick or in danger, we have a right to be informed of it, and Papa says it is a mistaken attempt at kindness to withhold the truth; for if the least suspicion crosses the mind that we are not informed of the worst, our imaginations torment us far more than any known evil could. Do you remember, William, when Louisa was ill and my father was in New York, and I kept him informed every day of her state?"

"O yes, I remember it; and I recollect, too, that Dr. Smith advised you not to tell my father anything about her illness, as he could not leave his business to return to her."

"I knew better what he would like. I wrote him every particular; and the confidence he had in me that I would do so saved him a great deal of suffering. He has often said that if he had had any suspicion of my trying to conceal the worst, he should have been miserable, and should have been tempted to return, though it would have ruined his affairs. But feeling sure that he knew the whole truth, from day to day, enabled him to continue in New York and perform the urgent duties that detained him there. Oh, there is nothing like truth, in all things! But now I must leave off talking with you, and make my additions to Louisa's letter. If you want something to read, Henry, you will find two very good fictitious letters in this excellent little book, *A Visit to the Seaside*."

Henry took the book and was soon wholly engrossed by it.

Chapter XI
Anna's Lessons in Letter Writing to
a Boy on Her Father's Farm

It was a rule of Mr. Price's house that all letters should be carried to and from the post office in a small leather bag or wallet with a spring-lock to it, provided for the purpose. When it was brought home and its contents distributed, it was hung up in the hall to receive the letters of the family which were going to the mail; and it was the business of one of the farming men to carry it every morning, at an early hour, to the post office, where it was left 'til the arrival of the next mail, that it might be ready to receive the next budget for Oakwood. In consequence of this arrangement, Mr. Price escaped the trouble of lost letters, of which he often heard his neighbors complain.

During his father's absence, it was William's privilege to go for the letters and distribute them, a business which he very well liked. One day there was found in the leather wallet a letter directed to James Williams. This was a boy of fourteen years of age who worked on the farm. He was so familiarly known as "boy Jem" that his name at full length was hardly recognized. When, however, it was ascertained that the letter was for him, John Price ran off with it to him, and, on his return, he told everyone that it was a letter from Jem's mother, and though very badly written and full of bad spelling, he had helped Jem to make out the greater part of it, and Jem was so pleased to hear from home that he could not help crying for joy. He said he had been away from home the greater part of a year, and had not heard a word about any of them 'til now. John had hardly finished his account when they saw Jem approaching the house with rapid strides. Anna suspected that he was coming to get further aid in deciphering the precious letter he held in his hand, and kindly put herself in his way. She was the very person whose help and sympathy he most desired, and they were soon to be seen standing under the shade of a spreading elm tree, Anna reading and Jem looking earnestly in her face. Nothing could be more incorrect than the composition, orthography, and penmanship of this letter, and yet, as a messenger of love and good tidings, it was a valuable and respectable performance; it certainly gave more real happiness than many a more elaborate composition. It must have cost the writer a great effort, but could she have seen the countenance of her son on hearing its contents, she would have felt amply repaid. None, therefore, should omit writing to their friends because they cannot do it well. Any letter is better than none. But all who have had any education ought to endeavor to acquire a facility in writing letters.

Anna found, on inquiring, that Jem had never written to his family since he left them; and yet he had had education enough to enable him to read with ease, and to write a tolerable hand. He said he had often wished to write, but thought it too great an undertaking for him. Anna offered to assist him, and encouraged him to reply immediately to his mother's letter. She perceived that his heart was full of feeling for his family, which he would find it extremely difficult to put on paper in any intelligible form; and, therefore, she proposed that he should tell her what he wished to say, when she would write it down for him and he could copy it in his own handwriting. Anna felt so much for the mother's anxiety for her son that she appointed an hour that very evening for writing Jem's letter. She had him alone with her in the schoolroom, and with a great deal of drawing out, questioning, and suggesting, she contrived to make him speak out some of the affectionate things he had in his heart, and to tell how he was situated, and what he had done ever since he left his father's house. When he was quite stuck fast, and could not think of anything else to say, Anna advised him to shut his eyes, and think how they all looked at home, to fancy himself there talking to them, and then he might think of something more to tell them in his letter. After pondering a long while with his hand over his eyes, he said he could not think of anything to say, only questions that he should put to them if he were really with them.

"Very well," said Anna; "tell me the questions, and put them all in your letter; perhaps your mother will answer them."

That was a new idea to Jem; he went on very fluently in this new track, and soon made his letter quite long enough, considering he had to copy it all.

Anna had written his sentences very plainly, and arranged his matter as it should be in a letter; and having put a sheet of ruled paper before him, and given him a good pen, she left him to make a literal copy of her manuscript. It was slow work for such clumsy, unpracticed fingers; and when Anna returned to the schoolroom at the end of an hour, he had but half completed his task and was very much tired, so she advised him to leave the rest 'til another time. She promised to take care of his unfinished letter, and not let anyone see it, as that was a point on which he was very sensitive.

On looking over her pupil's letter, Anna was surprised to find how many blunders he had contrived to make, notwithstanding he had hers before him as a model. He had paid no attention at all to her paragraphs, but had written it all close together. He did not know that words should be divided according to their syllables; so he put in as many letters of a word as he could crowd in at the end of a line, and added the remainder at the beginning of the next, whether they made a syllable or not. Sometimes he joined several words together, as if they were one; frequently he wrote the same word twice over; he put in and left out syllables; and what looked worst of all, he wrote the pronoun I with a small letter.

Anna felt rather discouraged at the sight of so many mistakes; but her benevolent wish that the boy's mother should hear from him made her resolve not to damp his energies by any criticisms, but encourage him to finish and dispatch this letter, and afterwards try to improve him in the art of letter writing. Accordingly, the next evening Jem finished copying out his letter; Anna sealed and directed it in his presence, and it was safely deposited in the family letter-bag. She found he was aware of having made numerous mistakes in copying from her manuscript and, on expressing a wish that he knew how to write a letter, Anna offered to instruct him, and appointed a meeting with him in the schoolroom, at the same hour the next evening.

On Anna's return to the parlor, the boys were eager to know all about Jem's letter, his mistakes and his difficulties. Anna told them he had the same fondness for a regular beginning that William had, for his first sentence was, "This comes to inform you that I am well, and hope you are the same."

William approved of this beginning, Henry thought it very stiff and old-fashioned, Anna objected to it as altogether superfluous.

"Every letter," she said, "comes to inform one of something; and therefore it is unnecessary to say that it does. And unless you have been ill, and there is great anxiety about your health, there is too much egotism in making that your first topic. Jem should have begun with saying that he had just received his mother's letter and that it had made him very happy."

After describing Jem's numerous difficulties to the boys, Anna told them of her promise to instruct him in the art of letter writing, and consulted with them on the best means. Jem's imperfect education in the first rudiments of learning and his want of familiarity with books made it necessary to teach him very differently from a well-educated boy. His ignorance of orthography was the first great difficulty to be overcome. The boys suggested his learning a lesson in the spelling book every evening; but Anna thought that would be very tedious to him, and of less advantage than writing from a book or correct manuscript, by copying which, other things might be learned at the same time, such as where to use capitals, how to divide words, etc. When, by this exercise, he had acquired some facility in putting words and sentences together, she would set him to writing original matter, in the shape of a diary of his own life. Noting down, each evening, what he had done during the day was the easiest of all composition, and would be a good introduction to letter writing. All were of opinion that it would be pleasanter to Jem to copy from manuscript than from print. And as Anna's handwriting was such a one as he could not hope to imitate, it was decided that he should copy one of the boys'. As William was willing to lend his aid, and his writing was very good, he wrote about ten lines in his best manner, making the farming operations of the day his theme. His manuscript was criticized, altered, and rewritten, that it might be as correct as possible, and Anna said Jem should copy it 'til he could do it without a fault.

The pupil liked his lesson very much, and did his best to imitate his model; but he was obliged to copy those ten lines four times before he could do it without a mistake, though he tried to imitate each word, as if he were writing a large-hand copy. When at last the task was accomplished, William wrote ten lines more in the same legible and correct manner, and these were copied with rather more facility than the first, which was encouraging to all parties.

By the end of a week's instruction, Jem's progress was considerable; and he even lengthened his exercise by adding a sentence of his own to the farming journal. The moment, however, that he attempted to go alone, he failed. The very words which he had written properly when copying, he spelled in a totally different manner when he wrote from his own head. This convinced him of the advantage of continuing still longer to copy from correct models, so, besides writing William's journal, he made long extracts from books.

When, by long practice, Jem had at last acquired some facility in writing and spelling, he began original composition under Anna's guidance, and soon learned to write a very good account of his day's occupations. He became fond of keeping a diary, and never failed to note down, in the evening, what he had been doing during the day. Being a youth of good abilities, he by degrees added a few reflections to the facts he recorded. The step from this sort of composition to letter writing was a very easy one; and what Jem had dreaded as the most difficult task proved so agreeable to him that he was in danger of making his friends pay too much postage,[2] and tiring them with long details of what could interest no one but himself. His kind instructress warned him against these errors, and he readily profited by her hints. It was more difficult to correct him of the fault which he next committed, that of writing in a flourishing, bombastic style, which is most especially to be avoided by young persons. Jem now aimed at making a fine, high-sounding beginning to his letter, such as the following:

My dear brother,
    My pen, which has lain so long in idleness, has now commenced its important task. It being my duty, and I trust, my interest, to inform you of my circumstances, I shall lead you to understand that I am in good health and prosperous condition. I have been, and still am, at work on Mr. Price's farm.

It was in vain that Anna hinted to her pupil that she thought all but the last sentence of the above paragraph superfluous. He valued himself very much upon it, and did not like to have it found fault with. Anna showed it to William, and it proved a good warning to him. This specimen of Jem's composition did more towards curing William of his fondness for formal beginnings than all the criticism he had heard on the subject. Another of Jem's errors was fancying that he showed his learning by using long words and expressing himself in a round-about way. Being troubled once by an inflammation in his eyes, he was informing his mother of it; and instead of saying in a simple way that his eyes were weak, and would not allow of his writing much at a time, he wrote thus: "At present, if I were to demonstrate on behalf of my eyes, I should say they were very poor."

He was very much surprised when Anna told him that he had written absolute nonsense, in trying to write elegantly, and that if she had occasion to mention such a thing, she should express herself in the plainest way.

It was long before Jem could be convinced that the simplest expression is the best. Many young persons err in this particular; but they need only examine the best models, to become sensible of its truth.

Notes for *The Youth's Letter-Writer*

These excerpts are taken from the Library of Congress copy of Eliza Farrar, *The Youth's Letter-Writer; or The Epistolary Art* (New York: H. & S. Raynor, 1840), 1–14, 134–43, 147–58. I have modernized spelling and punctuation in a few instances.

   1. On the siege of Dunkirk, see the biographical introduction.

   2. In the nineteenth century, postage was still paid by the recipient, not the sender, of a letter.

Hallie Quinn Brown

1849–1949

Hallie Quinn Brown was born in Pittsburgh, Pennsylvania, on March 10, 1849, to freed slaves Frances Jane Scroggins and Thomas Arthur Brown. Hers was a middle-class family; her father worked as a porter, conductor, and steward. While she was growing up, her house was a center for the A.M.E. (African Methodist Episcopal) Church and the Underground Railroad. Her family moved to Canada in 1864, as did many other black families during the Civil War, for safety. After the war, her family relocated to Wilberforce so that she and her brother could attend Wilberforce College. She was taught elocution by Bishop Daniel Payne at Wilberforce College and graduated in 1873, making her first public speech as salutatorian. For several years she taught at plantation schools in Mississippi and South Carolina. From 1874 to 1878 she taught in Dayton, Ohio, and she studied further there under Professor Robertson of the Boston School of Oratory. In the 1880s, she toured with the Lyceum as an elocutionist, and in 1882 joined the Wilberforce Concert Company, touring all over the United States and Europe. She graduated from the Chautauqua Lecture School in 1886. From 1885 to 1887, Brown was dean of Allen University in Columbia, South Carolina, and from 1892 to 1893, she taught at Tuskegee Institute in Alabama under Frederick Douglass. Brown taught public school again in Dayton, Ohio, from 1887 to 1891, and established a night school for migrants there. In 1893 Brown was appointed professor of elocution at Wilberforce College. She used her speaking tours from 1894 on to raise funds for Wilberforce College and spent five years touring Europe.

Hallie Quinn Brown was an able politician and a friend of Frederick Douglass. She was an activist in campaigns for temperance, women's suffrage, and equal rights for African Americans. She was a feminist, converted by Susan B. Anthony, whom she heard speak at Wilberforce. She campaigned for Warren Harding and Herbert Hoover, and used her influence to promote an antilynching bill. She was a founder of the National Association of Colored Women's Clubs, and from 1920 to 1924 she was president of the National Association of Colored Women. When Wilberforce College split from Central State University, Brown chose to stay with the institution of public education, Central State. She had lived most of her life in Wilberforce, at Homewood Cottage, with her parents. She died September 16, 1949, at age one hundred.

Many African American writers had trouble publishing with national white presses. Her elocution texts, *Bits and Odds: A Choice Selection of Recitations* (1880) and *Elocution and Physical Culture: Training for Students, Teachers, Readers, Public Speakers* (1910?), she had printed locally and then served as her own distributor, listing the publisher on the title page as "Homewood Cottage." Some biographies refer to a text titled *First Lessons in Public Speaking* (1920) by Hallie Quinn Brown. I have been unable to locate a copy of this work; perhaps the remaining copies were lost when a tornado destroyed the Hallie Quinn Brown Library at Central State University in 1970, or perhaps the early biographies renamed the pamphlet on *Elocution* by some mistake.

Bits and Odds is an undated collection of "pieces" to be spoken in elocutionary performances, with a short preface on elocution that I include in this volume. This preface celebrates elocution as a contemporary art that unites vocal training and spiritual uplift. I assume that Hallie Quinn Brown's repertory in her tours would be very like the selections she made for this volume: in that case, she performed a varied program that included classics (like Shakespeare and Mark Twain), political activist poems and speeches (like Frances Watkins Harper's "The Dying Bondman"), and dialect humor (Irish, German, Negro).

Brown's theory of elocution, expounded in *Elocution and Physical Culture*, is greatly influenced by the theories of Delsarte, the French actor who developed elocution as an art, but also by her reading in classical rhetoric (especially Cicero and Quintilian) and her personal experience as a speaker, singer, and teacher. Borrowing from Delsarte the notion that elocution allows vocal expression of the moral, intellectual, and spiritual, Brown outlines a course in physical training that also uses techniques from classical delivery. I have included most of Brown's pamphlet, since it is very rare. This work accomplishes three things at once: it describes a program of exercises for voice, posture, and gesture; it summarizes human physiology of speech and nineteenth-century theories of gesture as a "natural" language of emotions; and it provides excerpts from theories on rhetorical delivery from many theorists, from Cicero to Delsarte. Brown insists that expression be natural and conversational, that emotion inhabit every expression, that sincerity be the hallmark of the true artist, and that delivery depend as much on the "moral tone" as on physical technique and emotional inflection. Brown adds to the traditional elocution manual a chapter on the Bible; many of her students at Wilberforce became preachers in the A.M.E. church.

For further information, see "A Sketch of the Life of Miss Hallie Quinn Brown," *The AME Church Review*, 1889–90, 256–61; Annjennette S. McFarlin, "Hallie Quinn Brown: Black Woman Elocutionist" (Ph.D. diss., Washington State University, 1975); McFarlin, "Hallie Quinn Brown: Black Woman Elocutionist," *Southern Speech Communication Journal*, Fall 1980, 72–82; Jane Donawerth, "Textbooks for New Audiences: Women's Revisions of Rhetorical Theory at the Turn of the Century," in *Listening to Their Voices: The Rhetorical Activities of Historical Women*, ed. Molly Meijer Wertheimer (Columbia: University of South Carolina Press, 1997), 337–56; Susan Kates, "The Embodied Rhetoric of Hallie Quinn Brown," *College English*, January 1997, 59–71; Claire Strom, "Hallie Quinn Brown," in *American National Biography*, ed. John A. Garraty and Mark C. Carnes (New York: Oxford University Press, 1999), 3:676–77; and Susan Kates, *Activist Rhetorics and American Higher Education, 1885–1937* (Carbondale: Southern Illinois University Press, 2001), 53–74.

From *Bits and Odds* (1880?)

"Remarks on Elocution"

Thought cannot be transmitted from mind to mind. The human mind must cognize for itself. Words are the physical symbols of ideas. Mere words often cause the mind to form ideas.

173

Words expressed by the human voice form the best method of arousing lively thoughts or deep feelings. In the lower animal nature we find utterance, *utterance*, UTTERANCE, from the thrilling warble of the songster to the dreary low of cattle.

True expression is a simple interpretation of nature. Elocution is the art of expressing thoughts and sentiments in the most natural manner. But elocution is also a science. It embraces a study of the respiratory system and the construction and management of the vocal organs.

Oratory and elocution are kindred. Oratory is more ancient. Elocution is recent. It is truly one of the fine arts. It is one of the most popular arts and its popularity is increasing. The day will come when it will be as customary to listen to the rendition of a poem or a fine prose selection at an evening parlor entertainment as that of a vocal or instrumental solo.

Schools of oratory were not uncommon among the ancients. Aeschines,[1] self-ostracized from classic Athens, established a school of oratory at Rhodes and thrilled his pupils by the powers of his eloquence.

But oratory is limited. The province of the orator is to convey to the listener his own ideas and to convince the listener at will while he has his ear. The elocutionist has a broader field. He has not so much to do with giving forth the original thoughts and feelings of his own mind as he has in giving forth those thoughts and feelings he has created in his mind, suggested by the expressed words of another, and causing the listener on the other hand to start the kindred chords vibrating in unison with his own.

"Nascuntur poetae, fiunt oratores"[2] may be a truism, but the latter statement can be made no more truly concerning orators than singers. Had the statement been made with respect to elocutionists, it would be less doubted, for truly without thorough culture the reader has not power to play at will upon the chords of the popular heart.

Elocution embraces many of the elements of music. To it belong as truly harmony, rhythm, cadence, swell, pitch, volume, etc., as to music itself.

The elocutionist must attain the expression of nature. We say *attain*, and use the word advisedly. The varieties of natural expression are as many, perhaps, as the varieties of the human countenance. To possess these, the reader must reach a high perfection. And this can come through no channel but training. Yet the true elocutionist, like the true singer, does not show his training in his execution. He must have that semblance of artlessness which is the perfection of the art. In short, through culture he must make many varieties of expression his very own. This cannot be accomplished by self-training alone, nor by the study of books. He who would excel in this art, for art it is, must undergo a thorough course in elocution under a skilled master. Hence the art, like that of music, painting, or sculpturing, is a *lettre de cachet*,[3] and he who attempts to appear before the public as an entertainer, without having broken the seal by permit of the "king," will find himself ruled out of the profession as a *bore*.

The reader should naturally possess a flexible voice, with richness of tone, and considerable volume. He should have a sympathetic nature, but should be able to control his emotions. With such qualifications, drill and study alone are necessary to fit him to please an audience.

It is not essential for him to lose his individuality. The reader has more to do than to imitate. He must feel and then express those feelings. Should two persons, one of a nervous, the other of a lymphatic temperament,[4] render a piece exactly alike, there would at once be shown proof of a defect in one of them, for they could not *feel* exactly alike, even about the same facts. Hence one of them would be artificial. It is the cultivation of our own natures that is aimed at and not the imitation of the nature of another. The powers of our own mind are to be drawn out.

Nature is "true, beautiful, good."[5] By culture we are to find these perfections of nature, and by training we are to conceal the art by which we adapt ourselves to the creations of the author, and the creations of the author to ourselves.

We cannot connect thought and its verbal symbols by secret links with our own thoughts and emotions. To do this and interpret them to the listener is the sole province of the public reader.

Notes for *Bits and Odds*

This selection is taken from Hallie Quinn Brown, *Bits and Odds: A Choice Selection of Recitations, for School, Lyceum, and Parlor Entertainments Rendered by Miss Hallie Q. Brown*, with introduction and sketches by Faustin S. Delaney. First printed in the 1880s in Xenia, Ohio, by Chew Press, 1910 (?). I am assuming that the phrase "With an Introduction and Sketches by Faustin S. Delaney" on the title page refers to the biographical sketches, not the preface on elocution. My gratitude to the Hallie Quinn Brown Library, Central State University, Wilberforce, Ohio.

1. Aeschines (c. 397–322 B.C.E.), Athenian orator and ambassador, rival of Demosthenes, who opened a school of rhetoric in Rhodes. He chose exile when he was defeated politically by Demosthenes and was stripped of his right to prosecute.

2. Poets are born, orators made. Elsewhere attributed to Cicero, but Brown probably lifted this Latin phrase from L'Abbé Delaumosne's introduction to his work on Delsarte; see *The Delsarte System of Oratory*, 4th ed. (New York: Edgar S. Werner, 1893), xxiv.

3. *Lettre de cachet*: letter of introduction

4. Lymphatic temperament: sluggish, unenergetic personality.

5. These terms are standard terms for aesthetic values in the nineteenth century, attributed to Plato and especially common in Delsarte. See François Delsarte, in *Delsarte System of Oratory*, 524, 528; and Angélique Arnaud, in *Delsarte System of Oratory*, 218, 228; see also Victor Cousin, *The True, the Beautiful, and the Good* (1858).

From *Elocution and Physical Culture* (before 1910?)

Preface

This course of Elocution comprises fifteen lessons. They are not designed for public use, only so far as they are to be taught by the teacher who presents them.

There are many topics, facts, and ideas merely stated or suggested, which are to be discussed, proved, and enlarged under the direction of the living instructor.

It has been the aim, as far as possible, to simplify and omit much of the "dead-work" that would confuse and discourage. At the same time, care has been taken to give such instruction as will enable a conscientious, determined student to "follow up" the study of elocution.

These lessons are by no means as full and concise as desired; they are far from the standard to which the teacher aspires. But if these subjects (although incomplete) and kindred ones are examined and their principles applied to practice, the more will it be seen and felt that no one can become a good elocutionist, unless he studies body and mind, matter and spirit, and makes the results his own by actual appropriation.

Science and art, theory and practice must go hand in hand to develop, train, and perfect us for this life and the one to come.

The works of Delsarte, the master-teacher, and Guttman's *Gymnastics of the Voice*[1] have been consulted and a complete list of authors can be given to any student who wishes to inquire more thoroughly into this, the Art of Arts.

LESSON I

All Art must be preceded by a certain mechanical expertness—Goethe[2]

DECOMPOSING EXERCISES

HEAD AND NECK EXERCISES

Turning the head right and left.
Bowing the head forward and backward.
Let the head describe a circle.

TRUNK EXERCISES

Shoulders up and down.
Shoulders backward and forward.
Shoulders circle. Turning the trunk right and left. Inclination of trunk backward and forward. Elevating the trunk.

ARM EXERCISES

Lifting and moving the arm forward up, downward back, and sideways up. Turning and revolving the arms. Attraction and repulsion (downward, upward, forward, backward).

HAND, WRIST, AND FINGER EXERCISES

Raise the arm from the shoulder, hand limp and following the arm.
Raise the arm from the shoulder, float the hand like a feather fastened to a rod. Turn the hand over, palm upward as the arm descends.
Free the wrists. Free the fingers.

FOOT AND TOE EXERCISES

Foot forward and backward.
Foot sideways.
Foot forward, side, back, and instep.
Rise on toes—arms loose, neck and trunk relaxed.
Weight of the body on the right toes—hop twice.
Weight of the body on the left toes—hop twice.

POSITION OF THE BODY

Place the audience in the realms of the superior, inferior, and equal.
Discussion: Deportment, dress, attitude, walking.

LESSON II
GESTURE

Suit the action to the word, the word to the action, with this special observation, that you o'erstep not the modesty of nature.—Shakespeare.[3]

PHYSICAL EXERCISES (See Lesson I)

Gesture is a natural language. It is the language of the heart.—Delsarte[4]

Action is the language of the body and should harmonize with the spirit within.—Cicero[5]

In the evolution of human expression gesture preceded speech, and in speech voice preceded articulation, and this natural order should be observed in the study of elocution.

The study of gesture and the practice of well-directed exercises for its culture demands the student's first attention.

Gesture is motion expressive of thought. Gesture serves as a prelude to the voice, and informs an audience the nature of what is to follow.

The sentiment to be delivered may demand that the gesture shall accompany, precede, or follow the words of the speaker.

Cicero states that the best orator, without it, is of no value, and is often defeated by one in other respects his inferior.[6] Athletic training is the true remedy for ungainly manners on the platform and in private life.

Delsarte's dictum is "Strength at the center and freedom at the surface."[7] This power is the secret of grace in all bodily action.

The attitude and action will usually be fitting and significant where the avenues of expression are open—that is, the ankle and knee joints loose; the thigh, trunk, neck, fingers, wrist, elbow, and shoulders free and under perfect control. The voice open, pure, round, and full; the thought well arranged and properly appreciated—these will give ease and confidence to the speaker.

Gesture must be studied in order to render it elegant, but in such a perfect way as not to seem studied.

"True Art is to conceal Art."[8] The student who would become an adept must study and practice with untiring industry. Says Garrick: "I do not rely upon that inspiration which idle mediocrity awaits."[9] To reach the heights one must make a critical study of every picture or piece of statuary he sees.

The principles which govern great artists, like Phidias, Leonardo da Vinci, Michaelangelo, Rosa Bonheur, Burne-Jones, Henry O. Tanner[10] and others, lie at the basis of true oratory.

The three essential elements of grace are ease, precision, and harmony, which correspond to the vital, mental, and moral centers of man. In order that these be properly blended, the speaker must be genuine, and truth must radiate from the mental or spiritual, which is the final center. As long as man has a voice and body, body and voice must be coordinate in their action with the spiritual. It is important, therefore, that their growth and cultivation should be well directed; too much or too little of the one or the other of these elements will be a violation of the law of proportion.

Discussion: Divisions of Gesture.

The parts of a gesture are preparation, consummation, and return.—The ictus.[11]

Physical Exercises.
Opposition of Agents.
Parallel Movements.
Opposite Movements.

THE NINE LAWS OF GESTURE *(Delsarte)*[12]

1. That the look of the eye always precedes the gesture of the hand and the arm.

2. It precedes the sound of the voice. The law of succession has us begin with the eye and unroll the whole arm from the shoulder to the tips of the fingers. A gesture made after the sound of the voice is useless and, therefore, bad.

3. Its velocity is precisely proportional to the mass moved. Gesture is like a pendulum: if the distance is short, the motion is quick. The longer the distance described, the slower the movement.

4. A gesture out from the body is eccentric.

5. A gesture in toward the body is concentric.

6. Gestures of force should move in straight lines.

7. Beauty, love, affection, sympathy, and especially address to Deity should be described in curved lines.

8. A general gesture should be made across the body, so as to utilize the space in front.

9. The arm should always move in sections and never from the shoulder.

THE FUNCTIONS OF THE HAND

Quintilian affirms that the hands are almost as powerful as words and points out that they may be made to beckon or dismiss, to threaten or beseech, to ask or deny, to excite or restrain, to express doubt or proof, admiration or shame, confusion, penitence, devotion, submission, astonishment, honor, avarice, and many other ideas and passions—besides indicating time, space, distance—and declares that the use of the hand is the common language of mankind.[13]

There are three faces to the hand. The front or palm of the hand, which is vital in nature, expresses all that is pleasant and generous. It reveals. The back of the hand, which is moral, is mystic in expression. It conceals. The side of the hand, which is mental, is definitive in expression.

FINGERS

1. The forefinger is used in explanation.

2. The second finger and thumb denote power.

3. The third finger connects with the heart and is used to denote the utmost delicacy.

4. The fourth finger denotes subtlety.

5. The thumb is the thermometer of life.

Discussion: Position, Poise, Movement, Thermometers of Passion.

[Gestures for hands are given.]
Discussion: Pantomime.

LESSON III
MUSCLES

Physical Education is a factor of modern development.

[Exercises for parts of the body are given.]

Anatomy teaches, by the articulations of the bones and the arrangement of the muscles, that the human form was fashioned by the Creator to execute graceful curves. Awkward movements are natural to no one; therefore, to be natural is to be graceful.

Hogarth's "Line of Beauty" is a flowing curve,[14] while another learned scientist shows that all natural movements are in curves, that the wings of birds and the limbs of man describe in motion representations of the figure 8, which is formed of a combination of curves. Action should be something more than graceful; it should be intelligent. Every movement should have a meaning and every action the right meaning. The study of muscles will enable us to give expression through the body.

A well developed body is essential to a forcible and dignified voice. Nature demands a correct muscular movement from the singer and orator, as well as from the athlete and the dancer. Without the proper cooperation of the muscles, it is impossible to accomplish anything. The muscles of the body are divided into voluntary and involuntary. The heart, the diaphragm, and the intestines are voluntary; all the remaining muscles are involuntary. We will consider those muscles of the trunk that are chiefly used in respiration, viz.: the chest, the abdominal muscles, and the diaphragm. The muscles of the chest serve in breathing to move the chest, the arms at certain times, and to raise and lower the shoulders. They lie upon the front surface of the thorax. The abdominal muscles serve for expiration, shield the intestines, promote the bending of the body, and help to contract the abdominal cavity.

The midriff, or diaphragm, is a large, powerful muscle, fan-shaped, flat and sinewy. It forms the floor of the chest and serves as a partition dividing the upper or breathing, and the heart or circulatory organs in the chest, from the lower or digestive organs contained in the abdomen. That part of the muscle extending toward the chest cavity is arched. In the act of inspiration it flattens itself and thus increases the chest cavity.

The diaphragm, although considered an involuntary organ, can, owing to the diverse nature of its nervous fibers, be made voluntary to a certain extent. It is this which enables us to speak and sing, as far as inspiration and expiration are concerned. The costal and intercostal muscles are attached to the ribs and are used in the elevation and depression of the short ribs.

LESSON IV

[Exercises for parts of the body are given. The chest, oral cavity, nasal cavity, pharynx, larynx, lungs, and trachea are physically described.]

179

LESSON V
BREATHING WITH EXERCISES

He who cannot condescend to "small matters" in preparation will never be great in achievement, for nothing is trivial in which principle is involved.—Bell[15]

[Exercises for parts of the body are given.]

It is written that when the Creator formed man He "breathed into his nostrils the breath of life; and man became a living soul."[16] It is certain that breath is life, breath is speech. It is the chief source of power. No student of elocution can make substantial progress who does not give special attention to the exercises in breathing. It is highly important that we know how to form and utilize breath. It is not so much the amount of breath that is desirable, as the manner in which it is used. Economy is better than quantity. Breath should be taken through the nose—which is the front door of the respiratory passages—and not through the mouth.

Breathing takes place voluntarily and to a certain extent involuntarily. Involuntary breathing is divided into two parts—inspiration, and expiration. Voluntary breathing [is divided] into three parts—inspiration, holding the breath, and expiration. The latter is called artistic breathing. The singer and speaker should not begin a single sentence before having his lungs sufficiently inflated. The acts of inspiration and expiration should be done slowly and uniformly. Right use of the diaphragm and abdominal muscles will thus be secured.

Practice systematic breathing while walking. A good full voice is closely connected with good breathing.

[Topics to consider for breathing are given, and suggestions for vocal exercises.]

LESSON VI
VOICE BUILDING

Trifles make up perfection, and perfection is no trifle.—M. Angelo.[17]

[Exercises are given: poise, legs, arms, trunk, neck, reaching, respiratory, "Mouth Gymnastics," etc.]

Sound is the first language of the babe in the cradle. All languages grew sound by sound; as with the race, so with the individual.

The original vowel-sound, the primitive a (ah), the first, simplest, and easiest of all vocal utterances, is man's mother-tone. To intensify its verbal expression, man gave the prefix "m-ma"; and the children have sweetened it by repetition into "mama." This mother-tone may be heard from every baby of every nation under the sun. It may be heard in the voice of the animal kingdom as in the *Ba* of the kid, the lamb, and the calf. This cry comes from the mother-tone *a* whose musical notation is placed in the second space of the treble clef. It is the first cry of babyhood, of mother-love, of home-love, and home-longing.

This mother-tone runs like a scarlet thread through the lullabies of many primitive peoples. It is heard in the folk songs, in the simple ballads, and in the passion of the opera. It is cadenced in the works of great composers, and in the tone-paintings of the masters.

The study of voice begins with sound. By voice is meant all sounds uttered by the vocal mechanism, whether it be a hoarse whisper, a coarse grunt, a sweet coo, or any other musical or unmusical sound. Every person must listen to his own voice in order to understand it, must cultivate it by correcting its faults. He should aspire to a good, sweet, mellow tone of voice. He should seek purity in advance of fullness and power. God has placed a wonderful instrument at the disposal of the orator. But what avails its possession if we do not know its use or how to tune it?

This instrument or apparatus is composed of three parts:

The Motor, represented by the chest cavity, or air reservoir.

The Vibrating Element, represented by the larynx, or sounding-reed.

The Resonators, represented by the pharynx and mouth, or resonance-box.

A healthy vocal development depends upon a knowledge of the vocal apparatus, a natural adjustment, and skill in the management of the same. To obtain the highest results, great skill is necessary in taking the breath suddenly or gradually, in holding it, and in giving it out suddenly or gradually. You must become absolutely master of your diaphragm. The chest should be elevated, the mouth and throat in a state of easy elasticity. The chest, larynx, nasal, and mouth cavities should be utilized in order to secure resonance from them.

The voice should be handled very gently, never forced, yet frequently exercised in every possible pitch, in every degree of force, and all variations of time and quantity.

LESSON VII
VOICE BUILDING (cont.)

God's grandest gift to Man is—Voice.[18]

[Voice exercises are given.]

LESSON VIII
ARTICULATION

Raftered by firm-laid consonants, windowed by opening vowels,
Thou securely art built, free to the sun and the air.—Story.[19]

[Exercises for parts of the body are given.]

Delsarte, the eminent teacher, asserts that all arts are found in articulation. Sound is the articulation of the vocal apparatus; gesture, the articulation of the dynamic apparatus; language, the articulation of the buccal[20] apparatus. Therefore, music, the plastic arts, and speech have their origin and their perfection in articulation. It is, thus, of the utmost importance to understand thoroughly the elements of speech, which is at the same time a vocalization and a dynamic. Without this knowledge no oratorical art is possible.

Articulation is the process of molding voice and breath into syllables and words, by the action of the jaw, lips, tongue, and palate. In order that articulation may be perfect, there must be a prompt, neat, and easy action of these organs. Words are to be delivered from the lips as beautiful coins, newly impressed, perfectly finished and neatly struck by the proper organs.

Unless one is perfectly distinct in articulation, he cannot become an easy, graceful, effective, and natural speaker. A singer or speaker has no more right to present to an audience a faulty articulation than he has to appear in an unbecoming dress. The saving grace for the impetuous in speech is careful articulation.

Exercise the soft palate by gaping, and the jaws by a movement down, up, and a rotary movement.

Practice the following exercise to secure an elastic play of the muscles of the mouth and for expressiveness of the face:

Ah-e-oo it-ip-ik

Elementary sounds of the English language are: Vocals, which consist of pure tones; Subvocals, consisting of tones and breath, united; Aspirates, composed of breath only. . . .

LESSON IX
PRONUNCIATION

Speak the speech, I pray you, as I pronounced it to you, trippingly on the tongue: but if you mouth it as many of our players do, I had as lief the town crier spoke my lines.—Shakespeare.[21]

Pronunciation is more a matter of habit than of knowledge.

Faults in pronunciation early contracted are suffered to gain strength by habit and grow so inveterate by time as to be almost incurable. A mere knowledge of the right way will not correct the fault. There must be a frequent repetition of the right way until the correct form will root out the wrong way. By obtaining correct ideas of the sounds, their influences over each other, the meaning and pronunciation of words, and their power over the understanding and will of man when properly arranged into sentences filled with correct thought and genuine feeling, a student may, with proper application and exercise, become a good reader and speaker.

We are made to realize the perfection which the ancient Greeks attained in this branch of delivery from the fact that, when a public speaker pronounced a word incorrectly, the whole audience simultaneously hissed him.

Defects can be removed by individual attention to the first principles of our language, at the same time following a teacher who can give the true English pronunciation, for sounds can only be learned by imitation; and this is the way in which elocution and music must be taught.

Cicero copied and imitated everybody—the very mockingbird of eloquence; but that is not his disparagement, but his greatest distinction and glory, for who so various as Cicero, who so sweet, so powerful, so simply eloquent, or again so magnificently flowing, and each and all in tune?

In pronunciation, great care should be taken that there be a distinct and dignified enunciation of every letter in a syllable.

Practice words, phrases, and sentences silently and audibly with an over-done precision and action of the jaw, tongue, and lips. The student must let every word be begun, continued, and ended before he touches its successor. One thing at a time and that one thing done in its entirety.

In addressing an audience, the words must not be uttered too far apart, but the sentences as a whole should be swung smoothly and gracefully.

Avoid a too rapid, as well as a drawling style of speaking. It is necessary to practice the voice and articulating organs in quick, slow, and moderate time.

The organs of speech, voice, and the breathing apparatus should be thoroughly exercised or "oiled up" in advance of every public effort.

LESSON X
INFLECTION, ACCENT, AND EMPHASIS

The soul that stops to contemplate its wings will never rise. —Delsarte[22]

[Exercises for parts of the body are given.]

Inflection is the bending or the sliding of the voice upward or downward from a given pitch.

Inflections are of three kinds—the upward or rising inflection; the downward or falling inflection; and the compound or circumflex inflection, which combines the two.

Inflection varies with the sense in which words are used and the feeling with which they are charged. It is by means of inflection that we express the varying degrees of emotion that we experience under different circumstances. And our main care in speaking should be to feel what we say and, as a rule, we shall not fail to observe due inflection. People who are in earnest are seldom at fault in this respect and, if we are as earnest and sincere upon the platform as we are in private conversation, we shall overcome any difficulties of inflection that may trouble us.

Let us get rid of the idea that there is one kind of inflection for the home, another for the pulpit, and another for the platform. Those who are most successful in either sphere are those who are the most natural, provided we remember not to allow the strength of our feeling to carry us beyond our proper pitch and pace.

Inflection in gesture has been defined as a movement indicating a passing emotion. Inflection in voice also subtly indicates each passing thought. Your inflection may become pantomime to the blind; and your pantomime, inflection to the deaf. The inflections have great influence in expressing or perverting the sense according as they are correctly or incorrectly made.

While we have given rules for making inflections, or slides of the voice either up or down, yet it should be remembered that every sentence which has been read with the upward slide can, under other circumstances, be read correctly with the downward slide. The sense governs everything here, as in emphasis. The pitch of the voice should vary sufficiently in inflection to be agreeable to the ear and to preserve the melody of sentences. As the lights and shades are to the picture, so are inflections to expression in reading and speaking.

Accent means stress or quantity of voice on a certain letter or letters in a word; it is made by concentrating the voice on that particular place in the word, heavy at first, then gliding into silence. There are two ways of making it: first by stress, when it occurs on short vowels; secondly, by quantity, when it occurs on long vowels.

Intonations are opposite to monotones and mean the rise and fall of the voice in its natural movements through a sentence. In the intonations the voice steps up or down by discreet degrees; but in the inflections, it glides up or down by continuous degrees.

Emphasis is the same thing as accent, only more of it. Emphasis is to words in a sentence what accent is to letters or syllables in a word. It is inseparably connected with the pauses. There are only two ways of making emphasis, which are the same as accent, viz: by stress and quantity. But there are as many ways of exhibiting it as there are pitches, qualities, and modifications of the voice—in song and in speech—all of which are very simple and very easily acquired by the persevering student. Nature abhors monotony or sameness of sound as much as she does a vacuum; therefore, give variety in emphasis, inflection, and waves as often as they occur.

Emphasis is sometimes exhibited by changing the seat of accent—"What is done, cannot be undone."[23] It may be exhibited by stress and higher pitch—"I tell you, tho' you, tho' all the world; tho' an angel from heaven declare the truth of it, I could not believe it." It is made by prolongation of sound and stress of voice, on either high, low, or medium pitches—"Roll on thou dark and deep blue ocean roll."[24]

Emphasis is also known by a pause just *before* or *after* the important word. The pause before awakens curiosity and expectation; after, carries back the mind to what was last said. Great care must be taken to avoid a stiff and formal mode of reading and speaking. Never be enslaved to thought alone, but yield to feeling when it predominates.

Cadence is a descent, or fall of the voice. In reading it means the proper manner of closing a sentence. The best cadence, that which rests most pleasantly on the ear, is the fall of a triad; that is, a regular fall of three notes from the prevailing pitch of voice. Cadence, or full stop, is not limited to the grammatical sentence, but at the end of a clause, or an auxiliary sentence.— "One country, one constitution, one destiny."[25]

LESSON XI
TIME, PITCH, AND FORCE

'Tis not enough the voice be sound and clear,
'Tis modulation that must charm the ear.—Story[26]

TIME

Time relates to duration. Its elements are quantity, movement, and pause. We have moderate, slow, and quick time. The speed with which we read depends entirely upon the matter to be presented. When the matter is of a light, joyous nature, the manner of reading or speaking should indicate that fact. Grave and solemn thought takes a stately style of utterance. A slight pause before and after an important thought, quotation, or metaphor gives emphasis to the same.

PITCH

Pitch is defined as the elevation and depression of the voice on the musical scale. "Every manifestation in life is a song, every sound is a song."[27]

Modulation signifies the accommodation of the voice to every variety and shade of thought and feeling.

Elocution and music are inseparable in their nature. Good reading and speaking are *music*; and he who can sit unmoved by their charms is a stranger to correct taste and insensible to the beauty of this art.

Everyone, whether he is aware of it or not, uses all the elements of music in his daily intercourse with society. When we call to one at a distance, we raise the voice to the upper pitches; when to one nearby, we drop it to the lower pitches; and when at a medium distance, we raise it to the middle pitches.

No better exercise can be given for the strengthening of the voice than the daily practice of the musical scale. The four best notes upon which to exercise the voice are those from *mi* to *la*.

[Exercises for voice are given.]

FORCE

Force relates to the loudness and softness of the voice, to the degree of energy, not to the manner of applying it—the latter is the province of stress. We have moderate, gentle, loud, and very loud force. These include the intermediate degrees. In a natural mood, moderate force is appropriate. When boisterous passions stir the soul, loudness and intensity of voice will inform the audience of its existence.

The quality of the voice should always be in harmony with the thought.

Do not mistake Pitch for Force, a common error known to public speakers.

185

[Passages to be read with varying force are given.]

STRESS

Stress always falls upon the accented syllables of emphatic words. We have radical stress, medium stress, and terminal stress.

[Passages to be read for practice placing stress are given.]

LESSON XIII
TONES OF THE EMOTION

Our voice can speak with its many and wonderful voices.
Play on the soft flute of love, blow the loud trumpet of war,
Sing with the high sesquialtro, or, drawing its full diapason,
Shake all the air with the grand storm of its pedals and stops.—Story[28]

[Exercises for parts of the body are given.]

"Eloquence is wisdom speaking fluently."[29]

Of all the wonderful varieties of artificial instruments which give forth sweet music, there is none that can compare with the human voice. And where shall we find an instrument that is like unto the human mind, upon whose stops the musician, the poet, and the orator grasps and strikes the compass of its magnificent capacities? What were all the attributes of man, his personal accomplishments and his boasted reason, without the faculty of speech whereby he may give utterance to the mind's great thoughts? To excel in the use of speech is the highest of human arts. It enables man to govern whole nations and to enchant while he governs.

The aristocracy of eloquence is supreme and in the land of the free can never be suppressed; it is the pride of peace and the glory of war. It rides on the wings of the breeze and thunders in the storm.

There is eloquence in every object of taste, both in art and nature—in sculpture, landscape gardening, architecture, poetry, and music. All come within the scope and plan of the orator, that he may rightly comprehend that intellectual relation in the liberal professions which connects one with the other and combines the influence of all.

The soul is often moved with feeling. We touch the strings of our harp and run through the whole gamut of expression. We have pleasant, unpleasant, and indifferent emotions, which express themselves in the tones of the voice. If the mind is unimpassioned, the natural or unimpassioned tone will be used. If a feeling of sublimity possess the soul, the orotund, or full-mouthed tone will be used. Should love or beauty dominate the speaker, effusive voice will present the same to the hearers. If hatred, disgust, and like feelings prevail, the guttural or throat voice should be used. Secrecy muffles itself in the aspirates. Anger and danger are expressed in the abrupt or explosive tone.

Every word and every sentence should have its proper proportion of emotion equally distributed by the speaker. Pity, indignation, love, hatred, etc., may be seen by an audience, in the eye, attitude, and action of an orator if he be thoroughly imbued with his subject.

Says Cicero: "The emotions you would move in others, must first be moved in you. Would you make men indignant, be yourself indignant. Would you move their pity, let it first appear that you pity. Would you excite admiration, admire the thing that you would have others esteem."[30]

"If you would move others, put your heart in the place of your larynx; let your voice become a mysterious hand to caress the hearer."—Delsarte[31]

[Passages are provided for voice exercises.]

PHILOSOPHY OF EXPRESSION

"I sought God in many places, and came at last to find Him in myself."—St. Augustine[32]

"The principle of this system lies in the statement that there is in the world a universal formula which may be applied to all sciences, to all things possible."—Delsarte[33]

This formula, or the principle of our being, is the *Trinity*. Man, the image of God, presents himself to us in three phases—the sensitive, intellectual, and moral. Man feels, thinks, and loves.

Life is the sensitive state, mind the intellectual state, and soul the moral state. These elements, though distinctive, cannot be separated. They interpenetrate, correspond with, and embrace each other, and must be harmoniously cultivated to reach the best possibilities of human existence.

Man communicates with his fellow man in three ways—the voice, the gesture, and the word—the different expressions of life, mind, and soul. The vocal apparatus of man is sound, inflection, and voice. Human language is composed of gesture, speech, and song. The muscular machinery of man is composed of gesture, sentiment, and emotion. Eloquence comprises voice, gesture, and speech.

The three great factors in the universe are God, man, and matter. Wherever God has worked, He has left the impress of His wisdom, love, and power. We find these reflected on earth, in air, and sky; sun, moon, and stars present them to view.

Plato's hypothesis was infinite goodness, infinite wisdom, and infinite active power, uniting to make one Divinity.

Having three factors with which to lay the foundation of a philosophy of expression as applied to oratory, we shall find a trinity of ideas frequently crossing our pathway. The painter has three colors: red, yellow, and blue. The sculptor has straight, convex, and concave lines whereby he gives utterance to his thought. We have length, breadth, and thickness. The law of velocity gives us rhythm, melody, and harmony.

The three Kingdoms of nature are the mineral, the vegetable, and the animal. *Three* is a vital number; it was the sacred number among the ancients. The Chinese take the triangle to signify union and harmony, the chief good of man, the heavens and earth.

The body, in connection with the mind, speaks many languages.

The painter and the sculptor make the flat canvas and the rough block of marble utter every passion of the mind, and touch the soul of the beholder, as if picture and statue spoke the language of the immortal Bard of Avon.[34] When masterly action[35] is joined with powerful elocution, the effect is irresistible; for if poetry, music, and statuary are good, is not oratory more so, since these three are embraced in the latter?

The Creator has implanted in our natures the senses, the mind, and the heart, for pure and noble purposes which cannot be reasoned away. We cannot argue men out of their senses and feelings. We may discuss history, science, philosophy, and the arts until we are wearied, but let us stand on some noted battlefield, some cherished spot of home and country, and your heart swells within you. Reason and cold philosophy vanish; you feel the inspiration of the place. A language which letters cannot shape nor sound convey speaks not to the head nor understanding, but to the heart and affections.[36]

Cicero says, "The poet is born such, the orator made such."[37] Reading books of rhetoric, eloquent extracts, choice bits of poetry, and eloquence will never produce an orator; these are but the effects of oratory. Eloquence may be found only in the depths of the human mind—the true philosophy of man and the practice of the highest good and truth.

The orator must feel rightly, think wisely, and act accordingly; then grace, style, and eloquence will cover you as a robe does the body.

[Passages for practice are given.]

LESSON XIV
COLOR

[O radiant bow!]
Heaven still rebuilds thy span,
Nor lets the type grow pale with age,
That first spake peace to man.—Campbell[38]

[Marching exercises are given.]

Says the Koran: "The colors which the earth displays to our eyes are manifest signs for those who think."[39]

The painter has three primary colors with which to pour his soul upon canvas—red, yellow, and blue. Red is significant of love; yellow of intelligence; blue of action or use. These compounded in various proportions enable the painter to produce every shade and hue seen in nature and in art. Blue and red in proper proportions make purple, or violet; yellow and red make orange; blue and yellow make green, etc.

By a similar and more incomprehensible process, the mental, moral, and vital tones of the voice may be blended, giving an endless variety to the expressions of all the different states and emotions of which we are capable. The mental voice may be enriched by being mixed with the vital, while the vital can be refined by association with the mental. The moral can also be blended with either, or both of the other two; and all three can be blended and, as illustrated by colors, be equal to the expression of the many moods to which man is subject.

Colors had great significance among all the ancient people. The color language may be traced through Egypt, Persia, India, China, Greece, and Rome. It was revived in the Middle Ages. These wonderful colors are to be seen in the Gothic cathedrals of Rome and Venice, as well as in all great cathedrals of Great Britain and other parts of the Old World—those living, pulsating paintings on window and wall with "hues that have words and speak to us of heaven."[40] Ruskin, that apostle of beauty and truth, in describing the art of a bit of blue carried into the red, and a bit of the red into the blue, and in speaking of the wonderful blending of colors in a thousand ways—whether on the shield of the knight, or in the masterpieces of art in hall or temple, or in the soft and subdued panes of ancient cathedrals, says: "And I call it a magnificent principle, for it is an eternal and universal one, not in art only, but in human life. It is the great principle of *brotherhood*; not by equality, nor by likeness, but by giving and receiving; the souls that are unlike, and the nations that are unlike, and the natures that are unlike, being bound into one noble whole by each receiving something from and of the other's gifts and the other's glory."[41] There is a striking analogy between painting and delivery. We have seven primary colors and seven pitches of sound, though strictly speaking we have but three of each. In painting, red, yellow, and blue are the essential ones; the others are produced by overlapping. Each color has its distinctive attribute—the red is caloric, the yellow is coloric, and in the blue ray chemical action is found.

Letters are likened to uncompounded paints, words to paints prepared for use, and, when properly arranged into sentences, they form the pictures upon the canvas of our imagination. Again, words are paints—the voice, the brush; the mind, the painter. But study, science, practice, taste, judgment, emotion, genius are necessary in order to paint well.

There is as much difference between a good and bad reader as there is between a good painter and a mere dauber. A good reader may become a good orator, singer, painter, or sculptor, for there is nothing in any of these arts that may not be seen in true delivery. A good reader and a bad singer, and a bad reader and good singer are without excuse, for the same strength, purity, distinctness, flexibility, and smoothness of voice that either requires and promotes are servants to each other.

[Passages for practice are given.]

LESSON XV
BIBLE READING

Thy word is a lamp unto my feet, and a light unto my path.—Psalms[42]

189

The Bible reveals God to man and is the interpreter of the God of nature. In revealing God, it discloses the greatest mysteries of creation; and by this knowledge we penetrate the labyrinth of the universe and look "from nature up to nature's God."[43]

The Bible is the most wonderful of all books and worthy of the profoundest study. There is no other language so rich in meaning, so full of imagery and moral beauty, so varied in biography, history, poetry, great truths and sublimity as the Bible.

If you stand mid towering Alps, beside the great and rolling ocean, or mighty, plunging Niagara—they all speak in thundering tones of God. These are the thoughts of God, visible forms of the Deity, created in our minds by the study of His Word. But this study reveals the relationship between man and his Maker, and we see God, tender, loving, and cry, "Abba Father."[44] We behold Christ who died for a lost world and, like Thomas, exclaim, "My Lord and my God."[45]

The study of the Word becomes a power unto salvation to all who believe. It becomes the only basis on which a consistent, stable, Christian discipline can be erected. If the Holy Scriptures come in constant attrition[46] with the mind, the conscience will be polished as a mirror and from its face our own characters may be reflected as with light from above. Says an eminent writer, "A peaceable citizen may be brought up under the eye of the law; an orderly and useful citizen under the eye of society; but a good and true man can alone be brought up under the eye of conscience."[47]

For this reason we urge the study of the Bible in the homes, the schools, and colleges of our land, so that the heart, as well as the mind, shall be trained to the love and the practice of every virtue. With the mind of the youth early imbued with the pure, peaceful, and benevolent principles of the Bible, we may bid defiance to selfish and immoral men who seek to decoy and corrupt.

A well furnished minister is among heaven's most precious blessings to a free, self-governed people. He stands as a sentinel, to warn, to arouse at the first alarm of danger; as a teacher, to correct and instruct; as a minister, to unfold the sacred page and lead the thirsty soul to the waters of eternal life.

Wisdom and intelligence are called for in religious leaders. They must be able to direct, and capable of commanding respect and confidence. They must be men of attainments and students of scripture. The standard of attainments in medicine, law, and pedagogy is continually rising; that in theology must also advance. An enlightened people demand an enlightened ministry. But you say, "The spirit of truth will guide you into all truth."[48] While God is constantly pouring out blessings and the Spirit is teaching—yet man's exertions should be none the less. It is the diligent that is made rich. God will certainly carry on His own cause, but through human instrumentality; and when He is favoring, by removing all obstacles and spreading a noble field of endeavor, the call is, "Arise, go forth."[49] The greatest enterprises should be undertaken, and everything calculated to enlighten and elevate the people should be done.

What a high calling is here! God has made His word very plain. It should not be wrapped in mystery by a weird, professional tone.

Do not dwell in the clouds. The gospel was meant for man, not the angels. It is a message from our blessed Father in heaven. Do not read it as a decree from a tyrant. Yet it is God's word and His truth meant for men.

There must be no flippant, reckless reading. Read it as Nehemiah says: "So they read in the book in the law of God *distinctly, and gave the sense, and caused them to understand the reading.*"[50]

The law of the Lord must be written on the heart[51] of the minister if he would impress his people. This is paramount. However, his manner appeals to the eye, his voice appeals to the ear, and through the eye and ear gates the spiritual riches within are made manifest. It is his imperative duty to cultivate speech and action. He should be fully equipped. No person has a right to inflict upon a congregation a weak, thin, ragged, jagged voice. He should not impose upon them a faulty articulation and pronunciation any more than he would present a poorly arranged and badly constructed sermon.

All arrogance and self-consciousness should be rooted out. Sincerity, sympathy, emotion, soul—better these with no art, than the highest art without these qualities.

Pack every sentence and word with meaning and feeling. Do not pervert the true meaning. Avoid the trifling style—the inflated and professional styles. Shun the drawl and pious tone. . . .

HYMN READING

Hymn reading should be a part of worship in the House of God. The hymns should be read with feeling and reverence. The effect must be produced by the tones of the voice.

A sing-song, monotonous voice should be avoided. Intelligence, culture of the head and heart may have a wide scope in this part of the service. Attention must be given to the ending of each line of a verse.

Examples in Hymn Reading.

LESSON XVI
HYGIENE OF THE VOICE

[Movement exercises are given.]

Hygiene is a part of the science of sanitation. It treats of the preservation of health in the individual, the household, communities, and the nation. Hygiene is the science of health in its most practical sense, and vocal hygiene simply means voice-health. It has been termed the science of prevention.

Preservation of health means the prevention of diseases. We all know the important part played by the mucous membrane in voice preservation and should seek to know the substances and conditions which destroy it.

Public speakers ought to live longer and enjoy better health than other persons if they conform to the laws of life and health generally. The dependence of the vocal on the general health of the body is universally admitted. The general condition of the vocal apparatus to a large extent depends on the degree to which it is exercised, provided it is exercised rightly.

The voice is weak or strong in proportion to the less, or greater, number of organs and muscles that are brought into action. If one uses only the upper part of the chest, his voice will be weak; if he uses the whole body as he should do, his voice will be strong. Hence, to strengthen a weak voice, the student must practice expelling the vowel sounds, using all the abdominal and dorsal nerves and muscles, in addition to which he should read and recite when standing, sitting, walking on a level plane, and uphill.

Do not force the voice by loud speaking and shouting; it often leads to congestion of the membranes of the throat and voice-box. Daily physical and vocal exercises are essential to the best and quickest results in the study of elocution. More fail from lack of a systematic study than from lack of talent.

Never use the voice immediately after eating; the most suitable time for practice is in the morning before breakfast. *No exercise* must be taken on a full stomach. Hot and cold drinks are injurious. Avoid vigorous vocal exercises when suffering from a cold. Do not force the voice beyond its normal strength. Take plenty of outdoor exercise.

Temperance, at all times desirable in every individual, is far more to be insisted on in the case of the voice-user, no personal habit having a more baneful effect on the purity and power of the voice than indulgence of alcohol.

Tobacco is also detrimental to the voice. Instances are numerous where great orators and great singers have been great smokers, but it is quite certain that no voice has been improved by it. Smoke should not be inhaled into the lungs, nor blown through the nostrils. This practice produces irritation, dryness, and congestion of the mucous membrane.

The clothing should be selected with the view of preventing chill to the body and maintaining an equal temperature. All oppressive clothing must be removed. The neck, chest, and abdomen should be free from anything that tends to constrict them in the form of corsets or tight belts.

The mouth and nose should be protected from cold air, after the voice-user has been in a hot atmosphere, and from dust, damps, and smoke. Never wrap the throat in wool and furs; silk muffler is by far the best.

Do not seek for power in the throat, but in the diaphragm and abdominal muscles. Never speak with the throat, but through it. The tone should lay hold of the throat, and not the throat hold of the tone.

Speak to the individual, not to the multitude. Cultivate direct address.

Regulate the voice to the size of the auditorium. Begin in a low pitch, speaking slowly and distinctly, and gradually elevate the voice until you are conscious that the entire audience hears you. The old oratorical rule holds good—

Begin low,
Rise higher,
Low again,
Take fire.
Let your motto be heart-work not head-work.

[The pamphlet ends with several selections for performance.]

Notes for *Elocution and Physical Culture*

This selection is taken from Hallie Quinn Brown, *Elocution and Physical Culture, Training for Students Teachers Readers Public Speakers* (Wilberforce, Ohio: Homewood Cottage, 1908?), with gratitude to the Hallie Quinn Brown Library, Central State University, Wilberforce, Ohio. A few spelling errors have been silently corrected, and punctuation in a few cases has been regularized.

1. François Delsarte (1811–1871) was a French teacher of acting and voice who worked out an extremely influential philosophy of aesthetics of delivery. His many students published his philosophy after his death. Brown recommends Oskar Guttman, *Gymnastics of the Voice: A System of Correct Breathing in Singing and Speaking, Based Upon Physiological Laws* (Albany, N.Y.: E. S. Werner, 1882).

2. Johann Wolfgang von Goethe (1749–1832) was a famous German Romantic poet. I have been unable to locate this quotation.

3. Shakespeare, *Hamlet* 3.2.16–19: Hamlet's directions to the players.

4. Paraphrase, or different translation of L'Abbé Delaumosne on François Delsarte's theories in *The Delsarte System of Oratory*, 4th ed. (New York: Edgar S. Werner, 1893), 39–41.

5. Cicero, *De Oratore* III.lix.222–23: "Est enim actio quasi sermo coroporis, quo magis menti congruens esse debet." Brown's is a very accurate translation of Cicero's Latin.

6. Cicero, *De Oratore* III.lvi.213.

7. Although Brown attributes this maxim to Delsarte, I have been unable to find it in his published works; perhaps it was passed on orally, as was much of Delsarte's system.

8. This commonplace is at least as old as the seventeenth century.

9. Brown takes this quotation by David Garrick from the preface to L'Abbé Delaumosne's treatise on Delsarte: see *Delsarte System of Oratory*, xxv. Garrick was a famous eighteenth-century actor, a friend of Hannah More.

10. Phidias was an ancient Greek sculptor (born c. 490 B.C.E.) famous for his gigantic statues of Athena and Zeus, and his frieze and pediment designs for the Parthenon. Leonardo da Vinci (1452–1519) was a Renaissance Italian painter, sculptor, architect, and scientist, famous especially for his *Last Supper* and the *Mona Lisa*. Michelangelo Buonarroti (1475–1564) was a Renaissance Italian painter, sculptor, architect, and poet, famous for his sculptures, the *Pietà* and the *David*, and for his painting on the ceiling of the Sistine Chapel. Rosa Bonheur (1822–1899) was a French painter and sculptor noted for her depictions of animals. Edward Coley Burne-Jones (1833–1898), pre-Raphaelite artist in the circle of Dante Gabriel Rossetti (poet) and William Morris (designer), was at the center of the Aesthetic Movement. Henry O. Tanner (1859–1937) was an African American painter who was famous for his landscapes, animal paintings, depictions of African American life (as in *Banjo Lesson*), and biblical scenes.

11. Ictus: recurring stress or beat in a rhythmical series.

12. The "Nine Laws of Gesture," which Brown attributes to Delsarte, are not a direct quotation but can be found as principles throughout L'Abbé Delaumosne's treatise on Delsarte. Brown has selected and reworded these principles. See *The Delsarte System of Oratory*, especially 3–126. Delsartean elocution was primarily an oral tradition, passed on from teacher to master. Other theorists record quite different "nine laws of Delsarte" than Brown's; see, for example, the version of the "nine laws" in Ted Shawn's brief history of the Delsarte movement, *Every Little Movement: A Book about François Delsarte* (1910; rev. ed., New York: Dance Horizons, 1963), 47–49. Brown's "nine laws" are not wrong; they are simply her contribution to a growing body of theory.

13. Quintilian XI.iii.85–87.

14. See William Hogarth, *The Analysis of Beauty* (London, 1753), 38.

15. Perhaps James Madison Bell, the abolitionist?

16. Genesis 2:7.

17. On Michelangelo, see note 10. I have been unable to locate this quotation.

18. I have not found this quotation in Delsarte's published works; a similar sentiment (perhaps a matter of a different translation) occurs in L'Abbé Delaumosne's treatise on Delsarte: see *Delsarte System of Oratory*, 127.

19. William Wetmore Story, *The English Language* (1856), ll. 19–20.

20. Buccal: relating to the cheeks or cavity of the mouth.

21. Shakespeare, *Hamlet* 3.2.1–4: Hamlet's speech to the players.

22. Paraphrase of L'Abbé Delaumosne's treatise on Delsarte; see *Delsarte System of Oratory*, xiv.

23. Shakespeare, *Macbeth* 5.1.68.

24. George Gordon, Lord Byron, "Childe Harold," canto lv, sec. clxxix, l. 1 (l. 1603).

25. I have been unable to locate this quotation.

26. I have been unable to locate this quotation. It is not in *The English Language*, the source for Brown's other quotations from Story.

27. Delaumosne on Delsarte, in *Delsarte System of Oratory*, 33.

28. Story, *English Language* (1856), ll. 69–72.

29. I have been unable to locate this quotation.

30. I have been unable to locate this quotation by Cicero; it is very likely a passage in Horace's *Ars Poetica*, ll. 103–4, so perhaps Brown is misremembering.

31. Delsarte, *Delsarte System of Oratory*, 524.

32. I have been unable to locate this quotation by Augustine.

33. Angélique Arnaud on Delsarte in *Delsarte System of Oratory*, 199.

34. Shakespeare is the "Bard" (or poet) of Avon; Avon is the river in Stratford-on-Avon where Shakespeare grew up and raised his family.

35. Action: rhetorical delivery.

36. See Cicero, *De Oratore* III.lix.223, on the language of delivery as a language of emotions speaking to all people.

37. Although Brown attributes this quotation to Cicero, she probably lifted this Latin phrase from L'Abbé Delaumosne's introduction to his work on Delsarte; see *Delsarte System of Oratory*, xxiv.

38. Thomas Campbell, "To the Rainbow," ll. 50–52. Brown or an editor has added "O radiant bow!"

39. The Koran is the sacred scripture of Muslims.

40. I have been unable to locate this quotation (perhaps also from Ruskin).

41. I have been unable to locate this quotation from Ruskin.

42. Psalm 119:105.

43. Edward Bickersteth, "Hearts-Ease" (1848), l. 16.

44. Mark 14:36, Christ in the garden of Gethsemane, praying that he not undergo what has been ordained.

45. John 20:28, Thomas recognizing the risen Christ.

46. Attrition: contact, friction.

47. I have been unable to locate this quotation.

48. An allusion to 1 John 4:6, not a direct biblical quotation, but attributed speech.

49. Ezekiel 3:22.

50. Nehemiah 8:8.

51. A paraphrase of 2 Corinthians 3:2.

Genevieve Stebbins

1857–1914?

Genevieve Stebbins was born on March 7, 1857, to Henrietta Smith and James Cole Stebbins (a lawyer) in San Francisco, California. Her mother died when she was young. At eighteen, Stebbins traveled to New York to study acting with Rose Eytinge. Stebbins premiered on February 19, 1877, in *Our Boys* at the New York Broadway Theater. After acting for several years, in about 1876 she began study in Boston with James Steele MacKaye, the foremost American teacher of the Delsarte method. Stebbins joined MacKaye's Boston University School of Oratory to demonstrate for his Delsarte lectures and was eventually put in charge of the Delsarte program there. Stebbins formed a partnership with Mary S. Thompson, the school's vocal coach, and these two opened two private Delsarte schools, one in Boston and one in New York. The Delsarte system, based on the "laws" of human expressions taught by Delsarte, the aesthetic and gymnastic exercises added by Mackaye, and new exercises and information developed by Stebbins, was the basis of the curriculum, but now taught to an audience of upper- and middle-class women. In 1880, Stebbins and Thompson presented their first Delsarte matinee at the Madison Square Theater in New York. Their programs combined readings, dance, pantomime, statue posing, gymnastics, and dance dramas, and became a model for women's exercise groups and performance across the United States in the late nineteenth and early twentieth centuries. (Such a performance is parodied in the women's group theatricals of the mayor's wife in *The Music Man*.)

In 1881 and 1886, Stebbins traveled to Europe to meet teachers who had been associated with Delsarte during his life—the Abbé Delaumosne and Delsarte's widow. She also studied breathing with a Hindu at Oxford, and toured European museums to study the poses of Greek statues. She published *The Delsarte System of Expression* in 1885. After the third edition, it included a translation of a Delsarte manuscript she acquired from his widow. Stebbins was married to Joseph A. Thompson from 1888 to 1892. In 1893 she married journalist Norman Astley, who became her business manager when she founded the New York School of Expression at Carnegie Music Hall. Stebbins was director of the board of the National Association of Elocutionists in 1892, and, in 1893, a member of the Advisory Council of Physical Culture for the Chicago World's Columbian Exposition (so she probably met Hallie Quinn Brown). She taught, lectured, and gave exhibitions all over the East and Midwest. Through her students, she was an important influence on the development of modern dance. She also published *Dynamic Breathing and Harmonic Gymnastics* (1895); *The Genevieve Stebbins System of Physical Training* (1898, enl. ed., 1913); *Society Gymnastics and Voice Culture* (1888); and numerous essays in magazines concerning voice. She disappeared on her last research trip to India.

I have included excerpts from *The Delsarte System of Expression* and *The Genevieve Stebbins System of Physical Training* in this volume. The earlier volume explains and elaborates Delsarte's ideas for a United States audience. *The Delsarte System of Expression* begins with an address on art by Delsarte, and quotations by Delsarte or by Arnaud on Delsarte are sprinkled throughout. Several chapters explain Delsarte's theory of all life organized in trinities of mental, moral, and vital activity. This highly spiritual view of life lies behind the nineteenth-century middle-class willingness to adopt, even for girls and women, the theatrical and sensuous exercises advocated by a French teacher of actors. While Hallie Quinn Brown took Delsartean elocution in the direction of oratory and spoken performance, Genevieve Stebbins took the same philosophy in the direction of physical education, pantomime, and dance, minimizing the spoken word—in *The Delsarte System*, there are several chapters on pantomime. This early volume, like all of Stebbins's texts, is addressed directly to students and includes short dialogues or conversations to attract young readers and a popular audience. *The Later Genevieve Stebbins System of Physical Training* adapts and revises Delsarte more freely. In this volume, there are sections on home exercises and exercises for schoolrooms and private classes, and a final section of suggested "drills" for public performance on exhibition days. This volume incorporates Stebbins's further researches, including breathing and relaxation exercises that must owe something to her study of Eastern methods of meditative exercise, and posing exercises that owe something to her study of statuary, as well as something to her successful dramatic career in New York. The exercises cover the entire body, some specifically touted to "cure headache," to "invigorate the ovaries," or to "prevent consumption." The drills for public performance appeal to the late nineteenth-century appetite for "culture," with names like "Athenian Drill," "Eastern Temple Drill," and "Greek Drill—The Nymphs." They also demonstrate Stebbins's interest in dance and her connection to later developments in modern dance, with titles such as "Minuet Fan Drill," and "Spanish Drill—The Carmen." I have included a drill based on Stebbins's study of European statuary, but also demonstrating her feminism: "Roman Drill—The Amazon." While elocution has been much maligned as a mechanical and pretentious form of expression, in Stebbins we can see that Delsartean elocution advocated physical expression and exercise for women, goals worthy in themselves. In addition, these highly physical and theatrical activities were justified by a light introduction to the tradition of Western European philosophy and aesthetics while revising them for a more democratic and female audience.

For further information, see Nancy Lee Chalfa Ruyter, "Genevieve Stebbins," in *American National Biography*, ed. John A. Garraty and Mark C. Caines (New York: Oxford University Press, 1999), 20:598–99; Ruyter, *Reformers and Visionaries: The Americanization of the Art of Dance* (1979); and Ruyter, *The Cultivation of Body and Mind in Nineteenth-Century American Delsartism* (Westport, Conn.: Greenwood Press, 1999).

From *Delsarte System of Expression* (1885)

LESSON I
DECOMPOSING EXERCISES
AESTHETIC TALK

Dear pupil, will you accompany me, an invisible presence by my side, as we trace our way through a course of lessons? And if you practice faithfully, I can assure you that you will not regret the time and patience required in the study.

A lovely day in spring. You are before me. Listen to my words: the first great step in the study of this art is the attainment of perfect flexibility. This is acquired by diligent practice of the decomposing exercises, as witness:

I withdraw my will-power from fingers, then hand. Touch it. Do not shudder. Do you feel as if a dead thing had struck your living palm? Now I will show you the same phenomenon with forearm, entire arm, waist, spine, hips, knees, ankles, toes, jaw, eye-lids. Now I fall. Give me your hand and help me to rise. I did not mean to startle you so. I have not even bruised myself. I simply withdrew my vital force into the reservoir at the base of the brain.

The first great thing to be acquired is flexibility of the joints. These exercises free the channels of expression, and the current of nervous force can thus rush through them as a stream of water rushes through a channel, unclogged by obstacles. We name these exercises *decomposing*. I wish you to buy a mirror large enough to reflect your entire figure, and faithfully to practice many hours a day if you wish rapid results.

Delsarte required of his pupils a great deal of hard work. You cannot in an instant prepare the human body for the translation, through that grand interpreter, art, of the best possibilities of the soul. There is too much imperfection in our nature.

The order of practice is as follows:

AESTHETIC GYMNASTICS

Exercise I
Let fingers fall from knuckles as if dead; in that condition shake them. Vital force should stop at knuckles.

Exercise II
Let hand fall from wrist as if dead; shake it in that condition forward and back, up and down, sideways, rotary shake.

Exercise III
Drop forearm from elbow as if dead; shake it. Vital force arrested at elbow.

Exercise IV
Raise arms above head, decompose them, i.e., withdraw force. They will fall as dead weights. Arms still hanging decomposed from shoulders, agitate body with a rotary movement. The arms will swing as dead weights; now change and swing body forward and back; knee bends in this. The arms will describe a circle in their sockets; they must be decomposed.

Exercise V
Drop head to one side decomposed; it will gradually describe a half-circle, moving from its own weight as you have seen persons asleep nodding. Drop it back decomposed.

Exercise VI
Drop torso sideways decomposed; commence with the head. The head will draw the shoulder, and, by degrees, with no conscious effort, the torso will fall. Do this first on one side, then on the other.

Exercise VII
Lifting foot from the ground, agitate it as you do the hand. You had better seat yourself for this exercise. Be sure the foot falls from the ankle decomposed.

Exercise VIII

Decompose lower leg as forearm; agitate from knee.

Exercise IX

(a.) Stand on footstool on one leg, then swing free leg by a motion of the entire body; free leg decomposed.

(b.) Lift leg from ground as a horse does in pawing, then drop it decomposed. You have discarded the footstool for this last exercise.

Exercise X

Standing with your weight on back leg, bend that knee; also bend torso forward. The head should fall back. Withdraw the will from back leg; the body will drop to the ground.

Exercise XI

Let lids fall as if going to sleep.

Exercise XII

Let jaw fall so you feel its weight, i.e. decomposed.

You must practice these exercises for me many hours a day; and, let me see—yes, come Thursday at two; you shall then teach me all this. I shall expect you to show me everything as if you know all and I nothing. Good morning.

LESSON IV
THE LEGS
AESTHETIC TALK

Good day. Will you have this bunch of goldenrod?[1] Let me fasten it in your dress, an autumn greeting. I have come from a walk through the fields, and purple aster, and red sumac, and goldenrod look up to the grey-tinted sky. Have you made as much progress in your work as nature has in hers? Think of it! When first we met in June, the meadows were one white plain of daisies, earth's stars; now they seem to have drawn the glowing sunset tints into their fecund bosom, and sent them, quivering with life, upward into passionate blossoming.

What shall we study today? Draw your chair to the table; there you will find pen and paper. Copy as I dictate from our master Delsarte:

Aesthetics is the science of the sensitive and passional manifestations which are the object of art, and whose psychic form it constitutes. Semiotics is the science of the organic signs by which aesthetics must study inherent fitness. The object of art, therefore, is to reproduce, by the action of a superior principle (ontology), the organic signs explained by semiotics, and whose inherent fitness is estimated by aesthetics. If semiotics does not tell us the passions which the sign reveals, how can aesthetics indicate to us the sign which it should apply to the passion that it studies? In a word, how shall the artist translate the passion which he is called upon to express? Aesthetics determines the inherent forms of sentiment in view of the effects whose truth of relation it estimates. Semiotics studies organic forms, in view of the sentiment which produces them.[2]

Let us consider the third paragraph. . . . Look with me at this aster. Do you realize that the purple star is as much the result of its "superior principle" as you or I am of ours? The spirit in a plant is its power of gathering from the earth and the air dead matter, and shaping it to its chosen form. The flower is the sign, the end, the creature, that the spirit makes.

You see, then, dear pupil, two things to observe: one, the life-power and energy; the other, the form proceeding therefrom, and most perfectly adapted to bring them into outward manifestation.

What we produce is merely the form of what exists in our minds. Every stroke of the artist's brush is made within ere it glows on the canvas. In the actor, every accent, every inflection, every gesture, is but the outer reverberation of the still small voice within.

The idea, as separate from the object, exists prior to the object itself; and the outward work is but the material form, the effect of the spiritual idea or spiritual form.

> The certain and practical sense of this word "spirit." The sense in which you all know its reality exists as the power which shaped you into shape, and by which you love and hate when you have received that shape. . . . The "spirit of man" truly means his passion and virtue, and is stately according to the height of his conception, and stable according to the measure of his endurance.   —Ruskin[3]

Delsarte says:

> External gesture, being only the reverberance of interior gesture, which gives it birth and rules it, should be its inferior in development.[4]

He adds:

> A voice, however powerful it may be, should be inferior to the power which animates it.[5]

After reflecting seriously on the foregoing, how can one call the system of Delsarte mechanical? Do we consider the blossoming into beauty of a rose mechanical because we soften . . . the hard soil through which it must force itself into being? We make the ground flexible for the tender rootlets, as we aim to make the clay of which we are made plastic to the inner emotion, revelatory of the soul. The music of the spheres might be echoing in the brain of some inspired master; but without an instrument, how could he convey its wondrous vibrations to his fellow-souls?

Ontology deals with the inner impelling power, the individual will. Suppose I say in metaphor, "The Greeks achieved marvelous deeds, nurturing the gifts of the intellect like faithful gardeners, and making them bring forth marvelous fruit!" Aesthetics would determine the fitness of the simile; semiotics would determine the sign.

The science of semiotics is the science of signs, of correspondences. Correspondence is derived from three Latin words, *cor-re-spondeo*, and it means literally "to answer again from the heart." We use the word in common speech to show that written communication has passed between two people. It is only complete when the one written to has replied, has spoken to the other again *from the heart*. I am thus particular because a great deal is learned by a strict attention to the derivation of words.[6]

The material form should correspond to the inner form, should answer "thought to thought, heart to heart." "Correspondence is no arbitrary relationship like metaphor or figure, but one founded alike on the inward and outward nature of the things by which we are surrounded."[7] I see an outward manifestation, viz., a child laughs. I infer that the child is pleased; it cries, I know it is displeased. Remember: "If, from a certain organic form, I infer a certain sentiment, that is semiotics."[8] An example of which is the foregoing. "If, from a certain sentiment, I deduce a certain organic form, that is aesthetics."[9]

An artist wishes to model Coriolanus[10] exiled from Rome by the people for whom he had risked his life and shed his blood. Aesthetics would select the bearing, attitude, and expression. The marble must reveal the passion surging in the breast of the outraged hero.

Do you not now see at a glance the importance to the aspirant for dramatic laurels of a knowledge of semiotics and aesthetics? The two, combined with individual will, make art.

I have dwelt at some length on the inherent principle, as I wished you never to lose sight of the fact that "The spirit quickens, the letter kills."[11]

In a science monthly of last year, I read an interesting account of the hypnotic experiments made by French doctors. A gendarme, on guard in front of the Louvre, was selected (on account of his phlegm[12]) for the experiment. Thrown into a mesmeric sleep by means of a few passes, an artist, summoned from a neighboring studio, posed him as a model of fear. The unconscious soldier obeyed the artist's hand. But now comes the strangest fact. He *felt* the emotion, and described himself as experiencing the throes of terror. This seems to bear out an idea to be inculcated in these lessons, viz.: a perfect reproduction of the outer manifestation of some passion, the giving of the outer sign, will cause a reflex feeling within.

This is delicate ground, and will make some of you cry, "Mechanical." I feel like replying with Aunt Betsy Trotwood, "Donkeys, Janet, donkeys!"[13] Think seriously a moment. Certain attitudes, by extending or contracting the muscles, by compelling the breath to come and go more rapidly, by increasing the heart beats, cause physical interior sensations which are the correspondences of emotion. The motion is then slightly felt, but you must bear in mind that the sign is first formed within; so, after all, the exterior expression does not come first. . . .

The artistic idea within must form the outward expression, but that idea seems in genius to be unconscious; you cannot mentally plan it at the moment of its execution. Regnier[14] said to me, in speaking of Delsarte: "If you have to seek in the head what ought to be in the heart, you are not an artist." That is true in itself, but not true of Delsarte. The latter may be mystical; he is certainly not mechanical. I think we shall find the solution in this: all our study, all our observations, all our experiences, all our life, is mixed in the mystic alembic, which, for want of a clearer name, I will call our *interior memory*—that unconscious storehouse where inherited tendencies, traits, and aptitudes are also found. At the call of art this memory awakes from its lethargy, and, without your having to again feel the emotion, forms the expression, which expression affects you in a reflex wave.

How I have wandered! But, although these paths lead from the main road, they must be traversed by art's pilgrim, if he would know all the truth.

But to return. Semiotics is thus the science of signs, and so the science of the form of gesture. There are three types to be considered in man:

1. The constitutional type is that which is congenital.

2. The passional type is that produced under the sway of emotions.

3. The habitual type is one not inborn, but created by habit, which acts as a second nature, refashioning the material being.

Passional types explain habitual types, and habitual types explain congenital types. Thus we obtain a complete analysis of man.

There are three forms of expression for gesture:

1. The habitual bearing of the agent of expression

2. The emotional attitudes of the agent

3. The passing inflections of the agent.

The bearing is the most permanent. The attitudes are less so. The inflections are passing.

Have you not observed how a man's habits will color his every action? This is such a well-recognized fact that we often hear, "He tried to pass for a gentleman, but his bearing betrayed him," or, *vice versa*, "He disguised himself as a workingman and went among the people, but his habit of command betrayed him."

Continued indulgence in any one form of feeling will make that feeling the predominant trait. So beware, young sculptors, each day you are perhaps carving—for eternity.

Take your pencil again, and draw a chart containing nine squares similar to the one in our second lesson. Leave room in each square for writing the signification of the attitudes of the legs. Now lay your chart aside while you again listen.

The legs and arms form the vital division of the body, representing, as they do, the power of action. "Strong leg" signifies that the weight of the body is borne on that leg. "Free leg" signifies that the leg is free from weight. "*Ex.*" is an abbreviation of *excentric*, "*con.*" for *concentric*, "*nor.*" for *normal*.

AESTHETIC GYMNASTICS

Will you stand? I will call off the attitudes of the legs. . . .

Exercise I—Action nor.-nor.

Both legs strong and wide apart; standing in the breadths, knees straight.

Signification: vital repose, vulgarity, intoxication, fatigue. You see, one must always observe two things: an attitude may be a sign of a physical condition, or of a sentiment. The foregoing attitude indicates either a condition or a sentiment: a condition of fatigue, vertigo, or intoxication; or a sentiment of familiarity or vulgar boorishness.

A gentleman, in the privacy of his own household, might permit himself to stand, his hands under his coat-tails, his back to the fire in the nor.-nor. attitude. He would be a vulgar boor if he assumed the same position in society. . . .

Exercise II—Action con.-nor.

Standing in the breadths; both legs are strong and together; knees straight, that is unbent; heels together; toes turned out.

N.B. In all these attitudes the toes should turn out.

This attitude signifies a condition of feebleness, or a sentiment of respect. It is the one a child assumes, a valet, a soldier.

Gentlemen, in a formal introduction to ladies, or to those superior to themselves in station, take this position. It is taught to small cavaliers in dancing school, when, with bent head and proffered arm, they beg their little sweethearts to tread a measure. The young should always assume it before the old. It is the position of the inferior before the superior. . . .

201

Exercise III—Action ex.-nor.

Standing in the lengths; both legs are strong and apart, one directly in front of the other; the knees are straight.

Do you observe that in all the normal attitudes of the legs, the weight is born equally on both?

The condition signified is indecision, while the sentiment is deliberation. It is an action halfway between advance and retreat. A slight forward impetus would decide for advance; a slight backward movement would declare for retreat. A change of weight, however, would be necessary to indicate these two opposites. This attitude is agnostic—it decides for nothing, but hesitates and cries, "Who knows?". . .

Exercise IV—Action nor.-con.

Standing in the lengths; the back leg is strong; the knee of that leg is straight; the forward leg is free, while its knee is bent, thus bringing the foot in front near to the foot behind.

N.B. You will observe that in all three of the concentric attitudes, the weight is borne on the back leg. It is the final term which names the genus of the attitude. The first term serves as an attribute making a species in the genus.

The foregoing attitude signifies calm strength, reserved force, reflection, controlled emotions. It is an attitude which shows the mind as ruler, the attitude of the thinker, the scholar, the gentleman. It indicates concentration. . . .

Exercise V—Action con.-con.

Standing in the lengths; the strong leg is back, its knee bent; the free leg is in front, the knee straight.

The condition shown is prostration; the sentiment, despondent passion. . . .

Exercise VI—Action ex.-con.

Standing in the lengths; the strong leg is back, its knee straight; the free leg in front, the knee also straight.

The condition such a position represents is antagonistic; the sentiment, defiance, irritation, splenetic emotion. It also indicates self-assertion with an added element of defiance.

Many men erroneously consider this position a manly one to assume. Remember, these attitudes are types. They can run into each other, mix, overlap, as colors in the rainbow. An attitude midway between the nor.-con. and the ex.-con. is very common. The mixed attitude, then, partakes of the meaning of the two from which it is composed. . . .

Exercise VII—Action nor.-ex.

Standing in the lengths; strong leg is in front. Stand so firmly on the forward leg that the other leg is unnecessary for support; the knee is straight; free leg is behind, the knee bent; the ball of the foot rests on the ground; the heel should be raised.

This attitude signifies a condition of vigor, animation, intention, or attention. It represents sentiments of an ardent or passional tendency. There is no introspection in this attitude; it is essentially eccentric. . . .

Exercise VIII—Action con.-ex.

Standing in the breadths; the free leg is slightly in the rear of the strong leg; the knee of the strong leg is straight; the free knee is bent; the toe of the free leg is on a line with the instep arch of the strong leg; the foot of the free leg is very much turned out; the heel of the free leg is raised a little from the ground, while the ball rests on the ground.

The attitude should be unconstrained. It represents a suspensive condition, neutral, transitive, or colorless sentiments. It should be assumed when changing the direction of the lateral walk on the stage. . . .

Exercise IX—Action ex.-ex.

Standing in the lengths; both legs should be wide apart; strong leg in front, the knee bent; free leg behind, the knee straight; the heel of the foot is raised, the ball resting on the ground.

This signifies a condition of great excitement or exaltation, sentiments of an explosive nature.

You have done very well. Practice these attitudes before a mirror, strictly observing a harmonic bearing in each of them. Keep in mind your previous lesson on that subject, viz.: the head must sympathize with the strong leg, must incline to the side of the strong leg, while the torso inclines in the opposite direction, thus always preserving equilibrium and the line of beauty.

AESTHETIC TALK (cont.)

Again I will unearth some of my treasures for you. Look over my shoulder at this collection of photographed statues. We will select one for each of the foregoing attitudes.

See, here is a faun holding a huge bunch of grapes, high overhead. With upturned face he is dropping them one by one into his laughing mouth. One seems to share the grapes, so contagious is his enjoyment. Be quick, be quick, my faun. Do I not hear the songs of the wine god and his bacchantes?[15] Soon you must join their revelry. Still he stands in marble silence. Can you tell me in what attitude? Yes, correct, in the nor.-nor., that of vital repose.

What have you found? Ah, Hebe,[16] the bewitching little waitress on Olympus. She stands, with both lovely arms upraised. Her two dear little feet nestle close together. It is our second attitude.

Here in this frieze of the Parthenon[17] we find our third example. That beautiful youth in the procession turns and stops for one short instant. About what does he hesitate? His lips are dumb—we shall never know.

Pallas Athena, haughty child of Zeus,[18] reflection, control, reserve power is conveyed by your bearing. You do not need Medusa[19] of the snaky locks on your helmet to chill our blood. It freezes at your look. We enter your temple to worship, and Cupid and Bacchus[20] are left outside, twining their garlands of roses and grapes.

Ariadne, do not despair. The same wind that is filling the sails of Theseus,[21] and wafting his argosy from you, brings to your ear the chant of merry bacchantes. A hero has deserted, but a god comes to console. So courage. She still is despairing; the pictured stone changes not. She teaches us the fifth attitude.

Ah! Demosthenes,[22] my noble friend, well met; but why this defiant position? Why this self-assertion? You have been petrified in the midst of an oration and are there to illustrate our sixth attitude.

"The horn of the hunter is heard on the hill."[23] Diana! Diana[24] of the Louvre! quick, select your arrow, shoot your bow. My heart beats quicker, my blood bounds at the sight of your vital presence. I would be one of your nymphs, Diana! Diana!

Sweet Modesty. Chastely your robes fold around you; you stand in a neutral attitude. What shall I judge from that?

Ah! Fighting gladiator! You indicate to me explosion, with your excited air and forward-bent knee. I am told that you are striving to seize the bridle of rearing horses with that outstretched arm, and you are running, not fighting. You have been much maligned.

What is it, child? You would look at the others? Seek some gallery where you will find casts of the antique, and spend a profitable hour in discovering the attitude in which each statue stands. Then go home and essay[25] them before the glass.

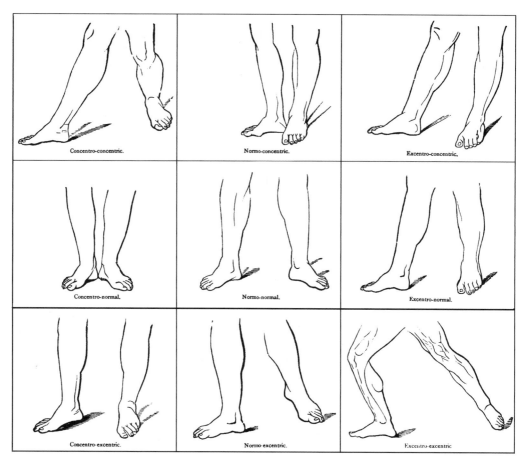

Concentro-concentric.	Normo-concentric.	Excentro-concentric.
Concentro-normal.	Normo-normal.	Excentro-normal.
Concentro-excentric.	Normo-excentric.	Excentro-excentric

Attitudes of the Legs

Notes for *Delsarte System*

This selection is taken from Genevieve Stebbins, *Delsarte System of Expression*, 5th ed. (New York: Edgar S. Werner, 1894), 11–14, 57–72; I gratefully acknowledge the Albin O. Kuhn Library, the University of Maryland–Baltimore County, for providing access to this work. I have silently corrected a few spelling errors and silently modernized spelling and punctuation in a very few cases.

1. Goldenrod was in Stebbins's time a popular flower, used in bouquets, embroidered on dresses; Stebbins's generation did not know it causes severe allergies.

2. Stebbins's note reads "Arnaud on Delsarte." These are actually Delsarte's own words, although somewhat rearranged. See *The Delsarte System of Oratory* (New York: Edgar S. Werner, 1893), 460–61.

3. John Ruskin (1819–1900) was an English essayist, art critic, and social theorist. I have been unable to locate this quotation.

4. Stebbins attributes these words to Delsarte, and they are, perhaps, her own translation from the French: for a different translation, see *Delsarte System of Oratory*, 468.

5. Stebbins attributes these words to Delsarte. Although the analogy to the preceding quotation from Delsarte is strong, I have been unable to find it in published materials by Delsarte and his French interpreters.

6. Stebbins cites Reverend Edward Madeley's *Science of Correspondences Elucidated* (1884) on this etymology: "*Correspondence*, compounded of two Latin words *con*, 'with,' and *respondere*, 'to answer.' Some

have thought that correspondence might be more properly derived from *cor*, 'the heart,' and *respondens*, 'answering'; but as the signification is the same either way it is of little consequence."

7. I have been unable to locate this quotation.

8. Delsarte: see note 2.

9. Delsarte: see note 2.

10. According to legend, Gnaeus Marcius Coriolanus, a Roman patrician noted for his great bravery defending Rome, was exiled because of his refusal to negotiate with the plebeians over grain, and he was prevented from capturing Rome at the head of an enemy Volscian army only by the influence of his wife and mother; he is the subject of one of Shakespeare's tragedies.

11. Paraphrase of Paul in 2 Corinthians 3:6: "for the letter killeth, but the spirit giveth life."

12. Phlegm: here, intrepid coolness or calm.

13. Aunt Betsy Trotwood is David Copperfield's great-aunt, disappointed that he wasn't a girl, disliking anyone riding a donkey over the green in front of her cottage, in Charles Dickens's *David Copperfield* (1850).

14. Probably Henri de Régnier (1864–1936), French symbolist poet, but possibly Marie Louise de Heredia de Régnier, his wife, also a poet.

15. In Greek mythology, the wine god is Bacchus; the bacchantes are his followers.

16. In Greek mythology, Hebe was daughter of Hera and Zeus, cupbearer of the gods.

17. The Parthenon was the temple sacred to Athena on the Acropolis at Athens; parts of the friezes remain in place, but many (known as the "Elgin Marbles") were brought by Thomas Bruce, Lord Elgin, to the British Museum, where Stebbins probably saw them.

18. In Greek mythology, Pallas Athena, daughter of Zeus, was goddess of crafts and wisdom and patron of Athens. She was usually depicted in armor.

19. In Greek mythology, Medusa was one of the Gorgons, killed by Perseus; her severed head, complete with snakes for locks of hair, so terrified men that they froze in fear.

20. Cupid was the Roman god of love. Often depicted as a naked child with bow and arrow, he represents passionate love. Bacchus was the Greek god of wine and represents intemperance.

21. In Greek mythology, Ariadne, who rescued Theseus, ran away with him but was abandoned by him on an island, where she was rescued by Dionysus (the bacchantes being the followers of Dionysus).

22. Demosthenes (384?–322 B.C.E.) is considered the greatest Greek orator, famous for his *Philippics*, orations warning of the dangers to Greek freedom of Philip of Macedon.

23. I have been unable to locate this quotation.

24. In Roman mythology, Diana was goddess of the moon and chastity, and was the patron of women.

25. Essay: to try.

From *The Genevieve Stebbins System of Physical Training* (1898)

LESSON II
DYNAMIC BREATHING

Several years ago, while in London, my attention was called to a peculiar method of recuperating brain exhaustion. The patients were tired brain-workers, some of them Oxford professors; the teacher was a Hindu pundit.[1] I made inquiry, and upon further research was rewarded by the discovery of what I have named "Dynamic Breathing," or the correspondence of breath and thought.

Few of us realize that we breathe as we think, and vice versa, we think as we breathe. The most interesting and at the same time the least understood of the functions of life is the phenomena of breathing. We need to dwell deeply upon the affinity which there certainly is between mental action and respiration. To the air we breathe, as well as to the food we eat, we owe every minute of our mundane existence.

It is quite possible for a man to exist in comparative health for forty or fifty days without a single mouthful of food, but we cannot keep body and soul together for half as many minutes without breathing. We all know this, and yet the fact seems to have escaped the general attention that its importance deserves. Every change of mental state is accompanied by a corresponding change in the power, force, and rhythm of respiration. Is it not legitimate to infer that certain ways of breathing, by reflex action, will produce certain trains of thought? If this be true, what power is really in our grasp! For breath is life,[2] and the power of breathing is the ability to draw in the invisible essence of continued existence.

Does not every [living] thing breathe—the plants by the roadsides, the trees of the forest, the birds of the air? Even the fishes depend for their existence and continued life upon the breath and the functions of respiration.

The atmosphere of the planets is the product of solar radiation. Apart from the physical elements of the atmosphere, the air we breathe is charged with nature's finer and more ethereal essences—magnetism, electricity, and ether.

Let us examine together a few of the correspondences of thought and methods of breathing.

First, the respiration produced by the state of the mind called "courage," when called upon to face danger. We find the inhalations long, deep, and vigorous, the lungs inflated to their utmost capacity. They are attracting the dynamic forces of the atmosphere, to supply the flashing fires, both mental and physical, which courageous action demands.

Compare this with its opposite emotion, fear. Fear reduces the breathing to the minimum. The greater the fear, the less the vigor of the inhalations. The action grows less and less until the muscles seem paralyzed and breathing stops.

We all know how exhausting is anxiety, but few realize that it is because we have not taken long breaths during our anxious periods. Continued, unhappy, pessimistic thought is a slow poison. We do not take in enough oxygen to purify the system, and we are literally poisoned.

On the other hand, hope produces a similar breathing to courage. It is more peaceful and easier than the breath of courage, requiring less grip and tension of the diaphragm. The emotional force of hope gives full expansion to the mind and, consequently, to the lungs. The nectar of the gods is quaffed.

"As the heart panteth after the water brooks, so panteth my soul after Thee, O God,"[3] expresses aspiration, that complete exaltation of soul and mind which is rewarded by the deepest inspiration, psychical and physical. The opposite mental state to hope is despair. What are its physical expressions? The muscles become relaxed, the brain energy subsides, the whole being becomes devitalized while the breathing is scarcely perceptible.

Anger and hate produce a short, hard, grasping respiration, as though each effort were the malicious signal for evil action. The opposites, love and peace, produce a gentle, long-drawn, peaceful, receptive respiration—a yielding, soft breath that speaks of joyful rest, of Paradise and the delicious aroma of summer flowers.

Have you not observed in yourself that you breathe most deeply in the presence of those objects which delight the mind and eye, and reverse this condition in the presence of those things which horrify the mind and displease the sight? How quick the brain and the lungs are to respond to the odors which delight, and to rebel against those which disgust.

By this time, I am sure that those who have followed this thought with me will admit that states of mind affect the respiration. How many will see the converse must also be true, viz., methods of breathing can affect and change states of mind. Loud, deep breathing, united with bright, happy pictures in the mind, will go far to counteract anxiety, fear, and despair. But, you reply to me, "All this is mechanical, not spontaneous. Are we machines?"

Do you not realize, that while much comes to man instinctively, he is still a creature of training? Instinct rises to reason, and there can be no lessening of effort if he would progress. Regeneration or degeneration is the law of all life. Thoughts and emotions are closely connected with sensations.

❧

The effect of the emotions and the body upon each other is reciprocal. The celebrated Frenchman, M. Alfred Fouillée,[4] says, "Reciprocally, the willful expression of an emotion which we do not feel generates it by generating the sensations connected with it, which, in their turn, are associated with analogous emotions. The actor who expresses and simulates anger ends by feeling it to a certain extent. Absolute hypocrisy is an ideal. It is never complete with a man. Realized in full, it would be a contradiction of the will with itself. In every case, nature is ignorant of it. Genuineness is the first law of nature as it is the first law of morals."

Admitting all this, it may still be urged: does not the imagination work first? Is it not the mind that first, through its fancied state of hope or joy, affects the body?

I answer gladly, yes; and to this very question I have been leading you, and now I, in turn, ask: what is the imagination? The imagination is the intrinsic action around which all mental movements cluster, and from which every other mental act is derived. It is the object-glass of the soul in which the human mind realizes and interprets all external forms and movements—symbolic when engaged with impersonal ideas and creative conceptions, and realistic when it reproduces the subjective images, the actual scenes and events of the past.

To come at once to a practical example—we have learned that hope has corresponding deep breathing, but how excite hope when low spirited and in despair? Deep breathing will do much, but it should, if possible, be natural. The close attention to the process of breathing will defeat your purpose. Instead, after a few deep breaths, fix the attention on something you hope for—a definite image. Realize it present, in your possession now. It is in your mind, and soon the joy of life, generated by the image and the breathing, will completely dispel the cloud of melancholy and doubt which sent despair to your very soul.

The logical conclusion, which we naturally derive from observation of the methods and emotions which dominate us, one and all, is:

First, that various states and conditions of respiration in the natural state are owing to certain manifestations of mind.

207

Second, that, seeing that certain states of respiration are the outcome of certain states of mind, we are led to infer that with the powerful aid of the imagination and a systematic rhythmic breathing we can stimulate the mental powers and through the ready response of the organism overcome many of the discords of life.

Surely all this is worth a trial, for air cannot injure one even if it does not help.

Patience and effort are necessary, for the system of culture advocated is not play. It will need attention and work; but this necessary training will result in a great art, viz., the art of being always able to express the true self, to elevate the soul to its highest aspirations, and the mind to its best thought. A thorough system of gymnastics must go hand in hand with the breathing-exercises, and the power of concentrating the attention upon an image in the mind must be slowly acquired.

The three principles of our being—mental, moral, and vital—are strictly correlated to and strengthened by breathing, mental imagery, and physical exercises.

BREATHING EXERCISES

Exercise I

(a) Completely empty the lungs.

(b) Allow the air to fill the air cells. Do not make any muscular effort; let the air pressure expand the lungs. Energy is wasted in making an effort to draw in the air.

Breathe rhythmically. The ingoing and the outgoing breath should be of exactly the same duration. For instance, if you count four for the incoming breath, hold it in two counts, then let it out during four counts. If the breathing be deeper, count seven for the incoming breath, three for holding, seven for letting out the breath. Even ten may be counted with impunity, always holding one-half as long as you inhale. Few people realize how unevenly they breathe. They take in air quickly and let it out slowly, so that we have less fresh air than bad air in the lungs. This is one reason why talking is so fatiguing unless one is also a good listener.

Exercise II

Lie or sit in any easy position—preferably, lie on the back—relaxing one knee and one arm, extending the other. Feel restful and dreamy. Put all the will into pressing out the air, then calmly wait until nature has filled you. The second time that you press out the air, you will not feel like emptying so much; again let nature replenish the loss. Each time you will find less and less air pressed out, for the lungs retain the oxygen much longer than we imagine, and it takes many exhalations to empty the lungs. At last the breathing is quite tacit—a deep exhalation— a deep sigh follows.

The foregoing breathing is the analysis of the kind of breathing that is the correspondent of states of mind when the soul is receptive to states or scenes of loveliness and beauty.

Exercise III

(a) Lie relaxed in any easy position.

(b) Breathe strongly, with a vigorous vertical surging motion, with the same rhythm as in Exercise I. This stretches the whole trunk like an accordion. Concentrate the mind as follows: (1) Imagine the ingoing and the outgoing breath being drawn through the feet, as though the legs were hollow; (2) direct the same mental idea to the hands and arms; (3) to the knees; (4) to the elbows. (5) Now breathe through the knees and the elbows together; (6) breathe through the lips; (7) breathe through the shoulders; (8) breathe through the abdominal and pelvic lumbar regions; (9) breathe through the upper chest; (10) complete this mental imagery by breathing through the head and the whole organism in one grand surging influx of organic life.

This breathing corresponds to energetic states of mind when the concentrated will is directed to the given parts of the body. Its value cannot be overestimated. It trains mind and body for strong, well-directed, energetic action, and rests the entire system by the distribution of nerve-force and quickened vigorous circulation, which ensues on its practice. It will almost cure nervous prostration. Fifteen minutes twice a day, about two hours after eating, is the prescription.

Exercise IV—*To Cure Headache*

(a) Lie in a relaxed, easy position.

(b) Fold the hands on top of the head.

(c) Breathe about four counts, heart rhythm.

(d) Hold one count.

(e) Breathe out four. Think that you are forcing the air out through your feet. The hands on the head lock the upper chest muscles and force deep breathing, while the hold of breath is only one. All this draws the blood from the head or stirs the circulation.

Exercise V—*To Invigorate the Base of the Brain*

(a) Stand and, holding the hands in front, shake them vigorously, relaxed from the wrist.

(b) Breathe deeply as you do so, gradually packing the air.

(c) When lungs are full, and the shaking has continued some time, suddenly stiffen the hands, and holding the breath, carry the hands to the base of the brain, pressing the thumbs on the soft part of the neck just under the bony structure; the fingers clasp and meet above. Press vigorously, holding the breath.

Exercise VI—*To Invigorate the Ovaries*

Take a good breath and hold it, while pressing the second finger vigorously on the abdomen in the region of the ovaries. Strain downward and will energy into that region.

Exercise VII—*To Invigorate the Entire Lung Region and Prevent Consumption*

(a) Fill the upper part of the lungs.

(b) Hold the breath and with the aid of the chest muscles force the air down into the lower chest, and then up. Do this for some little time.

Exercise VIII—*To Give Nerve Power*

Standing, take a good breath. Hold it and clenching the hands in front, draw them vigorously backward to the shoulder. Repeat several times with great rapidity.

These breathing exercises constitute physical culture for the diaphragm, the great center muscle, the roof of the stomach and the floor of the lungs. In its rise and fall, contraction and relaxation, it carries with it all muscles attached, and all the vital functions of life are toned and invigorated by its energetic action. The abdominal contents should be lifted upward toward the chest, so that the great expansion is at the waist, although a slighter outer swell of the abdomen begins the action. The chest muscles should always allow themselves to be passively raised. God's air is above and around us only awaiting an empty receiver to rush in and stimulate heart and brain and soul.

THE ROMAN DRILL
The Amazon.

This drill is called "The Amazon" from its generally athletic nature, and because its figures are principally studies from Amazon statues in the Vatican, Rome.

Figure I

Preliminary Exercise.

1. Bring both clenched hands to shoulders, and count one.

2. Raise elbows sideways, still keeping the hands at shoulders—count two.

3. Extend forearms sideways, clenched hand, palm down—count three.

4. Turn clenched hands palm up; this twists entire arm—count four.

5. Sink elbows to hips; this brings clenched hands to shoulders, palms in—count one—and proceed in a similar way, up, forward, and down—four counts to each direction. Repeat the four directions, and prepare for attitude.

(Do not jerk the foregoing, but perform it like a yawn or morning stretch, breathing deeply.)

Attitude: Amazon holding a spear on high, horizontal oblique.

1. Right leg forward and strong. Both arms up, with bent elbows and clenched hands, the left arm the more advanced at shoulder level, the right arm the highest, head turned to left forward oblique; fancy yourself hurling a spear. Hold the pose two counts.

2. On three return hands near shoulder level but well out, feet together. On four to sides, keep fist. Repeat on the same side. Perform 1 and 2 on opposite side.

With same arm motion carry the right leg back and stand on it, returning as from front position. Repeat on same side, and perform twice on opposite side.

Figure II

First Attitude: Running Amazon.

Second Attitude: Amazon drawing bow.

Perform the angular arm stretch as described twice, then take first attitude.

Forward right leg strong, right arm extended, and slanting up from shoulder level, palm down index hand, head looking to left oblique back, left arm bent back near hip, hand clenched. Hold this pose two counts. Return as described in Figure I. Repeat and perform twice on opposite side. Second Attitude: Retired right leg strong, knee bent, left arm forward, and extended slanting up, right clenched hand near right ear. Return as in Figure I. Repeat, and perform twice on opposite side. Take attitudes obliquely.

Figure III

Attitude: Amazon heaving a rock.

1. Perform the preliminary arm exercise as per diagram.

2. Attitude: Forward right leg strong, bent knee, both arms are held over the head with bent elbows, hands seem to hold a huge rock with intention of hurling it below. Finish the figure as previously described, and as per diagram.

Figure IV

Attitude: Wounded Amazon.

1. Preliminary exercise of arms.

2. Attitude: Forward right leg strong, right arm back of head, head bend to the back left oblique, left hand on heart. Hold two counts. Return as previously described. Repeat. Perform

DIAGRAM.

I.

(1) Ang. A. out, up, for., down		A. arms 2
(2) Ama., hurl spear	R. for. ob. l. 2	L. for. ob. l. 2
	R. bk. ob. l. 2	L. bk. ob. l. 2

II.

(1) Ang. A. out, etc.		B. arms 2
(2) Ama. running } Ama. draw bow)	R. for. ob. l. 2	L. bk. ob. l. 2
	R. bk. ob. l. 2	L. bk. ob. l. 2

III.

(1) Ang. A. out, etc.		B arms 2
(2) Ama. heave rock	R. for. ob. l. 2	T. for. ob. l. 2
	R. bk. ob. l. 2	L. bk. ob. l. 2

IV.

(1) Ang. A. out, etc.		B. arms 2
(2) Ama. wounded	R. for. ob. l. 2	L. for. ob. l. 2
	R. bk. ob. l. 2	L. bk. ob. l. 2

V.

(1) Ang. A. out, etc.		B. arms 2
(2) Ama. charge } Ama. retreat)	R. for. ob. l. 2	L. for. ob. l. 2
	R. bk. ob. l. 2	L. bk. ob. l. 2

VI.

(1) Ang. A. out, etc.		B. arms 2
(2) Ama. with bow } Ama. vow)	R. for. ob. l. 2	L. for. ob. l. 2
	R. bk. ob. l. 2	L. bk. ob. l. 2

Abbreviations used in " The Amazon Drill : " Ama., Amazon; Ang., angular ; R., right ; L., left ; l., leg ; bk., back ; for., forward ; ob., oblique.

Diagram for Amazon Drill

twice on opposite side. Perform with retired legs strong, same action of head and arms as per diagram.

Figure V

First Attitude: Amazon charging.

Second Attitude: Amazon retreating.

1. Perform the preliminary exercise.

2. Then take following. First Attitude: forward right leg strong, knee bent, right arm high over head holding battle-axe, left arm across body seeming to hold shield. Perform as per diagram.

2. Second Attitude: retired right leg, knee bent, left arm held high as if protecting head with shield, right arm, which is the battle-axe, held low. Perform as per diagram.

Figure VI

First Attitude: Amazon with broken bow.

Second Attitude: The Amazon's vow.

1. Preliminary exercise as per diagram.

2. Then, First Attitude: right leg strong, right arm up and bent at elbow, so that forearm is straight and level just above head, the right hand being thus carried to the left side, palm front. The left arm falls at left side, but not touching the side. The hand holds the broken end of bow. This is a study from the most celebrated Amazon statue in the world. Be sure to draw the figure well up under the arm on the right side. Repeat. Perform on the opposite side twice.

3. Second Attitude: Retired right leg strong, right arm up straight, clenched hand, palm in, left arm at side as if resting on shield, clench hand, head thrown up. Repeat. Perform twice on opposite side.

If musical phrase needs it, the heaving attitude can be taken at the end of each attitude, changed slightly by throwing the head back and broadening the arms.

Notes for *The Genevieve Stebbins System of Physical Training*

This selection is taken from *The Genevieve Stebbins System of Physical Training* (1898), enl. ed. (New York: Edgar S. Werner, 1912), 21–32, 110–14. I have silently corrected misspellings and modernized punctuation and spelling, although I have made very few such changes. I am grateful to the Lewis J. Ort Library of Frostburg State University for permission to reprint this material.

1. "Pranayama," or breath control, is a fundamental part of the discipline of yoga, an aspect of the Indian religion of Hinduism. A pundit is a sage or teacher.

2. This phrase also appears in Hallie Quinn Brown.

3. Psalm 42:1.

4. Alfred Fouillée (1836–1912) was a French philosopher and social theorist who wanted to make philosophy central to education and to modernize education by dropping Greek and adding modern languages and more mathematics. I have been unable to locate this quotation.

Jennie Willing

1834–1916

Jennie Fowler was born to Horatio and Harriet (Ryan) Fowler on January 22, 1834, in Burford, Ontario, Canada. Of Irish descent, the Willings took refuge in New York after the father, a founder of Canadian Methodism, participated in the failed rebellion of 1837. From there they moved to a farm in Illinois, where Jennie Fowler grew up. Her brother Charles was engaged for a brief time to Frances Willard. Fowler was mainly schooled at home because of her health, but she began teaching at the age of fifteen. She married William C. Willing, a Methodist preacher, in 1853. They had no children, and she became a licensed preacher with her husband's encouragement in 1877 (but the Methodist Church revoked all women's licenses in 1880).

Willing was an activist throughout her life, organizing for the suffrage movement, the WCTU (Women's Christian Temperance Union), the Women's Home Missionary Society of the Methodist Church, and many other causes. Like Frances Willard, she became a Christian Socialist. Willing helped to found the Illinois State Suffrage Association in 1869, and from 1869 on she was founding secretary of the Illinois Women's Foreign Missionary Society. She wrote for its paper, the *Heathen Women's Friend*, and published many essays on progressive themes. In 1872, Evanston College for Ladies (with Frances Willard as president) awarded her an honorary A.M. degree. In 1874, Willing helped to organize the national WCTU and became editor of its journal, the *Signal*. Also in 1874, Willing was appointed a professor of English language and literature at Illinois Wesleyan University, and her husband was given a law professorship. She lectured at chautauqua on temperance. Willing published *The Potential Woman* in 1886.

In 1889 the Willings moved to New York, and Jennie Willing took up work with immigrant women as a reform issue. After her husband's death, she founded the New York Evangelistic Training School and Settlement House in 1895, which devoted much time to work with immigrants. Willing authored seventeen books and hundreds of articles on missions, temperance, women's rights, education for women, theology, conduct, raising children, poverty, and women's role in the church. She died in New York on October 6, 1916, at age eighty-two.

In *The Potential Woman* Jennie Willing adapts the tradition of conduct book rhetoric for women to more radical ends—preaching and social reform. Willing's accessible, conversational style is aimed at a broader audience than many nineteenth-century conduct books, as the chapter on "Bread-Winning" implies: this audience includes not only middle-class but also working women (although perhaps only those women who work before marriage). In the chapter on "Talking," Willing begins with the radical proposition that men and women are equal, and that education in speech needs to be reformed to reflect women's status. Willing appends to this claim an analysis of the diplomatic role that women assume in conversation as a result of this discrimination. With a perceptive, parodic analogy, she critiques the expected role of woman as good listener: women "say 'Yes,' and 'No,' and keep up a gentle jingle of the small bells of assent and applause, hoping to gain by pleasing what they are not allowed honorably to claim; their hearts, meanwhile, hungering for the mental food of excellent, ennobling speech." This passage also calls into question the advice on conversation of the preceding fifty years of conduct book rhetoric for women. Women should not be sympathetic, agreeable, mainly good listeners, according to Willing, for it cramps their souls.

In her chapter on talking, then, Willing begins with the role of woman as conversationalist from the tradition of conduct book rhetoric, but expands that role considerably. Like Mary Astell and Hannah More before her, she argues that because they converse, women must be educated. She insists that they must be well educated in grammar, if only in self-help texts, and that they must read the classics so that they have something to talk about. Reading for Willing also means writing: in the classical and renaissance tradition, Willing wants her pupils to write down their summaries, selected quotations, and comments in a commonplace book.

This rhetorical program, however traditional, is immediately Christianized: "to talk well, it is necessary that the motive prompting our speech be right and pure; and we can be sure of that only as it is cleansed by the blood of Christ" "To talk well" is a translation of Quintilian's rhetorical dictum that only the good speaker speaks well. But the words are translated not only from another language, but also to another forum—conversation. In addition, Willing's Christian interpretation has roots in Augustine's famous transformation of rhetoric in *De Doctrina Christiana*. For Augustine, as well as for Willing, only the good Christian can be a good speaker. And finally, this program is also feminized: Willing combines these principles from the masculine tradition with the instructions from conduct book rhetoric for women not to gossip but instead to speak so no one is caused pain.

Willing reminds us that "Christianity could not at once overturn social customs," a rhetorical move that allows her to imply that the main purpose of Christianity was, in fact, to overturn and reform social customs, although not all at once. Willing is thus placing herself and her women who talk in an honored tradition, and she moves on to claim further privileges. Women must not only be educated but must also teach. And women who are called should also preach. The last third of her chapter, in fact, merges the defense of women's preaching into her chapter on women's conversation and conduct book rhetoric. Thus Willing seizes the conservative form of the conduct book and separates it from the separate spheres theory of women's rhetoric that had been promoted in that genre. Instead, Willing fully claims for women a private and a public voice.

For further information, see Theodore L. Agnew, "Jennie Fowler Willing," in *Notable American Women, 1607–1950*, ed. Edward T. James (Cambridge, Mass.: Harvard University Press, 1971), 3:623–25; Mark Edward Lender, "Jennie Fowler Willing," in *Dictionary of American Temperance Biography* (Westport, Conn.: Greenwood Press, 1984), 519–20; Carol Mattingly, *Well-Tempered Women: Nineteenth-Century Temperance Rhetoric* (Carbondale: Southern Illinois University Press, 1998), 70–71; Joanne Carlson Brown, "Jennie Fowler Willing," in *American National Biography*, ed. John A. Garraty and Mark C. Carnes (New York: Oxford University Press, 1999), 23:529–30; and Jane Donawerth, "Nineteenth-Century United States Conduct Book Rhetoric by Women," *Rhetoric Review*, forthcoming.

From *The Potential Woman: A Book for Young Ladies* (1887)

Chapter X: Talking

Philologists[1] may wrangle as they will, yet it is generally believed that articulate speech is a gift of God. Like thought or musical ability, it is given in rudimentary form; its recipient must develop it, and bring it to proper dignity and strength.

There are differences of linguistic endowment, as there are differences in musical talent. One may become a fine talker with less effort than another; yet no one can talk to good purpose unless he stirs up the gift that is within him. There are people who have left off trying to learn to talk before acquiring even a respectable skill in the expression of thought. Grant[2] was so slow of speech that he tells us with the utmost *naïveté*, how he suffered on a public occasion when a congratulatory address was made to him, to which he feared he would have to reply; and how the torture was relieved when the people began to shake hands, thus making it unnecessary for him to say anything. He thought out the campaigns that saved the Union and spoke in the victories of Vicksburg and Richmond. We would wish more earnestly that he had learned to talk, if he had not used those last, death-smitten months in giving the world the great, honest, generous thought that filled his silent soul. Many of gracious, richly-freighted spirits have been held in dumbness through the dolorous centuries because their speech was timid and gentle. When such are taught and encouraged to speak, we shall see the dawn of a better day.

The gift of speech has been bestowed alike upon men and women; but women have not been permitted the scope of theme, nor the practice that men have reserved to themselves. It has not been thought safe for them to discuss politics, philosophy, literature, or science, lest they become "strong minded." On account of this restriction, they may sometimes say, with all the more persistent fluency, what is allowed them. If a set of musical people were kept forever at a few little jingles, they might come to rattle them off with uncomfortable celerity. Men not infrequently make painfully apparent the fact that women are restricted to few subjects of conversation, by dropping into "small talk" when they address them, as if speaking to children or minors.

Women, like all who have not had a fair field, have fallen into diplomacy, carrying by favor points that they are not permitted to win by direct argument. They understand that nothing pleases an egotist more than to have one listen well to his talk. So they say, "Yes," and "No," and keep up a gentle jingle of the small bells of assent and applause, hoping to gain by pleasing what they are not allowed honorably to claim; their hearts, meanwhile, hungering for the mental food of excellent, ennobling speech. Consequently, their talk often has merely the flash and gleam, the shimmer and ripple of the shallows, lacking the sweep of the cataract, and the fullness of the sea.

A bad man sneers at a woman's tongue, because he has never known the sweet and serious words of a sister, the tender counsel of a mother, the whispered confidences of a wife who has surrendered all for the love of him. The men of the nobler Christian chivalry are above such paltriness.

The wonder is that women talk as well as they do, since they are not allowed their full share of practice. They do hardly a thousandth part of the public speaking. It is not they who talk against time at national expense, settling public affairs, as Lowell says of the blackbirds, "in windy congresses."[3] It is not they who turn the exchange into the veriest Babel[4] by their unearthly howls and shrieks. They are rarely called upon for speech-making on occasions of special interest. They do but little preaching or college lecturing. They are obliged to keep silence in most of the churches. It is not their voices that are heard at a dinner party, or above the rattle of the cars. Where they have been permitted to create a social order that has made fine talk possible to them, as in the palmy days of the French *salon*, they have reigned as queens of society; and under their rule, conversation has become one of the fine arts, making the free interchange of exalted thought a most delightful pleasure.

Women can talk, and they ought to learn to talk well. They train the children and make the home, the most important of all enterprises, demanding the clearest, steadiest thinking. Clear talking is usually necessary to clear thought. If one talks by jerks and hitches, starting out with a sentence that rattles off like an empty wagon, but that has to be drawn up and started back a half dozen times for a forgotten part of the load, you may be sure his thinking is quite as uncertain as his speech.

It costs thousands of dollars to teach young ladies music; yet it would be an infinitely finer and more useful accomplishment for them to speak well their own vernacular. If you can render skillfully one of Chopin's intricate polonaises, or Beethoven's grand symphonies, your effort may be understood by a few cultured people; but you need clear thought, simply and directly expressed, that you may be understood by yourself and your friends. You cannot be reliably truthful unless you state things plainly to yourself. If we have careless and inaccurate habits of speech, we may play rhetorical tricks upon ourselves, even in our approaches to God, and so our piety may rest upon an unsound basis. The love of friends must be short-lived, unless there is among them a free and honest interchange of thought.

To speak well, one must know the meaning and grammatical relations of words; and in these days of many books and cheap education, he is surely to blame who does not learn to use his own language correctly. It would save a world of misunderstandings, if we would always say just what we mean, and not something else. We must speak so as to give sensible people pleasure. I need not warn you against mannerisms, loudness, coarseness of voice or words, the giggling habit, the Auducia Dang-yer-eyes style as set forth by Mrs. Stowe,[5] offending good taste by its lack of modesty; the simpering and affected, the slangy, the haughty, the ostentatious; your own common sense protests against all these faults. If it has not done so, it may take severe discipline to bring you up where you can see that by them you hedge up your own way.

A woman ought to talk, as a real lady always dresses, simply, neatly, and with refined taste; her tones should be quiet, even, sure, and steady. So much for the mechanical part. Now for the matter: she must "read much," as Seneca says, "but few books."[6] Few and the best, wasting no time on that which is shallow and trashy—only so can she gather material for intelligent conversation. Going through a good book is like walking in a garden of flowers; even if you bring away not one blossom, you will carry its fragrance on your garments. But in that garden of spices—a noble volume—you must use pencil and commonplace book, so as to enrich your own thought with that which was planted for that very purpose.

After all, in talking, as in everything else, the motive is the mainspring of character. To talk well, it is necessary that the motive prompting our speech be right and pure; and we can be sure of that only as it is cleansed by the blood of Christ. Only when we know that it is whiter than snow through faith in him[7] can we be sure that we use this gift of his simply for his glory. We must consecrate it to him, determining never again to try to impress people with our own good qualities or attainments; never another word shall pass our lips to cause anyone a throb of unnecessary pain; never a syllable will we utter in violation of that love described by Paul in the thirteenth chapter of Corinthians. We will be "swift to hear, and slow to speak";[8] always gentle, always kind. If we will say: "never a word of gossip or enmity shall ever pass my lips, nothing to give a needless pang to any human soul, but rather that which is kind and helpful," we may talk to some purpose, and to God's glory.

The Pentecostal tongues of fire[9] were an object lesson, showing that the world is to be conquered for Christ through divine truth, uttered by human lips, that have been touched by hallowed flame.

There were women in that upper room, and the record says of the baptism of power: "It sat upon *all of them*; and they were *all* filled with the Holy Ghost, and began to speak with other tongues as the Spirit gave them utterance." Peter said: "this is that which was spoken by the prophet Joel, 'I will pour out of my Spirit upon all flesh, and your sons *and your daughters shall prophesy*. On my servants and on my handmaidens I will pour out in those days of my Spirit, and they shall prophesy.'"[10]

Philip, the evangelist, had four daughters, virgins, which did prophesy.[11]

On account of the corruptness of the Corinthians, and the fear that even converted men among them had not lost all memory of the abominable slums of licentiousness out of which Christianity had fished them, Paul directed that women among them who prayed and prophesied should cover their heads. In the same Epistle he defines prophesying as speaking "unto men to edification, exhortation, and comfort."[12]

When the great apostle ordered women to "keep silence in the churches," adding that it was "a shame for them to speak in the church," he gave them an injunction applicable only to their land and time.[13] As our Lord said about the old, easy divorce laws of the Hebrews—enactments the best that could be made for people in their low grade of civilization—they were given on account of the hardness of the people's hearts.[14] He could no more teach them the higher truth, than a professor of mathematics could give arithmetic scholars the formulae of trigonometry. He could lay down general principles, that could be developed into the higher teaching, as soon as they were able to receive it, like that saying of Paul: "There is neither male nor female, but ye are all one in Christ Jesus."[15]

Christianity could not at once overturn social customs. Neither Christ nor his apostles gave one clear, definite utterance against slavery. The slavery of their time was of the most cruel and barbarous type. For example: Epictetus was the slave of a Roman.[16] He was a man of genius, and taught his master the Stoical philosophy. To test the power of his theories, his master had both legs of his slave teacher broken. This incident illustrates the brutal, irresponsible character of the servitude of that day; yet the apostles felt the uselessness of an attempt at emancipation, and held their peace. Paul was often quoted in defense of our own Southern slavery, because he sent Onesimus back to his master, and enjoined upon slaves generally the duty of faithful obedience.[17]

The bulk of the world's teaching is done before children are ten years old; and, of necessity, by women. Yet when women began to teach in public schools, the "stupid good people" were alarmed, lest it was in violation of the Pauline injunction: "I suffer not a woman to teach."[18]

If other scriptures had been wrested out of their natural interpretation, and taught in their bald, false literalism, as have been those on the Christian use of a woman's tongue, ministers would all have had to give up drinking water, and take only wine. For does not Paul, in his letter to Timothy, the typical pastor, say: "Drink no longer water, but use a little wine, for thy stomach's sake, and thine often infirmities"?[19] And, indeed, the enemies of total abstinence are not slow to avail themselves of this apostolic advice, as well as of the silence of the Book on the theme that they oppose.

But shall women preach? Certainly, if God calls them to preach. He cannot make a mistake. He is not the author of confusion. But will it not subvert the existing social order? If the existing social order is not in harmony with the divine plan, it will have to be subverted. Will it not make havoc with domestic relations and duties? It did not seem to do so in the case of Susannah Wesley, whom the learned Adam Clarke pronounced "an able divine," and yet who held her *nineteen* children to a regimen as firm as that of West Point, though so gentle and tender that the same wise man writes of them: "They had the reputation of being the most loving family in the County of Lincoln."[20]

Catherine Booth[21] has solved the same problem. Hardly Spurgeon[22] himself is a better preacher, or has a wider influence than she; yet her nine children are so loyal to her and her work, they seem to think there is only one thing in the world worth the doing: that is, to get everybody to Christ as soon as possible.

"I am sorry I can't hear your mother preach tomorrow," I said to her son, as handsome and manly a young Englishman as ever a mother was proud of.

"Indeed, I regret it," he replied, as he handed me to my car. "It is a rare privilege to hear her preach the gospel."

Quaker women have never found the question a difficult one. They have always been free to obey "the Inner Voice"; and there are no lovelier women on the planet, than those same gentle Friends, with their free step and well-poised heads.

If one believes herself called of God to public work, she must "wait on the Lord" 'til he speaks clearly and distinctly. Then she must set about the matter with no question of its propriety. God could not possibly lead one to do an improper thing. If the call is genuine, she will, no doubt, have a high ideal of the service she ought to render, and a humility that will make her deeply distrustful of her own ability. She will have to steer her little tilting boat, between Scylla and Charybdis.[23] Without the self-distrust, she will fail through coarseness and a lack of reliance on God. With it, she will run great risk of utter discouragement. She need not hope to convince others of her call. "*Vox Dei*" will not be "*vox populi*."[24] Through false biblical interpretation the prejudices of the majority of the Lord's servants will bristle in her path like an *abattis*;[25] and she will soon learn that she cannot argue down a prejudice. She may as well take the advice of good, wise old Sojourner Truth: "What's de use o' makin' such a fuss about yer rights? Why dun ye jes' go 'long an' take 'em?"[26]

Aurora Leigh says:

> "And woman,—if another sat in sight,
> I'd whisper,—'Soft, my sister, not a word!
> By speaking, we prove only we can speak,
> Which he, the man here, never doubted. What
> He doubts is, whether we can *do* the thing

218

With decent grace we've not yet done at all.
Now do it; bring your statue,—you have room!
. . . .
    . . . there's no need to speak.
The universe shall henceforth speak for you,
And witness, 'she who did this thing was born
To do it,—claims her license in her work.'"[27]

Like Moses in Midian, God's best ministers have had to put forth the hand upon the mount of testing, and take by the tail the terrible serpent of certain failure.[28] They have cried to the Lord: "O, my Lord! I am not eloquent, neither heretofore, nor since Thou hast spoken unto thy servant; for I am slow of speech and of a slow tongue."[29] They have held back from the work 'til they have heard the Lord say: "I will be with thy mouth, and teach thee what thou shalt say."[30] Sometimes, as in the case of D. L. Moody,[31] the officiary of the church have informed them that they are mistaken. God could not have blundered so egregiously as to set them at such work. The only way for them, in that Golgotha of crosses,[32] is to make it a simple question between God and the soul, and follow where Christ leads, though they go as Esther went before the king, saying, "If I perish, I perish."[33]

Having settled the matter of the call, you need prayerfully to consider the preparation for service. You must not depend upon the novelty of a woman's public speaking to hold the attention of the people. Indeed, so many women are speaking now, that is quite worn off. Nor upon emotional appeals to sensibilities; people cannot live and grow robust on custards and whipped cream. You must study to show yourself approved workmen, that need not be ashamed. The mines of thought are as free to women as to men. They must learn to delve. One trouble with women in the past has been, they have had to use so much strength in breaking through the hedges with which prejudice has fenced them in, that they have had but little heart or leisure left for the digging out of thought with which to instruct and help their hearers. There is no excellence without labor. In these days, and in this land of many books and schools, they who will not work mentally, must work physically, among the scattered and starving on the frontier.

God saves souls by the foolishness of preaching,[34] but the very best is foolish enough. There is one book which you must study most carefully and constantly. You must get out of the Bible the bulk of what you say to people for their soul's help. Daniel Webster,[35] who was no saint, only a statesman, is said to have read it through once a year for mental stimulus. You must go to it as soldiers go to an arsenal, for weapons and ammunition. You can claim God's blessing upon its use, as you cannot hope to do upon the utterance of your own opinions. The Lord says: "So shall my word be that goeth forth out of my mouth; it shall not return unto me void, but it shall accomplish that which I please; and it shall prosper in the thing whereto I sent it."[36]

God, who has chosen the weak things of this world to confound the things that are mighty,[37] will use the simple utterances of any sincere, Spirit-taught soul. In the state of Maine a few years ago, he brought a whole village to himself through the words of an idiot who could only rap at each door and ask: "What will you do when eternity comes?" If we are moved by a fervent desire to save souls from eternal death, we may be used of God mightily, and we need not lack the very best furnishing for that service while we can read God's Word and commit it to memory.

Notes

My text is based on the Library of Congress volume, Jennie F. Willing, *The Potential Woman. A Book for Young Ladies* (Boston: McDonald & Gill, 1887), 110–27. I have modernized spelling and punctuation, but very few changes were necessary.

1. Philologists study the origins of words and the history of language.

2. Ulysses S. Grant was commander of the Union armies during the Civil War and president of the United States from 1869 to 1877. Although slow of speech, Willing suggests, he "spoke" through his deeds, his military victories at Vicksburg and Richmond. He wrote his memoirs during his last year when he was dying of throat cancer.

3. James Russell Lowell, "Once git a small o'mush," in *The Writings* (1890), l. 62.

4. Babel: metaphorically, a confusion of tongues, alluding to God's curse of many languages on the workmen who tried to raise the Tower of Babel to heaven, Genesis 11:1–9.

5. Harriet Beecher Stowe (1811–1896) was the famous author of *Uncle Tom's Cabin*, an antislavery and women's rights activist. I have been unable to locate the reference to Auducia.

6. Seneca the younger (c. 3 B.C.E.–65 C.E.) was a Roman philosopher, dramatist, and statesman, famous for his tragedies and Stoic essays. For this idea (although not a word-for-word quotation) see Letter II in *Letters from a Stoic*.

7. Paraphrasing Psalm 51:9.

8. Paul in James 1:19.

9. See Acts 2:3.

10. Peter in Acts 2:3–4, 16–17.

11. See Acts 21:8–9.

12. 1 Corinthians 11:5; 14:3.

13. 1 Corinthians 14:34–35.

14. See Matthew 19:8.

15. Galatians 3:28.

16. Epictetus, although a slave, was a famous Stoic philosopher who advocated indifference to external fortunes and attention to the true good within oneself.

17. Defenders of slavery cited Paul in 1 Timothy 6:1–4, suggesting that Paul's advice to be content with the lot of a servant gave biblical authorization to slavery.

18. 1 Timothy 2:12.

19. 1 Timothy 5:23.

20. Adam Clarke, *Memoirs of the Wesley Family* (New York: N. Bangs & T. Mason, 1824), 292; Clarke, *Memoirs of the Wesley Family*, rev. ed. (London: W. Tegg, 1836), 1:128.

21. Catherine Mumford Booth (1829–1890), a noted preacher, helped to found the Salvation Army; her children also devoted their lives to religion.

22. Charles Haddon Spurgeon (1834–1892) was a famous English Baptist preacher whose popularity required larger churches; he published many of his sermons.

23. Scylla, a sea monster whose six heads devoured six men at a time from passing ships, and Charybdis, a whirlpool opposite Scylla's cave in a narrow strait, in the *Odyssey*.

24. Latin: *Vox Dei*, the word of God, will never become *vox populi*, the word of the people.

25. *Abattis*: (French) a slaughterhouse.

26. Sojourner Truth (c. 1799–1883), a slave emancipated by New York state law, became an outstanding public speaker on abolition and women's rights.

27. Elizabeth Barrett Browning, *Aurora Leigh*, bk. 8, ll. 827–33, 838–41. The omission in this poem is Willing's.

28. See Exodus 3:2–4:4.

29. Exodus 4:10 (slightly misquoted, so perhaps from memory).

30. Exodus 4:12.

31. Dwight L. Moody (1837–1899), a famous evangelical preacher, headed a touring company of song leaders and preachers, including, briefly, Frances Willard.

32. Golgotha, the place where Christ was crucified; see Matthew 27:33.

33. Esther 4:16.

34. 1 Corinthians 1:21.

35. Daniel Webster (1782–1852), U.S. statesman, member of the House and the Senate, twice secretary of state, and brilliant orator.

36. Isaiah 55:11.

37. 1 Corinthians 1:27.

Sara Lockwood

1854–c. 1902

Sara Elizabeth Husted was born in Bridgeport, Connecticut, on September 13, 1854, to Alfred W. and Lucy (Northrop) Husted. She graduated from New Haven High School in 1873 and taught there from 1874 to 1890. On the title page of *Lessons in English*, Lockwood is identified as "Teacher of English in the Hillhouse High School, New Haven, Connecticut." She married Dr. William E. Lockwood on June 30, 1887; he died in 1897. It was quite unusual for a middle-class white woman to continue working after marriage before the 1940s; some schools forbade it. She was the author of a revision of *The Essentials of English Grammar by Prof. W. D. Whitney of Yale* (1891), *Lessons in English* (1888), and, with M. Alice Emerson (a professor of English at Carleton College), *Composition and Rhetoric* (1901). Lockwood and Emerson's *Composition and Rhetoric* seems to be a later revision with the help of a coauthor of the earlier *Lessons in English*, which Lockwood wrote by herself. Lockwood's last address was California.

Lockwood's *Lessons in English* is an all-purpose grammar and composition textbook suitable for high schools, academies that mixed secondary and junior college students, and college writing courses. It does assume that the teachers using the textbook will be women—in the introductory address, Lockwood terms the teacher "she." *Lessons in English* is representative of turn-of-the-century American composition studies in its breadth of sources—classical rhetoric, eighteenth-century belles lettres rhetoric, and nineteenth-century reformist education theory. It does not seem influenced by the turn toward correctness as a primary goal of composition studies.

Lessons in English begins with three chapters on the history of the English language, an overview, and explanations of both Anglo-Saxon and Latin contributions. Chapters 4–8 cover grammar, but from a rhetorical point of view, concentrating on figures of speech, errors, diction, rhetorical classifications of sentence structure and style, and punctuation. For this anthology, I chose selections from the chapter on sentence structure because it anticipates much recent work on sentences in contemporary composition studies, derived from the union of linguistics and rhetoric; in addition, Lockwood's exercises for writers include sentence combining, another popular late twentieth-century composition technique. While Lockwood is somewhat indebted to eighteenth- and nineteenth-century rhetoricians Blair and Hill, she is influenced even more by the classical tradition (the classification of periodic and loose sentences comes from that tradition). Thus Lockwood moves quite easily from exercises in the writing of long sentences based on qualities of style and rhetorical purpose, into other classical rhetorical preparations for speech composing: reproduction, paraphrase, abstract, and amplification.

While Lockwood borrows from empiricist rhetoric and Alexander Bain's classification of composition into four kinds, she deals only with two of them, description and narration, judged appropriate for this age level. But she further adds letter writing from the conduct book tradition of rhetoric. She teaches invention, but not according to classical dicta. Instead, she incorporates the nineteenth-century reform tradition of education and composition studies, based on Pestalozzi's emphasis on students' learning from direct observation of objects and personal experience. Lockwood even calls her section on collecting information for writing "Composition upon Objects," indicating the Pestalozzian emphasis in her approach, and she defines good writing topics within the bounds of sensory observation and personal experience—description and personal narrative.

Thus Lockwood is innovative in many ways, although she is not originating but borrowing from other reform-minded educators. Especially important is her patriotic concentration on composition combined with American "classics." Her textbook registers the increased importance of vernacular literature and its development as part of American culture. She is thus engaging in a debate that continues until today between advocates of courses in composition based on literature or readings, and courses in composition based on persuasion and argument.

For more information on Lockwood, see *Who Was Who in America* (Chicago: Marquis–Who's Who, 1968), 4:582.

From *Lessons in English* (1888)

CHAPTER VII
SENTENCES[1]

A sentence is such an expression of thought as makes complete sense, and is followed by a full pause.

GRAMMATICAL CLASSIFICATION OF SENTENCES

1. *A Simple Sentence* contains but one proposition.

Ex. The sun shines.

2. *A Complex Sentence* contains one independent proposition and one or more dependent propositions.

Ex. The sun shines, even when we do not see it.

3. *A Compound Sentence* contains two or more co-ordinate propositions.

Ex. The sun shines, and the earth is glad.

RHETORICAL CLASSIFICATIONS

As considered in Rhetoric, sentences are divided into three classes, according to their construction.

1. *A Periodic Sentence* does not complete the main thought until the close of the sentence.

Ex. Having been wrecked on the coast of Jamaica, during one of his voyages, and reduced to the verge of starvation by the want of provisions which the natives refused to supply, *Columbus took advantage of their ignorance of astronomy*.

2. *A Loose Sentence* is so constructed that it may be brought to a close in two or more places and in each case make complete sense.

Ex. We made our way up the mountain, | riding in the shade of lofty birches, | occasionally crossing the path of some clear mountain stream, | but hearing no human voice | and seldom even the chirp of bird or insect.

3. *A Balanced Sentence* is made up of two members which are similar in form, but *often* contrasted in meaning.

Ex. Train up a child in the way he should go; and when he is old, he will not depart from it. Worth makes the man; the want of it, the fellow.

EFFECTS OF DIFFERENT KINDS OF SENTENCES

Too many loose sentences give an impression of carelessness.

Too many periodic sentences make the style stiff and monotonous.

Balanced sentences are well suited to satire or to essays in which persons or things are contrasted. They are not suitable in narrative or description.

Antithesis[2] is commonly expressed by the use of the balanced sentence.

RULE AS TO KINDS OF SENTENCES

Study variety. The mind tires of any one style of construction carried to excess.

SECOND RHETORICAL CLASSIFICATIONS

For convenience, a more general classification of sentences is often made, all sentences being regarded as either SHORT or LONG.

EFFECTS OF THE TWO KINDS OF SENTENCES

Short sentences give animation to the style, but a constant use of them becomes tiresome and destroys the smoothness of expression.

Long sentences give a fine opportunity for climax,[3] but are commonly not so easily understood as shorter ones. They require closer attention on the part of the reader or hearer.

RULE AS TO LENGTH OF SENTENCES

Do not use either short or long sentences to excess. Vary the construction to prevent monotony.

EXERCISE

1. Novels, as a class, are injurious to young people. They destroy the taste for more solid reading. They cultivate the emotions to an undue extent. They convey false impressions of life. [Combine into one sentence.]

2. I was once an enlisted soldier, under the three months' call, and for three days was in camp at Hartford, sleeping in tents, rising at the tap of the drum, going through the routine of drill, and thrice daily marching to the Clinton House for rations, when the word came from Washington that no more three months' men were wanted in front, but three years, or for the war, it having at last penetrated the brains of the men in authority that the contest was no boy's play of two or three months, but man's work for an indefinite period.[4] [Divide into six sentences.]

RULES FOR THE CONSTRUCTION OF SENTENCES

Rhetorical Qualities of a Good Sentence—The most important qualities of a good sentence are *Clearness, Emphasis, Unity, Strength, and Harmony.*

CLEARNESS

General Rule—The arrangement of words should be such that the meaning cannot be misunderstood.

SPECIAL RULES

1. Position of the Adverb—Adverbs should be placed as near as possible to the words which they modify.

Ex. I *only* saw two birds.

Here the adverb *only* seems to modify *saw*; I saw them, but did not hear them sing; or, I saw them, but did not shoot them. If the thought is that there were two birds, *and no more*, the adverb is in the wrong place. The sentence should read, "I saw *only two* birds."

2. Position of Modifiers in General—All modifiers, whether words, phrases, or clauses, should be placed as near as possible to the word or words which they limit.

Ex. He went to town, driving a flock of sheep, on *horseback*.

The phrase *on horseback* modifies *went*; but from its position, it seems to refer to *sheep*. The proper order would be, "He went to town, *on horseback*, driving a flock of sheep."

Participial Construction—In the use of participial phrases and clauses, great care is needed to preserve clearness of thought.

Ex. *Being exceedingly fond of birds*, an aviary is always to be found within the grounds.

Here the participial phrase seems to refer to *aviary*; it should, of course, refer to some person previously named. For example, "*Sir Robert* being exceedingly fond of birds," etc.

3. Use of pronouns—Every pronoun should be so placed that its antecedent cannot be mistaken.

Ex. The figs were in small wooden *boxes*, *which* we ate.

The pronoun *which* seems to refer to *boxes* as its antecedent. It should refer to *figs*: "The *figs which* we ate were in small wooden boxes."

4. "Squinting" Construction—A word, a phrase, or a clause should not be thrown loosely into a sentence, so that it may be understood as referring to either the preceding or the following part.

Ex. Please tell my mother, *if she is at home*, I shall not hurry back.

The clause *if she is at home* may modify what precedes, the idea being *If she is at home*, please give her my message. But the clause may also be connected in meaning with the last part of the sentence—I shall not hurry back if she is at home. If she is away from home, my services may be needed, and I must hurry back.

EXERCISE

Correct the sentences, explaining which of the special rules is violated.

11. Then the Moor, seizing a bolster, filled with rage and jealousy, smothers her.[5]

25. The horses became fatigued, and after holding a council they decided to go no farther.

EMPHASIS

General Rule—The words of a sentence should be so arranged that the emphasis in reading will naturally come upon the main parts of the sentence, the Principal Subject and the Principal Predicate.

SPECIAL RULES

1. The Principal Subject—The principal subject, it must be remembered, is not, in all cases, the grammatical subject of the sentence. Sometimes it is in the objective case, as in the sentence, "You have heard the story of *Paul Revere's ride*."[6] Here the most important thing spoken of is not the grammatical subject *you*. The emphasis in reading will naturally come upon the last three words, which constitute the principal subject. Notice how the sentence loses its force if we say, "Of the story of *Paul Revere's ride*, you have heard."

The place of the principal subject is commonly at the beginning of the sentence, but stronger emphasis is often secured by inversion.

"Great is *Diana of the Ephesians!*" is far more emphatic than "*Diana of the Ephesians* is great."

Often, too, and especially in sentences which contain participial phrases or clauses, it is well to dispose of the modifiers first, and then to introduce the principal subject.

Ex. Allowing for the exaggeration of friendship and poetry, *Tennyson's tribute to his friend*[7] is just and well deserved.

2. The Principal Predicate—The same suggestions will apply to the principal predicate. Let the modifiers be so arranged that the principal subject and the principal predicate shall stand out clearly in the sentence.

Proper emphasis may often be secured by changing the verb from the passive form to the active.

EXERCISE

(a) Point out the principal subject and the principal predicate of each sentence.

(b) Reconstruct the sentence so as to increase the emphasis.

2. She, being ambitious to perform the same exploit, darted from her nest and fixed her talons in a large sheep.

5. The English language, spoken in the time of Elizabeth[8] by a million fewer persons than today speak it in London alone, now girdles the earth with its electric chain of communication,[9] and voices the thoughts of a hundred million souls.

UNITY

General Rule—The parts of a sentence should be so arranged that Unity of thought shall be maintained.

SPECIAL RULES

1. Change of Subject—The subject should be changed as little as is unavoidable. This rule does not, of course, mean that a sentence must never contain more than one subject.

Ex. The vessel made for the shore, and the passengers soon crowded into the boats, and the beach was reached in safety, where the inhabitants of the island received them with the utmost kindness.

This sentence contains four subjects: *vessel, passengers, beach,* and *inhabitants.* It is evident that the principal subject is *the passengers.* The sentence should read, "The vessel having made the shore, the passengers soon crowded into the boats and safely reached the beach, where they were received with the utmost kindness by the inhabitants of the island."

2. Relative Clauses—Unity of thought is often destroyed by a loose arrangement of relative clauses. A sentence may properly contain two or more relative clauses having a common dependence upon the principal clauses.

Ex. This is the most charming chapter in the story, which is full of pleasant incidents and which the reader will find well worth perusal.

Here both relative pronouns refer to *story.* But in the sentence, "We had no lack of entertainment during the time which we spent in the city, which seems very gay and attractive," the relative clauses are wrongly used. The second *which* refers to *city* in the preceding relative clause. The first *which* refers to *time.*

"And which." The following sentence illustrates a common error in construction.

Ex. His is a style abounding in strength and vivacity *and which* never transgresses the bounds of literary propriety.

It must be remembered that *and* is a coordinate conjunction, and that it should, therefore, join words or phrases or clauses which are of the same kind. In this sentence, *and* joins a participial phrase to a relative clause. Both modifiers may be made participial or both relative, as follows:

(a) His is a style abounding in strength and vivacity and never transgressing the bounds of literary propriety.

(b) His is a style which abounds in strength and vivacity and which never transgresses the bounds of literary propriety.

3. Too Many Ideas—Ideas which have no close connection should not be crowded into the same sentence. Long and rambling sentences are very likely to contain other faults besides lack of unity.

Ex. As we drove along, we met a young lady in full lawn-tennis costume, and passed a house where there was a handsome flower-garden and where Mr. Gray lives, who is the teller of the bank and who owns a superb St. Bernard dog.

4. Parentheses—Avoid the use of parentheses. A parenthesis is commonly a sign of careless construction.

Ex. One day last week (Wednesday, I think) we went nutting.

In the following sentence, the parentheses is allowable, but a division into two sentences would be a better arrangement.

Ex. Then said the Shepherds, "From that stile there goes a path that leads directly to Doubting-Castle, which is kept by Giant Despair; and these men (pointing to them among the tombs) came once on pilgrimage, as you do now, even until they came to that same stile."[10]

5. Supplementary Clauses—When the expression of a thought is apparently complete, no additional clause should be "tacked on" at the end.

Ex. There is to be a grand wedding next week, to which we are all to be invited; *or, at least, so I hear.*

EXERCISE

(a) Which of the special rules is violated?

(b) Correct the sentence so as to maintain unity of thought.

10. A violent storm drove me to the coast of Sardinia, which is free from all poisonous herbs except one, which resembles parsley and causes those who eat it to die of laughing.

11. Dr. Kane described the Arctic silence as sometimes almost dreadful; and one day at dinner, while Thackeray was quietly smoking and Kane was fresh from his travels, he told them a story of a sailor reading *Pendennis*.[11]

STRENGTH

General Rule—A sentence should be so constructed that the thought which it contains shall be expressed with all possible force. Energy and Animation are other names for this quality.

SPECIAL RULES

1. Unnecessary Words—Cut out all words which do not add anything to the meaning.

The error of using too many words has three manifestations: Tautology, Redundancy, and Circumlocution.

(a) Tautology consists in repeating the *thought*.

Ex. Silence reigned, and not a sound was heard.

(b) Redundancy consists in using words which are not necessary to the sense.

Ex. Collect *together* all the fragments.

(c) Circumlocution consists in using "round-about" expressions.

Ex. One of those omnipresent characters, who, as if in pursuance of some previous arrangement, are certain to be encountered in the vicinity when an accident occurs, ventured the suggestion. This is a round-about way of saying, "A bystander advised."

2. Words of Connection—The strength of a sentence is increased by careful use of the words of connection.

(a) Avoid "stringing" clauses together loosely with *and* as connective.

Ex. They were soon at home *and* surrounded by the family *and* plied with questions as to what they had seen *and* what they had heard *and* soon the neighbors came in *and* then the whole story had to be told again. In this sentence, there is lack of unity as well as lack of strength.

In a sentence containing a series of words or expressions in the same construction, insert conjunctions between each two words or expressions if the intention is to make the mind dwell upon each particular.

Ex. "And the rain descended, and the floods came, and the winds blew, and beat upon that house; and it fell: and great was the fall of it."[12]

But when the author's object is to give a many-sided view of a subject, or to convey the idea of rapid movement, the conjunction should be omitted.

Ex. Charity "beareth all things, believeth all things, hopeth all things, endureth all things."[13]

or

One effort, one, to break the circling host;

They form, unite, charge, waver—all is lost![14]

(b) Do not weaken the sentence by the omission of the relative pronoun. Such omissions are allowable in familiar conversation, but rarely in careful writing.

Ex. The idea [which] he is working on is fraught with great possibilities.

(c) Do not have two prepositions govern the same noun. This awkward construction is called "splitting particles."

Ex. He ran *by*, but did not look *into*, the windows.

Better: He ran by the windows, but did not look into them.

3. Contrasts—Contrasted members of a sentence should be similar in construction.

Ex. The President holds the executive power of the land, but the legislative power is vested in Congress. The contrast is more forcible if we say, "The President holds the executive power of the land; but Congress, the legislative power."

4. Conclusion—The mind naturally dwells upon the last part of a sentence. Care should, therefore, be taken to have the last word a forcible one. Avoid closing a sentence with an insignificant word or phrase; as, for example, an adverb or a preposition or such a phrase as *to it*, *by it*, etc.

Ex. That is a danger which young children are exposed *to*.

The sentence should read, "That is a danger to which young children are exposed."

Ex. None but capital letters were used *formerly*. The idea is more forcibly presented if we say, "*Formerly*, none but capital letters were used."

5. Climax—Whenever it is possible, arrange words and clauses so as to make an effective climax. The last clause of a sentence and the last paragraph of an essay should ordinarily be the strongest one.

Ex. of faulty climax: Where shall I find hope, happiness, a clear conscience, friends, money?

Ex. corrected: Where shall I find money, friends, hope, happiness, and a clear conscience?

EXERCISE

(a) Which of the special rules is violated?

(b) Change the sentence so as to increase its strength.

12. The freshet destroyed life and property and washed away thousands of hencoops.

14. It is a great privilege to assemble and meet together.

15. On account of the small number of seats available, no ladies will be admitted, only the men.

HARMONY

General Rule—A sentence should be constructed with due regard to a pleasing effect upon the ear.

It must be evident, that while Harmony is a very desirable quality of sentences, it is less important than Clearness, Unity, or Strength. In applying the special rules, therefore, care should be taken not to sacrifice the sense to the sound.

SPECIAL RULES

1. Pleasant Sounds—Pleasantness of sound, or Euphony, as it is called, is best secured by avoiding the use of words, or combinations of words, which are difficult to pronounce. The most melodious words are such as contain a blending of vowels and consonants, especially if some of the consonants are liquids. Compare the following, as to euphony:

Ex.: He arbitrarily singled out an inexplicably scrubby shrub and peremptorily repri-manded the giggling, but shame-faced Driggs for having haggled all the shrubbery instead of properly pruning it.

Ex.: I love the old melodious lays

Which softly melt the ages through,

The songs of Spenser's golden days,

Arcadian Sidney's silvery phrase,

Sprinkling our noon of time with freshest morning dew. *Whittier*[15]

Examples of disagreeable combinations of sounds:

He will wilfully persist.

I can candidly say. . . .

In an analogous case. . . .

2. Needless Repetition—Avoid repeating the same word in a sentence or a paragraph. Aim to secure variety of expression.

Ex. The general *ordered* the captain to *order* the soldiers to observe good *order*.

Better: The general directed the captain to see that the soldiers observed good order.

3. Rhythm—The words should be so arranged that the accents shall come at intervals convenient for the reader or speaker. The harmonious flow of sounds made by the rise and fall of tone is called Rhythm. No definite rules for the arrangement of accents can be given. The ear must be trained to recognize any interruption to the smoothness of sound.

Take the following sentence from Irving:

It is delightful, in thus bivouacking on the prairies, to lie awake and gaze at the stars; it is like watching them from the deck of a ship at sea, when at one view we have the whole cope of heaven.[16]

It is evident that there is something wrong in the sentence. "It doesn't sound right," would be a very natural criticism. If we examine the sentence, we shall find that between the words "watching" and "heaven" are nineteen successive monosyllables. Such a sentence may be greatly improved by inserting one or two longer words in place of the short ones. A succession of words of one syllable is very likely to destroy the rhythm of a sentence.

4. Cadence at the Close—Words should be so arranged as to give an agreeable Cadence at the close of a sentence. By "cadence" is meant the falling of the voice. Avoid closing a sentence with a small word or with a succession of unaccented syllables. Such a construction is lacking in strength as well as in harmony. Words of three syllables, accented on the second, and words of four syllables, accented on the first and third, make pleasant cadences.

Ex. de-light'-ful; in-ter-ces'-sion.

Example of faulty cadence: In the farming districts, where the people are fully as well educated as those of any rural district in the United States, the servants form part of the family circle at the table, around the hearth-stone, or in the pew at church; they share the best sleeping apartments of the family, wear just as good clothing as the master and mistress, and the maids, if they are pretty, get as much attention from masculine visitors as the daughters of the house, *too*.

5. Adapting the Sound to the Sense—Whenever it is possible, and particularly in description and narration, the Sound should be adapted to the Sense. The use of the figure onomatopoeia, which has already been explained,[17] gives vividness and animation to the style.

A fine example of this kind of harmony is given by Longfellow in "The Courtship of Miles Standish":

Silently out of the room then glided the glistening savage,

Bearing the serpent's skin, and seeming himself like a serpent.

Winding his sinuous way in the dark to the depths of the forest.[18]

EXERCISE

(a) Explain the lack of harmony.

(b) Correct the sentence.

3. To two tunes, I have made up my mind never to listen.

4. One cannot imagine what a monotonous being one becomes if one constantly remains turning one's self in the circle of one's favorite notions.

CHAPTER X
COMPOSITION WRITING

TO THE TEACHER:

The author's intention is to furnish in this chapter some practical hints concerning such a graded course in Composition Writing as may profitably be pursued in connection with the study of American classics. It must be evident that only an outline of the plan can be given within the limits of a single chapter. Each teacher is expected to adapt the work to the needs of her individual pupils, according to her own best judgment.

It will be noticed that the plan calls for but little original work during the first year. The wisdom of this arrangement will doubtless be apparent to all who have had any experience in teaching pupils from fourteen to sixteen years of age. The simple announcement that a composition of so many pages, upon a particular subject, must be handed in upon a certain day in the near future is enough to cast a gloom over the sunniest schoolroom.

If we inquire why this is so, we shall probably find that the chief reasons are the following:

1. The pupils have few ideas of their own.

2. They are now old enough to realize the crudeness of their own thoughts as compared with the thoughts of their elders. As a natural consequence, expression is less spontaneous with them than it was when they were younger. The ideas which they have seem to them not worth presenting.

3. They have but little command of words. The narrow limits of their vocabularies prevent their making a wise use of the help which they might otherwise, and very properly, get from books. They know that they should not copy the author's words, yet do not understand how to clothe the thought in a new dress.

It is, therefore, recommended that throughout the first year attention be devoted mainly to the reproduction of thought. By constant and varied practice of this kind, the pupils learn how beautiful and interesting even common things appear when sketched by a skillful word-painter. Their own powers of observation are quickened by noticing the results of the careful observation of others. Ingenuity, accuracy, and aptness of expression are developed. The taste is educated by a critical study of cultured idiom and graceful diction. Abundant material is provided, so that the pupil is not, at the outset, discouraged by having "nothing to write."

It is safe to say that no one will be successful as a teacher of composition who cannot do easily the work which she exacts from the class. She should be able not merely to *tell* them how to write, but to *show* them how. A little help of this kind over the hard places will rob composition writing of many of its terrors.

Most of the exercises which are quoted as examples were written by pupils, and appear with all their imperfections thick upon them. They are to be regarded, not as models, but as helps to the beginner.

COMPOSITION
FIRST YEAR

REPRODUCTION

Any expression of another's thoughts in our own words is a Reproduction. It may be only a phrase, a clause, or a sentence; and, on the other hand, it may be a long story or essay.

Varieties of Reproduction—There are three special forms of reproduction: Paraphrase, Abstract, and Amplification.

PARAPHRASE

A Paraphrase is a reproduction in which the same thought is expressed in equivalent words. If the original article be written in verse, the thought expressed in prose is a paraphrase. Retaining the original thought, we change the style by substituting our own expressions for the author's. A paraphrase is, therefore, a sort of translation from another's speech into our own.

Ex. From his half-itinerant life, he was a sort of walking gazette.

Paraphrase: He spent nearly half his time in going about from house to house, and so he became a kind of traveling newspaper.

How to Write a Paraphrase

1. Read the selection carefully, looking up the definition of any word whose meaning is not clear to you. You must understand exactly what the author means before you undertake to express his thought. If he uses figurative language, study his figures so as to be able to give the same idea in plain language.

2. Taking one sentence, or, if it be a story, one paragraph at a time, make a list of the expressions which you wish to vary. There will necessarily be some words which you cannot change without spoiling the sense. A little study will show you which words and phrases may safely be "translated."

3. Select other words and phrases to substitute for those on your list. The dictionary will help you in this. Try to select the best word. Take time to think whether the word will fit into the place which you intend it to occupy.

4. Reproduce the selection. It is proper, in translating from a foreign language into our own, to make what is called "a free translation," changing not merely the expression, but also the construction. So, in this kind of translation, we should not paraphrase word by word, imitating closely the author's construction. We may sometimes secure variety by changing from the form of indirect discourse to that of conversation, or we may change a declarative sentence to the interrogative or the exclamatory form.

Advantages of Exercise in Paraphrasing—This kind of reproduction furnishes excellent practice in writing.

1. It teaches us to notice how words are used by careful writers. It often happens that we have to let a word or a phrase stand just as it is in the original, because the author has chosen the best possible expression for his thoughts.

2. It increases the number of words at our command. If we learn three ways of expressing an idea where we knew only one before, we are richer by just so much.

3. It enables us to make a proper use of another's thought in our own writings.

[Exercises on paraphrasing sentences, paragraphs of prose or poetry, and whole poems are suggested.]

ABSTRACT

An Abstract is a *condensed* statement of another's thought. The most important ideas are presented and in the same order as in the original, but the details are omitted. A condensed report of a lecture or a sermon is an abstract. It differs from Outline in being expressed in complete sentences.

> Ex. "In the old days (a custom laid aside
> With breeches and cocked hats) the people sent
> Their wisest men to make the public laws;

And so, from a brown homestead, where the Sound
Drinks the small tribute of the Mianas,
Waved over by the woods of Rippowams,
And hallowed by pure lives and tranquil deaths,
Stamford sent up to the councils of the State
Wisdom and grace in Abraham Davenport." *Whittier*[19]

Abstract—More than a hundred years ago, it was the custom to choose the wisest men to make the laws; so Stamford sent Abraham Davenport to the Legislature.

This tells *who* was sent, *from where, to where, when,* and *why.* If we arrange these points in the proper order, we shall have an Outline.

1. When   3. From where   5. To where
2. Why   4. Who

Advantages Derived from Practice in Writing Abstracts—The chief benefit of this kind of reproduction is that it teaches us to select the really important ideas from the article which we have to condense. It helps us, too, to see clearly the relations between different parts of a sketch or story. A third advantage is that it helps us to cultivate a clear, concise, and forcible style. Young writers are likely to use too many words to express an idea. For this reason, practice in writing abstracts is of special importance in the early part of our work in composition.

How to Write an Abstract

1. Read carefully the whole of the sketch or story or poem which you have to condense. Be sure that you understand the relation of parts and the order of events, so that you can tell the whole story to a friend who asks what you have been reading.

2. Make an outline of the story. This should be brief, consisting of not more than five or six topics or heads, expressed as concisely as possible. Take care to select the most important topics and to arrange them in the right order.

3. Consider the relative importance of the topics, and decide about how much time and space you can afford to devote to each. A very common mistake, in the writing of abstracts, is that of reproducing too many details in the early part of the work and making the last part very much more condensed.

4. Express clearly, definitely, in complete sentences, but concisely, what you wish to say upon each of the topics. Avoid rhyme, and do not borrow the author's language except where it is unavoidable.

[Exercises on abstracting sentences, paragraphs, stories, and biographies are suggested.]

AMPLIFICATION

Amplification is the opposite of Abstract. An Amplification is an *expanded* statement of another's thought. Things left unsaid or only hinted at in the original are fully and positively expressed in the amplification. The details are carefully given and the imagination is allowed free play.

Ex. A ship was lost at sea.

Amplification: Many years ago, on a beautiful September morning, a ship sailed out of the harbor of New York, bound for the East Indies. She was loaded with the products of American industry and was expected to bring back a cargo of coffee and spices. The captain was a young man full of energy and ambition. He was the only son of a widowed mother. On board were two passengers, a boy and a girl, the children of a missionary in India. They had been at school in America, but had been summoned to their distant home by the news that their mother grieved so sorely over the separation from her children that her life was in danger. The days sped on and lengthened into weeks, but the good ship did not reach her port. Months passed, but no tidings of the missing vessel came to either shore. On one side, an aged woman, watching for a sail that never came, cried to the sea, "Bring back my boy." On the other side, a dying mother moaned, "Give back my dear ones." But the sea gave no sign. Years have rolled away, and both mothers have gone where there is "no more sea"; but still the waves hide their cruel secret.

Advantages of Amplification—The chief advantage of Amplification is that it is a step towards original composition. It *suggests* ideas and leaves us to think them out more fully—to develop the meaning in our own way. It is like taking a pencil sketch which someone else has made, and producing from it a finished picture, using our own taste as to the colors and tones, the lights and shades.

How to Amplify a Selection

1. Read the selection carefully until you are so familiar with the story that you can tell it in your own words.

2. Write an orderly list of the points or incidents of the story as told by the author.

3. Make a list of the things which are omitted; as, for example, place, time, name of person, occupation, history, events leading to the incident, consequences, conclusion. Try to supply in this way whatever the original story leaves to the imagination of the reader.

4. From the two lists, make a complete outline, observing the directions previously given.

5. Study the outline with reference to relative importance of the topics, and decide about how much space to devote to each.

6. Expand each topic in the best words at your command, carefully avoiding the forms of expression in the original.

7. Be careful to connect the topics in such a manner that the story shall not seem disjointed. Read over what you have written, noticing whether the transition from one topic to another seems abrupt. If it does, you must try to connect the parts more smoothly. This may often be done by using such expressions as "nevertheless," "on the other hand," "meanwhile," "however," "in spite of all this," "and so."

[Exercises in amplifying a sentence, a paragraph, and a story told in poetry are suggested.]

INVENTION

We may now attempt to invent thought for ourselves, instead of reproducing the thoughts of other persons, expressed in various ways. It will be easier at first to write upon subjects which will exercise the imagination.

Caution—In this species of composition, be careful not to give your imagination too much liberty. The charm of this kind of writing consists in making the story seem not only probable, but natural.

[Exercises in editing for spelling and punctuation, writing a paragraph from the teacher's dictation, writing a story based on an allusion, writing sentences with certain grammatical forms, writing a short story using a given list of words, writing an explanation of a quotation, writing on a topic of current local interest, writing an advertisement, writing a telegram, reproducing an anecdote, describing a character, and rewriting a passage to change figures of speech are suggested.]

I. COMPOSITIONS UPON OBJECTS

In most of your practice in composition thus far, you have used the thoughts of others as the basis of your work. Now you must learn how to write without so much help of this kind. It is well to begin by writing about simple things concerning which you have some knowledge. The first thing to be done is to find out how much you know about the subject.

Collection of Material—As soon as the subject is assigned, you should begin to study it, noting down your thoughts as they occur to you. One topic will naturally suggest another; and if you keep the subject in mind and make a memorandum of each thought, you will soon be surprised to find that you have more material than you can conveniently use. If you do not make a note of your thought at the time it occurs to you, you will be very likely to forget it when you are ready to write. As far as possible, depend upon your own knowledge. If you need to learn more than you already know about the subject, consult authorities concerning the points on which your knowledge is deficient, but never copy the language of those authorities. Make the information so thoroughly your own that you can easily express it in your own words. Then make brief notes which will help you in writing. You should, if possible, collect your material several days before writing the composition.

[A collaborative class exercise on the topic of "paper" is suggested. Further topics—such as almanacs, cats, heroes, slang, letters, iron, fireplaces, and the Indians—are suggested.]

II. NARRATIVE OR STORY

In this kind of composition, the writer relates some incident or series of incidents. We shall consider three special forms of Narratives:

1. Personal Narratives, founded upon incidents in the writer's own experience.

2. Historical Narratives, founded upon events in history.

3. Fiction or *Romance*, founded upon imaginary incidents.

Personal Narratives—As the easiest form of the personal narrative, you may now write some true story about yourself: something which you have seen or done. Remember that the interest of such a story depends almost as much upon the way in which it is told as upon the incident itself. Try to make it fresh and interesting instead of trite and commonplace. Remember that in order to do this you need not use "big words" or adorn your style with elaborate figures. In language, as in dress, a simple style is often the most elegant. The stories which make the strongest impression on us—whose humor awakens our mirth and whose pathos brings the tears to our eyes—are commonly those which are told in simple, unaffected style. Be clear, exact, and truthful in all your statements. Aim to tell the story in such a way that the incident shall be vividly presented to the reader. The frequent use of "I" in a personal narrative makes the writer appear egotistical. This effect may often be avoided by introducing a part of the story in conversational form.

[Topics—such as a journey, a dog, housekeeping, a ride in the streetcar, and "My Best Day Last Vacation"—are suggested.]

Historical Narratives—The Historical Narrative is, of necessity, a reproduction. It is commonly either an abstract or an amplification of what has been told by others. Imaginary incidents are often combined with historical events, making what is called an *Historical Romance*. Many of Sir Walter Scott's "Waverley Novels" are of this character. So, too, are James Fenimore Cooper's stories of Indian life.[20] In writing an abstract of a story taken from history, be careful to select the most important incidents and to make a clear and connected outline. In amplifying, be sure that the details which your imagination supplies are in keeping with the scene, the time, the characters, and the spirit of the story which you are relating. If you invent conversations, let the language be such as would be natural and appropriate for the persons whom you imagine to be talking.

[Topics—such as the Boston Tea Party, the flight of Mahomet, the Battle of Waterloo, the destruction of Pompeii, and the Salem witches—are suggested.]

III. DESCRIPTION

Description is a more difficult kind of composition than any which you have yet attempted. It aims to portray objects in such a manner that they shall appear to the reader exactly as they do to the observer. A good description is a clear, vivid, and accurate word-picture. If you notice how much your enjoyment of a book depends upon the author's power to make things seem real, you will understand how important it is to practice this species of composition. In our study of description, we shall consider the following varieties:

1. Description of Objects
2. Description of Scenery
3. Description of Persons

Description of Objects—In writing Descriptions of Objects, observe the following directions:

1. Select a subject which is attractive and about which you are well informed or which your imagination can easily develop.

2. Study the subject carefully, noting all the important points. You cannot expect to give others a clear and correct idea of the object which you are describing, unless you see it clearly for yourself. It is well to make a list of the elements which you wish to combine in your description.

3. Having chosen the most important elements, arrange them in such an order as to make the description most effective.

4. Combine the elements, aiming to make a *clear*, *vivid*, *truthful*, and *complete* picture.

Caution—Remember that the vividness of your description depends largely upon the language which you use. Let your adjectives be carefully chosen and not too numerous. Remember that *particular* terms are far more graphic than *general* ones. For example, if you write "A tree stood by the house," your word-picture is indistinct because you have not told what species of tree it is and what sort of a house you have in mind. Notice how the picture changes if we substitute particular terms:

(a) A great elm spread its protecting arms over the cottage.

(d) In front of the ruined house a single tall poplar stood like a sentinel.

[Topics—such as a ruined mill, an art gallery, a prison, a post office—are suggested.]

Description of Scenery—In writing descriptions of natural scenery, you should aim to make the picture appear to the reader as beautiful and interesting as it does to you. For this reason, it is best to begin by describing some scene with which you are very familiar or which has made a strong impression upon you. You must first be able to tell what are the most important features of the scene and to give a clear idea of their arrangement and their relations to one another. To this end, you must cultivate the habit of careful observation. It is an excellent practice to keep a notebook in which to record such facts and impressions as you would be likely to forget when the scene is no longer before your eyes. Hawthorne's notebooks show how good an observer he was, and what use he made of his observations.

Importance of Little Things—The charm of a description consists largely in the author's attention to little things, such as would escape the notice of the careless observer. Sir Walter Scott, wishing to write a graphic description of a ruined abbey, thought it worthwhile to take a long journey on horseback, on purpose to see for himself what species of flowers and weeds were growing about the ruin.

In addition to the features which are visible, you may properly mention the sounds which you hear and the thoughts which are awakened by the scene. You may mention also the circumstances under which you make your observations. You should first make a plan, showing what features you intend to embody in your description, as, for example:

Time—Early evening in August

Circumstances—Twilight of a hot day, the full moon just rising

Features of Scenery—Hills in the distance, sky, trees, shrubbery

Artificial Features—Buildings, etc.

Living Beings—Birds, bats, insects (Avoid use of general terms.)

Sounds—Children at play, barking of a dog, crying infant

Persons—Tell what people you see and what they are doing

Reflections—These may be interwoven with the several parts of the description, in the order in which they are suggested to the mind.

[Topics—such as a sunset, a waterfall, a volcano, a tropical forest—are suggested.]

Description of Persons—You are now to have some practice in the most difficult kind of Description. In this, as in the varieties which you have already studied, attention must be paid to the little things. The best way of learning how to describe persons is to notice how others do it and then to study the personal descriptions which seem to you most graphic.

Writing a Personal Description—Make a study of the peculiarities and characteristics of the person whom you wish to describe. Notice what are the strongest points of individuality, and reproduce these in your sketch. Do not be disagreeably personal, if you choose your subject from your own list of acquaintances. Remember that a portrait-painter should always place his subject in the best possible light. Some of the points which you may have in your outline are the following:

Form, features, manners, attitudes, dress, habits; peculiarities of gait, speech, and expression; habits of thought; disposition; traits of character; intellectual and moral capacities; influence; usefulness.

[Topics—such as a teacher, a miser, a homely but good woman, a doctor—are suggested.]

How to Choose Composition Subjects—Teachers sometimes find it difficult to select interesting subjects for compositions. One of the advantages of combining composition work with the study of literature is that many lines of thought and investigation are thus opened, affording fresh and varied topics for writing. Some of the most successful teachers of composition are in the habit of assigning subjects which are suggested to them by books and by newspaper and magazine articles. It is strongly recommended that the studies in literature be made the basis of the practice of composition.

Notes

This excerpt is taken from Sara E. Husted Lockwood's *Lessons in English, Adapted to the Study of American Classics: A Textbook for High Schools and Academies* (Boston: Ginn & Co., 1888), 179–209, 269–73, 279–332. The subtitle on the cover is different from the subtitle on the title page. The cover reads *Lessons in English: Language, Composition, Rhetoric, Literature.* The editor gratefully acknowledges McKeldin Library of the University of Maryland at College Park for providing access to this work. I have modernized spelling and regularized punctuation, although very little change was required.

1. References listed at the end of the chapter include Hugh Blair, *Lectures on Rhetoric* (1783), John S. Hart, *A Manual of Composition and Rhetoric* (1870), David J. Hill, *Elements of Rhetoric* (1878), Adam S. Hill, *Principles of Rhetoric* (1895), John S. Clark, *Practical Rhetoric* (1886), Alfred H. Welsh, *Essentials of English* (1884), Welsh, *Complete Rhetoric* (1885), and Bardeen, *Complete Rhetoric.*

2. Antithesis: a rhetorical figure consisting of contrasting ideas emphasized by parallel syntax.

3. Climax: the rhetorical figure in which a series (of words, phrases, or sentences) is arranged in ascending order of rhetorical impact (and also, usually, length).

4. An allusion to the Revolutionary War, when the United States troops were commanded by General George Washington.

5. An allusion to the ending of Shakespeare's *Othello.*

6. Paul Revere (1715–1818), a Boston patriot, is chiefly remembered, because of Henry Wadsworth Longfellow's poem, for his ride the night of April 18, 1775, to warn the countryside that British troops were being sent against them (a foray that began the American Revolution).

7. Alfred, Lord Tennyson's tribute to his dead friend, Arthur Henry Hallam, was the poem *In Memoriam* (1850), an epic elegy that traces his grief, doubt, despair, and ultimate faith in immortality.

8. Queen Elizabeth I ruled England from 1558 to 1603.

9. In 1888, the "electric chain of communication" that "girdles the earth" is the telegraph; the transatlantic cable was laid in 1866. Although patented in 1876, the telephone was not widely used yet in 1888.

10. An allusion to John Bunyan's *Pilgrim's Progress* (1678), an immensely popular religious allegory, thought especially appropriate for children.

11. Dr. Elisha Kane (1820–1857), American physician and Arctic explorer, was famous for his books on these explorations: *U.S. Grinnell Expedition* (1853), better known as *Adrift in the Arctic*, and *Arctic Exploration* (1856); William Makepeace Thackeray (1811–1863), British novelist, satirist, and cartoonist, born in India, most famous for his novel *Vanity Fair* (1848); *Pendennis* (1850) is his partly autobiographical novel.

12. Matthew 7:27.

13. 1 Corinthians 13:7.

14. George Gordon, Lord Byron, "The Corsair: A Tale" (1814), Canto 2.6.849–50.

15. From John Greenleaf Whittier's "Proem" (1849), ll. 1–5.

16. Washington Irving, *A Tour of the Prairies* (1835).

17. Lockwood defines the figure "onomatopoeia" earlier in *Lessons in English* as "adapting the sound to the sense" (86). A more precise definition might be "expressing a thing or action by constructing a word as a vocal imitation of it" (as in "buzz" for bees).

18. Henry Wadsworth Longfellow, *The Courtship of Miles Standish* (1858), Section IV, ll. 479–81.

19. John Greenleaf Whittier, "The Tent on the Beach" (1894), ll. 1398–1406.

20. Sir Walter Scott (1771–1832), a Scotsman, was one of the most popular nineteenth-century novelists, famous for such works as *Rob Roy* and *Ivanhoe*. James Fenimore Cooper (1789–1851), first United States author to use American and frontier settings, famous for *The Deerslayer* and *The Last of the Mohicans*.

Frances E. Willard

1839–1898

Frances Elizabeth Caroline Willard was born in Churchville, New York, to Mary Hill and Josiah Willard in September 1839. She was named after the English novelist Frances (Fanny) Burney, the American poet, Frances Osgood, and her sister, Caroline Elizabeth, who had died the previous year. She was nicknamed "Frank" and grew up in Wisconsin, where her father was a farmer, a naturalist, and, in 1848, a legislator. Both mother and father attended Oberlin College. Willard's mother was a teacher before marriage and ran evening classes for domestics during much of her life. Frances's brother was sent to school, but the girls (Frances and two sisters) were tutored at home. Willard had three years of formal schooling: in 1857 she attended Milwaukee Normal Institute, where her mother's sister taught; from 1858 to 1860, she and her sister attended North Western Female College in Illinois.

After graduating, Willard taught first at Harlem Public School in Cook County, Illinois, and then at Kankakee Academy, but her parents were embarrassed by her career, and she resigned to return home. She was briefly engaged to Charles Fowler, who later became a Methodist bishop, but she broke off the engagement. Willard's primary loyalties and emotional relationships throughout her life were with women. Frances's sister Mary died of typhoid in 1862, when she was nineteen, and Willard's first book was a commemorative life of her sister. Beginning in 1862–1863, Willard taught natural sciences (and arithmetic, geometry, algebra, history, and elocution!) at North Western Female College. In 1863–1864, Willard taught at Pittsburgh Female College, traveling in order to alleviate the depression resulting from her sister's death. In 1864–1865, Willard taught in Evanston, becoming corresponding secretary for the American Methodist Ladies Centenary Association in 1865–1866, where she first tried out her organizing skills. In 1866, Willard taught at Genesee Wesleyan Seminary, a coeducational school, in Lima, New York. Soon Kate Jackson, a friend from Evanston, joined Willard teaching at Genesee. These two women remained together as partners for ten years, touring Europe and the Middle East together from 1868 to 1870 (including six months of college in Paris to study French). Jackson's father financed their trip, Willard providing some money through journalistic accounts of their travels. By this point, Willard's family could provide no support for her because her brother, an alcoholic and a gambler, had squandered the family's money. In 1869, Willard participated in the founding of Evanston Ladies' College; in 1870, the college united with the former North Western Female College and Willard was appointed the president; after the first year, however, finances forced the college to merge with Northwestern University, and Willard became dean of women. Although Willard's position included life tenure, after her former fiancé, Charles Fowler, became president, his controlling tactics made her position untenable, and she resigned in 1874.

Willard turned to feminist and temperance organizations, and in the fledgling WCTU (Women's Christian Temperance Union) in Chicago, she found her calling. Willard spent several years as corresponding secretary of the WCTU and traveled as a lecturer. In 1876 she was president of the Chicago WCTU; she continued as the corresponding secretary of the national WCTU until 1877. She became president of the Illinois WCTU in 1879 and wrote a column for the WCTU newsletter. In 1876, Willard met Anna Gordon, who replaced Kate Jackson as her companion and became Willard's devoted private secretary. Willard remained on good terms with Jackson. Having become friends with Annie Dickinson in 1875, a female orator who supported herself handsomely by lecturing, Willard joined the Dwight Moody touring revival troupe in 1877 as an evangelist preacher, but the arrangement lasted only briefly because Moody disagreed with Willard on the issues of temperance and feminism. In 1878, when her brother died, Willard took over the editorship of his newspaper, *The Chicago Post*. Willard and her sister ran the paper and wrote most of it, but financial problems caused the paper to be sold at auction in less than a year. Throughout the 1870s, Willard worked to bring the WCTU to support women's suffrage, arguing that women needed to vote in order to protect the home. She and Jennie Willing both attended the Illinois WCTU convention that passed the home protection resolution in 1876.

In 1879, Willard achieved the national presidency of the WCTU, and for the next twenty years remained president, becoming the most famous woman in the United States. Under her leadership, the WCTU in the 1880s grew from 27,000 to 200,000 members, and Willard, touring the United States, averaged one organizing meeting a day during that decade. She supported herself and her whole household (including Anna Gordon) on her speaker's fees, for she was not paid a salary by the WCTU until 1886. Willard saw temperance as part of a larger program of social reform: she began her career in temperance as a feminist, and by the 1890s, she was also a socialist and a supporter of the labor movement. She developed the slogan "Do Everything" for the women of the WCTU, at first meaning methods of persuasion (lobbying, petitioning, preaching, publication, education), but eventually meaning utopian goals of social reform: labor-saving strategies for women and day nurseries, federal aid to education and free school lunches, unions for workers and the eight-hour day, work relief for the poor, municipal sanitation and boards of health, national transportation, strong antirape laws, and protections against child abuse. Willard was a committed abolitionist, and African Americans were welcome members of the WCTU from the beginning. Under Willard's sponsorship, Jews and Catholics were also eventually admitted. One of Willard's famous speeches from the 1890s was titled "Gospel Socialism."

In the early 1890s, Willard took her campaign to the world. She became great friends with Lady Isabella Somerset, president of the British WTA (Women's Temperance Association), and they became companions for the rest of their lives. They worked together and, despite ill health, alternated countries for the national conferences and organizational work. Willard's success was clouded by a long-running debate with the great African American antilynching campaigner Ida Wells. Willard sponsored an antilynching resolution at the national WCTU, but she worded it in such a way that the guilt of black men was assumed, to palliate the southern contingent of the WCTU. More successful was the resolution against Turkish genocide of Christian Armenians. During what was to have been a vacation in France in 1896, Lady Somerset and Willard established a center for refugee support, housing three hundred Armenians in an old hospital in Marseilles. After 1896, Willard's growing illness made regular speaking engagements impossible, and she returned home to the United States and retired to a sanatorium.

Frances Willard died on February 17, 1898, in New York City after several years of increasing debilitation because of pernicious anemia. She was one of the two or three most famous women in the world when she died. Her funeral was attended by thousands and her statue was placed in the U.S. Capitol. Children in Chicago named a lion cub after her at the zoo.

Willard contributed to the history of rhetorical theory in two ways. First, under Willard's leadership, the WCTU taught parliamentary procedure, organizational skills, and public speaking to its members, in order better to lobby for its wide-ranging social goals. WCTU handbooks and pamphlets that Willard had a hand in included instruction in these areas. In addition, Willard wrote a defense of women's preaching, a selection from which is included in this anthology.

In 1874, Willard was denied the privilege of conducting evening prayers by Charles Fowler, the Methodist bishop who was president of the college, who required male clergy to lead the service at the women's college. In 1880, Willard was refused admission to the Methodist Conference in Cincinnati, Ohio, which sparked a huge debate in the conference and in the church. In 1888, Willard was elected as a lay delegate to the national Methodist Conference, one of five women. Another debate erupted, and the women lost. These rejections led in 1889 to *Woman in the Pulpit*, a defense of women's preaching. It was not until 1896 that women were seated at Methodist conferences.

Woman in the Pulpit weaves together Willard's own words and letters and essays from male and female preachers to argue for the benefits of women preaching. Whereas Margaret Fell two centuries before had adopted inspirational style and collaboration with scripture to achieve authority, Willard devised a method more in keeping with nineteenth-century rationalism and American republicanism (although Willard, like Fell, also draws on anti-Catholic bias to argue that Protestants should allow women to preach since the misled Roman Church does not). In the first chapter, Willard refutes arguments against women's preaching, including Saint Paul's. In the second chapter, Willard argues that women demonstrate their faith as apostles in the scriptures, so that there is a kind of history of women preaching; that preaching is particularly appropriate to women, who by their natures appeal to moral sentiment; that women's voices are physically sufficient to be heard, with proper training; that motherhood is not in conflict with a life of spiritual guidance of others, but in keeping with it; and that God calls women as well as men to preach. Willard buttresses her own arguments with a collage of testimony and arguments of others. She begins her treatise with three letters by men in support of women preaching, offers a chapter of testimony from twenty male preachers, as well as a chapter of testimony from eleven women preachers, and concludes with publishing a debate between two men occasioned by her argument first published in a journal. Willard thus assumes that a great part of her audience will be hostile to the idea of women preaching. She constructs her argument not straightforwardly, but interwoven with refutation, and what Aristotle calls "inartistic proofs"—testimony from witnesses. She lets other voices speak along with her in order to be heard. Willard separates men and women into their own chapters—creating quite literally in her book the separate spheres of nineteenth-century Anglo American social life. Yet she argues against this doctrine for preaching. Willard is thus adapting her characteristic political strategy to this topic. Willard won her national following with the platform that women's domestic and moral role in the family requires her influence in politics; in *Woman in the Pulpit*, Willard tries to demonstrate that woman's domestic and moral role as mother makes her especially suitable for the role of preacher.

For further information, see Ruth Bordin, *Frances Willard: A Biography* (Chapel Hill: University of North Carolina Press, 1986); Bonnie J. Dow, "The 'Womanhood' Rationale in the Woman Suffrage Rhetoric of Frances E. Willard," *Southern Communication Journal* 56, no. 4 (Summer 1991): 298–307; "*Do Everything Reform: The Oratory of Frances E. Willard*, ed. Richard W. Leeman (Westport, Conn.: Greenwood Press, 1992); Carolyn DeSwarte Gifford, "Frances Willard and the Woman's Christian Temperance Union's Conversion to Woman Suffrage," in *One Woman, One Vote: Rediscovering the Woman Suffrage Movement*, ed. Marjorie Spruill Wheeler (Troutdale, Ore.: NewSage Press, 1995), 117–33; *Writing Out My Heart: Selections from the Journal of Frances E. Willard, 1855–96*, ed. Carolyn De Swarte Gifford (Urbana: University of Illinois Press, 1995); Carol Mattingly, *Well-Tempered Women: Nineteenth-Century Temperance Rhetoric* (Carbondale: Southern Illinois University Press, 1998); Martha Watson, *Lives of Their Own: Rhetorical Dimensions in Autobiographies of Women Activists* (Columbia: University of South Carolina Press, 1999); and Jane Donawerth, "Poaching on Men's Philosophies of Rhetoric: Eighteenth- and Nineteenth-Century Rhetorical Theory by Women," *Philosophy and Rhetoric* 33, no. 3 (2000): 155–62.

From *Woman in the Pulpit* (1889)

Chapter II
The Spirit Giveth Life

Christ, not Paul, is the source of all churchly authority and power. What do we find him saying? How did he deal with women? In the presence of the multitude, he drew from Martha the same testimony that he required of his apostles, and she publicly replied, almost in Peter's very words, "Yea, Lord, I believe that thou art the Christ, the Son of God, which should come into the world."[1] He declared his commission to the woman at the well of Samaria, with an emphasis and a particularity hardly equalled in any of his public addresses, and her embassy was abundantly rewarded. What pastor would not rejoice to hear such words as these: "Now we believe, not because of thy saying, for we have heard him ourselves, and know that this is indeed the Christ, the Savior of the world."[2]

It is objected that he called no woman to be an apostle. Granted, but he himself said that he chose one man who had a devil;[3] is this a precedent? One is half inclined to think so, when one reads the long record of priestly intolerance, its culmination being the ostracism of Christ's most faithful followers from their right to proclaim the risen Lord, who gave to Mary the first commission to declare his resurrection.[4] True, he did not designate women as his followers; they came without a call. From their sex he had his human origin; with the immeasurable dignities of his incarnation and his birth, only God and woman were concerned. No utterance of his marks woman as ineligible to any position in the church he came to found; but his gracious words and deeds, his impartation of his purposes and plans to women, his stern reproofs to men who did them wrong, his chosen companionships, and the tenor of his whole life and teaching—all point out precisely the opposite conclusion. Indeed, Luke explicitly declares that, as "he went throughout every city and village, preaching and showing the glad tidings of the Kingdom of God," "the twelve were with him, *and certain women*," among whom were "Joanna, the wife of Chuza, Herod's steward, and Susanna, and many others, which ministered unto him of their substance."[5]

What a spectacle must that have been for the "Scribes and Pharisees, hypocrites."[6] What loss of caste came to those fearless women, who, breaking away from the customs of society and traditions of religion, dared to follow the greatest of iconoclasts from city to village with a publicity and a persistence nothing less than outrageous to the conservatives of that day.

> Verily, Devotion, thy name is Woman![7]
> Not she with trait'rous kiss her Savior stung;
> Not she denied him with unholy tongue;
> She, while apostles shrank, could danger brave,
> Last at his cross, and earliest at his grave.[8]

Christ's commission only is authoritative. To whom did he give it after his resurrection, until which time the new dispensation was not fairly ushered in? If we are to accept specific statements, rather than the drift and spirit of the inspired book, as conclusive of a question involving half the human race, let us, then, here take our stand on our Lord's final words and deeds. It is stated (Luke 24:33) that the two disciples to whom Christ appeared on the way to Emmaus "returned to Jerusalem, and found the eleven gathered together, and *them that were with them*, saying, 'The Lord is risen, indeed, and hath appeared to Simon.'"[9] Be it understood that women used this language, the women "which came with him from Galilee." It was "them that were with them" (i.e. with the eleven), who were saying, "The Lord is risen indeed."[10]

While they were thus assembled and talking of the wonderful experience of that day, Jesus appeared again, saying, "Peace be unto you."[11] Let us turn to John 20:19–23, where we have an account of this same appearance of Christ to his disciples, for it says explicitly (after stating that Mary Magdalene came and told the disciples that she had seen the Lord), "Then the same day at evening . . . Jesus stood in the midst and saith unto them, Peace be unto you; as my Father hath sent me, even so send I you. And when he had said this, he breathed on them and saith unto them, Receive ye the Holy Ghost; whosesoever sins ye remit they are remitted unto them, and whosesoever sins ye retain they are retained."[12] These, then, are his words spoken to the eleven and "*them* that were with them." He then "opened their understanding that they might understand the Scriptures," and declared that "repentance and remission of sins should be preached in his name among all nations, beginning at Jerusalem," and "*ye are witnesses* of these things. And behold, I send the promise of my Father upon you, but tarry ye in Jerusalem until ye be endued with power from on high. And he led them out as far as to Bethany, and he lifted up his hands, and blessed them. And it came to pass, while he blessed them, he was parted from them, and carried up into heaven. And they worshipped him, and returned to Jerusalem with great joy."[13]

Does any reasonable person suppose that his mother was not there, or that the other Marys were not? or the great company of women that had ministered to him? But we are not left in doubt. Turn to Acts 1:13–14. After stating Christ's command that they should not depart from Jerusalem, but wait for the promise of the Father—"For ye shall be baptized with the Holy Ghost not many days hence"—after which "Ye shall be witnesses unto me unto the uttermost parts of the earth," and after giving a brief account of the resurrection, this passage occurs: "Then returned they unto Jerusalem, and when they were come in, they went up into an upper room where abode both Peter and James and John . . . these all continued with one accord in prayer and supplication *with the women*, and Mary, the mother of Jesus, and with his brethren. And when the day of Pentecost was fully come, they were *all* with one accord in one place. . . . And they were *all* filled with the Holy Ghost and began to speak with other tongues as the Spirit gave them utterance."[14] Then Peter said, "This is that which was spoken by the prophet Joel, I will pour out my Spirit upon *all* flesh, and your sons and *your daughters* shall prophesy, and on my servants and on my *handmaids* I will pour out my Spirit, and *they shall prophesy*."[15] Paul proves that prophesying may be preaching when he says (1 Corinthians 14:3), "But he that prophesieth speaketh unto men to edification and exhortation and comfort." Well said Gamaliel of this new dispensation: "If this counsel or this work be of men, it will come to naught; but if it be of God, ye cannot overthrow it, lest haply ye be found to fight against God."[16]

Let not conservative ecclesiastical leaders try to steady the Lord's ark; let them not bind what God hath loosed; let them not retain the bondage he hath remitted,[17] lest haply they be found to fight against God!

"We want the earth," is the world-old motto of men. They have had their desire, and we behold the white male dynasty reigning undisputed until our own day, lording it over every heritage, and constituting the only unquestioned "apostolic succession."[18] Only one thing can end the dire enchantment we are under, and that is to know the truth, for truth alone makes free.[19] And the truth of God, a thousand times repeated by the voice of history, science, and everyday experience, resounds louder today than in all preceding ages: "It is not good for man to be alone!"[20] Suppose it be admitted that the dual-natured founder of Christianity, in whose character the force that smote the money-changers of the temple[21] was commingled with the love that yearned to gather Jerusalem as a hen gathers "her chickens under her wings,"[22] chose as his apostles the only ones who in that barbarous age would be tolerated in preaching it. Be it remembered that Protestantism recognizes the apostles as having had no successors.[23] Hence, any argument built on man's primacy as related to them and the manner of their choosing falls to the ground. It is curious, considering certain exegetical[24] literalism, that their method of choosing by lot should not have been insisted upon as part of the divine order!

In the revolt from Roman license, the clergy early declared woman a delusion and a snare, banished her from the company of men who aspired to holiness and, by introducing the denaturalizing heresy of a celibate clergy, made it impossible for the doctrine of God's eternal fatherhood to be so understood by the preacher that it should become vital in the hearer's heart. It is *men* who have defrauded manhood and womanhood, in the persons of priest and monk and nun, of the right to the sanctities of home; men who have invented hierarchies, enthroned a fisherman as God's viceregent,[25] lighted inquisitorial fires, and made the Prince of peace a mighty man of war. It is men who have taken the simple, loving, tender Gospel of the New Testament, so suited to be the proclamation of a woman's lips, and translated it in terms of sacerdotalism, dogma, and martyrdom. It is men who have given us the dead letter rather than the living Gospel. The mother-heart of God will never be known to the world until translated into terms of speech by mother-hearted women. Law and love will never balance in the realm of grace until a woman's hand shall hold the scales.

Men preach a creed; women will declare a life. Men deal in formulas, women in facts. Men have always tithed mint and rue and cummin[26] in their exegesis and their ecclesiasticism,[27] while the world's heart has cried out for compassion, forgiveness, and sympathy. Men's preaching has left heads committed to a catechism, and left hearts hard as nether millstones. The Greek bishop who said, "My creed is faultless, with my life you have nothing to do," condensed into a sentence two thousand years of priestly dogma. Men reason in the abstract, women in the concrete. A syllogism symbolizes one, a rule of life the other. In saying this, I wish distinctly to disclaim any attack upon the clergy, any slighting allusion to the highest and holiest of callings; I am speaking only of the intolerant sacerdotal element that has handicapped the church from the earliest ages even until now, and which has been more severely criticized by the best element in the church than by any words that I have penned.

Religion is an affair of the heart. The world is hungry for the comfort of Christ's Gospel, and thirsty for everyday beatitudes of that holiness which alone constitutes happiness. Men have lost faith in themselves and each other. Boodlerism[28] and "corners" on the market, greed of gain, passion for power, desire for drink, impurity of life, the complicity of the church (Protestant as well as Papal) with the liquor traffic, the preference of a partisan to a conscientious ballot, have combined to make the men of this generation faithless toward one another. The masses of the people have forsaken God's house, and solace themselves in the saloons or with the Sunday newspaper. But the masses will go to hear women when they speak, and every woman who leads a life of weekday holiness, and has the Gospel in her looks, however plain her face and dress may be, has round her head the sweet Madonna's halo, in the eyes of every man who sees her, and she speaks to him with the sacred cadence of his own mother's voice. The devil knew what he was doing when he exhausted sophistry to keep woman down and silent. He knew that the only "consecrated" place on earth is where God's Spirit is, and that a Christian woman's heart enshrines that holy guest more surely than many a "consecrated" pulpit.

Men have been preaching well-nigh two thousand years, and the large majority of the converts have been women. Suppose now that women should share the preaching power, might it not be reasonably expected that a majority of the converts under their administration would be men? Indeed, how else are the latter to have a fair chance at the Gospel? The question is asked in all seriousness, and if its practical answer shall be the equipping of women for the pulpit, it may be reasonably claimed that men's hopes of heaven will be immeasurably increased. Hence, one who urges the taking-off of the arbitrary ruling which now excludes woman from a choice portion of her kingdom may well claim to have manifested especial considerateness toward the interests of men.

The entrance of woman upon the ministerial vocation will give to humanity just twice the probability of strengthening and comforting speech, for women have at least as much sympathy, reverence, and spirituality as men, and they have at least equal felicity of manner and utterance. Why, then, should the pulpit be shorn of half its power?

To the exegesis of the cloister, we oppose that of common life. To the orientalism that is passing off the stage, we oppose modern Christianity. In our day, the ministers of a great church[29] have struck the word "obey" out of the marriage service, have made women eligible to nearly every rank except the ecclesiastic,[30] and are withheld from raising her to the ministerial office only by the influence of a few leaders, who are insecurely seated on the safety valve of that mighty engine, Progress. In our day, all churches, except the hierarchical Presbyterian,

Episcopal, and Roman Catholic, have made women eligible as members of their councils, leaders in their Sunday school systems, in several cases have set them apart to the ministry, and in almost all have opened their pulpits to them—even the slow-moving Presbyterian having done this quite generally in later years, and the Episcopal, in several instances, granting women "where to stand" in its chapels, outside the charmed arc of its chancel rail.

Whoever quotes to the intelligent and devout women of the American church today the specific instructions given by Paul to the illiterate and immoral women of Corinth[31] does so at the expense of sound judgment, not to say scholarship. An exegesis so strained and so outworn is on a par with that which would pronounce the Savior of the world "a glutton and a wine-bibber," because the Pharisees, when he "came eating and drinking,"[32] declared him to be such.

The lifeless prayer meetings, from which women's voices are excluded, are largely given over to perfunctory, official prayers, and the churches that still quote "He shall rule over thee"[33] as a Gospel precept are deserted by the great humanity that beats its life along the stony streets. "Behold, your house is left unto you desolate"[34] is the requiem of empty pews that would be full if men and women stood side by side at the church, as they are now fast learning to do at the home altars. For the "man of the house" to do all the praying is to deprive the children of one of life's most sacred ministries—that of their mother's voice in prayer and in the giving of thanks for daily food. Observation in a great variety of homes convinces me that this joint leadership in household worship is being largely introduced. Probably the extreme of masculine prerogative in this regard was illustrated in an Eastern town some years ago, when a boy of twelve was called in from his play to say grace over the lunch prepared between meals for his young lady cousin, a guest newly arrived. The incident is perfectly authentic, and the act was entirely consistent and devout, upon the theory of man's divinely constituted primacy in matters spiritual.

"Behold, I make all things new"[35] was the joyful declaration of woman's great deliverer: "He hath sent me to heal the broken-hearted, to preach deliverance to the captives, and recovering of sight of the blind, to set at liberty them that are bruised."[36] Above all other beings these words must refer to woman, who, without Christ, lies prostrate under society's pitiless and crushing pyramid. Whether they perceive it or not, it is chiefly ecclesiasticism and not Christianity that Robert Ingersoll[37] and Elizabeth Cady Stanton[38] have been fighting; it is the burdens grievous to be borne that men have laid upon weak shoulders, but which they themselves would not touch with one of their fingers. Christ knew that this would be; he had to place the treasure of his Gospel in the earthen vessels of selfish human hearts. But that treasure is like the leaven that a woman took and hid in three measures of meal until the whole was leavened.

"Behold, I make all things new"; "the letter killeth, the spirit giveth life."[39] These are his words, who spake not as man speaketh; and how the letter killeth today, let the sectarianism, the sacerdotalism, and the woman-silencing of the church bear witness. The time has come when those men in high places, "dressed in a little brief authority"[40] within the church of Christ, who seek to shut women out of the pastorate, cannot do so with impunity. Today they are taking on themselves a responsibility in the presence of which they ought to tremble. To an earnest, intelligent, and devout element among their brethren they seem to be absolutely frustrating the grace of God. They cannot fail to see how many ministers neither draw men to the Gospel feast, nor "go out into the highways and hedges"[41] seeking them. They cannot fail to see that, although the novelty of women's speaking has worn off, the people rally to hear them as to hear no others, save the most celebrated men of the pulpit and platform; and that especially is it true that "the common people hear them gladly."[42] The plea, urged by some theologians with all the cogency of physiological illustration, that woman is born to one vocation, and one alone, is negatived by her magnificent success as a teacher, a philanthropist, and a physician, by which means she takes the part of foster-mother to myriads of children orphaned or worse than motherless. Their fear that incompetent women may become pastors and preachers should be put to flight by the survival of the church, in spite of centuries of the grossest incompetency in mind and profligacy in life, of men set apart by the laying-on of hands. Their anxiety lest too many women should crowd in is met by the method of choosing a pastor, in which both clergy and people must unite to attest the fitness and acceptability of every candidate.

Formerly the voices of women were held to render them incapable of public speech, but it has been discovered that what these voices lack in sonorosity they supply in clearness, and when women singers outrank all others, and women lecturers are speaking daily to assemblies numbering from one to ten thousand, this objection vanishes.[43] Lack of special preparation is but a temporary barrier. When we see Agnata Ramsay, an English lady but twenty years old, carrying off the Greek prize from the students of Cambridge University, Pundita Ramabai[44] mastering Sanskrit and four other languages, and Toru Dutt, another high-caste Hindu, writing choice verses in French and English before she was twenty-one; when we study the consensus of opinion from presidents of universities as to the equality and even the precedence of the girls in scholarship, we see how flimsy is this argument.

But some men say it will disrupt the home. As well might they talk of driving back the tides of the sea. The mother-heart will never change. Woman enters the arena of literature, art, business, what you will, becomes a teacher, a physician, a philanthropist, but she is a woman first of all, and cannot deny herself. In all these great vocations she has still been "true to the kindred points of heaven and home,"[45] and everybody knows that, beyond almost any other, the minister is one who lives at home. The firesides of the people are his weekday sanctuary, the pulpit is near his own door, and its publicity is so guarded by the people's reverence and sympathy as to make it of all others the place least inharmonious with woman's character and work.

When will blind eyes be opened to see the immeasurable losses that the church sustains by not claiming for her altars these loyal, earnest-hearted daughters, who, rather than stand in an equivocal relation to her polity, are going into other lines of work or taking their commission from the evangelistic department of the Woman's Christian Temperance Union? Or are they willing that woman should go to the lowly and forgotten, but not to the affluent and powerful? Are they willing that women should baptize and administer the sacrament in the zenanas[46] of India, but not at the elegant altars of Christendom? Are they aware that thousands of services are held each Sabbath by white-ribbon women, to whom reformed men and their wives have said, "We will come if you will speak. We don't go to church, because they have rented pews, and because we cannot dress well enough, but we'll come to hear you"? Have they observed that W.C.T.U. halls, reading rooms, and tabernacles for the people are being daily multiplied, in which the poor have the Gospel preached to them? Do they know that the World's W.C.T.U., with Margaret Bright Lucas of England at its head,[47] is steadily wending its way around the globe, and helping women to their rightful recognition as participants in public worship and as heralds of the Gospel?

To ministerial leaders who have been profoundly impressed by the difficulties of the question, "Shall women be ordained to preach?" another question is hereby propounded: "Shall women ordain themselves?" When Wesley urged the Bishop of London to send out a bishop to the Methodist societies in America, that functionary turned aside with disdain—the societies were so few and the country so far. Wesley, loyal churchman though he was, then yielded to demands he could no longer ignore, and consecrated Thomas Coke a bishop, who in turn consecrated Francis Asbury, the first Methodist bishop in America.[48] That decision of the intrepid founder of Methodism cost the Episcopal Church its future in the New World, as time has proved. History repeats itself. We stand once more at the parting of the roads; shall the bold, resolute men among our clergy win the day and give ordination to women, or shall women take this matter into their own hands? Fondly do women hope, and earnestly do they pray, that the churches they love may not drive them to this extremity. But if her conservative sons do not yield to the leadings of Providence and the importunities of their more progressive brothers, they may be well assured that deliverance shall arise from another place, for the women of this age are surely coming to their kingdom, and humanity is to be comforted out of Zion "as one whom his mother comforteth."[49]

The National Woman's Christian Temperance Union has departments of evangelistic work, of Bible readings, of Gospel work for railroad employees, for soldiers, sailors, and lumbermen; of prison, jail, and police-station work; each of these departments being in charge of a woman called a national Superintendent, who has an assistant in nearly every State and Territory, and she, in turn, in every local union. These make an aggregate of several thousands of women who are regularly studying and expounding God's Word to the multitude, to say nothing of the army in home and foreign missionary work, and who are engaged in church evangelism. Nearly all of this "great host" who now "publish the glad tidings"[50] are quite beyond the watch-care of the church, not because they wish to be so, but because she who has warmed them into life and nurtured them into activity is afraid of her own gentle, earnest-hearted daughters.

The spectacle is both anomalous and pitiful. It ought not to continue. Let the church call in these banished ones, correlate their sanctified activities with her own mighty work, giving them the same official recognition that it gives to men, and they will gladly take their places under her supervision.[51]

There is hardly an objector who does not say, "I would be willing to hear Mrs. or Miss Blank preach, but then they are exceptions; if we open the floodgates, we cannot tell what may happen." But have you ever opened the floodgates to men? And certainly your dread of the unseemly behavior of Christian women (the most modest and conservative of human beings!) will lead you to greatly increased caution when their cases are being passed upon. The dominant sex has proved itself able to keep women-incapables out of the medical and the teachers' professions, and surely it will stand on guard with double diligence lest they invade the place where are declared the holy oracles. The whole difficulty is one of the imagination and vanishes when individualized, as it would necessarily be in practice, by the separate scrutiny of Conference and Synod[52] upon each separate case.

"Oh, it must come, and let it come, since come it must, but not in our day." Why not in yours, my brother? The day in which it comes will be the most glorious one since Christ started the church based on his resurrection, by commissioning Mary to bear the gladdest tidings this dying world has ever heard: "Behold, he is risen!"[53]

The time is hastening, the world grows smaller; we can compass it a thousandfold more readily than could any previous generation. Within five years, so we are told by leading railroad authorities, we shall be able to go around the globe in forty days, and to go accompanied by all the security and comfort of our scientific and luxurious civilization. Women can do this just as readily as men. Then let us send them forth full-panoplied; let us sound in their gentle ears the "Take thou authority" of the church's highest tribunal, that untrammelled and free they may lift up the standard of Christ's cross on every shore, and fulfill that wonderful and blessed prophecy (Psalm 68:11, R.V.): "The Lord giveth the word. The women that publish the tidings are a great host."[54]

Of the graceless sights this is most graceless: the unseemly word-wrangle of a man against women, or of a woman against men. In all that I have herein said, I would be understood as speaking only of men as they were, and as they doubtless had to be in times passing and past. Few men are so great that official position does not diminish the sturdiness of their individuality and the fearlessness of their utterances. The air of libraries has less of ozone than that of outdoor life, and a great exegete is ofttimes made at the expense of a great man. But it would ill become me as a woman to forget that if men want the earth, women are enough like them to be content with nothing less than half of this bewitching planet; and that if we are coming to our kingdom, we have our brothers largely to thank, for is not possession nine points of the law, and did they not early foreclose the mortgage given at Eden's gate, and gain possession of the globe in its entirety?

It was our big brother, Man, who, at the banquet of Minerva,[55] said to his sister, "Sit down beside me." And since he said it, we have gone dutifully to school. It was he who read our books and encouraged us to write more. It was he who listened to us on the platform and applauded every good thing we said; it is he who invites us to his counsels, ministerial, educational, medical, and philanthropic; he who must let us into the pulpit if we enter, as we know we shall, and that ere long; he who must swing wide the door to the throne room of government, and bid us share his regal seat as joint rulers with him of this republic. In short, there are men—and men. Why should not those of largest magnanimity do all that they have done and more for us? Are not their wives and daughters women? Did not their earliest and holiest purposes dawn upon them in the mirror of a mother's loving eyes?

It has been my good fortune to be, by tradition and training, largely moulded in thought by two coeducation schools—Oberlin College, and the Northwestern University at Evanston, Illinois. Both of these institutions admit women to the study of theology, and Garrett Biblical Institute (the theological department of the latter) has women students now, and has given a woman its diploma, to whom her young ministerial classmates voted the valedictory. This Institute was founded by one woman, and its time-honored "Heck Hall" is named for another, who was the foundress of American Methodism.[56] Women have been proverbial for their financial liberality toward schools of the prophets, little dreaming that they were but "laying up in store for themselves a good foundation against the time to come," when they should be prophets themselves.

But even my dear old mother-church (the Methodist) did not call women to her altars. I was too timid to go without a call; and so it came about that while my unconstrained preference would long ago have led me to the pastorate, I have failed of it, and am perhaps writing out all the more earnestly for this reason thoughts long familiar to my mind.

Let me, as a loyal daughter of the church, urge upon younger women who feel a call, as I once did, to preach the unsearchable riches of Christ, their duty to seek admission to the doors that would hardly close against them now, in any theological seminary, save those of the Roman, Episcopal, and Presbyterian churches; and let me pleadingly beseech all Christian people who grieve over the world's great heartache, to encourage every true and capable woman, whose heart God has touched, in her wistful purpose of entering upon that blessed Gospel ministry, through which her strong yet gentle words and work may help to heal that heartache, and to comfort the sinful and the sad "as one whom his mother comforteth."[57]

Notes

This excerpt is taken, with gratitude, from the Library of Congress copy of Frances E. Willard, *Woman in the Pulpit* (Boston: D. Lothrop, 1888), 40–62.

1. John 11:27.
2. John 4:42.
3. The apostle rumored to have a devil in him before Christ chose him was John: see Matthew 11:18.
4. In John 20, Mary Magdalene greets the risen Jesus and takes the news to the other disciples.
5. Luke 8:1–3.
6. A refrain repeated throughout Matthew 23:13–29.
7. Paraphrase of Shakespeare's *Hamlet* 1.2.146: "Frailty, thy name is woman!"
8. Eaton S. Barrett, "Woman, A Poem" (1818), Part I, ll.183–86, on Mary Magdalene.
9. Actually, Luke 24:33–34.
10. Paraphrase and quotation from Luke 23:55–24:34.
11. Luke 24:36.
12. Actually, John 20:18–23.
13. Luke 24:33, 45–52.
14. Actually, Acts 1:4–5, 8–14; 2:4.
15. Acts 2:16–18.
16. Acts 5:38–39; Gamaliel is himself a Pharisee.
17. Reversing Matthew 16:19 and John 20:23, where Jesus is transferring the powers of the priesthood to his disciples, Willard is suggesting that priests' powers do not extend to undoing what God ordains.
18. Apostolic succession: the Roman Catholic tenet that the pope is the legitimate successor to the apostles and, in some functions, to Christ.
19. John 8:32.
20. Genesis 2:18, which promises woman as man's "help meet."
21. John 2:15.
22. Matthew 23:37.
23. Willard means that Protestants (as opposed to Catholics) do not believe in a pope, or in apostolic succession, but believe that God may call any person to preach, whether or not a church recognizes that person as a priest.
24. Exegetical: interpretive (exegesis is the art of biblical interpretation).
25. A reference to the Roman Catholic belief that Peter was the first pope.
26. Matthew 23:23: "Woe unto you, scribes and Pharisees, hypocrites! for ye pay tithe of mint and anise and cummin, and have omitted the weightier matters of the law, judgment, mercy, and faith."
27. Willard is a presbyterian (not to be confused with a Presbyterian, a member of a specific denomination) rather than an ecclesiastic: she believes that the organization of the church should be broad and collaborative or democratic, rather than hierarchical headed by bishops.
28. Boodlerism: swindling or accepting bribes.
29. Willard's footnote reads: "The Methodist Episcopal, with two million members."

30. The "ecclesiastic" office is that of a preacher.

31. Willard is referring to Paul's command in 1 Corinthians 14:34–35 that women not speak in church.

32. Matthew 11:19: "The Son of man came eating and drinking, and they say, Behold a man gluttonous, and a winebibber." (See also Luke 7:34.)

33. Genesis 3:16, where Adam is given dominance over Eve as her punishment for sinning.

34. Matthew 23:38.

35. Revelations 21:5.

36. Luke 4:18.

37. Robert Ingersoll (1833–1899), lawyer, attorney general of Illinois, famous for his antireligious speeches, such as "Why I Am an Agnostic" and "Superstition."

38. Elizabeth Cady Stanton (1815–1902), leader of the women's suffrage movement, orator, journalist, social reformer.

39. Revelations 21:5; 2 Corinthians 8:6.

40. Shakespeare's *Measure for Measure* 2.2.118.

41. Luke 14:23.

42. Mark 12:37: Willard is revising a passage on Jesus' preaching: "And the common people heard *him* gladly" (my italics).

43. Willard's footnote: "It is probably no more 'natural' to women to have feeble voices than it is for them to have long hair. The Greek priests of the East, not being allowed to cut their hair, wear it braided in long cues, even as our forefathers wore theirs. 'Nature' has been saddled with the disabilities of women to an extent that must make the thoughtful ones among them smile. The truth is clearly enough proved from the analogies of Creation's lower orders that this gracious and impartial dame has given woman but a single disability, viz: she can never be a father; and this she has offset by man's single disability, he can never be a mother. Ignorance, prejudice, and tyranny have put upon her all the rest, and these are wearing off with encouraging rapidity."

44. Pundita Ramabai: an Indian feminist whom Willard met in England and who became a special friend.

45. Bernard Barton, "A Poet's Memorial of a Departed Friend," in *Household Verses* (1845), l. 12.

46. Zenana: the part of the house in India and Pakistan reserved for women.

47. Margaret Bright Lucas (1819?–1890) was president of the British Women's Temperance Association from 1878 until her death.

48. John Wesley (1703–1791), English preacher, missionary to Georgia, founder of Methodism, famous for his belief in salvation by faith alone and his preaching in the fields and public places; Thomas Coke (1747–1814), English preacher and early bishop of the Methodist Episcopal Church in America; Francis Asbury (1745–1816), English missionary and superintendent of the Methodist Episcopal Church in America.

49. Isaiah 66:13.

50. Willard is here using biblical language rather than direct quotation: "tidings" refers to the news of the resurrection of Christ and the consequent salvation of humanity.

51. Willard's footnote: "The work of D. L. Moody and his associates is without a parallel in Christian annals, and constitutes the great exception to the rule of official church recognition. It is the writer's humble belief that the church would better lay her hand upon all these consecrated men for her own sake. What will India think of the importance of ordination if Mr. Moody, the most successful of preachers, comes to her without it? One thing seems certain: ordination will cease within a hundred years to hold the people's reverence, or the church will enlarge her borders to take in those whose whole lives are dedicated to ministerial work." Willard was the only woman to preach with Dr. Moody's traveling evangelists.

52. "Conference" and "Synod" are the regional governing bodies of Protestant denominations.

53. This quotation does not occur anywhere word for word in the Bible; closest is Mark 16:6, where the angel tells the Marys to tell the disciples, "he is risen; he is not here: behold the place where they laid him."

54. Psalm 68:11: although Willard marks this quotation as "R.V." (revised version), she is making a joke: this is quoted from the King James Version, but with the word "women" substituted because the Marys discovered the risen Christ and carried that news to the disciples.

55. Minerva: goddess of wisdom.

56. In 1853, with a gift of $300,000, Eliza Garrett, widow of the mayor of Chicago, founded Garrett Theological Seminary (at first the Garrett Biblical Institute), a Methodist theological seminary. Barbara Ruckle Heck (1734–1804), Irish American immigrant, known as the "mother" of Methodism, arranged the first Methodist meeting in the United States in her cousin's house in 1766.

57. Isaiah 66:13.

Anna Morgan

1851–1936

Daughter of Mary Jane Thornton Morgan and Allen Morgan, a New York farmer and legislator, Anna Morgan began the study of elocution in 1876, after her father died and her mother moved the family to Chicago. From 1880 to 1883, just as Hallie Quinn Brown was touring with the Wilberforce Concert Company, Anna Morgan was a professional elocutionist who toured throughout the Midwest and in some eastern cities, including New York and Boston. Like Genevieve Stebbins, she was trained by Steele MacKaye in the Delsarte method. Her repertoire included speeches from the serious drama of Schiller and Shakespeare, as well as poems by Browning, Rossetti, and Paul Laurence Dunbar. After 1884, as a member of the staff at the Chicago Opera House Conservatory, she focused on teaching drama.

Over the next twenty years, she and her students produced a variety of plays—Greek tragedy, Shakespeare, Ibsen, Shaw, Maeterlinck, Yeats, Synge, and local dramatists Alice Gerstenberg and Marjorie Benton Cooke—on the conservatory or the studio stage and to small, select audiences. In 1902, hers was the first American production of Shaw's *Caesar and Cleopatra*, and with an all-girl cast. In 1898 she opened her own school, the Anna Morgan Studios. She trained some professional actors but emphasized a general cultural curriculum that included literature, dramatic reading, theatrical and political history, playwriting, set design, costuming, and even etiquette. She was a central figure in Chicago culture and theater, and her studio became a salon where famous poets, editors, and actors (such as Ellen Terry and Henry Irving) were welcomed. She introduced a more natural style of acting into the American theater and helped to found the "little theater" movement. Besides the book from which a selection is taken for this volume, she published two others: *Selected Readings* (1909) and *The Art of Speech and Deportment* (1909). She retired about 1925.

Elocution eventually separated out into the strands of rhetorical delivery, dramatic training, and physical education and modern dance. While Hallie Quinn Brown emphasized oratorical delivery and Genevieve Stebbins focused on movement and dance, Morgan leaned toward dramatic training in her deployment of elocution. *An Hour with Delsarte* is an elegant volume with illustrations of graceful women in dramatic poses. It is dedicated to Morgan's students and addresses an audience of young women. Like Stebbins's and Brown's textbooks, Morgan's depends heavily on the Delsarte system of philosophical justification for physical training, emphasizing the trinity of moral, spiritual, and vital aspects of expression. The examples in the text, and the illustrations, however, show clearly that this is Delsarte adapted to training actors: most of the illustrations depict girls speaking a line from Shakespeare or a popular play of the period, with appropriate posture, gesture, and facial expression. The advice on how to apply Delsarte often concerns enacting emotions. A final chapter is titled "The Stage," suggesting the purpose of this version of Delsarte as an aid in acting.

For further information, see Joyce Sozen, "Anna Morgan," in *Notable American Women, 1607–1950*, ed. Edward T. James (Cambridge, Mass.: Harvard University Press, 1971), 2:577–79; and Anna Morgan, *My Chicago* (1918).

From *An Hour with Delsarte: A Study of Expression* (1889)

I
Introductory

Hitherto the subject of physical culture has suggested only the gymnasium, with visions of Indian clubs, dumbbells, and various other violent exercises for the development of muscle; but, thanks to the genius of Delsarte, we are in possession of means whereby we may obtain muscular strength, but not at the expense of flexibility, which is the basis of grace. He has given us a perfect method by which we may not only obtain freedom and elasticity of action, but one which adds force and meaning to our every movement. It frees the body from all restrictions, and renders it as it should be—subservient to the master, the will. It should be the training of every child from its cradle, and then there would be no bias of birth or custom to overcome in later years.

The purpose of this little book is to popularize this study by freeing it from the technical phraseology usually employed in treating the subject and, while endeavoring to interest the trained intellect, to present it in a manner comprehensible to the average mind. A suggestion to the intelligent is enough to convey the idea; but unless the mind possesses the attributes of taste and judgment, a living teacher is necessary to the execution of the plan.

III
Plea for Flexibility

"How beautifully you perform!" said I one day to a pianist; and she replied, "Yes, but my performing, beautiful as it appears, represents many years of patient practice under skillful masters; I have given five hours a day for several years to preliminary practice alone." If this be true of an art, the exercise of which requires trained fingers merely, with how much more force does it apply to one in which the entire body is concerned!

The lack of training in art is most apparent when there is the greatest absence of flexibility, which is the basis of freedom, and is essential to grace in expression. We have seen the enormities of physical bearing which vices of habit and custom have entailed upon us, and the necessity we are under of removing them before we are able to conform to a standard of natural grace.

In other words, we must free the body from the stiffness of individuality by yielding it up to the claims of universality. We must break down error before we can build up truth. This object is attained in physical training by surrendering the body to the discipline of an aesthetical gymnastic drilling.

Delsarte's inventive genius has furnished us a series of mechanical exercises which subject all the joints and muscles to a flexing or freeing process, which is the first step toward restoring them to the pliancy of unconscious freedom. They destroy that unbending muscular rigidity largely imposed by conventionality, and infuse an air of elastic independence—so fundamental an element in a graceful carriage. They correct all faults of negligent personal habit, and overcome hereditary tendencies which sometimes, if unchecked, result in

Arrogance, Defiance

257

grave consequences to health. These are among the purposes of Delsarte's scheme of mechanical movements. As every part of the body is concerned in expression, it should be uniformly cultivated throughout.

V
Philosophy of Delsarte's System

It was Delsarte's great discovery that the human soul, in its covering of flesh called the body, moves in obedience to universal law; that its efforts to manifest itself to the outer world are restricted to the conditions imposed by space, time, and motion, the three great elements by which its activities are inevitably environed; that the soul must express itself *in space, through time, by motion*—in other words, every agent of expression must appear in space by means of motion, and requires time in which to manifest itself; and finally, that the force by which this motion is produced is supplied by the soul, or psychic principle, and is of three different kinds, each corresponding to the three states of the being which it translates in expression.

Thus, when this force causes motion outward, or from the body, it is said to proceed from our physical nature, and is called Vital; when this force causes motion inward, or toward the body, it is said to proceed from our intellectual nature, and is called Mental; and when this force is poised—that is, when it neither causes motion from nor toward the body, but tends to hold the body in poise—it is said to proceed from the emotional nature, and is called Emotive.

In every human being one of these three natures, or states of the being, as they are called, is predominant, while the other two are tributary or subordinate; and the degree of this predominance of the one state, and the order of importance of the other two, are the root and source of all the various types and traits in mankind.

For example, a man of intellectual habit, or one in whom the mental is predominant, will reveal his nature through subjective motion, or motion which is mainly toward the body. On the contrary, in a man in whom the vital nature leads, the motion will be chiefly objective, or from the body; and if the emotional nature rules, the motion will be neither directly subjective nor objective, but may partake of either, according to the extent to which the emotional nature is invaded by the mental or the vital.

Thus we find the seat of sensation in the physical nature, which is also the source of vitality, and reveals itself through outward or objective motion. The seat of sentiment is in the emotive nature, which is the source of the highest emotions of the soul; it reveals itself through centered or poised motion. The seat of consciousness is in the mental nature, which is the source of thought, and is revealed through subjective or inward motion. It should be borne in mind here that this division of the soul into separate states is purely an arbitrary distinction, and is made for the purpose of facilitating analytical study. It is a matter of convenience merely, and has no existence in fact.

Now in the same way that the soul is divided, and for the same purpose of study, the body is arbitrarily separated into three grand divisions, each division corresponding to one of the three states of the being which it represents and which it selects as its favorite ground for display.

Thus, the head represents the favorite ground for the expression of the mental nature; the legs and arms the ground for the vital nature; and the trunk, or torso, the ground for the emotive nature. Each of these grounds, or divisions of the body, is subdivided, and again we have the three states of the being represented in these subdivisions.

" Well sir, what would you? "

In the domain of the head, the eyes and forehead are mental, the nose and cheeks are emotional, and the mouth and lips are vital. In the trunk the upper torso is mental; the heart region, or middle torso, is emotional; and the abdomen is vital. For the legs and arms, the feet and hands are mental, the forearms and lower legs are emotive, and the upper arms and upper legs are vital.

XI
Gesture

Gesture is the immediate revelation of the being. The most evanescent flashes of thought and temperament are first and immediately revealed in gesture. The quality of his gesture is the quality of the individual, and the touchstone to the character of the man. His speech can be attuned to the occasion; but he betrays himself in the quick surprises of involuntary gesture—the sudden tremor of the lip, the startled turn of the head, the dropping of the jaw, the spasmodic clutch of the hand, the blush and pallor of the cheeks, and the flashing and quailing of that sensitive mirror, the eye. And apropos of the sudden flushing and paling of the cheeks, the French philosopher, Descartes,[1] observes that while the will may have some control over the muscles, it has none over the blood.

Gesture is the language of nature, and is comprehensible to people of every tongue, whereas their different forms of speech must be laboriously learned before they can be employed or understood. The most pacific overtures, when couched in words, might be misinterpreted by a foreigner, but a conciliatory movement of the hand is readily appreciated by any race or condition of men.

XIII
Teachers—Exercises for Practice

A Greek writer has declared that "a man's mind is in his walk." Gracefulness in walking requires that the body be carried erect without stiffness, that the legs swing easily from the hip joints, and that the toes be turned slightly outward and carried on a level with the whole foot. In turning to retrace one's steps, or in making short turns, one should pivot lightly on the balls of the feet, not take three or four steps in a half circle, as many do.

The bearing and carriage of the body having been considered in this general way, we proceed to examine the members of the body in detail, beginning with the hand. Extend your arms forward with the palms down or prone, energize and move stiffly up and down; now surrender the hands at the wrist, shake them as before. The object is to take the mind out of the hands, to let the effort of the will cease at the wrists. The sensation of freedom or flexibility is obtained by repeatedly energizing the hand and then relaxing or surrendering it. Now, shake the hands laterally from side to side; forget them, let them go; remember that you have arms, but no hands, for the time being. Now turn the hands with the palms facing each other, give them up as before, and shake them back and forth, letting the energy cease at the wrist. Now, repeat the movement with the palms upward; imagine that you are shaking drops of water from the tips of your fingers. Now, the rotary movement: turn the hand round and round from right to left; now, reverse the movement and turn them from left to right. Next, hold the hands facing each other, the sides downward, and shake them freely as you would in a gesture of threatening. Next, rest your forearm on the arm of your chair; now cut the energy off at the wrist. We must obtain perfect flexibility of this agent, which in some people extends to the fingers, giving them the same freedom as at the wrist.

These movements we call flexing or freeing exercises, because they render flexible or supple the agent thus treated, and free it from the bias of customary forms of action. By this means the way is opened for the introduction of unaccustomed forms.

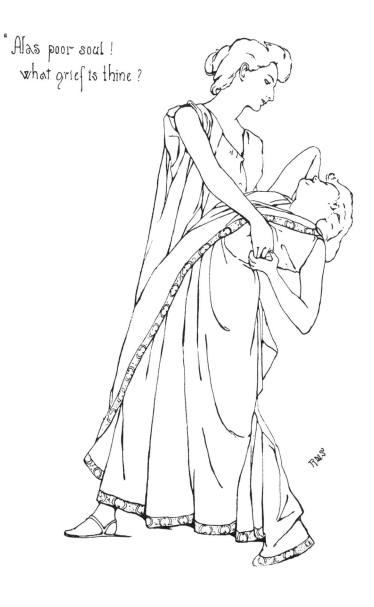

"Alas poor soul!
what grief is thine?

261

From the hands we proceed step by step to each division of the limbs and body, subjecting each to this freeing and flexing process, until the entire body becomes readily responsive to the slightest calls of the will.

Raise the arms and extend them laterally with the motion made in swimming. Free the forearms, letting the energy cease at the elbow; with the arms in this position, agitate the upper arm up and down, forward and backward, rotarily, or with a rotary motion, letting the forearm swing as if dead. This exercise frees the arms from the elbows down, and gives flexibility and suppleness to the muscles of the upper arm.

Standing in a position of perfect ease, allow the arms to hang naturally at the sides; now, energize or stiffen the arms and bring them slowly together with the backs of the hands meeting just before the hips at the lowest altitude; holding them thus for an instant, relax and let them fall back to their usual position. Again, energize the arms and carry them forward and upward, holding them extended at full length to a horizontal position before the chest; relax and let them fall into place as before. Repeat the movement, carrying the arms this time to a position just above or on a level with the eyes; relax as before, letting them drop lifelessly into place.

Again, stiffen the arms to a rigid tension, and holding them at full length, carry them up sideways until they meet, the backs of the hands together, directly over the head. Agitate the hands as in the preceding exercises for the hands, relax and drop them. Again this movement, carrying the arms above the head, but as far back as possible, and finally relax and allow them to fall into place.

Standing in the same position, elevate the shoulders as much as possible, relax them and, allowing the arms to hang lifelessly, freely agitate the rest of the body. Carry the shoulders forward as much as possible, neither raising nor depressing them; relax them, and agitate the body as before. Depress or slightly droop the shoulders, then slowly carry them backward and upward, and finally downward, expanding the chest to its fullest extent; relax and agitate the body as before. Rotate the shoulders forward several times, then backward; then swing the arms round and round, letting them revolve in their sockets.

These exercises, besides freeing the muscles of the chest and shoulders and relieving them of stiffness and angularity, will, if perseveringly practiced, materially expand and enlarge the chest, thus promoting the healthy action of the lungs.

XV
The Head, Eye, Nose, Mouth, and Mechanical Movements

A well-poised head is the fitting accompaniment of a shapely person, and usually bespeaks a well-ordered mind, and goes far besides to atone for the physical imperfections of other members, being the objective point of the line of vision and therefore most constantly under the criticism of the eye.

We admire an elastic step, a yielding curve of the pliant arm, and a supple grace in the carriage of the body; but add to these the charm of a nicely balanced head, and the picture is complete; we have the finished grace of an undoubted personal bearing.

A normal poise of the head requires that it shall be carried midway between the shoulders, neither raised nor depressed. The ruling state of the being is revealed through the various attitudes of the head. For instance, a person of a sympathetic nature who is full of trust and tenderness will habitually incline the head forward or toward the object of his esteem; while, on the contrary, a person who is cold, unsympathetic, and distrustful will habitually and naturally withdraw the head backward. Bearing in mind that motion is in obedience to the thought or emotion which created it, it will readily be seen that reflection, humility of spirit, subordination of self, and all kindred sentiments will concentrate or lower the head upon the chest; and if the sentiment be a complex one of humility, trust, and affection, we have the spiritual attitude of veneration or adoration, which is also complex in that it is first lowered and then inclined forward with an upward inflection.

In the same way, the complex feelings of scrutiny and distrust will produce an attitude of suspicion, jealousy, hate, or envy, which first lowers the head and then draws it backward. All emotions of exaltation throw the head upward; if the feeling of exaltation is invaded by that of trust and resignation, it first throws the head backward and then forward with an upward inflection. If the feeling of distrust and self-assertion is mingled with that of exaltation, we have the attitude of arrogance or defiance; the head is first thrown upward and then drawn backward. The study of the attitudes of the head and those of all parts of the body, especially the various expressions of the eye, nose, and mouth, should be carefully practiced before a mirror.

Most people consult their mirrors for the single purpose of seeing their attractiveness; we should study them for the purpose of seeing ourselves as others see us. The study of the profile view of the face and head should not be omitted: some features will bear a straight profile view; others of a warmer nature look best with a convex exposure of the features; still others require that the head be turned away.

XVI
The Stage—Conclusion

In the domain of art, the function of the body is to reflect the soul; it is the material expression of the immaterial part of us. It is only when the intellectual holds an undoubted supremacy over the physical, as in the case of the famous artist named above [Henry Irving],[2] that we lose sight of the material altogether and enjoy a feast of the spirit.

This is the test of greatness: those only are great who have so disciplined the body that it has become the servile creature of the soul, mirroring with equal truth its lightest fancies and its gravest thoughts, at the master's will. This is the end; to reach this end in the shortest possible time is the desideratum, and it is the *raison d'etre* of countless theories, systems, and speculations—all of which contain elements of truth and have contributed their quota to the sum of accumulated facts. To reach this end is of more importance to us than the means we shall employ to do it.

The possession of the thing is what we aim at, not the means of possessing it; and having obtained the thing, we enjoy the possession without troubling ourselves about how we came into it. To learn to express what we feel of human nature and know of human character—this is the primary consideration; how or by what process of training we shall attain to this knowledge is a secondary matter, but we must have training. No natural talent is sufficient of itself. No natural endowment can be exercised at its best without the discipline of experience to give it breadth and scope, and the wider the experience, the broader the result. The most gifted among us must learn to know himself, as it is only through this knowledge that he can know others, and therefore know how to affect others.

Delsarte's philosophy of physical expression enables the student to analyze and classify his own motions and their corresponding emotions. It places expression on a sure and certain footing; it makes the actor independent of his moods and delivers him from the thraldom of an untoward temperament. It enables him at will to put on the semblance of a feeling which he does not at the moment experience. For has he not already analyzed it, and is he not familiar with its source and stop? The real feeling cannot always be commanded at the moment when it is required, hence the necessity for a perfect simulation to preserve the illusion. Delsarte's methods are Nature's methods systematized for the purposes of art. When the formulae of the Delsartian principles first reached this country, they were seized upon by all manner of charlatans whose heralding of the "New System of Acting" and "Acting Made Easy" brought the subject into a disrepute from which it is but just emerging. From the announcements of these quacks one was given to understand that what Delsarte had discovered was a purchasable commodity, and that a term of twenty lessons with its dispensers would equip one with a supply of ready-made tragedy and compressed pathos which could be taken home and, as it were, turned on at will. And the spirit of guileless, aspiring youth rose to an exuberant state. The result was a storm of "Juliets," "Ophelias," and "Melnottes"[3] whose measured artificial woes carried unmeasured real distress to many innocent onlookers.

These absurdities—which are scarcely exaggerated—become transparent when it is remembered that Delsarte's reasoning is in perfect accord with the best monuments of tradition, and with the results of the most enlightened research. It fully recognizes the fact that the artistic, like the poetic, temperament is essentially a matter of inheritance, not of study; that its promptings are intuitive, not volitional; and that while cultivation can do much to hasten development and expansion, it cannot supply the material to be developed and expanded. It may broaden and enlighten; it was never intended to originate or create. This is all quite in keeping with Delsarte's teachings, which, while they recognize no school, prove their universality by comprehending all schools.

Other things being equal, the actor with a system has an infinite advantage over him who is without any. In preparing a character for representation on the stage, the former is able to keep constantly narrowing the plane over which his efforts are dispersed, from the universal and general going to the specific and particular, and by thus concentrating his thought, he effects an immense saving of time and labor. He applies a few simple tests and ascertains to which class his character belongs; knowing this, he is able to tell which of the three phases of the being is apt to predominate or rule, and the order of subordination of the other two. This enables him to disengage the salient traits and features of the character, and being already in pos-

"No tears can drown my passion of remorse"

session of their corresponding outward equivalents, he gives prominence to them, sinking the other by contrast. Thus his work is greatly simplified.

His methodless brother, on the other hand, is like the much-quoted rudderless ship; he is plunged at once into an infinite sea of doubt, where he is left experimenting and speculating, squandering his time and energies until some temporary harbor of thought is sighted in which he takes refuge. That student fails, however, to grasp the significance of Delsarte's labors in behalf of aesthetic science who imagines that a knowledge of the mere mechanics or the mere theory will suffice to give him command over his own resources in the interpretation of human character in art work.

No, this is not enough; it is the thoughtful merging of the two. It is the idea, feeling, or emotion speaking through cultivated mediums that touches the subtlest chords of harmony.

Notes

This excerpt is taken from my own copy of Anna Morgan, *An Hour with Delsarte: A Study of Expression*, illustrated by Rose Mueller Sprague and Marian Reynolds (Boston: Lee & Shepard, 1890), 8–9, 15–16, 25–28, 58–59, 73–76, 96–98, 110–14. Illustrations: opposite 18, 28, 72, 115. François Delsarte (1811–1871) was a French teacher of acting and voice, who worked out an extremely influential philosophy of aesthetics of delivery, and whose many students published his philosophy after his death.

1. René Descartes (1596–1650) was a French philosopher and scientist noted for his empiricist argument for the existence of God and his contributions to logic and mathematics.

2. Sir Henry Irving (1838–1905), English actor and manager of the Lyceum Theater in London who was famous for his realistic acting in Shakespeare and melodrama, especially opposite Ellen Terry; his theory of acting emphasized study of movement.

3. These are romantic young leads of popular plays: the female leads are Juliet of Shakespeare's *Romeo and Juliet*, and Ophelia of Shakespeare's *Hamlet*; the male lead is Melnotte, in love with Pauline in Edward Bulwer-Lytton's *The Lady of Lyons, or, Love and Pride* (1838).

Harriet L. Keeler
1846–1921

Emma C. Davis
c. 1891

Harriet Louise Keeler was born in South Kortright, Delaware County, New York, in 1846, to Burr and Elizabeth (Barlow) Keeler. She taught briefly in her teens in Cherry Valley, New York. She received an A.B. from Oberlin College in 1870 and an honorary A.M. in 1900, as well as an LL.D. from Western Reserve University in 1913. She must have studied classical rhetoric at Oberlin because her section on persuasion shows the marked influence of Aristotle and Cicero, the classical tradition (and Oberlin was one of the few colleges where a woman could achieve a traditional classical education). She served in the Cleveland public schools from 1871 until 1912—as superintendent of primary instruction from 1871 until 1879, as a teacher at Central High School from 1879 to 1909, and as superintendent of public schools from January 1912 to September 1912, when she retired. She was active in the women's suffrage movement.

Keeler was a prolific writer. Because of her connection to Oberlin, she wrote *The Life of Adelia A. Field Johnson Who Served Oberlin College* (1912). She was also a naturalist and published many studies of plants, her earliest on the flowers of Ohio, *Wild Flowers of Early Spring* (1894). She also published *Our Native Trees and How to Identify Them* (1900); *Our Northern Shrubs* (1903); *Our Garden Flowers: A Popular Study of Their Native Lands, Their Life Histories, and Their Structural Affiliations* (1910); *Our Early Wild Flowers* (1916), *The Wayside Flowers of Summer* (1917); and *Our Northern Autumn* (1920). Besides her coauthored textbook represented here, *Studies in English Composition with Lessons in Language and Rhetoric* (1891), which went through at least two more editions (1892, 1900), she also published *High School English* (1906) with Mary E. Adams, and *Ethical Readings from the Bible* (1915) with Laura Wild. She died in Clifton Springs, New York, on February 12, 1921; she was buried in Oberlin, Ohio.

I have not been able to find any information about Emma C. Davis, unless she is Emma Collett Davis (née Whitaker), who also published two genealogical family history volumes in 1929 and 1930. *Studies in English Composition* was under Keeler's copyright, and the preface was also written by Keeler. The preface does say that the volume resulted from experience teaching high school in Cleveland, Ohio, so we may infer that Emma Davis was a fellow teacher with Keeler.

Keeler and Davis's *Studies in English Composition* is one of many textbooks published by women for elementary or secondary pupils after the Civil War. It is short and eclectic, written in a delightfully plain and clear style. Underlying this volume is a thorough understanding of the classical rhetorical tradition of persuasion. It thus stands among the opponents of the educators' writing textbooks like Sara Lockwood's *Lessons in English*, which emphasized informative or expository rather than persuasive writing.

Keeler and Davis's textbook includes chapters on narration, diction, description, errors of usage, letter writing, the structure of sentences and paragraphs, rhetorical figures, American authors, style, historical writing, short stories, verse, Shakespeare, book reviews, persuasion, and public speaking. It is a textbook addressed to secondary students, and it is well suited to accompany students through all their years of secondary education. It is eclectic and student centered, borrowing from whatever works to help students learn to communicate. Keeler and Davis are influenced by empiricist rhetoricians in their view of narration and description as means to persuasion, because of the appeal to feelings and personal experience. Their example of successful emotional appeal is *Uncle Tom's Cabin*, placing them in Northern reform movements. Their rhetorical politics, rather than the elitism of the British empiricists, then, is closer to classical republicanism. They urge writers to be fair with their opponents and establish themselves on good terms with their listeners. They do not seek to dominate their audience but to respect them—they don't want writers to push the audience around or trick them. Although publishing their textbook in the 1890s, they are not at all influenced by the school of correctness, warning teachers in the introduction that they should never teach "technical dress" with more emphasis than "spirit and thought."

For further information on Harriet Keeler, see W. Stewart Wallace, *A Dictionary of North American Authors Deceased before 1950* (Toronto: Ryerson, 1951), 245; William Coyle, ed., *Ohio Authors and Their Books* (Cleveland: World, 1962), 349; and *Who Was Who in America*, vol. 1, 1897–1942 (Chicago: Marquis–Who's Who, 1966), 659.

From *Studies in English Composition with Lessons in Language and Rhetoric* (1891)

Chapter XIX
Persuasive Discourse
Lesson 72—The Art of Persuasion

A man convinced against his will
Is of the same opinion still. —*Old Proverb*

Not he is great who can alter matter, but he who can alter my state of mind. —Ralph Waldo Emerson[1]

There is probably no one, young or old, who has not at some time felt a desire to influence the opinion and conduct of others. The child tries to induce his parents to grant his request, the boy to lead his companions to do as he wishes, to think as he does, the man to influence his friends, the lawyer to win his jury, the minister to benefit his congregation, the politician to carry the people with him. Each one has attempted *to persuade*. If he has succeeded in doing this, he has, consciously or unconsciously, followed certain definite principles. It is to the study of these principles that this chapter is devoted.

Persuasion is an effort to influence the will, and through the will to affect the conduct. The will is influenced in two ways: through the emotions or through the judgment. In the first instance, the appeal is made to the feelings; in the second, to the reason. These appeals are named, respectively, exhortation and argument. Both are necessary to successful persuasion, but which is to be used depends upon the character of the person or audience to be influenced, as well as upon the character of the speaker. The following fundamental principles underlie all persuasive discourse:

It is best to decide at first whether you will use argument to influence the reason, or exhortation to move the feelings, or both.

No one would address an audience of lawyers as he would a mixed audience, or a group of children as he would a company of adults. Instinctively, in trying to persuade people, we appeal to their feelings or their reason, according as we think the one or the other will move them. It is well, usually, to use both methods, and the character of your listener will decide which one will predominate.

It is easier to move the feelings by narratives and descriptions than by direct appeals.

Persons are frequently armed against direct appeals, but a telling story or a pathetic description finds them quite unprepared to resist, and they yield at once. Attend a missionary meeting and see how the audience are brought into sympathy with the speakers by tales of foreign lands. *Uncle Tom's Cabin*[2] doubtless convinced thousands of the wrong of slavery, who would not have listened for one moment to a direct appeal for the slave.

The question to be discussed should be clearly stated. If necessary, define it.

It is the utmost importance that the point at issue should be perfectly clear. A great deal of useless discussion is often indulged in because the disputants do not understand what they are talking about.

Always be fair to those who oppose you.

Whatever temporary advantage may be gained by unfairness is usually lost in the end. Nothing helps a debater more than to be fair to his opponents. Mr. Lincoln's great success in debate[3] was largely due to his habit of stating his opponents' case quite as well as they could, and then, when he had overthrown it, there was nothing further to be said.

Put yourself on good terms with your listeners.

Experienced speakers do this in a variety of ways: sometimes by means of a story or an anecdote, to make their hearer good-natured; sometimes by agreeing with them as far as possible; sometimes by flattery more or less concealed. Especially if a speaker is addressing a person or audience prejudiced against his cause, it is necessary to win the willing attention of his hearers at any cost; otherwise, he might as well keep silent.

It is sometimes well to anticipate possible objections and answer these in the first part of your argument. This may free the minds of your hearers of possible prejudice.

State the arguments separately. It is well to begin with a strong argument and usually to end with one. Sometimes they may be arranged to a climax.

It is well to make a good impression at the beginning and also at the close of your argument. It is necessary to have clearly in mind what your arguments are before you attempt to arrange them.

Do not dogmatize. Let the conclusions follow from your arguments rather than from your personality.

Let the conclusions follow from your arguments, rather than state the conclusions first, and then give your reasons. People are willing to be convinced, but not so willing to be told beforehand what they should do or think. Arguments stated in the form of questions are frequently very effective, for the reason that they do not assert, but compel the hearer to draw the conclusion for himself.

Guard against the fallacy of supposing that because two events occur together, or in succession, one is the effect of the other.

It often happens that a statement seems to be true when it is not. When such a statement is used as an argument, it is called a fallacy. People often use fallacious arguments without recognizing them as such. This kind of argument is also used by speakers who know better, and is often heard in political debate. If "times are hard," it is often charged as the result of this or that political condition which in fact has nothing to do with it.

Guard against the fallacy of supposing that because one thing is true, another thing very much like it must be true.

This is the fallacy of reasoning by analogy. The error lies in supposing because two things are very much alike that they are necessarily exactly alike. The very point in which they differ may be the one which makes it impossible for them to be judged alike. Do not understand that no arguments by analogy are good ones—many are—but see to it that the cases compared are alike in that for which they are compared.

It is well at the end to make a summary of your arguments. State what you think you have disproved and what you think you have proved.

This is an assistance to the memories of your hearers. It impresses what you have said.

Notes

These excerpts are taken from my own copy of Harriet L. Keeler and Emma C. Davis, *Studies in English Composition* (Boston: Allyn & Bacon, 1892), 174–77. I have modernized spelling and punctuation in a very few instances.

1. Ralph Waldo Emerson, *The American Scholar: An Oration* (1837).

2. Harriet Beecher Stowe's novel, *Uncle Tom's Cabin* (1852), depicting the oppressive life of slaves and the cruelty with which escaped slaves were pursued, sold over 300,000 copies. It was made into a play and translated into dozens of foreign languages, and it aided in the campaign against slavery.

3. Abraham Lincoln (1809–1865) was sixteenth president of the United States during the Civil War. A self-taught lawyer, he was famous for his antislavery speeches in the Lincoln-Douglas debates in the Illinois senate race, as well as for numerous important speeches that he gave while president (including the Gettysburg Address).

Gertrude Buck

1871–1922

Gertrude Buck was born in Kalamazoo, Michigan, on July 14, 1871, to Anne Bradford and George M. Buck. She was educated at the University of Michigan, receiving her B.S. in 1894, her M.S. in 1895, and her Ph.D. in 1893. She studied under Fred Newton Scott, a pioneer in rhetoric and composition studies based on psychology and developmental education. Buck taught as a graduate teaching assistant at Michigan, as a public school teacher in Indianapolis, and at the normal school for teachers in Detroit.

In 1897 Buck became an instructor at Vassar College, where she was promoted to associate professor in 1901 and full professor in 1907. Laura Wylie, chair of English at Vassar, hired Buck to run the composition and rhetoric program. Buck also was liaison to secondary school teachers, and she served on committees for national organizations such as NCTE (National Council of Teachers of English, the professional organization for teachers of writing). As an associate professor, Buck taught seven courses a semester and, once promoted, four courses, most of them writing courses. Vassar's English program integrated study of history of language, literature, and writing.

Buck never married. From 1908 on, she shared a house in a committed relationship with Laura Wylie; they even considered adopting a child. Buck was a feminist and favored women's suffrage. She authored *A Course in Argumentative Writing* (1899); *The Metaphor: A Study in the Psychology of Rhetoric* (1899); *The Social Criticism of Literature* (1916); several plays published posthumously in *Poems and Plays* (1922); numerous journal articles on education and rhetoric; with H. M. Scott, *Organic Education* (1899); with Elisabeth Woodbridge, *A Course in Expository Writing* (1899) and *A Course in Narrative Writing* (1906); with Fred Newton Scott, *A Brief English Grammar* (1905); and with Kristine Mann, *A Handbook of Argumentation and Debating* (1906). She edited Ruskin's *Sesame and Lilies* (1906). Buck retired from Vassar in 1922 and died that same year.

Elisabeth Woodbridge Morris, who coauthored with Gertrude Buck *A Course in Expository Writing* (1899) and *A Course in Narrative Writing* (1906), was born in Brooklyn, New York, on June 16, 1870, and was educated at the Packer Collegiate Institute and Vassar College; she earned a Ph.D. from Yale University. She married Charles Morris in 1899. She wrote children's plays and contributed regularly to national magazines, including *Atlantic Monthly* and *Saturday Review*. She died in 1964.

Gertrude Buck and Elisabeth Woodbridge were part of a group of women who responded to the challenges of teaching a generation of new students at college level with new kinds of textbooks and, consequently, new theories of rhetoric. Buck, especially, was influenced by "scientific" progressive education theory like that of John Dewey and William James. She adapted this psychological theory to her own subject of composition, arguing for an organic, developmental model of learning language and writing, as well as a more socially collaborative view of making meaning. Her emphasis, like those of male theorists, was on formal composition and public speech, but she started in the classroom with informal dialogue and written exercises, and used conversation as a model for teaching and learning writing, a model adapted because of her new audiences of students at coed Michigan and female Vassar. Buck's textbooks on each of the "modes" of writing (narrative, expository—which combined description and definition—and argument) were among the first such specialized textbooks to be published.

Buck's theoretical approach to language and rhetoric is already evident in her earliest work, *The Metaphor—A Study in the Psychology of Rhetoric* (1899). In this study, Buck refutes the classical idea of metaphor as a word for one thing transferred to another similar thing because of the poverty of language or a desire to ornament. She shows that in many cases there is no transfer, the metaphor occurring spontaneously as the only word for a thing. Influenced by the new developmental psychology, Buck outlines a history of the development of metaphor that applies to both individual growth and also the growth of language: metaphor originates as radical metaphor, where two objects or experiences identified with each other are contained in a single word; in poetic metaphor, the two are beginning to be differentiated; and in the simile the process of abstraction and differentiation is complete and the resemblance can be specified. Thus the function of metaphor is neither clarity nor ornament, but communication and stimulation: either it is the only way the speaker can communicate an idea in the process of formation or it is stimulating to the reader (and the writer as reader) because of a release of tension when we perceive the resemblance in what was before inchoate. In this philosophical exploration of metaphor, Buck outlines several of the tenets on which she establishes all of her work: language is social, communication between a speaker and a hearer, or a writer and a reader; language is in the process of evolutionary development both for the entire society and also for the individual speaker; and understanding and, so, education are based on an evolutionary psychological model rather than a mechanistic one. Just as now "virtual reality" has become a schema for understanding experience beyond the computer, so in Buck's time, the recently developed concept of evolution was a schema for understanding many other human experiences besides biological development of species.

In her textbooks, this philosophy of language translates into pedagogical strategies that seem very contemporary. In *A Course in Argumentative Writing* (1899), for example, Buck teaches argument not as artificial techniques of dominance or manipulation, but as a means of communicating belief or understanding from one person to another, with full respect for the other person's ability to judge. She defines argument not as persuasion, but as "transplant[ing] your conviction into [the hearer's] mind," or "establishing in the mind of another person a conclusion which has become fixed in your own, by means of setting up in the other person's mind the train of thought or reasoning which has previously led you to this conclusion."

Buck advocates a developmental organization of what she teaches, in *Argumentative Writing*, urging argumentative strategies paralleling human development: from less abstract sensory experience (induction) to abstracted, more differentiated experience (classification, deduction, and analogy). In teaching, Buck attempts to help students see that reasoning is not imposed on experience, but arises from one's own experience and thought processes; logic is thus "a knowledge of those typical activities of mind common to all thinking people," while rhetoric supplements logic by considering the audience, and by allowing the speaker to "put himself imaginatively in the place of the person he addresses" in order to establish an appropriate train of reasoning for this different individual. In this textbook on argument, Buck encourages a progressive pedagogy: she recommends a subject matter for writing close to students' interests, and oral debate in class to establish a purpose and sense of audience for writing outside of class.

The textbook that Buck coauthored with Elisabeth Woodbridge, *Expository Writing*, covers description and definition. The two authors' approach to this subject is empiricist in the sense that experience is presented as the basis of knowledge. The work draws heavily on analogies from science, discussing the telescope, for example, in the section on definition. According to Buck and Woodbridge, the purpose of expository writing is to put the reader in possession of the experience of the writer. In this textbook, Buck and Woodbridge are concerned to teach students how to see thinking and writing as processes that they can break down into steps in order better to convey their own perceptions to their readers, thus to lead them by means of words through the same processes of perception. Description must follow the actual order of "sensual experience" that it describes. The "natural order" means, to Buck and Woodbridge, that a writer will follow an initial general impression with details in the order of perception. Unity, coherence, and accurate paragraphing will result from "honestly" and accurately expressing our sense impressions in the order of perception. To these sense impressions, we naturally add our interpretation of the significance of the experience. By means of interpretation, Buck and Woodbridge draw, under the fold of description, writing in the categories of history, and appreciation of art and literature. The authors see definition as related psychologically to description. They offer students the techniques of defining by classification into genus and species as a "natural" mental process, which depends for clarity on concrete illustration. This textbook encourages a "writing across the curriculum" approach because the examples of description and definition are drawn from the whole range of arts and sciences, especially history and biology.

In "The Present Status of Rhetorical Theory," Buck outlines her theory of discourse by means of an interpretation of Plato and the sophists. She accepts Plato's view of the sophists, as seeking to persuade for the end of personal power only, and criticizes them for lack of ethical purpose since they seek only to dominate the audience, not to better them. Buck then defines ideal discourse as a platonic process whereby the speaker communicates a "truth" to the hearer, and thus makes them equal (a slightly distorted view, since Plato's dialogues usually depend on the temporarily unequal relation of teacher and student). Buck nudges Plato's theory in the direction of modern relativism by admitting that her contemporaries no longer see "truth" as unequivocal, and that "temporary" and "practical" truths have value for the modern rhetor in ways Plato would not have approved. Still, Buck also argues that Plato grounds the subject matter of discourse in personal experience, which must seem to us a very strange reading of the idealistic Plato, especially after the recent feminist recovery of the relativistic sophists as a model for modern composition studies. This last move allows Buck to argue that discourse, for Plato, as for right-thinking moderns, must be viewed as a "function of the social organism." While Buck's interpretation of Plato seems quite distant from his purposes as modern scholars have described them, we still may prefer the materialist, socialist theory of discourse that Buck advances under the ostensible authority of the ancient Greek. Just as Buck used the schema of evolution to express her conception of metaphor, in this essay she uses the schema of electrical circuitry to express her conception of communication.

Historians of rhetoric have recovered Buck as a crucial figure in opposition to mainstream emphasis on grammatical correctness and forms of discourse in late nineteenth- and early twentieth-century composition theory, and as a precursor of pedagogical and theoretical reforms of the 1960s and 1970s. They point to Buck's inductive teaching of writing based on students' experience, her view of writing as a process, her respect for student writing, her advocacy of writing across the curriculum, her development of a psycholinguistic theory of metaphor, her opposition to "correctness" as the goal of writing, and her emphasis on cooperative social behavior—all as forerunners of current interests in composition theory. In addition, Buck shares with contemporary feminist pedagogues an emphasis on discussion and collaboration and an understanding of the hierarchies at work in persuasion.

For further information on Buck, see Rebecca J. Burke, "Gertrude Buck's Rhetorical Theory," *Occasional Papers in the History and Theory of Composition*, no. 1, ed. Donald C. Stewart (Manhattan: Kansas State University, 1978); Gerald P. Mulderig, "Gertrude Buck's Rhetorical Theory and Modern Composition Teaching," *Rhetoric Society Quarterly* 14 (1984): 95–104; Virginia Allen, "Gertrude Buck and the Emergence of Composition in the United States," *Review of Metaphysics* 39, no. 3 (March 1986): 141–59; Gertrude Buck, *Toward a Feminist Rhetoric: The Writing of Gertrude Buck*, ed. JoAnn Campbell (Pittsburgh: University of Pittsburgh Press, 1996); Jane Donawerth, "Textbooks for New Audiences: Women's Revisions of Rhetorical Theory at the Turn of the Century," in *Listening to Their Voices: The Rhetorical Activities of Historical Women*, ed. Molly Meijer Wertheimer (Columbia: University of South Carolina Press, 1997), 337–56; and Susan Bordelon, "Resisting Decline Stories: Gertrude Buck's Democratic Theory of Rhetoric," in *The Changing Tradition: Women in the History of Rhetoric*, ed. Christine Mason Sutherland and Rebecca Sutcliffe (Calgary: University of Calgary Press, 1999), 183–95.

For further information on Morris, see *Who Was Who among North American Authors, 1921–1939* (Detroit: Gale Research, 1976), 2:1038.

From *The Metaphor* (1899)

Chapter III
The Evolution of Plain Statement

We have traced the metaphor from its origin in a nebulous and undeveloped perception of a situation to its first tentative outbranchings from a state of perfect homogeneity to one of beginning differentiation. But our task is not yet ended. The growing perception does not at this point cease to develop. There is a sequel to the history thus far outlined. And this sequel is our present interest.

What becomes of the developing perception of a situation after it has passed the metaphorical stage? For instance, when the child says "moon" as he points to the lamp-globe, we know that "moon" represents to him a single physical sensation which he refers vaguely to any large, white, softly glowing object which is present to his consciousness. The moon and the globe are one for his undiscriminating mind. But little by little out of this hazy sense of something large, round, and softly glowing, emerge into half-distinctness the two objects lamp-globe and moon, probably first differentiated by the dawning sense of distance. When the two had become sufficiently separated in perception, they would doubtless be distinguished in speech. The lamp-globe might, for instance, become the "near moon" or "baby's moon." Later its proper name would be discovered and used, and the two objects would have become perfectly distinct in the consciousness, so that the common origin would as such be quite forgotten. The two objects would stand in the mind of the speaker almost as completely separated as if they had always been so. Not quite, however, for between the two exists a connection, recognized by the speaker, the vestige of their former identity. This connection might find expression in such a statement as the following: "That lamp-globe looks like a full moon." It no longer *is* the moon, nor is it the "near moon" or "baby's moon." It is not a moon at all, but only looks like one. The two elements in the metaphor have separated so widely that each is seen as distinct from the other.

So far, then, we have noted three stages of metaphor growth which may be briefly characterized as follows. The first represents that stage of perception in which the figure is still homogeneous. Teeth are pearls. The one name stands for a single sensation produced by a row of vaguely-perceived small objects, white, glistening, and all but translucent. The second is that representing the stage of perception at which it has begun to differentiate into two main constituents. This is expressed by saying "pearly teeth." The third represents a later stage of perception in which the two objects, just beginning to draw apart from one another in the second period, have separated so far that a connection is visible between them, this connection being commonly expressed in language by the words "as" or "like." At this stage of the developing perception, one would say "Her teeth are like pearls."

The development of a metaphor is strikingly like the process known as "fission" in the case of the lowest forms of life. The amoeba, for instance, at one moment apparently a homogeneous jelly-like splash of protoplasm, shows an hour later a slight elongation and a constriction near its middle. It is becoming dual. Two sections of its body are beginning to show themselves where before was but one. The constriction narrows little by little, the two parts of the once single-celled animal become more distinct. Finally, there is but a thread connecting them. It slowly parts, and there are two amoebae where one was before.

In the metaphor process, we have reached the stage at which the constricted portion has become visible as a connection between the two dividing sides of the figure. These two sides were at first indiscernible, united in the single homogeneous structure of the original perception. But as the perception developed, it divided, and a connection of resemblance was visible where complete identity had been.

This last stage of development might, perhaps, with a degree of propriety, be termed "conscious." The resemblance or analogy between the two elements in the metaphor, which at first existed only as a hazy sense of identity, has now, in psychological phrase, "come to consciousness." It is recognized as resemblance. When Swinburne says, "And fruit and leaf were as gold and fire,"[1] we know that the fruit and the gold are no longer included by him in the one large, undifferentiated class of things that make upon him the sensation later identified as yellow; that the leaf and the fire have become distinct from one another in his consciousness. They have so far separated that he sees them clearly as two, though recognizing that somehow they resemble each other.

In all these cases, however, this common quality, the exact point of resemblance, is not specified. The perception has not reached a stage of development sufficiently advanced for such specification. The analogy is felt rather than thought. It grows explicit, however, when the writer or speaker comes to perceive that not only two things are alike, but in what respect they are alike. This step is only the logical sequence of those which have preceded. The series of which we have hitherto spoken, beginning with the name "pearls" as applied to all small, white, glistening, translucent objects, and proceeding with "pearly teeth" and "teeth like pearls," is continued by the phrase "teeth white as pearls." Here the resemblance is particularized. That which at first constituted, in part at least, the identity of impression received from the two objects is now clearly perceived as a quality common to both.

The hair of the Blessed Damosel, "yellow as ripe corn,"[2] has reached this stage of perception. It is not vaguely assigned to the comprehensive class of things, making an impression of rich yellow color in the mind of the writer. Out of this class have already separated two distinct objects, the hair of the Blessed Damosel and ripe corn. They have drawn so far apart from each other that the writer cannot now say, though he might have done so an instant before, "her hair was ripened corn." He sees now that the one is not the other, but only resembles it. He might say that it is "like ripe corn" simply; but his thought-process has moved a step beyond this, and he sees in what respect the hair is like the corn. They are alike in color. Both are yellow, so he says her "hair was yellow like ripe corn."

The statement,

> Her eyes were deeper than the depths
> Of waters stilled at even,[3]

reveals the same stage of metaphor-development. "I wandered lonely as a cloud"[4] shows not only that the two objects are separated from one another, and that a connection is observed between them, but that this connection is recognized as being a resemblance in one particular, that of isolation, not whiteness, not transitoriness, nor any other quality whatsoever. Browning's characterization of a "fruit-shaped, perfect chin"[5] belongs to this family, as does Tennyson's

> But bland the smile that like a wrinkling wind
> On glassy water drove his cheek in lines.[6]

The shape constitutes the point of likeness in the one case; in the other, the effect produced by each element in the figure unites them.

We may, then, classify the developing metaphor as follows:

1. Radical metaphor, in which objects later recognized as two are represented by a single word or phrase which is equivalent to neither object, nor to the quality which they have in common, but to the one vague sensation or impression made by both objects upon the mind of the speaker, not yet defined or differentiated. Illustrations of this metaphor would be the term "cola" as applied by M. Taine's infant daughter to all sweetmeats, the word "moon," as including lamp-globe, the word "house" as used to designate a bird's nest, etc.[7]

2. Poetic metaphor, in which two objects or images are just beginning to disentangle themselves from this homogeneous sensation. Illustrations of this class are found in such examples as "the hoarse wind,"[8] "a sorrow-clouded eye,"[9] "Sorrow darkens hamlet and hall,"[10] etc.

3. Simile, including all cases in which the two constituents of the metaphor have so far separated themselves from the original homogeneous sensation and from each other that they are recognized as two objects slightly cohering by some resemblance or analogy. Of this there may be two species:

(a) That simile in which the connection between the two objects is recognized by the writer only as a resemblance, the particular point of resemblance not being specific.

> That face, like a silver wedge
> 'Mid the yellow wealth,[11]
> is an illustration.

(b) That simile in which the resemblance between the two objects is limited to a particular quality or characteristic common to both. This species may be illustrated by Keats's "jellies soother than the creamy curd" and "upon his knees he sank, pale as smooth-sculptured stone."[12]

Our conclusions, then, as to the relationship between metaphor and simile must be quite contrary to those commonly held by the rhetoricians. The simile is not the earlier figure, transformed into metaphor by the simple device of cutting out the connective "as" or "like,"[13] but it is a stage later than metaphor in the process of developing a vague sensuous impression into the clear-cut judgment upon a given situation. The relation between these figures is more than merely verbal. It is a fundamental relationship of thought. Simile is a half-way house for the metaphor-process on its way to plain statement. . . .

We have now reached a point beyond which the development of the metaphor cannot go. When the two constituents of the figure have been completely separated, their resemblance recognized as such and narrowly defined, no further separation can take place without a complete rending in twain, a disintegration of the metaphor.

Chapter IV
The Aesthetics of Metaphor

If an action felt as pleasurable is one which is symmetrical or harmonious, that set up in the reader by metaphor must be symmetrical or harmonious if it is to give pleasure. And so, indeed, it is. . . . It consists of a sudden tension in the mind between the two incompatible images introduced, a resolution of that tension in the perception of the single impression or sensation out of which the two images had emerged, the subsequent division of the original impression and its return to a distincter unity. This means, of course, in the technical phrase, an intellectual experience of unity in variety.

But this activity set up by the metaphor is not purely cerebral. Other parts of the body participate in it. The sudden tension brought about in the mind by the almost simultaneous introduction of the two elements in the metaphor means physically a sudden catching of the breath, a sense as if the lungs were being forced wide apart. Anyone who notes his sensations while reading metaphor will, I doubt not, discover something at least analogous to this experience. The breath cannot be released until the unity has been reached. Then, with a sigh or a laugh, it is let go, the lungs fall together, and one feels the pleasure that always accompanies a lifting tension, if it has not been unduly prolonged.[14]

This physical experience can be, I think, easily accounted for in terms of Dr. Dewey's theory, that all feeling is the subjective reaction of a bodily attitude once useful to the organism. It is a familiar fact that, as Dr. Dewey puts it, "All expectancy, waiting, suspended effort, etc., is accompanied, for obvious teleological reasons, with taking in and holding a full breath, and the maintenance of the whole system in a state of considerable tension. Now let the end suddenly 'break,' 'dawn,' let one see the 'point,' and the energy discharges. . . . This sudden relaxation of strain, so far as occurring through the medium of the breathing and vocal apparatus, is laughter." And later the statement is made that "The laugh is thus a phenomenon of the same general kind as the sigh of relief."[15] Either phenomenon may take place as the reader vividly experiences a metaphor. I should say, from my own experience and observation, that one is almost certain to occur. At any rate, the sense of strain and of relief, whether recognized in its physical manifestations or not, will be recalled by most sensitive readers as concomitant with their enjoyment of a metaphor.

But further, as soon as the embryo of the metaphor comes to consciousness, it begins straightway to branch and divide. Having found its beginning, the same process occurs in us that took place in the mind of the writer. The metaphor grows and branches into two main trunks. We follow this division with a symmetrical expansion of the two lungs, a bracing of the two feet on the floor, a sense of balance ever returning to a single center and ever distributing itself anew. We experience the metaphor, not only mentally but physically as well. Its reading brings about in our physical organisms harmonious action which is felt by us as distinctly pleasurable.

The effect of metaphor upon the reader is, then, agreeable, because metaphor stimulates him to actions, both of mind and of body, which fulfill the law of unity in variety, which offer an outlet for pent energies, which establish a symmetrical exercise, a moving poise for the physical functions, and which consequently are felt as pleasure.

Notes for *The Metaphor*

This excerpt is taken from the Library of Congress copy of Gertrude Buck, *The Metaphor: A Study in the Psychology of Rhetoric*, Contributions to Rhetorical Theory no. 5., Fred Newton Scott, series ed. (Ann Arbor, Mich.: N.p., 1899), 36–41, 58–59. In all these selections from Gertrude Buck's works, I have tried to include sections not already available in JoAnn Campbell's excellent edition, *Toward a Feminist Rhetoric: The Writing of Gertrude Buck* (Pittsburgh: University of Pittsburgh Press, 1996).

1. Algernon Swinburne, *Atalanta in Calydon* (1865), First Chorus, l. 101.
2. Dante Gabriel Rossetti, "The Blessed Damosel" (1891), l. 12.
3. Rossetti, "The Blessed Damosel," ll. 3–4.
4. William Wordsworth, "I Wandered Lonely as a Cloud" (1804), l. 1.
5. Robert Browning, "A Face" (1888–1894), l. 13.

6. Alfred Lord Tennyson, "The Princess" (1907–1908), ll. 353–54.

7. Buck's note here reads "See Ch. I."

8. Matthew Arnold, "The Forsaken Merman" (1849), l. 110.

9. Matthew Arnold, "The Forsaken Merman" (1849), l. 103.

10. Alfred, Lord Tennyson, "Ode on the Death of the Duke of Wellington" (1852), l. 7.

11. Robert Browning, "Gold Hair: A Story of Pornic," ll. 46–47.

12. John Keats, "The Eve of Saint Agnes" (1819), xxx, l. 266; and xxxiii, l. 297.

13. Buck's footnote reads, "Precisely this statement is made by the following writers: 'A metaphor is a simile with the words *like* or *as* left out.'—J[ohn] M. D. Meiklejohn, *The English Language* (1891), p. 190. 'The simile and the metaphor are . . . essentially alike: and a metaphor can be made from any simile by omitting the word *like* or *as*.'—W[illiam] E. Mead, *El[ementary] Comp[osition] and Rhet[oric]* (1894), p. 46. 'A metaphor differs from a simile in form only, not in substance.'—[Henry Home, Lord] Kames, *El[ements] of Crit[icism]*, Chap. XX, see 6. 'The metaphor is a shorter simile.'—Goldsmith, *Essay* (unacknowledged) *on the Use of Metaphors*. 'The metaphor is . . . an abridged simile.'—D[avid] J. Hill, *Elements of Rhetoric [and Composition]* (1878), p. 83. Metaphor is 'an abridged comparison.'—[Hugh] Blair, [*Lectures on Rhetoric and Belles Lettres* (1785)]. 'Metaphora brevior est similitudo.'—Quintilian, *Institutes*, Bk. VIII, Ch. VI, see 8. 'Eine abgekürzte Vergleichung.'—Brinkmann, *Die Metaphern*, p. 25. Metaphor is 'no other in effect than a comparison in epitome.'—G[eorge] Campbell, *Philosophy of Rhetoric* (1776), Bk. III, Ch. II, Pt. I. 'A metaphor is a simile in one word.'—[James Burnett], Lord Monboddo, *Of the Origin and Progress of Language* (1774), Vol. VI, Bk. II, Ch. I, p. 101. 'A metaphor is a brief similitude contracted into a single word.'—Cicero, *De Oratore*, Bk. III, ch. xxxix."

14. Buck's footnote reads: "Evidence of the existence of this tension and of the pleasurable effect of its breaking was furnished, outside my own experiences, in the course of some experiments made by me in the laboratory of psychology at the University of Michigan in 1895. In reading to several hundred students, taken singly, metaphors selected for the purpose, I noticed the grave, intent, expectant look, which was visible on the face of the individual while the first words were being read, break into a sudden smile or even a subvocal laugh, as the meaning of the figure flashed upon his mind—that is, when he had traced back the two conflicting images to their root in the speaker's mind and was thus enabled to 'see how he got it.'"

15. Buck's footnote reads, "*Psych[ology] Rev[iew]*, vol. I, p. 559." John Dewey (1859–1952), American philosopher, revolutionized education by his emphasis on adaptation to change in society and learning through practice.

From *A Course in Expository Writing* (1899)

Coauthored with Elisabeth Woodbridge

Preface

The English teacher, more perhaps than any other, is consciously aiming, not to give his students information, but to make them acquire capacity—capacity, in this case, for expressing their thought to others. But it is only by writing that the student can learn to write well, though much writing may not teach this, and one of the difficulties which an English teacher has to meet is a no less fundamental one than the difficulty of getting his students to write at all—to write, that is, not perfunctorily, but spontaneously, for this is the only kind of writing that counts.

This difficulty has its source, at least very largely, in the students' sense of the artificial character of his work. What is the use, he thinks, of writing about the birthplace of Hawthorne, or the character of Lady Macbeth?[1] His teacher knows all about them beforehand, and besides, he isn't writing to his teacher, he isn't writing to anybody, he is just "writing a composition" that is to be corrected for spelling, punctuation, paragraphing, or for its lack of certain qualities, such as "clearness," "precision," and "unity." No wonder he finds it hard to write. We ourselves, when alone, do not usually talk aloud about the things around us, describe the picture before us, or the desk, or the view. We should feel "silly" to be talking to nobody. Why should we expect a child to talk to nobody on paper? He feels "silly," too, or at least uncomfortable. But give him somebody to talk to, a real audience, and a subject that his audience is interested in, and his whole attitude will change. Tell him to "describe a game of basketball," and he will be lifeless enough; but find some classmates who like football better, and tell him to describe the game to them so as to convert them, or let each side try to convert the other, with the class as judge—then he has something worth doing. Evidently it is the subject, as well as the audience, that has been wrong; give a boy or girl something that he—not we—calls "interesting," and give him somebody who is interested, or whom he must make interested, and he will write for you. Not that "the character of Lady Macbeth" is in itself an unfit subject. Take a class studying *Macbeth* for college preparatory work and set them talking about the characters. Some will pity Macbeth and despise his lady; others will feel differently. Discussion will arise; sides will be taken. Before they have reached a decision, tell each student to defend his opinion in writing. The results will be spirited, and the effect of the writing, when read to the class, will be eagerly watched, while if a little argument creeps into the exposition, no harm is done.

All sorts of such devices can be found to provide the students with an audience, and of course it will be best of all if they feel that the teacher himself is a real, not a sham, audience, that he is listening for what they have to say, as well as holding himself ready to correct the way they say it. And when the students have got a little out of the old rut of writing compositions addressed to nobody, and have had some experience in writing to real readers, they will be able to imagine audiences for themselves, and write with vigor to these hypothetical hearers.

And in general it may be suggested that it is always best, not first to tell a student how to write a thing and then bid him do it, but first to get him to do it and afterwards to let him see how it was done. Take, for example, the various forms of the paragraph—the paragraph "by method of specific instance" or "by method of contrast." These forms have arisen because they were the best ones for the treatment of a given subject. Give the student such a subject, and he is more than likely to drop naturally into this form. Tell him to write a paper about the intelligence of his dog or cat or parrot, and if he does not do it by the method of "specific instance," he is a remarkable boy. Or tell him to discuss the comparative merits of setters and collies; he cannot help doing it by the method of "contrast." Having dropped into the form, he will be interested in seeing how better writers than he have used it, and will get hints from them as to ways of making his own work more effective, while at the same time he will come to realize that writing is not made from rules, but rules are discovered in writing.

Chapter I
The Basis of Exposition

All language, written or spoken, has one object, to put the person addressed in possession of certain ideas, to make him possess those ideas as firmly as though he had arrived at them independently. We have seen a beautiful orchid, our friend has not seen it, and we try to make language take the place of experience for him; in common parlance, we "try to make him see it." Or, there is a practical issue before us; our friend wants to go trout fishing, and we know a certain pool that has not been fished out. We could take him there, but that is not feasible, and we fall back upon language to put him in possession of the ideas he needs to have. Perhaps, however, he has never been trout fishing, and does not know a trout when he sees it. "How can I tell one when I catch him?" he asks, and we try to tell him how.

For all our own convictions have been gained through sense experience, and we unconsciously recognize this when we revert to experience in communicating with others. The farther removed we are from the direct testimony of the senses, the more liability there is to misunderstandings, and these can best be cleared up by reverting again to sense experience. When this cannot be done, we are lost indeed. Suppose that in discussing some question of beauty or taste, I find myself differing with my companion; to settle the trouble, we resort to a concrete instance, and at once I discover that my companion is partially color-blind. Instantly I realize that no matter how long I talk, I can never really communicate to him certain ideas whose foundation is in our color sense, for there is nothing more fundamental, where we can find a common meeting ground, and from which we can attempt an explanation. I may discover that his sense of hearing agrees with mine, and perhaps I may appeal to that and tell him that "red is like the sound of a trumpet," or I may appeal to his sense of temperature, and tell him that red is "hot" and green is "cool," but so long as he cannot practically tell green from red, what use is it? And how can I hope that the line,

> The multitudinous seas incarnadine,[2]

will ever have for him the associative meaning that it has for me? Such difference in sense perception is fundamental and insurmountable.

In the following discussion, therefore, one thing has been taken for granted: namely, that the impressions of our eyes and ears and other sense organs are the basis of our knowledge; rightly understood, they are our knowledge. Hence, although expository writing aims to communicate to others our interpretation of sense experience—which we may call knowledge or opinion according to the degree of our conviction—yet we shall understand its principles best if we approach it through a study of description, which is the communication of our immediate sense experience itself.

Chapter II
The Process of Description

When we describe anything to someone else, our prime object is, as has been said, to make him perceive a thing as we perceive it. If it be something seen, we try to make our words do the duty of his eyes; if something heard, we must find ways to make him feel that he, too, has heard what we have. This object is clear enough, but how may it be attained? Horace's rule, "If you wish to make me weep, you must weep yourself,"[3] was nearly right, but not quite. He should have said, "If you wish to make me weep, you must know what ideas were the ones that made you weep, and you must convey those ideas to me." That is, if we wish to make another person see or hear as we have seen or heard, we must know what our own experience has been, and try to reproduce its stages in their order.

It may be said, "When we see a thing, our experience has no 'stages' and no 'order.' We see it all at once, and that is the end." It was in this conviction that Lessing maintained the insurmountable difficulty inherent in descriptive writing to be that it required us to describe in sequence what had taken place simultaneously.[4] It was for this reason that he regarded Homer's method in describing the shield of Achilles as the right one, because instead of taking the shield ready-made, he took it in process of making, and thus turned description into narration.[5] To a certain extent, Lessing's view was right, inasmuch as words are slow things compared with the senses, and language is slow in reproducing what the senses have been quick in perceiving. But though there is this disparity in speed, it ought to be recognized for what it is—a difference in degree, not in kind. For our sense perceptions only appear instantaneous; they are not really so, but, as we shall see, follow a discoverable order and sequence. And it is this order and sequence which we must observe, that we may reproduce it in the mind of our listener. For if we have answered the question, "How did we see the thing?" we have gone a long way toward answering the second question, "How can we make someone else see the thing?"

First, then, how do we see? The initial difficulty in answering this question is that, in general, our seeing of things has through habit become so rapid a process that it does seem instantaneous, and when we try to discover stages, we find it almost impossible. It may, therefore, be of service to begin with cases where from the nature of the circumstances these processes are retarded and their consummation delayed. This is exactly what happens when the object seen is distant and our approach gradual, and here it is easy to recognize distinct stages in perception.

Evidently, the only effective way of accomplishing [making others see], which is the end of description, is by instituting in the minds of our hearers the same processes through which we have ourselves passed. Our general order of procedure is therefore established for us by what we have found out as to the order of our own experience. If, having seen a bunch of poppies ourselves, we wish to make another person see them, we shall not begin by mentioning the furry stems or the black centers, but by emphasizing the color masses, the slenderness and height, leaving details to be mentioned later.

❧

The question at once arises, "How shall we go to work, if we want to convey to someone else the whole of such a fully developed impression?" The difficulties are, indeed, great. It is not easy to make someone else share our first comprehensive perception of a thing, but it is perhaps even less easy to make him partaker in our final comprehensive perception, with its clear definition of parts, its fullness of detail. Here, as always, the only possible salvation is an appeal to our own experience, to discover how we ourselves perceived details.

In the earlier experiment we saw that, as we looked at the object, our perception gradually made explicit what was at first implicit; that it did not add new bits of perception, new fragments of details, as one might add fresh patches to complete a quilt, but that our first perception grew into our last by a process of defining what was always inherent in it. The secondary and tertiary impressions were not superimposed upon the first, or added alongside it; they grew out of it.

In conveying our experience to another person, we shall, therefore, naturally try to follow the order of our own experience. We shall first transfer to him our own general impression, which will contain in itself the main values; then we shall try to follow with him the development of our perception as these main values gain in definition. No amount of detail will confuse him if he has been already prepared for it, as we ourselves were—if he has the germ out of which it naturally grows.

The difference between the right and the wrong way of going to work may be illustrated by a case from common experience. Having never seen the moon save with the naked eye, we are taken to a powerful telescope and told to look. As we place our eye at the eyepiece, our vision is dazed and blinded by a confusion of lights and shadows; there seem to be meaningless masses, meaningless crags and chasms and peaks, and we withdraw in bewilderment, and look out with a feeling of relief at the little pale disk with its large familiar outlines of "eyes, nose, and mouth," of the "man and the dog," or of the "lady." There seems no connection between that comfortably intelligible moon and the chaos of lights we have just seen. But let us turn an ordinary field glass upon its surface: the "man" has disappeared, but we still see the conformations that made us think of him, and after a moment's adjustment to the new view, we are ready to look through the "finder" of the telescope and adapt ourselves to a yet bigger scale of vision. Here we see nearly the whole disk, much more magnified than in the field lens, but bearing about the same relation to the image which that had given us, as that image bore to the one furnished by the lens of our eye. Again we establish general relations, identify this and that crater or peak or crack, and now we are ready to return to the huge lens and to look with delighted appreciation at the details of crag and chasm which had at first baffled our understanding.

Elaborate description should in its general procedure follow the processes of experience just suggested; it ought to use the naked eye before it resorts to the "finder," and it ought to use both before it employs the high-power lens. But too often it leaves out all intermediate processes and the unfortunate observer finds himself before the eyepiece of the telescope where he must, in weariness and bewilderment, make out for himself the general values and relations which should first have been supplied him. He can sometimes do it, but it is not wise nor economical of energy to demand that he shall.

In detailed description, then, nothing ought to be presented to the listener for which provision has not been made, which has not been really implied or suggested in his first general view of the whole. The process should be one not of accretion, but of development.

Evidently by this method any amount of detail can be assimilated, because nothing is presented that has not some germ of suggestion out of which it grows. And if the result can be attained when dealing with this subject, it can be attained with any subject.

Description, then, is successful just so far as it follows the actual order of the sensuous experience it describes. In written description the process of perception will, moreover, be reflected in the structure; its paragraphs will possess the qualities of "unity," "coherence," "proportion." For paragraphs are not arbitrary groupings, made to break the page and assist the eye; they are the outer expression of thought-groups as they exist in the mind. And just as in determining the order of expression we found it necessary to appeal to the order of our own experience and reproduce that, so in determining the grouping of sentences which shall on the written page constitute a paragraph, we are in little danger of going wrong if we honestly follow the order of our own thoughts. For, as we have seen, we perceive things as wholes; our first impression contains in the germ all that is in our last, most detailed impression. If our expression conveys this, it will constitute a paragraph, which will be a whole as the experience it relates is a whole. It may be a single sentence giving merely the first general impression, or little more than this, as in Mr. Burroughs' columbine; or it may be many sentences, and be as complex as was the experience, as in Ruskin's description of St. Marks.[6] But so long as it honestly follows the real experience, it will be right. It will possess unity, because the experience it embodies possessed it; it will possess coherence or continuity, because the stages of perception themselves cohere, being continuously developed each out of the preceding; it will possess proportion, because no detail will have a place which did not also have its part implicit in the first impression, and the place and value of each detail is determined not arbitrarily, but by the fact of its real place and value in the perceptive stages.

We may illustrate this by the analogy of a tree, with its main trunk, its limbs, branches, and twigs. The tree is complex, but it is a coherent, proportioned whole: the size of the trunk determines the size of the limbs into which it divides; the branches and twigs have their number, size, and position determined by the size and position of the limbs from which they spring. In a description, the first general impression corresponds to the main trunk; the first set of details growing out of this impression corresponds to the large limbs; the later sets of details growing out of the earlier ones correspond to the branches and twigs. The relative elaboration of various groups of details will depend upon the relative importance of the impression out of which they grow, as the elaboration—if we may transfer the word—of the branch into branchlets and twigs is conditioned by the size of the branch.

The question "When shall a paragraph end and another begin?" is to be met by the same appeal to experience. The paragraph ends when the perception, whatever its scope, is complete. A new one begins whenever the perception dealt with is thought of as in some way new and different.

Chapter III
Description in Its Relation to Exposition

Thus we see that our impressions of the tangible world may have different values for us and we may in communicating them to others have different purposes. We may want to convey simply our immediate sense impression, or we may want to convey our sense of the meaning of the impression, our conviction as to the nature of the thing perceived. Not that any antithesis is assumed between appearance and reality. Appearance rightly understood is reality. But because this right understanding does not always inhere in the immediate sense impressions, because the reality is implicit rather than explicit in their sensuous appeal, the record of this appeal, where its full significance has been perceived, ought to be so made as to carry this significance with it. When the description subserves such an interpretative purpose, we call it "expository," since it has ceased to be a final end and has become a means. But there is naturally no definite boundary to be fixed between the one and the other kind of thing, and we may often be in doubt how to class a given bit of writing.

Chapter IV
Definition in Its Relation to Exposition

The word "definition" naturally brings to our mind the notion of such formal statements as this: "An animal is a living organism broadly distinguished from a plant by incapacity to convert inorganic into organic matter." What is the object of such a definition, and how is it attained? Evidently it aims to tell us exactly what an animal is, and this is accomplished by doing two things: first, by assigning the object to a large class, in this case, "living organisms"; and second, by distinguishing it from other members of that class, in this case, "plants." We might picture a tabular scheme of the result, thus:

$$\text{Living organisms.} \begin{cases} \text{Those which can convert} \\ \quad \text{inorganic into organic} \\ \quad \text{matter} \\ \text{Those which cannot} \end{cases} \begin{matrix} \Big\}....\text{Plants} \\ \\ \\ ....\text{Animals} \end{matrix}$$

This is the method pursued by all definitions: they, on the one hand, assign the subject defined to a class or genus, and, on the other, state what qualities it has which are not found in all members of the class and which therefore constitute a distinct species within the class. The two processes are respectively designated by the terms "classification" or "identification" on the one hand, and "discrimination" or "differentiation" on the other, and a definition is technically said to define an object by giving its "genus" and its "differentia."

Clearly, the aim of definition is identical with that of exposition as we have observed it in the preceding chapter: both aim to convey an adequate notion of the thing itself, of its real nature. Both, therefore, must be called "exposition." But do they pursue this common aim by totally dissimilar methods? Is exposition by definition, as a process, to be set absolutely apart from exposition by description? Or is it possible that this new form of exposition may be related to the other as that was to description?

The question which arose as to the relation between such exposition [by description] and exposition by definition is now answered. Not only do the two have the same end; they use the same method, the method of classification and differentiation; only, whereas in the formal definition the method is immediately apparent, in the cases we have just been considering, it is sometimes discernible only after some scrutiny, being obscured by the emphasis placed on the "differentia" of the subject instead of on the "genus." The manner in which the emphasis will fall will vary infinitely, being dependent on the writer's habit of mind, on his purpose, and on the nature of the subject.

That both processes must be at least implicit in any expository expression follows from the nature of our mental processes. We are aiming to convey what we conceive to be the true nature of a thing. But in reaching, ourselves, this perception of its true nature, we must consider something besides the individual thing; for we do not really know what it is until we know what it is not; we cannot recognize its characteristic traits as characteristic unless we know which traits are not characteristic but common to other things, as well. We cannot know the individual unless we also know the class.

Even in the processes of immediate sense perception—and therefore in description as the record of that process—this consciousness of the class is involved, although the emphasis is more consistently upon the individual than anywhere else. In Mr. Burroughs' description of the columbine,[7] for example, there is a recognition of the class, as well as of the individual; indeed, the significance of the passage depends on our perception of contrasts between class and individual. The thought implied is: the columbine belongs to that class of flowers which are most exquisitely beautiful. This particular columbine belongs to its class and possesses the class characteristics, but it also possesses individual characteristics, not shared by all columbines: it is also "magical and audacious." The classification, partly implied, partly expressed, and indispensable to the effect of the description, might be represented thus:

Familiar
wild-flowers. $\begin{cases} \text{Those which} \\ \text{are exquisitely} \\ \text{Beautiful.} \end{cases}$ Columbine $\begin{cases} \text{This columbine, whose} \\ \text{exquisite beauty was} \\ \text{further differentiated by} \\ \text{being magical and audacious} \end{cases}$

A little observation of one's own experience will show how inevitable is this process of classification as an accompaniment of all our sense perception. . . . The simple naming of a thing involves such classification, although it is so rapid and habitual that its nature is no longer recognized.

On the whole, however, all the writing we have thus far considered, except the formal definition quoted at the beginning of the chapter, is characterized by the fact that, while both processes are involved, it is the discrimination process which is given most scope. The genus is rather assumed, and the attention is invited to the differentia; our faces are set toward the individual. . . . It is easy to see how the relative proportion might be reversed, and the emphasis be placed on the genus instead of the individual, . . . on columbines instead of that columbine "I saw one spring day."

Both processes will in such cases [of exposition by definition] still be involved, but instead of assuming the generic qualities and elaborately discussing the individual, we shall assume the individual traits and elaborate the generic.

The traits that characterize the genus, then—keeping so far as possible free from the technical terminology—may be summed up about as follows:

Columbines are low herbs growing in delicately massed clumps, with finely cut leaves, and flowers nodding from slender stems. The flowers themselves, varying in color, are from one and a half to three inches long, and look something like a shuttlecock, with spurs instead of feathers.[8]

Notes for *A Course in Expository Writing*

This selection is taken from the Library of Congress copy of Gertrude Buck and Elisabeth Woodbridge, *A Course in Expository Writing* (New York: Henry Holt, 1899), iii–v, vii–viii, 1, 4, 6, 9–11, 13, 16, 21–23, 25–27, 29, 63, 156–57, and 162–66; I have modernized spelling and punctuation conventions.

1. The birthplace of an author (or at least a famous person's biography) and a character sketch of a character from a Shakespeare play (especially *Lady Macbeth*) were favorite theme topics for late nineteenth-century composition classes.

2. Shakespeare, *Macbeth* 2.2.59.

3. Horace, *Ars Poetica* ll. 103–4.

4. Gotthold Ephraim Lessing (1729–1781) was a German professor and literary critic, noted especially for his treatise, *Laokoon, or On the Limits of Painting and Poetry* (1766), in which he discussed literature (and thus description) as bound by temporal, consecutive order, and painting and sculpture, in contrast, as spatial and simultaneous; receiving a verbal description is thus much slower than perceiving a painting.

5. For the description of Achilles's shield, see Homer's *Iliad*, bk. 18.

6. Buck had discussed these descriptions by Burroughs and Ruskin earlier in her chapter. See John Burroughs, *Riverby* (1894); and John Ruskin, *The Stones of Venice* (1851).

7. See note 6.

8. A shuttlecock, hit back and forth in badminton, in Buck's day was made of feathers stuck in a cork.

From *A Course in Argumentative Writing* (1899)

Preface

This book arises out of certain beliefs concerning the study of argumentation, which, though perhaps not wholly novel, have as yet found no recognition in the literature of the subject. The first of these beliefs is that the principles of argumentation should be derived by the student from its practice before the practice is made to conform to the principles. In short—one may as well acknowledge it—a firm faith in the so-called "inductive method" as applied to argumentation lies at the root of this treatise. Such a faith implies, of course, that the student should be asked to dissect out logical formulae for himself from his own unconscious reasonings, using them, when discovered, to render those reasonings more exact. The construction and the rough analysis of arguments would, similarly, precede the formulation of any principles of persuasion.

From the conviction that the student should formulate his own principles of argumentation follows the second article of faith: that the subjects set for argument and the material used for analysis should be not remote from the student's natural interests, but interwoven with his daily experiences. If the student is to gain his principles from his unconscious practice, it follows that he will, for a time at least, be concerned with arguments about the probable score of the coming football game or the fairness of a certain examination, rather than the desirability of a high protective tariff for the United States or the iniquity of free silver. . . .

The third canon of which this book is exponent is also involved, though somewhat indirectly, in the first. This is the conviction that the logical basis of argumentation should be ultimately referred to psychology. This is an old word in philosophy, but it has not yet found a place in treatises on argumentation. The logical substructure of arguments is universally recognized, but seldom is the psychological stratum beneath that pointed out; and thus, cut off from its deepest roots, logic has come to seem rather like a dead tool than like a living expression of thought. Beginning, however, as this study of argumentation does, with the unconscious reasonings of the student, it is bound to see them as they are, not compositions carefully planned to exhibit logical principles, but natural outputs of typical mental processes. Each argument is referred not only to its logical but to its psychological antecedent, so that the maxims and formulae, usually regarded by the learner as malign inventions of Aristotle,[1] represent to our student rather the ways in which real people really think. In fact, he himself thinks and argues in these ways—he has often caught himself doing so. And from this fact, the abstract logical equations acquire a distinct flavor of personal interest. Knowing them thus inwardly, not as a mere external imposition upon his memory, he has them better in hand as a tool. He uses them not gingerly, but with the dash of intimacy.

Chapter I
Argumentation

Argumentation . . . is the act of establishing in the mind of another person a conclusion which has become fixed in your own, by means of setting up in the other person's mind the train of thought or reasoning which has previously led you to this conclusion.[2] Here we have a statement both of the end and of the means employed for attaining the end. The goal is the establishment of a certain belief or conclusion in the mind of the hearer or reader. But as soon as this goal is clearly recognized, the question arises—how is it to be attained? How can this conclusion be implanted in the mind of the reader or hearer? It is evident at first glance that no conclusion of a process of thought can be introduced bodily into any person's mind without the train of reasoning which naturally leads to it. A conclusion is not an isolated thing which can be thrown into another mind from without. A belief is not accepted by one who sees no justification for it. To convince any person of the truth of a proposition requires that he reach that proposition himself as the logical outcome of some process of thought. Hence it is necessary, if one wishes to persuade another person to a certain conclusion, that he set up in that person's mind a train of reasoning which is bound to issue in this conclusion.

This, then, is the problem of argumentation: given the conclusion which is to be established in the mind of the hearer or reader, to find the train of ideas which is bound to lead to this conclusion. The solution which at once presents itself is that of using the train of ideas which, in the speaker's mind, has already served to establish the conclusion in question. Let us say, for instance, that the speaker has come to the conclusion that teachers in the primary schools of this country receive very small salaries. If he wishes to convince another person of the truth of this judgment, he will naturally cite the various cases in which such teachers are poorly paid, which, coming to his knowledge, have induced him to this belief. . . .

This is the most obvious way of finding a train of reasoning pretty certain to issue in the conclusion to be established—looking into one's own mind and noting the series of ideas which there have actually established the conclusion for one's self. One feels assured that this series should lead to the desired conclusion in another person's mind simply because in his own it has already done so. And, in view of the fact that the mental processes of all normal people follow the same general laws, this assurance is by no means unreasonable.

Chapter II
Inductive Reasoning

We do not know all clergymen of the English Church; neither ourselves nor our friends have been able to observe that more than a hundred or so wear vestments while conducting the service, but we are nevertheless fully persuaded in our own minds that this is the habitual practice of all clergymen of the English Church. We return, then, to our question, as yet unanswered—whence comes our right to this conclusion?

It is evident that something lies back of this reasoning process to justify it, a principle too self-evident to be spoken of under ordinary circumstances. When we find a certain characteristic in several members of a class, we consider ourselves entitled to suppose its existence in all the other members of that same class, though we have not examined each of them separately. When we see that the leaves on one side of a tree are five-pointed, fine-textured, and pale green, we expect those on the other side to have these same characteristics. If we know that some chestnut burrs are brown and spiny, we cannot imagine finding others smooth and pink.

From this tacit expectation arises the principle[3] taken for granted whenever we reason inductively: *What is true of several members of a class is true of the class as a whole.* Starting with this assumption, we are enabled to reason as follows. Since whatever is true of several members of a class is true of the class as a whole, if I find it true of several buttercups that they are yellow, I can conclude that buttercups as a class are yellow. If all the Episcopal clergymen I know wear vestments in conducting church services, all Episcopal clergymen may be judged to do so.

Chapter III
Inductive Argument

When one has carried on a reasoning process such as that discussed in the foregoing chapters, and come to a certain conclusion about a class of things, he often has occasion to transfer this conclusion to the mind of some other person. He may wish, let us say, to make someone else believe, as he does, that college men are generally successful in business. In order to introduce this conclusion in the mind of another person, he will, it is certain, need to begin with a train of reasoning which logically leads to the conclusion. Such a train of reasoning has already passed through his own mind, leaving behind it this conclusion which he wishes to induce another person to accept. He therefore notes carefully what this train of reasoning has been, with a view to securing its entrance into the mind of his auditor.

Let us say that our believer in the success of college men in business has come to this faith through knowledge of several collegians whose financial success was marked. "All the men in my class," he says to himself, "who went into business, made a good thing of it. Some did better than others, of course, but nobody has failed to make a handsome living. Then there is my father, and his partner, and both my uncles, and Grant, and Tobey, and Rolf, and Stevens, and Van Tassel—all of them are college men who have made fortunes in business."

This being the course of reasoning which has brought him to the conclusion that college men are successful in business, he naturally attempts to start this same course of reasoning in the mind of the friend whom he would induce to his belief. Accordingly, he cites each of these instances of a college man's success in business, one after another, certain that if each fact be accepted by the hearer, the conclusion must obtain lodgment in his mind.

It may be, however, that in seeking to establish this conclusion in his friend's mind, he will not be content with the simple enumeration of the facts which have determined his own belief. These may have been very few in number, but successful in establishing the conclusion to his own satisfaction, either because uncontradicted by any opposing facts, or because in themselves peculiarly conspicuous. But he will not rely upon these few facts, although so effective in his own case, to accomplish the same conviction in the case of his hearer. To the hearer they may seem far less cogent, lacking, perhaps, the flavor of personal, first-hand knowledge; in which case the speaker must either increase very largely his number of supporting instances or furnish some from the common acquaintance of speaker and auditor. Then, too, it may be that the hearer is acquainted with certain collegians whose inefficiency in business matters is notorious. This case, however, demands a separate treatment.

It seems a matter of small difficulty to introduce an inductive conclusion into the mind of another person by citing the particular facts which have given rise to it, provided no opposing facts lurk in the consciousness of the other person. But when the entrance of the conclusion is resisted by an antagonistic conclusion, drawn from facts in the hearer's own experience or observation, the problem becomes doubly complicated. In this case the first necessity is plainly to uproot the opposing conclusion. How this is done we shall see if we inquire how any inductive conclusion is displaced from our own minds, after it has once obtained a foothold there.

We have repeatedly noticed in our own experience the overthrow of generalizations once implicitly credited. As children we believed that all dogs were ferocious beasts, because one had bitten a playmate; that all stepmothers were harsh and cruel, because one in a story was so; that all girls named Florence had blue eyes and yellow hair, because the only two Florences known to us happened to be of the blonde type. But we discarded these conclusions after a while, without argument. How did we come to do so?

These are the two ways, therefore, which are open to one who wishes to displace a similar conclusion by means of argument. One, which may be called the direct way, is by simply disproving the facts on which the conclusion rests. In doing this, new facts will inevitably arise which issue in a contrary conclusion, tending to supplant the original generalization. The other way is more indirect. The old conclusion is not openly attacked, but other facts are brought forward which compel a new generalization, exactly antagonistic to the old. The two conclusions cannot stand together in the same mind; hence, it becomes necessary to get rid of one, either by disproving its facts, as in direct refutation, or by setting it aside, its facts being allowed to stand, but regarded as exceptional and therefore not affecting the rule. The conclusion which is set aside, in this case, is of course altogether likely to be the one supported by the fewest or by the most disputable facts.

Exercises

1. Write a short argument inducing the person named in each case to accept any one of the following conclusions. Before writing the argument, set down, in this order, the particular assumption, the facts you mean to use, and the conclusion. If, when you have finished the argument, you find you have in any way deviated from your plan, as by using more facts or different ones, add a second skeleton of the argument, representing it as you actually wrote it.

(a) Great cities are located on large bodies of water. (To an inhabitant of Squedunk, who boasts that that inland town will become the metropolis of the state.)

(b) Literary men make unhappy marriages. (To a friend who has never noticed that fact.)

(c) Haste makes waste. (To a companion who exhorts you to hurry, when you are not disposed to do so.)

2. Having exchanged themes with some member of the class who has written upon another subject than the one you chose, take the point of view of the person to whom his argument is addressed, analyze the argument carefully, disprove the facts alleged in support of the conclusion, or cite a larger number of other facts leading to the contrary conclusion, or use both these methods of refutation.

Appendix A
Inductive Reasoning in Modern Educational Methods

The essential nature of inductive reasoning may be illumined by some illustrations of its more obvious uses, both practical and theoretic. One particularly interesting illustration on the practical side is here presented as a suggestion to the teacher. Similarly, the inductive process might be traced in the generalizations of popular philosophy, both those which have crystallized into proverbs and those which have not yet assumed an exact formulation, in superstitions (both primitive and more developed) and in the laws determined by every branch of science.

The inductive process of reasoning has recently become very conspicuous in our methods of education. The old idea of education was to give a student all the generalizations he needed, and let him only apply them to particular cases. Thus, in mathematics he would be told that the square of the hypothenuse in a right-angled triangle equals the sum of the squares of the other two sides, so that all he had to do when he wished to know the length of the hypotenuse in a certain right-angled triangle was to add the squares of the other two sides and extract the square root. In language study he learned from a book that a certain combination of letters always stands for a certain word, so that he needed only when he met this particular combination of letters, to conclude that here, as everywhere else, it had the meaning assigned to it by the dictionary. When studying literature, he would read in a book that the poetry of Milton[4] is sonorous and involved, so that he would be relieved of any obligation to do more than notice the involutions and the sonorities in that particular poem of Milton's which he chanced to be reading.

The introduction of the laboratory method in natural science has, however, changed all this. The laboratory method means nothing else but induction. It means that the student, instead of accepting the inductive conclusions of other people, reaches his own, from facts that fall under his personal observation. Instead of being told that an explosion always results when oxygen and hydrogen are brought together and ignited, the student learns that this is so by trying it several times for himself. He learns that a salt is formed by the union of an acid and a base, because he has found it so innumerable times; that a submerged body displaces its own volume of water, by submerging several bodies of known volumes and measuring the water displaced.

This method, transferred to language study, has given us the system by which the student, beginning to read before any grammatical principles have been imparted, formulates for himself the law that a certain combination of letters or sounds always means a certain definite thing, that the object of a verb always ends in certain letters, or that nouns with certain meanings are always neuter. These generalizations, formerly given to the student in the form of rules which he must apply, must now be discovered, as well as applied, by himself.

One of the most conspicuous instances of the use of the inductive method in education appears in the modern teaching of English. In this subject students are not now set to master general principles of composition from books of rhetoric, but are required to formulate these for themselves from particular pieces of literature which are given them to study, and from their own writing. For instance, after noting several times that a piece of prose which is easy to read has a distinct plan, the student is led to the generalization that all pieces of prose which are easy to read have a distinct plan. And such a generalization would be still further confirmed if several times, when the student has taken care to have a plan, his writing has proved easy to read.

In much the same way he determines laws for the employment of certain methods in the processes of description and exposition, for the use of unified paragraphs, clear sentences, and suggestive words. He is not told that concrete words produce a sharper effect upon the reader's mind than abstract ones, but discovers the truth for himself, to apply as he finds occasion for it.

Notes for *A Course in Argumentative Writing*

This selection is taken from the Library of Congress copy of Gertrude Buck, *A Course in Argumentative Writing* (New York: Henry Holt, 1899), pp. iii, iv–v, 3–5, 12–13, 26–34, 153–55; I have modernized spelling and punctuation conventions.

1. Aristotle (384–322 B.C.E.) discovered deductive reasoning and founded modern logic; the principles of the syllogism that he outlined in several treatises were taught as the basis of argumentation for two thousand years.

2. Buck's note reads: "In its statement of the end to be attained this definition agrees substantially with such as the following: 'Argumentation is the art of producing in the mind of someone else a belief in the ideas which the speaker or writer wishes the hearer to accept' ([George P.] Baker, *Principles of Argumentation* [1895], p. 1). 'Argumentation is the process of proving or disproving a proposition' ([Elias J.] MacEwan, *Essentials of Argumentation* [1898], p. 1). In both of these definitions, however, the means to attaining the end remains unspecified. It may further be noted that these definitions do not insist upon the speaker's having previously arrived at the conclusion he would establish in the hearer's mind. It is, however, manifestly impossible that a speaker should be able to conduct his hearer to a goal which he himself has not, at least in imagination, reached. Even when he wishes to convince another person of the truth of a proposition which he himself does not believe, he must imagine himself as having come to belief in it, and trace out the route thereto, in order that he may be able to act as guide."

3. Buck's note reads: "Sometimes called the principle of the uniformity of nature."

4. John Milton (1608–1674), radical Protestant poet who wrote *Paradise Lost*.

"The Present Status of Rhetorical Theory" (1900)

Two opposing conceptions of the nature of discourse bequeathed to us from classic times still struggle for dominance in our modern rhetorical theory—the social conception of Plato, and the antisocial conception of the sophists.[1] The latter, though known to us only fragmentarily from allusions and quotations in later treatises, can be, in its essential outlines, easily reconstructed. According to the sophistic teaching, discourse was simply a process of persuading the hearer to a conclusion which the speaker, for any reason, desired him to accept. Analyzed further, this familiar definition discloses certain significant features.

First of all it conveys, though somewhat indirectly, a notion of the ultimate end of the process of discourse. Why should discourse take place at all? Why should the hearer be persuaded? Because, answers the definition, the speaker wishes to persuade him. And, to pursue the inquiry still further, the speaker wishes to persuade the hearer to a certain belief presumably because he recognizes some advantage to himself in doing so. We should conclude, therefore, from examination of the definition before us, that discourse is for the sake of the speaker.

Nor is this conclusion threatened by further investigation into the pre-Platonic philosophy of discourse. It is true that the practical precepts of the sophistic rhetoricians pay great deference to the hearer, even seeming, at first glance, to exalt him over the speaker. Every detail of the speech is to be sedulously "adapted" to the hearer. Nothing is to be done without reference to him. His tastes are to be studied, his prejudices regarded, his little jealousies and chagrins written down in a book; but all this, be it remembered, in order simply that he may the more completely be subjugated to the speaker's will. As the definition has previously suggested, the hearer's ultimate importance to discourse is of the slightest. To his interests the process of discourse is quite indifferent.

But not only does persuasion, according to the sophistic notion, fail to consider the interests of the hearer; frequently it even assails them. . . . If [the hearer's] own advantage should chance to lie in the same direction with that of the speaker, the utmost that the process of discourse could do would be merely to point out this fact to the hearer. In such a case little persuasive art is demanded. It is rather when the interests of the hearer, if rightly understood by him, oppose his acceptance of the conclusion urged by the speaker that real rhetorical skill comes into play. Then is the speaker confronted by a task worthy of his training—that of making the acceptance of this conclusion, which is really inimical to the hearer's interests, seem to him advantageous. In plainest statement, the speaker must by finesse assail the hearer's interests for the sake of his own.

This is a typical case of discourse, according to the sophistic conception. Its essentially antisocial character appears both in its conscious purpose and in its unrecognized issues. We have seen that the end it seeks is exclusively individual, sanctioned only by that primitive ethical principle of the dominance of the strong. The speaker through discourse secures his own advantage simply because he is able to do so. The meaning of his action to the hearer, or to society as a whole, is purely a moral question with which rhetoric is not directly concerned. There is, in the rhetorical theory of the sophists, no test for the process of discourse larger than the success of the speaker in attaining his own end.

But further, the sophistic conception of discourse is antisocial in its outcome. Instead of leveling conditions between the two parties to the act, as we are told is the tendency in all true social functioning, discourse renders these conditions more unequal than they were before it took place. The speaker, superior at the outset by virtue at least of a keener perception of the situation, through the process of discourse comes still further to dominate the hearer. As in primitive warfare the stronger of two tribal organizations subdues and eventually enslaves the weaker, so in discourse the initial advantage of the speaker returns to him with usury.

This antisocial character of the sophistic discourse, as seen both in its purpose and in its outcome, may be finally traced to the fact that the process, as we have analyzed it, just fails of achieving complete communication between speaker and hearer. Some conclusion is, indeed, established in the mind of the hearer, but not necessarily the conclusion which the speaker himself has reached upon this subject. It may, in fact, oppose all his own experience and thought, and thus hold no organic relation to his own mind. But wishing the hearer to believe it, he picks it up somewhere and proceeds to insert it into the hearer's mind.

This absence of a vital relationship between the normal activities of the speaker's mind and the action by which he seeks to persuade the hearer breaks the line of communication between the two persons concerned. Conditions at the ends of the circuit cannot be equalized, as in true social functioning, because the current is thus interrupted.

This conception of the process of discourse might be graphically represented in figure:

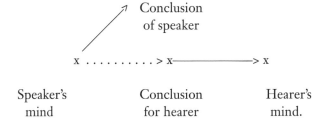

The sophistic account of discourse, then, makes it a process essentially individualistic, and thus socially irresponsible. It secures the advantage of the speaker without regard to that of the hearer, or even in direct opposition to it. Because this conception leaves a gap in the chain of communication between the minds of speaker and hearer, it fails to equalize conditions between peaker wins and the hearer loses continually. Discourse is purely predatory—a ression of the strong upon the weak. The art of rhetoric is the art of war.

Against this essentially crude and antisocial conception of discourse, Plato seems to have raised the first articulate protest. Discourse is not an isolated phenomenon, he maintained, cut off from all relations to the world in which it occurs, and exempt from the universal laws of justice and right. The speaker has certain obligations, not perhaps directly to the hearer, but to the absolute truth of which he is but the mouthpiece, to the entire order of things which nowadays we are wont to call "society." Discourse is, indeed, persuasion, but not persuasion to any belief the speaker pleases. Rather is it persuasion to the truth, knowledge of which, on the part of the hearer, ultimately advantages both himself and the speaker as well. The interests of both are equally furthered by legitimate discourse. In fact, the interests of both are, when rightly understood, identical; hence there can be no antagonism between them.

In respect, then, to the advantage gained by each party to the act of discourse, speaker and hearer stand on a footing of at least approximate equality. In fact, the ultimate end of discourse must be, from the Platonic premises, to establish equality between them. Before discourse takes place, the speaker has a certain advantage over the hearer. He perceives a truth as yet hidden from the hearer, but necessary for him to know. Since the recognition of this truth on the part of the hearer must ultimately serve the speaker's interests as well, the speaker, through the act of discourse, communicates to the hearer his own vision. This done, the original inequality is removed, the interests of both speaker and hearer are furthered, and equilibrium is at this point restored to the social organism.

It is plain that the circuit of communication between speaker and hearer is in Plato's conception of discourse continuous. The speaker having himself come to a certain conclusion does not set about establishing another in the hearer's mind, but simply transmits his own belief into the other's consciousness. The connection between the two minds is living and unbroken. The Platonic notion of the process of discourse may be thus illustrated as in this figure:

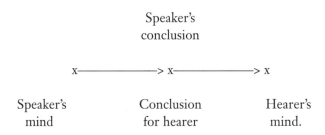

Thus have been hastily reviewed the two opposing conceptions of discourse delivered to us by the earliest rhetoricians. The changes which they have suffered in the lapse of centuries are surprisingly slight. We find implicit in many of our modern textbooks practically the same conception of discourse which was held by the pre-Platonic teachers of rhetoric—a conception which regards discourse as an act performed by the speaker upon the hearer for the advantage of the speaker alone. It is true that the present-day sophists include in the end of discourse not persuasion alone, but the production of any desired effect upon the hearer. This fact does not, however, modify fundamentally the nature of the process itself. The hearer (or reader as he has now become) is to be interested or amused, or reduced to tears, or overborne with a sense of the sublime, not indeed because the writer himself has previously been interested or amused and, in obedience to the primal social instinct, would communicate his experience to another, but because—well, because the writer wishes to produce this effect upon the reader. Thus wishing, and being able to gratify his desire, the act of discourse results, an act still individualistic and one-sided, serving no ends but those of the speaker himself. The effect to be produced upon the hearer, being wholly external to the experience of the speaker, leaves unjoined the old break between speaker and hearer in the process of communication. We have again, in but slightly altered guise, the sophistic conception of discourse.

But in spite of the persistence of this outworn conception in even some recent textbooks, there are not wanting many evidences that the Platonic theory of discourse is at last coming home to the modern consciousness. It is doubtless true that the later social theory of rhetoric would not venture to define the end of discourse as that of declaring to another the absolute and universal truth. There may be two reasons for this. In the first place, we are not nowadays on such joyfully intimate terms with the absolute truth as was Plato. And, again, the practical value of even a little relative and perhaps temporary truth has become clearer to us—such truth as touches us through our personal experiences and observations. Yet it must be remembered that Plato himself allowed the subject matter of discourse to be the speaker's own vision of the absolute truth, thus individualizing the abstraction until we cannot regard it as fundamentally alien from our modern conception of experience, in the largest sense of the word.

Granting this substantial identity, then, we have only to prove that Plato's idea of personal experience as the subject matter of discourse is a real factor in modern rhetorical theory. For this, no long argument is required. We find this idea theoretically expressed in rhetorical treatises even as far back as Quintilian,[2] in the implied definition of discourse as self-expression, a conception recently popularized by such writers as Arnold and Pater.[3] This notion of discourse, neglecting that part of the process of communication by which an experience is set up in the mind of the writer, emphasized exclusively that segment which develops the experience of the writer into articulate form. Being thus incomplete as was the sophistic theory of discourse, it served only to supplement that by bringing out into clear consciousness the Platonic truth that the subject matter of discourse has a direct relation to the mental processes of the writer.

On the practical side, this truth has appeared in the comparatively recent decay of formal instruction in rhetoric, and the correlative growth of composition work in our schools. This practical study of composition, insofar as it deserved its name, displaced the writing of biographical essays, largely drawn from encyclopedic sources, and of treatises on abstract subjects far removed from any natural interests of the student who wrote. Both these lines of effort proving relatively profitless, the experiment was tried of drawing the material for writing directly from the everyday experience, observation, and thinking of the student—an experiment whose results proved so successful that the practice has long been established in most of our schools. This is a piece of history so recent and so well-known that it need not be dwelt upon. Its import, however, is worth noting. It means the practical, though perhaps unconscious, acceptance of Plato's principle that the subject matter of discourse bears a vital relation to the mind of the speaker. And by virtue of this, it means the complete closing of the circuit of communication between speaker and hearer.

So far, then, the rising modern rhetorical theory agrees with the doctrine of Plato. It may, perhaps, differ from him in making discourse a process somewhat less self-conscious than he seems to have conceived it, arising from the speaker's primitive social instinct for sympathy, or (to put it more technically) for closer relations with his environment, rather than from any explicit desire to communicate his own vision of the truth to another. But this modification affects neither the nature of the process itself, nor its ultimate outcome. Both the Platonic and the modern theory of discourse make it not an individualistic and isolated process for the advantage of the speaker alone, but a real communication between speaker and hearer, to the equal advantage of both, and thus a real function of the social organism.

This conception of discourse is rich in implications which Plato never saw, and which no modern has yet formulated. To this formulation, however, our practical teaching of English, with all its psychologic and sociological import, is daily bringing us nearer. It cannot be long before we shall recognize a modern theory of discourse as large in its outlines as Plato's and far better defined in its details, a theory which shall complete the social justification which rhetoric has so long been silently working out for itself.

Notes for "The Present Status of Rhetorical Theory"

"The Present Status of Rhetorical Theory" by Gertrude Buck has been reprinted from the Library of Congress *Modern Language Notes* 15, no. 3 (1900): 84–87. I have regularized capitalization and punctuation conventions.

1. Buck's footnote at this point reads: "The use of the term 'social' in connection with rhetorical theory has been borrowed directly from Professor F[red] N[ewton] Scott of the University of Michigan; though for the interpretation here put upon the word, he is not necessarily responsible." Scott, an influential compositionist, was Buck's teacher at the University of Michigan.

2. Quintilian (c. 35–95) taught rhetoric in Rome and published the *Institutio Oratoria*, a major handbook of rhetorical education and practice; given Quintilian's emphasis on wide reading and imitation of great orators, it is strange to cite Quintilian as a proponent of writing from personal experience.

3. Matthew Arnold (1822–1888), English poet and critic, was extremely influential in aesthetics; in several volumes of literary criticism, he argued that education depends on teaching the "best" literature in order to reform society and counteract the "philistine" values of the middle class. Walter Pater (1839–1894) was an English essayist and critic who taught that the ideal life was founded on appreciation of the beautiful and the profound. Both writers emphasized creative self-expression rather than argumentative communication in their theories.

Mary Augusta Jordan

1855–1941

Mary Augusta Jordan was born in Ironton, Ohio, on July 5, 1855, to Augusta Woodbury Ricker and Edward Jordan. Jordan's father, a lawyer, served as solicitor of the Treasury under President Abraham Lincoln. She received an A.B. from Vassar in 1876, an A.M. from Vassar in 1878, an honorary doctorate in literature from Smith in 1910, and a Ph.D. from Syracuse University in 1921. She was the Vassar librarian from 1877 to 1880, and tutored undergraduates in English at Vassar from 1880 until 1884. She taught as a professor in the Smith College English Department from 1884 until 1921, living on campus in Hatfield House. Jordan was a challenging and opinionated teacher who failed to engage her students for the first year, and only slowly developed into one of Smith's most charismatic teachers. Her lectures, discussing world events and philosophies of life, as well as literature and composition, became a Smith tradition, and even her colleagues attended. She wrote that she thought of the "classroom [as] a spiritual powerhouse, whose builder and maker and engineer was God"—a description similar to the one she gives in *Correct Writing and Speaking* for all public speaking. Jordan required daily writing from her students, arguing that self-expression increased self-knowledge, and asked students to meet with her often in conference to discuss their writing. She was influential in establishing Smith's curriculum as a women's college, arguing that women should "cut loose from the traditions of men, not because they are men's nor indeed because they are traditions, but because the best men have no saving faith in them. . . . The work in a woman's college offers an ideal field for experiment" (*Atlantic Monthly*, October 1892, 540–46). Jordan also helped coordinate rhetoric with other departments. She held to high standards of learning for women, preferring the study of Greek for women to easier modern languages, but she also argued that standards should not be reduced to mere correctness, that never should "Definiteness, precision, and accuracy [be] taken out of their proper province—that of ever-present factors in the process of education—and made indispensable parts of the material results" ("Influential Fallacies about Education," *School Review* 12, no. 2 [1904]: 129–37). Jordan edited Goldsmith's *Vicar of Wakefield*, Edmund Burke's *On Conciliation* (1900), two volumes of essays by Ralph Waldo Emerson (1907), and John Milton's *Minor Poems* (1904). She also published many essays on education, as well as a pamphlet against women's suffrage (1921). She died in New Haven, Connecticut, on April 14, 1941.

Jordan's contribution to rhetorical theory is *Correct Writing and Speaking*, published in the Woman's Home Library Series in 1904. The *Harvard Report*, published in 1892, which criticized students' lack of knowledge of grammar and spelling, stimulated a rush toward correctness in the teaching of English in the United States. Despite its title, Jordan's volume argues against this standard. Citing the history of unstandardized English of the time of Chaucer, Tyndale, and More, and the rich diversity of peoples whose contributions to the language—English is the language of Irish, Australian, and Indian peoples, as well as United States and English people—Jordan argues that the best English is that of individual citizens, citizens well-read, familiar with dictionaries and spelling books, trained in elocution, but still speaking a language that combines dialect and book English into easy, colloquial, intelligent speech. Such language is acquired not by following rules of spelling, not by mimicking great actors, not even by going to college, but by being a good person who makes education a lifelong commitment. To women who read the home library, many far from colleges, without their husband's advantages of education in Jordan's times, this must have been a sensible and comforting message.

Influences on Jordan are many. She quotes long passages, trying to put the best of men's sciences of languages—the new linguistics and history of language, as well as the old belles lettres rhetoric—into her book for women. But she seems most influenced, overall, by Ciceronian republicanism and its emphasis on the eclectic style and knowledge of the great speaker and writer. She would have a dictionary for every American citizen. She supposes that her readers will approach letter writing and conversation with the same seriousness and sense of responsibility that they do formal composition, literary criticism, and public speaking. She exults in the social reform rhetoric of her day and, perhaps thinking of the success of abolitionists or the WCTU, imagines public speaking not as the manipulation of a crowd, but as the expression of the spiritual consensus of a group. She offers sensible advice, although not rules, on studying language, pronunciation, spelling, literary criticism, letter writing, conversation, and public speaking.

For further information, see Jane Donawerth, "Textbooks for New Audiences: Women's Revisions of Rhetorical Theory at the Turn of the Century," in *Listening to Their Voices: The Rhetorical Activities of Historical Women*, ed. Molly Meijer Wertheimer (Columbia: University of South Carolina Press, 1997), 337–56; Susan Kates, "Subversive Feminism: The Politics of Correctness in Mary Augusta Jordan's *Correct Writing and Speaking* (1904)," *College Composition and Communication* 48, no. 4 (December 1997): 501–17; Kates, *Activist Rhetoric and American Higher Education, 1885–1937* (Carbondale: Southern Illinois University Press, 2001), 27–52; and Kathleen Perkins, "Mary Augusta Jordan," in *American National Biography*, ed. A. Garraty and Mark C. Carnes (New York: Oxford University Press, 1999), 12:274–75.

From *Correct Writing and Speaking* (1904)

Chapter One
The Standard

The desire for rules and standards is an expression of human nature in one or more of its aspiring, its self-satisfied, or its despairing moods. Rules and standards may point to perfection, may rest in the easily attainable, or may make the best of a bad matter. Or, in still other words, rules and standards may be ideals, or conventions, or observed facts.

From this difference of meaning springs much confusion of thought in all subjects where rules and standards are applicable. Rule is made to stand for at once too much or too little. Standards are treated now as foot rules, now as ever-advancing aims. Nowhere is this confusion more fertile in mischief than in the practical interests of speaking and writing. It is not limited in its influence to those who instruct or to those who wish for instruction. Like a shifting mist, it sways and swings over both companies, and disguises not only one from the other, but the members of each from all the rest.

To a man satisfied in the faith that a rule at its best approximates to a moving and advancing ideal, the demand for easy and precise accuracy seems so unreasonable that it blinds him to the natural disappointment of those who believed that he would provide them with ascertained weights and measures. The stupid and the children of genius alike emancipate themselves from conventions, and yet the discussion about correct speech, good English, and faultless grammar goes on. It is at least encouraging to know that it goes on much as it has always gone on.

In this respect matters are no worse than they have been in the past. We are not forced to bring action against human nature in our generation, as more incompetent and more muddle-headed and tongue-tied than it was before our evil days. It is safe to say that we are not degenerate. There is some ground for belief that we are holding our own fairly well amidst a Babel of interests and words second only to the first great recorded confusion of tongues.[1] It is then with a spirit of good cheer that one undertakes to find out what is meant by correct English and how it is to be acquired in speaking and in writing.

There is a general impression that correct English is something that the ordinary, plain person may reasonably hope to secure. It is a well-defined, safe territory in which the painstaking need not err. It is believed that correct English is a passport to good society where, on a level plain of expression, the gently bred exercise their minds. To speak like persons of intelligence is the goal that most of us set up as reasonable and desirable. And certainly the aim seems within reach. But a little effort shows us that reaching our goal is about our only evidence that it is within reach. There are so many ways that persons of intelligence have of expressing themselves. Some of these ways have little in common; many of them are contradictory in method; most of them differ in the effect aimed at, or the impression made. In despair the student of English decides to adopt a classification that will relieve him from some of his embarrassment. He will use a self-consistent form of English that shall avoid what Dryden called "gross error";[2] and he will exact of others no more than he requires of himself. But the first effort that he makes to secure consistency brings him into open rebellion against the idioms that he has used all his life and that are as dear to him as his home, his church, and his dead. Is idiom part of correctness, or is it flat defiance of it, or is it better than correctness—a sort of Sunday-best, to be used for everyday when it is outgrown or threadbare?

The like happens to the inquirer concerning the typical English voice. Is it to be found in England, Scotland, Ireland, or Wales? In the United States, Canada, Australia, or India? With what authority does the voice speak when it is found? Is it that of natural, spontaneous charm—has it perchance a brogue? Or does it hold by a book, and measure its cadences by a scale? The seeker for the plain path is bewildered by the directions he gets. He asks so little—only a sure guide to his own improvement and a safe estimate of the probable serviceableness of the various models offered for his use. If the Londoner's English is cockney and vulgar, and the Scotchman's is provincial, and the Irishman's is Irish, and the Welshman's is impossible, and the Colonial's is just what you might expect, and the Pulpit, the Bench, and the Bar, and the University are slangy or pedantic, and the Yankee's is United States—where is the place of English, and where shall true pronunciation be found? If faith is put in the finding [of] lists variously entitled "Guide to Pronunciation," or "Some Thousand of Words Usually Mispronounced," it finds itself betrayed in the end because, while it is a small matter to avoid one form of erroneous speech, no rules are given for finding the one excellent way—which is taken

301

for granted as being a mere matter of choice, . . . the other way of two equally at the speaker's disposal.

The anxious inquirer knows only too well from bitter experience, that to eschew evil is far from being the same thing as learning to do well. Where one aggressively wrong emphasis or vowel sound justifies condemnation and avoidance, a half dozen inaggressive infelicities of tone and emphasis escape by their minuteness. To be made intelligent enough to see the fault in one instance is to be put in the way of noting others and of suffering from the knowledge that makes afraid. Avoiding flat "a's" does not qualify one to deal successfully with broad "a's," nor will omitting the letter "r" from the vocal alphabet in Massachusetts dispose efficiently of twisted "r's" in Michigan.

If finally we are willing to replace "United States" by "English," what English shall we choose? How shall we get it? The state of mind naturally following upon these questions instructs us concerning the folly of any demand for absolute precision. The desire for it is natural and, so, excusable, if not laudable, but satisfaction is no part of its history. In this condition of affairs inquirers often fall into the mistake of thinking that English is a tongue exceptional in its history and eccentric in its structure. It is often described as the spoiled child of the linguistic family. The result of the acceptance of this view of English speech and writing is unfortunate. The student can hardly fail to be depressed at the seeming necessity of dealing with his subject in a spirit quite apart from that directing his other efforts at expression. Nor can he readily get his own consent to study in an orderly way what is confessedly a realm of disorder. So whim will call out whim, and individuality which charms without rule will become eccentricity without rule or charm.

Clearly the case is a hard one for the seeker after truth about standard English. It has not precision enough to do his work without his will, but it has too much precision to let him have his will entirely with it. It is of course quite possible to put the whole matter out of mind as an overstrained counsel of perfection. It is possible to dispose of it as a pure abstraction, expensive and tantalizing, like the principle of life or the existence of the soul. But English speech and writing resist this treatment. They are so closely entangled with those social relations which make existence intelligible, endurable, or enjoyable that we hate to waste time and strength in costly experiment about the best way of employing them.

It is deplorable to make false starts, lose the clew,[3] and get into no-thoroughfares, when the right road would have led into the noble estate of self-mastery and the pleasant country of human brotherhood. We want to know, and we need to know, English. Must we then assume that it is a gift like that of personal beauty? That, therefore, its excellence is indeed a superlative which may not be acquired as such, but must be gratefully accepted and joyfully acknowledged as of the beneficence of nature? Is this the only English speaking and writing in which precision is possible; this all that affords the conditions of standard expression, beside which everything else is known by its defect? Must we adopt a "great man" theory in English expression, and explain all attainments of the less imposing representatives of the race by the much or little that they derive from him as he appears at intervals in history? This doctrine has not been without its supporters. The use of the masterpieces of literature and the influence of great orators and actors has been cited in evidence of its validity.

But the result has been the thing known as a school—a thing so definite and so much apart from the normal progress and development of expression, whether in English or in French, or Latin, or Greek, that a clear statement of the theory is all that is necessary for its refutation.

The teacher of speech or writing who imparts few or many of his own devices and makes a series of incomplete editions of himself does not, in the old phrases, "ascertain the tongue" or "extend the powers of language." He makes men into puppets and supplies them in their memory and habit with a superior sort of string to work themselves by. Likewise, if they unconsciously imitate him, their use of his powers is but mimicry unless they unconsciously or consciously use it as a point of departure for something in their own talent or genius. The accuracy with which a parlor "stunt" reproduces the well-known features of Mr. Henry Irving's rendering of the character in action of Louis XI does not give evidence of the vitalizing influence that Mr. Irving's dramatic art has exercised upon the mimic's habitual voice, manner, and gesture, so much as of the infectious nature of certain mannerisms. The conscious parody is a more remunerative piece of literary craft than is a direct imitation in miniature. The precision that is gained by imitation of the ancients, the classics, or the popular idol is misleading. The standard we are looking for is not a graduated series of lengths from the admirably great to the little admirable, whatever else it may be. Then it seems likely that what is ordinarily known as precision is not in any high degree characteristic of English speaking and writing.

❧

Most speakers naturally incline to agree with Ben Jonson's Morose: "All discourses but my own afflict me; they seem harsh, impertinent, and irksome."[4] Without too close scrutiny our own delivery passes for sweet, pointed, and entertaining, but only because we assume that our outward show is what we would have it, not because we aim intelligently at any precise effect, not because we know the means that we habitually employ to effect the results we actually secure.

So the theory of a standard pronunciation is kept for the most part in reserve for use when we wish to silence opposition or to confirm our own judgment in our own behalf. But otherwise the responsibility of it sits very lightly on our consciences and so it sat very lightly on the consciences of speakers in every decade before us. It is useless to try to maintain that the English-speaking public has ever neglected its beef and pudding, or its interest in the crops, or its devotion to the reigning monarch for anything so fine-spun and unsubstantial as purity of speech. It has always managed to get on with such powers as it had. Discussion on the subject has been as much a matter of course as intelligent interest in the weather and inspection of the barometer. But nobody intends to be interfered with by the weather, or bullied by the barometer.

❧

[Jordan offers first a history of English pronunciation and grammar showing it was never "standard," and then a survey of the development of pronouncing dictionaries emphasizing their contradictions.]

There certainly is at present, then, no standard English, either in writing or in speaking, that is easily and cheaply available. There is no one correct way of writing or of speaking English. Within certain limits there are many ways of attaining correctness. What these limits are and how they are to be employed and what their interrelations are, it is the purpose of the later chapters of this book to indicate.

303

Chapter Two
The Spoken and the Written Word

Closest to the personal character of the writer, the most direct record of his spoken word are his letters. Even the telegraph and telephone have not made away with letters or very much impaired their authority or their charm. It is asserted by some critics that the style of correspondence has deteriorated and that the ultimate effect of the typewriter will be to cheapen the expression of personality to the vanishing point. Thus far, however, the facts seem to point in the other direction. The peculiar vulgarity and impersonality of these machine-made or machine-helped productions intensify by contrast the characteristics of the autograph letter and make the recipient grateful not alone for the revelation of whatever is unusual or interesting, but for the time and pains spent in his behalf. More than ever today, letters are what Hamerton[5] urged his readers to consider them—a gift. There is an almost proportionate increase in the interest attaching to published letters, particularly if they are free from the suspicion of having been written for publication. Letters of friendship, of love, of hate, of business, of state, have come into new value within the last twenty-five years. Reading them has come to be one of the most alluring pleasures of a large class of persons. A new demand has grown up for the qualities of style and suggestiveness in contemporary letters. More attention is given, avowedly at least, to letter writing; the machinery of desks, paper, pen, ink, and so on, is more precisely adjusted in the average person's provision for his way of life. Nor can it be denied that a more critical attitude exists toward the result. It is not enough now that a letter should be full of good intentions in the matter and the manner. The performance is expected to contribute to the meaning or to the enjoyment of life.

Comparison with the machine-made products of print and typewriting brings a growing impatience with confusion, awkwardness, and illegibility, but these are almost put out of the question, and the real demand is made after these requirements are satisfied. The real demand is for skill in presentation, vividness of detail, choice of significant subject matter, evidence of delicate and precise knowledge of the reader's taste and character, and just so much revelation of the writer's self and interests as shall really serve the reader's.

At no time in the history of human intercourse has the letter been forced to carry itself so adroitly, or fail of its mission. Cheap postage has not brought easy letter writing. The letters of the average member of society are the only contribution he makes to literature. He would not so dignify them, but they are all that is left to him untouched by the paralysis of professionalism or the fear of ambition. The peculiar problem that every letter has to solve grows out of this complex and delicate function. It must be at once rigorously formal and easily spontaneous. The letter writer who spends his individuality in faddish paper, colored ink, and enigmatic paging, who "crosses" his manuscript or insists upon paper so thin that it is hard to know which side one is reading, will need large revenues of talent to keep him from living beyond his means in his claims on his reader's attention. When Esther Edwards wrote on the backs and uncovered parts of old envelopes, and the great Jonathan himself did not disdain the curved bits of paper left over from the fans his wife and daughters manufactured, paper was a luxury and letters a rare sending.[6]

The strictest conformity to the rules of the printer in the matter of copy is hardly too much to require of the writer who wishes to produce the best letters. Certainly a friend's eyesight, and convenience, and pleasure are as well worth consideration as are those of a compositor or the gentle reader. The rules for copy vary with improvements and changes in the mechanics of printing, the taste of the public, and the cost of material and process. The general principle is a simple one, however. Make the page legible and beautiful. It should be remembered that ink is easily blurred by handling; therefore, leave generous margins. It should not be forgotten that combinations of lines, full of significance for the writer, are meaningless or misleading often to the reader. The effort to make the page represent the speaker should not be entirely given up, however. If the handwriting is clear and "carries" well to the eyes, there is abundant room within the prescribed limits of formal "copy" for the exhibition of varied moods and tempers in dramatic force. It is surprising how slight are the details necessary for the display of character.

The most suggestive traits are not the biggest in face or mind. It is said by many observers of the times that English is being less and less used in public speech. So great has been the change in a quarter of a century that there are those who believe that the art of oratory is near its extinction. The place it once held is to be taken by the newspaper, by the pamphlet, or circular. The increasing influence of organization makes some persons think that the walking delegate, the boss, or the committee's rules, will eventually intervene successfully between any individual of however powerful will and the members of the community. This point of view is hardly possible except to one unduly influenced by the importance of the individual as contrasted with that of the group to which he is continuously related while he exercises his powers of oratory. It is precisely in organization that public speech should find its true field. The picture of the orator as a desert and solitude haunting soul, receiving his inspiration from some oracle, or his instruction from some divine Egeria,[7] is far from a faithful portrait. Or if it ever was a correct representation, times have changed and men with them. Public utterance is full as important as it ever was and perhaps more definitely an instrument of good, inasmuch as its methods are better understood and its effects judged of as being within the sphere of ordinary cause and effect. After-dinner speaking has for some years gone beyond the telling of old stories or the repetition of platitudes. Wit and wisdom are both expected at banquets, and the postprandial effort that is all froth is quite sharply resented by the eaters of well-planned, well-served, and well-paid-for dinners. Closer analysis reveals the underlying conviction that the community spirit, at its simplest, is real and significant enough to require some serious expression. Earnestness and purpose are an important part of the social experience; the individual in his public spirit must somehow or other draw upon the reserve of sympathy and common living which influences him more rather than less than it does the silent members of his audience. To vary a common expression, he does not give them his tongue, but finds their tongues for them. The cloven tongues, as of fire, that sat upon each of them,[8] are still necessary to make interest.

If it be true that the need for public speech still exists for those who have practiced it in the past, one feels no surprise at finding that the range of its employment has been extended to women. Indeed women may be said to have come into entirely new duties and new responsibilities. The question of their increased enjoyment is, perhaps, still open. The old teaching that women should not be heard in the congregation has given way before necessity. Probably few women who speak in public began by choosing to do so as the gratification of any taste or desire for publicity. But circumstances forced the effort upon them, repetition made its difficulties less formidable, and gradually the feeling has grown in the community that women ought to be able to do what public speaking naturally comes in their way. The attitude of conservatism in regard to the pleasure that they should display in the exercise of their powers is not retained when their success or skill is under discussion. A woman may be forgiven for saying nothing, or even for publishing her incapacity for public address, but nothing justifies or quite excuses her saying her say badly. She is often without training for the task laid upon her, but she is expected to use her mother-wit to take the place of technique and somehow make her voice heard. The resulting strain and distortion are regretted, are often considered necessary incidents to the transition state of women's social influence, but by degrees they are coming to be looked upon as indications of the exorbitant price following bad or no training. The fact is that public relations are as normal and as dignified and therefore, in their degree, as pleasurable as private or personal ones.

Few women are ignorant of the education they have undergone in the effort to fit themselves for the discharge of their purely private obligations. It probably takes as many years to learn to keep one's temper with an exasperating companion as it does to acquire control of the pitch and carrying tones of one's voice. Nor is it quite clear that it is one's duty to cultivate private sympathy at the expense of one's wider intelligence. It is at least conceivable that human beings out of pictures may need depth of background as much as do their counterfeit presentments in frames. The desired action may be secured better by reflected or transmitted influence through a group of persons, than by going straight at the person himself, though approached with all the tact in the world. There is a duty to the soul of society, as well as to the soul of one and of another. . . . There is increasing respect for well-directed preparation, for explicit training, for modest competence.

In an age of scientific contrivance, inefficiency and ineptitude are peculiarly distasteful; less and less is left to chance or to what used to be called inspiration, and less and less sympathy is felt for the sort of failure following trust in luck. As in the most individual form of literature, letter writing, the individuality is strengthened by contact with form and prescription, so here: there is a form for public address that is prescriptive. It has not the mechanical point-device accuracy of the old manuals of forty years ago, but it is nonetheless final in its authority. The audience is not to be dominated, cajoled, or bullied. It is to be interpreted, and made to know its own self in terms of something else than prejudice, or passion, or lazy self-indulgence. And to that end can one suppose nothing contributes but a general willingness to advance the cause of truth with an average power of articulation such as would serve one in ordering a luncheon at a restaurant or answering the telephone? The speaker must have as well-controlled powers as the actor has, but in one respect they are opposites. The actor must consciously exercise his art for the accomplishment of a definite end which he has predetermined and arranged. The successful speaker of the present, and of the future, will use his art to enable him to discern the signs of the spiritual forces coming into action in his presence. His aim will be to conserve them, to let as little as possible real energy go to waste, and to reduce to the lowest degree the inevitable friction of human motives by his own efficiency as a medium. To this end, no culture of his powers would be too expensive or too burdensome. The precise nature of this culture brings up a long series of practical considerations as special as these earlier ones have been general. Some of this culture is in lines markedly opposed to old methods, employed and advised, with unquestioning reliance upon their efficacy.

The study of foreign languages, alive or dead, was supposed to be a sure guide to a linguistic sense, of such accuracy and precision and comprehensiveness as to include English by a sort of first intention. The use of Latin grammar for this purpose has been time honored. But the day of that kind of Latin grammar is over. It is gone, never to return. The students who rested content with their memory of listed rules and a few picturesque exceptions have either been rudely shaken out of their repose or they find themselves more and more solitary in their easy Zions. For the facts of the Latin tongue, as exhibited in the Roman usage, do not bear out the old system and order out of which this desirable grammatical sense was to be derived. As Professor E. P. Morris says in his book, *On Principles and Methods in Latin Syntax*,[9] "irregularity and absence of system are not merely occasional but are the fundamental characteristics of Latin form-building. It is the regularity that is unusual and exceptional." With this characterization of the structure, study of which was once depended upon to introduce order where no order was, users of English may dare to admit that their standard usage is an ideal.

Chapter Three
The Office of Criticism

The disinterested effort to learn is the best that the plain man can get out of his own life, or hand on to others. Through it the humblest life takes on the splendor and the thrill of creative effort, and because its issues are of the spirit and of the spirit alone, some of its history must always remain untold.

But there is a homespun side to these skyey robes. The aim is spiritual and remote that men set before themselves for their improvement, but the means to it are definite and painstaking. They preclude all satisfaction with self-deluding blindness, they involve the most careful and even mechanical adjustments. The opponents of criticism find fault with it because of the disturbing effect of its attention to detail. They fear that sensitiveness to detail will finally prevent the due interest in results and effects. They place much emphasis on the grace of unconsciousness in speech and writing and advise what they call "being simply oneself." They deplore self-consciousness as the arch enemy of success in English expression. They point to the artless charm of the spontaneous word and accent as being far more attractive than the studied form of either. The columns of answers to questions about the best way of acquiring a pleasant speaking voice, or a refined pronunciation, and an easy epistolary style, are full of variations on the theme—"be yourself," "be natural." Nothing is more repellent than the appearance of effort. Sincerity is the first of literary virtues. Do not despise it.

And, so, all sorts of bad habits and unsuspected awkwardnesses are left to grow and increase while the owner mistakes negligence for nature and self-indulgence for charm. The novels of the day have not a little to answer for in this connection. With the indestructible white muslin, done up into style and starch by the wearer's own hands and spreading conquest in its cloudy path, ranks the unstudied sweetness of the fascinating one's curiously attractive tones. The hero of the people wins by his "characteristic manner," strongly contrasting, as it does, with the trained eloquence of his rival.

And certainly the task of getting a good voice and easy expression is not a light one, nor accomplished without some awkward and temporarily distorted effort. The analysis of speech, good in itself, into its processes, and the comparison of one manner with another, are necessary if definite improvement is to be made or intelligence to be secured. But such intelligence calls for choice and exclusion as the conditions of its existence, and choice and exclusion are not among the easy-going, hospitable virtues. . . .

The ardent admirer of "good style" commonly pays for his admiration by irritation at all the competing methods he has set aside in its interest. It is a high price to pay as looked at from the point of view of a student of things as they are and of plain humanity, but it seems hardly a price at all, but rather the crown of his success, to the industrious striver for perfection. The taste for the best may come to be as arrant a convention as the thoughtless preference for one's own way simply because it is one's own, and may be as unintelligently maintained. The charms of grace, flexibility, and variety cannot be had except as the expression of constantly renewed comparison of one's own methods with those of all sorts and conditions of men, for there can be no doubt that English expression, written and spoken, is a debtor to the Jew and the Gentile, the Greek and the Barbarian. In other words, mental alertness, catholicity of taste, rigid self-discipline, patient experiment, and humility in self-reference are absolute requisites in the work of the student of English. For while he may profit by the training given him by teachers, may even use to some advantage arbitrary habits imposed upon him, the best qualities and traits of English will never be his unless he can command its hospitality to ideas and its energy of self-development.

There is much to be observed, too. The provincial speaker can never feel the same unquestioning acceptance of his own vowels and consonants after he has heard Chaucer or Shakespeare read with attempt at a scientific reproduction of the vowels and consonants so differently sounded today. The user of citified speech, conventionalized and thinned, as it often is, will be the better for respectful association with accent and emphasis intensified by the slower utterance of the less voluble tongue of the countryside. Local peculiarities, survivals, and inaccuracies, not to mention variations and experiments—all contribute to the richness and possible range of expression.

This is true of the voice itself. It is possible that the voice should be interesting, as the character is interesting, for its suggestion, its attainments—for what, in a very real sense, it has gone through. Nor does this mean that mere persistence is any more creditable to a voice than to a human being, or that experience is the same thing as fatigue or dilapidation.

Quite within the limits of their musical structure, their freshness, or their strength, voices are capable of a wide range of character. The rarest form is the one most often taken for granted as the natural voice. Few observant listeners can call to mind a voice that really expresses the nature of its possessor. Most voices are arbitrarily associated with their owners. They are known as hats and gowns are known, by repetition of the personal connection. Like them, they are pitied and endured, too. The pity of it is that so much more might be accomplished in the way of pleasure and significance.

A few voice qualities have been worn threadbare by novelists. Who does not remember the mocking tone of certain accomplished villains, the imperturbable composure of others, the diplomatic insignificance of still others? But these are the exceptions, even in books, where for the most part the author is content to claim richness, sweetness, or evenness as the all-sufficing vocal traits.

It must be admitted that too many a voice is characterless or deformed. The low, sweet voice of the society woman bears almost as little relation to her real character as it does to her real voice without the restraints and conventions of social form. The full manly tones of the typical gentleman are so identified rather by courtesy than by the critical ear. But the rare exception to all this shows in what direction effort should be made. The English voice may take on good habits, as well as put off bad ones. It may acquire interest and fascination, and yet divest itself of nasality, snuffle, and mumble, of high pitch, forced tone, and jerked accent. It is perfectly possible to be impressive without emphasizing every word in the spoken sentence. It is equally possible to be polite in speech without so loose a vocal hold on words that the hearer is kept on the stretch to catch them.

But all these things cost. They are not to be had without the labor and the pain of study and self-knowledge. Bishop Spaulding has well expressed his sense of the importance of careful expression:

> The most marvelous monument of a people's genius is its language. . . . However true and profound one's thoughts may be, he may not hope to introduce them into circles which are capable of recognizing and appreciating their worth, unless he clothe them in a fitting garb of words, habit them in a style which shall commend and give them currency; and this skill they alone acquire who inure themselves to the labor and fatigue which genuine writing involves. . . . He who would attain beauty, force, and accuracy of verbal expression must keep his pen in hand day by day, and must not weary of subjecting what he writes to his own pitiless criticism. . . .[10]

Considerations of this sort insure one against the acceptance of a popular and dangerous teaching that unconscious models are the best. If one hears good English, it is asserted, good English will naturally come to his lips; if he reads the English classics, he will write classic English. Setting aside the difficulty of securing good English to hear, something must be allowed to the influence of novelty and the claim of the contemporaneous. Variety of expression dissipates and distracts attention and enforces temporary charms. In its worst form, because its most expensive, this influence is felt in school, where lisps and stutters and vulgarities of enunciation are far more infectious than good speech. Everyone probably remembers some experience of this sort. Some leading character in school affairs has marked mannerisms, or a quick ear for provincialism, and forthwith they go through the school like mumps and measles. The excellent models of the home speech, and the careful exclusion of all but the best from the home influences seem to go for nothing. In some cases, it is true, the young citizen manages to keep his privileges in both worlds and supports the luxury of two fashions of speech, one for home and parents and "grown ups" generally, the other for his mates. But such facility is exceptional. The ordinary person insensibly takes on the habitual sounds and the customary vocabulary of his closest neighbors, in almost exact proportion as they are different from his own, but mechanically, and without intelligent choice or well-directed effort to organized results of any kind.

The speech of even thoughtful persons of mature years is too often an unworthy, unrepresentative mixture of all sorts and conditions of vocal habits, whims, and accidents, but properly called "natural" only insofar as it is not art. Habitual misuse probably counts for more in the creation of the typical Yankee voice than any influence of climate. . . . This theory of the good effect of unconscious models makes it appear almost unreasonable to resent any form of assault on the ears, because the speaker may simply be speaking as he has been taught—a condition of things calling for combined respect and indulgence. So the public goes suffering on and the American speech grows less and less beautiful.

For many years our public school system gave no place to the formal teaching of English, on the ground that a taste for the best authors could be depended on to meet all requirements. A style formed on that of the English classics was a commonplace of biography, of criticism, and of pedagogic theory. Nor has all its influence departed even now. There are many persons who firmly believe that the acquisition of a good style must be by literary infection, and that mainly through reading for the interest of the subject matter. Somehow it is believed clearness, force, and beauty will make their way. The reader of the masterpieces of English literature will insensibly acquire the merits he enjoys until he commands a wide range of spoken and written expression. But the facts of history and biography fail to bear out this pleasant fable. The cited miracles of untaught and unpracticed skill invariably prove to have had the best of teaching and training, though perhaps of an unexpected or unconventional pattern.

Chapter Six
The Speller and the Copy Book

Not long ago a literary man of considerable pretense to reputation declared, with an air of easy detachment, that he did not see the use of all this pother about spelling: for his part he left it to his printer. And the businessman who "finances" great undertakings can hardly write ten lines of legible script—he leaves that sort of thing to his typewriter or stenographer, and travels with a staff of them—after the manner of a general at the seat of war. Doubtless much of this temper is pure reaction from over-worship of mint, anise, and cummin and consequent neglect of the weightier matters of the law.[11] Besides, it is much to be doubted whether the art of spelling has ever been widely practiced. Examination of autograph letters and the "admired" copy for masterpieces of literature leaves room for grave uncertainty about the attainments of the past in this particular. It must be taken into account that our standard editions of English authors of all ranks and periods have undergone "treatment" at the hands of editors and printers. Most of these persons had eccentric ideas on spelling or had no ideas at all; they simply did what they pleased on the impulse of the moment, and worshipped not at all at the shrine of consistency. Some of them had principles and no practice; others had practice of the most unprincipled sort.

The present spelling is mainly the creation of the printers, who are not entirely above fault or without whims. But the ground of the present demand for good spelling is not a simple assertion of the demands of a duty-loving, duty-doing generation in its solicitude for the workers and burden-bearers who are to follow in its van. Not at all does the average critic of bad spelling mean to attach much intrinsic importance to spelling in and of itself, or to compare it to their discredit with the realities of thought, life, or expression.

The point is that spelling has been avowedly reduced to system or to a few systems by the very printers to whom reference has been made; the systems have been put into a form suitable for popular use; books have been enormously multiplied and, at the same time, cheapened in price so that the systems are seen in everyday use and their details made familiar by constant exemplification. Meantime, the teaching of the schools has been similarly changed. The old methods of *memoriter*[12] learning have been discarded; the scientific spirit has been given its due place in the training of the mind, and one of the subjects formally accepted by the schools for the display of their skill is spelling.

The fact is that most of the students from the schools do not spell well. This does not mean that they always spell incorrectly or that they never by any chance hit a correct combination of letters. It means mainly that the products of these schools do not display any of the acknowledged results of school methods in their spelling. The impression they make is that of persons dealing with the subject as they might with any other requiring or courting their attention. So it is suggested by more than one able critic of education that this inefficiency may be the fault of the printer's system, and that one devised on sounder principles of etymology and historical record would prove more influential to teachers and seem better worthwhile to students. It is not necessary to settle the question of spelling reform here, fortunately. The subject recurs almost as periodically as the traditionally coldest winter or the hottest summer, and there are always great talents employed on both sides of the controversy.

The point really at issue seems a very different one and a very simple one. If the subject is taught, why are not the results of the teaching evident? The real ground of objection against the present spelling is that as a discipline it bears no proper relation to the arithmetical processes with which it is associated, and that it is likely to be joined in the educational limbo where it languishes by reading and writing. In other words, these three subjects have not faithfully reflected the changes and improvements supposed to have been made in the material and method of education.

Spelling, in the last resort, is a form of observational science. It is no more arbitrary, no more inconsistent, no more variable, than is the vocabulary and nomenclature of any science. As a field for training in the essentials of observation, nothing could be better suited to the purpose than the printed pages naturally coming in the way of the student in the grades. But the teaching is badly done. It lacks significance, accuracy, and suggestion. Probably not ten out of a hundred teachers of the children in primary grades know appreciably more about a book as a mechanical contrivance, or the printed page as a result of combined art and science, than do the children. The same thing is true in regard to the sound value of the letters and the varied histories they have undergone. It is considered hard work to teach children their letters and the so-called first principles of reading, but most of them fail to learn the principles, and so practice the art stumblingly and falteringly all their days.

Chapter Eight
The Dictionary

But the main use of the dictionary is, after all, exactly what it ought to be, in spite of the satire, amusement, and misunderstanding of critics and onlookers. The average citizen in the United States aims to have a mind of his own, and among other furniture for it, covets means of expression. The dictionary helps him to find out what he means and to say his mind. He has little sympathy with the spineless attitude of those who insist that life is a hopeless maze, or a barren desert, or a meaningless riddle. In any event, he fancies that better results are secured by living and thinking than by slouching and evading thought, and he more than suspects that something in the process of thought itself is a solution of his worst puzzles. For the rest, he patiently makes and remakes the experiments called for by a life that is to count for something in terms of itself, in courage and determination, in clearer views of the folly of selfishness, and in passionate attachment to the hope that maketh not ashamed,[13] since it gives courage for the duties of the passing day. The resources of the English speech, in big and little, as cause and effect, serve the average citizen to press on to his ideal aim of a man thinking, without wasting time in the stage of mere thought.

The Gist of the Whole Matter

Correctness in writing and speaking is no slight affair. It is not easy in the getting or the keeping. It is, first of all, dependent on personal character. It rises and falls in value with the personal and social virtues. It is no more to be acquired fully and finally than life, genius, or personal perfection. Too often it is identified with cheap and easy processes and uninteresting results. On the contrary, patience, fortitude, unselfishness, and a real interest in the world of men and things are only other names for what is called the sense for facts, which is always and everywhere demanded for the material of correctness.

To speak and write correctly, one must think, feel, and act correctly. If this is impossible in its entirety, then the only hope, humanly speaking, lies in keeping up the effort. The speaking and writing will be correct in precise proportion as the thinking, feeling, and acting attain, in their due degree, characteristic correctness. If it is discouraging to think that one never will be done, it is cheerful to reflect that one will always have something to do.

In the attainment of this ultimate end, use should be made of all the means suggested by the broadest as well as the most detailed criticism. Material of the greatest practical value exists in the passing comments of newspaper readers, play-goers, sermon hearers, and novel writers. The word *use* is employed advisedly. "Use" here implies examination, comparison, intelligent acceptance or rejection. It implies also accurate estimate of competing methods and resolute practice of the best. No so-called "authority" can be equally correct at all points, nor can any conclusion, however well founded, be forever correct. At best it must change; it may even be superseded or contradicted.

A few considerations in regard to the contemporaneous speaking and writing of English may be useful. English speech is at its best when the tones are full, free, varied in pitch enough to be flexible, but without cadence, or sing-song. Over-precision in separate sounds is not more nor less agreeable than suppression of them. Blurting and jerky emphasis is always offensive to the hearer, though affection for the speaker may make it tolerated. Careful speakers try to be as intelligent as possible about their voices. They ascertain if possible their exact range, their best points, and the causes of their faults and weaknesses. Knowledge on these points may be gained from doctors, singing masters, and good teachers of voice.

The use for a few minutes, ten or fifteen every day, of the exercises prescribed for the culture of the voice will do much to improve, mend, or develop the voice. Most voices in the United States are disfigured by bad habits in the use of throat, nose, mouth, and lips, by catarrh, by too high a pitch, by too rapid utterance, by too monotonous inflection, and by confirmed carelessness and indulged mannerisms and provincialisms. Here attention and practice will do much, but the criticism of teachers, doctors, and faithful friends should be invited and heeded.

While speech should never be slovenly, there should be a marked difference between the use of the voice in private and in public. Few persons can speak well in public without definite preparation for the effort. The services in criticism and direction of a good teacher or practiced speaker are almost essential to success.

Not only the manner but the matter of private speech is characteristic. While all perfections may be supposed to belong to every member of a given social group, still they cannot all be displayed by all at once. *Fair play* may be offered as the brief advice for the conduct of private conversation. Don't force the tone of your voice, nor your subjects, nor your interests on the company. If your voice is tired, at least consider whether you have given anybody else time for the proper exercise of hers.

Under no circumstances "gush," "enthuse," "spout," or "talk down." Avoid exaggeration of thought and expression, worn out or misapplied terms, like "grand," "elegant," and the phrases of the day, like "attractive." Avoid slang, abbreviations, legal terms, phrases whose meaning is not clearly understood, and coined words. Correctness does not require daring or surprise.

Speak only when there seems to be a fair chance of something to say, and then finish the sentence before starting another or another subject. Say one thing at a time. Never ramble or prattle or do your thinking aloud—at the expense of the company. Except with intimate friends who are known to enjoy your performance, never interrupt (with or without apology), never keep up an accompanying comment on another's talk, never supply a word to a hesitating speaker. All vague, ambiguous, puzzling, enigmatic speech and reference is unpardonable among any but intimate friends.

The familiar intercourse of intimate friends permits, by common consent, waste of time, display of personal weakness, or the expression of strong feeling that should never be imposed on general society, even in private.

The speech employed in private business should be explicit, direct, literal, brief, and considerate of the other person's time and interests. Mean a definite thing, say what is meant. Avoid the technical terms of business, unless you are expert in their use.

Personal peculiarities of speech should be sparingly indulged in except among intimate friends. Favorite quotations, characteristic or pithy sayings, "being funny," are out of place in formal, though private, intercourse. The difference between formal and informal private association lies mainly in the suppression of the purely individual way of putting things in favor of what is broadly human.

Rarely if ever, in public or in private, take the opinions or actions of other persons for granted by ascribing or imparting to them any course of behavior described in your own words. It is annoying to self-pride and that preference for being virtuously mysterious that marks even the most commonplace mortal.

Leave some conversational pickings for the next speaker. Don't try to exhaust even one subject that may have fallen to your share. Avoid all air of finality or authority, and all display of importance in voice and words. Don't be "bossy" or "fussy" in appearance or reality. Avoid trite little phrases like "it seems to me," "the long and short of it," "all the same," and "above all," "don't yer know," or "d'yer know," or even "don't you know," perforated and punctuated with confiding or killing glance. The monotony of "now," "then," "well," as the opening of sentence after sentence is very tiresome.

Be careful not to sacrifice to your own feeling of interest in what you are saying or thinking, or to the expression you are making of yourself, the convenience and pleasure of others in working out similar expressions of themselves. Under this general principle come the preferences you may feel for "pointing morals," "drawing lessons," giving descriptions of scenery and events, providing information, personating actors in little self-made dramas with "says he" and "says she" for the tiresome introduction to what seems likely to be endless. In short, don't be a bore; and if you can't help it, at least keep from talking like one. Avoid frequent reference to yourself and particularly to your feelings, habitual preferences, or dislikes.

Don't fear to speak politely and interestingly to those who happen to serve you. The relation might be reversed. In all cases, give one clear, unequivocal direction at a time. Remember the substance of your order and express intelligent satisfaction when it is carried out.

The expression of all respect, affection, and courtesy, as such, should be careful, painstaking, and explicit. Abbreviated endearment and admiration is absurd. The formal adoption of what was unconscious carelessness in the original user is vulgar. Trying to say "m'lud" will never make a plain citizen of the United States appear at home with the aristocracy of England. Never have the air of avoiding reference to persons, whether present or absent, by their names. Use "he," "she," and "they" as general, impersonal, conversational deities as little as possible. Keep the claptrap of empty allusion out of your talk and never descend to the vulgarity of real "secrets" under the guise of apparently simple reference.

Say what will give pleasure to your hearers, provided you can do so innocently. The requirements of jaded sensibilities and hysterical tempers constitute no obligation on sensible persons. Irreverence, vulgarity, impropriety, coarse vivacity are never correct, whatever else may be claimed for them. In formal intercourse avoid archness, playfulness, banter, and coyness. Keep all personality out of your expression, and to that end avoid all discussion that cannot be carried on in such a way as to interest everybody of mature years and proper feeling. Never complete a story or a remark that has to begin, "I hope there is nobody here who," etc.

Phrases of salutation and leave taking like "hello" and "so long," or "I must be getting along," need only their statement for their rejection. Introductions, congratulations, and expressions of sympathy should be explicit, literal, and direct. Never apologize for a civility, or explain a courtesy, or let either seem to be indistinguishable from an affront. "Having nothing better to do, I thought I would look in on you" is the type of these incorrect forms. They do not mean what they say or they were not meant to be said.

The written English of our time has suffered from some of the same causes that afflict our speech. They are hurry, carelessness, and a general delusion that comfort is increased by slovenliness. It is popularly supposed that people talk as well as they can, but are victims of natural weakness, malformation, or awkwardness when they write. Nearly everybody professes hatred of writing. Yet nearly everybody admires and enjoys good writing in others and depends upon it as one of the consolations or resources of life.

Because writing is not so necessary and inevitable as speech, the writer appears to be taking more on himself than does the talker. Writing and writers are judged by a severer code of morality and beauty than are talk and talkers. Since time goes to the performance of the voluntarily undertaken task of writing, the result is expected to be well considered, and what, in the United States, is meant by the term "responsible." What is true of written expression is still more so of what is printed. At each step the audience grows larger, and the obligation incurred weighs more. There should be no "spur of the moment" with baleful influence and sad results on pen or printing press.

The commonest form of private writing is undoubtedly the letter. Diaries and journals are so intimately associated, either with the writer's desire for secrecy or his intentions of printing and publishing his record, that they do not count as independent forms. In no case can ford to write what he ought to be ashamed to have read.

A familiar letter is a pious duty, a gift, a courtesy, an evidence of friendly affection. It should be explicit and painstaking. Its aim should be distinctly pleasure giving, its methods those likely to secure the greatest satisfaction to the recipient with the least effort on his part. The date and place of writing should be clearly written, preferably at the opening of the letter. The material should be paper and ink. The ink should be black and of even flow. The paper should never be thin enough to show the writing through nor blur the effect. The signature should be full, so as to serve for the return of the letter in case it goes astray, and to complete the impression of personal accountability. The handwriting should be clear and legible, with as much expression of character and individuality as is consistent with these qualities.

Any items of business occurring in a letter of friendship should be marked by all the care of business correspondence. The rest may be as "characteristic" as the writer's temper and ability permit, but the freedom of friendship does not include loose statement or inaccurate figures. Friendly self-expression is a form of art. Business statements are science or they are nothing.

In a letter, as in conversation, the other person should be left something of the topic to deal with. Letters should not be simply "unpublished works," but part of a pleasurable give and take, of suggestion, comment, interested question, and generous self-expression. The form might be after this sort: something about me, something about you, something about the wide world.

As far as possible, a letter should be complete in itself. It should not need reference to the rest of the series to make it intelligible, nor should it compel the reader to cudgel her brains for information about the writer's previous history or associations. Allusion should be avoided, and what cannot be told outright would be as well omitted. Vague references to "my brother," where the writer has several, and to "a friend," when the context only teases by its suggestion, are not correct. Tell the essential details or leave the reference out.

Letters have become an important part of classic English literature. Models may be found in the letters of Nathaniel Hawthorne to his wife, the letters of Lord Chesterfield, the letters of Lady Mary Wortley Montagu, the letters of Swift and the "Journal to Stella," the letters of Lord Byron. As models for formal letters intended for publication, nothing can be better from the point of style than the letters of Junius. Nothing can be worse as models for the letters of any serious and self-respecting person than the collections recently offered to the public as love letters of women of various nationalities, never sent, or accidentally discovered, or those, from time to time, put in as testimony in trials for divorce or breach of promise. If anything could justify the proceedings, they would seem to do so. The public letters of Abraham Lincoln, and of Grover Cleveland, of George Washington, and of Thomas Jefferson afford a library of reference for students of these forms who may desire to compare the "strenuous" expression of President Roosevelt with the style of Judge Parker.[14]

The careful writer will read and study the work done by successful writers of his own and other times. He will use all the means at his disposal in the way of dictionaries, grammars, rhetorics, and studies of style and structure in verse and in prose.

Nobody wishing to write well can afford to neglect the help given by good printers and publishers. Their published methods and manuals will help him to understand some of the forces most influential in English expression. The habit of conforming his practice to their standards will greatly improve his expression in precision and facility.

All students of correct speaking and writing should read the dictionary. They should master its full notation of sounds, and should practice the production of each until it becomes easy and precisely identified. They should study the history of words in etymologies and dialectical collections. They should study the associations of words in the writings of those who have taught, and warned, and pleased in English expression.

Finally, the only way to learn to write is—to write.

Notes

The selections are taken from Mary August Jordan, *Correct Writing and Speaking*, The Woman's Home Library (New York: A. S. Barnes, 1904), 7–15, 25–26, 36, 60–71, 193–98, 229–42, with thanks to Susan Joseph for finding Jordan, and to Smith College for access to Jordan's book. I have in a few instances modernized spelling or punctuation or corrected obvious printer's errors.

1. Babel: a confusion of tongues or noises, so called after the city stricken with confusion by God for its pride in building the Tower of Babel; see Genesis 11:1–9.

2. A reference to John Dryden, *Religio Laici*, l. 265: "Let in gross errors to corrupt the text."

3. Clew: the ball of thread that guides one through a maze.

4. Ben Jonson, *Epicoene, or The Silent Woman* (1609) 2.1.3–4.

5. Philip Gilbert Hamerton (1834–1894), a British art critic and essayist, was famous for his guide to *Etching and Etchers*. He was founding editor of *The Portfolio*, a leading art journal in England.

6. Esther Edwards (later Burr) (1732–1758), New England colonist who lived through the religious revival known as the Great Awakening, kept a diary from 1754 to 1757 that she sent to Boston as letters to her friend, Sarah Prince. Jonathan Edwards, her father (1703–1758), was an American theologian and Calvinist preacher, whose favorite themes were predestination and grace, instrumental in the Great Awakening; his treatise *The Freedom of the Will*, as well as his letters and sermons, have been published. In early modern England and New England, paper was so expensive that letters were crammed to the margins. Sometimes sentences were written one way, then the paper was turned and more sentences written across the other way; old letters were saved and the empty spots used for other household writing.

7. Egeria was the subject of the fifth-century Latin *Diary of a Pilgrimage* discovered in 1884. This early Christian woman, probably a nun, kept a diary letter for her "sisters" of a three-year journey to Jerusalem and other holy places of Egypt, Palestine, and Syria.

8. See the description of Pentecost, the gift of special abilities to the apostles, in Acts 2:3: "And there appeared unto them cloven tongues like as of fire, and it sat upon each of them."

9. Edward P. Morris, *On Principles and Methods in Latin Syntax* (1901).

10. Bishop Spaulding: I have been unable to locate this quotation.

11. An allusion to Matthew 23:23: "Woe unto you, scribes and Pharisees, hypocrites! for ye pay tithe of mint and anise and cummin, and have omitted the weightier matters of the law, judgment, mercy, and faith: these ought ye to have done, and not to leave the other undone."

12. *Memoriter*: literally memory method; learning by rote.

13. An allusion to Romans 5:5: "And hope maketh not ashamed; because the love of God is shed abroad in our hearts by the Holy Ghost which is given unto us."

14. Abraham Lincoln, Grover Cleveland, George Washington, and Theodore Roosevelt were all U. S. presidents. Judge Parker is perhaps Theodore Parker (1810–1860), famous American preacher and social reformer.

Bibliography

Allen, Virginia. "Gertrude Buck and the Emergence of Composition in the United States." *Review of Metaphysic* 39, no. 3 (March 1986): 141–59.

Aristotle. *Aristotle on Rhetoric: A Theory of Civic Discourse*. Translated by George A. Kennedy. New York: Oxford University Press, 1991.

Aronson, Nicole. *Mademoiselle de Scudéry*. Translated by Stuart R. Aronson. Boston: Twayne, 1978.

Astell, Mary. *A Serious Proposal to the Ladies for the Advancement of Their True and Greatest Interest*. Pts. 1–2. 4th ed. London, 1701.

Batigelli, Anna. *Margaret Cavendish and the Exiles of the Mind*. Lexington: University Press of Kentucky, 1998.

Baym, Nina. "Lydia Sigourney." In *American National Biography*, edited by John A. Garraty and Mark C. Carnes, 19:926–28. New York: Oxford University Press, 1999.

Berlin, James. "Revisionary History: The Dialectical Method." In *Rethinking the History of Rhetoric: Multidisciplinary Essays on the Rhetorical Tradition*, edited by Takis Poulakos, 135–51. Boulder: Westview, 1993.

Biesecker, Barbara. "Coming to Terms with Recent Attempts to Write Women into the History of Rhetoric." *Philosophy and Rhetoric* 25, no. 2 (1992): 140–61.

Bitzer, Lloyd. "The Rhetorical Situation." *Philosophy and Rhetoric* 1 (1968): 1–14.

Bizzell, Patricia. "Feminist Methods of Research in the History of Rhetoric: What Differences Do They Make?" *Rhetoric Society Quarterly* 30, no. 4 (Fall 2000): 5–17.

———. "Opportunities for Feminist Research in the History of Rhetoric." *Rhetoric Review* 11, no. 1 (Fall 1992): 50–58.

Bizzell, Patricia, and Bruce Herzberg, eds. *The Rhetorical Tradition: Readings from Classical Times to the Present*. 2d ed. Boston: St. Martin's, 2001.

Blair, Carole. "Contested Histories of Rhetoric: The Politics of Preservation, Progress, and Change." *Quarterly Journal of Speech* 78 (1992): 403–28.

Bloedow, E. F. "Aspasia and the 'Mystery' of the *Menexenus*." *Wiener Studien*, n.s. 9 (1975): 32–48.

Bordelon, Susan. "Resisting Decline Stories: Gertrude Buck's Democratic Theory of Rhetoric." In *The Changing Tradition: Women in the History of Rhetoric*, edited by Christine Mason Sutherland and Rebecca Sutcliffe, 183–95. Calgary: University of Calgary Press, 1999.

Bordin, Ruth. *Frances Willard: A Biography*. Chapel Hill: University of North Carolina Press, 1986.

Brink, Jean R. "Bathsua Makin: Educator and Linguist." In *Female Scholars: A Tradition of Learned Women before 1800*, edited by Jean R. Brink, 86–100. Montreal: Eden Press Women's Publications, 1980.

Brown, Hallie Quinn. *Bits and Odds: A Choice Selection of Recitations, for School, Lyceum, and Parlor Entertainments Rendered by Miss Hallie Q. Brown*. With introduction and sketches by Faustin S. Delaney. Xenia, Ohio: Chew Press, 1880[?].

———. *Elocution and Physical Culture: Training for Students Teachers Readers Public Speakers*. Wilberforce, Ohio: Homewood Cottage, 1910[?].

Buck, Gertrude. *A Course in Argumentative Writing*. New York: Henry Holt, 1899.

———. *The Metaphor: A Study in the Psychology of Rhetoric*. Contributions to Rhetorical Theory no. 5. Edited by Fred Newton. Ann Arbor, Mich.: N.p., 1899.

———. "The Present Status of Rhetorical Theory." *Modern Language Notes* 15, no. 3 (1900): 84–87.

———. *Toward a Feminist Rhetoric: The Writing of Gertrude Buck*, edited by Jo Ann Campbell. Pittsburgh: University of Pittsburgh Press, 1996.

Buck, Gertrude, and Elisabeth Woodbridge. *A Course in Expository Writing*. New York: Henry Holt, 1899.

Burke, Kenneth. *A Rhetoric of Motives*. Berkeley: University of California Press, 1969.

Burke, Peter. "The Art of Conversation in Early Modern Europe." In *The Art of Conversation*, 89–122. Ithaca, N.Y.: Cornell University Press, 1993.

Burke, Rebecca J. "Gertrude Buck's Rhetorical Theory." *Occasional Papers in the History and Theory of Composition*. No. 1. Edited by Donald C. Stewart. Manhattan: Kansas State University, 1978.

Butler, Marilyn. *Maria Edgeworth: A Literary Biography*. Oxford: Clarendon, 1972.

Campbell, Karlyn Kohrs. "Gender and Genre: Loci of Invention and Contradiction in the Earliest Speeches by U.S. Women." *Quarterly Journal of Speech* 81, no. 4 (November 1995): 479–95.

Campbell, Karlyn Kohrs, ed. *Man Cannot Speak for Her*. 2 vols. Contributions to Women's Studies, no. 101. New York: Greenwood Press, 1989.

Cavendish, Margaret. *Margaret Cavendish: The Blazing World and Other Writings*. Edited by Kate Lilley. London: Penguin, 1992.

———. *The Worlds Olio*. London, 1655.

Certeau, Michel de. "Reading as Poaching." In *The Practice of Everyday Life*, 165–76. Translated by Steven F. Randall. Berkeley: University of California Press, 1984.

Christine de Pizan. *The Book of the Body Politic*. Edited and translated by Kate Langdon Forhan. New York: Cambridge University Press, 1994.

———. *De Oratore*. Translated by E. W. Sutton. 1942. Reprint, Cambridge, Mass.: Harvard University Press, 1967.

———. *Le Livre du Corps de Policie*. Edited by Robert H. Lucas. Geneva: Librarie Droz, 1967.

Cicero. *De Inventione*. Translated by H. M. Hubbell. 1949. Reprint, Cambridge: Harvard University Press, 1968.

Connors, Robert J. "Women's Reclamation of Rhetoric in Nineteenth-Century America." *Feminine Principles and Women's Experience in American Composition and Rhetoric*, edited by Louise Wetherbee Phelps and Janet Emig, 67–90. Pittsburgh: University of Pittsburgh Press, 1995.

Delsarte, François. *The Delsarte System of Oratory*. New York: Edgar S. Werner, 1893.

Demers, Patricia. *The World of Hannah More*. Lexington: University Press of Kentucky, 1996.

Donawerth, Jane. "'As Becomes a Rational Woman to Speak': Madeleine de Scudéry's Rhetoric of Conversation." In *Rhetorical Activities of Historical Women*, edited by Molly Wertheimer, 305–19. Columbia: University of South Carolina Press, 1997.

———. "Conversation and the Boundaries of Public Discourse in Rhetorical Theory by Renaissance Women." *Rhetorica* 16, no. 2 (Spring 1998): 181–99.

———. "Hannah More, Lydia Sigourney, and the Creation of a Women's Tradition of Rhetoric." In *Rhetoric, the Polis, and the Global Village*, edited by C. Jan Swearingen, 155–62. Proceedings of the 1998 Rhetoric Society of America Conference. Mahwah, N.J.: Erlbaum, 1999.

———. "Nineteenth-Century United States Conduct Book Rhetoric by Women." *Rhetoric Review*, forthcoming.

———. "Poaching on Men's Philosophies of Rhetoric: Eighteenth- and Nineteenth-Century Rhetorical Theory by Women." *Philosophy and Rhetoric* 33, no. 3 (2000): 243–58.

———. "The Politics of Renaissance Rhetorical Theory by Women." In *Political Rhetoric, Power, and Renaissance Women*, edited by Carole Levin and Patricia A. Sullivan, 257–72. Albany: State University of New York, 1995.

———. "Textbooks for New Audiences: Women's Revisions of Rhetorical Theory at the Turn of the Century." In *Listening to Their Voices: The Rhetorical Activities of Historical Women*, edited by Molly Meijer Wertheimer, 337–56. Columbia: University of South Carolina Press, 1997.

———. "Transforming the History of Rhetorical Theory." *Feminist Teacher* 7, no. 1 (Fall 1992): 35–39.

Dow, Bonnie J. "The 'Womanhood' Rationale in the Woman Suffrage Rhetoric of Frances E. Willard." *Southern Communication Journal* 56, no. 4 (Summer 1991): 298–307.

Edgeworth, Maria. *Letters for Literary Ladies, To Which Is Added, An Essay on the Noble Science of Self-Justification*. London, 1795.

Eunapius. *Lives of the Philosophers and Sophists*. Translated by W. C. Wright. 1921. Reprint, Cambridge, Mass.: Harvard University Press, 1961.

Farrar, Eliza. *Recollections of Seventy Years*. Boston: Ticknor & Fields, 1866.

———. [By a Lady]. *The Young Lady's Friend*. Boston: American Stationers' Co.; John B. Russell, 1837.

———. *The Youth's Letter-Writer; or The Epistolary Art*. New York: H. & S. Raynor, 1840.

Fell, Margaret. *Women's Speaking Justified*. London, 1666.

———. *Women's Speaking Justified* [1667]. Published with *Epistle* and *A Warning to All Friends*, compiled and with an introduction by David J. Latt. Los Angeles: William Andrews Clark Memorial Library/University of California, 1979.

Field, Guy Cromwell. "Aristippus." *The Oxford Classical Dictionary*, 2d ed., edited by N. G. L. Hammond and H. H. Scullard, 111. Oxford: Clarendon, 1976.

Ford, Charles Howard. *Hannah More: A Critical Biography*. New York: Peter Lang, 1996.

Gifford, Carolyn DeSwarte. "Frances Willard and the Woman's Christian Temperance Union's Conversion to Woman Suffrage." In *One Woman, One Vote: Rediscovering the Woman Suffrage Movement*, edited by Marjorie Spruill Wheeler, 117–33. Troutdale, Ore.: NewSage, 1995.

Glenn, Cheryl. *Rhetoric Retold: Regendering the Tradition from Antiquity through the Renaissance*. Carbondale: Southern Illinois University Press, 1997.

———. "sex, lies, and manuscript: Refiguring Aspasia in the History of Rhetoric." *CCC: College Communication and Composition* 45, no. 2 (May 1994): 180–99.

Goldsmith, Elizabeth. *"Exclusive Conversations": The Art of Interaction in Seventeenth-Century France*. Philadelphia: University of Pennsylvania Press, 1988.

Goldsmith, Elizabeth, ed. *Writing the Female Voice: Essays on Epistolary Literature*. Boston: Northeastern University Press, 1989.

Haight, Gordon S. *Mrs. Sigourney: The Sweet Singer of Hartford*. New York: Yale University Press, 1930.

Hammond, N. G. L., and H. H. Scullard. *The Oxford Classical Dictionary*. 2d ed. Oxford: Clarendon, 1976.

Harden, Elizabeth. *Maria Edgeworth*. Boston: Twayne, 1984.

Hartley, Florence. *The Ladies Book of Etiquette and Manual of Politeness*. Boston: Lee & Shepard, 1870.

Henry, Madeleine. *Prisoner of History: Aspasia of Miletus and Her Biographical Tradition*. New York: Oxford University Press, 1995.

Herberg, Erin. "Mary Astell's Rhetorical Theory: A Woman's Viewpoint." In *The Changing Tradition: Women in the History of Rhetoric*, edited by Christine Mason Sutherland and Rebecca Sutcliffe, 147–57. Calgary: University of Calgary Press, 1999.

Hobbs, Catherine, ed. *Nineteenth-Century Women Learn to Write*. Charlottesville: University Press of Virginia, 1995.

Hobby, Elaine. *Virtue of Necessity: English Women's Writing, 1649–1688*. London: Virago, 1988.

Hopkins, Mary Alden. *Hannah More and Her Circle*. New York: Longmans, Green, 1947.

Hull, Suzanne W. *Chaste, Silent, and Obedient: English Books for Women, 1475–1640*. San Marino, Calif.: Huntington Publications, 1988.

Jarratt, Susan. "Speaking to the Past: Feminist Historiography in Rhetoric." *Pre/Text* 11, nos. 3–4 (1990): 190–208.

319

Jarratt, Susan, and Rory Ong. "Aspasia: Rhetoric, Gender, and Colonial Identity." In *Reclaiming Rhetorica: Women in the Rhetorical Tradition*, edited by Andrea A. Lunsford, 9–24. Pittsburgh: University of Pittsburgh Press, 1995.

Johnson, Nan. *Nineteenth-Century Rhetoric in North America*. Carbondale: Southern Illinois University Press, 1991.

———. "Reigning in the Court of Silence: Women and Rhetorical Space in Postbellum America." *Philosophy and Rhetoric* 33, no. 3 (2000): 221–42.

Jones, Kathleen. *A Glorious Fame: The Life of Margaret Cavendish, Duchess of Newcastle, 1623–1673*. London: Bloomsbury, 1988.

Jones, M. G. *Hannah More*. Cambridge: Cambridge University Press, 1952.

Jordan, Mary Augusta. *Correct Writing and Speaking*. The Woman's Home Library. New York: A. S. Barnes, 1904.

Kates, Susan. *Activist Rhetorics and American Higher Education, 1885–1937*. Carbondale: Southern Illinois University Press, 2001.

———. "The Embodied Rhetoric of Hallie Quinn Brown." *College English* 59, no. 1 (January 1997): 59–71.

———. "Subversive Feminism: The Politics of Correctness in Mary Augusta Jordan's *Correct Writing and Speaking* (1904)." *College Composition and Communication*, 48, no. 4 (December 1997): 501–17.

Keeler, Harriet L., and Emma C. Davis. *Studies in English Composition*. Boston: Allyn & Bacon, 1892.

Kempton, Daniel. "Christine de Pizan's *Cité des Dames* and *Trésor de la Cité*: Toward a Feminist Scriptural Practice." In *Political Rhetoric, Power, and Renaissance Women*, edited by Carole Levin and Patricia A. Sullivan, 15–37. Albany: State University of New York Press, 1995.

Kennedy, George. *The Art of Persuasion in Greece*. Princeton: Princeton University Press, 1963.

———. *Classical Rhetoric and Its Christian and Secular Tradition from Ancient to Modern Times*. Chapel Hill: University of North Carolina Press, 1980.

———. *Comparative Rhetoric: An Historical and Cross-Cultural Introduction*. New York: Oxford University Press, 1998.

Krueger, Christine. *The Reader's Repentance: Women Preachers, Women Writers, and Nineteenth-Century Social Discourse*. Chicago: University of Chicago Press, 1992.

Kunze, Bonnelyn Young. *Margaret Fell and the Rise of Quakerism*. Stanford: Stanford University Press, 1994.

Levin, Carole, and Patricia A. Sullivan, eds. *Political Rhetoric, Power, and Renaissance Women*. Albany: State University of New York Press, 1995.

Lockwood, Sara E. Husted. *Lessons in English, Adapted to the Study of American Classics: A Textbook for High Schools and Academies*. Boston: Ginn, 1888.

Logan, Shirley. *"We Are Coming": The Persuasive Discourse of Nineteenth-Century Black Women*. Carbondale: Southern Illinois University Press, 1999.

Logan, Shirley, ed. *With Pen and Voice: A Critical Anthology of Nineteenth-Century African-American Women*. Carbondale: Southern Illinois University Press, 1995.

Loraux, Nicole. *The Invention of Athens: The Funeral Oration in the Classical City*. Translated by Alan Sheridan. Cambridge, Mass.: Harvard University Press, 1986.

Lunsford, Andrea, ed. *Reclaiming Rhetorica: Women in the Rhetorical Tradition*. Pittsburgh: University of Pittsburgh Press, 1995.

Makin, Bathsua. *An Essay to Revive the Antient Education of Gentlewomen*. London, 1673.

———. *An Essay to Revive the Antient Education of Gentlewomen (1673)*. With an introduction by Paula Barbour. Publication 202. Los Angeles: William Andrews Clark Memorial Library and University of California, 1980.

Mattingly, Carol. *Well-Tempered Women: Nineteenth-Century Temperance Rhetoric*. Carbondale: Southern Illinois University Press, 1998.

McFarlin, Annjennette S. "Hallie Quinn Brown: Black Woman Elocutionist." Ph.D. diss., Washington State University, 1975.

———. "Hallie Quinn Brown: Black Woman Elocutionist." *Southern Speech Communication Journal* 46 (Fall 1980): 72–82.

Mendelson, Sara Heller. *The Mental World of Stuart Women: Three Studies.* Brighton, U.K.: Harvester, 1987.

Minnich, Elizabeth Kamarck. "A Feminist Critique of the Liberal Arts." In *Liberal Education and the New Scholarship on Women: Issues and Constraints on Institutional Change,* 23–38. Report of the Wingspread Conference. Washington, D.C.: Association of American Colleges, 1981.

More, Hannah. *Selected Writing of Hannah More.* Edited by Robert Hole. London: William Pickering, 1996.

———. *Strictures on the Modern System of Female Education.* London, 1799.

———. *The Works of Hannah More.* New York: Harper & Brothers, 1855.

Morgan, Anna. *An Hour with Delsarte: A Study of Expression.* Illustrated by Rose Mueller Sprague and Marian Reynolds. Boston: Lee & Shepard, 1890.

Mulderig, Gerald P. "Gertrude Buck's Rhetorical Theory and Modern Composition Teaching." *Rhetoric Society Quarterly* 14 (1984): 95–104.

Murphy, James J. "Conducting Research in the History of Rhetoric: An Open Letter to a Future Historian of Rhetoric." *Publishing in Rhetoric and Composition,* edited by Gary A. Olson and Todd W. Taylor, 187–95. Albany: State University of New York Press, 1997.

Nicholson, Linda. "Interpreting Gender." *Signs* 20, no. 1 (Autumn 1994): 79–105.

Palmer, Phoebe. *The Promise of the Father.* 1859. Reprint, New York: Garland, 1985.

———. *Tongue of Fire on the Daughters of the Lord.* In *Phoebe Palmer: Selected Writings,* edited by Thomas Oden, 35–57. 1859. Reprint, Mahwah, N.J.: Paulist, 1988.

Perelman, Chaim. "Rhetoric and Philosophy." *Philosophy and Rhetoric* 1 (1968): 15–24.

Perry, Ruth. *The Celebrated Mary Astell: An Early English Feminist.* Chicago: University of Chicago Press, 1986.

Peterson, Carla. *"Doers of the Word": African-American Women Speakers and Writers in the North (1830–1880).* New York: Oxford University Press, 1995.

Plato. *Menexenus.* Translated by R. G. Burys. 1929. Reprint, Cambridge, Mass.: Harvard University Press, 1961.

Plutarch. *Plutarch's Lives.* Translated by Bernadotte Perrin. 1916. Reprint, Cambridge, Mass.: Harvard University Press, 1951.

Quintilian. *Institutio Oratoria.* Translated by H. E. Butler. 1921. Reprint, Cambridge, Mass.: Harvard University Press, 1966.

Redfern, Jenny R. "Christine de Pisan and *The Treasure of the City of Ladies:* A Medieval Rhetorician and Her Rhetoric." In *Reclaiming Rhetorica: Women in the Rhetorical Tradition,* edited by Andrea A. Lunsford, 73–92. Pittsburgh: University of Pittsburgh Press, 1995.

Ross, Isabel. *Margaret Fell: Mother of Quakerism.* London: Longmans, Green, 1949.

Royster, Jacqueline Jones. *Traces of a Stream: Literacy and Social Change among African American Women.* Pittsburgh: University of Pittsburgh Press, 2000.

Royster, Jacqueline Jones, and Jean C. Williams. "History in the Spaces Left: African American Presence and Narratives of Composition Studies." *College Composition and Communication* 50, no. 4 (1999): 563–84.

Ruyter, Nancy Lee Chalfa. *The Cultivation of Body and Mind in Nineteenth-Century American Delsartism.* Westport, Conn.: Greenwood Press, 1999.

———. *Reformers and Visionaries: The Americanization of the Art of Dance.* New York: Dance Horizons, 1979.

Schilb, John. "Future Historiographies of Rhetoric and the Present Age of Anxiety." In *Writing Histories of Rhetoric,* edited by Victor Vitanza, 128–38. Carbondale: Southern Illinois University Press, 1994.

———. "The History of Rhetoric and the Rhetoric of History." *Pre/Text* 7 (1986): 11–34.

Schultz, Lucille M. *The Young Composers: Composition's Beginnings in Nineteenth-Century Schools*. Carbondale: Southern Illinois University Press, 1999.

Scudéry, Madeleine de. *Conversations nouvelles sur divers sujets: Dedie'es au roy*. La Haye, 1685.

———. *Les Conversations sur divers sujets*. Amsterdam, 1686.

———. *Conversations upon Several Subjects*. Translated by Ferrand Spence. London, 1683.

Sei Shonagon. *The Pillow Book of Shei Shonagon*. 2 vols. Translated by Ivan Morris. New York: Columbia University Press, 1967.

Sigourney, Lydia. *Letters to My Pupils: With Narrative and Biographical Sketches*. New York: Robert and Carter and Brothers, 1851.

———. *Letters to Young Ladies*. 1833. Reprint, New York: Harper & Brothers, 1852.

Smith, Hilda. *Reason's Disciples: Seventeenth-Century English Feminists*. Urbana: University of Illinois Press, 1982.

Sprague, Rosamond Kent, ed. *The Older Sophists*. Columbia: University of South Carolina Press, 1972.

Stanton, Domna. *The Aristocrat as Art: A Study of the Honnête Homme and the Dandy in Seventeenth- and Nineteenth-Century French Literature*. New York: Columbia University Press, 1980.

Stark, Ryan John. "Margaret Cavendish and Composition Style." *Rhetoric Review* 17, no. 2 (Spring 1999): 264–81.

Stebbins, Genevieve. *Delsarte System of Expression*. 5th ed. New York: Edgar S. Werner, 1894.

———. *The Genevieve Stebbins System of Physical Training*. Enl. ed. 1898. Reprint, New York: Edgar S. Werner, 1912.

Sutherland, Christine Mason. "Aspiring to the Rhetorical Tradition: A Study of Margaret Cavendish." In *Listening to Their Voices: The Rhetorical Activities of Historical Women*, edited by Molly Meijer Wertheimer, 255–71. Columbia: University of South Carolina Press, 1997.

———. "Mary Astell: Reclaiming Rhetorica in the Seventeenth Century." In *Reclaiming Rhetorica: Women in the Rhetorical Tradition*, edited by Andrea A. Lunsford, 93–116. Pittsburgh: University of Pittsburgh Press, 1995.

———. "Outside the Rhetorical Tradition: Mary Astell's Advice to Women in Seventeenth-century England." *Rhetorica* 9, no. 2 (Spring 1991): 147–63.

Sutherland, Christine Mason, and Rebecca Sutcliffe, eds. *The Changing Tradition: Women in the History of Rhetoric*. Calgary: University of Calgary Press, 1999.

Swann, Nancy Lee. *Pan Chao: Foremost Woman Scholar of China*. 1932. Reprint, New York: Russell & Russell, 1968.

Teague, Frances. *Bathsua Makin: Woman of Learning*. Lewisburg, Pa.: Bucknell University Press, 1997.

———. "The Identity of Bathsua Makin." *Biography* 16, no. 2 (Winter 1993): 1–17.

Watson, Martha. *Lives of Their Own: Rhetorical Dimensions in Autobiographies of Women Activists*. Columbia: University of South Carolina Press, 1999.

Wertheimer, Molly Meijer, ed. *Listening to Their Voices: The Rhetorical Activities of Historical Women*. Columbia: University of South Carolina, 1997.

Willard, Frances E. *Do Everything Reform: The Oratory of Frances E. Willard*. Edited by Richard W. Leeman. Westport, Conn.: Greenwood Press, 1992.

———. *Woman in the Pulpit*. Boston: D. Lothrop, 1888.

———. *Writing Out My Heart: Selections from the Journal of Frances E. Willard, 1855–96*. Edited by Carolyn De Swarte Gifford. Urbana: University of Illinois Press, 1995.

Willing, Jennie F. *The Potential Woman: A Book for Young Ladies*. Boston: McDonald & Gill, 1887.

Index

About the Editor

Jane Donawerth, professor of English and affiliate in Women's Studies at the University of Maryland, has authored *Shakespeare and the Sixteenth-Century Study of Language* (1984) and *Frankenstein's Daughters: Women Writing Science Fiction* (1995); she has co-edited two collections of essays on early modern women's writing and one on utopian and science fiction by women. She has also published widely in Shakespeare, early modern women's writings, pedagogy, and history of rhetoric. She has held NEH and University of Wisconsin Humanities fellowships, and won six teaching awards, as well as 1995–96 University of Maryland Distinguished Scholar-Teacher Award. She is also a member of the costume crew for her daughter's musicals, and roadie for her son's rock band. She is finishing a translation of Madeleine de Scudéry's rhetorical theory and writings, and a cultural studies analysis of the history of women's rhetorical theory, and starting a study of early modern women's reading and writing practices.